Lecture Notes in Computer Science 10309

Commenced Publication in 1973
Founding and Former Series Editors:
Gerhard Goos, Juris Hartmanis, and Jan van Leeuwen

AF738417

More information about this series at http://www.springer.com/series/7407

Simon K.S. Cheung · Lam-for Kwok
Will W.K. Ma · Lap-Kei Lee
Harrison Yang (Eds.)

Blended Learning

New Challenges and Innovative Practices

10th International Conference, ICBL 2017
Hong Kong, China, June 27–29, 2017
Proceedings

Springer

Editors
Simon K.S. Cheung
The Open University of Hong Kong
Hong Kong
Hong Kong

Lap-Kei Lee
The Open University of Hong Kong
Hong Kong
Hong Kong

Lam-for Kwok
City University of Hong Kong
Hong Kong
China

Harrison Yang
State University of New York at Oswego
Oswego, NY
USA

Will W.K. Ma
Hong Kong Shue Yan University
Hong Kong
Hong Kong

ISSN 0302-9743 ISSN 1611-3349 (electronic)
Lecture Notes in Computer Science
ISBN 978-3-319-59359-3 ISBN 978-3-319-59360-9 (eBook)
DOI 10.1007/978-3-319-59360-9

Library of Congress Control Number: 2017942987

LNCS Sublibrary: SL1 – Theoretical Computer Science and General Issues

Printed on acid-free paper

This Springer imprint is published by Springer Nature
The registered company is Springer International Publishing AG
The registered company address is: Gewerbestrasse 11, 6330 Cham, Switzerland

Preface

Welcome to the 10th International Conference on Blended Learning (ICBL 2017), which marks the 10th anniversary of ICBL with its predecessor the International Conference on Hybrid Learning. This year, ICBL 2017 was held at the City University of Hong Kong, Hong Kong, SAR China, during June 27–29, 2017.

Undoubtedly, blended learning has become one of the promising approaches to teaching and learning. It aims to integrate traditional learning with innovative means, such as e-learning and open online learning, in order to create a new learning environment to enhance learning effectiveness and enrich the learning experience. Like the previous conferences in the series, ICBL 2017 provided a platform for knowledge exchange and experience sharing among researchers and practitioners in this field.

The theme of ICBL 2017 was "Blended Learning: New Challenges and Innovative Practices." To cope with the recent technological advances, our focus was on the new challenges and innovative practices of blended learning. ICBL 2017 attracted over 100 paper submissions. After a rigorous review process, 42 papers were selected for inclusion in this volume. The selected papers cover various areas of blended learning, including the experience, assessment, and strategies of blended learning, computer supported collaborative learning, improved flexibility of learning processes, open educational resources, and pedagogical and psychological issues.

We would like to take this opportunity to thank the following parties who made the conference a success: (a) the conference Organizing Committee; (b) the international Program Committee; (c) the organizers and co-organizers; (d) the sponsors; (e) Springer, the publisher of the conference proceedings, and (f) all the conference participants.

We trust you will enjoy reading the papers.

June 2017

Simon K.S. Cheung
Lam-for Kwok
Will W.K. Ma
Lap-kei Lee
Harrison Yang

Organization

Organizing Committee

Honorary Chairs

Horace H.S. Ip	City University of Hong Kong, Hong Kong, SAR China
Kedong Li	South China Normal University, China
Harrison Yang	Central China Normal University, China, and State University of New York at Oswego, USA

Conference Chairs

Lam-For Kwok	City University of Hong Kong, Hong Kong, SAR China
Junjie Shang	Peking University, China

Program Chairs

Simon K.S. Cheung	The Open University of Hong Kong, Hong Kong, SAR China
Fu Lee Wang	Caritas Institute of Higher Education, Hong Kong, SAR China
Will W.K. Ma	Hong Kong Shue Yan University, Hong Kong, SAR China

Organizing Chairs

John Hui	City University of Hong Kong, Hong Kong, SAR China
Lap-kei Lee	The Open University of Hong Kong, Hong Kong, SAR China

Finance and Registration Chairs

Steven Ng	Caritas Institute of Higher Education, Hong Kong, SAR China
Raymond Wong	City University of Hong Kong, Hong Kong, SAR China

Publicity Chairs

Morris Jong	The Chinese University of Hong Kong, Hong Kong, SAR China
Shudong Wang	Shimane University, Japan

Web Master

Richard Li	City University of Hong Kong, Hong Kong, SAR China

International Program Committee

Oliver Au	The Open University of Hong Kong, Hong Kong, SAR China
Jinnong Cao	The Hong Kong Polytechnic University, Hong Kong, SAR China
Keith Chan	The Hong Kong Polytechnic University, Hong Kong, SAR China
Peter Chan	Brigham Young University, USA
Chih-Tsan Chang	National Chung Cheng University, Taiwan
Simon K.S. Cheung	The Open University of Hong Kong, Hong Kong, SAR China
David Delahunty	University of Oulu, Finland
Giuliana Dettori	Istituto di Tecnologie Didattiche del CNR, Italy
Min Eng	University of Toronto, Canada
Owen Hall Jr.	Pepperdine University, USA
Andreas Henrich	University of Bamberg, Germany
Yoko Hirata	Hokkai-Gakuen University, Japan
Yoshihiro Hirata	Hokkai-Gakuen University, Japan
Jenq-Muh Hsu	National Chiayi University, Taiwan
Ronghuia Huang	Beijing Normal University, China
Kenichi Kubota	Kansai University, Japan
Reggie Kwan	The Open University of Hong Kong, Hong Kong, SAR China
Lam-For Kwok	City University of Hong Kong, Hong Kong, SAR China
Ivan Lai	Caritas Institute of Higher Education, Hong Kong, SAR China
Jeanne Lam	HKU School of Professional and Continuing Education, Hong Kong, SAR China
Jun Le	Guangdong Radio and TV University, China
Lap-kei Lee	The Open University of Hong Kong, Hong Kong, SAR China
Victor Lee	City University of Hong Kong, Hong Kong, SAR China
Yan Li	Zhejiang University, China
Yi Li	Nanjing University, China
Kousuke Mouri	Kyushu University, Japan
Steven Ng	Caritas Institute of Higher Education, Hong Kong, SAR China
Hiroaki Ogata	Kyushu University, Japan
Diana Perez-Marin	Universidad Rey Juan Carlos, Spain
Petra Poulova	University of Hradec Králové, Czech Republic
Junjie Shang	Peking University, China
Liana Stanescu	University of Craiova, Romania
Jay Tashiro	University of Ontario Institute of Technology, Canada
Stefanie Trausan-Matu	University Politehnica of Bucharest, Romania
Aihua Wang	Peking University, China
Fu Lee Wang	Caritas Institute of Higher Education, Hong Kong, SAR China
Shudong Wang	Shimane University, Japan

Tak Lam Wong	The Hong Kong Institute of Education, Hong Kong, SAR China
Di Wu	Central China Normal University, China
You Ru Xie	South China Normal University, China
Harrison Yang	Central China Normal University, China, and State University of New York at Oswego, USA
Wing Lok Yeung	Lingnan University, Hong Kong, SAR China
Morris Jong	The Chinese University of Hong Kong, Hong Kong, SAR China
Liming Zhang	University of Macau, Macau, SAR China
Guodong Zhao	Peking University, China
Jianhua Zhao	South China Normal University, China
Ying Zhou	Beijing Normal University, China

Keynote Speakers and Panel Chairs

Keynote Speakers

Ronghuai Huang	Beijing Normal University, Beijing, China
Christian Wagner	City University of Hong Kong, SAR China
Kenichi Kubota	Kansai University, Japan
Petra Poulova	University of Hradec Kralove, Czech Republic

Panel Chairs

Harrison Yang	Central China Normal University, China, and State University of New York at Oswego, USA
Kedong Li	South China Normal University, China

Organizers

City University of Hong Kong

Co-organizers

Caritas Institute of Higher Education

Hong Kong Society for Multimedia and Image Computing

Sponsors

Hong Kong Pei Hua Education Foundation

Springer Science+Business Media

Contents

Keynotes

Experiences in Blended Learning

Keynotes

Blended Learning as Means of Support Within the Elderly People Education

Petra Poulova(✉) and Ivana Simonova

Faculty of Informatics and Management,
University of Hradec Králové, Hradec Králové, Czech Republic
{ivana.simonova,petra.poulova}@uhk.cz

Abstract. The article deals with the research conducted within the elderly people of Hradec Kralove region, Czech Republic, which works as a pilot research to the representative study of ways how the elderly reach and develop their IT skills, particularly how social relationships work as movers within this process. The method of questionnaire was applied to the research sample of 432 respondents attending the University of the Third Age and IT courses held by the Municipality of Hradec Kralove. The results, described and displayed in eight figures, clearly proved, the elderly people met the three predefined criteria for successful implementation of blended learning in this age group, as they both possessed modern devices and had skills to exploit them successfully for various purposes. There are no limits showing that blended learning could not be applied within this age group.

Keywords: Blended learning · Elderly · Information and communication technology · Device · Smart technology · Research

1 Introduction

Apart from others, the current society is characterized by penetrating modern technologies into all spheres of (human) life. This feature has been mentioned by numerous authors since 1990 (e.g. [1–3], etc.) and widely researched during the last decade, e.g. by [4–6] and many others. All age categories, from pre-school children to the elderly people have been affected by modern technologies to some extent.

If the elderly people are under the focus, the problem is even more appealing, from various reasons. Those interested in further education can see how modern technologies are exploited to support education (e.g. of their grandchildren) and, they would definitely appreciate to undergo such experience by themselves (e.g. [7]). To reach this, at least two pre-conditions should be reached: (1) having modern devices available as well as (2) master the skills required for their effective exploitation for educational purposes. Below, two educational activities are mentioned – courses of the University of the Third Age and IT courses towards developing skills for using modern devices and technologies. Within these activities e.g. links to additional sources of information (in the form of texts, presentations, audio- and video-recordings, blogs and discussions, samples of good practice etc.) could be provided to the participants, sample of good practices, pictures of historical places, pieces of arts, medical schemes and many others. Moreover,

S.K.S. Cheung et al. (Eds.): ICBL 2017, LNCS 10309, pp. 3–14, 2017.
DOI: 10.1007/978-3-319-59360-9_1

the didactic guide how to apply this information in the educational process should be provided by course lecturers. Reflecting the above mentioned, three main areas (preconditions) are under the focus of this research: (1) the ownership of modern (i.e. ICT/smart) devices, (2) their exploitation of modern devices and technologies by the elderly people and (3) the ways how they reached the skills necessary for their exploitation. If these preconditions are fulfilled, the blended learning could be successfully implemented in the process of the elderly people education.

Therefore, this paper aims at presenting results of the research, the objectives of which are to answer three questions: (1) What modern devices do the elderly people possess?, (2) What purposes do they exploit them for? and (3) How have they reached the skills required for using modern devices and technologies?

2 Theoretical Background

Having worked during the whole life, the worker becomes a retired person one day. This fact brings substantial changes into his/her life, both in the personal and professional areas. The professional career is suddenly, or step-by-step closed, in personal field social and/or health problems may appear. To stay active in this age period is one of the recommendations provided to this age group. Moreover, modern devices and technologies can help substantially in this field.

Most countries have accepted the chronological age of 65 years to define the retired, mostly also called the 'elderly' person. This approach is based on a retirement age; however, the age classification varies between countries and times, reflecting in many cases functional ability related to the workforce, and/or even more frequently the current political and economic situation. Many times the definition is linked to the retirement age, which often is lower for women than men. This transition in livelihood became for decades the basis for the definition of old age which occurred between the ages of 45 and 55 years for women and between the ages of 55 and 75 years for men [8].

In the Czech Republic the chronological retirement age also varies – been based on social circumstances in the past, 53 years used to be the starting level for the retirement age (or it was even lower in some professions), up to the current times, when 60+ limit is applied reflecting the gender, profession and number of children born. For the purpose of this research the age of 55 years was selected to be the start of the retirement age and minimum age limit for the group of elderly people [9].

According to the Czech Statistical Office the age structure of the Czech Republic is of the regressive type, which means the category of children does not cover the category of post-productive age group, i.e. the elderly people, which reaches 28% [10]. The importance of this fact calls for both the support and necessity to carefully monitor this age group and the correlation to their skills towards acquiring latest development in information and communication technologies.

The group of retired/elderly people (which sounds irrationally in some cases) has been defined by numerous authors and various criteria have been applied. According to the World Health Organization (WHO), in most developed West European and North American countries the chronological age of 65 years has been accepted as a definition of 'elderly' or older person. However, it does not adapt well to e.g. Africa, South America or East Asia. Whereas this definition may seem arbitrary to some extent, in fact it is connected with the age at which the person can begin to receive pension benefits. At the moment, the standard numerical criterion agreed by United Nations is 60+ years to refer to the older population. On the other hand, although there exist widely accepted definitions of old age, there is no general agreement on the age at which a person becomes old. The calendar age assumes equivalence with biological age, yet at the same time, these two are not necessarily synonymous. Various approaches have been applied, however, they differ substantially, e.g. in 1875 in Britain any age after 50, yet pension schemes mostly used age 60 or 65 years for eligibility of the old age [11]. Lacking an accepted and acceptable definition, in many instances the age at which a person became eligible for statutory and occupational retirement pensions is of 60 and 65 years [8].

Moreover, adding to the difficulty in establishing a definition, actual birth dates are quite often unknown because many individuals in Africa, South America, East Asia do not have an official record of their birth date. As Gorman states "The ageing process is of course a biological reality which has its own dynamic, largely beyond human control. However, it is also subject to the constructions through which each society makes sense of old age. … In many parts of the developing world, chronological time has little or no importance in the meaning of old age. Other socially constructed meanings of age are more significant such as the roles assigned to older people; in some cases, it is the loss of roles accompanying physical decline which is significant in defining old age. Thus, in contrast to the chronological milestones which mark life stages in the developed world, old age in many developing countries is seen to begin at the point when active contribution is no longer possible" [12].

Within this research, the definition of elderly people follows the cultural environment of the central Europe. The elderly people are defined as those not been active in the working process any more (i.e. they retired) and draw the old age pension. Despite the retirement age is generally higher, as mentioned above, in the Czech Republic it used to start from the age of 55 years. Consequently, the research group starts at this age.

Whether they can have the same quality of life in this new period is one of the fears of newly retired people, i.e. those who became the elderly, when referring to the above presented definitions. The 'same' often does not mean 'identical' but 'not lower' quality. In practice, it means the elderly people are afraid of loss of social contacts, becoming lonely, reaching worse (lower) financial affordances, and last but not least, not been able to acquire/held all the technical/technological competences which are/will be necessary for living in the e-society. Therefore, the social relationships are so important for the new life, either in the family, with friends, or in both areas.

The sociological survey has indicated that more than 42% of elderly people have the appropriate skills to using modern Information Technologies. [13] However, on the other side, numerous studies have shown that elderly people deal with difficulties in using ICT, despite the great benefits that mobile sensing and social computing could provide to increase elderly's quality of life. [14] From the view of social life on the elderly people, evidence indicates that contemporary ICT have the potential to prevent or reduce the social isolation of elderly people via various mechanisms, e.g. for communication, sharing photos etc. [15] Modern technologies offer many facilities; however, the elderly people are often unable to enjoy them, from minimum to maximum extent. Consequently, or because of the lack of ICT skills they feel discouraged or intimidated by modern devices, and thus become progressively isolated in the society where the Internet communication and ICT skills are essential [16].

Moreover, latest ICT and mobile devices, particularly smartphones and tablet, are able to carry out the noninvasible and unnoticed monitoring activities and assess the user's health status at the same time. Therefore, they enable frail health users to live in their own home environment and to receive remote assistance, if needed [17].

In the current time of e-society, where modern devices and technologies play an important role, the ownership as well as mastering skills to exploit them are highly required. From this point of view, this research is expected to discover crucial findings which can help the elderly people to cope with the new life and spend this time period fruitfully, without frustration.

3 Research Objectives

The main objective of this research is to collect data and thus answer the question whether the blended learning can be applied within the elderly people education, particularly with special focus on three areas:

(1) what modern devices the elderly people possess,
(2) what purposes the elderly people exploit them for,
(3) how the elderly people reached the skills required for using modern devices and technologies.

3.1 Methodology and Tool

The method of questionnaire was applied to focus on selected fields of elderly people's exploitation of modern devices and technologies. The questionnaire included twelve items. Data on respondents were collected in items 1–3, their opinions and experience in the questioned fields were monitored in items 4–12. The respondents' feedback was provided in the open answer format, multiple-choice format with one, four or all choices and in the dichotomous format (Yes/No). The respondents filled in the printed questionnaire by handwriting immediately on the site, as described below.

3.2 Research Sample

The data collected by the questionnaire were processed by the IBM SPSS Statistics software. Totally, 432 questionnaires were administered. At the beginning of the process, questionnaires were provided to 437 respondents, i.e. five questionnaires were not included in the final amount. Those ones which were not fully completed, were considered in two ways: if questions 1–3 were answered and only one answer to questions 4–12 was missing, it was replaced by the group mean value. In other cases, if more answers were missing, the questionnaire was not included in the research sample (the above mentioned five ones).

The questionnaires were distributed within two groups: (1) participants of the University of the Third Age courses (U3A) and (2) IT courses held by the Municipality of Hradec Kralove (MHK). This approach means that only those elderly people who are interested in self-education were included in the research sample. Reflecting this fact, the research sample is not representative but the convenient one – it is limited (a) to active-in-education respondents, (b) dwelling in Hradec Kralove region. The authors are aware of this fact and reflected it in conclusions. The collected data and research results will be exploited for the purpose of the pilot study towards the further research within the representative sample of elderly people in the Czech Republic.

The research sample was analyzed under the respondent's age, gender and level of education. The sample consisted of 26% of male (M) and 74% of female (F) respondents, i.e. 115 men and 317 women. The distribution follows the demographic curve of the Czech population of this age group [10]. Within a detailed analysis of the research sample we can see that:

- the oldest respondents were in the group of 85+ years – they were 15 ones (12 female and 3 male respondents, the oldest respondent was a 94-year-old male),
- the higher amount of respondents was born in 1942–51 (59%),
- most respondents were female in the 1942–51 age group (n = 188), i.e. 65–74 years old.

This distribution also follows the demographic structure of the Czech Republic [13] (Fig. 1).

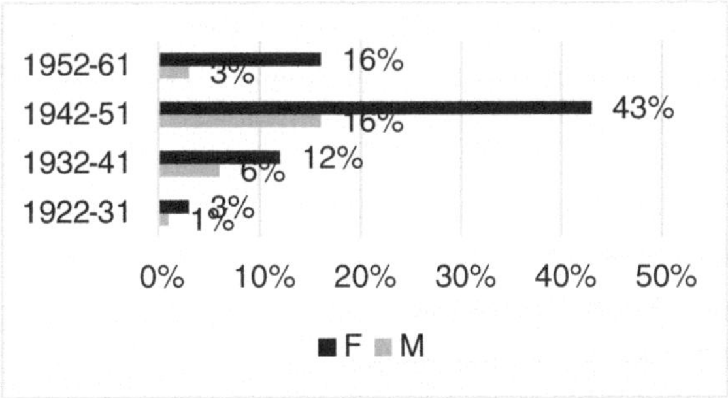

Fig. 1. Respondents: age/gender structure (F: female, M: male).

Level of education reached by the respondents was structured into three groups:

- vocational (i.e. three-year upper level secondary education without school leaving examination, mostly required for working class and crafts professions; 13%; 55 respondents),
- upper secondary (i.e. four-year education graduating with school leaving examination; 66%, 287 respondents),
- tertiary (i.e. university, higher; 21%; 91 respondents) education.

Most respondents reached upper secondary level of education (Fig. 2).

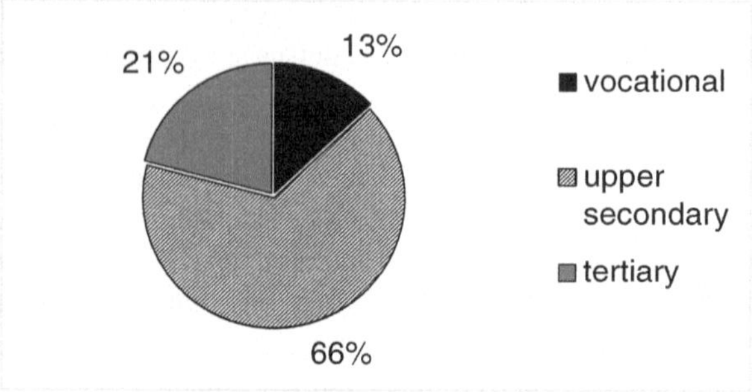

Fig. 2. Respondents: level of education

4 Research Results

The collected data were structured under the three research questions presented above. Moreover, additional data for deeper analysis were gained from multiple choice answers to items 4–12.

4.1 What Modern Devices the Elderly People Possess

The collected data show that most respondents own and explore mobile phones (383; 89%), followed by PC owners (217 respondents; 50%) and notebook owners (167 respondents; 39%), 59 respondents own smartphones (14%) and 45 ones are tablet owners (9%). Two respondents do not possess any device (Fig. 3).

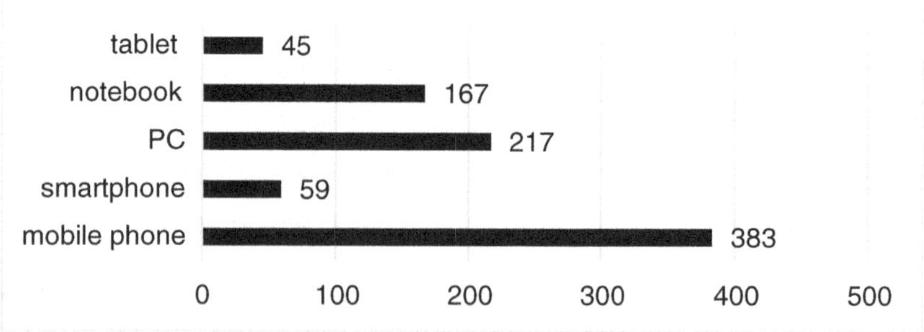

Fig. 3. Possession of mobile devices (n)

4.2 What Purposes the Elderly People Exploit Modern Devices for

Respondents expressed rather a large range of purposes they exploit modern devices and technologies for, e.g. for e-services (e-mailing, 73%; e-banking, 40%; e-shopping, 34%), but also for socializing purposes (e.g. skyping and sharing photos, writing documents including letters, 38% each; collecting information (e.g. from newspapers, 25%;

information on health, 33%; playing games (16%), active participation in discussions, or even writing blogs (3%) etc. The complete list of activities is displayed below (Fig. 4).

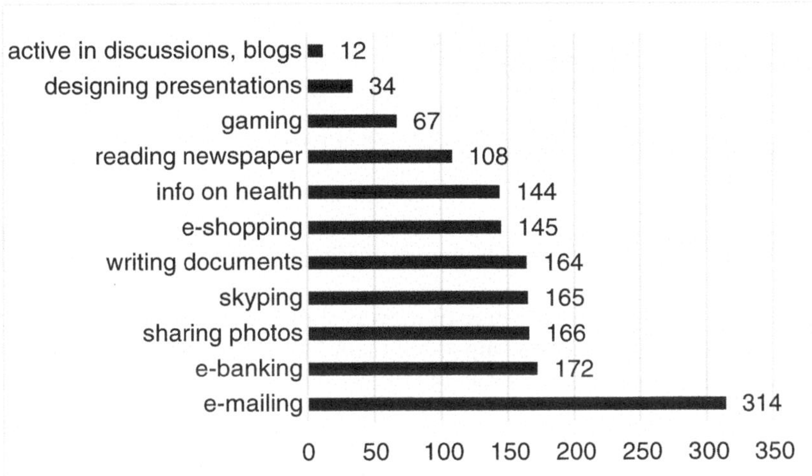

Fig. 4. Purposes of working with devices (n)

4.3 How the Elderly Reached the Skills Required for Using Modern Devices and Technologies

When answering the question what the ways and approaches lead the respondents to acquiring the skills on how exploit the modern devices and technologies, following ones were detected:

- self-learning (i.e. respondents acquired the competence by autonomous learning),
- other people helped them (their children, grandchildren, friends),
- participation in IT courses.

As displayed in Fig. 5, most respondents attended IT courses (193; 26%) where they learned how to use modern devices, PC, notebook, and related (smart) technologies. Authors are aware of the fact the data were (among others) collected also from attendees of these courses, which explains the high score in this criterion. However, the role of family members is also important because children and grandchildren helped them substantially (children: 183; 24%; grandchildren: 78; 10%). Reflecting the social relationships of the elderly people, friends also played the role of movers in this process, as 131 respondents (17%) declared them to be those who helped them within the process of acquiring the IT competence (Fig. 5).

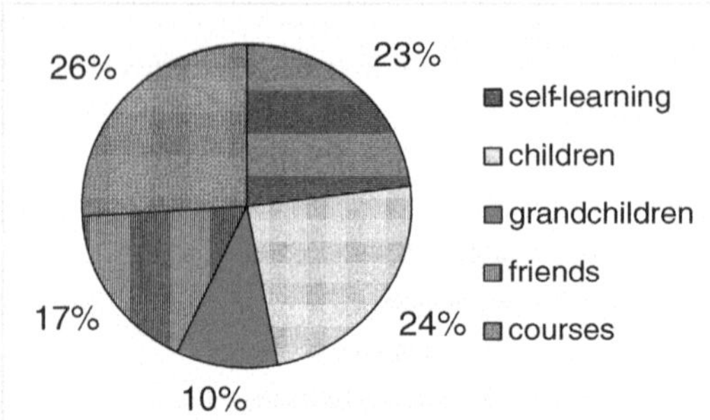

Fig. 5. Movers to the process of acquiring the IT skills

The detailed insight in the structure of movers shows that they were mostly friends younger than the respondents who supported them (83; 63%). However, friends of the same age also played an important role (42; 32%) and even older ones helped in some cases (6; 5%) (Fig. 6).

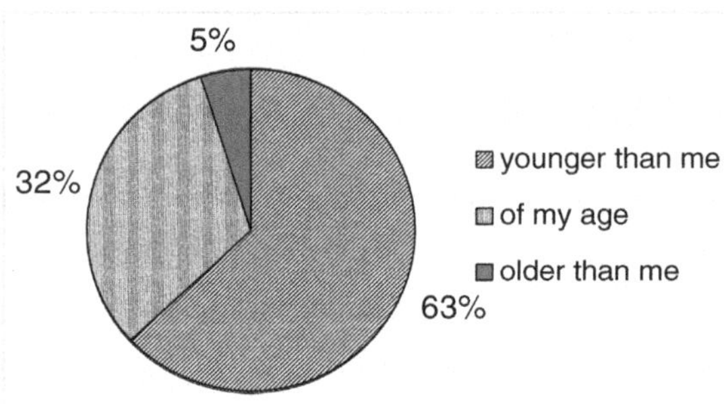

Fig. 6. Movers to the process of acquiring the IT competence: respondent's friends

As mentioned above, IT courses performed the role of strong mover towards development of IT skills. They differed from the view of learning content and the organizer. Most respondents (101; 23%) attended the Introductory courses, which focused on basic work with the computer/notebook and the Internet. Several of them continued with the Advanced courses, where they learned how to explore MS Excel, Power Point etc. (12; 3%), or they attended Complex courses, which dealt with e-mailing, skyping, participating in discussions, reading/writing blogs etc. (20 respondents; 10%). A small group of respondents attended the course dealing with digital photographs.

The IT courses were held either by the Municipality of Hradec Kralove (123 respondents; 29%; free of charge), or by the University of the Third Age (22 respondents; 5%; paid courses). Some respondent also mentioned IT courses held and paid by their last employer (42 respondents; 10%).

The length of the courses varied from several to tens of hours. Most courses took from 10 to 19 h, usually taught two hours per week – these were attended by 14% of respondents, some courses were even much longer (from 20 to 99 h; 9% of respondents).

The efforts of elderly people resulted in the fact that after successful graduation from the courses, self-learning, consultations with family members and friends, they are able to work with modern IT and smart devices. Most of them exploit them daily (53%), the others once or several times per week (7%; 4%; 11%), or less frequently (9%; 4%). This question was not answered by 12% of respondents; their answers could not be replaced by the group mean (Fig. 7).

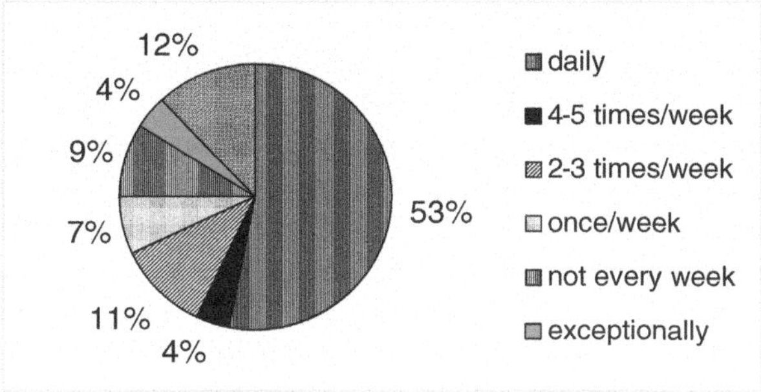

Fig. 7. Frequency of working with devices

When considering the above presented data, we can sum up all three criteria defined as preconditions for starting the blended learning in the elderly people education were fulfilled:

(1) a large scale of mobile devices is possessed by the nearly all respondents (a few exceptions were detected only (see Fig. 3), as well as
(2) the elderly people exploit the modern devices and technologies for rather a wide scale of purposes (see Fig. 4) so we can expect they will be able to do so in the field of education as well,
(3) the elderly people used various ways how to reach IT skill so as to benefit from modern technologies (see Figs. 5, 6).
(4) Last but not least, these conclusions should be also considered from the view of convenient research sample limited to respondents dwelling in Hradec Kralove region and being interested in their further education which is expressed by attending the University of the Third Age and/or IT courses. Some prognoses on lifelong education (including the period of retirement) have been made which expect that people who were used to continuing their education during their whole period of work will do so in the retirement times as well Czech Statistical Office [18]. Moreover, these people, when becoming the elderly ones, will have their IT skills developed from the previous period of work. So, they will "only" update them following the latest developments in this field.

Considering all the above mentioned we assume there is no reason why not to believe the blended learning can be successfully implemented in the elderly people education to make it easier and more interesting, as within other age groups.

5 Conclusions, Discussions

As being in contact with other people belongs to human features, a gratifying correlation was discovered within this research – under the conditions of e-society, which is often considered to be destroying face-to-face contacts and communication, the elderly people's skills in IT/smart tools and technologies are being developed with the support and help of family, friends and face-to-face courses. These results have been proved by other authors, e.g. [19–22]. Reflecting these works it can be concluded that the quality of life of elderly people, both from the view of social contacts and health state, can be supported through the ICT/smart devices and technologies.

Partial attention should be paid to the Veelken study originating nearly three decades ago and focusing on the topic of the elderly people education. The author proposed a model of retirement scientific continuing education for elderly adults [23]. He referred to the "… changing situation of "older adults" within a changing society, … and ran the research studies stating it is the universities' task to develop education models and prototypes for cooperation with elderly people within the field of applied education and socialization research for tertiary socialization (sociogeragogy) … This kind of study, as further education for elderly persons, is closely connected with teaching and research. Aspects of education and socialization reflecting the progress of the elderly persons, as well as methods of such educational work, explain this connection, including the development of a transpersonal identity" (abstract).

From numerous other studies, the one by Friebe and Schmidt-Hertha, in our opinion, should be emphasized. [24] Authors present identical opinion as we do, i.e. the adult education at higher age can play an important role, as it preserves the autonomy and encouragement of the elderly people in social participation in this period of life. They mainly highlight this fact from both the individual and social view stating it is important to enhance mainly educational activities which help developing their positive perception of themselves (reflecting their physical and mental levels). During the process of ageing the engagement and participation in further education of (the elderly) people decreases, partially because of the lack of learning opportunities, predominantly in rural areas and those with low standards of living. In later ageing the decrease in general social ability may also occur. These are selected criteria of the elderly people education process [25]. They clearly show that the support to the learning potential of the elderly people can contribute to active and participatory lives via education, particularly if they are interested in education before the process starts, been motivated and moved e.g. by their grandchildren, as mentioned above. Naturally, the pre-conditions for this process in their age cannot be identical with those of young and adult people [26]. However, it may bring some contribution.

Last but not least, The Open University continues the process of dealing with this topic and asks a crucial question whether there is enough being invested in education for older people [27]. Within the e-discussion with counterparts of this process, the higher age is recommended to be understood as a challenge, both form the learners' and teachers' part, and one of the social care assistants [28] proposes it to be systematically applied in care homes.

Not only topics from the field of health care are often dealt [29] but also foreign languages, or the highly required modern information technologies.

Acknowledgments. This work and the contribution were supported by project of Students Grant Agency. In addition, the authors thank Monika Borkovcova for her help with the survey.

References

1. Martire, L.M., Schulz, R., Mittelmark, M.B., Newsom, J.T.: Stability and change in older adults' social contact and social support: the Cardiovascular Health Study. J. Geronthology Ser. B Psychol. Sci. Soc. Sci. **54**(5), 302–311 (1999)
2. van Tilburg, T., Aartsen, M.J., Knipscheer, K.: Effect of changes in physical capacities upon personal social network in aging people. Tijdschr. Gerontol. Geriatr. **31**(5), 190–197 (2000)
3. Shaw, B.A., Krause, N., Liang, J., Bennett, J.: Tracking changes in social relations throughout late life. J. Geronthology Ser. B Psychol. Sci. Soc. Sci. **62**(2), 90–99 (2007)
4. Kunal Sinha, O., Mather, S.: The future of technology and its impact on our lives. In: WPP (2004). http://www.wpp.com/wpp/marketing/digital/the-future-of-technology/. 24 Sept 2016
5. McLuhan, M., Brdicka, B.: The influence of technology on the human mind. http://it.pedf.cuni.cz/~bobr/hmind/. 21 Sept 2016
6. European Parliament. Surveillance and censorship: the impact of technologies on human rights (2015). http://www.europarl.europa.eu/RegData/etudes/STUD/2015/549034/EXPO_STU(2015)549034_EN.pdf. 18 Jan 2017
7. Simonova, I., Poulova, P.: Level of education and previous experience in acquiring ICT/smart technologies by the elderly people. In: Accepted for the ACIIDS 2017 Conference to be held in April 2017 in Kanazawa, Japan (2017)
8. Thane, P.: The muddled history of retiring at 60 and 65. New Soc. **45**(826), 234–236 (1978)
9. Eurostat. https://www.czso.cz/csu/czso/seniori. 18 Jan 2017
10. Past and future population ageing trends in EU. http://ec.europa.eu/eurostat/statistics-explained/index.php/Population_structure_and_ageing#Past_and_future_population_ageing_trends_in_the_EU. 20 Jan 2017
11. Roebuck, J.: When does old age begin? The evolution of the English definition. J. Soc. Hist. **12**(3), 416–428 (1979)
12. Gorman, M.: Development and the rights of older people. In: Randel, J., et al. (eds.) The ageing and development report: poverty, independence and the world's older people, pp. 3–21. Earthscan Publications Ltd., London (1999)
13. Ivankina, L.I., Trubchenko, T.G., Krukovac, E.M., Shaidullina, A.R., Shaftelskaya, N.V., Chernyak, V.K.: The use of information and communication technologies by elderly people. Eur. Proc. Soc. Behav. Sci. **19**, 235–242 (2017)
14. Marcelino, I., Laza, R., Fdez-Riverola, F., Pereira, A.: Removing barriers to promote social computing among senior population. Int. J. Distrib. Sensor Netw. **36**(1), 1–13 (2015)
15. Chen, Y.R.R., Schulz, P.J.: The effect of information communication technology interventions on reducing social isolation in the elderly: a systematic review. J. Med. Internet Res. **18**(1), e18 (2016)
16. Saracchini, R., Catalina, C., Bordoni, L.: Augmented reality assistive technology for the elderly. Comunicar **45**, 65–73 (2015)
17. Borrelli, G., et al.: Care@Home: methodology, goals and project experimentation activities. Andò, B., Siciliano, P., Marletta, V., Monteriù, A. (eds.) Ambient Assist. Living: Italian Forum 2015, pp. 307–3016 (2014)

18. Czech Statistical Office, Seniors. https://www.czso.cz/csu/czso/seniori. 16 Jan 2017
19. Eneanya, N.D., Winter, M., Cabral, H., Waite, K., Henault, L., Bickmore, T., Hanchate, A., Wolf, M., Paasche-Orlow, M.K.: Health literacy and education as mediators of ratial disparities in patient activation within an elderly patient cohort. J. Health Care Poor Undeserved **27**(3), 1427–1440 (2016)
20. Liyanagunawardena, T.R., Williams, S.A.: Elderly learners and massive open online courses: a review. Interact. J. Med. Res. **5**(1), 41–50 (2016)
21. Modad, R.G.H., Encinas, K.L.P., Arriaga, L.G.L.: Permanent education for older adult. In: Gomez Chova, L., Lopez Martinez, A., Candel Torres, I. (eds.) EDULEARN15: 7th International Conference on Education and New Learning Technologies. EDULEARN Proceedings 2015, pp. 5866–5871 (2015)
22. Grigoryeva, I., Dmitrieva, A., Vdovenko, T.: Elderly in Russia: between medicine, consumption and life-long education. In: SGEM 2015, Book 1: Psychology and Psychiatry, Sociology and Healthcare, Education Conference Proceedings, vol. 1, pp. 471–478 (2015)
23. Bujnowska-Fedak, M.M., Pigorowicz, I.: Support for e-health services among elderly primary care patients. Telemedicine e-health **20**(8), 696–704 (2014)
24. Veelken, L.: Senior studies–a model of retirement scientific continuing education for elderly adults. Zeitschrift fur Gerontologie **21**(4), 198–205 (1988)
25. Friebe, J., Schmidt-Hertha, B.: Activities and barriers to education for elderly people. J. Contemp. Educ. Stud. **1**, 10–26 (2013)
26. Baltes, P.B.: The aging mind: potential and limits. Gerontologist **33**(5), 580–594 (1993)
27. Findsen, B., Formosa, M.: Lifelong Learning in later Life. A Handbook on Older Adult Learning. Sense Publishers, Rotterdam (2011)
28. Stevankova, E.: Discussion. http://www.open.edu/openlearn/health-sports-psychology/health/health-studies/education-older-people. 11 July 2014
29. Kececi, A., Bulduk, S.: Health education for the elderly. Geriatrics, pp. 153–178

Promoting Citizen's Learning Experience in Smart Cities

Ronghuai Huang(✉), Rongxia Zhuang, and Junfeng Yang

Smart Learning Institute, Beijing Normal University, Beijing, China
{Huangrh,zhuangrx}@bnu.edu.cn, yjf@hznu.edu.cn

Abstract. Lots of research has been done on smart cities, however, only few studies can be found on smart cities from the educational perspective. This paper will discuss the framework of building smart city from educational perspective to identify the importance of promoting smart learning in smart cities. Then the characters of smart learning are elaborated, and the difference of traditional classroom learning, digital learning and smart learning are analyzed. After that, the paper analyzes the typical learning environments in cities: school, family, community, workplace, and museum. Based on the analysis, we develop indicators to evaluate learning environments in smart cities, which was used to evaluate the learning environments in the selected 68 cities in China.

Keywords: Smart learning environments · Smart cities · Digital learning · Smart learning

1 Framework for Smart Cities from Educational Perspective

Smart cities are nowadays widespread all over the world to tackle urban sustainability issues. In the initial stage, both academic research and the practice of the smart city focused on how to utilize information technology to improve economic and political efficiency (Röller and Waverman 2001). With the development of smart city, the focus was no longer limited to the hardware facilities, but more attention was paid to the availability and quality of knowledge communication, as well as to social infrastructure (human and social capital).

Nam, T. and Pardo (2011) identified and clarified the key dimensions of smart cities, and re-categorized them into three categories of core factors: technology (infrastructures of hardware and software), people (creativity, diversity, and education), and institution (governance and policy). The most often cited dimensions of smart city appeared in the report of "Smart Cities-Ranking of European Medium-Sized Cities" by Vienna University of Technology, University of Ljubljana, and Delft University of Technology, in which Giffinger (2007) identified the six characteristics as a roof for the further elaboration of smart cities: smart economy, smart people, smart governance, smart mobility, smart environment, smart living.

The new citizens will have vital roles in building smart cities to promote all the innovations, who should be hyper connected, creative, entrepreneurs, and also actively participate in the cities' activities and decisions (Ljiljana and Adam 2015). With smart city technologies emerging and gradually contributing to a more sustainable and green

S.K.S. Cheung et al. (Eds.): ICBL 2017, LNCS 10309, pp. 15–25, 2017.
DOI: 10.1007/978-3-319-59360-9_2

future, it is becoming apparent that creative skills to deal with these innovations in smart city must be taught to upcoming generations (Wolff et al. 2015). Education should become a vital part of the future of smart cities (Hall et al. 2000), and learning dimension is becoming more central within smart city discussions. However, they are often ignored in the construction of smart learning.

From educational perspective, we proposed a framework of smart city, as shown in Fig. 1. On the macro level, the construction of smart cities covers three aspects: The first one is smart economy, which involves urban enterprise creativity, the "internet +" economic form and its employment entrepreneurship atmosphere. The second aspect refers to smart environment which covers the planning of urban buildings, green energy and green city. The third aspect relates to smart governance (management) which mainly involves urban service policies, openness and transparency of data, as well as the popularization of e-government. In another words, the smart features of a city could be represented by "the vitality for urban innovation" which includes the three characteristics of smart economy, smart environment and smart governance.

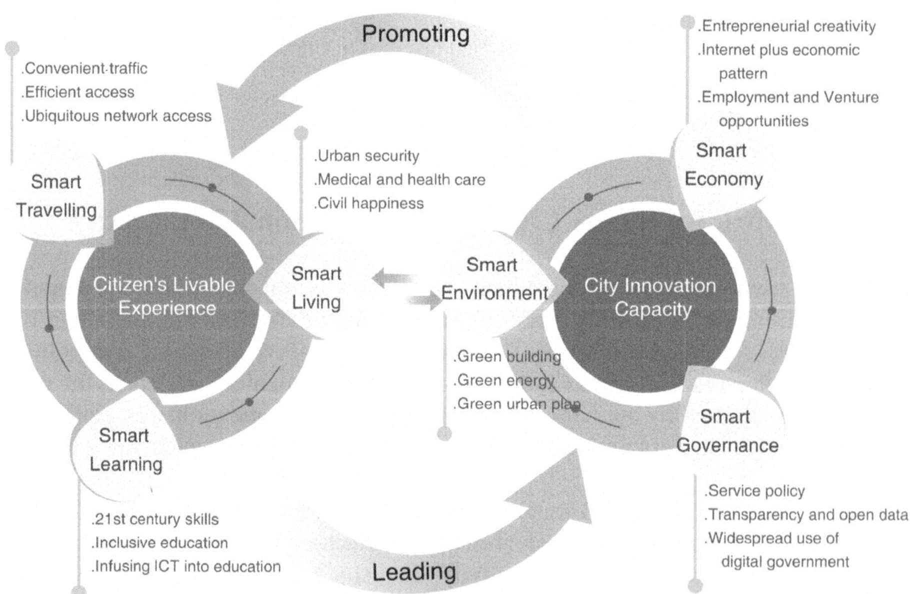

Fig. 1. Dual-core framework of smart city

On the micro level, the construction of smart cities could also be considered in three aspects. The first one is smart mobility (travelling) which aims at providing the citizens with convenient transport facilities and efficient, ubiquitous access to internet. The second aspect includes smart living, which refers to people's sense of security of urban life, medical and health conditions, and the citizen's sense of happiness. The third aspect refers to smart people (learning), that should provide skills that the citizens should master in the 21st century. This can be achieved by accepting inclusive and technology integrated education.

Therefore, smart city construction mainly consists of city-oriented macro level construction and citizen-oriented micro-level construction. The smart features that citizens can feel is "citizens' livable experiences" which cover smart travelling, smart living and smart learning. The concept of "smart citizens" in the context of "smart city" ultimately refers to smart learning.

It could be indicated from the above analysis that the mean of smart cities construction is diversified with many aspects centering on the two cores: "Citizen's livable experiences" from the micro-level and "City Innovation Capacity" from macro-level. On the left of Fig. 1, the core of citizen's living experience includes smart travelling, smart learning, and smart living which together provide bountiful living experience for citizen. Smart learning takes 21st century skills, inclusive education, infusing ICT into education, etc. into consideration; smart living takes urban security, medical and health care, civil happiness, etc. into consideration; smart travelling takes convenient traffic, efficient access, ubiquitous network access, etc. into consideration. On the right of Fig. 1, city innovation capacity includes smart environment, smart economy and smart governance which together provide the vitality of innovation. Smart environment takes green building, green energy, green urban plan, etc. into consideration; smart governance takes service policy, transparency and open data, widespread use of digital government etc. into consideration; smart economy takes entrepreneurial creativity, internet + economic pattern, employment and venture opportunities, etc. into consideration.

2 Characteristics of Smart Learning

The two cores of smart cities construction serve as the basic drive to promote a city's development, the main aim of which is to improve a city's benign operation and sustainable development. Advocating "smart learning" plays a cultural leading role for stimulating vitality for urban innovation and it also provides scientific support for citizens' livable experiences. In fact, it is the ultimate target of smart city construction to let humans have better urban living environments. The two cores that represent features of a smart city indicate that smart learning is the fundamental driving force to enhance citizens' wisdom and the basic solution to improve people's livable experiences. Therefore, it is necessary to understand the character of smart learning.

In smart learning, a learner can learn at anytime, anywhere, in any way and at any pace, which is short for "4A". The learning environment is capable of supporting "Easy Learning", "Engaged Learning" and "Effective Learning" (Huang 2012), which is short for "3E". In such smart learning environment, the easy, engaged, and effective learning (3E) at anytime, anywhere, in any way and at any pace (4A) could be regarded as smart learning. The character of smart learning was shown in Fig. 2, which is short for DEEE@4A with D stands for diverse.

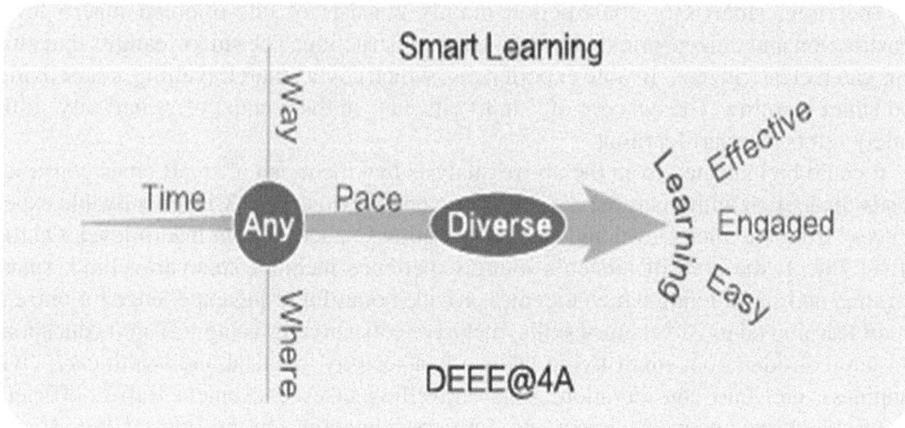

Fig. 2. Characteristics of smart learning

Table 1. Comparison of traditional classroom learning, digital learning and smart learning

	Traditional classroom learning	Digital learning	Smart learning
Learning result and forms	Precision processing of knowledge, In unified forms	Knowledge interconnectivity, in diverse forms	Knowledge interconnectivity, self-adjustment
Learning task	Homogenization	Diversity	Personalization, differentiation
Learning method	Listening and teaching based	Blended learning (listening and teaching + online learning)	Seamless learning
Teaching strategy	Teaching based, but complemented with asking questions and discussion	Application of multiple strategies	Personalized learning instruction
Learning support	Face-to-face Q&A and tutoring	Online communication and support	Multi-channel communication and intelligent system support
Learning assessment	Standardized tests and exams	Online tests at anytime	Adaptable tests
Learning community and ways of participation	Groups and class, School arrangement	Virtual community oriented towards themes, Apply for participating	Virtual community oriented towards themes, Automatic matching and recommendation
Learning space	Fixed physical space	Physical and virtual space	Intelligent learning space
Learning pace and time sequence	Relatively unified	Relatively flexible	Arbitrary pace
Learning goal	Relatively unified	Diverse goals	Personalized goal
Learning resources and source	Textbooks and tutorial materials in hard copies, arranged by teachers	E-textbooks and network resources, recommended by teachers	Diverse digital resources free choice and intelligent recommendation
Learning media	Paper media only	Paper media, internet media	Across terminals, rich media

The differences of smart learning, traditional classroom learning, and digital learning are shown in Table 1. Traditional classroom learning refers to learning in traditional classroom environments with chalks and blackboard as teaching aids; digital learning refers to on-line learning environment or classrooms equipped with multiple technologies; smart learning is learning with the character of DEEE@4A in smart learning environments.

Face to face learning in traditional classrooms mainly involves refined knowledge learning processes which stress unified standards, unified learning paces and unified examinations. The learning paths that students take are linear and of the same nature, which results in monotonous, relatively rigid learning methods which further impedes the cultivation of creative capabilities among students. Learning in smart environments emphasizes the interconnection between knowledge nodes and aims to build a variously-typed, diversified, pluralistically-evaluated teaching and learning ecology. In such a learning method, learners are provided with diversified learning paths such as the linear type, point to surface type or whole to part type paths (Huang 2014).

Smart learning environments provide learners with room for deep-level communication. It can expand innovation spaces, enrich the depth and breadth of learner's knowledge structures, and create diversified supporting environments for them. The new model of instruction based on smart learning environments will incline towards the "4A" model under which smart learning pays more attention to students' diversities and individual variations. This makes it possible to carry out the educational concept of "people first".

Smart learning has three basic characteristics. First is Easy Learning, that is the prerequisite for engaged learning; smart instruction makes the learning process become easy and fun. Second, Engaged Learning, is the precondition for effective learning; only through engaged learning that students are able to perform good communication and cooperation with their fellow students and achieve designed learning objectives. Third, Effective Learning, is the target of smart learning, which means smart learning shall bring the desired learning results effectively.

3 Typical Learning Environments in Smart Cities

With the advancement of learning society, citizens could learn life-wide, and life-wide learning includes not just learning in formal contexts, but also learning in different contexts such as in the home, school, work, community and others (Desjardins 2003; Cambridge 2008). Therefore, smart learning could happen in school, family, community, workplace, museum and others. The following section will analyze these typical learning environments in smart cities.

School Learning Environment

During the whole life, school education gives people an overall, systematic and in-depth influence, and this period is the important process for learning and self-shaping of people (Wang 2007), and school learning environment is the primary tools and learning environment for people's socialization. Specially, a classroom learning environment is a combination of social and physical qualities that create the classroom experience. There are several instruments used in prior research to assess perceptions of classroom learning environment. The implication from prior research is that student outcomes might be related to perceptions of classroom learning environment; in other words, student's achievement might be improved by creating better classroom learning environment (Fraser 1986; Madu 2010; Tas 2016). In addition, with integrating technology into education, growing number of researchers focus on smart classroom learning environment and new forms classroom learning environment like flipped CLE in recent years (Butzler 2014; Jena 2013).

Family Learning Environment

The family, as the first group of individuals, provides the most basic conditions for people's socialization (Wang 2007), is the basic field of people's social life. The family learning environment is also the basic learning environment for people. Family learning environment consists of a series of characteristics, including language stimulation, learning materials available at home, such as books and computers, as well as parenting behaviors, such as engaging children in learning activities and providing children with learning experiences (Bradley and Caldwell 1995). Present researches pay more attention to the influence of family learning environment to children in cognitive abilities, learning performances and socio-emotional development (Melhuish et al. 2008; Foster 2005).

Community Learning Environment

Community is the most basic social living base for majority social members, with multiple functions including politics, economy, culture and social management (Zhou 2002). Communities play important roles on supporting learning and teaching that occur outside of schools, and the cultural education activities in communities have significant influence on the teenagers, the adults and the elders. Community learning occurs when the knowledge created in the integrative "community process" is fed-forward and embedded at the level of community structure (Morse 2004). Moreover, the development of the Internet induces greater living space to the community with emerging a lot of online learning community.

Workplace Learning Environment

The development of work tasks, the promotion of performance, the workplace training and so on, have an important role in promoting the individual development of in-service staffs, and workplace learning environment is one of the important fields for adult learning activities. Watkins and Marsick (1993) suggested that key components of the workplace environment include creating continuous learning opportunities, promoting equity and dialogue, supporting individuals in maintaining an openness towards new experiences, reflection, and translating the learning into practice, encouraging team learning and collaboration, empowering people towards a collective vision and connecting the organization to its environment. Zhao and Zhu (2015) considered that relying on new technology has very important value to workplace learning due to eliminating the conflict between working time and learning time. It benefits employees proceed informal learning and form the good habit of learning anytime and anywhere.

Museum Learning Environment
In public places, people can conduct multiple social activities such as working, learning, culture, social communication, entertainment, sports, rest and traveling, and public place learning environment is the important constituting part of learning environments for citizens; it is a window reflecting the social material conditions and spirit civilization of a country or a nation. In this study, museum learning environment is represented the learning environment in public places. We use "museum" as a generic term that includes all kinds of science museums, historical museum, planetarium, and other interpretative centers for science learning. Museums are an integral part of the broader learning and provide education to the public that called 'museum learning', playing a key role in 'lifelong learning' and educational leisure. Museum learning is an important research topic in the field of informal learning. Currently, research on technology-assisted museum learning focuses on developing a learner-centered method and applying technology to assist learners in exploring and learning in a museum (Wishart and Triggs 2010; Hou et al. 2014).

4 Evaluating Learning Environments in Smart Cities

The above five typical learning environments provide the atmosphere for learning in a city, which is vital for cultivating talents with creative skills to deal with all the innovations in smart cities. Citizen's learning experience, livable experience and city innovation development, are all connected with these learning environments. Therefore, it is important to understand the typical learning environments in smart cities, that is why we create the following indicators to evaluate these learning environments.

For school learning environment, it is normally evaluated from these aspects: the proportion of the number of students and the number of computers, the proportion of the number of teachers and the number of computers, network coverage, network equipment, multimedia classrooms, and so on (Liu et al. 2014). In this research, we chose computer resource allocation in primary and middle schools, multimedia classrooms and digital resource of primary and middle schools as sub-level indicators for the school learning environment indicator (Table 2).

For family learning environment, the Home Observation of the Measurement of the Environment (59 items version) is formed of eight subscales: (1) Emotional and Verbal Responsivity of Caregiver; (2) Encouragement of Maturity; (3) Emotional Climate of the Home; (4) Growth-Fostering Materials and Experiences; (5) Provision for Active Stimulation; (6) Family Participation in Developmentally Stimulating Experiences; (7) Paternal Involvement with Child; and (8) Aspects of the Physical Environment (Bradley et al. 1988). As reference, we chose family digital devices, family book possession and satisfaction with family learning environment as sub-level indicators for the home learning environment indicator.

Based on the research for the evaluation method of the effect of learning community construction, we can evaluate the effectiveness of the learning community construction from the organizational management, carrier design, learning activities, and the achievement of the construction. Thus, utilization of learning places in community, utilization of community's information platform, participation of learning activities in community, and development of community education were chosen as sub-level indicators for the community learning environment indicator.

Table 2. Indicators for the five typical learning environments in smart cities

Indicator	Sub-level indicators
1 School learning environment indicator	1.1 Indicator of computer resource allocation in primary and middle schools
	1.2 Indicator of multimedia classrooms
	1.3 Indicator of digital resource of primary and middle schools
2 Family learning environment indicator	2.1 Indicator of family digital devices
	2.2 Indicator of family book possession
	2.3 Indicator of satisfaction with family learning environment
3 Community learning environment indicator	3.1 Indicator of utilization of learning places in community
	3.2 Indicator of utilization of community's information platform
	3.3 Indicator of participation of learning activities in community
	3.4 Indicator of development of community education
4 Workplace learning environment indicator	4.1 Indicator of Internet environment in workplace
	4.2 Indicator of learning engagement in workplace
	4.3 Indicator of online learning in workplace
5 Museum learning environment indicator	5.1 Indicator of the number of museums
	5.2 Indicator of utilization of the museum for learning
	5.3 Indicator of informationization in museum

On the basis of a review of the literature, Clarke pointed out the factors which influence workplace environment for learning outcomes: (1) supportive learning and development infrastructure; (2) particular types of learning opportunities; (3) empowerment and effective communication; (4) support for reflection and job challenge; and (5) support for learning transfer (Clarke 2005). We chose Internet environment in workplace, learning engagement in workplace, and online learning in workplace as sub-level indicators for workplace learning environment.

Referring to the characteristics of learning environment proposed by Chuang (2005) and Tsai (2008), Tsai et al. (2012) have constructed the evaluation structure of characteristics of learning environment in digital venues, which was composed of three dimensions: study subject, situation, and digital exhibits. Therefore, we chose the number of museums, utilization of the museum for learning, and infomationization in museum as sub-level indicators for museum learning environment indicator.

According to the indicators, a survey was conducted to evaluate typical learning environments in cities. 68 cities in China were assessed, including Beijing, Shanghai, Tianjin, Chongqing, Guangzhou, and so on. Data are collected from China Statistical Yearbook, China City Statistical Yearbook, and statistical yearbooks related to the 68 cities. The results were presented in Table 3, in which the ranking of the 68 cities was listed according to the indicators of learning environments.

Table 3. Ranking of cities according to the learning environments indicators (Top 10 cities were listed).

Cities	Indicators for typical learning environments		School learning environment indicator	Family learning environment indicator	Community learning environment indicator	Workplace learning environment indicator	Museum learning environment indicator
	Rank	Score	Score	Score	Score	Score	Score
Shanghai	1	0.8547	0.9292	0.8340	0.7175	0.8880	0.9047
Yichang	2	0.7892	0.5597	0.9807	0.7500	0.9159	0.7396
Beijing	3	0.7733	0.7869	0.7944	0.7286	0.6890	0.8676
Qingdao	4	0.7720	0.4227	0.9615	0.8551	0.9560	0.6650
Dalian	5	0.7550	0.6587	0.8353	0.8312	0.8343	0.6156
Wuhan	6	0.7532	0.4599	0.9029	0.9140	0.7782	0.7112
Jinan	7	0.7378	0.5648	0.9149	0.7082	0.8494	0.6519
Hangzhou	8	0.7369	0.5911	0.8721	0.7578	0.7761	0.6875
Shenzhen	9	0.7362	0.7084	0.7468	0.6740	0.7034	0.8482
Wulumuqi	10	0.7289	0.7200	0.9602	0.6083	0.7431	0.6126

The results showed that there were differences on the development levels of five typical learning environments in different cities. Few differences existed in the 68 Chinese cities in the family learning environment and workplace learning environment. Huge differences existed in school learning environment. The results indicated that there was relatively large space for improvement in learning environment construction in some cities.

The top ten cities include 2 municipalities directly under the Central Government, 3 cities enjoying the provincial-level status in the state economic plan, 4 provincial capitals and 1 prefecture-level city (Yichang ranks as the second.). The indicator of home learning environment and working place learning environment are both higher than 0.9 in Yichang, which is the only prefecture-level city. Although the development of smart learning environments in cities is connected to some objective factors (e.g., economic level, city size, areal of distribution, etc.), some prefecture-level cities are at the forefront of the development as they provide their citizens with good smart learning experiences.

The indicators of learning environments of cities can reflect the status of the construction of a learning society, which also can reflect the development level of the construction of smart cities. The construction of a city's learning environments is based on the city's innovative capacity, with the goal is to improve the citizens' smart learning experiences.

The construction of learning environments in smart cities needs top-level design and support by the government. In addition, there is a need for participation of multiple parties including enterprises and a social commitment to gradually build a sound long-term environments to support smart learning.

The aim of learning environments in smart cities is to support smart learning. Smart learning should become an important part of the construction of smart city. Smart learning provides strong support for citizens' life-long learning, which is also the key feature of self-evolution of the urban system. Development of smart learning can improve the citizens' livable experiences, enhance the city's innovative capacity, and present the intelligence quality of a city.

Acknowledgments. This research work is supported by the 2016 National Natural Science Fund Youth Project: Blended synchronous cyber classroom supporting educational balanced development (No. 71603067).

References

Bradley, R.H., Caldwell, B.M.: Caregiving and the regulation of child growth and development: Describing proximal aspects of caregiving systems. Dev. Rev. **15**(1), 38–85 (1995)

Bradley, R.H., Caldwell, B.M., Rock, S.L., Hamrick, H.M., Harris, P.: Home observation for measurement of the environment: development of a home inventory for use with families having children 6 to 10 years old. Contemp. Educ. Psychol. **13**(1), 58–71 (1988)

Butzler, K.B.: The effects of motivation on achievement and satisfaction in a flipped classroom learning environment. Dissertations & Theses – Gradworks (2014)

Cambridge, D.: Audience, integrity, and the living document: eFolio Minnesota and lifelong and lifewide learning with ePortfolios. Comput. Educ. **51**(3), 1227–1246 (2008)

Chuang, S.C., Tsai, C.C.: Preferences toward the constructivist Internet-based learning environments among high school students in Taiwan. Comput. Hum. Behav. **21**(2), 255–272 (2005)

Clarke, N.: Workplace Learning Environment and its Relationship with Learning Outcomes in Healthcare Organizations. Hum. Resour. Dev. Int. **8**(2), 185–205 (2005)

Desjardins, R.: Determinants of literacy proficiency: a lifelong-lifewide learning perspective. Int. J. Educ. Res. **39**(3), 205–245 (2003)

Foster, M.A., Lambert, R., Abbott-Shimm, M., McCarty, F., Franze, S.: A model of home learning environment and social risk factors in relation to children's emergent literacy and social outcomes. Early Child. Res. Q. **20**(1), 13–36 (2005)

Fraser, B.J.: Classroom Environment. Groom Helm, London (1986)

Giffinger, R.: Smart cities-Ranking of European medium-sized cities (2007). http://linkinghub.elsevier.com/retrieve/pii/S026427519800050X

Hall, R.E., Braverman, J., Taylor, J., Todosow, H.: The vision of a smart city. In: 2nd International Life Extension Technology Workshop, Paris, p. 28 (2000)

Hou, H.T., Wu, S.Y., Lin, P.C., Sung, Y.T., Lin, J.W., Chang, K.E.: A blended mobile learning environment for museum learning. Educ. Technol. Soc. **17**(2), 207–218 (2014)

Huang, R.: Three realms of smart education: smart learning environment, ICT teaching model and modern educational system. Mod. Distance Educ. Res. **6**, 3–10 (2014)

Huang, R., Yang, J., Hu, Y.: From digital to smart: the evolution and trends of learning environment. Open Educ. Res. **1**, 75–84 (2012)

Jena, P.C.: Effect of smart classroom learning environment on academic achievement of rural high achievers and low achievers in science. Int. Lett. Soc. Humanistic Sci. **03**, 1–9 (2013)

Ljiljana, M., Adam, S.: Building a gamified system for capturing MOOC related data: smart city learning community as its most precious source of intangible cultural heritage. In: 2015 International Conference on Culture and Computing (Culture Computing), pp. 175–182 (2015)

Liu, X., Wang, Y., Wang, X., Ren, G., Jiao, J.: Research on the development strategy of ICT infrastructure in education in the process of educational informatization. J. Distance Educ. **2**, 13–24 (2014)

Madu, N.E.: Associations between teachers¢ interpersonal behaviour, classroom learning environment and students¢ outcomes. Ph.D. Curtin University of Technology, Science and Mathematics Education Centre (2010)

Melhuish, E., Belsky, J., Leyland, A.H., Barnes, J., NESS Reasearch Team: Effects of fully-established sure start local programmes on 3-year-old children and their families living in England: a quasi-experimental observational study. Lancet **372**(1), 1641–1647 (2008)

Morse, R.S.: Community learning: Process, structure, and renewal. Doctoral dissertation, Virginia Tech (2004)

Nam, T., Pardo, T.A.: Conceptualizing smart city with dimensions of technology, people, and institutions. In: Proceedings of the 12th Annual International Digital Government Research Conference: Digital Government Innovation in Challenging Times, pp. 282–291 2011. doi: 10.1145/2037556.2037602

Röller, L.H., Waverman, L.: Telecommunications infrastructure and economic development: a simultaneous approach. Am. Econ. Rev. **91**, 909–923 (2001)

Tas, Y.: The contribution of perceived classroom learning environment and motivation to student engagement in science. Eur. J. Psychol. Educ. **31**, 1–21 (2016)

Wang, R.: Huamn Behavior and Social Envirionment, 2nd edn. East China University of Science and Technology Press, Shanghai (2007)

Watkins, K.E., Marsick, V.J.: In Action: Creating the Learning Organization. American Society for Training and Development, Alexandria (1993)

Wishart, J., Triggs, P.: MuseumScouts: exploring how schools, museums and interactive technologies can work together to support learning. Comput. Educ. **54**, 669–678 (2010)

Wolff, A., Kortuem, G., Cavero, J.: Towards smart city education. In: 2015 Sustainable Internet and ICT for Sustainability, SustainIT 2015 (2015). doi:10.1109/SustainIT.2015.7101381

Tsai, C.C.: The preferences toward constructivist Internet-based learning environments among university students in Taiwan. Comput. Hum. Behav. **24**(1), 16–31 (2008)

Tsai, P.S., Tsai, C.C., Hwang, G.J.: Developing a survey for assessing preferences in constructivist context-aware ubiquitous learning environments. J. Comput. Assist. Learn. **28**(3), 250–264 (2012)

Zhao, M., Zhu, S.: The problem domain and the development tendency of practice in workplace learning. J. Soochow Univ. Educ. Sci. Edit. **3**(4), 53–60 (2015)

Zhou, P.: Social Work of Community. Social Sciences Academic Press, Beijing (2002)

International Collaborative Project-Based Learning: How Did US and Japanese Students Learn Together at a Distance When Supported by ICT?

Kenichi Kubota(✉)

Kansai University, 2-1-1 Ryozenji-cho, Takatsuki, Osaka 569-1095, Japan
kubota@kansai-u.ac.jp

Abstract. Technological advancement, for example Web 2.0, has supported new learning paradigms such as blended, distance, collaborative, and cross-cultural learning. However, instructional methods in Japanese universities are still traditional. ICT, as a collaborative media incorporated into learning activities, is a possible direction for 21st century education. The author introduces two cases of distance collaborative learning between University of Hawaii campuses in Honolulu, USA and Kansai University, Osaka, Japan. The first case is a year-long program for undergraduate students studying environmental science. Starting with video conferencing between US and Japan, the students became acquainted with each other. Then, Japanese students visited Hawaii and worked together to investigate invasive algae along the seashore. Next, US students came to Japan to study a "*Satoyama*" ecosystem. This program consisted of both distance and face-to-face collaboration to prepare reports and produce video products. The second case is a semester-long graduate course. Japanese and US students collaboratively produced short video programs while working in teams at a distance. Teams from both countries encountered difficulties, but overcame them at the end of the program. Overall, most students were satisfied with their collaborative experiences.

Keywords: Project-based learning · Web 2.0 · Environmental science · Invasive species · International collaboration

1 Introduction

Technological development and globalization have changed societies from industrial into knowledge-based. While learners were required knowledge and skills to follow manuals in an industrial society, leaners in today's knowledge-based society need broader knowledge, self-regulated skills, communication skills, and improvisation to solve unexpected problems. OECD (2000) defined these new abilities as "key competencies" using three categories: (1) Use tools interactively. (2) Interact in heterogeneous groups. (3) Act autonomously (Soparat et al. 2015). The author insists that International Collaborative Project-Based Learning (ICPBL) is better learning strategies to develop the key competencies.

S.K.S. Cheung et al. (Eds.): ICBL 2017, LNCS 10309, pp. 26–37, 2017.
DOI: 10.1007/978-3-319-59360-9_3

In this paper, the author introduces two cases of ICPBL that describes how students learn together in heterogeneous groups to acquire key competencies through collaborative activities. The ICPBL case 1 is a yearlong undergraduate program named "Kai Yama Program," which is a collaboration between University of Hawaii, Kapi'olani Community College (KCC) and Faculty of Informatics, Kansai University (KU). "Kai" is named after the native Hawaiian word for ocean, and "Yama" is named after the Japanese word for mountain. Both US and Japanese students study natural and social environments of the sea and mountain collaboratively in face-to-face situations and at a distance through the Internet.

The ICPBL case 2 is a semester course for graduate students. In this course, US graduate students in a course of the College of Education, University of Hawaii, Honolulu, USA, and Japanese graduate students of Faculty of Informatics, Kansai University, Osaka, Japan collaboratively produce video programs. It is named the "Collaborative team Video Project (CVP)." This collaboration has no direct face-to-face sessions. Instead, US and Japanese students meet synchronously through video conferencing and communicate using SNS asynchronously. They discuss how to develop video scripts collaboratively, shoot video for each site, and combine the videos into one video product.

Traditional lecture type education is still pervasive at most universities today in Japan. However, if students were to develop key competencies that are required in the 21st century, university education needs to incorporate active learning activities. ICPBL is one example where students can strengthen key competencies. Collaborative online technologies will play an important role in this context. In order to analyze the two cases of ICPBL, the author discusses the strengths and weaknesses of each case.

2 Key Competencies Through PBL with ICT

2.1 Project-Based Learning (PBL) with ICT

Project-based learning (PBL) is designed to engage students to investigate authentic problems in real-life situations. PBL allows student learners to investigate more about a topic by constructing a meaningful artifact (Harris and Katz 2001). PBL is based on constructivism, which explains that students can construct their own knowledge from the current knowledge through interactions with their environment (Piaget 1969; Perkins 1991).

PBL is an effective way for students to develop and integrate skills during small group collaboration because they are learning while they are using their knowledge. The more they work collaboratively, the more they are inspired to understand in-depth what they are learning (Bautista and Escofet 2009; Richards 2005).

Technological advancements, for example video conferencing and SNS, can support students collaboratively in face-to-face and in distance situations. Web learning tools can be accessed by everybody today. Learners can use and share information. These days, web learning tools are not distinguished from education anymore. Learners should have a chance to learn at an age that is not too different from adults as in the past (Jonassen et al. 2003; Richards 2005). Focusing on the understanding of project-based learning, there are still different understandings among teachers. Many teachers are familiar with designing a science project. To do a science project, a student must begin with questions and progress through the scientific method for seeking answers that might or might not be artifacts or products in the end. Project-based learning is focused on the "products" as the target.

2.2 Project-Based Learning (PBL) with ICT

The world has been changing rapidly. Globalizations and modernization are creating an increasingly diverse and interconnected world. In order to make themselves successful, students may need to adjust to changing technologies and make sense of large amounts of available information. Students need to acquire key competencies to accomplish goals.

The OECD report classified key competencies in three broad categories. First, students need to be able to use a wide range of tools for interacting effectively with the environment. Tools refer to both physical and socio-cultural ones. The physical tools include the Internet, computers, and software. Students handle the physical tools interactively to process information. The socio-cultural tools include language, symbols and texts. Students make sense of and become competent in the word interacting with socio-cultural tools. Second, students need to engage with others. Since they will encounter people from a range of backgrounds, it is important that they are able to interact in heterogeneous groups. Third, individuals need to be able to take responsibility for managing their own lives, situate their lives in the broader social context and act autonomously.

2.3 Place-Based Learning

In ICPBL case 1, students learn environmental issues. They have to visit sites they study in the sea and on the mountain through their own experiences. They also meet people working at these sites to learn how those people interact with environment. Place-Based Learning is a part of ICPBL in the case 1. Students, teachers, and adults in the community work together to investigate the problems in the community (Sobel 2005). With Place-Based Learning, students can learn more about the natural world in which they live.

A Place-Based curriculum fundamentally changes the traditional curriculum framework. The PBL framework shifts the educational system from an outdated industrial input-output linear model to a more dynamic interdisciplinary approach of the 21st century digital age based on action research. In PBL, the goal is to create opportunities for students to think collaboratively, collect, analyze, synthesize, and critique data, address community opportunities and concerns, and create knowledge and innovative ideas. Another major goal of PBL is enhancing communication skills. In PBL students develop communication skills by reporting their research findings through publications and presentations to their peers and the community. PBL creates an environment that fosters genuine relationships not only between teachers and students, but also between the community and students (Lawson et al. 2016).

Place-based learning includes the following elements:

- Interdisciplinary Study: Students learn to pull together ideas and concepts from many subject areas, which enables them to tackle real-world issues in all their complexity.
- Collaborative Learning: Students develop knowledge and skills through shared learning, rather than learning in isolation and in competition with others.
- Learning Across Significant Differences: Students learn to recognize, respect and bridge differences, which are critical skills in an increasingly diverse world.
- Personal Engagement: Students develop their capacities to judge, speak and act on the basis of their own reasoned beliefs.
- Linking Theory with Practical Applications: Students understand abstract theories by applying them to projects and activities and by putting them into practice in real-world situations. (Fly 2010, p. 3).

Recently, educators have valued outcomes from collaborative learning activities because it provides authentic tasks that lead to deeper learning, and higher levels of cognition. Reeves et al. (2004) describe learning from collaboration on authentic problems as having outcomes "of the highest order, including improved problem-solving abilities, enhanced communication skills, continuing intellectual curiosity and robust mental models of complex processes inherent to the performance contexts in which their new learning will be applied."

Authentic learning through collaboration has components of using knowledge in real life, supporting collaborative construction of knowledge, promoting reflection to enable the formation of abstraction, articulating ideas to enable the explicit formation of knowledge and assessing the learning of tasks (Reeves et al. 2002).

3 Research Design and Methods

Data have been collected through participant observation, reflection records, and students' field notes. Based on the grounded theory (Charmaz 2014), the authors coded the texts. The purpose of this study is to identify the effectiveness of the ICPBL programs in order to improve the programs for next implementation. Based on Kirkpatrick's evaluation model (Kirkpatrick and Kirkpatrick 2016), the author obtained the Level 1 evaluation of student feedback about the program.

4 Case 1: Kai Yama Program

4.1 Overview

The Kai Yama Program was envisioned as a true educational, cultural, and intellectual exchange that involved two site visits, Kansai university (KU) students going to Hawaii and Kapi'olani Community College (KCC) students coming to Kansai, Japan. Students and faculty would be engaged in a yearlong conversation using collaborative online technologies. During each site visit, students were involved in fostering people-to-people understanding on local issues and developing contacts that would promote future partnerships. The target audience were undergraduate students in Japan and Hawaii who had a deep interest in learning more about how environmental science connects to local communities, both locally and across the globe, and who wanted to employ international partnerships and collaboration to face environmental challenges.

Hawai'i and Japan share similar environmental challenges. Both are island ecosystems and are especially vulnerable to the impacts of urbanization and introduced species. Over a yearlong collaboration, students and faculty from each region shared their experience and expertise addressing these challenges and developing sustainable futures, especially through the lens of community-based restoration and environmental science.

The exchange program involved two site visits, Kansai students to Hawai'i and KCC students to Japan. Over the yearlong exchange, students and faculty also interacted collaboratively via technology. Students learned through active place-based research and developed leadership skills as they served as peer colleagues and assisted with site visit.

4.2 Participants

Twelve junior students in a seminar class of Kansai University, and six students who took Environment and Ecology Lab course (Biology 124) of KCC, participated in the Kai Yama program. Starting January 2015, they held video conference sessions every Wednesday for an hour to introduce each other and discuss activities of the program.

Five faculty members, two from KCC, one from KU, and two American faculty members who had experiences with Japanese and American cultures, were involved in the program. In addition, one graduate student served as a program assistant. The faculty members periodically conducted video conferencing to coordinate activities at different times from students' video conferencing.

4.3 The First Period: Initiation (November 2015 – March 2016)

The Kai Yama program started in November 2015. Twelve students joined a seminar class in Japan. English communication classes were held every Wednesday for 90 min. In January, six KCC students, enrolled in a class met the KU students through video conferencing every Wednesday for 50 min to introduce each other and explain their culture and environmental conditions.

4.4 The Second Period: Visiting Hawaii (March 2016)

For the Japan to Hawaii portion of the exchange, the visit was modeled on the current Kapiolani Community College (KCC) Biology 124 lab course which includes an active learning based lab and a collaborative partnership between KCC and a local community group, Mālama Maunalua. The KU Students stayed at the University of Hawaii dormitory during spring break. During the five-day exchange students were introduced to ecology and environmental science skills and then applied those skills to real-world support for community initiatives. KCC students shared their learning of basic ecological sampling skills and their participation in support of a local community initiative to restore Maunalua Bay. During the Hawaii portion of the exchange, the students worked with the community to collect and analyze data on invasive algae abundance before and area removal.

KCC students also shared the Hawaiian cultural understanding of the environment, including the traditional Hawaiian land concept of the Ahupua'a, which manages resources from the mountains to the ocean. A framework of sustainability and the importance of environmental science to both local and global issues supported learning across the exchange. Six groups were composed to work together and produce video clips.

4.5 The Third Period: Preparation for Visiting Kansai (April – July 2016)

After visiting Hawaii, KU and KCC students met through video conferencing until the end of the spring semester, April 2016. KU students introduced environmental issues in Japan. The KU students were informatics majors and not majors in biology or environmental science. They need to learn about environmental issues in Japan, such as invasive spaces and wild animal attacks so that they in turn shared knowledge of Japanese environmental issues. They also visited a marginal village in the mountains and the Biwako museum to understand local environmental changes.

"*Satoyama*" is a key concept of harmonizing inhabitants and nature in Japan. However, since the general population has decreased and the percentage of elderly people has increased in villages, people cannot take care of *Satoyama*. Farm fields were discarded, and wild animals, such as deer, monkey, and boar came down to marginal villages and damaged the fields. KU and KCC students learned about this situation before visiting the fields.

4.6 The Fourth Period: Kansai Visit (August 2016)

For the second site exchange, KCC students and faculty visited Kansai, Japan at the beginning of August. They met with their peers from Kansai University and continued their collaboration. As part of the exchange, students learned about the ecology of Lake Biwa, marginalized villages, and *Satoyama* on site. They produced video clips to demonstrated what they learned during the fieldwork.

4.7 The Fifth Period: Summing Up (September – October 2016)

After visiting two sites, the students produced a report in the form of documents, video clips, and web pages to summarize what they learned during the field trips. They also presented what they learned to junior students and others, such as high school students and families. As a capstone project, students from both campuses were required to work collaboratively over the Internet to produce a final presentation on their research results, which will be shared with the community-based organizations and a wider online audience.

4.8 The Second Round of the Program (December 2016 – October 2017)

The second round of Kai Yama started in December 2016 after establishing a new seminar class of 13 sophomore students at Kansai University. Four junior students and two senior students from KCC will visit Japan first to conduct fieldwork on *Satoyama* and *Satoumi* in Mie prefecture. Japanese students will visit Hawaii in August, 2017. Video conferencing sessions started in January for students to introduce themselves and exchange information about their countries and natural environments.

5 CASE 2: Collaborative Team Video Project (CVP)

5.1 Overview

CVP was conducted in a graduate course, "ICT for learning." The course is a one-semester long where students met once a week. It was designed for students to learn about Web 2.0 technologies as applied to education. Web 2.0 has brought new services, tools and user-created content to the Internet. It is changing teaching, learning, and creativity in education. The instructor designed the course for collaboration and authentic learning pedagogical principles. Each class includes readings, demonstrations, use of technologies, and a group discussion. In this course, students use these technologies and discuss how such technologies will help students gain 21st Century learning skills. Additionally, English is a medium of instruction in this class to enable improvement in written and spoken English. The students also gained familiarity with English terms used in modern technology.

Collaborative team video project (CVP) is one of the learning assignments in this course. US and Japanese students collaboratively work and produce a short video related to the use of modern technologies among students in Japan and Hawaii as end products. The students employ a variety of Web 2.0 technologies such as Skype, Dropbox, Google Hangouts, Google Docs and Facebook to communicate each other.

Students received an orientation about local time differences, different academic schedules, technology access, levels of technology skills, language proficiency, cultural differences in communication techniques, decision-making and problem solving styles at the beginning of the CVP. For example, students are informed that difference between Japan and Hawaii standard time is 19 h.

5.2 CVP Process

The instructor provided an orientation about Google Hangouts, and Japanese students practiced using it to collaborate during in-class activities before meeting with Hawaii students. The students gained self-esteem to use the technology and communicate in English. Students became more aware of difficulties when communicating online, such as microsecond delays when speaking, awkwardness of seeing their faces as they spoke English and the need to prepare before each meeting.

Initial videoconferences were held during a class session on Google Hangout. Students in both sides introduced themselves. The students were required to create a team name, decide on a topic for their video and drafted a short storyboard. Following meetings were scheduled by students themselves outside of class. After agreeing on a topic and video script, US and Japanese students prepared video clips independently. They were then edited into a single video based on the script developed collaboratively.

The student teams uploaded the final video to YouTube after five weeks. They linked the video to a Google+ community in which students reviewed and commented on the final video products produced by other teams and provided feedback asynchronously.

Faculty assessed student progress and difficulties by reviewing a progress reports and weekly oral reflections by students. The project provided students with authentic learning experiences where they used Web 2.0 tools to increase their knowledge and utilize skills learned in class in real-life situations. Students found that ICT in real contexts increased their consciousness of the advantages and disadvantages of collaborating online with people from a different culture.

Although Japanese students encountered difficulties by collaborating in English, these activities provided authentic situations for students to use Web 2.0 tools to increase their intercultural awareness and enabled researchers to observe how online communities evolve. The Japanese students overcame these difficulties through perseverance, effort, and the desire to communicate in English.

6 Discussion

These collaborative projects will continue this year, 2017, as the programs have been improved by evaluating the previous outcomes. Overall, students who participated in the activities were satisfied with collaborative activities. The authors received feedback that all students were satisfied with the program. International exchanges between Japan and US help both students understood each other. They had unique experiences to become motivated and to be actively involved in the program. Visiting Hawaii in case 1, students called each other first names and became more familiar with each other through Facebook and LINE after returning to Japan.

In both cases 1 and 2, US and Japanese faculty closely communicated to design the curriculum. US and Japanese faculty also periodically discussed how to design, implement, and evaluate the curriculum.

6.1 Logistics

Time management is one of most important factors to make ICPBL successful. The difference in time between Japan and Hawaii is 19 h. When students communicate through video conferencing, they need to consider when both groups can meet at the same time.

In the case 1, video conferencing is held in class time at KCC so that it was operated at a fixed time. The KCC class started on Tuesday at 17:00, which is lunch time on Wednesday at 12:00 Japan time.

Kai Yama is a year-long with activities that start on November for one year, including video conferencing, field studies in US and Japan, and reporting activities. However, the academic calendars are different between the US and Japan. KCC starts spring semester in January, while KU starts in April. Therefore, KU students were assembled as a seminar class in the previous year and started English communication class in November. KCC students enrolled in biology class in January and then started video conferencing with KU students.

Kai Yama includes site visits to both countries. KU students visited Hawaii at the end of March which is spring break at KCC while KCC students came to Japan in the beginning of August, summer break for both students. Reserving accommodation is not easy because inexpensive accommodations such as dormitory and seminar houses are full during semesters. Students need to visit each other during semester breaks so that both groups can fully participate in the program.

In the case 2, the period of CVP is 5 weeks which is shorter period compared to Kai Yama program. However, when they produce video programs collaboratively, they have to spend time outside of class. It creates some difficulties in managing the students' schedules.

When a formal survey was conducted in the fall 2010 semester, 17 US and 14 Japanese students participated in the CVP. Since US graduate students were part-time students working as full time staff, such as high school and college teachers, administrators, and instructional designers, Japanese students as full time students had difficulties to find time for communicating through Hangout. Because of their busy personal schedules and the difference in time zones, both US and Japanese students answered that the time to communicate synchronously was the biggest challenge.

When working in virtual teams, effective time management is important. Busy schedules with full-time jobs, family responsibilities and differences in time zones often resulted in lack of timely response from group members. Students stated that "time management" and "team management" were important when collaborating online. Nevertheless, the students adopted various strategies for effective communication based on available group resources. All seven groups cleared the initial project objective successfully.

6.2 Budget

Budget is also one of important factors for implementing the Kai Yama program. To receive funding for educational programs is difficult in Japan so that KU students spent their own money to participate in the program while KCC students obtained financial support from a non-profit funding organization. Kai Yama is considered as STEM education for which there are a variety of funding sources. Students stay at inexpensive accommodations such as a university dormitory and seminar house to reduce the budget. For continuity, stable funding sources are needed.

On the contrary, CVP does not require any budget. The students use existing resources and shoot video near-by. To observe two cases, students would become more friendly and learn in greater depth, if they had opportunities to meet each other in real-time, face-to-face situations.

6.3 Language

It was difficult for KU students to communicate in English in the Kai Yama program. At the beginning, they were not used to speaking English nor listening to it. They were afraid that they could not speak in English when met KCC students through video conferencing. However, as they participated in an English oral communication class, they gradually gained confidence to speak in English. After visiting Hawaii, they confirmed that they could do it. KU students wished that they could speak English better. KU students have studied English communication for a year so that they can communicate well enough with KCC students, not only verbally but also with non-verbal communication. Motivation is important for language learning. Since Japanese students meet US students through video conferencing and onsite face-to-face, they were motivated to improve their English conversation skills.

Although research literature showed that the difficulties with technologies generally inhibit participation in online communities and thus negatively influence performance (Guldberg and Mackness 2009), our data indicated that the Japanese members' English language proficiency as well as satisfaction with the levels of interactions with other group members were two important factors influencing their motivation.

One Japanese student stated that learning to speak English actively and without fear aided her communication. Another stated that the project provided a "nice practice to improve my ability to use English and Web 2.0 tools." When synchronous communication proved difficult, some students resorted to asynchronous tools that allowed for language translation and provided more time to compose replies. However, one student stated that sending text messages and email lessened the sense of community and involvement with the project.

6.4 Collaboration

The Kai Yama program, involved two types of collaboration: Working together onsite and at a distance. At the beginning, both students met each other through video conferencing. They were rather shy at first. Japanese students hesitated to speak in English and did not understand US students' English. They gradually became accustomed to participating in the video conference and to be more pro-active. When both students physically meet onsite and spent a week together to conduct fieldwork, it was the first time that both groups of students really felt that they could collaborate to achieve common goals. After the first fieldwork session, they felt closer and were more likely to communicate with each other.

In contrast, students do not physically meet each other in case 2, CVP. The CVP is more task-oriented so that time management is crucial. However, US students are part-time to study at graduate school so that agreeing on a video conference time for both groups of students to participate is difficult. They made schedules, but the conferences were sometimes cancelled because both groups of students did not show up.

Students realized the need for good leadership, time management, scheduling in different time zones and selecting tools that best facilitated communication. A good leader helped to facilitate teamwork and provided direction for the project. One Japanese student expressed the desire "to study English more so I can be a leader of this project." The quality of the final product often reflected the leadership and ability of the group to work as a team (Kimura et al. 2012).

6.5 Technology Support

Technology plays an important role for ICPBL. Especially, ICT is indispensable for ICPBL to communicate both synchronously and asynchronously. For educational settings, students are required to combine different kinds of applications to meet their goals. They use facebook, hangout, LINE, twitter, iMovie, Skype, etc. These combinations enable students to communicate better and also accumulate data for portfolio purposes as activities are undertaken.

In addition to the technology supported communications, students enjoyed communicating and working together with local residents. Students learned more in authentic situations. A balance between digital and analog contexts must be considered. Overall, students were actively involved in activities to develop key competencies through the program.

7 Future Direction

A significant amount of time and labor was spent to implement ICPBL. If teachers do not recognize its educational value, they tend to avoid this type of program. However, students are more autonomous than what teachers usually think. Therefore, if teachers provide more freedom and control to student learners, they can bemore self-directed and responsible individuals.

The cases that the author introduced in this paper will continue in 2017. After every program is implemented, it is reviewed and revised. The Kai Yama program is in its second year with students soon to complete fieldwork in Japan. Japanese students will visit Hawaii in August 2017 with senior students who have participated in the previous program. The Kai Yama program will be much improved with support from senior students.

References

Bautista, G., Escofet, A.: Project-based learning with ICT: changes in ecology classroom in primary school. Res. Reflections Innovations Integrating ICT Educ. **1**, 108–112 (2009)

Charmaz, K.: Constructiong Grounded Theory. Introducing Qualitative Method Series. Sage Publications Ltd., London (2014)

Fly, J.M.: A Place-Based Model for K-12 Education in Tennessee (2010). http://web.utk.edu/~markfly/documents/Place-Based%20K-12%20Education%20Proposal%205_10_10.pdf

Fullan, M., Langworthy, M.: A Rich Seam: How New Pedagogies Find Deep Learning. Pearson, London (2014)

Guldberg, K., Mackness, J.: Foundations of communities of practice: enablers and barriers to participation. J. Comput. Assist. Learn. **25**(6), 1–26 (2009). doi:10.1111/j.1365-2729.2009.00327.x

Harris, H., Katz, G.: Young Investigators: The Project Approach in the Early Years, New York (2001)

Jonassen, D., Howland, J., Moore, J., Marra, R.: Learning to Solve Problems with Technology: A Constructivist Perspective, 2nd edn. Prentice Hall, Upper Saddle River (2003)

Kimura, B.Y., Kimura, M.E.O., Ho, C.P., Kubota, K.: Authentic learning and collaboration with web 2.0 technologies. Japan Association for Educational Media Studies Kenkyukai (2012)

Kimura, B.Y., Kimura, M.E., Ho, C., Kubota, K.: ICT & Collaborative Learning: Collaborative Learning between Kansai University & University of Hawaii. Kansai Univ. Joho Kenkyu **41**, 25–39 (2014)

Lawson, M.A., Alameda-Lawson, T., Richards, K.A.: A university-assisted, place-based model for enhancing students' peer, family, and community ecologies. Educ. Sci. **6**, 1–15 (2016)

OECD. The definition and Selection of Key Competencies. OECD (2000)

Perkins, N.: What constructivism demands of the learner. Educ. Technol. **31**, 18–23 (1991)

Piaget, J.: Science of Education and the Psychology of the Child. Viking, New York (1969)

Reeves, T.C., Herrington, J., Oliver, R.: Authentic Activities and Online Learning. Higher Education. Research and Development Society of Australasia, Inc. (2002). http://researchrepository.murdoch.edu.au/7034/1/authentic_activities_online_HERDSA_2002.pdf

Reeves, T.C., Herrington, J., Oliver, R.: A Development Research Agenda for Online Collaborative Learning, p. 53. Wilson Education Abstracts (2004)

Richards, C.: The design of effective ICT-supported learning activities: exemplary models, changing requirements and new possibilities. Lang. Learn. Technol. **9**(2), 60–79 (2005)

Sobel, D.: Place-Based Education: Connecting Classrooms & Communities, With Index, 2nd edn. The Orion Society (2005)

Soparat, S., Arnold, S.R., Klaysom, S.: The development of Thai learners' key competencies by project-based learning using ICT. Int. J. Res. Educ. Sci. (IJRES) **1**(1), 11–22 (2015)

Stein, B.A., Kutner, L.S., Adams, J.S.: The Status of biodiversity in the United States. A joint project of the Nature Conservancy and Association for Biodiversity Information. Oxford University Press, New York (2000)

Experiences in Blended Learning

A Review of Learning Behaviors in Using E-Schoolbag: Enhancing Academic Performance in Primary Chinese

Yan Keung Hui[1(✉)], Bo Mai[2], Sheng Qian[1], and Lam For Kwok[1]

[1] City University of Hong Kong, 83 Tat Chee Avenue, Kowloon, Hong Kong
{john.ykhui,sqian9-c,cslfkwok}@cityu.edu.hk

[2] The Shaxuyi Primary School, Panyu District, Guangzhou, China
997065001@qq.com

Abstract. The trend of using e-schoolbag in blended learning environment in basic education in China is increasing but the impact on academic performance is yet to be verified. In this paper, we conducted a preliminary review through expert interview and a quantitative analysis on e-schoolbag usage against the Primary Chinese performance in a primary school. The finding shows that the usage pattern of e-schoolbag on Primary Chinese can be treated as a direct indicator of learning behavior which in turns shows the learning attitudes including active learning and engaged learning. These learning attitudes affect the academic performance in a positive way. It also highlighted the importance of incorporating proper learning activity design when using e-schoolbag.

Keywords: E-Schoolbag · Blended learning · Active learning · Engaged learning

1 Introduction

E-schoolbag, formerly called "e-textbook" which simply digitizes learning materials from hardcopy to digital format composing texts, videos, and voices, has been enhanced to become a more comprehensive learning platform, with similar functions and features as a learning management system, is commonly termed as "e-schoolbag" in mainland China. On top of digitizing learning materials, it also provides various tools to facilitate teaching and learning activities such as homework assignment management, forum discussion, group project collaboration, questionnaires, and tests. However, arguments on whether e-schoolbag should be promoted to basic education and whether the academic performance can be enhanced through adopting the e-schoolbag are still non-stopping [1].

According to an expert interview that was conducted in December 2016 by the authors with learning-activity design experts, an e-schoolbag supplier, and experienced Primary Chinese teachers, it was believed that most of the e-schoolbag adoption in recent years focuses only on introducing e-schoolbag to replace traditional textbooks without integrating the corresponding learning activity design. It also failed to consider the learning activity, teachers' and students' capability in using the e-schoolbag, and the quality of learning materials provided in the e-schoolbag. They also pointed out that

S.K.S. Cheung et al. (Eds.): ICBL 2017, LNCS 10309, pp. 41–52, 2017.
DOI: 10.1007/978-3-319-59360-9_4

previous research failed to linkup the behavioral pattern of using the e-schoolbag, learning attitudes, and academic performance.

With the limitation of the number of teachers, small class approach cannot be adopted in most of the primary schools in China. Therefore, student-centric learning methodology, with teachers playing the role of a facilitator, supported by blended learning environments is being introduced. This allows teachers to put efforts in helping students-in-need. It relies heavily on students' learning attitudes such as active learning and engaged learning to enhance their academic performance [2–6].

In this paper, by using the behavioral information captured in e-schoolbag and the actual Primary Chinese performance provided by the school, we conducted a review of the e-schoolbag usage pattern against students' actual Primary Chinese performance through tight integrating the e-schoolbag with the learning activity design.

The rest of this paper is organized as follows. Section 2 reviews learning attitudes being reflected from learning behavior as recorded in the e-schoolbag platform. Research method and result are summarized in Sects. 3 and 4 correspondingly. Discussion and implication are in Sect. 5 while conclusion will be followed in Sect. 6.

2 E-Schoolbag Usage Behavior and Learning Attitudes

2.1 E-Schoolbag in Basic Education

The fast development of technology has changed our daily life significantly, including education. From traditional classroom instruction with physical textbooks, teaching and learning are now more interactive with the help of technology. Examples include remote classroom, combined classrooms which are far away in the physical distance, videos and voices learning materials, and the recently introduced e-schoolbag which rides on tablets into flipped classroom and can be used anytime and anywhere [7].

Since the twelve five-year plan of mainland China, digital education has been promoted quickly [8]. China has become one of the countries with highest mobile learning growth rate [9]. Network infrastructure and equipment are the basic and the initial phase. The introduction of e-schoolbag is the second phase while building the national centralized cloud platform for maximizing data sharing and data analytics is the ultimate goal which is expected to be completed by the year 2020 [10].

Despite the technological support, introducing e-schoolbag faces certain challenges including the lack of communication between teachers and parents on the benefit of e-schoolbag to students, licensing issues, and the lack of evidence in verifying the positive impact on students' academic performance [11]. The first two challenges can be solved by having a significant amount of schools participating in pilot experiments of using e-schoolbags with supports from the Government, from the learning activity design experts in designing learning activities for the specific blended learning environment, and from e-schoolbag suppliers to the involved teachers. However, the positive impact on academic performance is yet to be verified.

E-schoolbag does not simply digitize learning materials from textbooks as what an e-textbook normally does. It is in fact a learning management system which creates a platform for collaboration and promotes self-learning and personalized learning [1].

E-schoolbag serving as a tool does not have direct impact on academic performance. It is useful when it is embedded in a blended learning environment such as flipped classroom. Before the class, teachers can assign/upload related learning materials for students to read and explore for more related knowledge. In the class, teachers can make use of the platform to conduct interactive demonstrations or even quiz. After the class, students can further digest the learning materials as well as continue the discussion in the forum.

Academic performance is influenced by learning attitudes, which in turn can be reflected and be changed by learning behaviors. In a blended learning environment using e-schoolbag with purposely designed learning activities such as flipped class room, the usage patterns as recorded in the e-schoolbag platform may partially represent the learning behaviors of students and in turn reflect their learning attitudes.

In this preliminary study, it was observed that the e-schoolbag under investigation did not capture much of activity logs. However, we observed that two activities in e-schoolbag were well recorded, which represent students learning behaviors affecting the corresponding learning attitude. The usage outside class measures how active students perform self-learning before and after classes, and forum responses measures how students being engaged in the learning by sharing and exchanging knowledge with others. These may reflect the learning attitudes of active learning and engaged learning correspondingly. In this paper, an overview is conducted to observe the impact of e-schoolbag on academic performance indirectly through observing the two learning attitudes as reflected from the e-schoolbag usage in the learning activity design for Primary Chinese of the selected classes of the primary school.

2.2 Active Learning

Active learning is defined as "students participate in the process and students participate when they are doing something besides passively listening" and is "anything that involves students in doing things and thinking about the things they are doing" [12]. In addition to simply listening to a teacher, students are expected to read, write, discuss, gather and analyze data, and involve in problem solving processes [13] with higher-order thinking tasks such as analysis, synthesis, and evaluation [14, 15].

Active learning is opposite with passive in learning [15]. Traditionally, Primary Chinese is taught in one direction from teachers to students. Students receive knowledge passively through listening and practicing. With the introduction of e-schoolbag, and with the supporting learning activity design of flipped classroom, students can have learning by themselves before the class. They can conduct information gathering, analysis, and discussion in the e-schoolbag platform with teachers acting as a facilitator. They can continue the discussion in the forum even after school without the intervention or instruction from teachers. Therefore, we classify the learning behavior of "e-schoolbag usage outside classroom" as an indicator of the learning attitude as the degree of active learning.

2.3 Engaged Learning

Students' engaged learning occurs when "students make a psychological investment in learning… in understanding the material and incorporating or internalizing it in their lives" [16] and refers to a "student's willingness, need, desire and compulsion to participate in, and be successful in, the learning process promoting higher level thinking for enduring understanding" [17]. Engaged learning is one of the active forms of learning focusing on both problem and process [18].

Engagement can be identified from three domains namely cognitive, emotional and social [19]. In the cognitive domain, students construct knowledge and demonstrated the ownership and self-regulation. In the emotional domain, learners feel curious yet secure and confident. In the social domain, information sharing, acceptance, and collaboration are demonstrated by students.

In Primary Chinese, the use of the forum features in e-schoolbag in a flipped classroom design enables students to construct knowledge by themselves with collaboration, sharing and being owned by themselves. Active responses to topics and questions in discussion forum demonstrated students' problem solving and promoting higher level thinking. Therefore, we define the learning behavior of "number of response in forum discussion" as an indicator of the learning attitude as the degree of engaged learning.

3 Methods

3.1 Research Context

In this paper, learning behavior data including the usage of e-schoolbag outside a class and the number of response in forum discussions of grade four students in the school year of 2015/16 of the Shaxuyi Primary School in Panyu of southern China was captured in the e-schoolbag system and is used for clustering analysis. Their corresponding academic performance in the Chinese subject in the school year of 2014/15 and 2015/16 were collected for verifying the clustering results.

3.2 Expert Interview

In order to know more about the selected group of students, an expert interview was conducted in late 2016, which involves the subject teacher of Primary Chinese of the selected group of students during the school year of 2015–16, three education design experts who provide consultation services to the school in blended-learning by combining classroom design such as flipped classroom and the use of e-Schoolbag, and two technical experts in developing the e-schoolbag platform.

3.3 Data Collection and Pre-processing

Among the 95 samples, 7 was dropped due to data incompletion. Thus, the rest 88 valid samples are included in the analysis. As shown in Table 1, the two classes consist of a relatively even distribution in both the number of students as well as the gender in each class. Multiple data pre-processing were applied, including dropping incomplete records, deprivatizing student identifiers, performing feature extraction, and normalizing values through Z-score normalization. Some variables were removed due to high Pearson Correlation and immature activity logging ability of the e-schoolbag platform.

Table 1. Descriptive statistics of student records

Class	Gender	Count	Sub_total	Total
1	Male	21 (50%)	42 (48%)	88 (100%)
	Female	21 (50%)		
2	Male	25 (56%)	46 (52%)	
	Female	21 (44%)		

3.4 Techniques for Data Analysis

Deploying the software of Alteryx Designer (version 10.6) for data cleansing, pre-processing and clustering analysis and Power BI Desktop (Version 2.4) for data visualization, we perform data analysis to identify the relationship between students' learning behaviors, the usage outside classes and number of responses in the forum, against their performance in Chinese. K-Centroids cluster analysis using K-Means was performed to identify clusters of learning behaviors. Then, scatter plot was used to visualize the distribution of academic performance in each cluster.

4 Result

In this section, a result of the qualitative analysis based on the expert interview conducted in late 2016 is described, followed by the results of quantitative analysis.

4.1 Qualitative Analysis

Non-biased Class Assignment: Every student was assigned to a particular class randomly at the time he/she enrolled in the school and will not be moved to another class for subsequent school years. The random class assignment process will try to preserve an even distribution of gender, minorities, and month of birth without assessing their academic ability. Therefore, we can assume that it is a non-biased process.

For School Year 2014/15: There were two classes in grade four that we selected. In the school year 2014/15, the performance and learning attitude of Class 1 were relatively poor in the teacher's point of view, while those of Class 2 were relatively better and had a better experience in using e-schoolbag.

For School Year 2015/16: Both classes were taught by the same teacher for the Chinese subject. Given the relatively better learning attitudes, higher performance and ability in using e-schoolbag in Class 2, and the constraint of teacher's resources, the teacher adopted the following approach:

- Learning Activity Design: Flipped classroom was used. Useful learning materials were posted to the e-schoolbag for students to perform self-study and discussion in the forum before the class. Interactive discussions, presentation, demonstration, and short tests were conducted in the class. Follow up forum discussion was carried out after class. These applied to both classes.
- Special treatment to Class 1: Majority of Class 2 students are familiar with the e-schoolbag as a result of training in the previous year as well as have better learning attitudes. Therefore, the teacher spent more times and efforts in helping Class 1 students in changing their learning attitudes and getting better understanding in using the e-schoolbag.

Well-trained Teachers: With supports from the government and senior management of schools, teachers in Panyu district received regular training on how to apply e-schoolbag with purposely designed learning activity design, one of the objective is to enhance teaching quality with the very limited teaching resources.

High Quality Teaching Materials: Third party supplier, learning-activity design experts and teachers can prepare and upload good quality teaching materials to the e-schoolbag to facilitate students self-learning.

Strong Government Support: Schools of Panyu district receive strong government support in setting up not only the information technology infrastructure and networks but also supporting students in procuring the required tablets for running the e-schoolbag system. It also organizes various sharing sessions on how to integrate the e-schoolbag and learning activity design in a more effective way for the purpose of raising up students' performance as well as reducing teachers' efforts in order to allow more teaching resources for the students in need.

Personalized Learning: It is common to have about 45 students in each class. Even with the help of information technology, personalized learning is not feasible with very limited number of teachers in each school. Students may have different levels of presentation skills, comprehension skills, writing skills, and social communication ability. With the e-schoolbag platform, the teacher prepares short learning materials based on the knowledge points of a particular topic and allows students to collect related information and to discuss in the forum. Teachers can understand what common issues are being faced by the majority and what particular difficulties are faced by some students leading to more discussions within and after a class. The use of e-schoolbag as a platform for discussion can also remove the boundary of time and space so that communication between students and teachers may happen anytime and anywhere. Students can express themselves in text, graphs, voices and videos.

Common View Point: In the expert interview, all members pointed out that e-schoolbag is just a tool which can make the modern learning activity design, such as flipped classroom, be more effective. The outcome should not depend only on the platform itself, but also on the learning activity design, teachers' ability in integrating their teaching activity with the e-schoolbag platform, teachers' intervention to different students in different ways (which is also a kind of personalized learning), the quality of the learning materials, the close collaboration between various stakeholders including but not limited to the teachers, students, learning activity design experts, e-schoolbag supplier, the government and parents.

4.2 Quantitative Analysis

Initial Observation – Differences between Two Classes: As shown in Table 2, the usage outside classroom and response in the forum of Class 1 is obviously much less than that of Class 2 and with lower variation. However, it also shows that Class 1 has a significant improvement in Chinese from P3 to P4 and with narrow deviation when comparing with Class 2. Another observation is that the average of the two classes in P4 is actually relatively the same (very close to the zero mean) but Class 2 has a higher deviation. It matches what the teacher mentioned in the expert interview that Class 1 was original with a lower performance than Class 2 but eventually be improved to almost the same as that of Class 2. At the same time, Class 2 has a higher deviation due to the differences in learning behavior.

Table 2. Summary statistics

Items	Average (Standard deviation)	
	Class 1	Class 2
Usage outside classroom	−0.37(0.39)	0.34(1.23)
Forum – number of response	−0.23(0.18)	0.21(1.33)
Chinese performance in P3	−0.32(0.94)	0.29(0.95)
Chinese performance in P4	0.04(0.82)	−0.04(1.13)

K-Means Analysis – Multiple Clustering Analysis: Further to the initial analysis, we performed further analysis by using the two identified learning behavior variables ("Usage outside the class" and "Forum – Number of response") to perform clustering analysis using the K-Means algorithm. By using Alteryx's K-Centroids Diagnostics function, we identified $K = 4$ is the best classification using K-Means. While Fig. 1 shows the distribution of academic performance of the four clusters generated in three scenarios (two classes students together, Class 1 students only and Class 2 students only), Fig. 2 shows the corresponding clusters.

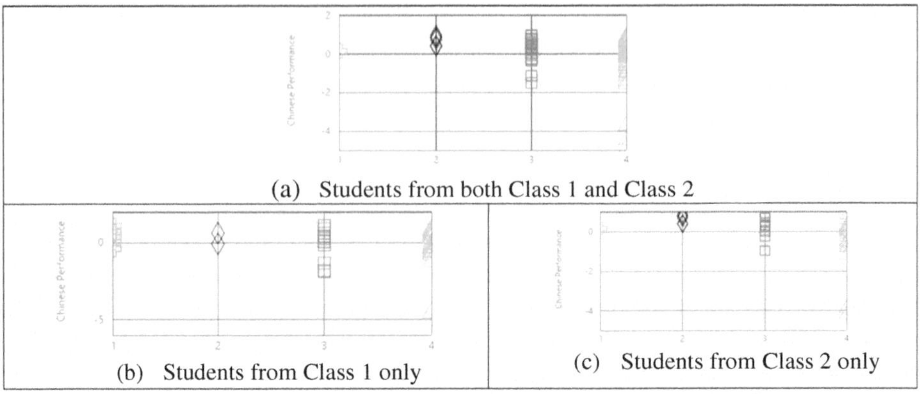

(a) Students from both Class 1 and Class 2

(b) Students from Class 1 only

(c) Students from Class 2 only

Fig. 1. Chinese performance in each cluster of different student groups

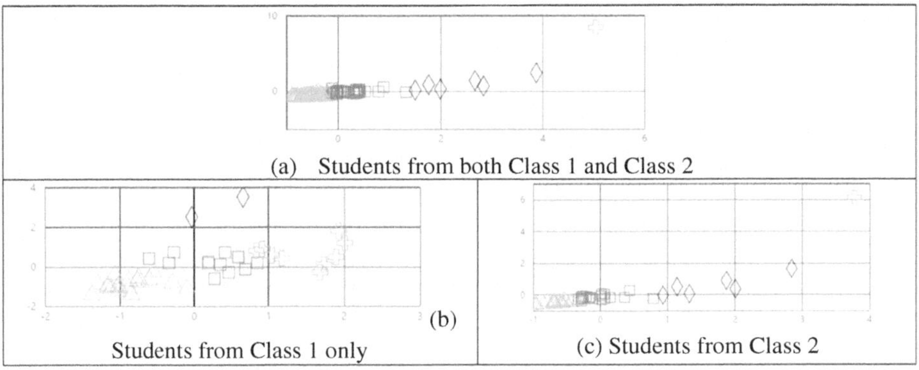

(a) Students from both Class 1 and Class 2

(b) Students from Class 1 only

(c) Students from Class 2

Fig. 2. Cluster distribution ("Usage outside the class" Vs "Forum response")

From the diagrams in Figs. 1 and 2, we can observe that the usage outside classroom and number of response in the forum are associated with the performance positively as summarized in Table 3.

Table 3. Performance of the Cluster Analysis

	Academic performance of Chinese			
	Cluster 1	Cluster 2	Cluster 3	Cluster 4
Usage	Very high	High	Average	Low
Performance	Above the mean	Above and close to the mean	Across but close to the mean	Naturally distributed

5 Discussion and Implication

5.1 Discussion

From the expert interview and analysis results, we can observe the following:

1. Learning Activities Influence Learning Behavior
   The learning behavior (usage of e-schoolbag) is highly related to the learning activity design. For example, students in Class 2 use e-schoolbag more significantly than that of Class 1, as purposely designed by the teacher. Those learning behaviors reflect the corresponding learning attitudes.
2. Learning Attitudes Affect Performance
   The usage of e-schoolbag outside class, which implies the level of active learning, positively affects the performance. The forum response, which implies the level of engaged learning, also positively affects the performance.
3. Replicability
   The result is similar in all the three scenarios, which show that the impact of active learning and engaged learning on performance can be observed in different classes with proper use of e-schoolbag and learning activity design.

The logical model is shown in Fig. 3, which summarizes our findings. First, learning behavior can be recorded in the e-schoolbag platform based on a careful learning activity design. Then, learning attitudes can be reflected from the corresponding learning behavior. Finally, academic performance can be enhanced through positive learning attitudes.

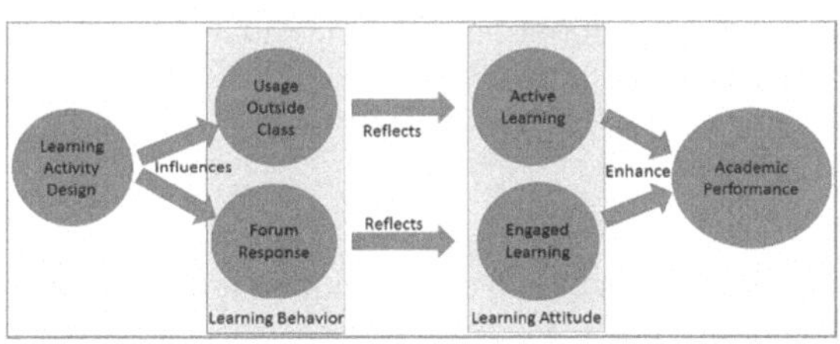

Fig. 3. The observed logical model

5.2 Theoretical Implication

While there were discussions on academic performance influenced by enhancing learning attitudes such as active learning and engaged learning, the way of enhancing these attitudes through e-schoolbag is not well analyzed. Even the data shows a positive relationship between the three variables and performance in the Chinese subject, we believe that learning activity design is another important element as mentioned in the expert interview. An e-schoolbag, as a tool, will not be useful without proper learning activity design and high quality learning materials. Future studies may put more focus on how to combine the blended learning environment together with proper learning activity design for better understanding on the relationship between learning behaviors and learning attitudes, and then to the performance.

5.3 Practical Implication

The findings in this paper may bring positive impact to students, teachers, and learning activity design experts in following areas:

1. Learning Behavior Reflects Learning Attitudes Affecting Academic Performance
   From our findings, there is a positive relationship between usage on e-schoolbag and performance in Primary Chinese. Students are encouraged to participate actively and extensively on using the e-schoolbag to explore useful learning materials for self-learning, to participate actively in forum discussions with classmates and response to topics and questions from both teachers and classmates.
2. Teachers Can Focus on Students-in-need
   Since students in Class 2 have significantly higher performance than that of Class 1 in P3, the teacher decided to adopt blended learning with heavier usage of an e-schoolbag platform for Class 2 to facilitate active learning and engaged learning. The teacher can focus more in helping students-in-need particularly those in Class 1 for enhancing the very basic elements in order to catch up with Class 2.
3. Learning Activity Design is Important in Adopting e-schoolbag
   It is observed that the performance in Chinese is positively related to active learning and engaged learning of students on the e-schoolbag environment with flipped-classroom design. Students can actively learn by themselves, with classmates/teacher before the class, as well as conducting revision after classes through the e-schoolbag platform. Future adoption of e-schoolbag should have proper plan and design of learning activities.

5.4 Limitation

This paper, being a review of e-schoolbag adoption in a particular grade of a particular school, obviously has limitations:

1. Sample Size and Data Volume
   Although the analysis looks replicable between Class 1 and Class 2 of grade four students in the school under investigation, both the sample size and volume of usage data is not large enough to have better attestation on replicability to other grades or other schools. It is suggested that more types of schools and different grades of students should be considered in the future analysis in order to identify a generic model that can explain the behaviors of majority of students.
2. Number of behavioral variables
   Only a few of behavioral variables were identified to be useful for analysis in this study. Limitations are due to insufficient data available from the platform such as login count, total online duration, average online duration. It is suggested that the

developer of the e-schoolbag platform should put efforts in collecting more behavioral information instead of focusing only the functions and features that are related to teaching and learning.

3. Available data of existing behavioral variables
   Some of the variables collected in the e-schoolbag platform were ignored due to low usage in the corresponding features, and immature system in capturing comprehensive user behavior information. Further enhancement of the e-schoolbag is encouraged to capture more user behavior information for further analysis.
4. Missing non-behavioral variables
   In this review, we focus mainly on the behavior usage in e-schoolbag. However, other factors such as students' demographic information, family backgrounds, psychological parameters, learning histories, technology acceptance level and learning materials …etc. may also influence their performance. It is suggested that more types of variables should be considered in the future study.
5. Side effects of using e-schoolbag
   Other effects of using e-schoolbag such as on eyes, are not covered in this study.

6 Conclusion

One of the most challenging factors in promoting e-schoolbag in basic education is the uncertainty of its effectiveness in enhancing academic performance. In this paper, we perform an overview on how e-schoolbag can enhance students' academic performance indirectly through enhancing their learning attitude.

It is observed that learning activity design is critical before adopting the e-schoolbag environment. The usage of e-schoolbag can reflect certain types of learning attitudes such as active learning and engaged learning in this review. Subsequently, these learning attitudes can positively affect the academic performance. In addition, teachers can place their efforts to help students-in-need.

Acknowledgements. We thank for the management supports from the Shaxuyi Primary School in Panyu, and times and efforts of teachers in verifying our results.

References

1. Li, S.G.: Is it time to popularize eschoolbags? Bejing Review (2017)
2. Soltanzadeh, L., Hashemi, S.R.N., Shahi, S.: The effect of active learning on academic achievement motivation in high schools students. Arch. Appl. Sci. Res. **5**(6), 127–131 (2013)
3. Freeman, S., Eddy, S.L., McDonough, M., Smith, M.K., Okorafor, N., Jordt, H., Wenderoth, M.P.: Active learning increases student performance in science, engineering, and mathematics. Proc. Natl. Acad. Sci. U.S.A. **111**(23), 8410–8415 (2014)
4. Sadik, A.: Digital storytelling: a meaningful technology-integrated approach for engaged student learning. Educ. Technol. Res. Dev. **56**(4), 487–506 (2008)
5. Kusano, S.M., Conger, A.J., Wright, M.C.: Development and assessment of collaboration, teamwork, and communication. In: Center for Research on Learning and Teaching Occasional Paper, vol. 35 (2016)

6. Brill, J.M., Park, Y.: Facilitating engaged learning in the interaction age taking a pedagogically-disciplined approach to innovation with emergent technologies. Int. J. Teach. Learn. High. Educ. **20**(1), 70–78 (2008)
7. Ni, M.S., Kwok, L.F., Zhen, L.Z., Xie, Y.R., Long, H.P., Zheng, X., Li, W.: A study of an E-schoolbag supporting flipped classroom model for junior mathematics review class. In: Cheung, S.K.S., et al. (eds.) ICHL 2015. LNCS, vol. 9167, pp. 243–254. Springer, Switzerland (2015)
8. Wu, Y.H., Lin, L., Ma, X.L., Zhu, Z.T.: Research on the E-textbook and E-schoolbag in China: constructing an ecosystem of E-textbook and E-schoolbag. In: IADIS International Conference on Cognition and Exploratory Learning in Digital Age (2013)
9. Long, T.T., Liang, W.X., Yu, S.Q.: A study of the tablet computer's application in K-12 schools in China. Int. J. Educ. Dev. Inf. Commun. Technol. (IJEDICT) **9**(3), 61–70 (2013)
10. KPMG: The 13th Five-Year Plan – China's Transformation and Integration with the World Economy: Opportunities for Chinese and Foreign Business (2016). https://assets.kpmg.com/content/dam/kpmg/cn/pdf/en/2016/10/13fyp-opportunities-analysis-for-chinese-and-foreign-businesses.pdf
11. Zhu, S., Shi, Y., Wu, D., Wang, J., Yang, H.H., Kwok, L.F.: To Be or Not to Be: using tablet PCs in K-12 education. In: 2014 International Conference of Educational Innovation Through Technology (2014)
12. Weltman, D.: A comparison of traditional and active learning methods: an empirical investigation utilizing a linear mixed model. Ph.D. thesis, The University of Texas at Arlington (2007)
13. Bonwell, C., Eison, J.: Active learning: creating excitement in the classroom. ASHE-ERIC Higher Education Report No. 1 (1991)
14. Renkl, A., Atkinson, R.K., Maier, U.H., Staley, R.: From example study to problem solving: smooth transitions help learning. J. Exp. Educ. **70**(4), 293–315 (2002)
15. Bean, J.C.: Engaging Ideas: The Professor's Guide to Integrating Writing. Critical Thinking and Active Learning in the Classroom. JosseyBass Publishers, San Francisco (2011)
16. Newmann, F.: Student Engagement and Achievement in American Secondary Schools, pp. 2–3. Teachers College Press, New York (1992)
17. Bomia, L., Beluzo, L., Demeester, D., Elander, K., Johnson, M., Sheldon, B.: The Impact of Teaching Strategies on Intrinsic Motivation. ERIC Clearinghouse on Elementary and Early Childhood Education, Champaign (1997)
18. Hung, D., Tan, S.C., Koh, T.S.: Engaged learning: making learning an authentic experience. In: Hung, D., Khine, M.S. (eds.) Engaged Learning with Emerging Technology, pp. 29–48 (2006)
19. Wang, M., Kang, M.: Cybergogy for engaged learning: a framework for creating learner engagement through information and communication technology. In: Hung, D., Khine, M.S. (eds.) Engaged Learning with Emerging Technologies, pp. 225–253. Springer, Dordrecht Netherlands (2006)

Blended Learning in the University English Courses: Case Study

Blanka Klimova(✉), Ivana Simonova, and Petra Poulova

University of Hradec Kralove, Hradec Kralove, Czech Republic
{Blanka.klimova,ivana.simonova,petra.poulova}@uhk.cz

Abstract. At present, thanks to the development of modern information and communication technologies, the higher education institutions run most of their courses also online. In foreign language teaching/learning the blended form is widely applied. Therefore, the aim of this article is to show through a case study how the blended learning form of instruction can be effective in practice. This is illustrated at the example of seven English courses taught in a blended form at the Faculty of Informatics and Management, University of Hradec Kralove. The authors describe the current blended English courses and analyze data collected from online evaluation reports. They demonstrate in figures how effective students' learning in these courses is. In the final part, the crucial didactic conclusions are presented.

Keywords: Blended learning · Online courses · English courses · ESP · Case study · Full-time students · Part-time students · Students' performance

1 Introduction

The teaching of foreign languages reflects the current paradigmatic changes which can be seen in all spheres of human activities by moving from positivism to post-positivism. The emphasis is rather put on social character of teaching than on students as individuals. Learning is not directed anymore but

- it is aimed at a student, not at a teacher;
- students are actively involved in the decision-making process;
- learning is more and more based on cooperation.

Attention is paid to student's specific needs because students are perceived as individuals with their specific needs and learning style preferences. Moreover, it is the student's creative potential which is being considered being expressed in following features:

- language skills and knowledge are being integrated across curricula;
- pedagogy works together with other related sciences in order to help students in their learning.

Teaching is enhanced by different teaching methods, strategies or techniques [1], which enables students of various cultural backgrounds to attend the same class. In addition, learning is perceived as a lifelong process than just preparation for an exam.

S.K.S. Cheung et al. (Eds.): ICBL 2017, LNCS 10309, pp. 53–64, 2017.
DOI: 10.1007/978-3-319-59360-9_5

Therefore the main factors of the learning process are autonomy, integration of knowledge and skills, continuity, creativity, multiculturality and cooperation [2]. These features and changes are defined in the Common European Reference Framework for languages (CERF), whose aim is to increase the quality of communicative competences of the EU citizens who speak different languages and come from different cultural backgrounds. This document provides a wide range of pedagogical recommendations on how to achieve this target.

One of the recommendations also concerns the implementation of modern information and communication technologies into education, including the teaching of foreign languages, which can support the factors of the learning process described above. Most higher education institutions run e-Learning courses to enhance students' studies in the most effective way [3]. This is also true for the Faculty of Informatics and Management (FIM), University of Hradec Kralove (UHK), Czech Republic, where e-Learning courses have been running since 1999. Nowadays, at FIM more than 250 online e-courses are run. They are exploited in different ways; either as the distance courses, or as blended courses (see [4]) serving as an additional support for students after their regular face-to-face classes. Thus the students can fix the information already obtained during the lecture. Several surveys and research studies have been conducted at the faculty confirming that students welcome the possibility to exploit online courses but preferably as the blended learning courses (cf. [5–7]).

Therefore, the aim of this article is to show through a case study how the blended learning form of instruction can be effective in practice. This is illustrated at the example of a few English courses taught in the blended form at FIM. The authors of this article have the following goals:

- to introduce the current blended English courses and the methods used for the research;
- to use online evaluation reports and figures to demonstrate how effective students' learning in these courses is; and
- to draw relevant didactic recommendations.

2 Research Questions

The purpose of this study is to examine issues with respect to the blended learning concept in practice. To attain this research objective, the authors used a case study approach [8], i.e. an empirical inquiry that investigates a contemporary phenomenon within its real-life context when the boundaries between phenomenon and context are not clearly evident and in which multiple sources of evidence are used.

- The following questions were set to be analyzed:
- How is the process of blended learning in English courses designed at FIM?
- What does learners' performance in online courses look like?

The method of frequency analysis, online evaluation reports and figures were exploited to demonstrate how effective students' learning in these courses was. Consequently, relevant conclusions and didactic recommendations were drawn.

3 Materials and Methods

The authors chose seven representative English blended courses, which are attended by students enrolled in Bachelor study programme Applied Informatics and Tourism Management and in Master study programme Information Management.

3.1 English for Specific Purposes Courses

The ESP courses for students of Applied Informatics (AI) and Information Management (IM) were taught for six semesters focusing on:

- summary of grammar so that the starting level of knowledge was B1 as minimum (courses ESP1, 2);
- written communication (ESP3) and oral communication (ESP4);
- reading comprehension and presentation of the acquired information from English professional texts, i.e. those relating to the field of study–Informatics) (ESP5, 6).

Method of ESP instruction

Within the 12-week-long semester students attended 24 lessons organized in four six-hour blocks. Students were divided into groups of 17–20 according to their schedule preferences and taught by the same teacher who tutored the online courses. Each semester started with the entry tutorial where core information and training on how to study the course were provided to students, and it was closed by the final assessment tutorial where students sat for written tests (in ESP 1–6) and additional oral exams (in ESP 2, 4 and 6 only). Within the semester another two optional tutorials were held (90 min each where students could consult their problems with acquiring the learning content in groups with the tutor; and individual student-tutor consultations were available during the whole semester. After the entry tutorial and face-to-face lessons, each week students worked individually according to their time, place, and pace preferences. Every year since 2008/9 academic year surveys have been conducted among students, focusing on the online form of ESP learning. The entry level of students' English usually ranges from A2 to C2 but nearly all students express their agreement with the study in online courses supporting the face-to-face instruction, which is both suitable for them from the point of time management and efficiency of foreign language learning. Being aware of the importance of direct conversation, they either do not miss it, if working e.g. in companies where English is the language of communication (these students usually have language certificates of C1 or C2 levels), or those who reached lower levels of knowledge, attend private (paid) lessons with native speakers/teachers in the place of residence (mostly saying the time/financial savings work as strong compensation for financial means spent on this activity).

Research sample

Totally, 591 students in six ESP courses (ESP 1–6) described above were monitored. These students were enrolled in IT study programmes (Bachelor programme Applied Informatics and Master programme Information Management in 2013/14 academic year. The number of students is decreasing as they left the study; either they failed,

Table 1. Research sample structure (authors' own source)

Course	ESP 1	ESP 2	ESP 3	ESP 4	ESP 5	ESP 6
Students (n)	151	137	92	78	65	68

or for private/work reasons. An increase in ESP 6 is rather regular, usually caused by the fact that students in the present form of study are offered a good work position before graduation, they accept it and study the final semester in the part-time form of study. A number of students in individual subjects are displayed in Table 1.

Methods of data collecting and processing

Data concerning six ESP courses were collected by tracking learners' performance in six online courses (ESP 1–6) in the learning management system (LMS) Blackboard. The data were processed by the method of frequency analysis by the NCSS2007 statistic software and analyzed according to the criteria monitoring the amount of hits: visit rate to the course; learners' performance on weekdays; learners' performance in weeks of semester; and learners' performance in daytime.

Time spent in courses was not intentionally included in monitoring criteria although the LMS closes if no activity is performed within 30 min, i.e. if no hits are made. This interval is long enough to have rather strong impact on the collected data. The visit rate is expressed by the amount of hits (n) in single tools of the Course Content structure–Syllabus, Study Materials (SM), Tests, Assignments, Communication tools (Discussions, E-mail), Announcements and Calendar. A detailed description of tools exploited in each course is displayed in Table 2.

Table 2. Tools exploitation in the course structure (authors' own source)

Tool/Course	ESP1	ESP2	ESP3	ESP4	ESP5	ESP6	Total
Chapters in study materials (n)	18	35	10	11	30	30	134
Tests (n)	12	29	9	10	0	0	60
Assignments (n)	2	2	1	1	1	1	8
Threads in discussions (n)	12	25	5	4	3	3	54

Tools exploited in the course design

As Table 3 illustrates, eight tools were implemented in the structure of each course.

In Syllabus the learning content of each course was summarized, obligatory and optional assignments displayed, teaching methods described, learning objectives introduced, required reading and additional sources listed, requirements for the credit/exam test and its form described.

In Announcements a welcome message was sent at the beginning of each course, followed by three announcements of credit/exam dates and test scores reached by the learners. After each assignment was corrected, the message was sent to students via the Announcements tool.

In Calendar deadlines for submitting assignments were displayed, and other data, if in need.

Study materials were structured into chapters; each chapter was devoted to one topic. Although the number of chapters was different in single courses, a total quantity of learning content was comparable, i.e. the learning content in individual courses was scheduled for 12 weeks (i.e. one semester). If the number of chapters in a course was high, they were shorter. The Welcome chapter was included in each course providing basic information about the course and instructions on how to study efficiently, sample tests with keys were available to students, animations presenting tenses in ESP 2, samples of excellent motivation essays in ESP 4, professional texts with translated vocabulary in ESP 5 and 6.

Learners' knowledge was tested by various types of tests; multiple-choice tests with one or more correct answers were largely used, as well as dichotomic of Yes/No and True/False types. Jumbled sentences, fill-in-gaps and the open-answer tasks, i.e. translations, which are suitable for testing foreign language skills, were also applied. In each course different numbers of tests were included, one test per grammar topic as minimum.

Assignments were planned as learners' independent homework on a topic going deep into the learning content acquired in the course. Two assignments showing how the grammar items were acquired by learners were required in ESP 1 and 2 courses; one assignment was included in ESP 3 and 4, and no assignments were set in ESP 5 and 6 courses.

In Discussion tool two threads with topics reflecting the course content were inserted by the tutor to support the development of communication skill. Students' participation in discussing these topics was voluntary but supported by extra points included in student's total assessment after the course. Other threads were devoted to particular problems in each course, e.g. Quantifiers in ESP 1, or Conditionals in ESP 2 and only those students who needed some support participated in discussions, either actively (by asking questions), or passively (by reading what had been said).

E-mails could be used for student-tutor and student-student communication. This tool was exploited if necessary.

3.2 A Course of Academic Writing

As Frydrychova Klimova says, the course Academic Writing (AWT) attempts to help both Czech and foreign or overseas students of the faculty [2]. It is a one semester course which students can attend either in the winter or summer term. The course focuses on the process of writing from beginning to end, and gives advice on how to write professionally. It shows the component parts of writing process which cover envisaging what to write, planning an outline, drafting passages, writing the whole thing, revising and rewriting it, and finishing it in an appropriate form, together with publishing all or parts of a text. In addition, it concentrates on those features which are different in English and Czech, such as citations, compiling a bibliography or using appropriate English. As for the last aspect, there are independent sections on grammar structures in written English, lexical structures, and punctuation. Moreover, the course provides students with ready-made materials, including templates for such text types as the Letter of Application or C.V. In addition, students can access the Guide to

Dissertations Written in English [9], which provides a clear sample with ample evidence on how academic writing works in practice. The main course topics are Summary of a lecture or a seminar; Argumentative essay; Professional essay 1 (including references and bibliography); Professional essay 2 (including references and bibliography); Writing an article for Wikipedia; and Final consolidation and evaluation of the course by both the teacher and the students. The entry level of students' English usually ranges from B1 to C1 according to CERF.

Method of AWT instruction

This one-semester optional course lasts 12 weeks. The reason why this course was chosen as the case study sample was that it has been successfully used since 2005 and it has been continuously modified to meet students' specific needs and also to comply with the institutional requirements as far as the format, structure and content are concerned. The course exposes students to blended learning. That means students meet a teacher once every two weeks to discuss and clarify the mistakes they made in their assignments, while at the same time, students are expected to undertake self-study of the materials that form their online e-Learning course. Students also receive double feedback on their assignments; one in the face-to-face class and the other online after submitting their assignment. There are usually five assignments during the course: a one–paragraph summary of a lecture/seminar; an argumentative essay without bibliographies and references; two essays including bibliographies and references and writing an entry for Wikipedia.

Research sample

Altogether 14 full-time students of Management of Tourism and one of Information Management participated in the winter term 2014/15 in the course. Eleven students were in the first year of their study and three students in the second year of their study. Although the sample of the respondents might seem small, it is a maximum for this course since students have to write long essays which the teacher must correct within a relatively short period to provide students with timely feedback.

Methods of data collecting and processing

The data were collected at the end of the term in form of evaluation reports generated from the Blackboard online course and focused on the following aspects: the most exploited tools in the course (given in percentage); learners' performance on weekdays; learners' performance during the whole semester; and learners' performance in daytime (per hour).

In addition, the findings from these evaluation reports were then expanded by students' opinions from their self-reflective essays for which students were given a few guiding questions (cf. [10]) by the course teacher such as What did I actually achieve while attending this course?, How have I developed my knowledge and skills?, What were three greatest challenges in doing this course?, Did you find the online course useful, not useful?, or What have I learned about myself while doing this course?

As it has been described in the ESP courses, similar tools were employed in the online component of the AWT course. These tools include syllabus, study/learning materials, assignments, communication tools (discussion, e-mail), announcements and

Table 3. Visit rate in tools of ESP 1–6 (authors' own source)

Hits/tool/Student	ESP1 (n = 151)		ESP2 (n = 137)		ESP3 (n = 92)		ESP4 (n = 78)		ESP5 (n = 65)		ESP6 (n = 68)	
Syllabus	347	2.29	244	1.78	96	1.04	82	1.05	62	0.95	37	0.54
Announcement	370	2.45	321	2.34	211	2.29	176	2.25	160	2.46	148	2.17
Calendar	302	2.0	297	2.16	224	2.43	192	2.46	131	2.01	159	2.33
SM	9,241	3.39	17,741	3.69	2,636	2.86	3,260	3.8	3.315	1.7	3,061	1.51
Tests	4,892	2.69	12,316	3.09	1,821	2.19	2,106	2.7	0	0	0	0
Assignments	327	1.08	301	1.09	107	1.16	89	1.14	95	1.46	80	1.17
Discussions	356	2.34	458	3.34	320	3.47	233	2.98	89	1.36	33	0.48
E-mails	177	1.17	182	1.32	76	0.82	32	0.41	14	0.21	27	0.39
Total hits	16,012		31,860		5,491		6,170		3,866		3,545	
Average hits/student/tool	*2.17*		*2.35*		*2.03*		*2.09*		*1.26*		*1.07*	

calendar. In comparison with the ESP courses, the AWT course does not contain tests. The reason is that students have to write a written assignment/essay every second week.

4 Results and Discussion

The data collected both in ESP and AWT courses are displayed and discussed below. First, they are presented in separate subchapters; then, they are compared and discussed.

4.1 ESP 1–6 Courses: Results and Discussion

As it has been mentioned in 4.1.3, the amounts of hits were monitored under four criteria:

- visit rate to the course;
- learners' performance on weekdays;
- learners' performance in weeks of semester;
- learners' performance in daytime.

ESP 1–6: visit rate

The results received from ESP 1–6 courses monitoring the visit rate to the courses are displayed in Table 3.

Totally, 66,944 hits were made in all ESP courses by all students. The Study Materials reached the highest visit rate of all tools, followed by Discussions. Students in ESP 4 course were the most active of all in hitting the Study Materials. The ESP 4 course deals with oral communication, therefore such a high visit rate was not expected. The reason for this could be that within the Job Interview topic students are to write a Letter of Motivation to show their prospective employers that they are the best choice for the position. In the Study Materials numerous samples of essays are available to provide inspiration to students so that they are able to write an impressive text which would hit the employer and they would succeed on the job market. ESP 2 course reached the second highest visit rate; this result was expected as the learning content was demanding (English tenses), as well as in ESP 1 (nouns, adjectives, adverbs, numerals, or quantifiers) on the third position. As it has been mentioned above, the results are expressed in hits per student per tool, therefore they are not impacted, e.g. by the fact that 35 chapters were included in ESP 2 course which was attended by the second highest amount of students (n = 137), compared to ESP 1 (18 chapters, n = 151). The Discussion tool reached the second highest amount of hits after the Study Materials. This tool was most frequently exploited in ESP 3 course (written communication), followed by ESP 2 (English tenses) and ESP 4 (oral communication). As it has been expected, tests were the third frequently used tool, particularly in ESP 2 course where English tenses call for much practicing. But in other courses the visit rate was also high. Announcements and Calendar were similar and reached a rather stable visit rate in all ESP courses, compared to Syllabus where the high visit rate was performed in ESP 1 course only, and it was gradually decreasing in follow-up courses. The reason might be students found another way how to share information provided by this tool; one can only assume that they started to use a social network, most probably Facebook. Assignments were used as needed, i.e. for learning the task and submitting the assignment. This frequency might support the designers' objectives that the assignments were clearly set and recurring hits would be redundant. E-mail was the least frequently visited tool, which can be explained by the high visit rate of discussions. It is likely that the problems were consulted there.

To sum up, learners in ESP 1–6 courses performed various activities expressed by a different average number of hits per course/student/tool: ESP 2–2.35; ESP 1–2.17; ESP 4–2.09; ESP 3–2.03; ESP 5–1.26; ESP 6–1.07.

ESP 1–6: performance in weekdays

Apart from the visit rate, other three criteria were applied for the analysis. Learners' performance on weekdays is displayed in Fig. 1. This figure clearly shows (the amount of hits is displayed on vertical axis) that Wednesdays are the weekdays, when learners most frequently visit the course and study. As the research participants were the students of part-time studies, one would expect that they would be most active during weekends. However, against all expectations this was not true. As their activity is concentrated in one day in the middle of the week, the reason might be that they do a great deal of their week load in two days (Mondays, Tuesdays) and they spend Wednesdays on studying. Then, before the weekend starts, they work in their profession. Weekends are not devoted to studying, but probably to private/family activities. This design can be supported by the fact that the period of three/five years (in Bachelor/Master study programmes) is long and the time management for this period must reflect students' private matters; they often start their family life and have children. Some activity was detected on Fridays, but hardly any student visited the ESP courses on Sundays and Thursdays. It is interesting that the identical result showing Wednesdays as a day of study was detected in another research conducted at FIM. This research focused on the online course of Library services–Information competence in education [11]. Neither in this course any reason to support this finding was discovered.

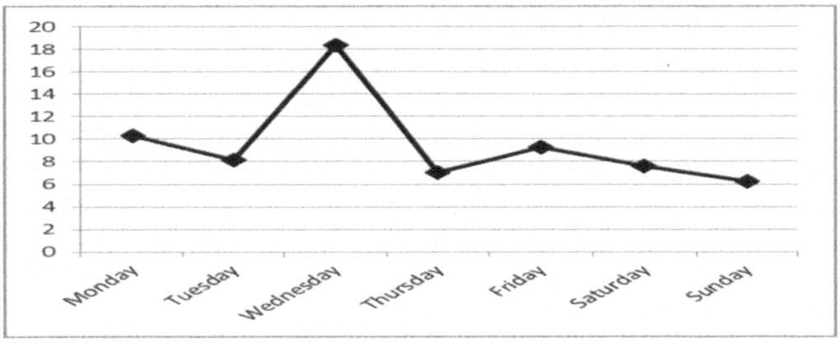

Fig. 1. Learners' performance on weekdays (authors' own source)

ESP 1–6: performance during the semester

Learners' performance during the semester is presented in Fig. 2 where in 12 weeks (horizontal axis) the total amounts of hits are displayed on vertical axis. As expected, a high activity was monitored at the beginning of these courses, when students are eager to find out what the requirements and deadlines are. Then, their activity sharply decreases although it is widely accepted that foreign languages should be studied on a daily basis. Some increase was detected in weeks when assignments were submitted, i.e. in weeks 6 and 10 in ESP 1 and 2, and in week 8 in ESP 3 and 4. The identical, even a sharper, increase in their activity is then performed in the final two weeks before the examination period starts. This fact supports the importance of continuous activation of learners during the whole semester–if no home or independent work is required, neither spontaneous activity, nor learning appears.

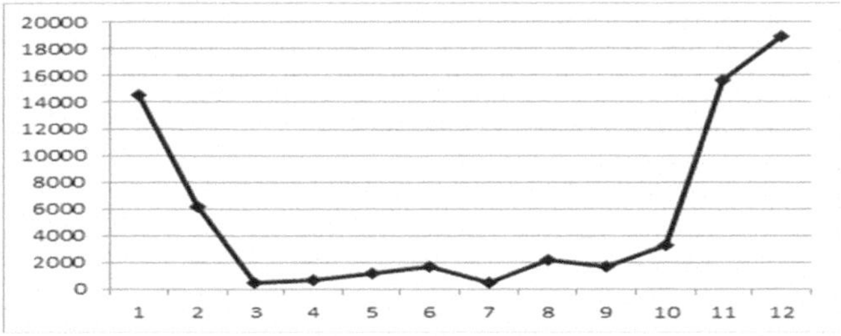

Fig. 2. Learners' performance in weeks of semester (authors' own source)

ESP 1–6: performance in daytime

As expected, two peak times were detected, i.e. 8 p.m. and 11 a.m., each of them having approximately a two-hour increase in study activity before the peak and two-hour period after it. Between the peak times a rather active period was detected from 2 p.m. to 5 p.m. Several students made hits late nights, probably in the time close to the examination period. No activity appeared late-night/early-morning hours, i.e. from 2 a.m. to 7 a.m. As for the time management and productivity of the learning process, this period is of very low efficiency (e.g. [12, 13]).

4.2 AWT Courses: Results and Discussion

The evaluation reports from the online course provide a course leader with useful information. One of the reports gives details of an overall summary of user activity in the course. Students were the most active in the content areas (77%). In fact, students did not need to use any other tools because they met their course teacher every second week and therefore they did not have to use calendar, announcements, e-mail or discussion tools.

Therefore, the authors of this article took a closer look at all user activity inside these content areas. Students were the most active in reading the course syllabus (330 hits/46%) and in the assignment area (283 hits/39%), whereas using the Study materials came last (109 hits/15%). The reason was that students mostly searched for the course structure, its requirements and compulsory reading in order to obtain credits. Since this course is mainly aimed at developing formal writing skills, students have to write on a regular basis. Therefore the second most exploited tool was Assignments. Finally, they accessed the study materials to complete the information from their face-to-face classes and when necessary to use it in the preparation of their written assignments.

Mondays and Tuesdays were the most active days in this course. The reason is that Tuesday was the deadline of submitting their assignments.

As far as the additional information from students' self-reflective essays is concerned, students stated that they had been satisfied with the course being held just once in two weeks since as they said, they had enough free time to think about their written assignment not only at school, but also at home where they had more free time and could write when it fitted them most. In addition, they appreciated the online support which had been fast, clear and useful, particularly when speaking about the feedback on their assignments. They also reported that the online support had helped them revise new material at home. However, they found very important to attend the face-to-face classes because they got a lot of information about the issues of each topic. They think it is essential not to miss these classes since then they do not have so many difficulties with writing if they are not present in class.

5 Conclusion

As it can be seen from the findings of the ESP and AWT courses, students exploit those tools which are relevant to their studies [14]. Thus, in case of the ESP courses they use study materials, they are enrolled in discussions since they do not have so frequent face-to-face classes as it is in the case of the Course of Academic Writing [15]. And they also do tests to prepare for the final exams. On the contrary, students of the AWT course meet their teacher every second week and therefore they do not need to use the discussion, calendar or emails tools. The course is aimed at their written production and therefore the AWT students exploit the assignments tool at most. Both groups also access the syllabus, particularly at the beginning of the terms in order to discover the course requirements for receiving a credit and/or an exam.

Although the proportion between the face-to-face classes and their online studies are different in the ESP courses and the AWT course, it is obvious that blended learning form of instruction works in both cases. Students efficiently and independently work according to their needs in order to succeed in their studies, either full-time or part-time. The online component enables them to study independently on location and time. In both groups students mostly prefer to study in the evening between 7 p.m. and 10 p.m. when they usually finish their daily/family commitments and can focus on their studies. Interestingly, the part-time/distance students prefer to study on Wednesdays since they probably want to spend weekends with their families. The AWT full-time students work in the online course mainly before the deadline of their assignment, as well as the ESP students.

Nevertheless, all the students are able to take on responsibilities for their own studies, to work independently and efficiently. The blended form of instruction can make such a study possible and students in this form of study can display greater engagement when they are exposed to such an instruction which is much more relevant to their learning preferences (cf. [16]).

Acknowledgement. This research was financially supported by the SPEV. In addition, the authors thank Jan Freiberg for his help with the data.

References

1. Wong, L.L.C., Nunan, D.: The learning styles and strategies of effective language learners. System **39**(2), 144–163 (2011)
2. Frydrychova Klimova, B.: Teaching formal written English. Gaudeamus, Hradec Králové (2012)
3. Ke, I., Cahyani, L.: Learning to become users of English as a Lingua Franca (ELF): How ELF online communication affects Taiwanese learners' beliefs of English. System **46**, 28–38 (2014)
4. Frydrychova Klimova, B.: Blended learning. In: Vilas, A.M., Martin, A.S., Gonzales, J.M., Gonzales, J.A.M.: (eds.) Research, Reflections and Innovations in Integrating ICT in Education, pp. 705–708. FORMATEX (2009)
5. Frydrychova Klimova, B., Poulova, P.: ICT in the teaching of academic writing. Lectures Notes in Management Science, vol. 11, pp. 33–38 (2013)
6. Frydrychova Klimova, B., Poulova, P.: Forms of instruction and students' preferences - a comparative study. In: Cheung, Simon K.S., Fong, J., Zhang, J., Kwan, R., Kwok, L.F. (eds.) ICHL 2014. LNCS, vol. 8595, pp. 220–231. Springer, Cham (2014). doi:10.1007/978-3-319-08961-4_21
7. Simonova, I., et al.: Klicove kompetence a jejich reflexe v terciarnim e-vzdelavani [Key competences and their reflection in tertiary e-education]. Milos Vognar Publishing House, Hradec Kralove (2011)
8. Yin, R.K.: Case Study Research: Design And Methods. Sage, Newbury Park (1984)
9. Frydrychova Klimova, B.: A Guide to Dissertations Written in English. Gaudeamus, Hradec Kralove (2006)
10. Race, P.: Evidencing reflection: putting the 'w' into reflection 2006. http://escalate.ac.uk/resources/reflection/02.html, Retrieved 2 Dec 2014
11. Simonova, I., Poulova, P.: Individualized online learning: tracking students' performance in the online course. In: Proceedings of the CTA 2015, Bangkok (in press 2015)

12. Baker, D.P., Fabrega, R., Galindo, C.: Mishook, J: Instructional time and national achievement: cross-national evidence. Prospects Q. Rev. Comp. Educ. **34**(3), 311–334 (2004)
13. Kolbe, T., Partridge, M., O'Reilly, F.: Time and Learning in Schools: a National Profile. National Center on Time & Learning, Boston (2011)
14. Simonova, I., Poulova, P.: Learning and assessment preferences in the ICT-enhanced process of instruction. In: 2014 Proceedings of the 7th International Conference (ICHL 2014), pp. 281–288. Springer (2014)
15. Poulova, P., Simonova, I.: Flexible e-learning: online courses tailored to student's needs. In: Proceedings of the 9th International Scientific Conference on Distance Learning in Applied Informatics (DIVAI 2012), pp. 251–260. UKF, Nitra (2012)
16. Yair, G.: Educational battlefields in America: the tug-of-war over students' engagement with instruction. Sociol. Educ. **73**, 247–269 (2000)

College Students' Computer Self-efficacy, Intrinsic Motivation, Attitude, and Satisfaction in Blended Learning Environments

Yanhong Li[1], Harrison Hao Yang[2,3(✉)], Jin Cai[1], and Jason MacLeod[2]

[1] Collaborative & Innovative Center for Educational Technology, Central China Normal University, Wuhan, China

[2] School of Educational Information Technology, Central China Normal University, Wuhan, China
harrison.yang@oswego.edu

[3] School of Education, State University of New York at Oswego, Oswego, NY, USA

Abstract. The purpose of this study was to examine the relationships between students' computer self-efficacy, intrinsic motivation, attitude, and satisfaction in blended learning environments. The participants were 239 college students enrolled at Hubei University in China. A survey including four existing instruments was used for data collection. The results of structural equation modeling analysis suggested students' attitudes toward online and face-to-face classes were the most influential toward to satisfaction in blended learning environments. Higher levels of intrinsic motivation were seen to be influential toward satisfaction in blended learning environments. Computer self-efficacy was seen to influence intrinsic motivation and attitudes, but not found to influence satisfaction in blended learning environments.

Keywords: Blended learning · Computer self-efficacy · Intrinsic motivation · Attitude · Satisfaction

1 Introduction

Blended learning (BL) is a learning approach that utilizes a combination of online and face-to-face learning processes [1]. Although various advantages of BL are widely acknowledged [2–5], insufficient levels of student satisfaction have been noted among the literature as being a negative aspect of BL [6]. As a result, researchers have focused on student satisfaction in BL environments [6, 7]. Among the related studies, Wu, Tennyson, and Hsia [8] identified students' computer self-efficacy, interaction, performance expectations, system functionality, content features, and learning climate were important factors determining students' satisfaction in BL environments. Wu *et al.* [8] also suggested other determinants might influence students' satisfaction in BL environments which have not yet

S.K.S. Cheung et al. (Eds.): ICBL 2017, LNCS 10309, pp. 65–73, 2017.
DOI: 10.1007/978-3-319-59360-9_6

been explored. Accordingly, our research focused on students' satisfaction in BL environments by exploring two new factors: intrinsic motivation and attitude.

2 Related Work

2.1 Intrinsic Motivation

Intrinsic motivation relates to participation and engagement that is derived from personal interest and enjoyment [9]. Intrinsic motivation has also been noted as being internationally regulated, and associated with one's inherent satisfaction [10]. Ryan and Deci [11] stated, "because intrinsic motivation results in high-quality learning and creativity, it is especially important to detail the factors that engender versus undermine it." Generally speaking, students' motivation to learn was found to be enhanced in BL environments [12]. However, few studies have focused more specifically on students' intrinsic motivation in BL environments. Consequently, this study includes intrinsic motivation as a research variable.

2.2 Computer Self-efficacy

Computer self-efficacy has been defined as, "judgment of one's capability to use a computer" [13]. In other words, computer self-efficacy refers to the level of conviction someone has in their ability to be effective. Computer self-efficacy has been found to be a significant predictor of students' satisfaction in BL environments [14, 15], however, Wu *et al.* [8] found computer self-efficacy only provided an indirect relationship to student satisfaction. Therefore, conflicting results have been documented for this variable. In an effort to provide clarity on this issue, computer self-efficacy was included as a research variable in this study.

2.3 Attitude

An attitude, as it relates to this study, refers to an affective response toward the performance of some type of BL related behavior [16]. Research has suggested that students' attitudes toward the computer plays an important role in BL environments [17, 18]. Students' attitudes have also been suggested to be particularly important in online learning environments, as one's attitude influences technology acceptance and participation [19, 20]. Despite previous investigation of students' attitudes in BL environments, few research has individually explored the influence of attitude toward the online and face-to-face components of BL separately. Therefore, students' attitudes toward the online and face-to-face BL environments were included as variables in this study.

2.4 Research Model and Hypotheses

Figure 1 illustrates the research model and corresponding hypotheses for exploring the relationships between students' motivation, computer self-efficacy, attitude, and satisfaction in a BL environment. Nine research hypotheses are show in Fig. 1, the tenth hypothesis is not shown, as it relates to gender influence toward the research model. The ten research hypotheses are as follows:

H1: Computer self-efficacy will positively influence intrinsic motivation.
H2: Computer self-efficacy will positively influence online attitude.
H3: Computer self-efficacy will positively influence BL satisfaction.
H4: Intrinsic motivation will positively influence online attitude.
H5: Intrinsic motivation will positively influence face-to-face attitude.
H6: Intrinsic motivation will positively influence BL satisfaction.
H7: Online attitude will positively influence face-to-face attitude.
H8: Online attitude will positively influence BL satisfaction.
H9: Face-to-face attitude will positively influence BL satisfaction.
H10: Males will show higher levels of computer self-efficacy, intrinsic motivation, attitudes, and BL satisfaction than females.

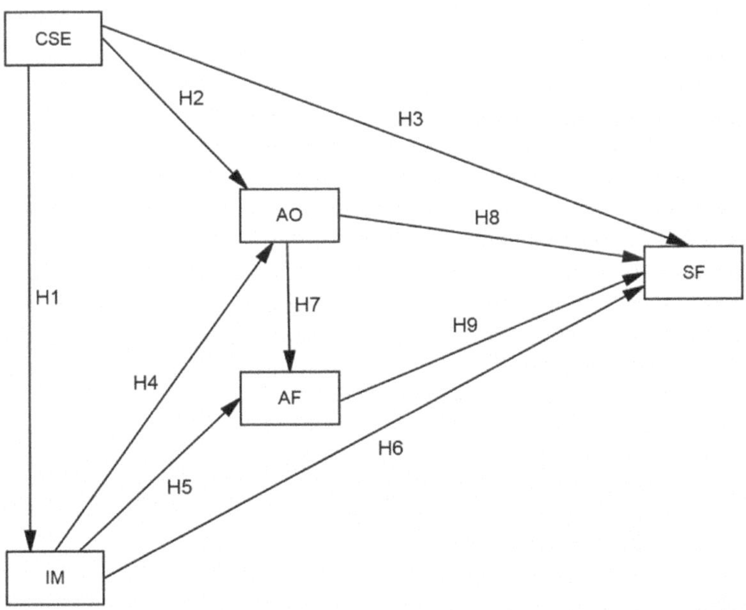

Fig. 1. Research model and hypotheses *Note:* CSE (Computer self-efficacy); IM (Intrinsic motivation); AO (Online attitude); AF (Face-to-face attitude); SF (Satisfaction).

3 Method

3.1 Participants

Participants of this study were purposely selected based on enrollment in college-level courses utilizing a common online platform for BL, Ruanko, which is the learning management system of the Hubei University of Education. 367 online surveys were sent to the targeted participants. 251 surveys were returned. 12 participant responses were omitted due to incompleteness. This left 239 valid responses for statistical analysis. The majority of participants were between 18 and 20 years of age. The female-to-male ratio was about 4-to-6.

3.2 Instrumentation

The computer self-efficacy, intrinsic motivation, attitude, and satisfaction (CMAS) survey included 43 items. All items were adopted from existing instruments. The computer self-efficacy (CSE) scale was a single construct adopted from Compeau and Higgins' [13] instrument. The intrinsic motivation (IM) scale was a single construct adopted from Pintrich and Groot's [21] instrument. The attitude scales were two constructs adopted from Akkoyunlu and Yılmaz-Soylu's [22] instrument. The two constructs of the attitude scale included online learning attitude (AO) and face-to-face attitude (AF). The satisfaction (SF) scale was adopted from So and Brush's [4] instrument. All survey items were measured on a 5-point Likert scale ranging from 1 (strongly disagree) to 5 (strongly agree).

3.3 Data Collection and Analysis

Before administering the survey, approval was granted from teachers to distribute collect data from their BL course students. All participations were voluntary and anonymous. The survey was administered online at the end of the fall semester of 2016. In order to administer the survey in the participants' native language, all items were parallel translated into Chinese by two researchers. Then, the complete CMAS survey was assessed by a bilingual educational technology expert to ensure content validity of the translation. Based on the expert's comments, some items were revised to improve overall readability. The data was imported into Microsoft Excel. Then, Statistical Product and Service Solutions (SPSS) was used for *t*-test analysis. Meanwhile, the sample size of this study is more than 5 times per variable, so Analysis of Moment Structures (AMOS) was suitable for data analysis [23]. Confirmatory factor analysis (CFA) and correlation analysis tests were used to analyze the research model.

4 Results

The results of this study are presented in two stages. First, an overview of the CMAS survey construct validity and reliability is provided. Then, analyses relating to the research model hypotheses are discussed.

4.1 Validity and Reliability

As shown in Table 1, all constructs' composite reliability (CR) coefficients were greater than 0.9 and all the average variance extracted (AVE) were greater than 0.5. These results indicate that all constructs of the CMAS survey have more than satisfactory convergent validity [24–26]. Table 2 showed the square root of all AVEs were above 0.50 [27] and larger than the respective correlation coefficients [25], which validate discriminant validity for the CMAS survey constructs. In addition, as for the multi-collinearity, despite the correlation coefficient between SF & IM, SF & AO, and SF & AF being higher than 0.8, their *t* values were 6.23, 7.52, and 6.63, respectively. In addition, their variance inflation factor (VIF) scores were 3.13, 3.00, and 3.05, respectively. When all *t* values are above 2 and all VIF scores are below 10, multi-collinearity makes no difference [28].

Table 1. Validity and reliability analysis.

Constructs	Item	Mean	SD	CR	AVE	*a*
CSE	10	3.74	0.86	0.928	0.567	0.923
IM	9	3.80	0.87	0.956	0.707	0.955
AO	6	3.55	1.01	0.958	0.793	0.958
AF	7	3.82	0.93	0.964	0.794	0.964
SF	11	3.72	0.86	0.968	0.735	0.968

Table 2. Correlation analysis.

Constructs	CSE	IM	AO	AF	SF
CSE	0.753[a]				
IM	0.640**	0.841[a]			
AO	0.589**	0.773**	0.891[a]		
AF	0.536**	0.777**	0.766**	0.891[a]	
SF	0.578**	0.831**	0.840**	0.831**	0.857[a]

Notes: [a] square root of the AVE; ** $p < 0.01$.

Table 3. Fit measures for the research model.

Fit index	This study	Recommended value
Chi-squared (χ^2)	0.73	–
Degree of Freedom (df)	2	–
χ^2/df	0.36	≤5.00
Goodness of Fit Index (GFI)	1.00	≥0.90
Adjusted Goodness of Fit Index (AGFI)	0.99	≥0.90
Root Mean Square Error of Approximation (RMSEA)	0.00	≤0.08

Furthermore, Table 1 shows all Cronbach's alpha (*a*) values were greater than 0.9, which indicate the CMAS survey has high levels of reliability. Accordingly, the CMAS survey is a valid and reliable instrument.

4.2 Analysis of the Research Model

AMOS was used to explore causal relationships between constructs of the research model. As shown in Table 3, the results indicate that the model has a more than satisfactory level of fit. Figure 2 illustrates the relationships of constructs in the research model. The results indicate that all hypothesized relationships were significant except for one. No significance influence was identified between CSE and SF.

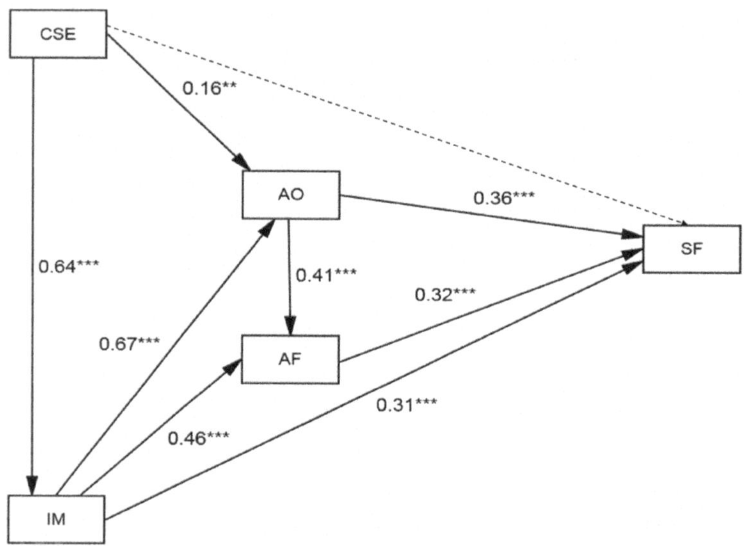

Fig. 2. Relationships between research model constructs *Notes:* ** $p < 0.01$; *** $p < 0.001$.

CSE was found to significantly influence IM and AO, however, CSE showed no direct effect on SF. The results indicated students with higher levels of CSE tended to also possess higher levels of IM and AO. Thus, H1 and H2 were supported; H3 was rejected.

IM was found to significantly influence AO, AF, and SF. These results indicate higher levels of IM influences both types of student attitudes and SF. Thus, H4, H5, and H6 were all supported. In regards to students' attitudes, AO was found to significantly influence AF, and both AO and AF were found to significantly influence SF. Thus, H7, H8, and H9 were all supported.

4.3 Analysis of Gender Influence

As shown in Table 4, male students showed significantly higher levels of IM and SF than female students. As for the constructs of CSE, AO, and AF, no significant difference was observed between genders, however, male students showed higher scores in all these aspects. Thus, H10 was partially supported.

Table 4. Analysis of gender influence on the research model constructs.

Constructs	Male		Female		*t*
	Mean	SD	Mean	SD	
CSE	3.86	0.88	3.59	0.82	2.47
IM	3.92	0.92	3.65	0.77	2.44*
AO	3.67	1.04	3.39	0.95	2.13
AF	3.87	0.98	3.75	0.86	1.00
SF	3.81	0.95	3.61	0.73	1.73**

Notes: * $p < 0.05$; ** $p < 0.01$.

5 Discussion and Conclusion

The purpose of this study was to explore the relationships between college students' computer self-efficacy, intrinsic motivation, attitude, and satisfaction in the context of the self-blend model of BL. The results of this study showed that students' attitudes toward online and face-to-face classes were the most influential variable that related to students' satisfaction in the BL environment. Higher levels of intrinsic motivation were also seen to be positively influential toward students' satisfaction. Computer self-efficacy was seen to influence intrinsic motivation and attitudes, however, computer self-efficacy was not found to directly influence satisfaction.

The results imply that instructors should consider students' attitudes in both environments, as students' attitudes were most influential toward satisfaction in BL. Furthermore, instructors should apply more emphasis toward students' attitudes toward the online components of the BL, as this aspect was seen to be the strongest relationship to students' satisfaction. In regards to the previous inconsistencies among computer self-efficacy research, our results were aligned to Wu *et al.* [8] findings which suggested computer self-efficacy only acted as a mediator of satisfaction.

Gender was seen to provide influence on the variables of intrinsic motivation and satisfaction within this sample of participants. However, no significant difference was found on either computer self-efficacy or perspective of students' attitudes, as hypothesized in the research model. These results indicate that instructors may need to consider specifically encouraging female students' in order to ensure females and males obtain the same levels of satisfaction in the self-blend model of BL environments.

It should be noted that this study only focused on the relationships between college students' computer self-efficacy, intrinsic motivation, attitude, and satisfaction in BL. In order to completely capture the dynamics of blended learning, future research should explore other related variables such as socioeconomic status and cultural background in a BL context.

Acknowledgments. The work was supported by the Key Project of Philosophy and Social Science Research, Ministry of Education of China (14JZD044).

References

1. Garrison, D.R., Kanuka, H.: Blended learning: Uncovering its transformative potential in higher education. Internet High. Educ. **2**, 95–105 (2004)
2. Singh, H.: Building effective blended learning programs. Educ. Technol. **43**(6), 51–54 (2003)
3. Osguthorpe, R.T., Graham, C.R.: Blending learning environments: definitions and directions. Q. Rev. Distance Educ. **3**, 227–233 (2003)
4. Yang, H., Wang, S.: Cases on Online Learning Communities and Beyond: Investigations and Applications. Information Science Reference/IGI Global, Hershey (2012)
5. Yang, H., Wang, S.: Cases on e-Learning Management: Development and Implementation. Information Science Reference/IGI Global, Hershey (2012)
6. So, H.J., Brush, T.A.: Student perceptions of collaborative learning, social presence and satisfaction in a blended learning environment: relationships and critical factors. Comput. Educ. **51**, 318–336 (2008)
7. Abrantes, J.L., Seabra, C., Lages, L.F.: Pedagogical affect, student interest, and learning performance. J. Bus. Res. **60**, 960–964 (2007)
8. Wu, J.H., Tennyson, R.D., Hsia, T.L.: A study of student satisfaction in a blended e-learning system environment. Comput. Educ. **1**, 155–164 (2010)
9. Deci, E.L., Ryan, R.M.: Intrinsic Motivation and Self-determination in Human Behavior. Plenum, New York (1985)
10. Ryan, R.M., Deci, E.L.: Self-determination theory and facilitation of intrinsic motivation, social development, and well-being. Am. Psychol. **55**, 68–78 (2000)
11. Ryan, R.M., Deci, E.L.: Intrinsic and extrinsic motivations: classic definitions and new directions. Contemp. Educ. Psych. **25**, 54–67 (2000)
12. Chao, C.Y., Chen, Y.T., Chuang, K.Y.: Exploring students' learning attitude and achievement in flipped learning supported computer aided design curriculum: a study in high school engineering education. Comput. Appl. Eng. Educ. **4**, 514–526 (2015)
13. Compeau, D.R., Higgins, C.A.: Computer self-efficacy: development of a measure and initial test. MIS Q. **19**, 189–211 (1995)
14. Lim, C.K.: Computer self-efficacy, academic self-concept, and other predictors of satisfaction and future participation of adult distance learners. Am. J. Distance Educ. **2**, 41–51 (2001)
15. Holley, D., Oliver, M.: Student engagement and blended learning: portraits of risk. Comput. Educ. **3**, 693–700 (2010)
16. Ajzen, I., Fishbein, M.: Understanding Attitudes and Predicting Social Behavior. Prentice Hall, New Jersey (1980)
17. Lu, Y., Zhou, T., Wang, B.: Exploring Chinese users' acceptance of instant messaging using the theory of planned behavior, the technology acceptance model, and the flow theory. Comput. Hum. Behav. **1**, 29–39 (2009)
18. Teo, T.: Assessing the computer attitudes of students: an Asian perspective. Comput. Hum. Behav. **4**, 1634–1642 (2008)
19. Mitchell, A., Honore, S.: Criteria for successful blended learning. Indust. Commer. Train. **3**, 143–149 (2007)
20. Dahalan, N., Hassan, H., Atan, H.: Student engagement in online learning: learners attitude toward e-mentoring. Procedia-Soc. Behav. Sci. **67**, 464–475 (2012)
21. Pintrich, P.R., De Groot, E.V.: Motivational and self-regulated learning components of classroom academic performance. J. Educ. Psych. **1**, 33–40 (1990)
22. Akkoyunlu, B., Yılmaz-Soylu, M.: Development of a scale on learners' views on blended learning and its implementation process. Internet High. Educ. **1**, 26–32 (2008)

23. Bentler, P.M., Chou, C.P.: Practical issues in structural modeling. Sociol. Methods Res. **16**(1), 78–117 (1987)
24. Gefen, D., Straub, D.W.: A practical guide to factorial validity using PLS-graph: tutorial and annotated example. Commun. Infor. Syst. **5**, 91–109 (2005)
25. Chin, W.W.: The partial least squares approach to structural equation modeling. In: Marcoulides, G.A. (ed.) Modern Methods for Business Research, pp. 298–336. Erlbaum, New Jersey (1998)
26. Shevlin, M., Miles, J.N.: Effects of sample size, model specification and factor loadings on the GFI in confirmatory factor analysis. Pers. Indiv. Differ. **1**, 85–90 (1998)
27. Fornell, C.D., Larcker, F.: Evaluating structural equation models with unobservable variables and measurement errors. J. Marketing Res. **2**, 39–50 (1981)
28. Chatterjee, S., Hadi, A.S.: Regression Analysis by Example. Wiley, New York (2000)

A Survey on Teachers' Ability to Apply Electronic Schoolbag into Teaching

Qinlei Wang(✉), Jing Bai, and Rui Yao

School of Educational Science and Technology,
Guangdong Polytechnic Normal University, Guangzhou, Guangdong, China
klwqlei@163.com

Abstract. With the introduction of Electronic Schoolbag (E-bag) into education, teachers' information technology teaching ability (TITTA) to use E-bag has been influenced obviously. In this study, a questionnaire was developed for figuring out the current situation of teachers' ITTA to apply E-bag and the potential influence factors, then a survey was carried out in some sampled schools in Pearl River Delta. It turned out that teachers were confronted with some challenges, such as resources and tools development, various teaching activities based on E-bag, though operations and functions of E-bag had been grasped early. In addition, the foundation of teaching reforming in school and the duration of E-bag application were the most obvious influence factors for instructional design based on E-bag. Teachers should participate in all kinds of teaching reforming activities to use E-bag more effectively.

Keywords: Electronic schoolbag · Information technology teaching ability · Influence factors

1 Introduction

Since 2010, there have been many Electronic Schoolbag (E-bag) experimental units in a number of regions across the country, especially the Pearl River Delta - such as Guangzhou, Foshan, Shenzhen and other places. There is widespread concern about teaching by using E-bag in many pilot schools. With the continuous popularization, application and in-depth study, e-bag teaching application plays an important role in promoting the transformation of teaching methods and learning styles. On the other hand, it also puts forward more requirements for teachers' information technology teaching ability (ITTA). It is directly related to the teaching effectiveness of E-bag in primary and secondary schools. Therefore, we designed a questionnaire for analyzing the improvement of ITTA promoted by E-bag and for discovering the existing problems and deficiencies. This questionnaire was developed by integrating some investigations and interviews about E-bag application with the *Information Technology Application*

Project of Distinguished Young Talents in Higher Education of Guangdong, Smart Learning Innovation Based on Electronic Schoolbag, Grant No. HS2015008.

S.K.S. Cheung et al. (Eds.): ICBL 2017, LNCS 10309, pp. 74–83, 2017.
DOI: 10.1007/978-3-319-59360-9_7

Ability Standard for Primary and Middle School Teachers (Trial). Then, a questionnaire survey was carried out.

2 Related Work

Teachers' information technology application capability contains two parts, which are respectively the ability to use information technology (IT) to optimize the original teaching, and the ability to use IT to innovate the original teaching [1]. Teachers' ability to apply E-bag into teaching refers to the TITTA to use E-bag. Compared to TITAC, it tends to emphasize the ability to apply E-bag to achieving individualized learning, changing original teaching methods, and developing learning tools. In order to carry out the study more smoothly, a review on related work is necessary.

Through exploring literatures about teachers' literacy or ability to use E-bag from China National Knowledge Internet and WanFang Data, it was found that the correlational study has been emerging since 2013. The related work focused on three aspects. Firstly, some studies [2, 3] analyzed teachers' emotional acceptance (understanding, needs, attitudes, satisfaction) of E-bag through questionnaire or interview, and proposed effective educational policy measures or improved original functions of E-bag. Secondly, teachers' technical literacy of E-bag was studied increasingly. These studies [4–6] elaborated on the influence factors of literacy to use E-bag, such as teachers' age, gender and TITAC, and explored the corresponding E-bag application technical literacy to innovate teaching effectively, in which the method of investigating and interviewing were often adopted. Thirdly, researchers intended to study how to improve the teaching method based on E-bag. It mainly explored the current situation and existing problems in the subject teaching based on E-bag and analyzing differences of subjects teaching between different disciplines based on E-bag [7, 8], or proposing new teaching modes based on E-bag, such as flipped classroom teaching based on E-bag, individualizing learning on E-bag [9, 10].

From analyzing the current related research, some revelations were available for this study. Survey was a good way to discover the existing problem in TITTA to use E-bag. And the influence factors of teachers' applying E-bag provided some references which contributed to building the connection between TITAC and TITTA to use E-bag. Lastly, few studies tended to explore teachers' applying E-bag on the foundation of TITAC, which made it possible to innovate study perspectives.

3 Research Design

3.1 Research Objective

This research tries to find out the status quo and influence factors about the development of teachers' ITTA promoted by E-bag in the Pearl River Delta through survey data. On this basis, it revealed problems appearing in application of E-bag and took some measures to improve teachers' ITTA to use E-bag. Finally, we aim to improve the application effect of E-bag.

3.2 Research Subject

Teachers of nine primary and secondary schools, in which E-bag was regarded as effective tool in teaching reform, were chosen as the research subjects. These schools contained 5 primary schools and 4 secondary schools, which were located in the cities of Guangzhou, Shenzhen, and Foshan.

3.3 Research Process and Method

The research was carried out mainly by using literature analysis and survey research methods, which included four parts in the process: theoretical analysis, questionnaire design, survey implementation, and data analysis. First of all, it analyzed and summed up three aspects of teachers' ITTA, including technical literacy, instructional design, teaching implementation and teaching evaluation based on E-bag. In this stage, the main task was to consult a great deal of literatures and the corresponding policy standards by using literature analysis. Then, the questionnaire design, survey implementation, investigation and analysis were carried out in turn according to the research process of the questionnaire survey.

4 Questionnaire Preparation

4.1 Questionnaire Development

This study clarified and defined the teaching application fields of E-bag according to Information Technology Application Ability Standard for Primary and Middle School Teachers (Trial). Furthermore, the questionnaire was developed to include two sections. The first section was to explore teachers' ITTA to use E-bag. The second section was designed to analyze influencing factors from the teacher individuals who were interviewed.

Indicators of teachers' ITTA based on E-bag. This section was made up of three parts, including technology literacy, instructional design, teaching implementation and evaluation (Table 1).

This section was the core part of the questionnaire, including the technical literacy, teaching design, teaching implementation, teaching evaluation. There are 15 items in total. These items would be implemented by using Likert, which covers five scales. They respectively were "Strongly agree", "Agree", "Neither agree nor disagree", "Disagree", "Strongly disagree", which would be converted to respectively 5, 4, 3, 2, 1 (or 1, 2, 3, 4, 5 if the topic is opposite). Then a higher score represents a higher information-based teaching ability to use E-bag.

Characteristics of respondents. The characteristics of respondents were divided into individual factors and basic factors of the school in which they were working. Individual factors cover age, teaching qualifications and information literacy, while basic factors include information construction foundation and the level of teaching reform [11]. They were presented in the form of multiple choice questions in the questionnaire (Fig. 1)

Table 1. Indicators of teachers' ITTA based on E-bag

Item	Content
Technology literacy	1. Teachers should be actively applied information technology to support effective teaching (TL1)
	2. The introduction of E-bag can improve traditional learning environment (TL2)
	3. The emerging concepts and ideas should be integrated into the teaching application of E-bag (TL3)
	4. I am unfamiliar with e-bag teaching functions and support (TL4)
	5. I can collect, develop and manage the materials and resources needed for e-bag teaching (TL5)
	6. I can discover or design learning tools (APP software) that are applied to specific disciplines (TL6)
Instructional design	7. I can analyze learning needs based on data records of E-bag (ID1)
	8. I fail to write effective and achievable teaching objective (ID2)
	9. I can appropriately use e-bag to solve key points and difficult points in teaching (ID3)
	10. I can collect or develop the teaching resources and tools needed for E-bag (ID4)
	11. I can design effective teaching activities by using a variety of teaching strategies (ID5)
	12. I fail to design evaluation questions such as test questions and measure gauge (ID6)
	13. I can optimize your instructional design through collective preparation of a lesson (ID7)
Teaching implementation and evaluation	14. I can stimulate students' interest in learning and guide them to actively participate (TIE1)
	15. I can adjust the teaching behavior according to the students' feedback (TIE2)
	16. I fail to use tools of E-bag to evaluate students in a shorter time (TIE3)
	17. I can record and analyze various evaluation data to support comprehensive quality assessment of learning (TIE4)

.

This section was mainly for understanding the background information of teachers, such as gender, age, information technology literacy. Differences in these factors resulted in differences in the ITTA to use E-bag. For example, the younger teachers tended to use information technology more frequently in teaching than senior teachers. More male teachers tended to apply new technology into teaching [12]. In general, this section laid the foundation for analyzing current problem occurring in using E-bag, which allowed us to design option variable to compare different results.

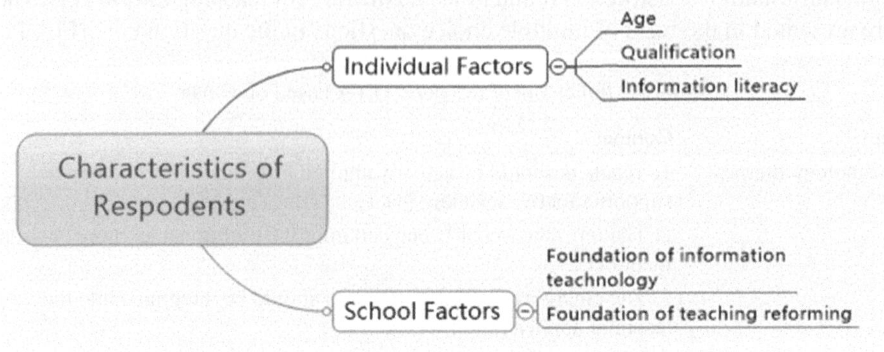

Fig. 1. Characteristics of teachers

4.2 Questionnaire Test

In order to examine the reliability of the questionnaire, 30 teachers who used the E-bag for teaching were selected and tested. Through statistically analyzing the data, the scale of Alpha coefficient was 0.8 or more, which indicated that the reliability of the questionnaire was acceptable. On the other hand, in order to examine its content-related validity, five experts were invited to criticize every item of questionnaire. Statistics suggested that the S-CVI/AVE was 0.91, which mean that the validity of the questionnaire was reasonable.

5 Implementation of the Survey

5.1 Investigation Sample

This study selected 90 teachers from 9 schools as survey object by Random sampling method. These schools were located in Yuexiu District and Panyu District of Guangzhou, Longgang District of Shenzhen, Nanhai District of Foshan. We determined the quantity of questionnaire according to application scale in the corresponding regions: 20 questionnaires were distributed in Yuexiu District of Guangzhou, 10 questionnaires were distributed in Longgang District of Shenzhen, 30 questionnaires were distributed in Panyu District of Guangzhou, and 30 questionnaires were distributed in Nanhai District of Foshan.

5.2 Questionnaire Distribution

In the course of the survey, paper questionnaires were distributed in combination with online electronic questionnaires. Due to the distance, respondents out of Guangzhou filled in the electronic questionnaire online, mainly through questionnaires star (http://www.sojump.com/jq/4438147.aspx). Meanwhile, paper questionnaires were distributed to teachers working in Guangzhou.

6 Data Analysis

In this study, SPSS data analysis software was used to statistically analyze the data. Among the 90 distributed questionnaires, 85 questionnaires were returned and 81 questionnaires were valid. The effective rate was 95.3%. According to the analysis, most teachers were mainly in the age group of 25–35 years old, while female teachers account for about 80%. About the information literacy, more than half of them have passed the National Educational Technology Ability Test for Primary and Secondary School teachers. Among the investigated teachers, 37.0% of teachers have used the E-bag for 1 semester, 33.3% for the 2 semesters, and 14.8% for 3 semesters or longer. On the basis of above analysis, the current situation of teachers' ITTA to use E-bag would be evaluated from technological literacy, capability of instructional design, capability of teaching implementation and evaluation.

6.1 Technological Literacy Analysis

This section was to investigate teachers' technological literacy, including techniques consciousness and the operation skills to use E-bag [13] (Fig. 2).

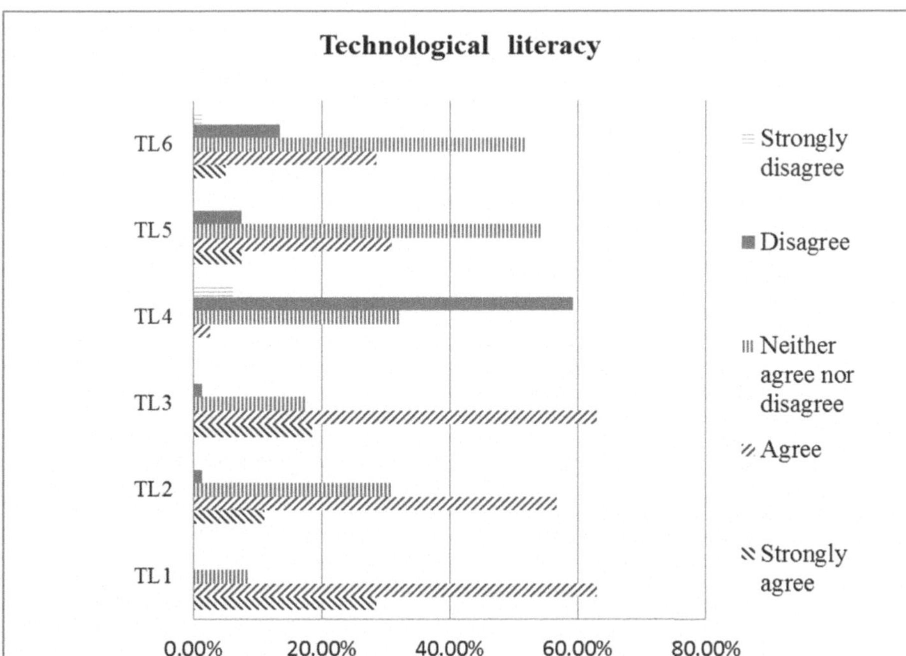

Fig. 2. Technological literacy analysis

More than 90% of respondents believed that information technology should be actively used to support teaching, and 80% of teachers approving that new instructional concept should be introduced, which indicated that most teachers hold positive attitude to applying

E-bag to teaching. From the rest of the collected data, we could find teachers' ability to develop resources and learning tools was still low. Compared to other items, less than 40% of respondents could choose and develop proper materials and tools used for E-bag. Furthermore, it was shown that foundation of school teaching reform affected teachers' information technology operation and resource application capability. Accordingly, 68% of teachers who believed to be familiar with functions and supports of E-bag were from schools with well reforming foundation. Consistently, 68% of teachers who could get materials and tools needed for E-bag were from schools with well reforming foundation.

From the above analysis, it indicated that foundation of schools reforming teaching was one of the significant influencing factors of teachers' technology literacy. Meanwhile, the problem of teachers' capacity to design and develop resources and tools was to be solved urgently.

6.2 Instructional Design Ability Analysis

It was significant to develop teachers' capability of instructional design to improve the application effect of E-bag. In this section, the capability of instructional design based-on E-bag would be analyzed from learning needs, instructional purpose, resources and strategies (Fig. 3).

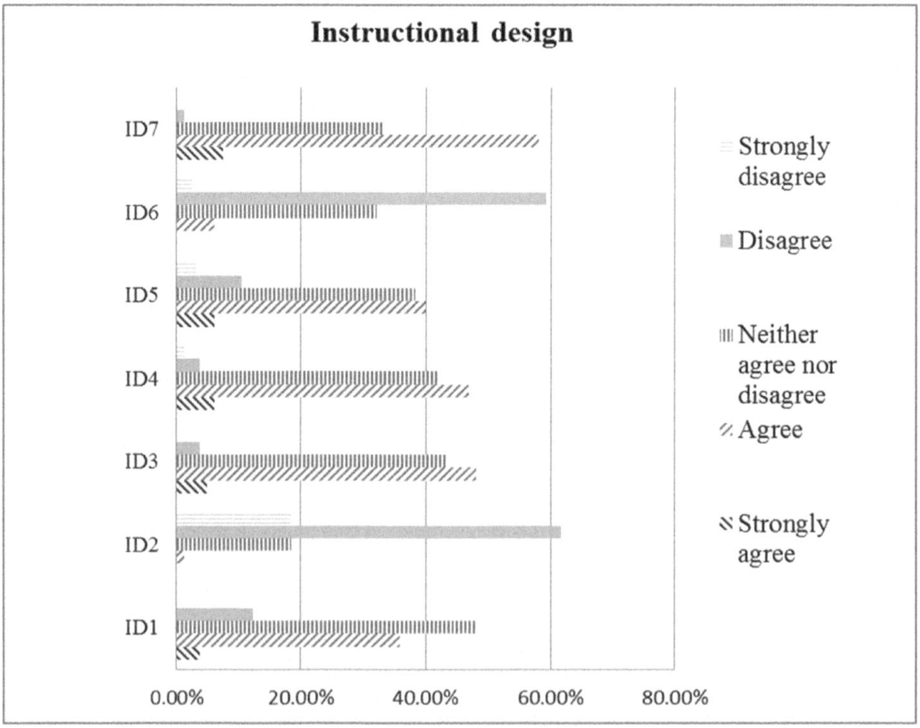

Fig. 3. Instructional design ability analysis

According to the statistics, more than 80% of teachers could use proper functions of E-bag in connection with instructional objectives, and more than 60% of teachers tended to plan teaching through the collective lesson preparation. From the above analysis, it was shown that teachers have grasped some application scenario of E-bag which contributed to some specific teaching purpose. In addition, teachers' feedback about teaching strategies and activities was not so satisfactory. Less than 50% of teachers thought they could choose a variety of teaching strategies based on E-bag according to analysis of learning needs.

It was found that two factors had a significant impact on the development of instructional design based on E-bag, which are the duration of E-bag application to teaching and the foundation of information-based teaching in school. In terms of duration, 82.35% of respondents who could design instructional objectives with E-bag have been using E-bag in teaching for more than 2 semesters, and 90.17% of teachers who could chose teaching resource and tools effectively have been using E-bag for more than 2 semesters. Regarding the foundation of information-based teaching in school, 83% of respondents who could design test questions, scales, portfolio to evaluate students' learning were from schools with good foundation of information-based teaching.

6.3 Teaching Implementation and Evaluation Ability Analysis

With the introduction of E-bag, the range of teaching interaction has been expanded [14]. However it also increased the difficulty of teaching implementation and evaluation, which

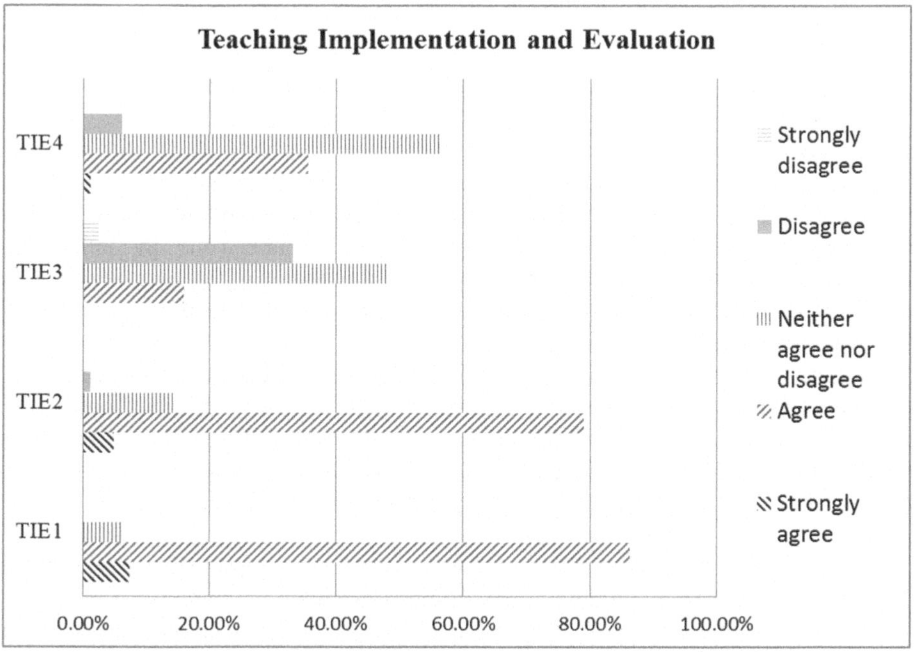

Fig. 4. Teaching implementation and evaluation ability analysis

was the core of teaching. In this section, teachers' ability to implement and evaluate teaching was investigated (Fig. 4).

Through the analysis, it can be found that teachers have reached the level of flexible operation on E-bag in a certain range, in which they could deal with some teaching problems in using E-bag. Almost all teachers believed that they can use E-bag to effectively stimulate students' interest in learning and guide them to actively participate. About 50% of teachers strongly agreed that they could flexibly handle the teaching incident caused by the unexpected situation in using e-bag, and 43.21% of teachers agreed basically they could handle some relative events.

Teachers were not so satisfied with the teaching evaluation effect of E-bag, which was not considered to lead to better evaluation effect or enhance the efficiency of evaluation. 48.15% of the teachers thought that the advancement of evaluation efficiency was not significant, and 16.05% of the teachers didn't think that it could enhance the evaluation efficiency completely. Furthermore, more than half of the teachers thought that application of E-bag could not provide support for students' comprehensive quality evaluation.

In conclusion, the survey was carried out based on the questionnaire. In terms of the current situation of teachers' ability to apply E-bag to teaching, we can draw the following points. The functions and operations were not so hard for teachers, who could even handle some E-bag operating problems agilely in classroom. The development of resources and tools used in E-bag was a challenge for more than half of respondents. Furthermore, teachers still expected to enhance diversity of teaching strategies and activities based on E-bag. In addition, teachers were not satisfied with the evaluation of E-bag, which were thought not to improve the efficiency of evaluation.

7 Conclusion

In this paper, the questionnaire comprised E-bag application ability index and influence factors, which were assigned a weight through Richter scale method. It not only fit the actual situation of teaching, but also was in line with the value orientation of Chinese information-based teaching ability development. On the other hand, the influencing factors of teaching with E-bag were discussed. The foundation of teaching reforming in school and the duration of E-bag application were the most obvious influencing factors for instructional design based on E-bag.

Summarizing the data analysis, the application of E-bag to teaching had higher demands for teachers. E-bag as a new learning tool, like other existing information technology, demanded new changes for teachers, such as the ability to develop resources and to evaluate student's performance based on E-bag. It is suggested that the following areas should be enhanced to exploit the full potentials of teacher who applied E-bag into teaching [15].

Firstly, more resources in training should be targeted at supporting staff in schools. They should at least be given training at a comfortable level to use E-bag.

Secondly, regular training should be provided for school personnel to update them with latest IT technology.

Thirdly, mobile learning should be explored to capitalize its advantages to benefit teachers by giving them greater flexibility to attend training workshops.

Fourthly, the Government should have a strategic plan to help schools, especially principals, on how to capitalize the full potentials of E-bag.

At last, it was important that teachers should participate in all kinds of teaching reforming activities to advance their capability of integrating emerging information technology into teaching.

References

1. Ministry of Education: Ministry of education's opinions on enhancing teachers' information technology application capability in primary and secondary schools. J. Inservice Educ. Training Sch. Teachers **12**, 3–4 (2013)
2. Zhang, L.C., Jiao, J.L.: A study on teachers' understanding and attitude towards E-schoolbag. J. e-Educ. Res. **5**, 46–52 (2015)
3. Jiang, F.G., Zheng, J.: The survey of degree of satisfaction and requirements towards E-schoolbag: a Chinese teachers' perspective. J. Open Educ. Res. **4**, 68–73 (2013)
4. Wang, F., Fu, G.S.: Research on the affection of teachers' perceived technology to the behavioral intention of using E-bag. J. Modern Educ. Technol. **23**(12), 36–41 (2013)
5. Zh, H.Y., Qian, D.M., Ren, Y.Q.: Advancing the application of E-bag: an empirical study of teachers' acceptance. J. e-Educ. Res. **10**, 92–97 (2015)
6. Guan, Y.Q., Su, X.B., Qian, D.M.: Study on current situation and strategy of application of E-bag by analysis of teacher's interview. J. e-Educ. Res. **10**, 53–59 (2014)
7. Jiao, J.L., Zhou, X.Q.: One-to-one digital learning BA4C model based on pad. J. e-Educ. Res. **1**, 9–17 (2015)
8. Guo, T.F., Duan, Y.S.: A comparative study on cognition of E-bag based on q method. J. e-Educ. Res. **8**, 73–79 (2015)
9. Sh, S.S., Liu, Q.: A flipped classroom teaching mode based on Electronic schoolbag. J. China Educ. Technol. **12**, 107–111 (2013)
10. Upon the personalized learning supported by electronic schoolbag technology. J. Ningbo Univ. **6**, 94–97 (2014)
11. Li, Y.B., Liu, H.Y.: The present situation of the information technology teaching ability of teachers in primary and secondary school. J. Chin. J. ICT Educ. **10**, 72–74 (2015)
12. Zh, Y., Ma, J.S.: The status and training advices of teacher's ICT competency in primary and secondary schools in Central China Area. J. China Educ. Technol. **1**, 104–110 (2015)
13. Williams, P.J.: Technological literacy: a multilayered approach for democracy. Int. J. Technol. Des. Educ. **3**, 19 (2009)
14. Xie, Y., Wang, Q., Li, Y., Kwok, L., Yang, Y., Guo, F.: Research on problem-oriented instruction mode supported by electronic schoolbag. In: Cheung, S.K.S., Kwok, L., Yang, H., Fong, J., Kwan, R. (eds.) ICHL 2015. LNCS, vol. 9167, pp. 231–242. Springer, Cham (2015). doi:10.1007/978-3-319-20621-9_19
15. Kwok, L.-F., Lam, K.-W.: A survey on using IT in administration and management in Hong Kong primary schools. In: Liu, W., Li, Q., Lau, R.W.H. (eds.) ICWL 2006. LNCS, vol. 4181, pp. 300–312. Springer, Heidelberg (2006). doi:10.1007/11925293_27

The Findings of Multi-mode Blended Learning in K-12: A Case Study of V-China Education Program

Yushun Li[1], Meiqin Wu[1(✉)], Jinrui Dai[1], and Shengri Chen[2]

[1] Faculty of Education, School of Education Technology, Beijing Normal University, Beijing 100875, China
1655962374@qq.com

[2] Shanghai QiBao High School, Shanghai 201101, China

Abstract. Blended learning, which combines the advantages of face-to-face learning and online learning, brought new life to the field of education. However, blended learning faces many challenges in junior middle schools. This paper is based on the findings of study on V-China Education Program, which carried out a pioneer initiative program of temporary open online courses for K-12 in China. The team surveyed teachers and students nationwide who joined open online courses provided by the initiative program. The survey shows that there are three types of blending modes based on these open online courses: Pure Online Model, Macro blended Model, Multiparty Collaboration Blended Learning Model. Each mode features different learning and teaching activities. Furthermore, teachers and students experienced with 7 multi-mode courses were surveyed by questionnaires and interviews, and students hold positive attitudes towards blended learning. Besides, high-level experiences such as interactions and experiences of learning-supportive services were required for more successful and more popular blended learning. Based on these findings, the paper put forward a number of suggestions for the implementation of more practices on blended learning in K-12 in China.

Keywords: Blended learning · V-China education program · Online learning · Elementary education

1 Background

1.1 About the V-China Education Program

The V-China Education Program is an Open Education program with considerable influence in Mainland China and Southeast Asia. The program explores the modes of Open Education in Internet era, and tends to promote the participation of teachers who are working in junior middle schools, and to enhance the spreading and sharing of high quality educational resources. The V-China Education Program was also committed to spreading advanced educational notions and booming abundant practices in the area of online learning. In this way, the program demonstrates its value in its efforts to organize and coordinate educational resources across geographical regions and different cultures, and its efforts to offer students a better platform with sufficient resources for e-learning and collaborative learning.

S.K.S. Cheung et al. (Eds.): ICBL 2017, LNCS 10309, pp. 84–96, 2017.
DOI: 10.1007/978-3-319-59360-9_8

The development of the V-China Education Program has gone through 3 stages.

The first stage: Originated from Hong Kong to promote Educational Cooperation. The V-China Education Program is funded by Quality Education Fund of Hong Kong (http://vchina.icampus.cn/). Started in 2004, the program was designed and directed by Professor Huang Baocai from the department of Information Engineering, the Chinese University of Hong Kong. At the beginning of the program, the interactions between Pairing Schools from Shanghai and Hong Kong were carried out through video conference systems and other real-time systems based on Internet. With the development of technology and the improvement in network bandwidth, member schools of the program were extended to Beijing, Shanghai, Zhejiang, Guangdong, Hubei, Shandong, Sichuan, Jiangsu, Jiangxi, Anhui and other provinces in Mainland China as well as Malaysia and Singapore.

The second stage: Rooted in Mainland to advance Open Education.

To achieve a continuous and favorable development, the V-China Education Program set up the Remote Education Institute of Hong Kong with the purpose of promoting the study and application of distance learning. In November 2011, the V-China Distance Education Development Center is established with its daily affairs handled by Shanghai QiBao High School. A cooperation pattern is formed in this stage, in which the Quality Education Fund of Hong Kong worked as the leader while Minhang District of Shanghai, Nanhai District of Foshan, Jiangdong District of Ningbo, and Nanshan District of Shenzhen as its core partners. After years of development in the mainland, the V-China Education Program has achieved three types of its services, that is, distance courses, distance learning activities and cultural communication.

The third stage: To continue promoting Online Education through more practices with a leading philosophy.

The program is determined to see the future developments such as innovative learning experiences, the transmission of cultures and the spread of philosophies as well as the formation of interpersonal networks. Since the beginning of 2012, the V-China Education Program has begun its leader work based on online courses and launched its collaboration with Beijing Normal University, Nanjing University, Henan University and other universities. This paper is based on the research and practice during the collaboration process. By the end of the Autumn Term of 2016, online courses provided by the V-China Education Program has gone through up to 5 rounds in member schools. Students that have selected courses come from 34 middle schools in cities like Shanghai, Ningbo, Foshan, Shenzhen, Qingdao and Nanchang. The number of participating students from the above 6 cities has reached 3232.

1.2 Literature Review

1.2.1 Potential Performance of Blended Learning

Blended learning provides a learning environment where students are placed at the center of learning and it makes use of modern technology on the basis of traditional classrooms to make the class more participatory, more efficient and success-oriented. In blended learning, students are able to maximize learning effectiveness under the face-to-face learning scenarios but also get their particular learning needs fulfilled [1]. It is proved in the study that students studying in the way of blended learning had better performance than those who adopted only a single way [2].

1.2.2 The Development of Blended Learning

According to study in this area at home and abroad, the comparison of the effects of online learning and traditional learning, and that of the students' preparation and maintenance of learning effects, were the dominant issues of the blended learning study in the 90 s. From the late twentieth Century to the early twenty-first Century, the focus of the study has transformed to concisely describing the practices and the effects. This empirical research approach was rarely adopted in the past few years. As time went by, later researches have turned to the presentation of maximized online teaching strategies, and those characteristics of students that affect their online learning effectiveness, and the ways to promote the online and offline interactions between teachers and students, as well as the evaluation of the quality of students' learning experiences [3].

1.2.3 Focus of Blended Learning Study

In the past ten years, the domestic study has focused on the empirical research of blended learning mode and on the students' satisfaction. Zhansheng Mou, Dongmei Zhao, Weihong Kong, et al. have respectively discussed the learning modes and educational practices based on different platforms like Coursera, Blackboard, Moodle, Windows Live Spaces, WeChat and other platforms [4–8]. Lei Huang, Yu Zhao, Ze Wang, Saihong Li, Lifang Gong and other researchers have explored possible blended learning modes in specific disciplines [9–13]. Guodong Zhao has launched his study on the factors affecting blended learners' satisfaction and constructed a satisfaction model for blended learning. In this model, students' adaptability to computer learning, perceived usefulness, prompt feedback and perceived ease of use, and the applicability of the curriculum, are considered as the significant factors that affect students' satisfaction in blended learning [14].

Wulin Ma has explored the blended learning mode of College English through empirical research and proposed a three-stage mode. His study found that the contradiction between the limited capacity of class and the individual needs of students can be solved in blended learning. Thus, the quality of English teaching in university is improved [15]. Yi Jin has put forward a hierarchical teaching mode in blended learning for people to do further study [16].

1.2.4 Status of Blended Learning Practice in Mainland

One of the challenges in the blended learning development is that schools open for online learning frequently encountered programs without careful design. The phenomenon has hurt the enthusiasm and confidence of participants from administrators of schools, teachers, to parents and students. Thus, keeping good communication with teachers and students so as to learn about their needs and make careful plans for online learning have become an essential part for the implementation of blended learning.

As mentioned earlier, the V-China Education Program has set its goal to promote the online learning based on online courses for junior middle schools since 2012. In the process, the Action Research carried out under the program layout has gone through different periods and now has turned to blended learning models and practices. Taking cognitive and psychological characteristics of students into consideration, the blended learning model, no matter how it is specifically constituted, will be the overwhelming future of online learning model in junior middle schools. However, research on the application of blended learning mode in junior middle schools is rare to see and long-time study haven't been conducted on a large scale. In this case, the paper is supposed to complete this kind of empirical research through continuous exploration into member schools in V-China Education Program.

1.3 Research Topics

The purpose of this study is to present the achievements of the blended learning based on ongoing practices for nearly 4 years. In the V-China Education Program, the application modes of blended learning in junior middle schools were explored, and the experiences and feelings of teachers and students involved in this program were tracked, so as to foster further development of the courses under the V-China Education Program.

The study focuses on the following two topics.

The first topic is to explore and develop the **application models** of blended learning in junior middle schools as well as its characteristics through 4 years' study of online courses.

The second one is exploring and evaluating the **effectiveness** of blended learning from the perspective of both teaching and learning respectively. To learn about the effectiveness, conversations and questionnaires were carried out to collect users' comments and feedback.

2 Study 1: Application Modes of Blended Learning Practice in Junior Middle Schools

2.1 Research Methods

This study adopts the method of Action Research. Under the support of Beijing Normal University, Nanjing University and Henan University, a set of online courses were designed and opened to users, such as the courses of *Discover yourself* and *Discover external reality* for Career Planning Theory, courses of *Explore careers: aviation and Explore careers: aerospace* for Career Planning Practice, introductory courses of *Touch the forefront of information technology* and *E-learning* for Information Literacy, and the curriculum of *My show* for Clothing Science.

Take the course *Discover yourself* as an example, the course was designed and implemented by a team of program assistants from the above-mentioned universities.

They carried out the study by working as curriculum instructors and followed the general procedure of Action Research, referring to the four steps of planning, acting, observing and reflecting. They analyzed students' actions and performances during the blended learning process of *Discover yourself*, and tried to abstract the possible blended learning models and characteristic of these models, and to improve the learning activities planning in the blended learning in return.

Based on nearly 4 years of curriculum design, application and improvements, three models of blended learning are formed: Pure Online Model, Macro Blended Model and Multiparty Collaboration Blended Learning Model (refer to Fig. 1). We have explored these three models in different periods respectively.

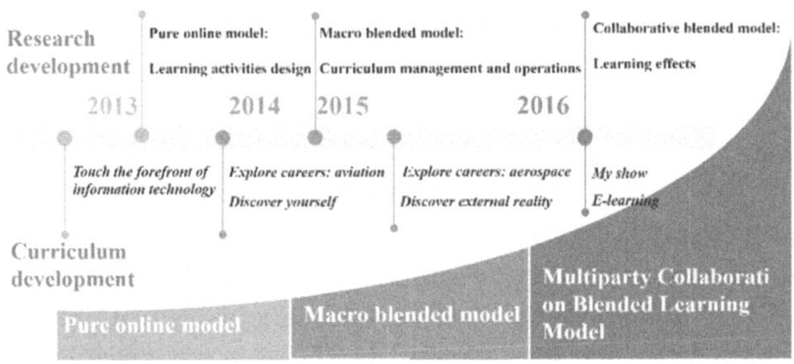

Fig. 1. Development of blended courses study

2.2 Stage 1: Pure Online Model

From 2012 to 2014, the research team mainly surveyed the implementation of online courses in junior middle schools when students could only follow the courses line. In order to arouse students' interest in and enthusiasm for this kind of pure online learning, the team focused on the design of interesting and interactive learning activities, and the development of more intelligible courses.

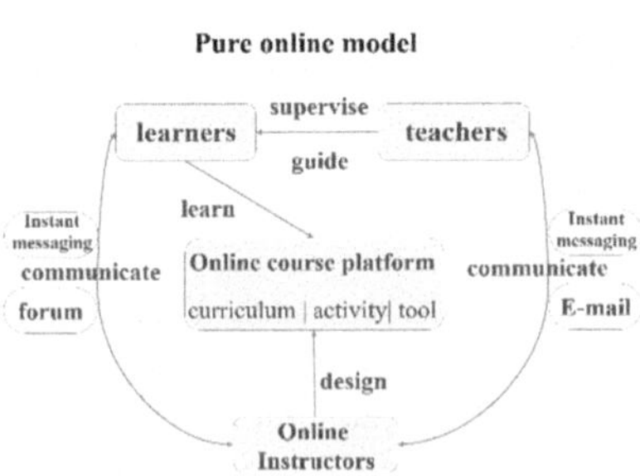

Fig. 2. Pure online model

In this model (refer to Fig. 2), instructors, learners and teachers have their different roles. Online instructors are responsible for course and activity design, the presentation of course through tools, and the online forums. Learners(students) carry out their learning by accessing the online courses. Teachers supervises the learning actions of their students and provide necessary guidance. The instructors and learners communicate through instant messaging service and online forum while instructors and teachers get in touch with each other through E-mail and instant messaging service.

At this stage, learners picked the courses spontaneously. Learners arranged their study with the support of online courses and corresponding activities. This kind of model is named as Pure Online Model. The main features of this model are that all the learning activities are carried out online, which means there are no offline activities.

2.3 Stage 2: Macro Blended Model

During the period of 2014 to 2016, the focus of blended learning has been turned to the management aspect which refers to the blended management from universities, schools and program managers. The study of this period attaches great importance to the design, management and relevant supporting services of the online courses.

Specifically speaking, the V-China Distance Education Development Center, which serves as the program manager, is responsible for the management of the courses. The three universities, which are Beijing Normal University, Nanjing University and Henan University, are responsible for the design and development of courses. And schools are responsible for curriculum implementation. In the process of curriculum implementation, online instructors from universities and offline teachers from schools provide learning-supporting services collaboratively (Fig. 3).

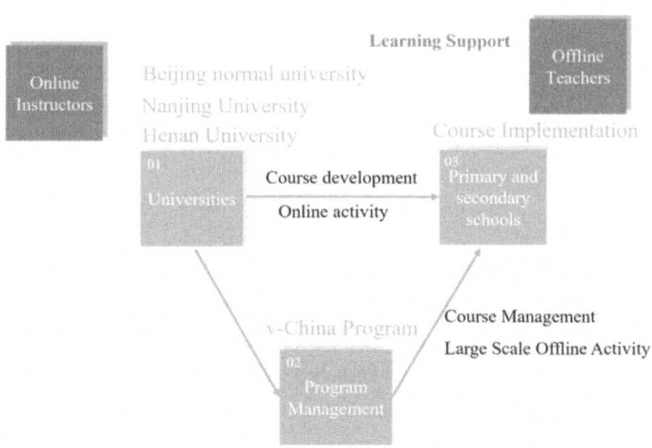

Fig. 3. Macro blended model

In this period of blended learning, some changes should be noticed the study group began to stress the significance of learners' participation. The cooperation among universities, schools and program managers has been strengthened. Large scale offline activities were planned and implemented as supplements to the online courses. This model is called Macro Blended Model. The main feature of this model is the introduction and expanded learning of offline activities.

2.4 Stage 3: Multiparty Collaboration Blended Learning Model

The blended learning has entered a new period since 2016. In this period, the study group not only focus on the fulfillment of students' and teachers' needs, but also attach great importance to the effectiveness of the program. From the perspective of application scenarios, 3 types of learning models could be derived, which are Pure Online Model, Assistance Model and Multiparty Collaboration Blended Learning Model.

As what has been introduced in the Pure Online Model (refer to Fig. 2), online instructors mainly play the role of guide and supervisor.

In the Assistance Model online curriculum resources are picked up by teachers as extended resources. Teachers are still the ones who are responsible for teaching in classrooms while students only select online curriculum resources according to their needs during the after-school time. And the online instructors and students never communicate with each other. Instead, teachers communicate with online instructors through E-mail and other means of instant communication to get appropriate teaching resources and better assistant services (Fig. 4).

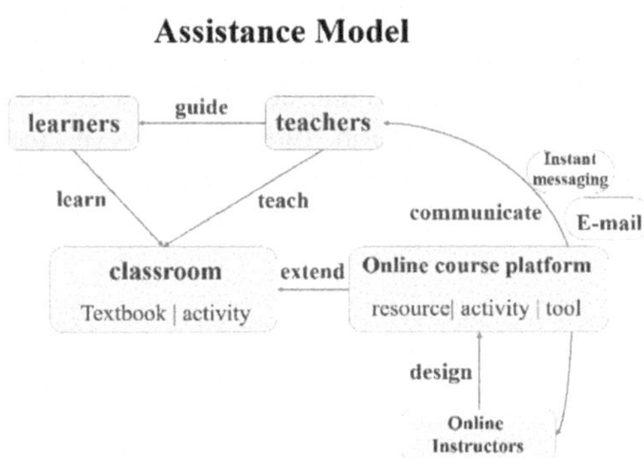

Fig. 4. Assistance model

In the Assistance Model, online instructors are responsible for online courses. Learners adopt a mixed way of learning, in which they access online course resources such as videos and texts. Participating in offline activities become the added task for students in the model. Thus the role of teachers is more complex than before, not only as school teachers whose major job is to teach in the classroom, but also as guides and supervisors.

There are three aspects of "blending" in the Multiparty Collaboration Blended Learning Model. **The first one is the blending of online courses and offline activities.** In the implementation process of courses for *career planning*, the study found that courses of this kind focus more on practices and experiences than knowledge or theory. The successful implementation of these courses needs offline activities and interactions among peers and between teachers and students. This explains the reason why the blending of "online and offline" is necessary and how the educational objectives could be achieved. **The second is the blending of learning services, namely, the "blending" of online instructors and teachers.** The online instructors, who are familiar with the online environment, provide supporting services for students. They are committed to optimizing online learning resources and tools. At the same time, teachers serve as the best offline activity planners and implementer. This combination could stimulate students' interest in learning and standardize their learning process. **The third one is the blending between online learners and face-to-face learners**. Learners of the same curriculum may come from different regions or schools. As learners not only have face-to-face peers, but also have online peers from afar, the abundance in course resources could make learning more dynamic, interesting, and valuable.

In the third period, the study group began to pay more attention to learners' learning effects. On the one hand, they tried to transform teachers' notions, stimulate their initiative and improve their skills. On the other hand, they tried to improve online instructors' services for students and teachers. This model is called the Multiparty Collaboration Blended Learning Model (Fig. 5).

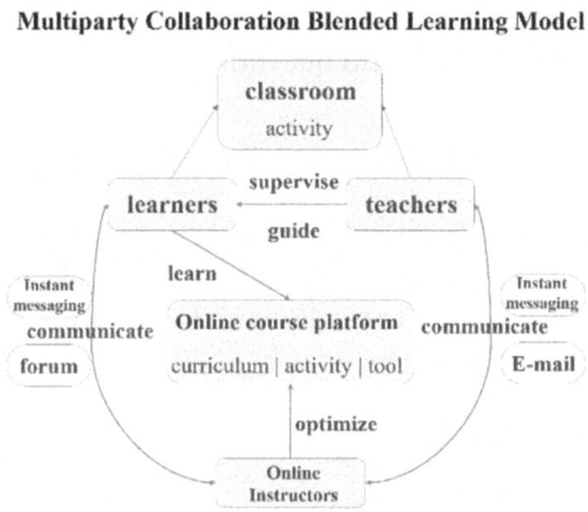

Fig. 5. Multiparty collaboration blended learning model

3 Study 2: Research on Students' Experience of Blended Learning

During the practice of the three periods, we found that students' attitudes of blended learning are changing. In order to improve the blended learning effects, we make a research on the students' and teachers' course experience to get more suggestions for this blended learning program.

3.1 Research Object

The object of this study is teachers and students in use of blended learning. Based on 7 courses from the V-China Education Program, 7 teachers and 81 students are selected as samples of the essay under the principle of convenient sampling and purposive sampling. Depth interviews were conducted with teachers and a semi-open questionnaire is distributed to 81 students from 3 schools.

3.2 Research Tools

To make it clear what blended learning experience is like, the thesis adopts self-compiled *Questionnaire on Middle School Students' Blended Learning Experience.*

According to the experience of students' learning process and blended learning, the questionnaire is designed to cover **19 single choice questions** from **7 dimensions**, namely students' learning attitude, knowledge and ability, teaching, interaction, learning resources, learning activities and learning support, as well as **2 multiple-choice questions** and **2 open questions** from the aspect of course optimization.

3.3 Research Process

In September 2016 before the beginning of the fall semester, 7 teachers that have selected courses in 2014 or 2015 are visited and interviewed. Based on the discussion, in December 2016, the researchers handed out questionnaires to students on the course of *Discover yourself* and collected 81 valid questionnaires.

3.4 Statistical Analysis——Questionnaires on Blended Learning Experience

After coding of the collected 81 questionnaires, the data was processed by SPSS to check the reliability and validity of the questionnaire. The Cronbach's alpha coefficient is 0.881, and the value of KMO is up to 0.848, which indicate that the questionnaire has high reliability and validity (Table 1).

Table 1. The statistics of the answers on students' learning attitude

Title	Percentage of items (%)				
	Strongly agree	Agree	General	Disagree	Strongly disagree
Degree of satisfaction with online course	69.41	27.16	3.7	0	0
Learning online course is very fruitful, and will be of great help in your future study	59.26	32.1	8.64	0	0
Through online course, you will use Blended Learning approach in your future study	43.21	48.15	8.64	0	0
Your overall feeling on blended learning	53.09	41.98	4.94	0	0

3.4.1 Analysis of Students' Learning Attitude

Through the analysis of the data on the students' learning attitude, we can find that the learners have a high degree of recognition towards blended learning. More than 90% of the students clearly express their appreciation of blended learning, and nearly 91% interviewees agreed that taking blended courses is helpful in promoting learning. Over 90% respondents exhibited a high degree of recognition and learning enthusiasm towards our courses, which indicates that the design and implementation of the curriculum is effective. 91% of the students expressed their willingness to adopt blended learning later on continuously, in proof of that the development and promotion of blended learning in junior middle schools is promising.

3.4.2 Analysis of Students' Interaction

Statistics in Table 2 shows data about student interaction. 37.04% of the learners often communicate with their classmates through online learning platform, and 29.36% learners sometimes discussed in this way.

Table 2. Statistics of survey on student interaction

Title	Percentage of items (%)				
	Strongly agree	Agree	General	Disagree	Strongly disagree
The classmates are helpful for pushing you	45.68	34.57	13.58	2.47	3.7
You always use the online learning platform to communicate with others	37.04	29.36	20.99	11.11	1.23

3.4.3 Analysis of Learning Resources

From the aspect of learning resources, data in Table 3 exhibits that our course resources on the platform is recognized by 69.14% of the learners. There are a few learners holding the idea that the resources on the course are not rich. This kind of feedback proves the necessity to enrich and improve the learning resources in these courses.

Table 3. Statistics of survey on learning resources

Title	Percentage of items (%)				
	Strongly agree	Agree	General	Disagree	Strongly disagree
Overall, *discover yourself* has rich content	69.14	23.46	6.17	0	1.23

As shown above in Fig. 6, the difficulties encountered by the learners in the blended learning are concentrated on time, learning methods, supervision for self-learning and the online learning skills. The main purpose of blended learning is not only to help learners complete the learning of knowledge, but also to cultivate the learner's information literacy and awareness of self-learning. Therefore, in the process of blended learning, instructors and other supporters should pay attention to the guidance of methods and strategies, and insist on cultivating students' ability and information literacy at the same time.

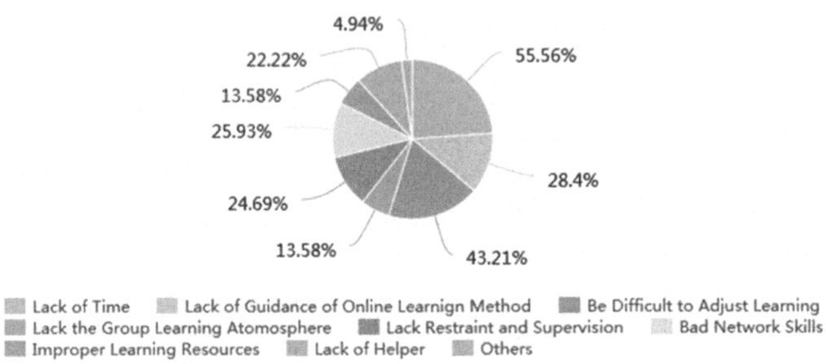

Fig. 6. Difficulties learners encountered in blended learning

4 Conclusion and Suggestions

The nearly four-year practice of blended learning in junior middle schools indicates the need of taking various factors into account when carrying out blended learning. For example, the design of blended learning environment and various types of learning resources, the design and organization of blended learning activities and support from experimenting schools and the related skills and competences of teachers. Only by recognizing and solving these problems can blended learning be put into practice effectively.

4.1 The Construction of Online-and-Offline Blended Learning Environment Is the Prerequisite for the Implementation of Blended Learning

Blended learning is a combination of online and offline learning which should be implemented in both online and offline environments. Thus the scientific and effective integration of the online and offline environments is the key to achieve learning objectives and solve learning difficulties in respect of blended learning. The online learning environment, which is also refers to the online learning platform, is not only expected to support self-learning, but also to support collaborative learning and inquiry-based learning in order to form an online learning community. Offline learning environment, apart from traditional classrooms and computer rooms, also includes various other places which could be helpful for learning, such as the practice bases, science and technology museums and so on.

4.2 The Design of Integrated Online and Offline Learning Activities Is the Key to the Implementation of Blended Learning

The design and organization of learning activities are the core of the implementation of blended learning as how to design and how to integrate online and offline learning activities are the key to effective learning. Online and offline learning activities have their own advantages and disadvantages as well as difficulties in the implementation. Normally, students study by accessing digital learning materials through online platform such as videos, texts and cases. And they also discuss and communicate with each other, give comments and reflections through the platform. While under the offline circumstances, students carry out in-depth learning under the guidance of teachers, such as more knowledge intake and face-to-face discussion and experiment participation.

4.3 Learning Tools and Other Learning-Supportive Elements Are the Guarantee of Effective Blended Learning

The complexity of blended learning environment makes it more demanding for teachers' competences and students' self-learning abilities. Although the employment of ICT in curricula is highly recommended, most teachers still use the traditional teaching ways in classrooms. And students have few opportunities to have access to the Internet. Therefore, to guarantee the organization and effective implementation of blended learning and to make sure that students can actively take part in and benefit from blended learning, the involvement of all communities and relevant supporting materials are needed. For instance, teaching manuals and teaching cases for teachers and, digital learning materials, learning activity lists, learning strategies for students as well as technical support, prompt feedback and frequent communications are really helpful.

Acknowledgments. This work is supported by online education fund from MOE Research Center for Online Education (QTONE EDUCATION grant NO. 2017ZD103).

References

1. Powell, A., Watson, J., Staley, P., et al.: Blending learning: the evolution of online and face-to-face education from 2008–2015. Promising practices in blended and online learning series. Int. Assoc. K-12 Online Learn. (2015)
2. Means, B., Toyama, Y., Murphy, R., Bakia, M., Jones, K.: Evaluation of evidence-based practices in online learning: a meta-analysis and review of online learning studies. US Dept. Educ. **115**(100), 93 (2009)
3. Cavanaugh, C.S., Barbour, M.K., Clark, T.: Research and practice in K-12 online learning: a review of open access literature. Int. Rev. Res. Open Distance Learn. **10**(1), 239–287 (2009)
4. Mou, Z., Dong, B.: Exploration of blended learning mode based on MOOC——taking coursera platform for example. Mod. Educ. Technol. **24**(5), 73–80 (2014)
5. Zhao, D., Yin, Y.: Study on the teaching practice of blackboard-based B-learning model. Mod. Educ. Technol. **22**(9), 41–44 (2012)
6. Kong, W., Gao, R.: Design and practice of blended learning based on moodle. China Educ. Technol. **2**, 80–83 (2008)

7. Jiang, L., Huang, L., Zhang, D.: Research on the application of blended learning platform based in windows live groups. China Educ. Technol. **10**, 136–140 (2012)
8. Yuan, L., Chen, X., Zhang, Y.: A study of blended learning supported by WeChat– basic photography technology as an example. China Educ. Technol. **7**, 128–132 (2012)
9. Huang, L., Yang, J., Li, W.: Construction of blended learning model based on free web service——take modern educational technology as an example. E-education Res. **8**, 103–108 (2011)
10. Zhao, Y.: Study on the effect of blended curriculum design and development in secondary vocational education. E-education Res. **5**, 91–96 (2014)
11. Wang, Z., Zhang, S.: Research and practice of blended learning in liberal arts curriculum in universities– a case study of visual culture and media literacy. E-education Res. **10**, 37–41 (2010)
12. Li, S., Hu, J.: Exploration and practice of the blended models of MOOC based on information technology. Comput. Knowl. Technol. **12**(27) 2016
13. Gong, L.: Research of blending learning mode based on flipped class ——taking financial accounting: course comprehensive training as an example. J. Jincheng Inst. Technol. (6) (2016)
14. Zhao, G., Yuan, S.: Factors affecting students' satisfaction in blended learning: the case of peking university. Distance Educ. China **6**, 32–38 (2010)
15. Ma, W., Zhang, X.: Research and practice on college english blended learning model. Comput. Assist. Foreign Lang. Educ. **3**, 50–57 (2011)
16. Jin, Y., Wang, Y., Liu, J.: Hierarchical instructional design and its practice based on the blended learning theory. Mod. Educ. Technol. **23**(1), 37–40 (2013)

E-learning in Accounting Programmes in Hong Kong: Evolution and Effectiveness

Billy Tak-Ming Wong[1(✉)], Kam Cheong Li[1], Beryl Yuen-Yee Wong[1], and Joseph Shiu-Wing Yau[2]

[1] The Open University of Hong Kong, Hong Kong, China
{tamiwong,kcli,byywong}@ouhk.edu.hk
[2] Centennial College, Hong Kong, China
joseph.yau@centennialcollege.hku.hk

Abstract. This paper reviews the evolution of e-learning in accounting programmes in Hong Kong and, as a case study, reports an evaluation of the effectiveness of e-learning in one of the programmes. The fast pace of economic development in Hong Kong since the 1960s has created an increasing demand for qualified professional accountants, who have been facing rapid challenges from the global socio-economic changes. To equip the future professional accountants to cope with the required competences, the tertiary institutions in Hong Kong have been employing e-learning as an important blended learning mode of knowledge-sharing and motivating the accounting students to develop lifelong learning skills. This paper covers the historical background and adoption of e-learning in accounting education during the past decades, showing how its evolution has been in line with the overall technological developments in education delivery as well as the accounting industry. On this basis, the e-learning practice of an accounting programme was evaluated for its effectiveness. The findings showed that students were satisfied with the overall quality of the e-learning facilities provided on campus, but technical support was an area which may hinder the effective use of the facilities.

Keywords: E-learning · Accountancy profession · Accounting education · Blended learning

1 Introduction

The rapid advances in technological innovation have enhanced the quality of e-learning in accounting education around the world. This paper aims to review the adoption and application of e-learning as a blended learning mode in Hong Kong since the 1990s in the accounting programmes offered by the local universities and tertiary institutions. It begins with the initial development of accounting education and the teaching and learning mode in these early programmes. Next, following the changing focus of accounting education and professional accounting practices, e-learning elements were introduced, which also facilitated the tailoring of blended learning for students' diverse needs.

S.K.S. Cheung et al. (Eds.): ICBL 2017, LNCS 10309, pp. 97–105, 2017.
DOI: 10.1007/978-3-319-59360-9_9

As a case study on the effectiveness of e-learning in accounting education, a survey was conducted to investigate the e-learning experience of students in a self-financing tertiary institution in Hong Kong which has adopted the blended learning mode in its accounting programme. The results indicate the way forward for e-learning and blended learning in accounting education in the territory.

2 Teaching and Learning of the Early Accounting Education Programmes in Hong Kong

2.1 Early Accounting Education Programmes

In parallel with the economic expansion in Hong Kong in the 1960s and 1970s, the accountancy profession developed rapidly in the ex-British colony. As early as the 1950s, when the Hong Kong Society of Accountants (HKSA) [the predecessor of the present Hong Kong Institute of Certified Public Accountants (HKICPA)] [1] had not yet been established, a few overseas professional accountancy bodies — including the CPA Australia (formerly known as the Australian Society of Accountants [2]), the Association of Chartered Certified Accountants (ACCA UK) [3] and the Association of International Accountants (AIA UK) [4] — were offering their professional examinations in Hong Kong. On completing one of these qualifying schemes and becoming full members of these professional accountancy bodies, these overseas qualified accountants could apply for the practising licence issued by the Hong Kong Government and become Certified Public Accountants (CPAs).

The Hong Kong School of Commerce (HKSC), established in April 1959, was the first accounting school in Hong Kong [5]. It mainly offered part-time accounting education programmes to assist working adults in undertaking professional accountancy examinations, such as the LCC&I, HKIAAT, AIA, and ACCA [6].

Due to the rapid increase in Hong Kong accounting practitioners undertaking the ACCA professional examinations from the 1950s, the Hong Kong Technical College (the predecessor of the Hong Kong Polytechnic University) launched its part-time, and then full-time, Diploma in Accountancy programmes in the 1960s [7], the curricula of which were highly geared to the ACCA examination syllabi.

At that time, Hong Kong had only two government-funded universities — the University of Hong Kong (HKU) and the Chinese University of Hong Kong (CUHK); but they had not yet offered bachelor's degree in accounting, except within the HKU Bachelor of Social Sciences programme which included an accounting major. Therefore, many A-level matriculated students in the 1970s, who intended to become qualified professional accountants, chose to pursue the three-year full-time Higher Diploma in Accountancy programme (HDAC) offered by the Hong Kong Polytechnic (which was upgraded to the Polytechnic University of Hong Kong in 1994).

The Hong Kong economy speeded up its development in the 1970s and 1980s, mainly driven by the financial and servicing industries, which had also created a great demand for professional accountants. In order to cope with this demand, the Hong Kong Polytechnic increased the new student intakes for its full-time and part-time certificate and diploma in accounting programmes in the late 1980s. Also, the five Technical

Institutes under the auspices of the Hong Kong Vocational Training Council (VTC) launched their two-year full-time Diploma in Accountancy (DAC) programme in 1982, which was geared to the examination syllabi of the Association of Accounting Technicians (AAT) in the UK.

2.2 Teaching and Learning Mode

The early accounting programmes were tailor-made to the professional examination syllabi. They focused on delivering the knowledge in the classroom as required by the respective syllabus. The students relied on the prescribed textbooks and handouts distributed in class for preparing individual assignments, mid-term tests and final examinations. The interactions between the teachers and students were rather limited: the teachers focused on covering the examination syllabus for the external professional examinations. Basically, the teaching and learning mode was mainly one-way delivery of programme knowledge. Accounting internships or work placements were rather limited, not to mention the adoption of the blended learning mode [8].

In the 1970s, the business world was using mainframe computers (e.g. IBM), and so did the public sectors, including the Hong Kong higher education institutions. The computer courses studied in the second- and third-year curriculum of the Hong Kong Polytechnic's HDAC programme were related to electronic data processing, the syllabus of which included writing and processing simple Common Business-oriented Language (COBOL) computer programs, by using the "punch card" as the data input and processing medium. Therefore, the e-learning in accounting programmes during that decade was confined to the principles and practices of computer hardware configurations and software applications.

3 The Start of E-learning in Accounting Education

3.1 Changing Focus of Accounting Education

Most of the Hong Kong Government-funded universities have established their self-financing extension arms for providing professional and continuing education with academic programmes pitched at different Qualification Framework (QF) Levels for the different age levels and backgrounds of students — the ultimate mission being "Life-long learning" and "Education for all". Accounting is one of the most highly sought after academic disciplines that those continuing education institutions offered at various QF Levels, ranging from certificate, diploma and bachelor's degree to postgraduate diploma and master's degree. For example, the School of Professional and Continuing Education of the University of Hong Kong (HKU SPACE) offered 130 part-time accounting programmes in early 2017 [9], ranging from short courses to master's programmes (i.e. QF Levels 3 to 6). Of these 130 programmes, 42 (or 32%) are preparatory courses for the examinations of various professional accountancy bodies, including the HKICPA, ACCA, CIMA, CPA Australia, AIA, HKIAAT and TIHK. It shows that the majority of the full-time and part-time accounting programmes offered by the tertiary institutions in Hong Kong are oriented to professional examination, with the objective of assisting the students to eventually become professional accountants.

The HDAC programme, offered by the Hong Kong Polytechnic since the 1960s, was converted to BA (Hons) in Accountancy programme in 1988, partly motivated by the fast-changing socio-economic developments in Hong Kong. This required a new breed of professional accountants, who possess only technical knowledge and skills but also a broader scope of soft skills and analytical abilities to cope with the ever-changing business, social and economic environments [10–12]. As such, the first bachelor's degree in accounting programme emphasized the knowledge and skills which were identified as important for professional accountants in relevant studies, such as English and Chinese communication [13, 14], information system analysis [15], Excel software [16], business and professional ethics [17–19], research and case studies [20], group discussion and presentation [21], and group projects [22].

3.2 Adoption of E-learning and Blended Learning

The changing focus in accounting education, coupled with the advances in information technology, facilitated the adoption of an e-learning mode across the accounting courses [23]. For example, the three-year full-time BA (Hons) in Accountancy (BAA) programme offered by the Hong Kong Polytechnic has included management accounting as a core course since the academic year 1989/90. In addition to the traditional mass lectures and tutorials taught in lecture theatres and classrooms respectively, the course teachers have developed assignments by using the Excel software, and required students to work out and submit them using a floppy disk. In the early 1990s, the Hong Kong Polytechnic started to offer hundreds of personal computers in computer laboratories opened for students' use. Soon other BAA courses — such as financial accounting, auditing, taxation, and management information system — adopted types of e-learning, despite the Disk Operation System (DOS) was in use with complicated operating procedures. In addition, the accounting software Peachtree was taught and practised by the BAA students.

In addition to the advancement in terms of e-learning, accounting education has been moved out of the conventional classroom to a more dynamic blended learning mode [24]. Elements of blended learning, such as the combination of the internet and digital media with conventional classroom teaching, have been incorporated. Teachers and students are thus free from the constraint of their physical presence in the classroom, and have more control over time, place, path, and pace [25].

For example, in the early 2000s, the College of Business and Finance of the HKU SPACE developed a tailor-made e-learning platform to offer online supplementary learning materials to students of its part-time Advanced Diploma in Accounting (ADAC) programme. The platform was helpful for those unable to attend a specific lecture(s) for work or personal reasons. This e-learning platform was later extended to support the full-time Higher Diploma in Accounting programme (HDAC) and the part-time Postgraduate Diploma in Accounting programme. Also, the popular accounting software MYOB has been taught and practised by the HDAC students since the mid-2000s.

The HKU SPACE has been implementing blended learning with e-learning features in part of its accounting and related courses. It has proved to be effective in terms of catering for different student proficiencies and motivating students in self-learning. Students can learn at their own pace; classroom time can be reserved for more interaction; and teachers can focus on giving comments on students' work. It also enhance peer sharing among students whose writings are posted on the e-learning platform, as preferred by the students instead of being hand-written on paper. From the early 2010s, part of the e-learning features has been migrated to the mobile-learning mode [26].

4 Evaluation of E-learning Effectiveness in an Accounting Programme

As a case study, the effectiveness of e-learning in an accounting programme offered by the Centennial College — a self-financing tertiary institution in Hong Kong established by the HKU — was evaluated. The following introduces the e-learning practice of this programme and the evaluation.

4.1 E-learning in the Centennial College's Accounting Programme

The Centennial College launched its four-year full-time Bachelor of Professional Accounting (Hons) programme (BPAcc) in the year 2012/13. The programme emphasizes both liberal and professional education by adopting a blended learning mode inside and outside the campus. Its students can undertake the Accounting Internship Programme, which is a credit-bearing 12-week full-time work placement in a large accounting firm or business organization.

As another crucial blended learning component to facilitate the learning process of students, the Centennial College has a web-based learning platform — WISE (Web-platform for Interactive Study Experience) — for on-line teaching and learning support to students. This platform serves as an interactive access point for learning activities. It supports the following features:

1. Distribution of handouts and assignments posted by teachers
2. Notices posted by administrators
3. Chat room sharing among students and teachers
4. Discussion forum initiated by teachers as a virtual tutorial.

The WISE platform has been employed by most of the accounting and related courses. Students are also strongly encouraged to make use of this platform to promote effective learning.

4.2 Evaluation of E-learning Effectiveness

Since the WISE learning platform has been employed by the Centennial College for five years, an initial tracking study has been started to evaluate the effectiveness of the platform in helping students on the BPAcc programme in their studies. A questionnaire survey was conducted, covering the effectiveness of the e-learning facilities in general and the WISE platform in particular.

Data Collection

BPAcc final-year students participated in the survey in February 2017. An online questionnaire was distributed to 62 students of the accounting programme, with the background and purpose of the study introduced to them. A total of 36 valid questionnaires were received. The questionnaire instrument was developed based on a questionnaire used for the annual evaluation of e-learning in HKU, which was modified to cope with the context of the present study. It contains two parts, covering (1) the effectiveness of hardware and software provision in e-learning in general (9 items), and (2) the effectiveness of the WISE platform (7 items). A five-point Likert scale was used, ranging from 5 ('Strongly agree') to 1 ('Strongly disagree'). There was also one open question for the students to share their e-learning experience and give suggestions for improvements.

Hardware and Software Provision for E-learning

Table 1 presents the students' rating on the effectiveness of the hardware and software provision in e-learning. They gave a higher rating on the provision of internet access on campus (3.86) and appropriate e-learning technologies to facilitate learning (3.70). However, they had reservation about the technical support for e-learning, especially when they had encountered problems and did not know how to seek assistance (3.18). The availability of prior training on raising their awareness of and skills on the use of e-learning technologies also received a relatively low rate (3.09). In this regard, the College can offer more training workshops and online training guides for the students.

Table 1. Effectiveness of e-learning on hardware and software provision

	Mean	SD
1. Appropriate e-learning technologies have been put in place in teaching and learning spaces to facilitate students' learning	3.70	0.81
2. Appropriate e-learning technologies have been put in place on campus to enable access to information and resources	3.51	0.78
3. I have been able to easily get access to the internet on campus	3.86	0.81
4. I have been able to get effective technical support when I encountered technical problems during my course(s)	3.18	0.80
5. The e-learning promotion activities on campus have raised my awareness of the integration of e-learning technologies in teaching and learning	3.09	1.09
6. I have been able to obtain helpful guidance and support/training on technology-enabled resources to enhance my e-learning skills	3.09	1.01
7. The e-learning technologies have opened up new opportunities for my learning	3.26	1.22
8. Overall, I am satisfied with the quality of the e-learning technologies provided on campus	3.42	0.84
9. Overall, I am satisfied with the technical support for e-learning technologies provided on campus	3.44	0.88

The WISE Platform

Table 2 shows the participants' feedback on the effectiveness of the WISE platform. The students were overall satisfied with the WISE platform in terms of its ease of use (3.71). They however did not agree very much with the objective that WISE provides a more flexible environment for their learning (3.27), and the availability of effective technical support in using the platform (3.26). The results suggest that the students concern as well about flexibility and technical support for using the e-learning platform.

Table 2. Effectiveness of the WISE platform

	Mean	SD
1. I have found WISE easy to use	3.71	0.80
2. The features on WISE have supported my learning	3.54	0.70
3. I have experienced little or no technical problems when trying to access WISE	3.50	0.75
4. I have been able to obtain effective technical support in using WISE	3.26	0.75
5. WISE provides a more flexible environment for my learning	3.27	0.69
6. Overall, I am satisfied with the WISE features that I use	3.26	0.86
7. Overall, I am satisfied with WISE as the central e-learning system	3.44	0.68

The students also recommended improvements to the WISE platform. One of those lies in upgrading the platform to support mobile learning to allow greater flexibility for students. It was also suggested that more interactive features be provided for communication among teachers and students. For the use of the platform, it was suggested that the learning materials could be posted onto the platform early for students to review them in advance.

5 Discussion and Concluding Remarks

There has been a significant transformation of accounting education from a one-way classroom teaching and learning mode in the 1960s to computer-aided learning in the 1980s and 1990s, and then blended learning in the 2000s, as well as e-learning and mobile-learning in the 2010s. This evolution follows, on the one hand, the development of information technology in general and that in the accounting industry in particular; and on the other hand, the changing learners' needs over time, place, path, and pace [25]. The extensive application of e-learning in accounting education has enhanced the blended learning approach which is crucial for accounting programmes, as it has an important role in nurturing future accounting practitioners, who can cope with the ever-changing challenges in the accountancy profession.

This research showed that adequate and high-quality computer hardware and software provision are the prerequisites for e-learning in accounting education, and they have to be upgraded in view of the rapid advances in information technology, especially support for mobile learning and web-based interactive applications. The finding is in line with relevant research that the effectiveness of e-learning technologies in enhancing teaching and learning experiences depends on keeping up-to-date with latest education trends and technological advances [27, 28]. In addition, on-going training and support for the e-learners is of paramount importance, with the benefits exceeding the costs in the long term.

Technology is widely seen as an enabler rather than a threat. In an ACCA member's survey conducted in 2016, 57% of the respondents agreed or strongly agreed that technology will replace many entry-level roles in the accountancy profession; and 84% believed that technology will enable accounting and finance professionals to focus on much higher value-added activities. This is encouraging, given the growing expectations that many employers, clients, regulators and other stakeholders have of professional accountants. To equip themselves for meeting these challenges, continuing professional development through various technological means, or e-learning, has become essential [29].

This paper has reviewed how e-learning has evolved and been adopted in accounting education to facilitate flexible learning and teaching; and it has presented an evaluation of the effectiveness of e-learning in an accounting programme in Hong Kong. It contributes to filling the gap in the literature addressing the influence of technology on accounting education in Hong Kong [28]. Despite having been an integral part of education delivery in virtually all accounting programmes, the effectiveness of e-learning is also influenced by factors such as institutional technical support and continuous investment on upgrading infrastructure to cope with latest technological developments. Future work will lie in the extent to which the current e-learning provision helps students to catch up with professional practices and technological use in the accounting industry.

Acknowledgement. The work described in this paper was partially supported by a grant from the Research Grants Council of the Hong Kong Special Administrative Region, China (UGC/IDS16/15).

References

1. Hong Kong Institute of Certified Public Accountants. http://www.hkicpa.org.hk
2. Australian Society of Accountants.: History of the ASA. The Society, Melbourne (1982)
3. Association of Chartered Certified Accountants. http://www.accaglobal.com/hong-kong
4. Association of International Accountants. http://www.aiaworldwide.com/hong-kong
5. Hong Kong School of Commerce. http://www.hksc.edu.hk
6. Lui. O., Yau, J.: Accounting, education & training. SCMP Education Post (2015). (in Chinese)
7. The Hong Kong Polytechnic University. http://www.polyu.edu.hk/web/en/about_polyu/history
8. Chen, T.T.: University accounting education in Hong Kong: An analysis of tri-partite perceptions. (Thesis). University of Hong Kong, Pokfulam, Hong Kong SAR (2010). http://dx.doi.org/10.5353/th_b4588182
9. HKU School of Professional and Continuing Education. http://hkuspace.hku.hk
10. Ng, A.: Accounting education in Hong Kong: suggestions for change. HKIER. Educ. J. **21**(1), 53–58 (1993)
11. Boyce, G., Greer, S., Blair, B., Davids, C.: Expanding the horizons of accounting education: incorporating social and critical perspectives. Account. Educ. **21**(1), 47–74 (2012). doi: 10.1080/09639284.2011.586771

12. Chen, T.: Is Hong Kong ready for accounting education reform: an analysis of tri-partite views. Account. Res. J. **27**(3), 249–265 (2014). doi:10.1108/arj-11-2013-0078
13. Riley, T.J., Simons, K.A.: The written communication skills that matter most for accountants. Account. Educ. **25**(3), 239–255 (2016). doi:10.1080/09639284.2016.1164066
14. Siriwardane, H.P., Durden, C.H.: The communication skills of accountants: what we know and the gaps in our knowledge. Account. Educ. **23**(2), 119–134 (2014). doi: 10.1080/09639284.2013.847329
15. Bloun, Y., Abedin, B., Vatanasakdakul, S., Erfani, S.: Integrating enterprise resource planning (SAP) in the accounting curriculum: a systematic literature review and case study. Account. Educ. **25**(2), 185–202 (2016). doi:10.1080/09639284.2016.1138136
16. Rackliffe, U.R., Ragland, L.: Excel in the accounting curriculum: perceptions from accounting professors. Account. Educ. **25**(2), 139–166 (2016). doi:10.1080/09639284.2015.1126791
17. Dellaportas, S., Kanapathippillai, S., Khan, A., Leung, P.: Ethics education in the Australian accounting curriculum: a longitudinal study examining barriers and enablers. Account. Educ. **23**(4), 362–382 (2014). doi:10.1080/09639284.2014.930694
18. Jorge, M.L., Peña, F.J.A., Muriel de los Reyes, M.J.: Factors influencing the presence of ethics and CSR stand-alone courses in the accounting masters curricula: an international study. Account. Educ. **24**(5), 361–382 (2015). doi:10.1080/09639284.2015.1051562
19. Cameron, R.A., O'Leary, C.: Improving ethical attitudes or simply teaching ethical codes? The reality of accounting ethics education. Account. Educ. **24**(4), 275–290 (2015). doi: 10.1080/09639284.2015.1036893
20. Wynn-Williams, K., Beatson, N., Cameron, A.: The impact of unstructured case studies on surface learners: a study of second-year accounting students. Account. Educ. **25**(3), 272–286 (2016). doi:10.1080/09639284.2016.1165125
21. Daly, A., Hoy, S., Hughes, M., Islam, J., Mak, A.S.: Using group work to develop intercultural skills in the accounting curriculum in Australia. Account. Educ. **24**(1), 27–40 (2015). doi: 10.1080/09639284.2014.996909
22. Huff, P.L.: The goal project: a group assignment to encourage creative thinking, leadership abilities and communication skills. Account. Educ. **23**(6), 582–594 (2014). doi: 10.1080/09639284.2014.974198
23. Kiboss, J.K., Tanui, E.K.: Effects of e-learning program in accounting on students' achievement and motivation to learn double entry bookkeeping. J. Educ. Pract. **4**(9), 50–57 (2013)
24. Osgerby, J.: Students' perceptions of the introduction of a blended learning environment: an exploratory case study. Account. Educ. **22**(1), 85–99 (2013). doi: 10.1080/09639284.2012.729341
25. López-Pérez, M.V., Pérez-López, M.C., Rodríguez-Ariza, L.: Blended learning in higher education: students' perceptions and their relation to outcomes. Comput. Educ. **56**(3), 818–826 (2011). doi:10.1016/j.compedu.2010.10.023
26. Hon, S.: Innovative teaching and online course development in HKU SPACE. In: HKU SPACE E-learning Workshop (2017)
27. Zhuang, Y., Ma, H., Xie, H., Leung, A.C.M., Hancke, G.P., Wang, F.L.: When innovation meets evolution: an extensive study of emerging e-Learning technologies for higher education in Hong Kong. In: Wu, T.T., Gennari, R., Huang, Y.M., Xie, H., Cao, Y. (eds.) SETE 2016. LNCS, vol. 10108, pp. 574–584. Springer, Heidelberg (2017)
28. Lam, J.Y.C., Chan, R.K.H., Yan, K.Y.K.: A report on the online learning experience of students in accounting course. Int. J. Serv. Stand. **10**(4), 192–210 (2015)
29. ACCA.: ACCA survey. Accountancy Futures 13 (2016)

Japanese Students' Utilization of Courseware in a Blended Learning Environment

Yoko Hirata(✉) and Yoshihiro Hirata

Faculty of Engineering, Hokkai-Gakuen University, Sapporo, Japan
hira@eli.hokkai-s-u.ac.jp, hirata@hgu.jp

Abstract. This paper outlines research conducted into what Japanese undergraduate students think about utilization of commercial online courseware in a blended language learning course; I also demonstrate apparent benefits and problems with introducing courseware in Japanese educational settings. A brief introduction of the concepts of CALL and availability of ICT in Japan is provided, followed by a short description of English language teaching in Japanese educational settings. The present study and its results are then explained. The findings show that different students had different opinions of the effectiveness of the courseware – less than half of them appreciated the benefits of the courseware, while the rest raised computer-related problems with learning English through it. It is crucial for teachers to determine how to construct face-to-face learning environments in order to accommodate students' different demands and requests in blended learning classrooms.

Keywords: Courseware · Japanese · Blended language learning

1 Introduction

E-learning has played an important role in language classes as computers have become readily available for use by both teachers and students [1]. E-learning derives from Computer Assisted Language Learning (CALL) which "covers a diverse area of study not only in terms of the range of technologies and software available for language learning" [2]. When the concept of CALL was initially developed, the technology for language learning was limited to "grammar drills, lexical games, transformation exercises, and language-learning software designed mainly for autonomous student-computer interaction" [3]. Conventional paper-based materials were simply converted to online materials without any reference to the needs of students and teachers. However, as time has progressed a variety of relevant computer-related systems and tools have become available [2]. There are various web resources such as free educational sites (for example, *Khan Academy*), internet tools (for example, computer-mediated communication, blogs and wikis) and networking system (for example, Learning Management System) (ibid).

Japan is not an exception. While the original concept of CALL still exists, the above computer resources have been introduced into the classroom. Cowie and Sakui

S.K.S. Cheung et al. (Eds.): ICBL 2017, LNCS 10309, pp. 106–117, 2017.
DOI: 10.1007/978-3-319-59360-9_10

[4] report on the use of computer technology implemented in Japanese educational settings as follows.

> "There are … few higher education institutions that do not use some kind of Learning Management System (LMS) in which students can register for courses, check their curriculum, download materials, and take quizzes or tests online. Most students would expect to use a digital device to carry out an internet search when they write a paper or look for an appropriate website to practice a language skill. Many teachers, too, use these same online opportunities as their students to create and carry out their lessons."

However, according to a survey conducted by the National Institute for Multimedia in Education (NIME) the ratio of Japanese universities providing regular e-learning courses was only 20.7% [5]. In addition, according to Lockley research on 105 Japanese university students' skills in using ICT [6], not all of them had received computer training when they were at high school. These numbers are surprising considering the fact that high school students are required to take ICT courses by the Ministry of Education in Japan [7]. Furthermore, the majority of households in Japan (87.2%) are able to access a computer and 67.1% of households have Internet access [6]. In addition, mobile phones and social networking play a vital role for younger generations [8].

Although there are some "online for-profit universities" available to students in Japan, utilization of e-learning systems in higher education is relatively sporadic. In addition, in many language learning classes in particular, commercial courseware, which does not take full advantage of electronic capabilities, including lexical and grammatical drill exercises to supplement textbooks and materials, are widely used. On the bright side, students are able to access these via a smartphone; this helps them extend their language learning even outside the classroom, which teachers often think important to provide them with opportunities to be exposed to English [9]. As yet, however, there has been little in-depth research on how Japanese students evaluate computer-based courseware. Study should also be conducted to explore how newer technologies in courseware can be integrated into the language classroom [2].

2 English Education in Japan

How Japanese students use e-learning closely depends on their educational background. Students learn English as a school subject and to pass entrance examinations. In order to get into both public and many private universities, the majority of students in secondary schools study English to take standardized university entrance examination (National Center Test for University Admissions) and get a good score. This examination exclusively includes multiple choice questions. Similarly, the STEP (Society for Testing English Proficiency) Eiken, another test students in secondary schools are required to take, includes multiple choice questions. When students get into a university they are then highly encouraged to take standardized English examinations, especially TOEIC (the Test of English for International Communication). Aspinall [10] states TOEIC has been widely implemented in Japan's colleges and universities because its scores play an important role in getting a good job after graduation and then getting promotions at work. In order to help students prepare for taking TOEIC tests and improve their scores, TOEIC test preparation classes are provided in many universities.

Since Japanese university students are accustomed to multiple choice exams, there is a wide variety of commercial courseware available which is intended to improve their English skills. When this is introduced into classes, students are usually required to work on it as additional online materials or after-school supplemental tasks; students study English in the blended learning environments. However, there are two major problems with effective implementation of courseware in blended learning classroom. Firstly, as those in many other Asian countries, students in Japan are required to take classes passively and teachers are respected as authorities who provide them with considerable knowledge [11]. This culture-specific style of language learning is seen at all levels of education in Japan and contradicts the concept of e-learning, which requires students to become more responsible for their own study. Another challenge to be considered when implementing blended learning in English language classes is that conventional stereotypical characteristics of Japanese students have been changing. There are many university students who are convinced that the importance of learning English is to communicate with other people in English [12]. Therefore, examining how students perceive courseware (whether it supplements classroom instruction or is extra follow-up practice) and determining how to fulfil students' needs to develop their communication skills is indispensable.

3 The Study

3.1 Purpose

The primary aim of this study is to determine how Japanese students who are used to passive learning approaches perceive blended learning in a language course. This study sought to answer the following two questions:

1. In their quest to improve their English skills, how do students evaluate the benefits and problems of multiple choice exam courseware?
2. Which characteristics of the courseware do students evaluate highly?

Answering these questions will provide teachers with new and considerable insights into determining how to implement e-learning into language learning courses and what kind of blended learning is suitable for students.

4 Procedure and Settings

4.1 Participants

Seventeen full-time Japanese undergraduate students participated in this study (16 males and 1 female, aged 19–20 years). They all were majoring in economics and engineering and accustomed to traditional large lecture-type language classrooms in secondary schools, where they were assigned exam-oriented multiple choice and gap-filling exercises with limited speaking opportunities [13]. All the students had learned English for six years and had attained a beginners' or a lower-intermediate level of proficiency. In addition, all the students were experienced smartphone users and had some experience in using computers. Unfortunately, however, they had no experience in online language learning in or beyond the classroom.

4.2 Courseware Description

The courseware described in this study was 'Practical English 6' [14] which provides a wide variety of English language learning exercises and systematic practice activities students are required to engage in for the purpose of gaining comprehensive knowledge of English and passing standardized English tests. One of the major characteristics of this courseware is its program, called Learning Path (see Fig. 1), which contains personalized lessons which help students be assigned to the language exercises and activities and tests appropriate to their proficiency levels. At the beginning of this program students were required to take its diagnostic test, including grammar, listening and reading components. Based on the results of the test students were specifically directed to the appropriate language lessons, therefore they did not have control over which exercises and materials to select. This courseware contained 330 lessons in total (i.e. 125 listening lessons, 125 reading lessons, and 80 grammar lessons). The time students normally take to finish a lesson is approximately 45 to 60 min (ibid). The lessons include a variety of fundamental communicative functions which are important for students to acquire in various English speaking contexts (e.g. a conversation with a bank clerk and

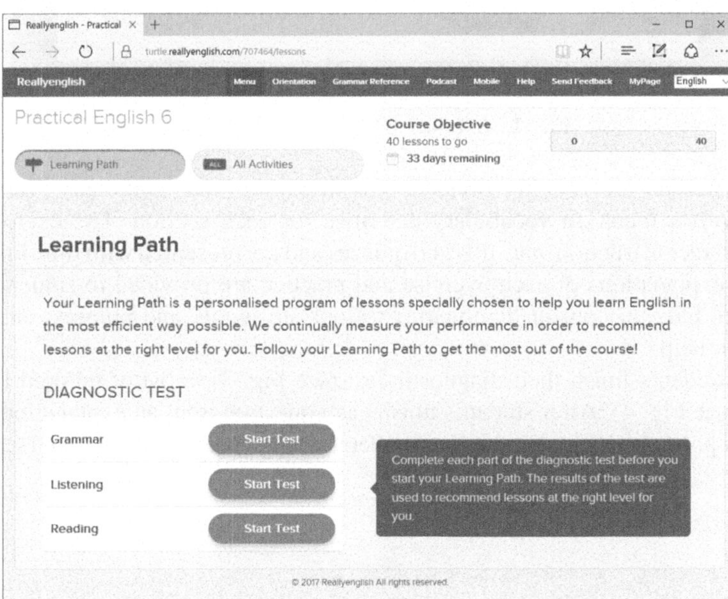

Fig. 1. Interface at the beginning of learning path

a talk with a neighbor). This courseware also enables teachers to monitor how far students have progressed with their studies.

Another notable characteristic includes customer support services which students can access through email via the interface. By clicking the Help button in the bar above in the interface (see Fig. 1) students are able to make direct contact with teaching and technical staff to solve their own problems with the program. Students are also regularly encouraged by Learning Path teaching staff to work on the courseware by email notification.

As shown in Fig. 2, the exercises presented to students look similar to those they do using paper-based materials. Students are required to do exercises with time restrictions (shown in the left hand side of the screen, see Fig. 2). This allows them to get accustomed to completing multiple choice examinations under time limits.

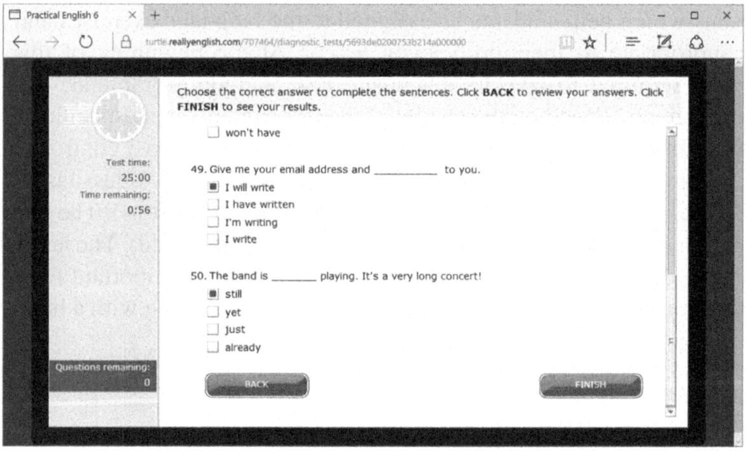

Fig. 2. Interface from a grammar lesson

The materials are roughly divided into three sections: grammar, listening and reading, with a focus on vocabulary activities for each section. The exercise types include text reconstruction, gap-fills and quizzes and are presented with time limitations. Thorough explanations of each exercise and practice are provided to students so that they do not have to consult dictionaries to look up words and phrases, or even ask teachers for help.

When students finish their diagnostic test (see Fig. 3), a list of tailored lessons is provided (see Fig. 4). After students finish each question item an explanation relevant to the item pops up to supplement their understanding each language item (see Fig. 5).

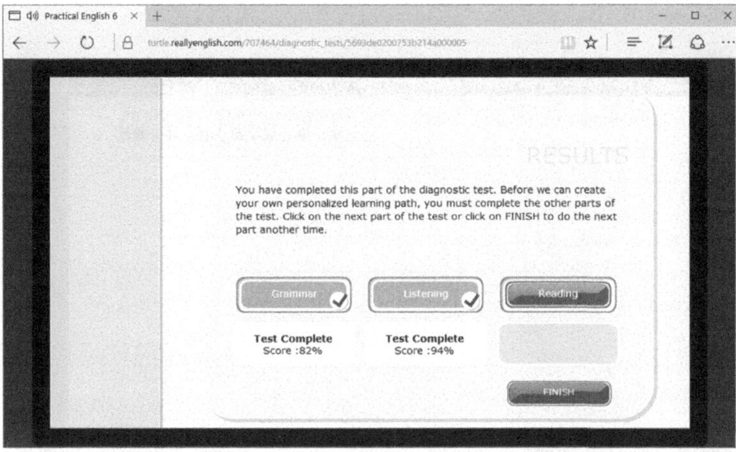

Fig. 3. Interface from the results of the diagnostic test

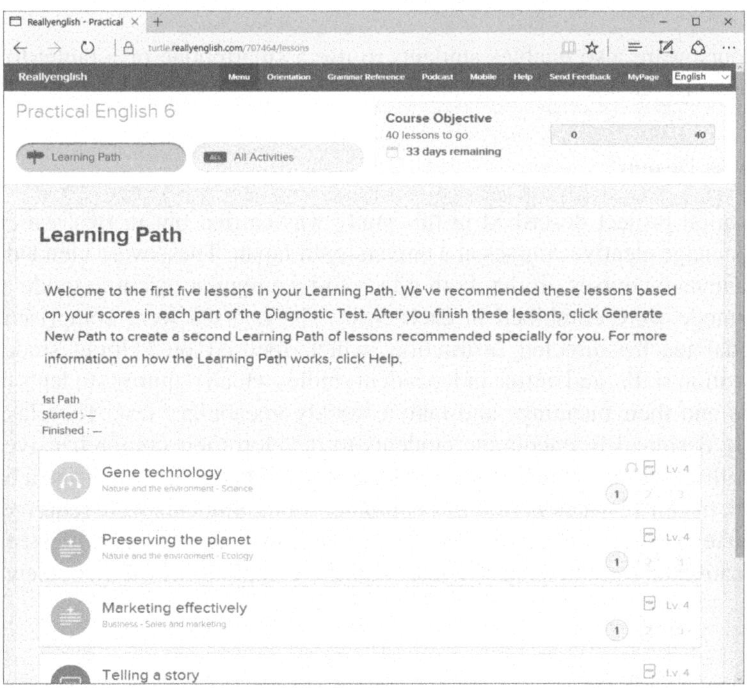

Fig. 4. A list of exercises students do after the diagnostic test

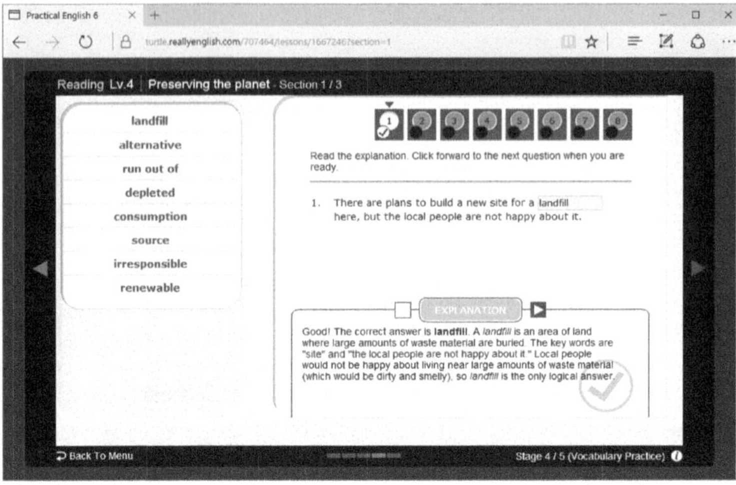

Fig. 5. An example exercise after the diagnostic test

The courseware also enables students to use a smartphone or a tablet to do their assigned lessons outside the classroom.

4.3 Course Design

The evaluation project described in this study was carried out in two semester-long English language elective courses at a university in Japan. These were blended learning English language courses, in that both a face-to-face regular teaching mode and an e-Learning mode were combined in each class. The courses were comprised of both conventional teacher-directed instruction, which focused on helping students gain communication skills, and online independent studies which required students to memorize words and their meanings and take a weekly vocabulary test. The classes were specifically designed to encourage students to develop their comprehensive English abilities with a focus on TOEIC tests. Each class was scheduled for one and a half hours every week over a 15-week period in a computer room. Students were required to work on the courseware both inside and outside the classroom. The scores from weekly tests, communicative tasks, end-semester tests and the completion of the courseware were assessed.

4.4 Student Feedback

Data was collected from a 20-item questionnaire, which was distributed to the students after the course had been completed. The purpose of this data collection was to seek opinions on the courseware and evaluate how effectively students were able to use it and what they thought about its advantages and disadvantages. The students were required to answer the questions anonymously. The rating scale used in the questionnaire was a 10-point Likert Scale with 1 representing "strongly disagree" and 10 representing "strongly agree". The responses were totaled and averaged to attain a mean response for each question. A standard deviation was also obtained to examine statistically significant differences between students' responses. The data is presented in this study as mean ±SD. Furthermore, students were encouraged to answer open-ended questions and report the benefits and problems of the courseware.

5 Findings

The results exhibited the students' both positive and negative responses to the use of the courseware. One of the major findings of this study is, despite the fact that students were provided the lessons appropriate to their English proficiency levels after they took the initial diagnostic test, only approximately 30% of the students were satisfied or relatively satisfied with them (Table 1).

Table 1. Results of the questionnaire: students' satisfaction with the courseware

Questions	Average (±SD)
1. The lessons in the courseware were appropriate to my English level	5.0 (2.5)
2. The courseware satisfied my study needs	6.3 (2.1)
3. The courseware provided me with various exercises	6.0 (1.8)

There was one student who thought the lessons were extremely inappropriate to his English level, three students who thought the lessons were perfectly appropriate to their levels and seven students who scored the question between 6 and 10. This indicates a weakness in the diagnostic test conducted at the beginning of the courseware. Similarly, with regards to the match between students' needs and teaching methods and materials in the courseware, the overwhelming majority of students were on neither side.

With regard to the enjoyment of studying TOEIC exercises through the courseware, approximately 40% of the students thought the courseware provided this. None of the students thought the courseware gave them very practical advice on TOEIC test taking skills. Similar to this question number 5, except for one student who highly rated the exercises provided by the courseware, almost none thought the courseware provided comprehensive explanations of the exercises. As shown in Table 2, the average (±SD) of this response was 5.5 (±1.6). Therefore, the students who were negative about the

Table 2. Results of the questionnaire: students' satisfaction in studying for TOEIC exercises

Questions	Average (±SD)
1. The courseware helped me enjoy studying the TOEIC exercises	6.2 (2.0)
2. The courseware gave me practical advice about studying for the TOEIC test	5.5 (1.6)
3. The courseware had comprehensive explanations of exercises	5.5 (1.6)
4. The courseware was effective in studying for the TOEIC test	5.7 (2.0)
5. The courseware helped me understand the importance of studying for the TOEIC test	5.5 (1.5)

exercises provided by the courseware reported in question 7 that it was not effective in helping them study for the TOEIC test. The average (±SD) of this response was 5.7 (±2.0). Similar results were gained from question 8.

With regard to the interface and the system, while approximately 47% of the students were satisfied or relatively satisfied with the courseware's simple screen layout, only 35% thought it was easy to navigate. The average (±SD) of these responses was 6.1 (±1.7) and 5.5 (±2.2) respectively. With regard to the presentation of the materials and audio files, almost none of the students highly rated their usefulness. Some thought the courseware was easier to use than the textbook and others did not. The average (±SD) of these responses was 5.5 (±2.3) as shown in Table 3.

Table 3. Results of the questionnaire: students' satisfaction with the system

Questions	Average (±SD)
4. The courseware had a simple and clear screen layout	6.1 (1.7)
5. The courseware was easy to navigate	5.5 (2.2)
6. The courseware was well-laid-out	5.6 (1.7)
7. The courseware had an easy-to-use audio playback system	5.4 (1.9)
8. The courseware was easier to use than the textbook	5.5 (2.3)

Students in this study used the courseware both inside and outside the classroom. However, many of them did not follow my instructions to work on the exercises concurrent with the weekly lessons. A few completed all of the exercises in the first several weeks in the semester (question 20), while many likely worked on them too infrequently (question 16). Those who worked on the courseware once a week usually finished them at the last minute just before their due dates, according to my observations. Their erratic approaches to the exercises are emblematic of issues with unsupervised online learning (Table 4).

Table 4. Results of the questionnaire: students' satisfaction with the overall assessment

Questions	Average (±SD)
6. The courseware should help me improve my TOEIC score	5.3 (1.6)
7. I enjoyed the courseware very much	5.4 (2.4)
8. I worked on the courseware about once a week	5.8 (2.0)
9. I was able to complete the exercises in a more meaningful manner in the classroom than outside the classroom	5.5 (1.9)
10. The courseware required lot of time and effort, but it didn't bother me	6.1 (1.6)
11. The courseware assisted me to reflect upon what and how much I had learned	5.8 (1.6)
12. I didn't work on the exercises at the last minute, but rather finished them in the first several weeks	4.9 (1.6)

6 Student Comments

As stated in the previous section, students' reaction to the courseware enormously varied and their feedback was shown in their comments on its benefits and problems. When asked about the benefits of the courseware, on average students reported that they were ambivalent about its effectiveness in preparing them for TOEIC test, which probably might result from the ineffectiveness of the diagnostic test they were required to take at the beginning of the courseware before they started working on their assigned exercises. Although it was difficult for lower proficient students to begin studying for the tests by themselves, the courseware did engage them in a wide variety of exercises intended to help them achieve good TOEIC scores. Many students favorably commented on the opportunities to listen to various speeches and talks conducted by native speakers of English, obvious considering the fact that they do not have any opportunities to speak and listen to English outside the classroom at all. Only a minority of students prized the efficiency and effectiveness of using the courseware in this blended learning course. These students appreciated the importance of the explanations of words and phrases as supplemental materials presented in the courseware and its user friendliness, which allowed them to do exercises repeatedly.

The students also expressed distinct opinions about the problems with using the courseware in the classroom. These were all relevant to computer-related issues they encountered when working on the exercises. For example, students expressed their difficulty in maintaining concentration on the exercises for a long time. This resulted from the physical problems (e.g. extreme fatigue, sore eyes and neck pain) they experienced after reading texts on the computer screen. I had no choice in the courseware I used (this was assigned by the university to all its TOEIC teachers), but do recommend for future improvement that courseware be broken up into smaller modules that can be completed within 30 min.

Working individually on the exercises also made them feel isolated and was laborious, and therefore discouraged them from understanding that they were learning a language. In addition, a minority of students lamented that the exercises provided them were too difficult to accomplish within a limited time frame.

7 Discussion and Conclusions

In this study the sample size was too small to allow any generalizations. However, its findings provide useful information teachers should take into consideration when implementing courseware into blended language classes.

Firstly, students perceive courseware in different ways. This is in accordance with the study conducted by Jung and Suzuki [15] who suggest the importance of accommodating different student proficiency levels in e-learning classrooms. To determine these levels the diagnostic test provided by the courseware was fairly ineffective. To address this issue, teachers should additionally assess students through direct interaction. In addition, although all the students were familiar with playing games using a smartphone or computer, not all of them engaged in doing the courseware exercises – they were not having fun with working on them. These students completed the required lessons at the last minute simply because they were required to do so to pass the course.

Secondly, teachers need to carefully consider what kinds of language activities students in a face-to-face learning component in blended learning classes should engage in, in addition to the exercises presented by the courseware. They should not rely on too much on electronic exercises (including the diagnostic test). Teachers need to determine the role commercial courseware will play in the courses they are in charge of; while commercial courseware is easy for teachers to implement because it saves the time and energy needed to develop online materials on their own, it in general does not allow customization to accommodate students' needs and preferences. Therefore teachers need to change included face-to-face classroom activities to make them more suitable for students' study needs.

Lastly, in order to be aware of different students' needs and interests, teachers need to regularly evaluate the effectiveness of courseware. As Hubbard [16] states, comprehensive courseware evaluation is important for teachers to understand its strengths and weaknesses and help students effectively maximize their computer-based independent learning opportunities. Careful evaluation conducted regularly by teachers will substantially contribute to the development of successful blended language learning courses and whole language learning approaches.

References

1. Naidu, S.: Learning & Teaching with Technology: Principles and Practices. Routledge Falmer, London (2003)
2. Gitsaki, C.: Course design to promote student autonomy and lifelong learning skills: a Japanese example? In: Anderson, H., Hobbs, M., Jones-Parry, J., Logan, S., Lotovale, S. (eds.) Supporting Independent Learning in the 21st Century. Proceedings of the Second Conference of the Independent Learning Association, pp. 9–12. Independent Learning Association Oceania, Auckland (2005)
3. Brett, D., Gonzalez-Lloret, M.: Technology-enhanced materials. In: Long, M.H., Doughty, C.J. (eds.) The Handbook of Language Teaching, pp. 351–369. Wiley-Blackwell, Oxford (2009)
4. Cowie, N., Sakui, K.: Assessment and e-learning: current issues and future trends. JALT CALL J. **11**, 271–281 (2015)
5. Suzuki, K.: E-learning in Japan: past, present, and future. In: 2009 KAEN and the 4th BK21 GGRTE International conference: technology and future learning space, Proceedings, pp. 9–17 (2009). http://citeseerx.ist.psu.edu/viewdoc/download?doi=10.1.1.394.2809&rep=rep1&type=pdf
6. Lockley, T.: Japanese students' experience of ICT and other technology prior to university: a survey. JALT CALL J. **7**, 93–117 (2011)
7. Murray, A., Blyth, A.: A survey of Japanese university students' computer literacy levels. JALT CALL J. **7**, 307–318 (2011)
8. Boase, J., Kobayashi, T.: Kei-Tying teens: using mobile phone e-mail to bond, bridge, and break with social ties — a study of Japanese adolescents. Int. J. Hum Comput Stud. **66**, 930–943 (2008)
9. Mindog, E.: Apps and EFL: a case study on the use of smartphone apps to learn English by four Japanese university students. JALT CALL J. **12**, 3–22 (2016)

10. Aspinall, R.W.: International Education Policy in Japan in an Age of Globalisation and Risk. Global Oriental, Leiden (2013)
11. Kennedy, J.: Perspectives on cultural and individual determinants of teaching style. RELC J. **22**, 61–78 (1991)
12. Fushino, K.: Students' reactions to a group project in a university English-as-a-foreign-language class for cultural understanding. Intercultural Educ. **22**, 301–316 (2011)
13. Humphries, S., Burns, A.: 'In reality it's almost impossible': CLT-oriented curriculum change. ELT J. **69**, 239–248 (2015)
14. Practical English 6. Reallyenglish, Tokyo
15. Jung, I., Suzuki, K.: Blended learning in Japan and its application in liberal arts education. In: Bonk, C.J., Graham, C.R. (eds.) The Handbook of Blended Learning, pp. 267–280. Pfeiffer, San Francisco (2006)
16. Hubbard, P.: An integrated framework for CALL courseware evaluation. CALICO J. **8**, 51–72 (1988)

Blended Learning as a Mover in the Tourism&Management Study Programme?

Ivana Simonova(✉)

University of Hradec Kralove, Rokitanskeho 62, 50003 Hradec Kralove, Czech Republic
ivana.simonova@uhk.cz

Abstract. The article deals with the bachelor Tourism&Management study programme taught at the Faculty of Informatics and Management, University of Hradec Kralove, Czech Republic. Reflecting various reasons and changing accreditation criteria, the level of students' knowledge of English was decreasing within 25 academic years. So as to reach the original level as a minimum, the blended learning design was step-by-step implemented. However, no improvements appeared. Therefore, other movers within the process of teaching/learning must be discovered and applied. The article is structured in three parts describing (1) changes within the development of study programme, (2) relating statistic data and (3) providing pedagogical interventions in the form of blended learning. In the final part, a brief review of solutions selected from the world experience is introduced. Their consideration and implementation is expected to result in changes in both the learning content and methodology of the study programme.

Keywords: Blended learning · Tourism · Management · Study programme · Foreign languages · English

1 Introduction

Resulting from political and economic development after 1989, within the last decade of the 20th century the fields of management and tourism became important branches of the Czech economy. Instead of others, this fact was also reflected in the area of education. A new structure of education was developed which followed the Bologna process and new competences were required from graduates on all levels of education, paying–instead of others–strong emphasis of teaching/learning foreign languages, development of managerial skills and the industry of tourism in general.

On the tertiary level of education, new study programmes were accredited which reflected latest demand for specialists in these fields. Therefore, the main objective of this article is to introduce the Tourism&Management study programme at the Faculty of Informatics and Management (FIM), University of Hradec Kralove (UHK), particularly (1) its development within decades considered from five criteria: subjects included in the learning content, compulsory and optional subjects, amount of students enrolled in the study programme, amount of state exam takers and their grades, (2) apply the

S.K.S. Cheung et al. (Eds.): ICBL 2017, LNCS 10309, pp. 118–128, 2017.
DOI: 10.1007/978-3-319-59360-9_11

blended learning as a mover which might have provided significant impact on the development and (3) reviewing selected world solutions consider how to improve the analyzed study programme.

2 Tourism&Management Study Programme

This study programme has been accredited for bachelor degree since the very beginning of the institution history. The faculty was established in 1992/3 academic year been called the Faculty of Management and Information Technologies (FMIT). It focused on preparation of specialists in the fields of Applied Informatics, Information Management, Financial Management, Sports Management and Health Management. Instead of others, it also offered a study programme *Tourism with Extended Foreign Language Learning* (ToEFLL).

In 1990s, when the Czech Republic opened gates to tourists from all over the world and Czech inhabitants were allowed to travel to any country, the demand for experts in the field sharply increased. Their education was mostly conducted on the upper secondary level at that times. Moreover, lifelong education courses of different quality and length appeared to prepare guides for tourists from foreign countries coming to the Czech Republic as well as for clients of Czech travel agencies going for stay and explore tours. Step-by-step, study programmes were accredited within the higher (tertiary, university) education on public and private institutions, e.g. Tourism&Management study programme in the full-time and part-time form is taught at Charles University, Prague, Institute for Language and Preparatory Studies; Masaryk University, Brno, Faculty of Economics and Administration; Mendel University, Brno, Faculty of Business and Economics; College of Polytechnics, Jihlava; College of Entrepreneurship and Law, Prague; University College of Business, Prague, etc. In all institutions, blended learning is implemented to some extent. The model of presenting study materials at web pages and conducting teacher-student or student-student communication through e-mail messages was widely exploited at starting phases. Nowadays, LMS Moodle is the most frequently used environment in the Czech Higher education environment, excluding FIM where LMS Blackboard is used. And, as FIM has been the leader in e-learning in the Czech Republic for two decades, the strongest support to blended learning is provided at this institution, as described below.

2.1 Original Content of the Study Programme at FMIT

As the name of study programme shows the learning content had strong focus on foreign languages. At that times, two languages within three combinations could have been studied: English/French, English/German, or French/German. During the first decade (1992/3–2002/3), the amount of applicants was 6–10 times higher compared to the amount of students who could have enrolled at this programme. This fact meant, that only the best applicants with high level of knowledge in both foreign languages had been accepted. Their starting knowledge was on rather similar level (B2–C1 according to CEFR [1]) and they were developing it during three years of study towards successful passing the state exams in two languages. The description and analysis of the state relates to English language, however, identical structure of the study programme was in German (and French language, as long as it was taught). Compulsory subjects, each of them taught 90 min per week, were as follows: English grammar in practice (GRAM1-6), Culture of English-speaking countries focused on literature, music, arts etc.) (CESC1-4), History, Geography, tourism and sights of English-speaking countries (HGTS1- 6); whereas Conversation in English with native speakers (CONV1-6), Translation and interpretation in practice (TRAN1-3), Seminars on English for specific purposes with focus of tourism and management (SESP1-4, SESP5-6), Business English (BE1-2), Business Russian (BR 1-6), Academic writing (AW), and general German, Spanish, Italian, Chinese language belonged to optional subjects.

2.2 Changes in the Original Study Programme

At the end of 1990s, many secondary-school graduates were expressing strong interest in managerial studies. From this and other reasons relating to the success in re-accreditation process, these trends were reflected in the Czech system of education and in the content of education, e.g. new managerial studies were accredited and conducted at numerous institutions.

As for the FMIT, following important changes were introduced:

- In 2003/4 academic year the faculty was renamed to Faculty of Informatics and Management (FIM). This was recalled by changes in the learning content of all study programmes taught at the institution. As for the ToEFLL study programme, it was renamed to *Tourism and Management* (TM) and following changes were made:
  - managerial part of the study programme was emphasized and new management-related subjects were added in the learning content;
  - not only two-foreign language combinations, but also single-language studies were offered to applicants (i.e. students could enroll in either English/French, English/German, or French/German, or they could also study English or German language only, and French language had not been taught any more).
- Since 2005/6 HGTS1-6 have become optional subjects.
- Since 2006/7 SESP1-4 have been added as optional subjects.
- Since 2007/8 one-language (English, or German) study programmes have been provided only and taking the state exam in a foreign language was not compulsory any more.
- Since 2008/9 academic year the part-time form of study has been open and compulsory subjects CESC1-4 have become optional ones (up to 2011/12 academic year).
- Since 2012/13 the subjects CESC1-4 have been included in the group of compulsory ones for part-time students.
- Since 2013/14 other changes have been made (e.g. SESP5-6 have been compulsory subject for part-time studies).
- Since 2014/15 other changes have been added (subjects TRAN1-3 have been compulsory for part-time studies).

– Business Russian language, German, Spanish, Italian, Chinese languages and other subjects were offered as optional ones reflecting the teaching staff availability in various academic years.

Table 1. Amounts of students enrolled in Tourism&Management study programme (n). (*(-): the study programme was not accredited in the academic year; (0): the study programme was not open in the academic year*)

Academic year	**English/ French**	**English/ German**	**French/ German**	***Academic year***	**English**		**German**	
	Full-time	Full-time	Full-time		Full-time	Part-time	Full-time	Part-time
1992/3	20	20	20	***2003/4***	20	-	20	-
1993/4	20	20	20	***2004/5***	20	-	20	-
1994/5	20	20	20	***2005/6***	20	-	20	-
1995/6	20	20	20	***2006/7***	20	-	20	-
1996/7	20	20	20					
1997/8	20	20	20	***2007/8***	40	-	20	-
1998/9	20	20	20	***2008/9***	40	40	20	20
1999/0	20	20	20	***2009/10***	40	40	20	20
2000/1	20	20	20	***2010/11***	40	40	20	20
2001/2	20	20	20	***2011/12***	40	40	20	20
2002/3	20	20	20	***2012/13***	40	40	20	20
2003/4	20	20	20	***2013/14***	40	40	20	20
2004/5	20	20	20	***2014/15***	40	40	20	0
2005/6	20	20	20	***2015/16***	40	40	20	0
2006/7	20	20	20	***2016/17***	40	40	20	0

Table 2. Development in the learning content: compulsory and optional subjects in Tourism&Management study programme 1992/3–2007/8). (*C: compulsory subject; O: optional subject; (-) means subject was not taught*)

	ToEFLL	TM	TM	TM	TM
	1992/3-2002/3 Full-time	2003/4-2004/5 Full-time	2005/6 Full-time	2006/7 Full-time	2007/8 Full-time
GRAM1-6	C	C	C	C	C
CESC1-4	C	C	C	C	C
HGTS1-6	C	C	O	O	O
CONV1-6	O	O	O	O	O
TRAN1-3	O	O	O	O	O
SESP1-4	-	-	-	O	O
OBAJ12	O	O	O	O	O
AWT12	-	-	-	O	O
SESP5-6	-	-	-	-	-

As the above mentioned changes were crucial for the learning content development of the study programme, they are summarized in Table 1 displaying the amounts of students enrolled in TM in single years (academic years, when both two-language and one-language combinations were taught, are highlighted in grey).

The learning content development is displayed in Tables 2 and 3. Compulsory subjects are highlighted in light grey, the crucial changes (HGTS1-6 in 2005/6 and CESC1-4 in 2008/9 are in dark grey.

Table 3. Development in the learning content: compulsory and optional subjects in Tourism&Management study programme (2008/9–2015/16).

	ToEFLL 2008/9-2011/12 Full-/Part-t.	ToEFLL 2012/13 Full-/Part-time	ToEFLL 2013/14 Full-/Part-time	ToEFLL 2014/15 Full-/Part-time	ToEFLL 2015/16 Full-/Part-time
GRAM1-6	C/C	C/C	C/C	C/C	C/C
CESC1-4	O/O	O/C	O/C	O/C	O/C
HGTS1-6	O/O	O/O	O/O	O/O	O/O
CONV1-6	O/O	O/O	O/O	O/O	O/O
TRAN1-3	O/O	O/O	O/O	O/C	O/C
SESP1-4	O/O	O/O	O/C	O/C	O/C
OBAJ12	O/O	O/O	O/O	O/O	O/O
AWT12	O/O	O/O	O/O	O/O	O/O
SESP5-6	-/-	O/O	O/O	O/O	O/O

3 Pedagogical Consequences

Changes in the learning content of the study programme in the field of foreign languages and the emphasis on managerial subjects were appreciated neither by the enrolled students, nor by those secondary school graduates who planned to apply for, as they intended to develop mainly their foreign language knowledge and skills and gain the tourist guide licence of higher quality within this study programme compared to various short-time courses. In other words, changes in the name and learning content of the study programme caused (1) the increase of lessons devoted to management-related subjects, (2) the decrease in amount of lessons related to foreign languages and (3) moreover, numerous language subjects, belonging to compulsory ones were included to the group of optional (GRAM1-6 have been the only compulsory subject up to now, others previously compulsory subjects became optional (CESC1-4, HGTS1-6 in 2005/6). Consequently, the total amount of applicants to this study programme decreased substantially: been 6–10 times higher in the past (as mentioned above), it has decreased sharply to 1.5–2 times since the 2003/4 academic year. In reality, this fact meant (1) the first-year students were selected from significantly *fewer applicants who did not have such a high level of knowledge in foreign language/s compared to previous academic years*. The main reason was they did not consider foreign language/s to be of their main interest, (2) *from the reason of lower level of knowledge and motivation to learning, fewer of the third-year students applied for sitting for the state exam in a foreign language (English)*, (3) average *grade at state exam in the foreign language (English) was worse* compared to previous academic years, as displayed in Fig. 1.

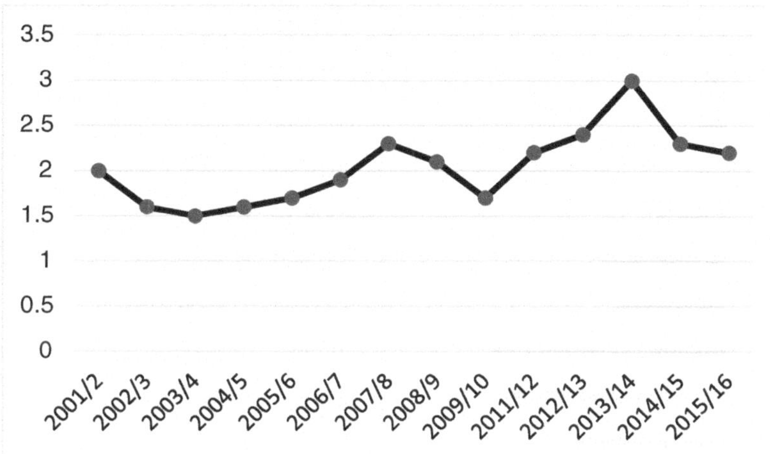

Fig. 1. Average grades in English state exams within the period of 2001/2–2015/16 academic years.

The observation started later in the field of state exams (i.e. sitting for the exams and gained grades) because a new system has been used since 2001/2 academic year and all previous data were lost (1992/3–2000/1). Until 2014/15 grading was made in the form of Fig. 1 (1 = A, 2 = C, 3 = E, 4 and 5 = F on the tertiary level of education in the Czech Republic; levels of B and D were not used). Starting from average grade 2 (i.e. C) in 2001/2 the results improved during the five-year period, reaching 1.5 (B) in 2003/4; however, they reached 2 (C) again in 2006/7 and were even getting worse in following two academic years. The improvement was detected in 2009/10. Unfortunately, the grades have been worse since, reaching even 3 (C) in 2013/14 (it should be mentioned that it is the result of the only one student who sat for the state exam in that year). Data from 2016/17 academic year are not available at this moment; however, latest results from 2015/16 show a slightly worse average grade compared to 2001/2. The 2010/11 academic year was not included in the figure, as not a single student sat for the English state exam (Fig. 2).

In Fig. 2 amounts of students sitting for the state exams in English are displayed (in the left column); the grades assessing their knowledge are in the right column. As mentioned above, grades A, C, E and F were used only. The upper parts of both figures show the decrease in amounts of students sitting for state exams and worsening their knowledge expressed in grades starting from *2010/11 academic year, which was the third year since the changes in the learning content of the study programme described above were implemented bachelor studies*. Not a single student sat for the English exam in that year.

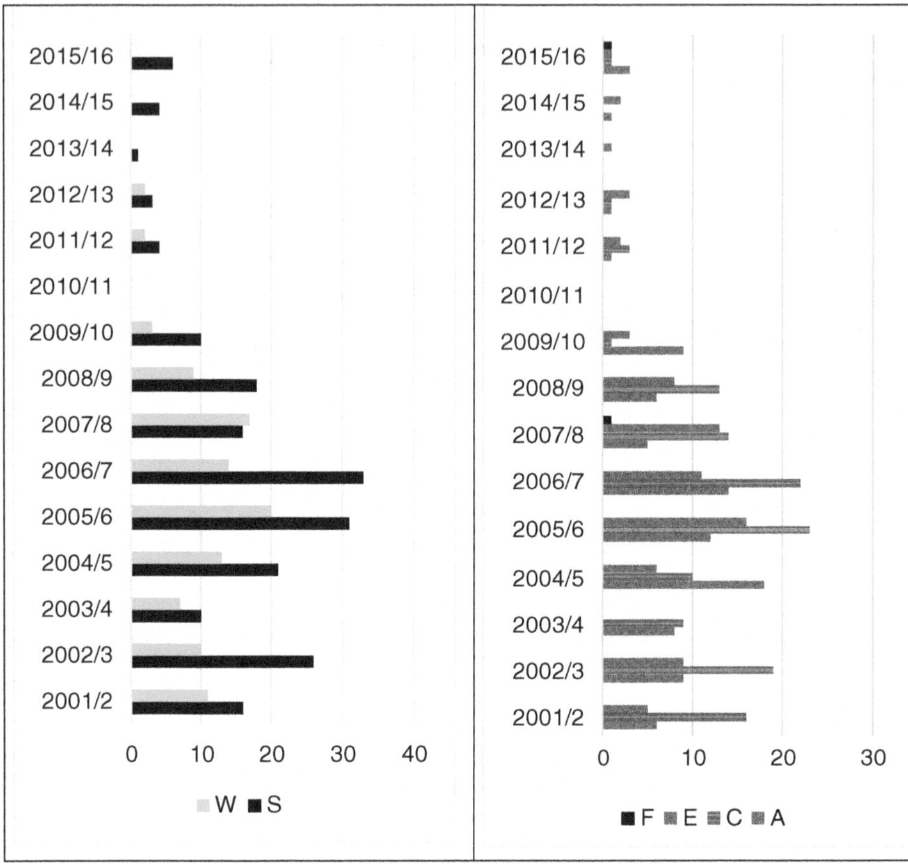

Fig. 2. State exams in English. Left column: amounts of students in winter terms (W; September–January) and summer terms (S; February–June); Right column: grades in state exams: A, C, E, F.

4 Pedagogical Interventions

Therefore, three main measures were taken within the content development of the study programme against the detected state: in face-to-face teaching of foreign language subjects, in online teaching of foreign language subjects and in online teaching of all subjects within the TM study programme.

- In face-to-face teaching of foreign language subjects), particular– teachers made greater didactic efforts towards enabling students to reach the level of knowledge developed in previous years–they applied new teaching methods, approaches, teaching/learning strategies.
- In online teaching–online courses in LMS WebCT were designed for subjects of CESC1-4, HGTS1-6 and GRAM1-6, and the blended learning was applied in these subjects. The first courses were designed in 2005/6 for compulsory GRAM1-6 subjects, then for HGTS1-6 ones, when these subjects became optional, followed by

CESC1-4 in 2008/9 from the same reason. There were two main reasons why online courses were designed to support teaching these groups of subjects. First, teachers of these subjects had got experience in other study programmes so that they were able to design and conduct such courses in TM study programme; second, the passing of these groups of subjects was a pre-condition to sitting for the state exam in the foreign language. Unfortunately, the latter fact was not sufficiently emphasized in sample study plans and some students discovered just before the end of their studies, when preparing for the state exam, that they did not meet all the requirements as they did not pass all compulsory subjects marked as optional in sample study programmes, and consequently, they could not sit for the state exam. Therefore, in some academic years the amount of students passing the state exam is very low, or even not a single student could sit for it.

- To support the online teaching of all subjects within the TM study programme, the IKLIM project was conducted in 2012–2015 [2]. Within the IKLIM (Interdisciplinary, Information, Cognitive, Linguistic and Modular support to the TM study programme) innovations in 22 subjects of the TM study programme were implemented, including 18 modular online courses in LMS WebCT(Blackboard), database of good samples of sustainability in tourism and management was established and supported, the conference on Tourism &Management was held, English and German courses for academic staff were conducted and study materials for student were published.

Moreover, special attention is paid to researching various instructional activities within the study programme, e.g. by Simkova [3], Simonova and Kostolanyova [4], Styrsky and Kacetl [5], Cech and Bures [6], etc.

5 Summary, Interpretation and Conclusions

Within the 25-year long development of the Tourism with Extended Foreign Language Learning/Tourism&Management study programme accredited at the Faculty of Informatics and Management, University of Hradec Kralove, Czech Republic, various changes were made, either reflecting the accreditation criteria of that time, and/or been instigated by 'good' intentions towards improving the quality of the study programme. The main changes were made in 2005/6 and 2008/9 academic years, when (1) several–crucial for the complete learning content–subjects changed their status from compulsory to optional ones, (2) the combination of two-foreign language studies was limited to one-language study programme and (3) more managerial subjects were included. Reflecting these interventions, the knowledge of enrolled students in foreign language/s was lower, as those interested in this field did not apply for the programme any more, and amounts of students focusing in management did not reach the numbers of the lost ones. Consequently, this state was reflected in (a) decrease of amounts of students who sat for state exam in English (which was not compulsory since 2008/9 academic year and resulted in no students taking state exams in 2010/11), and (b) in worse grades gained in English state exam of those who sat for it.

The above described pedagogical interventions did not help in supporting the students' knowledge of English, interest in the study programme, foreign language/s study and sitting for state exams and other related criteria. Unfortunately, neither the blended learning worked as a mover under these conditions.

To consider the state in a complete view, the fact of emphasizing managerial subjects might have caused this state, as the management has not belonged to the top fields any more, that the secondary school graduates are interested in [5]. As the new re-accreditation is approaching, it is high time to adjusting the study programme to currents requirements of the market and thus make it more attractive for applicants.

Moreover, experience collected abroad should be implemented. Cruz and Guardia [7] conducted analyzed feedback of tourism&management students on the quality of their education within a higher education institution. Having analyzed students' surveys they discovered that educators introduced a narrow view of the concepts on tourism, particularly limiting the practical skills of students. The application of a dynamic modular curricular system driven by typical work tasks was researched by Liu [8] from the view of tourism as the major subject within the curriculum. Reflecting this fact the traditional 'subject' curriculum was de-constructed and a specific career scene was included in the model, been supported by web technologies. Educational standards in tourism were researched by Russian scientists Agranovich et al. [9] from the view of business circle. They designed the modular learner-centred model of higher education in which the theoretical (university-based) knowledge was projected through business (i.e. practical) aspects of the field. Moreover, entrepreneurship and latest innovations were emphasized within the Malaysian approach introduced by Heo and Lee [10].

On the other hand, Min [11] paid more attention to the development of educational strategies within the higher tourism education and training, dealing with gifted students in theoretical and practical training, particularly focusing on constraints and limits. Within Chinese students he discovered strong motivation arising from the rapid development of this industry and the hospitality which he considered to be a national characteristics.

In the Czech Republic, Repik [12] started the discussion on the settings, structure of actors, learning content and ways of acquiring the learning content by the learners at higher education institutions. He emphasizes that numerous professional in the field of tourism got their formal education within lifelong and other types of courses; however, he considers the institutional training to be of higher quality, both in the field of theory and practice. In Slovakia, a neighbouring country to the Czech Republic, where the state is comparable, the emphasis is also paid to higher education conducted at state universities in this sector, despite the accreditation criteria do not provide much support to this solution [13].

Last but not least, the role of English language was highlighted by Rahayu [14] who consider mastering the language not only the necessary pre-condition for the work in the field of Tourism&Management and a tool towards reducing communication barriers but also cultural constraints.

Despite been a strong supporters of blended learning, in this case the blended learning did not prove to be the mover towards solving the above described state. From the listed (and other) verified concepts, a new one will have to be created in a short time period, so as the Tourism&Management study programme was successfully re-accredited, and appreciated by the enrolled students during their studies and later on in Tourism&Management practice [15].

Acknowledgments. The paper was supported by project of Students Grant Agency–FIM, University of Hradec Kralove, Czech Republic (ID: UHK-FIM-SP-2017). The author expresses thanks to Jiri Forman for help with statistic data processing.

References

1. CEFR (Common European Framework of Reference for Languages: Learning, Teaching, Assessment). http://www.coe.int/t/dg4/linguistic/cadre1_en.asp
2. IKLIM project, CZ.1.07/2.2.00/28.0104. http://fim2.uhk.cz/iklim/
3. Simkova, E.: Current Issues in Tourism Research. Czech Hospitality and Tourism Papers **VIII**(6), 82–97 (2012)
4. Simonova, I., Kostolanyova, K.: The blended learning concept: comparative study of two universities. In: Cheung, Simon K.S., Kwok, L.-F., Shang, J., Wang, A., Kwan, R. (eds.) ICBL 2016. LNCS, vol. 9757, pp. 302–311. Springer, Cham (2016). doi:10.1007/978-3-319-41165-1_27
5. Styrský, J., Kacetl, J.: Možné pojetí přípravy odborníků v cestovním ruchu, zvláště v přírodním turismu [Possible concepts of training for the professionals in tourism, particularly in nature tourism]. In: Conference Proceedings Dobrá praxe v udržitelnosti cestovního ruchu [Good Practices in Sustainability of Tourism Industry], pp. 83–90 (2012)
6. Cech, P., Bures, V.: Advanced technology in tourism. In: ACS 2009: Proceedings of the 9th WSEAS International Conference on Applied Computer Science, pp. 85–92 (2009)
7. Cruz, M.V., Guardia, M.S.: Eduaction for tourism: caiso's multicase study. Tourismo-estudos e Practicas **5**(2), 275–299 (2016)
8. Liu, Y.: Development of dynamic modular curriculum system driven by typical work tasks–a case of tourism major of high vocational college. In: Proceedings of the 2016 International Conference on Education, Management and Computer Science (ICEMC 2016). Advances in Intelligent Systems Research, vol. 129, pp. 1126–1132 (2016)
9. Agranovich, V.B., Kiryanova, L.G., Zavyalova, M.P., Melnikova, V.G., Arlyapova, P.A.: Techniques for upgrading educational standards in tourism: how to integrate business circles into university research. In: Ardashkin, I., Martyushev, N. (eds.) International Conference on Research Paradigms Transformation in Social Sciences (RPTSS 2015), SHS Web of Conferences, Vol. 28, Article number: UNSP 01111, 5 p. (2016)
10. Heo, C.Y., Lee, S.: Examination of student loyalty in tourism and hospitality programs: a comparison between the United States and Hong Kong. J. Hospitality Leisure Sport & Tourism Educ. **18**, 69–80 (2016)
11. Min, W.: A study on higher tourism education training status and development startegies. In: Yingying, S., Guiran, C., Zhen, L. (eds.) Proceedings of the 2016 International Conference on Education, Management, Computer and Society. ACSR-Advances in Computer Science Research, vol. 37, pp. 667–670 (2016)
12. Repik, O.: On the issue of education within the context of tourism in the Czech Republic. In: 19th International Colloquium on Regional Sciences, pp. 1109–1118 (2016)
13. Misunova, E.: Development of higher education in tourism sector in Slovakia. In: 19th International Colloquium on Regional Sciences, pp. 1119–1127 (2016)

14. Rahayu, A.U.: The mastery of the english language in reducing cultural and communication barriers in tourism world. In: Proceedings of the Asia Tourism Forum 2016–The 12th Biennial Conference of Hospitality and Tourism Industry in Asia, vol. 19, pp. 574–578 (2016)
15. Vadkertiova, A., Mistina, J.: Effective knowledge transfer as a condition for the applicability of secondary school graduates in labour market. In: Mistina, J., Hrmo, R. (eds.) Key Competences and the Labour Market, pp. 189–213. Management University Publishing House, Warsaw (2016)

A Blended-Experiential Learning Model: An Action Research Case Study

Ivan Ka-wai Lai(✉), Kwan-keung Ng, and Joseph Shi-piu Fong

School of Business and Hospitality Management,
Caritas Institute of Higher Education, Tseung Kwan O, Hong Kong
{ilai,sng,jfong}@cihe.edu.hk

Abstract. This research proposed a blended-experiential learning model for the higher education. Participatory action research method was selected in order to validate the proposed model. Eight students were invited to participate in this project to develop a live case that demonstrated how students operating a restaurant 'Café de Music' in spring 2016. The thematic concern for students was 'how to improve food quality, service quality, and atmosphere quality of the Café de Music'. The results of three action research cycles showed how the blended-experiential learning model successfully worked in a hospitality education case and how students learned by reflection in this case setting. Furthermore, recommendations for educators to implement the proposed model were provided based on the findings.

Keywords: Blended-experiential learning · Action research · Hospitality education case

1 Introduction

Many scholars believed blended learning is a learning which combines online and face-to-face approaches [1]. However, Procter [2] argued that blended learning is the effective combination of different modes of delivery, models of teaching, and styles of learning. Therefore, the learning styles of blended learning are not limited to formal face-to-face lectures with online supporting resources; the learning styles of blended learning can be any kinds of learning include informal and non-formal learning.

In the higher education, most of the students' learning activities are intentional, organized, and structured within a formal curriculum that aims for certain learning outcomes. However, students in different disciplines (such as art and science) exhibit different learning preferences, so there is no unique learning style that is suited for all the students. For some of the programmes such as journalism, 'reading and writing' are essential. On the other hand, for some programmes such as hospitality management, students may effectively gain certain knowledge and skills in informal and non-formal contexts. The informal and non-formal learning helps students integrate theories learned from formal lectures with on-hand practices learned from informal and non-formal learning activities. Therefore, in order to have an effective learning, some teachers tend

S.K.S. Cheung et al. (Eds.): ICBL 2017, LNCS 10309, pp. 129–138, 2017.
DOI: 10.1007/978-3-319-59360-9_12

to arrange some informal and non-formal learning activities for their students especially for students in the hospitality management.

Most of existing blended learning research focuses on studying different modes of delivery and models of teaching, therefore the research tends to be centered at technical or didactical or evaluation issues [3]. This study aims to introduce a blended-experiential learning model that is suitable for students who like to have informal learning to supplement their formal studies. Experiential learning is a common type of informal learning that means learning from experience or learning by doing [4]. Field-based experiential learning provides students the benefit of having hands-on practices to bolster their formal learning [5]. In this study, a blended-experiential learning model is constructed that emphasizes learning through reflection on doing with online resources. An action research will be conducted to explain how this model works in a hospitality education case and investigate how students in hospitality management learn in this case setting.

2 Research Background

2.1 Blended Learning

In recent years, blended learning has become common for universities in conducting teaching and learning sessions [6]. There are several definitions of blended learning given by different researchers. Singh [7] focused on delivery media and defined blended learning as a combination of multiple delivery media designed to complement each other and promote learning and application learned behavior. Kudrik et al. [8] focused on the learning environment and defined blended learning as a combination of physical classroom learning and online learning to enhance the learning outcomes. Harona et al. [9] provided a broader definition and stated that blended learning is a process of incorporating many different ways in which people learn (learning style) through the use of "blended" virtual and physical resources that include a variety of learning activities and the use of technology. Educators have developed 6 models for blended learning. They are: face-to-face driver model, the rotation model, the flex model, online lab school model, self-blend model, and online driver model [10].

There are several reasons for the rapid growth of the adoption of the blended learning in higher education. Collis and Moonen [11] and Jusoff [12] explained that blended learning is a flexible approach that goes beyond time, location, and cultural constraints. Azizan [13] and Poon [14] stated that blended learning can improve pedagogy, increase access or flexibility, and increase cost-effectiveness. Means et al. [15] even claimed that on average, blended courses have higher success rates and lower withdrawal rates compared to face-to-face courses and fully online courses. Othman et al. [16] considered the benefits for stakeholders and stated that the development and delivery of blended courses can be used to address a variety of institutional, faculty, and student needs. For universities, blended courses can be part of a strategy to compensate for limited classroom space, as well as a way to think differently about encouraging faculty collaboration. For faculties, blended courses can be a method to infuse new engagement opportunities into established courses or, for some, provide a transitional opportunity between fully face-to-face and fully online instruction. For students, blended courses offer the conveniences of online learning combined with the social and instructional interactions that may not lend themselves to online delivery (e.g., lab sections or proctored assessments).

Although many scholars agreed that blended learning can maximize the best advantages of face-to-face and e-learning approaches [17]. However, Dunlap and Lowenthal [18] found that instructors in a blended learning format struggle to find an effective balance between the face-to-face instruction that is high in fidelity but perhaps not as flexible, and online instruction that is high in flexibility but perhaps low in fidelity. Therefore, educators should find their ways to make a good balance between face-to-face and online portions when conducting blended learning.

On the other hand, scholars claimed that blended learning develops students' capacity for reflection, hence, improving their learning experience [19]. But very little cases have been found in the literature to show how blended learning facilitates learn by a reflection. Furthermore, scholars stated that blended learning offers flexible learning to students to accommodate diverse learning styles [20, 21]. Similarly, very little cases have been found in the literature to show how blended learning accommodates different learning styles. Thus, this study attempted to fill these gaps and to provide a successful case to show how students learned by reflection under blended learning setting.

2.2 Experiential Learning

Kolb [22] defined experiential learning as the process whereby knowledge is created from the combination of grasping and transforming the experience. Figure 1 shows Kolb's experiential learning cycle which involves four learning modes — concrete experience, reflective observation, abstract conceptualization, and active experimentation. Also, the experiential learning cycle portrays two dialectically related modes of grasping experience (concrete experience and abstract conceptualization) and two dialectically related modes of transforming experience (reflective observation and active experimentation). The immediate or concrete experiences are the basis for observations and reflections. These reflections are assimilated and distilled into abstract concepts from which new implications for action can be drawn. These implications can be actively tested and serve as guides in creating new experiences.

During the last three decades, researchers have examined experiential learning in different areas such as education, management, computer/Information science, psychology, medicine, nursing, accounting, and law. For the educational research, the experiential learning studies covered k-12, higher education, and adult learning. Experiential learning has been widely accepted as a useful framework for learning-centered educational innovation, including instructional design, curriculum development, and life-long learning [23]. As college faculties recognize a need to provide experiential learning opportunities into their courses and programs to make learning more relevant for their students [24], so higher education institutes are using experimental learning.

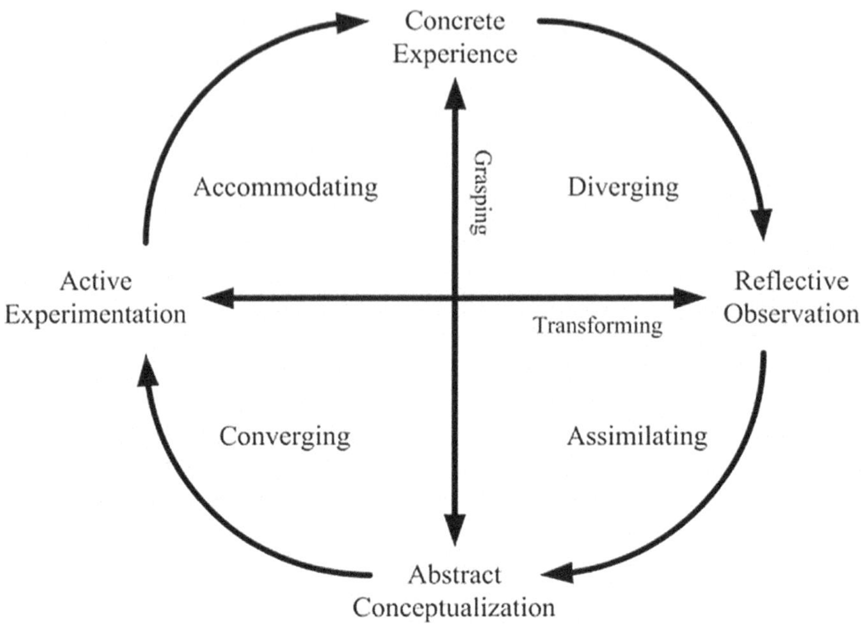

Fig. 1. Experiential learning cycle [22]

3 Blended-Experiential Learning Model

For the above 6 blended learning models, there is a key component - the teachers. Although different models require different levels of teachers' participation, the learning practices are based on the information transferred from teachers to the students. But for the proposed blended-experiential learning model, it aims for an informal learning, so no teacher is involved. Figure 2 shows the proposed blended-experiential learning model with six components. In this blended-experiential learning model, there are two types of stakeholders: students and facilitators. One of the roles for facilitators is to provide an advice to students when they have a difficulty in making a decision. However, students should make the final decision themselves and select the way or method to complete the task. Other than this, students should (1) share the knowledge with other students and (2) collaborate together to complete a task. For doing a task, they need to search information online once they do not know how to do it. Upon students' request, facilitators would support necessary offline resources (such as tools) for them to complete the task. After completing the task, students can learn by reflection.

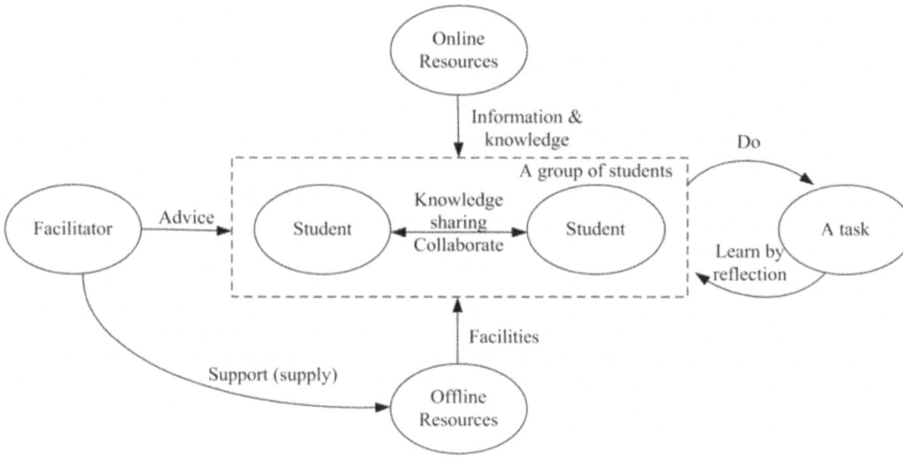

Fig. 2. Blended-experiential learning model

4 Research Method

4.1 Participatory Action Research

In order to validate the proposed blended-experiential learning model, action research method was selected because action research is a systematic self-reflective scientific inquiry by practitioners to improve their own practices [25]. In this study, Kemmis and McTaggart's [26] participatory action research was adopted which involves a spiral of self-reflective cycles that consists of plan, act & observe, and reflect as shown in Fig. 3.

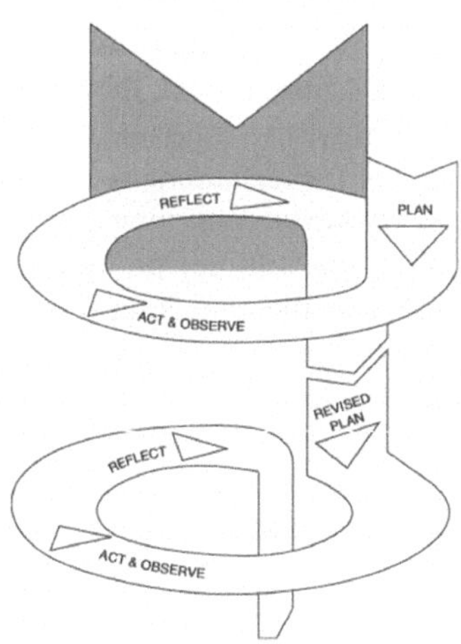

Fig. 3. The action research spiral [26]

4.2 Case Background

In order to promote blended-experiential learning, Prof. Joseph Fong proposed to develop a live case to demonstrate how students operating a restaurant in November 2015. The name of the restaurant was ‘Café de Music’ where clients (students and teachers) could enjoy their meals and listen to music. The restaurant was opened every Friday afternoon. Students would post its operations include menus and photos in the Café de Music’s Facebook such that audiences (other students) could get a participation feeling in this case. Eight students in hospitality management were invited to participate in this project. A student committee was formed where Prof. Fong was acted as a facilitator to support students. Caritas Bianchi College of Careers was the host of the project. International Hybrid Learning Society was the sponsor of the project. The thematic concern for students was ‘how to improve food quality, service quality, and atmosphere quality of the Café de Music’.

5 Results

After a month of preparation, the Café de Music was opened in February 2016. Due to the limitation of pages in length for publication, this paper only reported the results of the 1st three action research cycles.

5.1 The 1st Action Research Cycle

In the 1st action research meeting, students (referred to as participants) identified two major problems that they needed to address. They found that they needed to have an effective promotion plan for the Café de Music because students and teachers might not be aware the restaurant was opened. Second, the image of student training restaurant was a Western-Style restaurant that provided sandwiches, coffee, cake, pizza, and Italian cuisine. Although they could cook Chinese food, they were a lack of Western cooking experience and there was no a short way to train up students to cook Western food. So, they decided to change the image of the restaurant as to provide Hong-Kong-Style food. For adapting the new image of the restaurant, they also decided to adopt low pricing strategy and use multiple (online and offline) promotion channels (posters, leaflets, Instagram, and Facebook) to promote the restaurant (Fig. 4). After few weeks of operations, participants evaluated the performance of the restaurant in terms of a number of customers, the amount of revenue, and a number of likes on the Café de Music’s Facebook. They learned by a reflection that online social media is a cost-effective way to reach potential customers. They also understood that low pricing and multiple promotion channels are effective marketing strategies to attract customers for a new business.

Fig. 4. Café de music's Facebook

5.2 The 2nd Action Research Cycle

Although the Café de Music was marketed well, participants recognized (observed) three consequential problems in the 2nd action research meeting. First, there were too many customers in the peak hour. Second, meal production speed was low so many customers complained the long waiting time. Third, due to a lack of manpower, customers also complained the speed of service. Prof. Fong suggested recruiting new helpers. Then, members posted the recruitment posters in the college and asked friends for help. After the recruitment process (interview and cooking test), they found that applicants, who got the recruitment information from the posters, were not really interested in the restaurant operations. Since it was a voluntary job, only friends were willing to give a help. Participants learned by a reflection that business is a business, there is no free lunch. They also recognized that friendship is a most important asset for doing business.

5.3 The 3rd Action Research Cycle

In the 3rd action research meeting, participants observed that having the new blood did not mean the problems recognized in the 2nd action research meeting had been solved. Participants found that even they had enough manpower but without having an appropriate training for new participants and standard operating procedures, the outcome of the action in the 2nd action research cycle was not as expected. Prof. Fong invited Mr. Joe Chan (the chef) to conduct a cooking training for the new comers. The members also standardized the ordering, food and beverage delivery, and payment processes. After few weeks of operations, participants evaluated the service performance of the restaurant in terms of a number of customers' complaints and the messages posted on the Café de Music's Facebook (Fig. 5). They learned by a reflection that staff training is essential for improving service quality in the hospitality industry. They also understood that for ensuring a consistent level of service quality to the customers, hospitality firms should develop standard operating procedures to help workers carry out routine operations.

Fig. 5. Facebook (online) and poster (offline) promotion

5.4 Post-case Interviews

Post-case interviews were conducted with all the participants for investigating how they learned in the case. Participants stated that they would like to seek solutions from online resources themselves rather than asking facilitator's help when they were facing a problem; Internet could provide them all kinds of information; Facebook is a good social media to do online marketing; and they could obtain responses and feedbacks about the Café de Music from the Facebook. This case showed that students tended to solve problems in their way; they liked to try a new way to do their tasks; they solved problems by taking actions; they took actions collaboratively; and they solved problems creatively.

For the learning method, participants said that they liked this informal learning method because they didn't like to sit in a classroom for a long period of time (say two hours), so blended-experiential learning was a good learning method for them. They also stated through the blended-experiential learning, they shared the success with each member, they worked happily, and they liked this kind of learning.

6 Discussions and Conclusion

For the extant blended learning models, the teaching and learning process takes place both in the classroom and online, where the online portion becomes an expected extension of traditional classroom learning [12]. However, the experiences outside of the classroom provide the increasingly growing numbers of non-traditional learners with valuable opportunities to apply theory to practice [27]. The results of the study indicated that the blended-experiential learning model is an appropriate learning method for students who like to take actions. The result of the study indicated that blended-experiential learning provides students an environment to improve their critical thinking for problem-solving. Since students' academic achievement is directly related to their problem-solving ability [28], so the enhancement of students' problem-solving ability can improve their academic achievement. Therefore, the study suggests that the vocational-based higher education in Greater China and Hong Kong should transform their passive learning and a teacher-centred approach into a blended-experiential learning and an active learning by a reflection approach. Eventually, this study has contributed the theory of blended learning by introducing another type of blended learning methods that is favours for vocational-based higher education.

References

1. DET: Blended Learning. NSW Department of Education and Training (2003)
2. Proctor, C.: Blended learning in practice: education in a changing environment. In: Proceedings of the Inaugural Education in a Changing Environment Conference, University of Salford, 17–18 September 2003 (2003)
3. Derntl, M., Motschnig-Pitrik, R.: A pattern approach to person-centered e-learning based on theory-guided action research. In: Proceedings of the Networked Learning Conference 2004 (2004)
4. Lewis, L.H., Williams, C.J.: Experiential learning: past and pesent. In: Jackson, L., Caffarella, R.S. (eds.) Experiential Learning: A New Approach, pp. 5–16. Jossey-Bass Publishers, San Francisco (1994)
5. Cantor, J.A.: Experiential Learning in Higher Education. ASHEERIC Higher Education, Washington, D.C., Report no. 7 (1995)
6. Zaini, A.A., Noradzan, H., Salim, A., Sadjirin, R., Nordin, N.M.: Blended learning mode: an analysis of the practices among UiTM pahang lecturers. In: Luaran, J.E., Sardi, J., Aziz, A., Alias, N.A. (eds.) Envisioning the Future of Online Learning, pp. 203–212. Springer, Singapore (2016). doi:10.1007/978-981-10-0954-9_18
7. Singh, H.: Building effective blended learning program. Educ. Tech. **43**(6), 51–54 (2003)
8. Kudrik, Y., Lahn, L. C., Morch, A. I.: Technology-enhanced workplace learning: blended learning in insurance company. In: Proceedings of the 17th International Conference on Computers in Education. Asia-Pacific Society for Computers in Education, Hong Kong (2009)
9. Harona, H., Abbasa, W.F., Rahman, N.A.A.: The adoption of blended learning among Malaysian academicians. Procedia Sco. Behav. Sci. **67**, 175–181 (2011)
10. Thompson, J.: 6 Blended Learning Models: When Blended Learning Is What's Up For Successful Students, eLearning Industry (2016). Accessed from https://elearningindustry.com/6-blended-learning-models-blended-learning-successful-students
11. Collis, B., Moonen, J.: Flexible Learning in a Digital World: Experiences and Expectations. Kogan Page, London, UK (2001)
12. Jusoff, K.: Preliminary study on the role of social presence in blended learning environment in higher education. Int. Educ. Stud. **2**(4), 79–83 (2009)
13. Azizan, F.Z.: Blended learning in higher education institution in Malaysia. In: Proceedings of Regional Conference on Knowledge Integration in ICT. pp. 454–466 (2010)
14. Poon, J.: Use of blended learning to enhance the student learning experience and engagement in property education. Property Manag. **30**(2), 129–156 (2012)
15. Means, B., Toyama, Y., Murphy, R., Bakia, M., Jones, K.: Evaluation of Evidence-Based Practices in Online Learning: A meta-analysis and Review of Online Learning Studies (2010). Accessed from https://www2.ed.gov/rschstat/eval/tech/evidence-based-practices/finalreport.pdf

16. Othman, C.N., Bakar, M.S.N.A., Muda, M.R., Farooqui, M., Muhsain, S.N.F.: Development of a One Stop Distance Virtual Learning (DVL) Program for Diploma of Pharmacy Students During Hospital Attachment (2015)
17. Graham C.R.: Emerging practice and research in blended learning. In: Handbook of Distance Education, 3rd edn. (2013)
18. Dunlap, J., Lowenthal, P.: The power of presence: our quest for the right mix of social presence in online courses. In: Mizell, A., Piña, A. (eds.) Real Life Distance Education: Case Studies in Practice, pp. 41–66. Information Age Publishing, Greenwhich (2014)
19. Cooner, T.S.: Creating opportunities for students in large cohorts to reflect in and on practice: lessons learnt from a formative evaluation of students' experiences of a technology enhanced blended learning design. Br. J. Educ. Tech. **41**(2), 271–286 (2010)
20. Christensen, L., Evamy, S.: MAPs to success: improving the first year experience of alternative entry mature age students. Int. J. First Year High. Educ. **2**(2), 35–48 (2011)
21. Pelliccione, L., Broadley, T.: R U There Yet? Using virtual classrooms to transform teaching practice. In: Steel, C., Keppell, M., Gerbic, P., Housego, S. (eds.) Curriculum, Technology & Transformation for an Unknown Future. Ascilite Conference Proceedings 2010, 5–8 December 2010, Sydney, Australia, pp. 749–760 (2010). Accessed from http://espace.library.curtin.edu.au/cgibin/espace.pdf?file=/2011/02/18/file_1/152536
22. Kolb, D.A.: Experiential Learning: Experience as the Source of Learning and Development. Prentice-Hall, New Jersey (1984)
23. Kolb, A.Y., Kolb, D.A.: Experiential Learning Theory: A Dynamic, Holistic Approach to Management Learning, Education and Development (2009)
24. Cantor, J.A.: Experiential Learning in Higher Education: Linking Classroom and Community. ERIC Clearinghouse on Higher Education, Washington DC. (1997)
25. Carr, W., Kemmis, S.: Becoming Critical: Education, Knowledge and Action Research. Palmer Press, London (1986)
26. Kemmis, S., McTaggart, R.: The Action Research Planner, 3rd edn. Deakin University Press, Geelong (1988)
27. Rolls, J.A.: Gendered evaluation responses to experiential learning as an adjunct to a basic communication skills course. Can. J. Comm. **22**(1), 41–60 (1992)
28. Perveen, K.: Effect of the problem-solving approach on academic achievement of students in mathematics at the secondary level. Contemp. Issues Educ. Res. **3**(3), 9–14 (2010)

Prior Knowledge Dwarfs Hard Work in Achieving Academic Performance

Oliver Au(✉), Raymond So, and Lap Kei Lee

The Open University of Hong Kong, Ho Man Tin, Kowloon, Hong Kong
{oau,rso,lklee}@ouhk.edu.hk

Abstract. In a final-year undergraduate course, study effort has insignificant positive influence on student performance. Prior knowledge alone accurately predicts student performance. We conjecture that prior knowledge gradually increases its influence on performance as students progress through a 4-year undergraduate program. To benefit students in latter study years, universities should allocate resources for freshmen to build solid study habits and background knowledge. Finally, our study shows that individual's choice between face-to-face lectures and recorded lectures has no bearing on student performance and cram study has limited benefits.

Keywords: Background knowledge · Academic performance · Cram study · Study effort · Study habits · Blended learning · Effective study hours

1 Introduction

Educators constantly look for recipes for students to achieve academic success. For example, we want to know the usefulness of cram study before a test versus the usefulness of weekly study. Is there a perfect ratio between the two for optimal results? How much does attentiveness during study time affect performance? Does the choice between face-to-face lectures and recorded lectures affect performance? These questions have been asked by researchers before though sometimes resulting in conflicting answers. We ask the same questions in a blended learning environment where roughly half the students attended the face-to-face lectures and the remaining half viewed the recorded lectures through YouTube.

Our most interesting finding is that prior knowledge dominates study effort in the prediction of student performance. In our study, students got poor results if they started the course with a poor background regardless of the amount of work they put in. The lack of influence from study effort may be in part due to the technical nature of the final-year undergraduate computing course in which we conducted the study.

Some of findings concern effective study habits for students. There is one lecture per week. There is up to one week for students to review before the next lecture. We found that students who reviewed in the first half of week performed better than those who reviewed in the second half. We went on to find that cram study is only useful to get a student into the middle performing group. The habit of top-performing group is to study more in a regular week.

S.K.S. Cheung et al. (Eds.): ICBL 2017, LNCS 10309, pp. 139–147, 2017.
DOI: 10.1007/978-3-319-59360-9_13

Some of our findings concern educators. The choice to attend face-to-face lectures or view recorded lectures has no influence on student performance. The trend of Canadian universities introducing small seminar courses to first-year students is well-supported by our main finding that prior knowledge is key. Other universities should consider to follow suit.

Section 2 of the paper has a literature review on variables that influence student performance. Section 3 describes our hypotheses and research method. Section 4 discusses the findings. Section 5 has a discussion of possible actions for students and educators and future work.

2 Literature Review

Expanded learning time is a school-wide strategy to improve student performance by lengthening the school day or the school year. Rocha advocates for expanded learning time because it broadens the choice options for learning activities and can be beneficial in many situations. When coupled with blended learning, expanded learning time encourages students to self-manage their study [1]. The choice of the learning mode, be it face-to-face, online or blended, does not affect the observed benefits of lengthening the learning time [2–4]. As a specific example, Liu and Cavanaugh found that time spent in an online learning environment had a positive influence on student performance in an online Algebra course for high school [5].

The work cited above stated that study effort is the key factor on student performance. But it is worth noting that they were all based on K-12 students. For university students, Li found a positive correlation between attitude, self-efficacy, effort and performance though effort was found to be more of an indirect factor instead of a necessary factor for the relationship between the other three variables [6]. In other words, effort matters but is not as important for undergraduate students as it is for K-12 students.

Other than study duration, attentiveness also affects performance. Fried found that the use of laptop computers has negative influence on learning [7]. Duncan et al. found that the use of mobile phone reduces learning [8]. Au et al. simultaneously investigate the influence of study duration and attentiveness on performance [9]. They found that increased study time improves weak students' performance up to the middle in the class. But for students already achieve the middle level of performance, they do not improve any further with an increase of study time. However improved attentiveness was found to be beneficial regardless of the current level of student performance.

3 Research Questions

3.1 Research Hypotheses

We have identified several variables, controllable by students, that we expect to have influence on student performance. They are: regular week-to-week study, cram study just before the test, attentiveness while studying and prior knowledge in the subject matter. The model of our hypotheses is shown in Fig. 1.

H1: There is a positive relationship between regular study and performance
H2: There is a positive relationship between cram study and performance
H3: There is a positive relationship between prior knowledge and performance
H4a: Attentiveness moderates the relationship between regular study and performance
H4b: Attentiveness moderates the relationship between cram study and performance
H5a: Prior knowledge moderates the relationship between regular study and performance
H5b: Prior Knowledge moderates the relationship between cram study and performance.

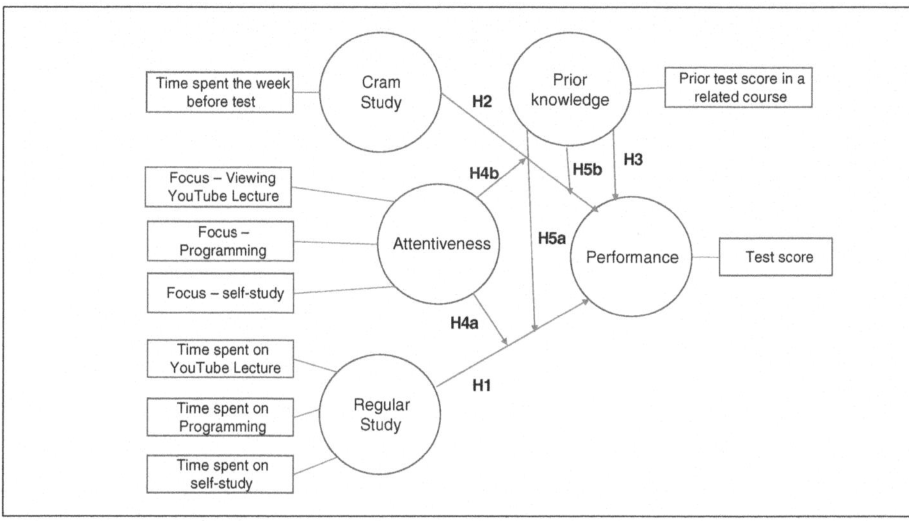

Fig. 1. Regular weekly study (H1), cram study before test (H2) and prior knowledge (H3) may have a positive influence on the test score. Attentiveness (H4a, H4b) and prior knowledge (H5a, H5b) may moderate the relationship between study effort and performance.

3.2 Research Method

Our research was conducted in a final-year computing course on distributed systems. Students learned a programming language called Erlang and write concurrent programs in it. This was their first course that required heavy application of recursion and functional programming even the two concepts were not new to them. Student performance was measured by their mid-term test scores. Prior knowledge was measured by mid-term test scores in another programming course students had just completed in the previous semester.

A question in the current mid-term test asked students to report their study habit and level of attention while studying. We allocated 4 marks out of 100 to give students an incentive to complete the survey question. The meagre 4 marks were intended not to distract students from spending sufficient time on other questions in the test that were used to measure students' current performance.

There were 55 students on the course; all took part in the survey. We eliminated 12 responses for incomplete answer in the survey. We eliminated another 7 responses for students not having completed the previous course which was our basis of prior knowledge. We have 36 valid responses in total.

4 Findings

We used RapidMiner version 7.4 to analyse the data.

4.1 Prior Knowledge Have More Influence Than Study Effort

Shown on Table 1, we found the correlation to be insignificant at 0.069 between regular study hours and performance (H1), moderate at 0.233 between cram study hours and performance (H2) and significant at 0.582 between prior knowledge and performance (H3). Prior knowledge dominates regular study and cram study to have a noticeable positive influence on student performance.

Table 1. Correlation Matrix.

	Regular study	Cram study	Prior knowledge	Performance
Regular study	1	0.150	−0.003	0.069
Cram study	0.150	1	0.153	0.233
Prior knowledge	−0.003	0.153	1	0.582
Performance	0.069	0.233	0.582	1

4.2 Studying Before Laboratory is Associated with Better Performance

The face-to-face lectures were conducted on Fridays, one lecture per week. The laboratory sessions took place on Tuesdays. The laboratory sessions evenly split the days between two consecutive lectures. Students applied what they had learned from the lecture to solve programming problems in the laboratory. We asked students to report their weekly study hours before and after the laboratory session respectively. We observed that some students came to the computer laboratory unprepared. Many needed tutor's assistance to complete the laboratory programming exercises. We want to find out whether it is more beneficial for students to spend their study time before or after the laboratory. This information also enables us to learn the influence of the study timing on their performance. It is possible that study timing affects understanding and memory retention.

Since the efficacy of study time depends partly on learner's attentiveness, we adopt the simplistic notion of effective study hours defined by Au et al. [8]. For an example, if a learner spent 2 h studying with 70% (self-reporting and self-assessed) attentiveness, the effective study hours would be 1.4 h based on Eq. (1). The study hours below by default would have been adjusted for the imperfect attentiveness unless prefixed with the qualification of raw.

$$\text{Effective Study Hours} = \text{Raw Study Hours} \times \text{Level of Attention.} \quad (1)$$

We employed k-means clustering to divide data into 3 groups as shown on Table 2. The prior knowledge score and current performance score correspond closely and rank in the right order for the top, middle and bottom performing groups. This is consistent with the finding of Sect. 4.1 that prior knowledge dominates other variables in their influence on student performance.

Table 2. k-Means Clustering (k = 3).

	Top	Middle	Bottom
Performance	69.9	48.5	44.7
Prior knowledge	69.5	59.1	36.5
Effective weekly hours before lab	1.75	0.84	0.83
Effective weekly hours after lab	1.38	1.47	1.44
Effective cram hours	6.65	10.74	7.20

The average time spent before the laboratory by a student in the top performing group was 1.75 h which doubles the corresponding numbers 0.84 and 0.83 for the middle and bottom groups respectively. On the other hand, the average time spent after the laboratory was consistent among the three groups at 1.38, 1.47 and 1.44 from top to bottom. This confirms our conjecture that more study time spent before the laboratory correlates to better performance.

Based on the curve of forgetting [10], studying before the laboratory means shorter lapsed time from the lecture. The well-paced learning and studying retain the new knowledge more effectively. Studying before the laboratory sessions prepares students to learn productively doing the programming exercises in the laboratory. It is reasonable for top-performing students to have adopted this strategy.

4.3 Cram Study is Only Useful to Reach Middle-Level Performance

From Table 1, we see that cram study has moderate positive influence on performance. Table 2 shows cram hours spent by the top, middle and bottom performing groups to be 6.65, 10.74 and 7.20 respectively. The middle performing group spent considerably more cram hours than the top and bottom groups. It suggests that cram study may have helped weak students to get into the middle performing group.

Top students doubled their weekly average study time of 3.13 to 6.65 just the week before the test. Middle students more than quadrupled their weekly study time of 2.31 h to pre-test cram study time of 10.74. Bottom students roughly tripled the 2.27 weekly study hours to 7.20 before test. Bottom and middle students spent roughly the same weekly study hours but the middle students cram more study hours than the bottom students a week before the test. Even cram study before test may have benefited performance, it does not help students get to the top performing group.

4.4 Miscellaneous Findings

Insignificant Correlations. Through multiple regression analysis, we found that regular study hours (std. coefficient = 0.089) and regular focus (std. coefficient = −0.053) explain an insignificant amount of variance in the value of Performance ($R^2 = 0.008$). Given the weak regression relationship, we see no support for H4a. In a similar way, there is no support for H4b, H5a and H5b.

Face-to-face and Recorded Lectures Suit Different Learners. Roughly half of the students attended face-to-face lectures and the remaining half viewed recorded lectures on YouTube. We found student's choice between face-to-face lectures and recorded lectures has no influence on performance. Figure 2 shows effects of face-to-face and non-face-to-face study efforts on performance. There is no pattern of student's choice of face-to-face and non-face-to-face affecting the performance. It does not mean that offering one learning medium is enough because we cannot rule out that students have their preferred medium. If the choice is given to students, they will not be penalized for preferring a learning medium not being supported.

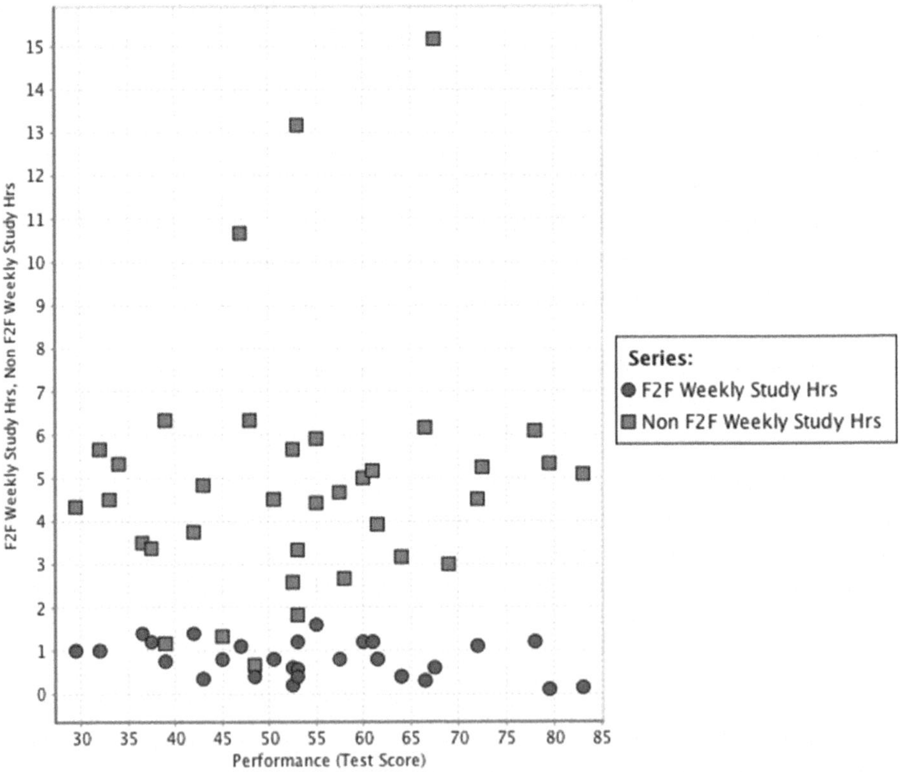

Fig. 2. Effects of face-to-face and non-face-to-face study hours on performance.

5 Discussion

We shall discuss how our findings may be related to the trend of abundant small first-year seminar courses in Canadian universities. We shall also discuss support and advices to learners in line with our findings. Finally, we will conclude with the limitations of our study, future work and a summary of our contributions.

5.1 Educators Should Increase Resources for Freshman Year

It is common to see universities running large classes for freshmen and sophomores. Class sizes of 300 and above are common in publicly funded universities in Canada. It seems to be a convenient cost-cutting decision for students who do not need to specialize early. The unit cost per student-course would be lower due to the economy of scale.

Coming out of high school, freshmen are ready to adopt new study habits. Freshman year is also the best time for students to acquire an inquisitive mind to meet the new demands in universities where they are expected to learn on their own and at a greater depth than in high school.

Instead of allowing the class size to grow in all freshman courses to cut costs, University of Toronto introduced seminar courses specially for first-year students to learn in a small-class setting. With a maximum class size of 24 students, a seminar course provides an excellent environment for students to discuss, interact and learn from each other. Instructors can also give close attention to students. Many other Canadian universities are providing first-year seminar courses to help their students [11]. Studies prove the benefits of first-year seminars across gender, ethnicity and study discipline [12, 13]. Instructors also have great satisfaction teaching first-year seminar courses. Padgett et al. went further to suggest that first-year seminar courses are pervasive in the overall development of a holist student and citizen [14].

The first-year seminar courses getting popular in Canadian universities improve motivation and student engagement. According to our finding, the background knowledge acquired in seminar courses will benefit students in latter courses. Prior study supports the benefits of freshman seminar courses. Our finding further justifies the empirical evidence in previous work.

5.2 Undergraduates Should Work Hard from the Beginning

Not all students attribute to the freshman year the importance it duly deserves. Many students do not work particularly hard in first year. If their first-year grades are low, they think that they can always catch up later. According to our findings, their increased effort in latter years would not take them very far for their weak background. We must advice our undergraduates to work hard right from the beginning. Appropriate first-year seminar courses can also equip them with effective study habits.

5.3 Limitations, Challenges and Future Work

The data we collected may not be accurate given its self-reporting nature. If we measure learners' behaviour from their usage of a learning (software) application or website to access our learning materials, we cannot measure study time spent on printed notes. For students who enjoy reading from printed pages, forcing them to read on an electronic device would affect their enjoyment and likely performance as well.

How do we interpret learner staying on the same page for 3 min using a tablet? She could be multi-tasking on the same or a different device. Measuring learner behaviour on a device has its limitations. We want to wait until we see a better solution before moving on to software-enabled automatic data collection method.

Our discovery of the dominance of background knowledge among variables that affect student performance was based on data collected in a final-year course. A future project can be a longitudinal study to follow students over their four years of undergraduate study. We expect to see the influence of study effort on performance to gradually decrease while the influence of background knowledge increases gradually.

5.4 Conclusion

We always encourage students to work harder with the belief that they will subsequently perform better. Teachers in less competitive institutions often complain about their students not working hard. Our finding suggests that there may be a deeper reason for that behaviour. Students may not perform better by increasing their effort beyond a certain point. We should reconsider how to coach our students and allocate our education resources. Is the trend of first-year seminar courses in Canada a solution for other countries? In our final-year computing course, we found that hard work has very little effect except to place a student in the middle-performing group. How will the picture differ in other year-level and discipline? More study is in order.

Is this phenomenon only applicable to universities? Is the same problem happening in primary school and high school perhaps to a different extent? Primary school education in Hong Kong employs a cookie-cutter approach. Every student is expected to have the same learning style progressing at the same pace. The underlying message of this paper is for policy makers to shift more resources to early stage of education. For universities, it entails a focus on first year students.

In the setting of weekly lecture, we found that students perform better by studying within the first-half of the week after the lecture rather than waiting until the second-half of the week. We also found that once you are a middle-performing student, the next improvement requires you to forgo cram study and increase your regular weekly study time. The ratio of study time of the testing week and of a regular week is 2:1 for top students, 4:1 for middle students and 3:1 for bottom students. Finally, we see no difference in performance in the choice of face-to-face and online learning as long as the choice was given to students.

References

1. Rocha, E.: Choosing More Time for Students: The What, Why, and How of Expanded Learning. Center for American Progress, Washington, DC (2007)
2. Cavanaugh, C.: Student achievement in elementary and high school. In: Handbook of Distance Education, vol. 2, pp. 157–168 (2007)
3. Cavanaugh, C.: Getting Students More Learning Time Online: Distance Education in Support of Expanded Learning Time in K-12 Schools. Center for American Progress, Washington, DC (2009)
4. Devadoss, S., Foltz, J.: Evaluation of factors influencing student class attendance and performance. Am. J. Agr. Econ. **78**(3), 499–507 (1996)
5. Liu, F., Cavanaugh, C.: Factors influencing student academic performance in online high school algebra. Open Learn. J. Open Distance e-Learning **27**(2), 149–167 (2012)
6. Li, L.K.Y.: A study of the attitude, self-efficacy, effort and academic achievement of city U students towards research methods and statistics. Discovery–SS Student E-J. **1**(54), 154–183 (2012)
7. Fried, C.B.: In-class laptop use and its effects on student learning. Comput. Educ. **50**(3), 906–914 (2008)
8. Duncan, D.K., Hoekstra, A.R., Wilcox, B.R.: Digital devices, distraction, and student performance: does in-class cell phone use reduce learning. Astron. Educ. Rev. **11**(1), 1–4 (2012)
9. Au, O., So, R., Lee, L.K.: Attentiveness and self-studying are keys to academic performance. In: International Symposium on Educational Technology (ISET), pp. 61–64. IEEE Press, New York (2016)
10. Finkenbinder, E.O.: The curve of forgetting. Am. J. Psychol. **24**(1), 8–32 (1913)
11. Murray, J., Wolf, P.: Faculty experience teaching in an interdisciplinary first-year seminar program: the case of the University of Guelph. Can. J. Scholarsh. Teach. Learn. **7**(1) (2016). Article 4
12. Starke, M.C., Harth, M., Sirianni, F.: Retention, bonding, and academic achievement: success of a first-year seminar. J. First-Year Exp. Students Transit. **13**(2), 7–36 (2001)
13. Sidle, M.W., McReynolds, J.: The freshman year experience: student retention and student success. NASPA J. **36**(4), 288–300 (1999)
14. Padgett, R.D., Keup, J.R., Pascarella, E.T.: The impact of first-year seminars on college students' life-long learning orientations. J. Student Aff. Res. Pract. **50**(2), 133–151 (2013)

Strategies in Blended Learning

Research on Blended Learning Model Based on Electronic Schoolbag

Min-sheng Fan(✉), Ming Liu, and Yu Wang

Faculty of Education, School of Educational Technology, Beijing Normal University, Beijing, People's Republic of China
{xmanfms,roverlium,Wangyu}@126.com

Abstract. This paper introduced the system structure and function advantage of electronic schoolbag, and carried on the literature investigation and analysis to the application situation of the Chinese electronic bag at present. It found that there were still many problems in the teaching application of the electronic schoolbag. On the basis of these problems, this paper combined the advantages of electronic schoolbag, put forward the application model of the electronic schoolbag under the blended learning environment and its corresponding teaching strategies, analyzed and combined the characteristics and implemented measures of these models. This study further discussed and summarized the characteristics and application trends of blended learning based on electronic schoolbag environment.

Keywords: Electronic schoolbag · Blended learning · Model

1 Introduction

With the rapid development of information and network technology, Modern science and technology with computer network as the core, has brought unprecedented opportunities and challenges to mankind, especially the continuous integration of information technology and education. Its influence overturned the traditional concept of human cognition completely, and simple classroom teaching has been unable to meet the needs of learners. Thus blended learning has become a common trend in the field of high education and k-12 education development [10]. Some scholars have found blended learning is more effective than face-to-face teaching or online learning through the relevant data analysis [1]. Blended learning, combining the advantages of two of them to integrate the learning resources, learning environment and learning styles, provides more targeted tutoring, more flexible learning arrangements and more learning materials so as to achieve better learning effects.

2 Research Background and Research Questions

How to use technology to promote blended learning is a research hotspot now; so electronic schoolbag is a good support to blended learning. In the current state of blended learning environment, the research on the teaching based on the electronic bag is still at

S.K.S. Cheung et al. (Eds.): ICBL 2017, LNCS 10309, pp. 151–165, 2017.
DOI: 10.1007/978-3-319-59360-9_14

the initial stage. Xie [22] conducted a statistical analysis of interactive teaching in the current domestic electronic schoolbag environment by means of questionnaires, and put forward some strategies for the development of interactive teaching of electronic schoolbag. Huang [9], from the perspective of the combination of electronic schoolbag and school classroom, analyzed and summed up how to change the classroom learning model by electronic schoolbag. Gao [5] concluded the specific learning models supported by the electronic schoolbag through practical teaching, and provided explanations to each model. Other scholars put forward a variety of teaching models based on the environment of electronic schoolbag from the teaching practice combined with the characteristics of various disciplines. Designing and adopting a variety of research methods, they verified the effectiveness of the proposed models through data collection, analysis, classroom observation and other means, and they refined and analyzed characteristics of all kinds of teaching models as well as explored the specific application model of electronic schoolbag in different disciplines [12, 15, 27].

However, the current models are not well described on how to support the development of blended learning in mixed learning environment, which didn't highlight the distinction between blended learning classroom supported by electronic schoolbag with general blended learning classroom, ignoring particularity and advantages of the electronic schoolbag and failing to provide a clear direction for better teaching and learning services in a blended learning environment. So this paper first analyzes the system structure and function advantages of the electronic schoolbag. Combining with the current teaching applied model of the electronic schoolbag, the paper also summed up and combed several teaching models based on the electronic schoolbag platform in the blended learning environment through classroom practice, as well as explored the characteristics of these models and their implementation.

3 System Structure and Function Advantages of Electronic Schoolbag

3.1 The System Composition of Electronic Bag

Gauthier [4] believed that Electronic Schoolbag was a digital collaborative learning space, which supported synchronous or asynchronous communication and resource sharing between teachers–students and students- students based on the network environment. Brusilovsk [2] regarded electronic schoolbag as a digital device, in which students could log to manage their own digital resources any time and any place over the wireless network. The paper believes that the electronic schoolbag system is a learning environment that integrates education cloud service and personal terminal application platform to provide learners with teaching support service in the way of "cloud + terminal" [20], shown as Fig. 1.

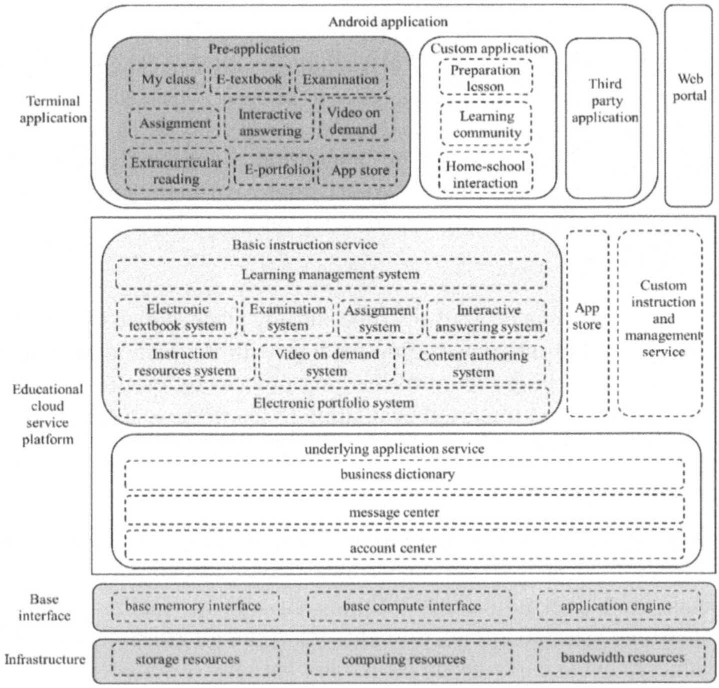

Fig. 1. The system architecture of electronic schoolbag

The electronic schoolbag terminal based on the education cloud can well support the development of blended learning. Individualized and flexible needs will be met by using electronic schoolbag through the introduction of custom applications and third-party applications. These basic applications are based on the cloud service platform core function modules, including electronic teaching materials, resource library, assignment and examination systems, interactive systems and electronic portfolio. These core functional modules will support the most common teaching and learning activities.

3.2 Functional Advantages of the Electronic Schoolbag

The electronic schoolbag is a mobile learning terminal with rich digital education resources, network supports and services, which supports the interaction among the elements of the schools, families and social education systems, and simultaneously meets with the needs of learners' individual learning [19]. Nowadays, the teaching function of the electronic schoolbag is so abundant that it makes a great contribution to create a learning organization which is the new form of online and offline. In addition, the electronic schoolbag provides a strong support to establish a teaching model which is based on digital and individualized subject.

(1) Abundant teaching resources

Electronic schoolbag integrates digital teaching resource packages including various types of teaching materials, teaching reference, reference books, and so on. At the same time, electronic schoolbag can be easily and quickly access to excellent learning resources with the help of network. The integration of various types of resources in teaching can fully mobilize the students' senses, improve the efficiency of the classroom, create a vivid and visualize learning situation for students [25].

(2) Convenient learning ways

Electronic schoolbag can be used any time and any place, which is a future - oriented educational products that integrate digital reading with internet communication function. In addition, the tracking record of learning process by electronic schoolbag can achieve comprehensive and impartial evaluation to learners, so as to encourage, diagnose, and promote learner's learning [8].

(3) A variety of interactive ways

Using the classroom interactive function of the electronic schoolbag can establish the interaction between the teachers and each student; teachers will master the teaching situation better, and then adjust the teaching strategy to realize the high-efficient teaching. Electronic schoolbag also provides a tool for interaction between students, which is conducive to the study group for inquiry learning, discuss experience between groups and share their learning experiences. Strong interaction created a teaching and learning environment which is co-existence of cooperation and individuation, achieve a new breakthrough in teaching and learning.

(4) Individualized learning

The emergence of electronic schoolbag, build a student-centered learning progress, which is learning-process-oriented, it supports different learning styles and realize the learning environment of different learning path [28]. Students can choose learning content, set the learning rate and formulate learning plan according to the learning progress or personal habits. Teachers can real-time grasp student's learning process and effectiveness, thus develop a hierarchical learning plan to give students individualized guidance through the electronic schoolbag. At the same time, the electronic schoolbag can timely push related learning resources according to students' learning habits and ways to support individualized autonomous learning of students.

4 A Blended Teaching Model Based on Electronic Schoolbag

Blended learning is a learning approach that uses different delivery methods to reduce costs and optimize outcomes. The blended learning is defined by some scholars as: at the right time, for the right object, the right delivery media, through right learning methods to provide right learning content, with minimal investment to obtain higher learning gains [16]. That is 5R definition. Under the environment of electronic schoolbag, learning resources become richer and learning forms are diversified [14].

The new learning environment can cultivate learners' knowledge construction, critical thinking, collaboration, and communication ability. In blended learning environment, with the aid of electronic schoolbag platform, teachers and students are liberated from a single relationship of "impartment to acceptance", which forms a diversified role relationship, thus contributing to the common development of teachers and students. In secondary school, the advanced digital learning environment based electronic schoolbag provides a new learning experience and major changes for middle school students for in the period that students are thirst for knowledge with strongest curiosity and the most active thinking. In the process of electronic schoolbag employed in schools, the author works closely with the front-line teachers to summarize their application experience and outstanding cases in the teaching and learning process, and to construct the feasible and controllable electronic bag application patterns in the blended learning environment for the goal to improve teachers and students' interaction in blended learning classroom, training students' ability in three dimensions: learning ability, innovation ability and information ability. Three kinds of innovative teaching models are constructed based on electronic schoolbag, which are theme-inquiry teaching model, flipped class teaching model and interaction teaching model.

4.1 Theme-Inquiry Teaching Model

The theme-inquiry teaching model is the model that students conduct self-exploration for the core learning topics under the guidance of teachers with rich digital education resources in the electronic schoolbag digital teaching environment [26]. The teaching model integrates teaching content with knowledge unit and the student's life facts, building knowledge topics. Students can explore and collaborate independently through the platform of electronic schoolbag, which can give full play to the students' creativity and cooperation in this process [21]. The students' learning ability and information ability are developed.

(1) The teaching process

A complete theme inquiry activity cannot be fully completed in limited class time. Therefore, the class is divided into three periods: pre-class, class and post class with electronic schoolbag platform, as shown in Fig. 2.

Pre-class: Teacher designs themes and releases tasks with the aid of electronic schoolbag platform. After receiving the tasks, students need to analyze them, clarify the problems of inquiry, and then use the electronic schoolbag to collect the relevant data. The teammates gather the whole data to facilitate the completion of the class activity. This process needs the teacher to provide the online instruction for responding promptly when students encounter problems.

Class: This stage is the core of the theme inquiry, in which teacher is just tutor and students are the main learning body, for teacher and students carry out interaction inquiry around the themes of the task. The key following steps are:

(1) Activities completion. Students analyze the themes in small groups as unit, set research plans intra-group division of labor, using the pre-class collection of

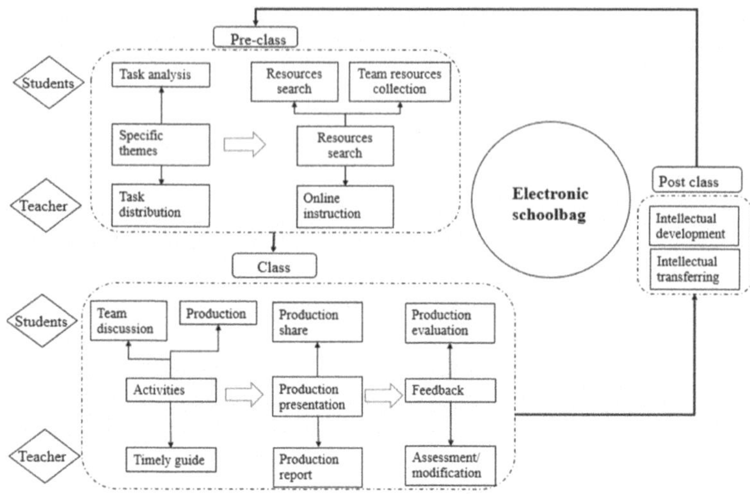

Fig. 2. The theme-inquiry teaching model based on electronic schoolbag

learning materials for group discussion, and form the final inquiry achievements according to the results of the discussion. In the whole process of complete activity, the teacher needs to guide students specifically, organize all students to participate in the activities, and ensure the inquiry activity carries on smoothly.

(2) Production presentation. While the task is completed, the group as a unit will form learning outcomes, exchange and display learning outcomes with the aid of electronic schoolbag platform, teachers should give students opportunities to show their results, it will contribute to cultivate the share awareness and expression of students.
(3) Evaluation and feedback. Evaluation is one of the most important links in teaching. After the students show the results of the research, teachers should evaluate the results and give appropriate suggestions for improvement. At the same time, teachers should organize students to evaluate the works of other groups.

Post class: Expanding the pre-class and class knowledge, as well as do the knowledge transferring applications in classroom inquiry learning process while encounter new problems and new tasks.

(2) Characteristics analysis

The theme inquiry teaching model has certain requirements for the knowledge points and learning objectives, and not all knowledge points can use the theme inquiry teaching model. It is oriented by learning tasks, solve the problem as the starting point to carry out teaching. The entire teaching process is led by teachers and students are the main body. The whole teaching process requires students to carry out self-exploration and cooperative inquiry to cultivate students' inquiry ability, cooperation ability, expression ability and problem solving ability.

The emergence of electronic schoolbag breaks the time constraints of traditional classroom. Teachers can extend the duration of activities before, during and after class, allowing students to have sufficient time to explore and solve problems. The three stages of theme inquiry that before class, in class and after class need the active participation of students require students to have strong subjectivity.

Inquiry learning is conducive to the development of students 'advanced cognition. The whole process of inquiry can cultivate students' ability of problem solving, group collaboration, evaluation and so on.

Theme inquiry teaching model needs students participate during the whole process, contribute to students' learning, meanwhile, put forward higher requirements to teachers, the successful implementation of inquiry model requires teachers to design a suitable task of exploration, and guide through the process.

4.2 The Flipped Class Teaching Model

Flipped class originated from the United States, with the rapid development of Khan Academy, the educational "flipped revolution" detonated [7]. In China, Chongqing JuKui middle school has been using the model that electronic schoolbag combined with flipped class for a long span, which reforms high school new curriculum, and summarized a set of flipped class teaching model that have their own characteristics, the model based on the "four steps before class" and "five links in class" of electronic schoolbag environment, On the basis of detailed analysis of "JuKui model", combining with the team's experience of using electronic schoolbag to flipped the class teaching in Qingdao second middle school, Guiyang no.6 middle school and other schools, the author summarized the flipped class teaching model based on electronic schoolbag, that is "directive study task-driven students autonomous learning" before class"; hierarchical problem-driven students cooperation research" in class; "evaluation and sharing of knowledge-driven internalization" after class. At the same time, under the support of e-book environment, teachers can use the analysis of learning data to achieve on-demand teaching, students can use learning data analysis to achieve on-demand learning.

(1) Teaching process

Teachers use electronic schoolbag individualized services platform to quickly release pre-class learning tasks and materials, students can learn new knowledge through electronic schoolbag before class, and then solve problems in the classroom through the exchange of discussion and use of new knowledge with teachers and students, communicate and rethink after class to enhancing themselves, as shown in Fig. 3.

Pre-class: Teachers prepare for teaching on electronic schoolbag platform, on the platform of electronic schoolbag ready for teaching making digital direct learning case which mainly includes learning task requirements, micro videos, online tests, etc. And the digital direct learning case provides channel of communication between student-student and teacher-teacher. Students watch videos to complete learning tasks by using electronic schoolbag through digital direct learning case under the guidance of teachers, prepare and detect through electronic schoolbag, electronic schoolbag learning platform can judge and give feedback for the question-answered situation immediately.

Class: teachers can create electronic lessons electronic schoolbag, multimedia electronic lessons integrate learning links and learning resources, which will help improve

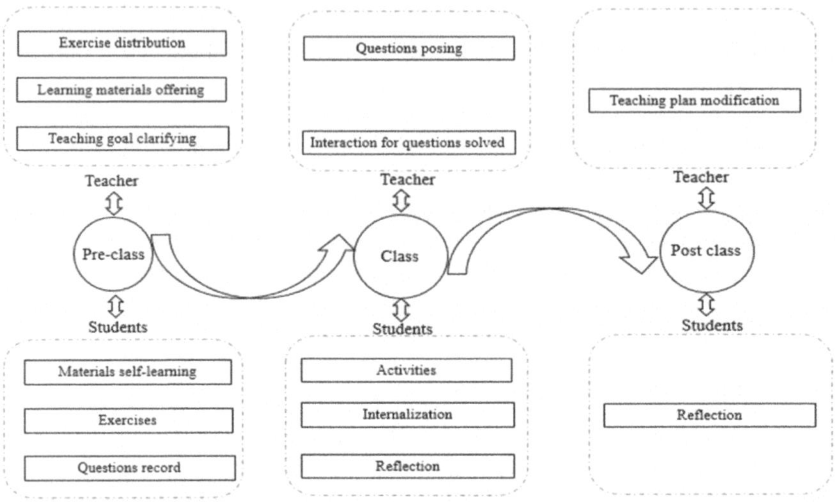

Fig. 3. Flipped class teaching model based on electronic schoolbag

the efficiency of teachers and students in the classroom, students can complete the tasks made by teachers in the classroom under the guidance of teachers independently or in groups. Teachers can give students the necessary guidance.

Post class: Students can view the answers in electronic schoolbag platform or watch the videos of teachers to analyze the exercises to correct the errors and consolidate the knowledge, communicate and discuss with the teachers and other students in the aid of Q & A platform of electronic schoolbag interactive environment, consolidate and internalize the knowledge and skills.

(2) Characteristics Analysis

"Flipped class teaching model" takes the students as the center, and electronic schoolbag provide students with a platform for viewing instructional videos, enabling students to connect with tools and resources and gain more learning support [17].

Students break the limited time constriction of classroom so that students can study fully before learning in the class, and the classroom will become the place that "interactive and communicate, cooperation and learn together" between teacher-student and student-student. At the same time, the use of electronic schoolbag makes students understand the knowledge more profound and thorough. The introduction of technology extends the students' brains, changing the way students think [24].

The flipped class teaching model under the electronic bag environment breaks through the limitations of the original classroom teaching in terms of time, space, content, manner, etc. The model creates a learner-centered atmosphere, allowing students to have more opportunities for autonomous learning and inquiry. Teachers will record the teaching content into video before class and provide it to students, save teaching time in the classroom; the feedback that uses learning platform for excise is timelier, increases the chances of interaction between teacher-student and student–student, it can meet individualized learning needs of different levels students. From the point of practice, the model is applicable to all subjects in middle school. For the flipped class of electronic schoolbag environment, the majority of students and teachers have given affirmation, for learning interest, and it has good promotion effect for the degree indexes of interest in learning and task completion.

The blended teaching model that combine online learning with classroom needs teachers and students to do a lot of teaching and learning jobs before the class, which will bring some pressure for teachers and students. In the process of teaching, teachers and students should use the electronic schoolbag platform skillfully to complete the relevant tasks, and adapt themselves to the new identity of "leading-subject [7] " in the flipped class model, these all not only have put forward higher requirements on teachers' organization ability and guidance ability, but also on students' learning ability, information ability, and so on.

4.3 Interaction Teaching Model

Interaction is the core of classroom teaching. Interactive teaching model is a classroom teaching activity based on the implementation of electronic schoolbag in the blended learning environment. Teachers and students make full use of the strong interaction of electronic schoolbag in the classroom, such as carrying out a variety of interactive communication and building up a two classroom model which combines "virtual classroom" based on the electronic schoolbag and cloud platform with "real classroom" that teachers and students face to face [11].

In this model, the "virtual classroom" constructed by electronic schoolbag fully utilizes the advantages of technology and resources to improve the efficiency of teaching and learning in "real classroom", and realizes students' "real classroom" through real-time sharing and timely evaluation. "In the level of participation and concentration, it promotes the degree of student's participation and attention in "real class" through the real-time sharing and timely evaluation functions.

(1) The teaching process

Constructing a strong interactive teaching environment helps teachers and students to carry out efficient face to face interaction and human-computer interaction. Constructing knowledge through different forms of interaction promotes meaningful learning. Interactive teaching model under the electronic schoolbag environment realizes the good interaction between four dimensions of human, technology, environment and resources, to develop the teaching effect [3], as shown in Fig. 4.

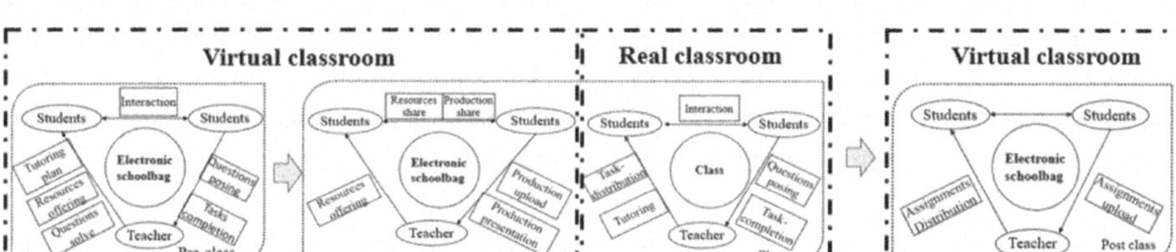

Fig. 4. Interactive teaching model based on electronic schoolbag

Pre-class: Teachers use electronic schoolbag library resources to extract or design and product multimedia teaching resources, extract classroom interactive exercises from the question bank, and develop pre-study case, guide students to self-preview.

Class: Teachers and students develop a multi-directional interaction by using "interactive classroom system" of electronic schoolbag, in the "virtual classroom" created by electronic schoolbag, teachers set a series of learning tasks, students use a variety of tools in electronic schoolbag to complete the task, after that, the results of everyone's feedback presented instantaneously through the electronic schoolbag or whiteboard, active the degree of participation in the "real classroom". When teachers are in teaching, multimedia resources stored in the cloud of electronic schoolbag, can be easily and timely push to the class for each student.

Teacher-student and student-student discuss the problem, the process and the result can be uploaded to electronic schoolbag cloud platform by using electronic drawing board, teachers display it through the electronic whiteboard one by one, select and enlarge the typical answer on the whiteboard for students to resolve or teachers to explain.

Post class: Instructors deliver digital assignments on the platform of electronic schoolbag, and after students submit homework on electronic schoolbag system, the objective questions will be timely feedback, wrong titles are included in the wrong title notebook to convenient students review the error-prone knowledge points and solve it. Teachers are responsible for correcting subjective questions, and give feedback to make the answers of students for helping students to fill gaps. Teachers can also grasp students' learning situation according to the feedback of the student's answers, and then make targeted collective or individual counseling. At the same time, electronic schoolbag can save generated resources of the entire learning process for helping students and teachers to review the learning content and learning reflection.

(2) Characteristics analysis

When the interactive instructional model supported by electronic schoolbag is implemented, teachers and students, instructional media, learning contents and classroom interaction are interrelated. Teachers are the leaders of the classroom, and the electronic schoolbag is the key tool to ensure the smooth flow of the "information flow" in the classroom teaching process. Teachers prepare electronic learning plan, and micro courses pre-class, and students use e-learning case and other resources to learn and display learning outcomes [6]. Compared with the traditional classroom, the "virtual classroom" constructed by electronic schoolbag environment integrates learning resources, teaching contents and teaching activities well, and solves the problem of "pass" between the learning content and knowledge points by combining the "reality classroom" whiteboard and PAD. On the basis of "pass", teachers, students and other elements in the classroom can effectively interact, and the classroom "move" up, making the atmosphere active, easy to teach and students can learn happily.

5 Characteristics and Application Trends of Blended Learning

5.1 The General Features

(1) Constructive learning

Blended learning is formally a mix of online learning (On-line) and off-line learning. But at a deeper level, it includes a mix of teaching models based on different teaching theories, such as constructivism, behaviorism and cognitive. Blended learning emphasizes that learning is a process of meaning construction, and a process of forming, enriching and adjusting one's own cognitive structure through the interaction of old and new experiences [13]. The leading role of teachers is emphasized in teaching process, thus effectively ensuring the imparting and mastering of scientific knowledge in the learning process.

This paper summarized several teaching application models based on electronic schoolbag, all broke the traditional cramming teaching model, and use a variety of interactive media technology to provide a specific learning environment for the learners, in which teachers fully play the role of teaching instructor, help and encourage learners to actively explore and construct knowledge by themselves. They focus on putting learning into the society and the situation, and focus on solving the problem in the situation of specific areas, pay attention to the students' learning initiative, the learner actively selects information and constructs the meaning of information.

(2) Self- inquiry

Learning in a blended learning environment can be combined with classroom learning and online self-learning without any restrictions or time on location by using electronic schoolbag, it can extend the time and space of learning, and cultivate students' good habits of self-learning. At the same time, the several application models above fully embody "learner-centered" concept, needing students to inquiry - based learning autonomously before class, cooperative, explore and self-learning in the classroom. Compared with the classroom of traditional model, the use of electronic schoolbag can easily collect data and create the situations, then analyzes the collected data. The above several class models based on electronic schoolbag give autonomy to students, emphasis self-exploration better.

(3) Union of on-line and off-line and pre- class and post class

Blended learning based on electronic schoolbag pays more attention to combining online and offline. Teachers and students can interact online through electronic schoolbag, so that teachers understand the situation of students' mastery at the first time, as the formation of online interaction with students. At the same time, the electronic schoolbag makes classroom more lively and interesting, makes more offline interaction between teachers and students, stimulate students' learning enthusiasm, arouse the enthusiasm of students, and enhance students' attention and participation in class.

At the same time, the "knowledge transfer" stage was put pre-class through the electronic schoolbag, students through the electronic schoolbag online courses and video materials to complete the initial acceptance and construction of knowledge, teachers check the "actual self-learning situation" of students through pre-class learning and testing, grasp the students' "existing developing level" [23]. The electronic schoolbag provides students with the function of repeatedly watching and discussing at any time, so as to realize the full learning of knowledge before class. At the same time, the classroom focuses on "knowledge internalization", students can solve the deep questions by the way of collaborative innovation with the help of teachers in class. The class and after class flipped improves the students' learning ability, analysis and problem-solving ability, cultivate students' ability of collaborative innovation, stimulate students' interest in learning.

(4) Guidance under teachers

Blended learning based on electronic schoolbag let the teachers transferred from the imparter and the indoctrinator to the helper and promoter of knowledge. So that students from passive acceptor, passive indoctrinator into active learners, active knowledge constructors. Whether in the pre class, in class or after class, in the process of students from traditional acceptance learning to inquiry learning, the teacher's important responsibility is changed to pay more attention to the students' aid and guidance, which teachers can better help students to achieve their learning goals, help students find the path for personalized learning, inspire students' enthusiasm for learning, set learning situations for students, guide students to learn, love learning, and interact with students, answer the problems of students encounter at any time in the process of students' learning by using electronic schoolbag environment.

5.2 The Developing Trends of the Application Model

(1) Electronic schoolbag will achieve deep integration of information technology and teaching

The development and popularization of digital and information technology have already affected education and teaching activities in a great extent and level, the trace of digital and information technology almost everywhere in education field [18]. The National Policy Document has defined the status and influence of information technology in the future education. The Outline of National Medium and Long-term Educational Revolution and Development Plan (2010–2020) states that "information technology has a revolutionary impact on the development of education, we must attach great importance to it", so in the next period, information technology will become an important part of the education development strategy, and electronic schoolbag plays a key role in integration of information technology and education teaching.

Electronic schoolbag is the product of the information technology environment, and now the relationship between electronic schoolbag and education is similar with nature to the ancient abacus and education, similar to the previous computer and education. The role of electronic schoolbag is not to complete the existing model and method of knowledge indoctrination, but to promote the education reform in the technological era. In the future, with the popularity of cheap, portable electronic schoolbag technology, information technology will have an all-round impact on education, not only the supporting role, but also the leading and transforming function.

(2) Electronic schoolbag will break the classroom space-time limitation

Electronic schoolbag will break through the boundaries of time and space of instructional materials, and transformed the original paper textbook and simple picture into a more lively audio, video, 3D animation and so on, this transformation can make students understand the learning difficulties more intuitively and magically; Electronic schoolbag can extend the theme from the instructional material to extra-curricular, so that students' knowledge is not limited to the classroom, which will help students master more extra-curricular knowledge. The use of electronic schoolbag can make some learning methods across time and region, such as the use of electronic schoolbag to carry out inquiry learning, this form of inquiry learning does not confine to the classroom, but from class to extra-curricular, internal school to the external school. Students in the process of autonomous learning and inquiry learning are often required to interact with other students, and the application of electronic schoolbag facilitate students' communication, and achieve the communication process for resource sharing, making the inquiry activities more smoothly, this open-ended, location-based inquiry learning method will be more and more applied to teaching.

(3) Electronic Schoolbag will change the existing teaching model, promote teaching and learning revolution

The basic form of blended learning is the combination of online learning and classroom teaching, which is the combination of teacher-led and student-centered. The emergence of electronic schoolbag fully integrates the advantages of online learning and classroom teaching. At the same time, promote the revolution of traditional teaching model through "blending". The new teaching model no longer confined to the tradition, it makes the role of teachers and students have major shift, which makes students from passive acceptance into the main and teachers from the classroom core into a classroom leader, in such a model of education, teachers prepare the resources and activities carefully, and students use mobile devices such as tablets to complete tasks assigned by the teacher, so that students can better understand the knowledge, and enhancing their ability to think and solve problems.

Provided information is not the core value of electronic schoolbag enter into the classroom, promote the development of students' thinking ability is the core pursuit. The most important role of the electronic schoolbag into the classroom is to transform the model of teaching, not only to expand the breadth of class and classroom participation, so that each student can participate, but also to expand the depth of the classroom. Through the use of electronic schoolbag, you can put the space of learning and thinking back to the students, making students to achieve a deep understanding for the knowledge while let capacity and thinking ability to develop. The traditional model of teaching and learning is brewing a major breakthrough, education is facing the most profound changes ever, and electronic schoolbag will play a vital role in such a change.

6 Conclusion

Through the application of electronic schoolbag in the project school, we can see that the electronic schoolbag embodies its advantages and functions in the process of blended teaching, and the learners construct knowledge continuously by focusing on theme teaching from the blend of the media such as electronic schoolbag and whiteboard, it also needs a variety of teaching organizations that media support to make learning more efficient. At the same time, we notice that electronic schoolbag has the content need to be completed. The author believes that with the popularity and penetration of information technology, electronic schoolbag and other products under the environment of information technology will gradually change the ecological environment of the education.

The application of electronic schoolbag is not to complete the existing model and method of knowledge indoctrination, not only develop the efficient of the existing model, its core value lies in the transcendence and change of existing teaching model, lies in creating new models and methods. In the future education, we can try to use the electronic bag to solve the problem of restricting the development of education, from this point of view, the electronic bag has very good application prospect, and it will play its unique and important role in advancing the educational revolution.

References

1. Allen, I.E., Seaman, J., Garrett, R.: Blending in: The Extent and Promise of Blended Education in the United States. Sloan Consortium (2007)
2. Brusilovsky, P., Cooper, D.W.: Domain, task and user models for an adaptive hypermedia performance support system. In: Proceedings of the 2002 International Conference on Intelligent User Interfaces, pp. 45–52. ACM Press, New York (2002)
3. Chen, W.-D., Ye, X.-D., Zhang, J.-P.: A research on the interactive forms and characteristics of future classroom. E-education Res. **8**, 91–97 (2011)
4. Gauthier, G., Frasson, C., van Lehn, K.: Adaptive Hypermedia: From Intelligent Tutoring Systems to Web-Based Education. http://link.springer.com/chapter/10.1007/3-540-451080_1#page-1. Accessed 4 Jun 2012
5. Gao, Z.-L.: Current situation and counter-measures of e-Book package promotion. Inf. Publ. **24**, 08–09 (2010)
6. Hao, Q.-L., Li, J.-N.: A study on the classroom teaching culture of "double platform" problem-guided learning model. Contemp. Educ. Cult. **5**, 49–54 (2016)
7. He, K.-K.: The future development of "flipped classroom" in china from the perspective of "flipped classroom". E-education Res. **7**, 5–16 (2014)
8. Hu, X.-Y., Zhu, L.: Research on the application model of electronic schoolbag in the view of digital. China Educ. Technol. **5**, 66–72 (2013)
9. Huang, M.-Y.: An application model of blending electronic school-bag with classroom learning. Mod. Educ. Technol. **23**, 28–31 (2012)
10. Johnson, L., Adams Becker, S., Estrada, V., et al.: NMC Horizon Report: 2015 Higher Education. The New Media Consortium, Austin (2015)
11. Ma, H.-C., Mie, Y., Xu, Q.-Q.: Research on "double classroom" teaching model based on electronic schoolbag in cloud environment. Chin. J. ICT Educ. **7**, 21–25 (2014)

12. Niu, X.: The application research of electronic schoolbag based flipped classroom in middle school English teaching. J. Nanchang Coll. Educ. **1**, 120–122 (2016)
13. Pan, H.-J.: Teaching "three dimensional knowledge" and achieving "three dimensional goals". Contemp. Educ. Cult. **7**, 30–36 (2016)
14. Peng, P.: The exploration of 6E teaching model in primary school English under the normal application environment of e-schoolbag. Chin. J. ICT Educ. **16**, 04–07 (2015)
15. Ren, Z.-D.: The application of e-schoolbag in history inquiry teaching in middle school. Educ. Inf. Technol. **5**, 75–77 (2015)
16. Singh, H., Reed, C.A.: Whitepaper: Achieving success with blended learning. http://www.docin.com/p-204705652.html
17. Shen, S.-S., Liu, Q., Xie, T.-X.: A flipped classroom teaching model based on electronic schoolbag. China Educ. Technol. **12**, 107–111 (2013)
18. Wang, J.-H., Li, S.: The hot and frontier research areas in digital instruction in china: a literature review of the visualized mapping of knowledge domains based on CSSCI (1998–2013). Contemp. Educ. Cult. **3**, 49–54 (2016)
19. Wu, F.-T., Mou, Z.-J.: The model construction and implementation path of students' personality analyzing based on big data. China Educ. Technol. **3**, 63–69 (2014)
20. Wu, F., Mou, Z.: The design and development of electronic schoolbag system based on educational cloud service platform. In: Chen, G., Kumar, V., Kinshuk, Huang, R., Kong, S. (eds.) Emerging Issues in Smart Learning. LNET, pp. 313–319. Springer, Heidelberg (2015). doi:10.1007/978-3-662-44188-6_43
21. Xiang, H.: The Integration of Information Technology and Middle School Physics Teaching. Beijing Normal University Press, Beijing (2013)
22. Xie, L.: The Research of Interactive Teaching Based an E-Bag. Unpublished Master thesis. Shanghai Normal University, Shanghai (2012)
23. Yin, D.: Rethinking "flipped classroom". Contemp. Educ. Cult. **2**, 64–67 (2014)
24. Yu, S.-Q.: Technology innovation education. China Educ. Technol. **7**, 01–06 (2011)
25. Yu, S.-Q., Li, X.-Q.: What is the core value of electronic schoolbag for education. People's Educ. **4**, 26–29 (2014)
26. Zhai, X.-M., Xiang, H., Mu, M.: S-WebQuest based on theme inquiry model. China Educ. Technol. **5**, 130–134 (2015)
27. Zheng, J., He, P.: Analysis of english teaching model and behavior in primary school under the environment of E-Book Package. China Educ. Technol. **12**, 112–117 (2013)
28. Zhong, Q.-Q.: The design of learning environments: framework and projects. Educ. Res. **24**, 08–09 (2015)

Learning Analytics for Monitoring Students Participation Online: Visualizing Navigational Patterns on Learning Management System

Leonard K.M. Poon(✉), Siu-Cheung Kong, Thomas S.H. Yau, Michael Wong, and Man Ho Ling

Department of Mathematics and Information Technology,
The Education University of Hong Kong, Tai Po, Hong Kong SAR, China
{kmpoon,sckong,shyau,mywwong}@eduhk.hk, alphaisfishing@gmail.com

Abstract. With the increasing use of blended learning approaches in classroom, various kinds of technologies are incorporated to provide digital teaching and learning resources to support students. These resources are often centralized in learning management systems (LMSs), which also store valuable learning data of students. The data could assist teachers in their pedagogical decision making but they are often not well utilized. This paper proposes the use of data mining and visualization techniques as learning analytics to provide a more comprehensive overview of students' learning online based on log data from LMSs . The focus of this study is the discovery of frequent navigational patterns by sequential pattern mining techniques and the demonstration of how presentation of patterns through hierarchical clustering and sunburst visualization could facilitate the interpretation of patterns. The data in this paper were collected from a blended statistics course for undergraduate students.

Keywords: Learning analytics · Blended learning · Sequential pattern mining · Hierarchical clustering · Navigational pattern · LMS · Moodle

1 Introduction

In Hong Kong, the integration of digital technologies to teaching and learning in a wide range of subjects is growing rapidly. Most higher education institutions in Hong Kong adopt Learning Management Systems (LMSs) as the digital learning environment to support the development of novel e-Learning practices such as blended learning. Despite successful cases showing the new pedagogical approaches are effective in enhancing students learning (e.g. [9]), not many previous studies have fully exploited the learning data of students from digital environment such as LMSs, which reflect the limited usage of these data to inform teaching and learning.

Reimann et al. [18] recently summarized three reasons contributing to the limited usage of learning data. First, large-scale assessment data available to teachers and students are not linked to the learning processes and outcomes of students. Another reason is that even the data reporting students learning in the system are available, the focus of the data is often on activity tracking rather than knowledge tracking, which

S.K.S. Cheung et al. (Eds.): ICBL 2017, LNCS 10309, pp. 166–176, 2017.
DOI: 10.1007/978-3-319-59360-9_15

provide limited insights for teachers to identify learning problems of student. Lastly, teachers are reported that neither do they feel themselves sufficiently qualified nor do they possess enough time to make good use of the learning data for teaching. These points corresponded to some major problems mentioned by Gómez-Aguilar et al. [4] regarding the information provided by learning platforms (e.g. LMSs), which is only available in text files format or with some basic charts in general. They are not effective and interactive for users to understand the actual usage situation in the system. Also, the massive amount of learning data without effective processing could lead to information overload to users, which drives them away to make use of these valuable data. Furthermore, advanced and pedagogically useful information such as those highlighting various patterns of usage on the system is often not available. In sum, the high complexity of available data and the lack of means to translate these data into comprehensible output on current learning platforms are also part of the reasons contributing to the limited usage reported by Reimann et al. [18].

In view of this, researchers have proposed using learning analytics based on educational data to strengthen teaching and learning in a digital environment. Learning analytics refer to the collection, organization, analysis and reporting of a wide range of data produced by students in the learning context in order to generate information and identify potential issues for prediction and pedagogical decision-making [2]. There is a close relationship between learning analytics and data mining as different data mining methods are also applied in learning analytics. For instance, *sequential pattern mining* (SPM) is one of the most popular methods which study the temporal association between variables, and one of its applications in education is the discovery of common action sequences conducted by users in the online learning environment such as LMSs. The use of data mining methods in learning analytics could better inform teachers about the overall learning processes of students online for them to determine if any interventions are needed, especially in the context of blended learning where a significant portion of time is allocated for students to study online.

This paper attempts to show the use of online learning data to better inform teaching and learning in a blended learning context. Essentially, we will demonstrate the way to effectively discover the frequent navigational patterns through SPM and present the results with hierarchical clustering and sunburst visualization, to show that how learning data could be better used for learning analytics, which still sees a lack of literature support. Results will be illustrated based on the data from a blended statistics course.

2 Previous Work

In common blended learning strategies, the provision of effective learning materials is an indispensable component for successful learning of students. The delivery of these materials is mostly by LMSs in current higher education institutions where students could perform different learning tasks or activities online during their time outside classroom. However, the behaviors of students online and their interactions with the learning materials, peers or teachers could also contribute to our understanding of the learning processes involved. This is the area where learning analytics could best help in revealing different sorts of relations in the online learning environment.

To study the navigational behavior of learners or access patterns of the resources online, analysis could be done by statistical methods (e.g. [5, 10]). However, more often data mining methods are adopted due to its ability to handle large amount of learning data, such as the log files from LMSs. *Sequential pattern mining* (SPM), which is a process of discovering and showing the hidden interrelationships, clusters and data patterns within data for supporting better decision making [23], would be a suitable approach for the investigation of access patterns. Although it is not initially designed for educational purposes, different researches have applied it for pattern discovery in learning data with some valuable insights offered (e.g. [7, 8, 17]). In a recent work by Ziebarth et al. [24], their analysis of the resource usage pattern of students during the exam preparation period in a blended learning course with SPM has discovered the association between the patterns and grades of students in the course. Some other studies have also used both the clustering method and sequential pattern mining on learning data to analyze the behaviors and performance of students online. For instance, Perera et al. [16] integrated these two methods in studying online collaborative activities to distinguish student groups in terms of performance based on the activity patterns of students.

On the other hand, the application of data mining in education has been criticized for the difficulty in the interpretation of results for users due to the complexity. Therefore, developing an effective mean to deliver the results is also vital. Visualization techniques were commonly adopted in the delivery of data mining results to highlight the overall trends and patterns [20]. Zhou et al. [23] further suggested that the implementation of intuitive graphic charts, tables or diagrams could facilitate users' understanding of the pattern based results generated from data mining algorithms, while a possible incorporation of interactive elements for user to explore the results is also desirable [21]. The visual representation of analytics results is sometimes referred as visual analytics, which uses interactive visual interfaces for systematic and analytical reasoning [4].

3 Sequential Pattern Mining

In this section, we review some technical details and introduce algorithms for SPM.

Consider a set of items such as resources on an LMS. A *sequence* is an ordered list of items. It may indicate the order of which resources are accessed by a student. An item can occur multiple times in a sequence. The number of items in a sequence is known as its *length*. A sequence $\alpha = \langle a_1\, a_2\, \ldots\, a_n \rangle$ is called a *subsequence* of another sequence $\beta = \langle b_1\, b_2\, \ldots\, b_m \rangle$, or α is *contained* in β, if there exists integers $1 \le j_1 \le j_2 \le \cdots \le j_n \le m$ such that $a_1 = b_{j_1}, a_2 = b_{j_2}, \ldots, a_n = b_{j_n}$. In other words, the subsequence α can be formed by removing some items from β with the order of the remaining items preserved. For example, the sequence $\langle a, c, d \rangle$ is a subsequence of the sequence $\langle a, b, c, d, e \rangle$, where a, b, c, d, and e are items. Due to brevity, we do not consider the general case where an element of a sequence can be a set of items.

Let S be a set of sequences. We refer to the number or proportion of sequences in S that contain a sequence α as the *support* of α in S. We denote the support as $support_s(\alpha)$ and omit the subscript when it is clear from context.

Sequential pattern mining (SPM) aims to discover frequent subsequences among a set of sequences. The frequent subsequences are also called *sequential patterns*. Specifically, given a set of sequences S and a real number $\xi \in [0, 1]$ as threshold, the problem of SPM is to find all the sequences α such that $support_s(\alpha) \geq \xi$. The threshold ξ is also known as the *minimum support*.

Many algorithms have been developed to mine sequential patterns efficiently. Some of the earliest attempts, e.g. [1], are based on the well-known Apriori algorithm for association rule mining. However, Apriori-like algorithms needs to consider an exponential number of candidate sequences in the worst case and they require repeated scanning of the data set to check the support of candidate sequences [12]. Those problems make Apriori-like algorithms infeasible for large data sets or when the sequential patterns are expected to be long.

PrefixSpan [14], on the other hand, avoids those problems by taking another approach. Its main idea is to project the database of sequences into a set of smaller databases based on a set of frequent subsequences. The frequent subsequences are then grown and checked in the smaller projected databases separately. The projection step and the growth step are done recursively until no more longer frequent sequences are found. PrefixSpan has been shown empirically to be considerably faster than another Apriori-like algorithm.

SPM may result in a large number of sequential patterns. This may lead to a long processing time and make the mining results hard to understand. Therefore, constraints have been imposed to limit the mining results to those more interesting to users [15]. One constraint used in our work is the gap constraint. It requires the time difference between two items in sequential patterns to be shorter or longer than a given gap. To support the gap constraint, along with other constraints, Hirate and Yamana [6] proposed an algorithm based on PrefixSpan. Their algorithm was further extended by Fournier-Viger et al. [3] to give only closed sequential patterns, meaning that those patterns contained by another patterns with at least the same support are not included in the output.

In the current study, we used a SPM algorithm adapted from that by Fournier-Viger et al. [3]. The adaptions were described in [13]. The adapted algorithm allows gap constraint to be specified and produces only closed sequential patterns.

4 Preliminary Study

In this section, the proposed methods are demonstrated through a blended statistics course in a university. The study context is first described followed by the overall trend in the course. Next, the discovered patterns from SPM are discussed and more detailed explanations with regard to the hierarchical and sunburst visualization of patterns are provided in the last two parts.

4.1 Study Context

The blended statistics course used Moodle as the LMS and the available digital resources on it were statistical simulations, online videos and online quizzes. These resources focused on four fundamental topics in statistics, which were sampling distribution, the central limit theorem, confidence interval and hypothesis testing. Two groups of undergraduate students enrolled in this course, with one group of 70 students who major in Mathematics (major group) and another group of 41 students who minor in Mathematics (minor group). The course length was 8-week long for the major group and 14-week long for the minor group. The major and minor groups had a double and single 3-hour lecture per week respectively, with an examination scheduled at the last week of the course. Students were encouraged to access the resources before and after the lessons for self-learning and knowledge consolidation. Although the course also covered other topics in statistics in addition to the focused topics by the digital resources, students were free to visit the platform in any period during the course. Some additional learning activities were given by teachers on the platform with additional bonus points as incentive. The interface of the platform and the digital resources could be seen in Fig. 1.

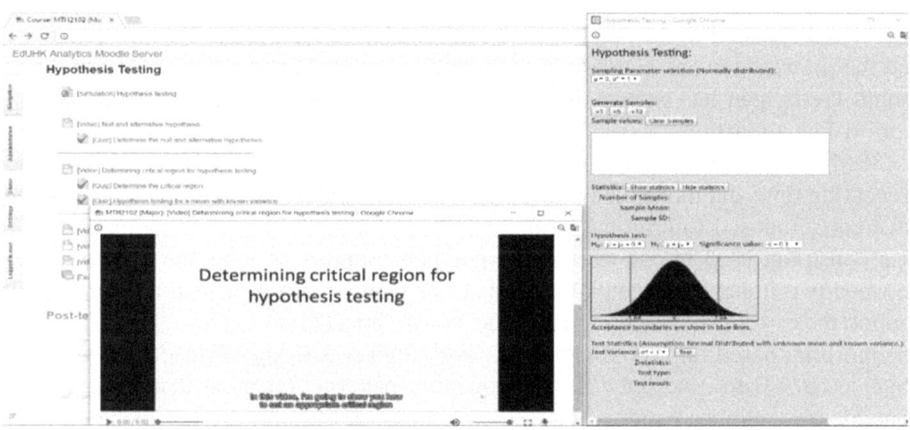

Fig. 1. Screenshot of the learning platform and the associated resources. The platform provides three types of digital resources, which are statistical simulations, online videos and online quizzes, for students to learn.

4.2 Overall Trend

The general usage situation on the platform could be illustrated by the average number of access across different time periods. Figure 2 provides an example of the overall trend based on the major and minor group. The class for major group started 3 weeks earlier than the minor group. The overall trend indicates that students from the major group were more engaged than the minor group in using the resources available on the platform outside lecture time to support their learning. The access of the platform surged rapidly during the last few weeks of the course in both groups, mainly because these periods were the preparation time for the final exam during near the end of course, so students accessed the platform more frequently for revision. Through the result in Fig. 2, we could identify the general students' behavior pattern over time. However, more advanced information would be needed to further understand how students make use of the resources online. Results from SPM could provide such information by finding and displaying the frequent navigational patterns of students on Moodle.

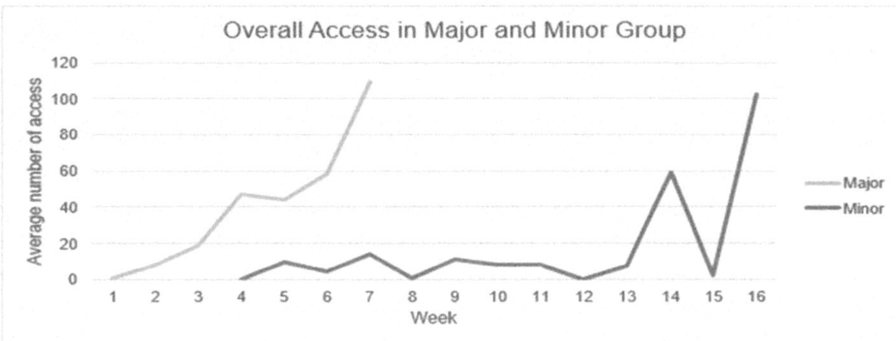

Fig. 2. Overall access to the digital resources on Moodle over time. The red curve represents the major group while the blue curve represents the minor group. The major group had a generally higher number of accesses to the platform. Both groups demonstrated a higher number of accesses near the end of the course.

4.3 Pattern Discovery

Before the pattern discovery process with our modified SPM, one further preprocessing step was conducted concerning the Moodle log data. Moodle contains fine-grained information about the behaviors of student on the system. In the case of quiz activity, there are different descriptions used by Moodle to record each action of students when they complete the quizzes. If all of them are included, many trivial patterns would be generated. In view of this, those consecutive quizzes related actions (or items) are aggregated into a single quiz action to improve the quality of patterns for better interpretation. The log data on Moodle of both major and minor group students were processed by the algorithm to discover the common access patterns of resources on the platform. We used the adapted method described in Sect. 3 for SPM. The algorithm returned 83 patterns for the major group on the support level of 0.5, and 52 for the minor group on the same support level. These patterns could help teachers to identify the most common patterns adopted by students when they learned online. The results could also show what kind of resources students prefer and the order of which these resources were used.

4.4 Visualization Based on Hierarchical Clustering

Results from SPM could be ordered in different ways, for instance according to the support level of the mined sequences or a specific position within the sequences such as the first or second item. However, we propose that further grouping and visualization of patterns with clustering technique could provide a more coherent presentation of results. This section will first briefly explain the clustering techniques used and explain the way to interpret the associated results, then comparison would be made with the first and second action alphabetical sorting. The mined patterns from minor group are used as an example for the following discussion due to space limitation.

Hierarchical clustering is chosen in the current study for the pattern grouping process. Hierarchical clustering assumes that structure of cluster appears as nested structural level and the results are usually visualized through a graph called dendrogram. In the consideration of distance measure, Levenshetin distance is adopted to calculate the similarity index between pairs of sequences. The definition of Levenshetin distance is the minimum number of operation required to transform a single sequence into the other using insertion, deletion, or substitution of an action in a sequence [22]. Figure 3 presents a row dendrogram based on SPM results from the minor group. Each pattern in the vertical axis is represented by the leaf nodes, which are the right most nodes in the diagram. Each node also represents a corresponding cluster of patterns located at the right of it. The horizontal axis represents the distance or dissimilarity between clusters and the horizontal position of the node shows the dissimilarity between two clusters, as illustrated by the vertical bar. For instance, pattern 2 and pattern 5 share a high similarity, indicated by the short distance between the two leaf nodes and their parent node.

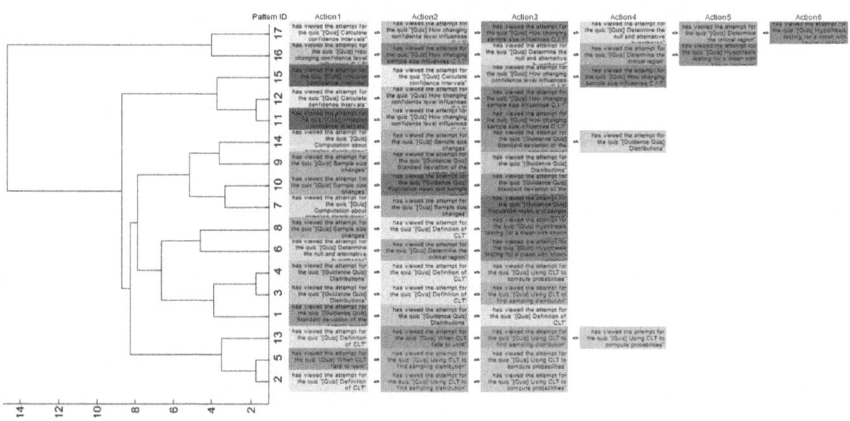

Fig. 3. Arrangement of patterns based on hierarchical clustering visualized by a row dendrogram. By the end of each leaf node, the pattern ID is indicated to represent the corresponding pattern on the right. All identical actions in the results are highlighted with the same colors.

Patterns from the minor group are compared under the arrangement of hierarchical clustering visualized by a dendrogram (Fig. 3) and first and second action alphabetical sorting in the sequence (Fig. 4). To aid readers' interpretation, all actions within the patterns are colorized and the identical actions are highlighted with the same colors across patterns. Those actions which accessed the resources within the same topic in the course were represented by different depth levels of the same color. The result shows that hierarchical clustering could effectively group similar patterns together in the presentation, especially for those patterns with a long length.

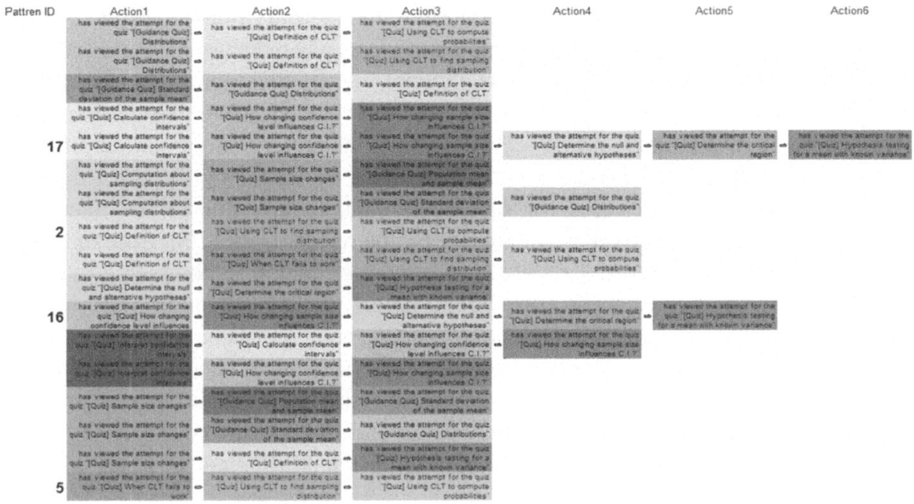

Fig. 4. Arrangement of patterns based on first and second action alphabetical sort. Using the pattern pair 16 & 17 and pattern 2 & 5 as comparison with Fig. 3, similar patterns are not grouped together under this sorting criterion.

For example in Fig. 3, pattern 17 with length 6 and pattern 16 with length 7 share a high similarity with only one different action between them. The processing of hierarchical clustering successfully arranges these two patterns together. In contrast, they are not put together under alphabetical sort in Fig. 4. This is because these two patterns contain a different first action and hence even though they have a similar composition of actions, they are not ordered close to each other. Similar situation happens to the pattern with identical and relatively short length such as pattern 2 and pattern 5 with length 3. They are arranged closely by hierarchical clustering but not by alphabetical sort.

In addition, judging from the distribution of colors in the results, the arrangement under hierarchical clustering could effectively group those patterns which focus on a similar topic together, even though the topic information is not used in the clustering process. For instance, actions highlighted with different color depth of blue showed they were actions within the topic of "Confidence Interval". Figure 3 showed that these patterns were concentrated in the upper part of the results while Fig. 4 showed that patterns highlighted with blue were separated under alphabetical sort.

4.5 Sunburst Visualization

The patterns discovered by the SPM algorithm have a text format output. The lack of visual element would cause difficulties during the interpretation process of patterns and this would not be favorable to users such as teachers, who are technically less sophisticated and could not afford to spend a large amount of time for analysis of the patterns. Visual analysis was found to be effective in this situation since it allows for an interactive exploration of the results and satisfaction of curiosity, which were both essential to exploratory analysis [4]. Furthermore, interactivity is an important element to the interpretation as users might spot interesting facts when the visual display changes which drive them to manipulate the visualization or the underlying data for further exploration of such changes [11]. Therefore, an effective visual representation of the discovered patterns would be necessary to facilitate the pattern interpretation process.

This study adopted the D3 sunburst visualization by Rodden [19] out of different available visualization packages for sequential data, mainly due to the interactive elements in it and the effectiveness in presenting the results from SPM. Similar visualizations were mostly designed for sites from industries such as e-commerce to understand the discovery of products by customers. The sunburst visualization was originally designed to display the webpage navigation sequences on YouTube to study the video discovery process of users and only focused on those sequences occurred at the start of a user's visit to the website. However, the navigation patterns in the current study context are frequent sequences of visit, which may occur at different time points during user's visit under the specified time gap. This major definitional difference to sequence leads to modifications in the package.

The visualization can display all sequences in a coherent manner which was concrete and easy to understand the patterns as reported by Rodden [19]. When the pattern discovery process was completed by the algorithm, the results could be visualized automatically. Figure 5 presents the sunburst visualization based on the results from the major group in the current study as an example. The legend is placed on the right hand

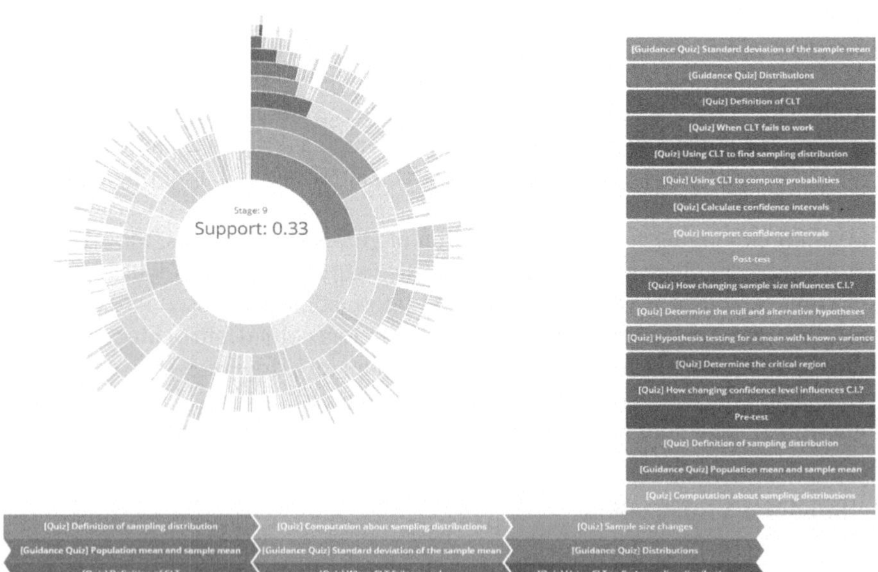

Fig. 5. Sunburst visualization of patterns.

side of interface and each action has its own corresponding color for easier differentiation. Using a mouse to hover any segment will highlight the entire associated pattern and desaturate all other segment in the visualization, with the display of support value at the center of the graph and detailed information about each action in the sequence below the graph. The size of the color block represents the proportion of total number of visit on that level of action. Comparing to the text-based output, the visualization could increase the effectiveness in delivering the results of discovered patterns from the mining process. For instance, teachers could easily find out which digital resources is the most popular among students and all other connected resources as revealed by the mined sequences. The graphical and interactive output also allows them to explore the results with higher flexibility and reduces the possible anxiety induced when facing a large quantity of information regarding the patterns. The sunburst visualization could make the analysis of navigational patterns easier to approach and use. More teachers could therefore be benefited to gain a more concrete understanding on the learning processes of students online.

5 Conclusion

This paper uses SPM to discover the navigational patterns of students on LMSs and presents the results through hierarchical clustering and sunburst visualization. The results are transformed into a more interactive and interpretable format for learning analytics, which aims to lower the difficulties in understanding the patterns for end users such as teachers. We hope that this paper could address the issues raised by Reimann et al. [18] and Gómez-Aguilar et al. [4] and promote further usage of learning data in a digital environment such as on LMSs, which contains valuable information of students which could facilitate the pedagogical decision making of teachers, especially with the prevalence of blended learning approach in instruction.

Acknowledgement. The study was funded by Teaching Development Grant (Ref: HKIED7/T&L/12-15) under the Hong Kong University Grants Committee.

References

1. Agrawal, R., Srikant, R.: Mining sequential patterns. In: ICDE (1995)
2. Ferguson, R.: Learning analytics: drivers, developments and challenges. Int. J. Technol. Enhanced Learn. **4**(5–6), 304–317 (2012)
3. Fournier-Viger, P., Nkambou, R., Nguifo, E.M.: A knowledge discovery framework for learning task models from user interactions in intelligent tutoring systems. In: MICAI 2008, pp. 765–778 (2008)
4. Gómez-Aguilar, D.A., Hernández-García, A., García-Peñalvo, F.J., Therón, R.: Tap into visual analysis of customization of grouping of activities in elearning. Comput. Hum. Behav. **47**, 60–67 (2015)
5. Graf, S., Liu, T.C.: Analysis of learners' navigational behaviour and their learning styles in an online course. J. Comput. Assist. Learn. **26**(2), 116–131 (2010)

6. Hirate, Y., Yamana, H.: Generalized sequential pattern mining with item intervals. J. Comput. **1**(3), 51–60 (2006)
7. Kang, J., Liu, M., Qu, W.: Using gameplay data to examine learning behavior patterns in a serious game. Comput. Hum. Behav. **72**, 757–770 (2016)
8. Kerr, D.: Visualizing changes in strategy use across attempts via state diagrams: a case study. Int. J. Comput. Games Technol. **2016**, 4 (2016)
9. Kong, S.C., Song, Y.: An experience of personalized learning hub initiative embedding BYOD for reflective engagement in higher education. Comput. Educ. **88**, 227–240 (2015)
10. Mahajan, R., Sodhi, J., Mahajan, V.: Usage patterns discovery from a web log in an Indian e-learning site: a case study. Educ. Inf. Technol. **21**(1), 123–148 (2016)
11. Mazza, R.: Visualization in educational environments. In: Romero, C., Ventura, S., Pechenizkiy, M., Baker, R.S.J.D. (eds.) Handbook of Educational Data Mining, pp. 9–26 (2010)
12. Mooney, C.H., Roddick, J.F.: Sequential pattern mining — approaches and algorithms. ACM Comput. Surv. **45**(2), 19:1–19:39 (2013)
13. Poon, L.K.M., Kong, S.C., Wong, M., Yau, T.: Mining sequential patterns of students' access on learning management system. In: The Second International Conference on Data Mining and Big Data (DMBD 2017) (2017)
14. Pei, J., Han, J., Mortazavi-Asl, B., Pinto, H.: Prefixspan: mining sequential patterns efficiently by prefix-projected pattern growth. In: ICDE (2001)
15. Pei, J., Han, J., Wang, W.: Constraint-based sequential pattern mining: the pattern-growth methods. J. Intell. Inf. Syst. **28**, 133–160 (2007)
16. Perera, D., Kay, J., Koprinska, I., Yacef, K., Zaiane, O.R.: Clustering and sequential pattern mining of online collaborative learning data. IEEE Trans. Knowl. Data Eng. **21**(6), 759–772 (2009)
17. Psaromiligkos, Y., Orfanidou, M., Kytagias, C., Zafiri, E.: Mining log data for the analysis of learners behaviour in web-based learning management systems. Oper. Res. **11**(2), 187–200 (2011)
18. Reimann, P., Hesse, F., Freebody, P., Cierniak, G., Imhof, B., Wasson, B., Hansen, C., Utz, W., Vatrapu, R., Bull, S., et al.: Supporting teachers in capturing and analyzing data in the technology-rich classroom. In: Future of Learning: Proceedings of the 10th International Conference of the Learning Sciences (ICLS 2012), pp. 33–40. International Society of the Learning Sciences (2012)
19. Rodden, K.: Applying a sunburst visualization to summarize user navigation sequences. IEEE Comput. Graph. Appl. **34**(5), 36–40 (2014)
20. Srivastava, J., Cooley, R., Deshpande, M., Tan, P.N.: Web usage mining: discovery and applications of usage patterns from web data. ACM SIGKDD Explor. Newsl. **1**(2), 12–23 (2000)
21. Van Barneveld, A., Arnold, K.E., Campbell, J.P.: Analytics in higher education: establishing a common language. EDUCAUSE Learn. Initiative **1**(1), 1–11 (2012)
22. Zhou, M.: Using traces to investigate self-regulatory activities: a study of self-regulation and achievement goal profiles in the context of web search for academic tasks. J. Cogn. Educ. Psychol. **12**(3), 287–305 (2013)
23. Zhou, M., Xu, Y., Nesbit, J.C., Winne, P.H.: Sequential pattern analysis of learning logs: methodology and applications. In: Handbook of Educational Data Mining, pp. 107–121 (2010)
24. Ziebarth, S., Chounta, I.A., Hoppe, H.U.: Resource access patterns in exam preparation activities. In: Design for Teaching and Learning in a Networked World, pp. 497–502. Springer (2015)

Construction of the 3L5G Task-Driven Instructional Model: Fostering Computational Thinking of Junior High School Students in an Application Software Course

Yi Fan[1] and Xiaotong Yang[2(✉)]

[1] Baoyuzhi Primary School, Haizhu District, Guangzhou, China
452090989@qq.com
[2] South China Normal University, Guangzhou, China
seasonyxt@gmail.com

Abstract. The focus of this research is to develop and verify the 3-level-5-guidance (3L5G) Task-driven Instructional Model aimed at fostering Computational Thinking (CT) of junior high school students in an application software course. As one of the most popular pedagogies in Informational Technology (IT) instruction, the task-driven learning approach is receiving increasing attention as it facilitates the development of CT among junior high school students. Instructional problems existed in task-driven learning applications as well as the status quo of the development of CT in IT courses were reviewed through document analysis. After the development of the framework of CT in application software learning, an empirical investigation was conducted to develop and refine the 3L5G Task-Driven Instructional Model from the perspective of task levels and cognitive guidance guiding. This investigation was conducted over two iterations of an action research effort with 8th-grade students of a public junior high school in Guangzhou. The model was verified through a practical study with students ($N = 301$) from two junior high schools in Guangzhou, China.

Keywords: Task-driven learning · Computational thinking · Junior high school

1 Introduction

Basic computer science knowledge and skills, programming, application software and so on, are taught in the IT course in the junior high schools in China [1], while application software accounts for an overwhelmingly large percentage. For example, it represents 50% of the whole teaching content according to the IT Course textbook used in Guangzhou (2013 edition). However, many teachers, nowadays, are used to teach the application software course in an inflexible mechanical way and treat students as the workers in the factory, which not only imperatively results in high operational error rate and superficial memory of the basic operational skills as the learning outcomes, but also overlooks the development of students' problem-solving ability, CT, and other higher-order thinking. Jeannette Wing firstly used the term CT in the article "Computational Thinking" appeared in the Viewpoint section of the March 2006 edition of the Communications of the ACM with the pronouncement: "It represents a universally applicable

S.K.S. Cheung et al. (Eds.): ICBL 2017, LNCS 10309, pp. 177–186, 2017.
DOI: 10.1007/978-3-319-59360-9_16

attitude and skill set everyone, not just computer scientists, would be eager to learn and use" [2]. While task-driven learning, which was proven by a large number of researches, is perceived as a justified effective way to foster CT in IT course [3].

The research questions investigated through the paper are below:

1. How to design the application software instructional model considering Task-driven learning to contribute to the cultivation of CT of junior high school students?
2. What is the change in the CT among students as a result of the model?

This paper focuses on the construction and verification of the 3L5G Task-driven Instructional Model aiming at fostering CT in application software instruction. A review of related work is presented concerning previous researches on CT cultivation as well as Task-driven learning in junior IT courses. In the Theoretical Framework part, the preliminary design of the 3L5G Task-driven Instructional Model is built on the basis of the framework of CT in application software instruction in the junior IT courses. Following is the description of the research methodology, including an action research over two iterations on model reflection and refining and an empirical study to examine the validity of the model. The paper ends with a synthesis of the main findings of the research as well as some existing limitations.

2 Related Work

2.1 Research on CT

There are some extensive literature tackling issues of conception, rationale, and value of CT. Royal Society (2012) offered a succinct and tractable definition that captures the essence of CT — "Computational thinking is the process of recognizing aspects of computation in the world that surrounds us, and applying tools and techniques from Computer Science to understand and reason about both natural and artificial systems and processes [4]." Barr and Stephenson (2011) provided a similar "operational definition of CT" aimed at K-12 teachers that comprised an explanatory checklist for what CT means along with an enumeration of core CT concepts and capabilities [5].

The focus is also on undertaking the more practical questions of how to promote and assess the development of CT in K-12. Nancai Yang from Shanghai Luodian Middle school proposed an Algorithm learning strategies for CT development [6]. Despite its growing popularity for promoting many 21st century competencies in K-12 (NRC, 2012), video gaming as a platform for examining CT among children has been underutilized in recent research [7]. Less attention, however, is paid for the empirical research on fostering CT in application software instruction in junior high schools.

2.2 Research on Task-Driven Learning

Task-driven learning has been applied in the IT education since the end of 20th centuries and caught the attention of a broad teacher community. There are mainly three understanding of the task itself: the transformation of the specific knowledge [8], being comprehensive and expansive [9], and being multiform [10]. A consensus on the general ideas of it have been reached: tasks acting as mainline, with teachers' guidance, and students being the subject of learning. However, taking the fact into account that abundant and interactive content has to be delivered in such a limited time in the junior IT course, it seems impossible to merely guide students to learn and investigate independently and collaboratively to complete the tasks. Thus, refinement and adjustments have to be employed to the original task-driven learning strategies to make it more adaptable to the specific context. The paper will redefine and classify "task" and design an operational instructional model aiming specially at fostering CT of junior high school students in application software courses.

3 Theoretical Framework

3.1 Framework of CT in Application Software Course

Comparing to the instruction of basic knowledge, basic skills, or programming in IT courses, the application course is featured by solving real-world problems with the use of digital tools, which makes it the target of New Curriculum Revolution concerning employing new instructional models like task-driven learning. The instructional objectives of the application software course include knowledge of the nature and features of the different software, application knowledge and ability to use and apply it in real-world problem solving [1]. Taking the three dimensions of instructional objectives in New Curriculum Revolution, and the nature of this kind of courses into consideration, the paper analyzed the construction of CT of junior high school students in application software course, including three elements - Thinking skills, Thinking methods, and Think habits (Fig. 1).

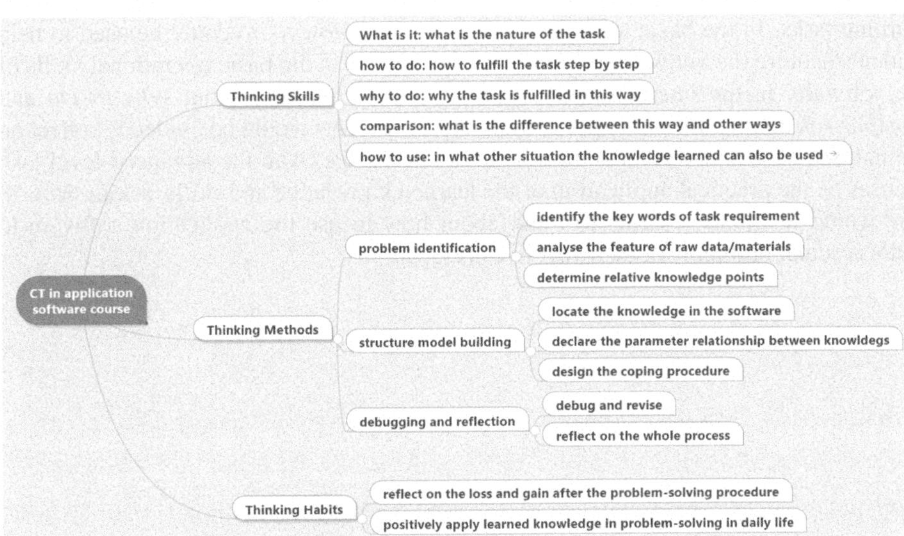

Fig. 1. Framework of CT of junior high school students in application software course

3.2 The Preliminary Model Design

The preliminary 3L5G Task-Driven Instructional Model design was based on the problem-solving process: (1) Problem identification; (2) Features abstraction; (3) Structure model building; (4) Problem-solving plan development, that contributes to the cultivation of CT among students (Fig. 2).

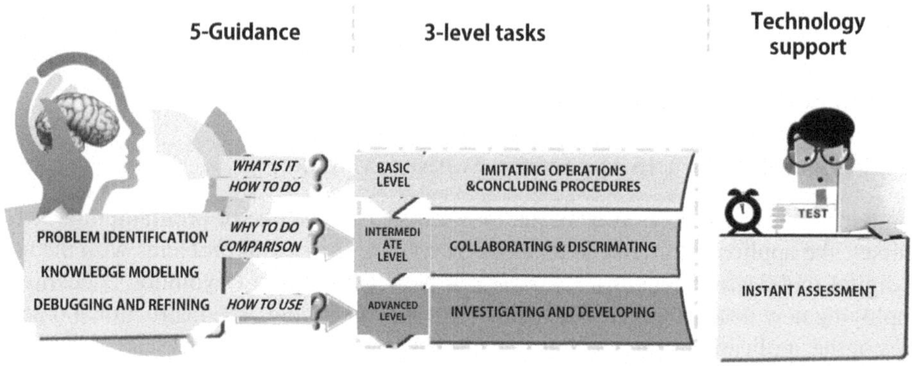

Fig. 2. The preliminary design of 3L5G Task-Driven Instructional Model aiming at fostering CT

3L means the classification of learning tasks from basic, intermediate to an advanced level by the instructional objectives of the task. While 5 Guidance means five practical tips guiding students' thinking to a deeper understanding throughout the three-level learning tasks. In the basic level task, *What is it* and *How to do* could be used to help students acquire the knowledge of the concept as well as the basic operational skills of the software. In the intermediate level task, led by thinking about *Why to Do* and *Comparison* among different operation methods, students would be guided to reflect on the nature of the software operation-relative knowledge. And the advanced level task focuses on the practical application of the learned knowledge and skills, asking *How to Use* would facilitate students to think about how to use the application software to address actual problems in their real lives (Fig. 3).

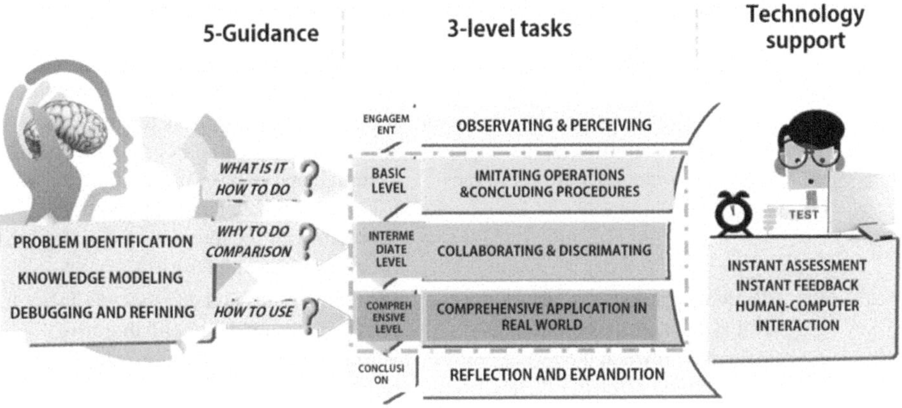

Fig. 3. The 3L5G Task-Driven Instructional Model aiming at fostering CT

At the same time, there is no doubt that feedback and reflection play an essential role in each level before students move to the next level. Based on VBA language, instant assessment system would provide instant feedback after finishing each level of learning tasks for both teachers and students to facilitate reflection and refine in the whole problem-solving process they have experienced.

4 Research Methodology

4.1 Action Research

An action research was conducted to facilitate the development of the 3L5G Task-driven Instructional Model by working through a series of instructional practice and reflective stages. The sample of students was from two 8th grade classes (96 in all) in a junior school in Guangzhou with similar mid-term exam scores mean and they are taught by the same teacher. The action research consisted of two iterated cycles and four stages: planning, acting, observing, and reflecting. The objectives, problems found and refinement accordingly of the preliminary model of each cycle are shown in Tables 1 and 2 respectively.

Table 1. Action research design

Teaching content	Cycle	Objectives
Excel data filtering	1st cycle	Analyzing the proposed problems in the preliminary draft of the model
Excel data filtering	2nd cycle	Revising and refining the model

Table 2. Problems found in action research and refinement

Cycle	Problems found	Reflection and refinement
1st cycle	The orientation of the advanced level task was ambiguous, either extending too much or limiting to the required learning content according to the textbook	Transforming advanced to comprehensive level, which means transferring focus from development in depth to breadth. In comprehensive level tasks, students are asked to solve an actual integrating problem with the integrating use of all the previous knowledge
2nd cycle	Students presented a lack of the ability of identifying the key information when they were required to self-study referring the textbook	Providing clues and advance organizer to guide explorative and collaborative learning align with the difficulty level of tasks

After the reflection and refinement of the problems found throughout two iterations, the 3L5G Task-driven Instructional Model was improved on the basis of the preliminary draft.

When going through the 3-level tasks, students could experience the progressive problem-solving processes rather than only acquiring knowledge, during which their CT would be developed. Taking the 5H2 W analysis into consideration, 5-guidance tips in the model, including *What is it, How to do, Why to Do, Comparison* and *How to Use,* could be perceived as a quite practical method to practice students' thinking with clearly defined objectives during the different level of tasks. When applying this model in the application software instruction, students would be solidly equipped with the thinking skills as well as the thinking methods from problem identification, knowledge modeling to debugging and reflection. What's more, chances are that the model would facilitate advanced thinking like evaluation, reflection and contribute to self-regulated learning among students. At the same time, by concluding, extracting, and discriminating knowledge behind the problem-solving processes, students would be able to learn to grasp the nature of new knowledge as well as construct their own knowledge system with the interaction with the contexts. The technology is properly used to provide needed information and instant feedback for the teachers to adjust instructional activities and to put the students in charge of their own learning.

4.2 Assessment

4.2.1 Participants and Procedure

An empirical study was conducted in two junior high schools (School A and School B) in Guangzhou to test the validity in CT development of the 3L5G Task-driven Instructional Model. Teaching content in the classes in the empirical study are Powerpoint, Excel and a photo editing software. Information on the student sample was shown in Table 3.

Table 3. Student sample in the empirical study

School	Average age	Gender (N)	
		Male	Female
A	15	54	36
B	15	110	101
Total		164	137
		301	

4.2.2 Instrument

Questionnaire and in-class observation were both used in the assessment part. Based on the analysis of the CT in the application software course among junior high students and Informational Technology Curriculum Plan of the compulsory education in Guangdong Province of China, the CT development in application software course self-reporting inventory was developed to measure three elements of CT among students receiving the model.

5 Results and Discussion

The CT development in application software course self-reporting questionnaire, with a five-point Likert-type scale ranging from "strongly disagree (−2)" to "strongly agree (2)" was used to measure the scores of Thinking skills, Thinking methods, and Thinking habits among sample students. The data was processed by the formula of two-dimensional scale: $Fi = \sum a_j n_{ij}/2N$.

5.1 Analysis of Thinking Skills

As shown in Table 4, the Fi scores of the five questions on thinking skills are positive. Students were gradually getting used to understand the nature of knowledge and foster some thinking skills as well with the guidance of the five thinking tips. Most students did a good job in understanding the concepts, acquiring operation steps and the underpinning rationale. So did someone in transferring of learning and knowledge application. But given the relative upset scores of differentiating between similar knowledge, according to the statistics, more attentions should be paid to related instructional strategies.

Table 4. Thinking skills data analysis

No.	Item	Fi value
1	*I can understand what I am truly asked to do in the task*	0.50
2	*I know the procedures to accomplish the task*	0.57
3	*I know the reason why I do these operations to accomplish the task*	0.54
4	*I can determine the knowledge related to the task*	0.39
5	*I know which other real-world situations that I can apply the knowledge I learned*	0.48

5.2 Analysis of Thinking Methods

According to Table 5, students basically had the thinking methods in the application software course and could focus on the interaction between the computer and the steps through problem solving. At the same time, students displayed the initial competency of analysis and knowledge system construction, while there was still some deficiency in their thinking and design before the operation, and they were not accustomed to it as well.

Table 5. Thinking methods data analysis

No.	Item	Fi value
1	*I can determine the relative knowledge using to accomplish the task through the key words and features of it*	0.46
2	*I can infer the location of specific operation command by observing the layout of the software*	0.44
3	*I will think about the meaning and relation of different options when I open a command dialog box*	0.42
4	*I will determine the order parameter and sequence before I make any operations*	0.33
5	*I will pay close attention to the reflective information of the software*	0.55
6	*I will conclude the operation procedure when I finish it*	0.50

5.3 Analysis of Thinking Habits

For the Thinking habits, the Fi scores are all positive. The score of item 2 in Table 4, in cooperation with the item 5 in Table 3, shows that the students had already got the idea of applying what they learned in addressing actual problem in their real lives. However, the score of item 1 in Table 6, which is not as good as the others exhibited the inadequacy in reflection on the problem-solving processes among students. The whole scores of Thinking habits are lower than that of Thinking skills and methods, which means that there is still a long way to go for the development of Thinking habits of CT among junior high school students.

Table 6. Thinking habits data analysis

No.	Item	Fi value
1	*I sometimes reflect on the whole problem generating and solving process*	0.33
2	*I usually try to apply what I learned in IT classes to solve real-world problem I meet*	0.45

Besides the quantitative statistics shown above, in-class observation from the teachers also indicated the positive empirical result of the students from these three perspectives. Forty percent students in the class could follow the problem-solving procedure of "defining-analyzing-observing-generating alternative solutions-implementing and reflecting" rather than trying to fix it immediately without a second thought when encountering a task. Along with the 5 Guidance, students gradually paid more attention to the nature and the rationale of the knowledge and they would think about the relationship between different knowledge in a critical manner after fulfilling the task. The best part is that more and more students tend to hold a positive attitude to the challenge instead of being reluctant to embracing it. The Thinking habits combining Thinking methods contribute to the improvement of the Thinking skills collaboratively, while they as a whole boosted the development of students' CT and problem-solving abilities with the application of IT tools.

6 Conclusion

This research makes several unique contributions. It is perhaps the first empirical study focusing on the specific declaration and analysis of CT of junior high school students in application software course based on the analysis of the instructional goal of the application software course and the nature of CT. Instead of mechanically repetitive practice, learners must be taught with the core disciplinary ideas, knowledge, and skills for problem-solving as well as its general applications in the application software course.

The explicit attention devoted to building the 3L5G Task-driven Instructional Model is also a unique aspect of this research, which could be gainfully employed in other pedagogical practice for the IT course.

First being applied in IT curriculum in 1998 [11], Task-driven learning has been developing and enriching for dozens of years. Document analysis and the action research were used to develop the 3L5G Task-driven Instructional Model to foster CT, characterized by leveled tasks, problem-guiding, and technology-support. It serves as a breakthrough overcoming the ambiguity of the definition of learning tasks as well as providing an explicit thinking path for students to follow for the development of CT.

The empirical studies justified CT development and some crucial points when applying the model. Sample learners showed a high level of the three elements of CT of junior high school students, Thinking skills, methods, and habits, after the intervention. When it comes to the cultivation of thinking skills, learning how to differentiating knowledge points on application software acted as a hard point. And students might need more strategical guidance on pre-thinking and pre-design ability development. Besides, guidance on the cultivation of the Thinking habit in applying what the students learned in IT courses in solving real-world problems should go through the whole teaching procedure.

Nonetheless, this research has demographic and research design limitations. Pre and Post quasi-experimental research design would be helpful in order to enhance the internal validity of the research. Besides, more samples from different levels of schools and background are supposed to be involved to testify the validity of the model.

Acknowledgment. Fund project: Education scientific research project of "Twelfth Five Year Plan" in Guangzhou "research on the instructional model supported by the instant assessment technology" in 2015 (NO. 1201532733)

References

1. Computer Teaching & Research Committee in Primary and Middle Schools in Guangzhou. Research on the IT course types in primary and middle schools. In research on the instructional model and course types of IT courses in primary and middle schools. New century, Guangzhou (2002)
2. Wing, J.M.: Computational thinking. Commun. ACM **49**(3), 33–35 (2006)
3. Fan, Y.: Focusing on thinking, action research on optimizing the multimedia products teaching in high school IT courses. J. China Educ. Inf. **5**, 30 (2011)
4. Royal Society. Shut Down or Restart: The Way Forward for Computing in UK Schools. http://royalsociety.org/education/policy/computing-in-schools/report/
5. Barr, V., Stephenson, C.: Bringing computational thinking to K-12: what is involved and what is the role of the computer science education community? ACM Inroads **2**, 48–54 (2011)
6. Yang, N.C.: Investigation on algorithm and programming teaching in senior IT teaching. Master's thesis. Shanghai Normal University, Shanghai (2013)
7. Holbert, N.R., Wilensky, U.: Racing games for exploring kinematics: a computational thinking approach. In: Paper Presented at the Annual Meeting of the American Educational Research Association, New Orleans, Louisiana (2011)
8. Dong, J.F.: Research on the task-driven in IT courses in primary and middle schools. J. China Educ. Inf. **10**, 28–31 (2007)
9. Qian, X.J., Ma, Y.J.: Comments on task-driven learning. J. China Educ. Technol. **9**, 35–36 (2002)
10. Guo, S.Q.: The nature of task-driven pedagogy. J. China Educ. Technol. **7**, 57–59 (2006)
11. Tao, Z.Z.: Task-driven facilitating self-study: an introduction of the senior school elective courses textbook computer courses for windows. J. Curriculum Textbook Pedagogy **8**, 48 (1998)

The Enlightenment of Learning Sciences to Blended Learning

Rong Miao(✉) and Qian Dong

Department of Educational Technology, Graduate School of Education, Peking University, Beijing, China
miao@gse.pku.edu.cn

Abstract. In recent years, the development of learning sciences causes more people's attention. The purpose of this paper is to analyze the impact of learning sciences to blended learning. With literature research, interviews and other forms of domestic survey, we study learning sciences from the perspective of four aspects: research fields, research hotspots, research institutions, and case study. The authors believe the core issue of learning sciences and blended learning research is how to promote learning. Both is closely linked, learning sciences can provide theoretical basis for teaching and learning methods, application of hybrid technology; blended learning research can also enrich learning sciences research and provide specific ways for a more effective learning. Learning sciences will have an important impact on blended learning, and promote blended learning progress in learning method, learning content and technical applications etc. to contribute to more effective educational reform and innovation.

Keywords: Blended learning · Learning sciences · Study

1 Introduction

In recent years, with the establishment of learning sciences research organization, academic journals and conferences, learning science researches have achieved fruitful research results and pushed forward the reform of education teaching practice. As a high-speed developing interdisciplinary field, learning sciences have attracted more attention.

With literature research, interviews and other forms of domestic survey, the authors explore the enlightenment of learning sciences research to the blended learning research from research fields, research hotpots, research institutions and research cases.

2 The Research Fields of Learning Sciences

While retrieving "learning sciences" as keywords in Baidu academic, Fig. 1 shows the rapid development of learning sciences in interdisciplinary research.

S.K.S. Cheung et al. (Eds.): ICBL 2017, LNCS 10309, pp. 187–198, 2017.
DOI: 10.1007/978-3-319-59360-9_17

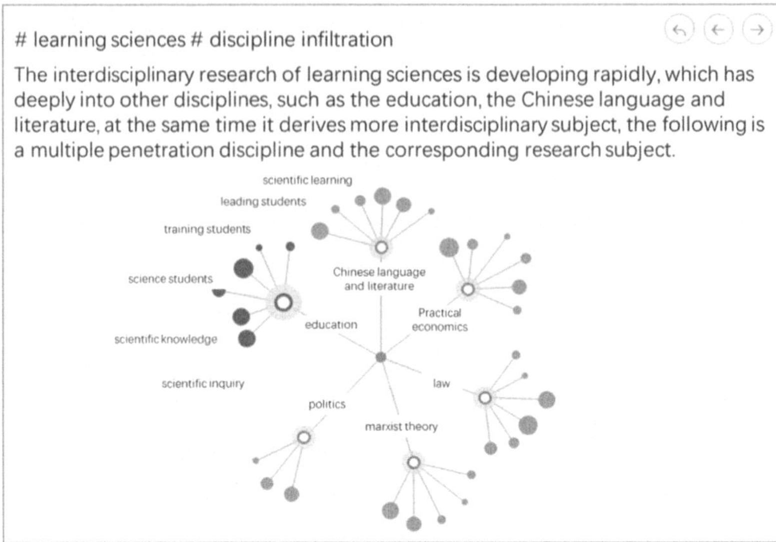

Fig. 1. Discipline infiltration of learning sciences

As a cross discipline, learning science covers research fields including psychology (including cognitive psychology, developmental psychology, educational psychology), computer science, neuroscience, brain science, pedagogy, anthropology, sociology etc.

In the Cambridge Handbook of learning science, the definition of learning sciences is an interdisciplinary field of research in teaching and learning. The scientists of learning sciences study the learning in a variety of fields, including not only the formal learning in the classroom, but also the informal learning that occurs in the family, while working and in the company. The goal of learning sciences is to learn how to understand the social cognition and the most effective process of learning, and to redesign the classrooms and other learning environment to make people more in-depth and more effective learning [1]. In short, the study of learning sciences mainly studies "how do people learn and how to promote effective learning?" [2]

Different scholars have different views on the specific research fields of learning sciences. In the Cambridge handbook of the learning sciences, the authors have regarded learning theory, design based research, expert learning and conceptual change, knowledge visualization, computer supported collaborative learning, learning environment, etc. as a set of focus fields [1]. Professors Jian Zhao, etc. from Learning Sciences Center have summarized the fields of learning sciences for constructivism, cognitive science, information technology, social-cultural studies, sociological research on knowledge. [3] As a representative of scholars, professor Jian li Jiao from South China Normal University thinks that learning sciences research mainly included ten aspects: situation and situated cognition, research on technology promote learning, visual language and visual intelligence, spatial intelligence and learning, learning excellence based on neuroscience, dynamic time of learning, informal and formal learning environment, robust learning and deep learning, research connectionist learning, learning environment design research [4].

Above different views, we think that learning sciences are widely studied in many fields, the main disciplines include cognitive neuroscience, technology, sociology and pedagogy and the major research fields include situation and situated cognition, research on technology promote learning, learning excellence based on neuroscience, informal and formal learning environment, robust learning and deep learning, research connectionist learning, learning environment design research and so on. Scholars from different disciplines keep a watchful eye on different aspects of learning sciences.

Learning sciences has absorbed a variety of theoretical perspectives and paradigms of learning, used many research methods to analyze the learning mechanism, and explored the human perception of the real world. Learning sciences not only studies the teaching and learning issues in the regular school situation, but also the informal learning environment. Therefore, the fields of learning sciences include not only the scientific research in general, but also the design and development of learning [4].

In this way, researchers in the field of learning sciences study the learning issues from different perspectives. However, the traditional blended learning cares more about the combination of various teaching methods to promote the learning effect. But could we extend the concept of blended learning not just in learning method? Is it possible the way of using a multi-perspective to learn knowledge also known as blended learning? Take air study for example, we can discuss its physical properties, chemical properties, but also the harm of the air pollution to human beings.

3 The Research Hotspots of Learning Sciences

The research in learning sciences is expanding since its birth, therefore, there are fruitful research in this field. But as a new subject, what are the hotspots of its research and how will it develop in the future?

Professor Junjie Shang from Graduate School of education Peking University believes, the most attractive or prominent research seems to be the following two categories: one is based on the research of neuroscience and learning (also known as neural education study), the other is research under the support of technology [2]. Based on literature analysis of "the journal of learning sciences" in these ten years, Haifeng Li and Yonghua Mo have summarized knowledge and cognition, learning environment, research tools and methodology, design, cooperative learning and community five categories as the research hotspots of learning sciences [5]. Youqun Ren & Yi Zhan have found that domestic scientific research hotspots are in four aspects: cognition and learning, scientific design in learning, social and cultural factors in learning, research methods [6].

For a better understanding of development and breakthrough in learning sciences research, the authors have interviewed Professor Dongchuan Yu from the research Learning Sciences Center at Southeast University, and Professor Youqun Ren from Learning Sciences Center at East China Normal University.

Learning Sciences Center at Southeast University pay attention to the children's science education, Professor Dongchuan Yu concentrates on three aspects: a. family education: provide more help for the parents of the students; b. school education: help school administrators and teachers solve practical issues; c. students: understand students more and help them improve learning efficiency.

Learning Sciences Center(LSC)at East China Normal University cares more about how to apply scientific research results to educational practice. Professor Youqun Ren indicates that it is still relatively weak in China at the mention of fundamental research on learning sciences, and it needs more investment. As for research methods of learning sciences, it needs more efforts, especially how to use technical methods to design the complex learning (rather than repetition) and enhance the depth understanding. Besides, more research needs to be done on the field of learning mechanism of the Chinese cultural context which can promote innovation and development.

In conclusion, learning sciences is a synthesis of many subjects, such as constructivism, cognitive science, educational technology, social and cultural research etc. Different scholars care for different parts. However, it can be seen that the research is focused on a great many areas of knowledge, and more cooperative scholars.

The core issue of learning sciences and blended learning research is how to promote learning. These two researches both pay attention to the fusion in multiple perspectives, the appropriate way of specific learners using to promote learning. The hotspots of learning sciences concentrate on the integration of knowledge in multidisciplinary, however, blended learning pays more attention to the fusion of using equipment (such as blackboard, books, etc.) tools (such as tablet computer, APP etc.), technology (such as audio, video, text, etc.) under a variety of teaching methods (such as constructivism, cognitivism etc.). On this occasion, the hotspots of learning sciences research can provide a reference for the study of blended learning, such as how to carry out the blended learning at home. Moreover, with the continuous study of learning sciences deeper and deeper, the cutting-edge results in this field may further expand the blended learning, such as teaching methods, learning content, technical equipment, to promote a wider and more multi-dimensional learning.

4 The Research Institutions of Learning Sciences

As a new interdisciplinary subject, the researchers of learning sciences have crossed many disciplines to understand the nature of learning from a broader perspective. On the whole, researchers are experts from psychology, education, computer science, anthropology and other disciplines in nation and abroad [1].

Learning sciences have first originated in the United States, germinated in 70 s, after 90 s moved towards maturity [7]. Researchers in the United States are mainly from cognitive science, neuroscience, computer science, educational psychology and others. Since 2004, the National Science Foundation (NSF) announced the allocation of $100 million to create learning science centers, aiming to draw the latest research results related to learning sciences into teaching and learning practice in the United States [8]. With the help of the NSF, six learning science centers have been established, such as

Centre for Education, Science and Technology, Informal and Formal Learning Center, Center for Cognitive and Educational Neuroscience, Pittsburgh Science of Learning Center etc. Here is a case study of Pittsburgh Science of Learning Center.

Pittsburgh Science of Learning Center(PSLC for short)was jointly established by Carnegie Mellon University, University of Pittsburgh and Carnegie company. Using cognitive theories and models, they have been committed to find the reasons how to promote students' robust learning and boost a better scientific understanding of robust learning. With the goal in mind, the center has established a Learning Lab which was jointly managed by Carnegie Mellon University and University of Pittsburgh, mainly to study the cognitive factors, metacognition and motivation, social communication, computational modeling and data mining.

Researchers in the center, including executive committee, advisory committee, research institute, postdoctoral, staff, etc. are various from different disciplines, such as psychology, computer science and computer engineering, education, linguistics, statistics, machine learning, philosophy and so on. Researchers in different disciplines distribute different parts, for example, Human-Computer Interaction Institute, Learning Research and Development Center, Institute of language technology, Institute of education and human development, Institute of intelligent systems etc. With the interaction, collaborative learning, fluency and refining in their research, researchers and staff work together to build a core theory to promote the development of the project, and gradually realize a more significant integration and achieve fruitful results.

Although there is still a gap between the domestic and European and America countries in learning sciences research, as a representative of the domestic colleges and universities, Southeast University, Beijing Normal University, East China Normal University have established research centers for learning sciences or related academic institutions. In 2002, the first center of learning sciences in Southeast University was established by Professor Yu Wei, the Former Vice Minister of education, Chinese Academy of Engineering, as a supporting institution of the Key Laboratory of Child Development and Learning Science, Southeast University. In July 2004, under the guidance of Qi Dong, the current president of Beijing Normal University, Beijing Normal University Institute of Brain and Cognitive Sciences (formerly the Research Institute of Cognitive Neuroscience and Learning) was set up, as a base of Cognitive Neuroscience and Learning State Key Laboratory. In October 2006, Dr. Wen Gao, a famous scholar in the field of learning and teaching and a tenured professor of East China Normal University, led the establishment of Learning Sciences Center at East China Normal University.

Key Laboratory of Child Development and Learning Science (Southeast University), Ministry of Education, is the first research center for learning sciences in China. The key laboratory has high-level researchers with a wide range of academic backgrounds, including neuroscience, psychology, education, biology, and engineering. There are currently more than 60 researchers and postgraduate students in the lab [9]. As far as the establishment of the laboratory, Professor Dongchuan Yu from Key Laboratory of Child Development and Learning Science said, the lab was originally created by researchers from biomedical engineering, computer, education, psychology, neuroscience, medical science and other disciplines, emphasizing multidisciplinary and interdisciplinary integration. Now all the researchers working in the laboratory in the same location, besides, each research team is close to the other, which causes natural fusion research.

Key Laboratory of cognitive neuroscience and learning at Beijing Normal University has established five research directions, that is the basic cognitive process and the interaction between learning, language cognition and mathematics cognition and learning, emotion and cognition, the psychological development and brain development, the methodology of cognitive neuroscience. Professor Wang Wenjing, from Key Laboratory of cognition and learning said, what the lab focused is not just fundamental research, but educational applications as well. The formation of teams is from disciplines emphasizing the integration of different viewports. Taking the laboratory of brain and language learning research for example, there are three teams in this research: neuroscience, cognitive science and education which have the same goal. Besides, each team with loose alliance has close ties and makes mutual communication and collaboration to promote research advance. Neuroscience team focuses on the brain mechanism of Chinese who learn a second language. Cognitive science team studies learning and its rules from the cognitive level, through carefully design of the teaching process of intervention, observation and analysis of the behavior on students under the intervention of education. The neuroscience and cognitive science teams seek evidence from the domestic and international research results to support the design and implementation of educational practice. From the perspective of educational practice, the education team draws the application of neuroscience and cognitive science into practical teaching.

In general, learning sciences researchers focus on interdisciplinary integration. Different research directions of the field form different teams. According to the specific research content, they make the most suitable team carry out research and present research results. At the same time, they concentrate on the communication, collaboration, integration among multiple teams so that they find evidences from different field to make the research more perfect.

Learning sciences research teams lay emphasis on interdisciplinary integration. They make the most suitable team carry out research for specific research content, at the same time, a number of teams interact with each other. Maybe it's difficult to set up a special blended learning research institution, but for a long-term development and better research of blended learning, we need multilateral participation, such as school teachers, product development team, learners.

5 The Research Cases of Learning Sciences

"Learning by doing" project was established in 2001 by the Ministry of Education of the People's Republic of China and China Association for Science and Technology. Under the understanding the educational background of promoting inquiry learning in the United States, France and other countries, this project sums up the experience of science education in China, and puts forward suggestion on the basis of absorbing the advanced ideas of foreign education. Besides, the project is committed to give all preschool, primary and secondary school children a chance to explore the mysteries of nature, moreover, experience scientific inquiry and construct fundamental knowledge through various activities, such as, observation, asking questions, ideas, hands-on experiments, communication activities. In this way, children can get scientific research ability, scientific attitude, scientific spirit, scientific thinking preliminarily so that children can form a scientific outlook of the world and promote the all-round development and high-quality talent.

The project has carried out a series of studies combined with many researchers, for instance, domestic and foreign experts, universities and research institutions, school teachers. From a perspective of neural theory and methods of education research for kindergarten and primary school education scientific, it emphasizes the development of inquiry science education on the basis of empirical research. Consequently, it established regional resource centers, "learning by doing" science education website, named as Han Bo——Chinese children's Science Education.

Take a study of doctoral thesis on the evaluation of children's empathy ability in the process of science education inquiry by Dr. Yuankui Yang for example, based on the relevant research results of neuroscience, the author first analyze the importance of the cultivation of social emotional ability, on this foundation, the author chooses the "learning by doing" as research platform. In this paper, it explores children empathy ability evaluation to explore the tools and methods of empathy assessment in children through the psychological mechanism, influence factors of empathy (internal factors and external factors), the neural basis of empathy (perception action model, mirror neuron model), behavior identity (the cooperative behavior, listening behavior), and then apply to the process of scientific education. With the help of evaluating the children's empathy in the process scientific education inquiry, it finds the scientific education impact on children's empathy.

The research has been conducted to develop the children's empathy ability scale (parent scale, child scale) which is used to test the students between scientific inquiry and traditional education. The results show that scientific inquiry can significantly improve the empathy of children, especially boys; the research has been also conducted to develop the evaluation scale of children's empathy ability which is applied for teaching activities. With the scale and behavior schema for the experimental group and control group, research shows that inquiry based science education helps children improve their cooperative and listening behavior. For skin conductance level of children's emotional condition, it shows that the children with higher empathy ability are significantly lower than children with lower empathy ability. [10]

Led by Wei Yu, "learning by doing" project has a great influence in the field of science education in primary schools. Over the past decades, the project has trained a number of excellent teachers. More than 2000 schools and nearly 200 thousand students benefit from it through the teaching and training exchanges in China. "Learning by doing" has been widely recognized and received high praise from home and abroad.

Climbing English is a project which devotes to issues on the shortage of English teachers in rural primary schools in China. [11] Based on current situation and practical needs of English education, the research is carried out on account of cognitive neuroscience, educational technology, psychological behavior science. For example, with functional magnetic resonance imaging (fMRI), a series of studies find the effects of brain mechanism on the switching of a second language. A comparative study of different learning support conditions shows that combination of Chinese translation and thematic prompts can significantly promote children's English vocabulary learning. On the basis of these researches, they have designed plans on learning of English learners, teaching experiments of teachers and so on. They have published a series of books, such as the "Climbing English Reading Series", "Guide to English learning", "A guide to English teachers", etc. Among them, Climbing English Reading series include two parts: "key reading skill training" and "graded reading" aiming at meeting different levels of English reading needs and providing effective methods and strategies of English learning resources for children. The story picture book effectively enhances the children's interest in English reading, writing and speaking ability which improves the efficiency of English learning.

In order to verify the Climbing English project effects, in July 2004, 140 students from 10 primary schools were selected in Beijing and then assessed English reading skills, learning attitudes and other aspects of comprehensive evaluation. The result reveals that the experimental group is better than the control group in the aspects of listening, speaking and reading. The experiment of Climbing English project provides a feasible scheme for students of primary and middle schools in our country to create high quality learning opportunities and resources [12].

Through the above research, we can find that the research of learning sciences focus on a specific topic. Many experts and scholars in the field set up a team from a number of disciplines to conduct joint research, in order to have a more in-depth understanding of a specific issue, and to achieve understanding of the principles, interpretation of humanities, social significance, and put the promotion into educational practice ultimately.

From a variety of views, learning sciences carries out interdisciplinary research. On one hand, research on learning mechanism and rules of neuroscience, cognitive science and others can be used as the theoretical basis and evidence of blended learning. On the other hand, learning sciences research from an application prospective can be combined with blended learning to jointly promote the reform and innovation of education.

6 Discussion

Blended learning is a concept put forward by western developed countries in enterprise training and it means a combination of various learning styles. For example, combine the use of audio-visual media with the use of traditional chalk and blackboard, combine the computer assisted with the traditional learning methods, combine autonomous with collaborative learning mode.

At present, there is no authority definition in the field of blended learning, and the followings are some of the definition of blended learning:

A typical definition of Blended Learning in the world is "Blended learning focus on optimizing achievement of learning objectives by applying the "right" learning technologies to match the "right" personal learning style to transfer the "right" skills to the "right" person at the "right" time."

Learning Circuits defined it as a learning approach in the ASTD'S Online Magazine Covering E-Learning glossary. This combination of learning methods are made up of the rational use of various information technology, audio video conference, network, CD-ROM and other media, as well as the rational use of knowledge and technology, online activities and learning support system.

In 2002, India NIIT published white paper of blended learning on the website of American Society for Training and Development where teaching design experts suggest that blended learning should be defined as a way of learning. This learning method consists of face-to-face learning, real-time E-learning and self-regulating step learning. In most cases, blended learning is also used to describe a wide range of blended applications, such as transmission media, intelligent learning instructors (ILT), and a variety of technologies. These technologies include E-learning, electronic performance support system (EPSS), and knowledge management practice, etc.

Michael Orey demonstrates that blended learning should be defined from three aspects: learners, teachers or instructional designers, as well as teaching administrators. From a perspective of learners, "blended learning" is a kind of ability which can be obtained from all the options of equipment, tools, technology, media and materials to match their previous knowledge and learning style so that help themselves reach learning objectives. From the view of teachers or teaching designers, it is the organization and distribution of all available equipment, tools, technology, media and materials to achieve teaching objectives. From the point of view of teaching managers, it is possible to organize and distribute all the valuable equipment, tools, techniques, media and teaching materials in order to achieve the teaching objectives. Proceeding from the aspect of teaching administrators, Michael Orey also points out that these equipment, tools, technology, media and materials include books, computers, learning groups, teachers, classrooms, virtual classrooms, non-traditional classrooms, teaching guide etc.

Margaret Driscoll (2002) believes that blended teaching consists of four different concepts: First, combine or mix a variety of networking technologies (such as real-time virtual classroom, self-paced learning, collaborative learning, streaming video, audio and text) to achieve educational goals. Second, combine a variety of teaching methods (such as constructivism, behaviorism, and cognitivism) and then use or not use teaching techniques to produce the best learning outcomes. Third, combine any of teaching techniques (e.g. video tape, CD-ROM, web based training, film) with face-to-face teacher training (ILT). Fourth, combine or mix teaching technology and actual task so that make learning and work stay in harmony.

Kekang He believes that blended Learning is to combine the advantage of traditional learning method and E-learning (digital or network learning). With this method, the teachers not only play a leading role, such as guide or inspire their students, monitor teaching process, but also fully reflect the initiative, enthusiasm and creativity of students to take them as the center of the learning process [13, 14]

Zhiting Zhu and Qi Meng (2003) put forward a three-dimensional integration framework of blended learning in distance education, like the following Fig. 2. It exhibits three dimensions in blended learning which are teaching media, learning mode and learning content. Media determines the level of dialogue can be achieved to a large extent and structural aspects are very important to learning content, the nature of different learning modes depend on the power control of teachers and students, namely learner' control over their learning in this figure [15].

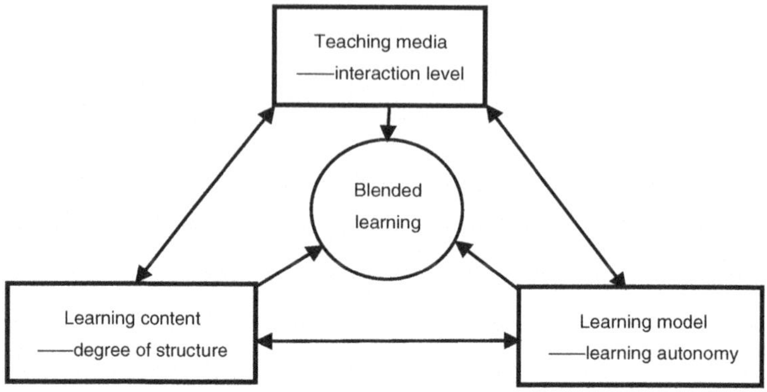

Fig. 2. Three-dimensional integration framework of blended learning (Zhiting Zhu, Qi Meng, 2003)

From the perspective of learning form to see the dimension of blended, it mainly includes five kinds of mixture: first, online and offline learning; second, self-paced learning and collaborative learning; third, structured learning and unstructured learning; fourth, specific learning materials and flexible learning materials; fifth, "work" and "learning".

With the above definition of scholars, the authors realize that blended learning is based on such a premise, that is learning is not a one-time process but a continuous process, blended forms of learning is better than single learning methods. After analyzing on the research of learning sciences, the authors believe that the study of learning sciences provides a theoretical basis and research theme for the study of blended learning.

First, from the aspects of research fields and hotspots, it demonstrates that there are many research fields of learning sciences, including situation cognition, technology research on promote learning, robust learning and deep learning, learning environment design research and so on. Scholars from different disciplines pay close attention to different aspects of learning sciences. These multiple prospective of research in learning sciences, not merely lay the theoretical foundation for blended learning research, but also provide enlightenment for research theme of blended learning.

Secondly, as to research institutions, it includes experts from pedagogy, psychology, computer science, anthropology and others disciplines. Scholars' diversity forms multi-perspective study of research issues. In the process of blended learning, attracting researchers from different fields can help improve the research quality.

Finally, as for case study, learning sciences research involves multiple disciplines. According to specific research issue, multi-disciplinary teams choose the most suitable team to carry out research. Moreover, there is mutual communication among disciplines, teamwork, identifying proof from multi-dimension and present research results. The research is in depth exploration from understanding to interpretation of principles of humanistic and sociological and then put forward promotion of educational practice. It also provides a useful enlightenment for the study of blended learning.

7 Conclusion

The authors believe that the core issue of learning sciences and blended learning is how to make students learn better and both of which should pay attention to the fusion of multi-views and to use more appropriate way to promote students' learning for specific learners. In addition, learning sciences can become a scientific theoretical basis of blended learning and provide theoretical basis and support for teaching methods, learning methods, application of hybrid technology; research of blended learning can also enrich learning sciences research, and provide specific ways and approaches for a more effective learning.

With the development of research, learning sciences has produced a series of cutting-edge achievements in technology, platform development. These results can be further expanded to connotation of blended learning to promote the fusion of learning content and methods. Learning sciences will have an important impact on blended learning, and promote blended learning progress in learning methods, learning content, learning environment, technology application and so on. Researchers from learning sciences and blended learning will contribute more educational reform and innovation.

References

1. Keith Sawyer, R.: The Cambridge Handbook of the Learning Sciences. Education Science Press, Beijing (2010)
2. Shang, J., Zhuang, S., Chen, G.: Learning science: promoting the reform of education. China Educ. Technol. **1**, 6–13 (2015)
3. Zhao, J., Zheng, T., Ren, Y., et al.: A review of research in learning sciences. Open Educ. Res. **13**(2), 15–20 (2007)
4. Jiao, J., Jia, Y.: Research field and new progress in learning science——"new progress in learning science" the introduction of a series of papers. Open Educ. Res. **17**(1), 33–41 (2011)
5. Li, H., Mo, Y.: Looking and thinking: The latest research progress and hotspot in the study of learning science——a case study of the Journal of Learning Science (JLS) in recent ten years. China Educ. Technol. **1**, 7–15 (2013)
6. Ren, Y., Zhan, Y.: Research progress and development trend of learning science at home and abroad. Chin. Educ. Sci. **2** (2013)
7. Huang, D., Jia, Y.: Research on the development of learning science in the United States. Stud. Foreign Educ. **5**, 91–96 (2011)
8. Qin, X.: Construction plan of "learning science center" funded by National Science Foundation. Softw. Guide (Educ. Technol.) **11**, 5–7 (2009)
9. Southeast University. Introduction to the center for learning science [EB/OL]. http://rcls.seu.edu.cn/introduction.aspx
10. Yang, Y.: Evaluation of Children's Empathy in the Process of Inquiry Based Science Education. Southeast University (2011)

11. Wang, W., Li, Y., Luo, L., Pei, M., Dong, Q.: System design and implementation innovation of educational experiment——a case study of Climbing English learning experiment. China Educ. Technol. **01**, 16–20 (2009)
12. Wang, W., Dong, Q.: A creative solution to the problem of the shortage of English teachers in rural primary schools——the application of modern information technology in Climbing English learning experiment. China Educ. Technol. **12**, 77–80 (2007)
13. He, K.: New development of educational technology theory from Blending Learning (Part I). China Educ. Technol. **3**, 5–10 (2004)
14. He, K.: New development of educational technology theory from Blending learning (part II). China Educ. Technol. **4**, 10–15 (2004)
15. Zhu, Z., Meng, Q.: Blended learning in distance education. China Educ. Technol. **19**, 30–34 (2003)

The Design and Development of Intellectual Skills Assessment App of Pupils in U-Learning Environment

Qiwen Guan[1], Jiaxin Liu[2(✉)], Xiaoling Huang[1], Jiehua He[2], Wei Li[2], and Chuangxin Sheng[2]

[1] GuangZhou PanYu Experimental Primary School, Guangzhou, China
1153740571@qq.com, 514792534@qq.com
[2] South China Normal University, Guangzhou, China
284762808@qq.com, 343723895@qq.com,
627540195@qq.com, 1499689643@qq.com

Abstract. Learning environment and learning style have had great changes In the "Internet+" age. Intellectual skills are regarded as students' the skills, and have become significant for one to carry out objective investigation, solve problems and develop critical thinking ability. In order to better evaluate the intellectual skills of pupils, this study puts forward an evaluation index system of primary school students' intellectual skills, through the literature research. On this basis, we developed an intellectual skills assessment app (ISA). It provides convenience in use for measuring the students' intellectual skills. The evaluation index system has theoretical significances and practical values to help develop students intellectual skills.

Keywords: Intellectual skills assessment · Design and development of the app · Ubiquitous learning environment · Primary school students

1 Introduction

In the "Internet+" age, a new stage of educational informationization is entering the smart education, great changes have taken place in the learning environment and learning. We gradually step into ubiquitous learning (u-Learning) from the digital learning (e-learning). In 2012, the organization for economic cooperation and development (OECD) released a research report pointing out that students in twenty-first Century must master the core skills of four areas, including the way of thinking, the means of work, work tools and life skills. Among them, the way of thinking includes creativity, critical thinking, problem solving, decision-making and learning ability. From a macro perspective, the way of thinking is considered to be the core skills that students must master in the twenty-first Century.

Psychological research shows that "the right way of thinking is the essential characteristic of intellectual skills". Grasping the scientific and rational way of thinking and having a certain intellectual skills level are the necessary core skills for every student to achieve a successful life and adapt to individual and social development. The intellectual skills refer to pupils' process of understanding specific things and solving specific

S.K.S. Cheung et al. (Eds.): ICBL 2017, LNCS 10309, pp. 199–210, 2017.
DOI: 10.1007/978-3-319-59360-9_18

problems. Students can take the initiative to adjust and control the intellectual experience which is the rule of activities formed by learning.

Children developing psychology believes that high-grade primary school students are in the best period of intellectual skills development. If teachers consciously assess student's intellectual skills and carry out targeted training according to the actual level of students, the development of students' intellectual skills will be faster. ubiquitous learning means that a person can learn in any time, any place, with any computing device, obtain any required learning resources and enjoy the learning process [1]. Ubiquitous learning environment includes sensor, server, mobile learning devices and basic components of wireless communication network. The mobile learning device provides a broad platform for the designing and using of Application for the evaluation of intellectual skills of pupils. Teachers and students can download App at anytime and anywhere.

As has been said, this study develops the evaluation application of pupil's intellectual skills, which can be widely used in learning environment for teachers and pupils and provide technical convenience for measuring the intellectual skills of pupils. This study has important theoretical significance and practical value to promote the development of pupils' intellectual skills.

2 Review

2.1 Review of Pupils' Intellectual Skills Training

Gagne, a representative scholar of intellectual skills, proposed that intellectual skills are the interaction between the individual environment and through the application of a symbol or idea [2]. Soviet psychologist Gary Perrin (1989) believes that intellectual activity is essentially derived from the internalization of external physical activities, which is a reflection of the external activities and their objects. He also put forward five-stage theory of the formation of intellectual skills, namely the intellectual skills formation process can be divided into five stages: "directional stage of activities" "arterial activities or material stage" "vocal stage" "silent external speech stage" "internal speech stage" [3]. Feng, Z.l. is an educational psychologist in China, thinks that intellectual skills are experience of regulating and controlling intellectual activities or a form of intellectual activity that formed by learning [4].

Most of the research on intellectual skills training is combined with the formation of intellectual skills. Gagne had a fine division of human intellectual skills. He believes that intellectual skills obtained from the order from low to high in turn, which can be divided into five levels: to identify specific concepts, definitions of concepts or rules, advanced rules and problem solving [2]. Soviet psychologist Gary Perrin put forward the five stage theories of intellectual skills formation, including "directional stage of activities, material activities or material stage, vocal stage, silent external speech and internal speech stage" [3]. American scholar Johnson put forward six teaching principles for the acquisition of intellectual skills and twenty-nine teaching strategies and pointed that teachers can guide students to develop their intellectual skills through formal learning and informal learning [5]. Xie, Y.R. et al. proposed an pupils' science inquiry intellectual skills training mode under the wisdom learning environment [6].

2.2 Review of the Dimensions and Evaluation of Pupils' Intellectual Skills

Foreign scholars have more researches on the composition and dimension of intellectual skills. Different scholars have different division, but generally, they contain a lot of common elements. In terms of the components of intellectual skills, Marzano believes that it has four aspects: Meta-cognition, core thinking ability, critical and creative thinking, and thinking process [7]. Linda et al. proposed that critical thinking is an essential ability standard of intellectual skill training [8]. Paul et al. put forward we can evaluate pupils' intellectual skills from five dimensions including analytical thinking, critical thinking, comprehensive thinking, creative thinking and problem solving ability [9]. In terms of evaluation of intellectual skills, questionnaires and paper-pencil tests are mainly used. For example, Li J.Z. uses test papers for the college students' teaching ability and practice scores so as to analyze the improvement of students' intellectual skills [10]. Zhu X. uses test papers to test and evaluate the intellectual skills of writing and judging the complex decomposition reaction [11]. In "the study on the cultivation of students" Flash animation skills under the informational environment", Ma Z.Y.'s evaluation method is to rate the works and questionnaire on the current situation of students' intellectual skills [12]. In addition, there are few researchers evaluating students' intellectual skills through technology. For example, Vagale V. & Niedrite L. added a test module in the MOODLE platform to evaluate the intellectual skills of students, which can get accurate test results of each student [13].

To sum up, there are a lot of researches on the classification, components and evaluation dimensions of intellectual skills in foreign countries, but there is no mature evaluation index system. However, the evaluation methods of intellectual skills in China are single, we mainly use paper-pencil test, questionnaire survey and so on. Generally speaking, there are few researches on the evaluation of intellectual skills, especially for the development of the evaluation tools for intellectual skills. Therefore, this research develops a App to evaluate pupils' intellectual skills. This App has the following advantages: firstly, it breaks through the limitations of the paper-pencil test to make the evaluation of intellectual skills more convenient and quick. Secondly, it makes sure that pupils can implement the test autonomously under ubiquitous condition and they will not confine to the classroom stress. This is conducive to the normal performance of pupils' intellectual skills and to avoid the Hawthorne effect so as to improve the effectiveness and accuracy of the evaluation. Thirdly, this App can give students a timely feedback, so that students can understand their intellectual skills development situation and their shortages quickly, which is beneficial to self-correction and adjustment in follow-up learning.

3 Requirement Analysis

Requirements analysis is to extract and analyze the information from the user, and finally describe the function and performance. The requirements of the evaluation in this research come from two aspects: first is to obtain the requirement of the pupils' intellectual skills evaluation from the literature investigation and analysis, second is according to the requirement of evaluation methods and the use of the role to the system function.

3.1 Requirement of Evaluation for Pupils

Through the study of literature, we found that the high-grade students of primary school are in the best period of the development of intellectual skills. If the teachers cultivate and train it consciously in the teaching process, the development of students' intellectual skills will become faster and faster. The teachers can detect the intellectual skills level of the individual or the whole class through the evaluation system, so they can train the students' intellectual skills pertinently.

3.2 Requirement of System Functions

Through clearly understanding applications of the ISA's tests in teaching practice, we divide the ISA's users into two sorts: students and teachers. Alongside that, there are five major function modules: basic information management, question bank management, Inference, report auto generation, and system management. We describe the specific requirement of each function as follow:

a. System management function: System can manage password and permission of the logged-in users.
b. Basic information management function: The information about the users who participate in the test embracing name, grade and class and so on will be included into the database to manage.
c. Question bank management function: The users can add or delete subject, edit titles, serial number and weight assignments, etc.
d. Inference function: According to the user's answers, the system offers corresponding interpretation, instructions and suggestions. The inference mechanism is designed to draw a conclusion according to the corresponding dimensions of the tests, the weight of dimensions, etc.
e. Report auto generation function: According to the test's result, the final evaluation report is generated automatically by inference mechanism.

4 Design of the ISA

4.1 Theoretical Basis

4.1.1 Metacognitive Theory

Stanford University psychologist Flavell [14] considered that metacognition is the cognition of cognition, specifically meaning that metacognition includes three aspects: the first is the metacognitive knowledge, namely the individual on his own or another person's cognitive activity, process, results and related knowledge. The second is the metacognitive experience, meaning that the produce of the emotional or cognitive experience in the process of cognitive activities. The third is metacognitive monitoring, namely the individual cognitive activities in the process of actively monitoring their cognitive activities, and accordingly to carry on the adjustment to achieve the target. In the actual cognitive activities, metacognitive knowledge, metacognitive experience and metacognitive monitoring are interrelated, influenced and restricted by each other [15]. In the process of learning, metacognition is the dynamic system of learning strategies [16], playing the "leader" and "prosecutor" in the whole learning process role, constantly activating learning interaction, analyzing to understand the learning situation and obtaining evaluations of learning, monitoring and regulation. As a consequence, the learners successfully complete the task of learning.

Intellectual skills training is a complex process of students' thinking mode and method change. In this process, students need to use the meta cognitive strategies to adjust their cognitive strategies and ways of thinking. Therefore, the theory has a certain guiding role in the development of primary school students' intellectual skills evaluation index system.

4.1.2 Educational Statistics Theory

Educational statistics is the theory and method of how to collect, organize and analyze the digital data reflecting the general information of the object in the field of education. Statistical methods include a large number of observation, statistical grouping method, comprehensive index method. Educational statistics adhere to the principle of combining qualitative analysis with quantitative analysis. In the process of education research, the quantitative method is mainly used for quantitative description and the data statistics and analysis of some characteristics of the research object. In this study, we use the principle of educational statistics to evaluate the intellectual skills of students, and make a quantitative description of the students' intellectual skills through the results of data statistics.

4.1.3 The Components and Evaluation Index System of Pupils' Intellectual Skills

Psychological research shows that "the right way of thinking is the essential characteristic of intellectual skills" [17]. Intellectual skills are mainly regard the thinking as the core. It's the regulation of operation skills and the process with the help of the language of the image of transformation in the human brain [18]. James M.R. [18] combined with the stages of intellectual skills to obtain the three stage proposed by the United States educational psychologist to propose the intellectual skills of the evaluation of the three dimensions: metacognitive skills; thinking development; knowledge acquisition, organization and institution [19]. Intellectual skills is one of the evaluation framework of the quality of higher education in Thailand. Therefore, Khon Kaen University proposed framework, to evaluate students' intellectual skills, including analysis of normal thinking, critical thinking, comprehensive thinking, creative thinking and problem solving. [8] Marzano et al. provides a comprehensive framework for thinking of intellectual skills, which is widely recognized [20]. The comprehensive framework includes: core thinking, thinking processes, critical and creative thinking, and Metacognition. Among them, the core thinking ability includes understanding ability, information acquisition ability, memory ability, organization ability, analysis ability, generative ability, integrating ability and evaluating ability. However, in the process of knowledge acquisition and Application, we need to adopt eight kinds of thinking process in practice, including "concept formation", "principles", "understand", "problem solving", "decision making", "survey", "creation", "oral narrative". As for the critical thinking, researchers at home and abroad have reached an agreement on the structure of critical thinking, identified that critical thinking is composed of two dimensions: critical thinking spirit and critical thinking skills. Torrance [21] developed the creative thinking test (TTCT), consisting of three parts: the speech test, the picture test, and the sound and word test. A total of 12 quizzes were applied to the kindergarten to adults, mainly examining fluency, flexibility, originality, and accuracy. This is the most widely and frequently used creative thinking test. Based on TTCT, we considered that the dimension of creative thinking evaluation should include four dimensions: fluency, flexibility, originality and precision.

Therefore, this study evaluated intellectual skills from the five dimensions including metacognitive ability, core thinking ability, thinking process, creative thinking and critical thinking. And based on this, the evaluation system and scale of primary school students' intellectual skills were developed as shown in Fig. 1.

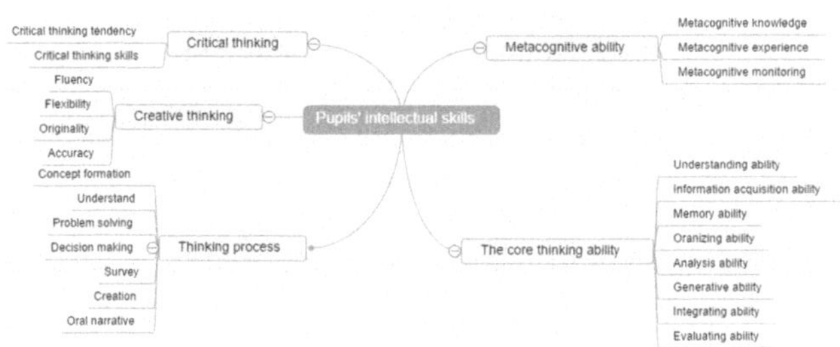

Fig. 1. Intellectual skills evaluation index system of pupils

In order to examine tests' effectiveness and reliability, we have been applied it into trial testing. Besides, we revised the system for evaluation index according to the result of examination. We chose 138 students in random respectively from the experimental primary school grade four, five, six at Panyu District, Guangzhou. Finally, we gained 131 effective reports.

The analysis tools are EXCEl2016, SPSS21.0, AMOS21.0. This research adopts Cronbach's alpha to examine the reliability of index system. Then the results show that the scale has good reliability because the five dimensions' sub-scales of Cronbach's alpha are between 0.658 to 0.837, and the coefficient of full scale's internal consistency is 0.956 (>0.9).

Furthermore, we via AMOS measure structure validity of the questionnaire that has been examined by confirmatory factor analysis. The Fitting index of the measurement model as shown in Table 1.

Table 1. Fitting index of the measurement model

RM-SEA	GFI	NFI	CFI	IFI
0.072	0.931	0.924	0.922	0.940

It is generally believed that when the RM-SEA below 0.08, GFI, NFI, CFI and IFI above 0.9, the fitting index of the measurement model is good. The table shows that structure validity of the scale is good because the fitting index of the measurement model meets the conditions. As a result, the index system can be used to measure pupils' intellectual skills.

4.2 Design of the ISA

The design of the ISA in this research is based on APP Inventor. As a result, the features of this program have been taken into account during the design phrase. The design consists of three parts: systematic framework design, interface design and logic function design.

4.2.1 Design of Systematic Framework

Basing on the analysis of functional need, the systematic framework, as shown in Fig. 2, involves five parts: system administration, elemental information administration, testing database administration, reasoning mechanism administration and result administration.

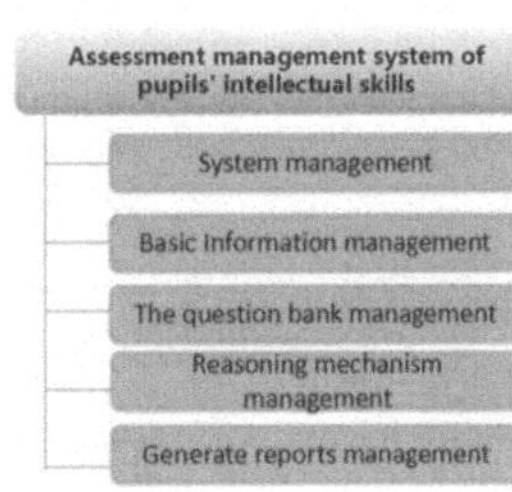

Fig. 2. System framework of ISA

Testing questions in the database are designed based on the evaluation index of Pupils' intellectual skills. The content is about basic information and skills assessment, which is tested in the form of multiple choice questions. There are five choices to each evaluation question, the design of which is inspired by the typical five-level Likert-type scale. Every item is assigned with different values. For example, in the test of metacognitive ability, five choices are provided in the range started from "strongly disagree" to "strongly agree" with respective values assigned from 1 to 5. as shown in Table 2.

Table 2. Design of Metacognitive ability test

Indicators dimension	The test subject	Subject options
Metacognitive ability	When I am in a new lesson, I often know what is the main content to learn.	◎strongly agree ◎a little agree ◎generally agree ◎a little disagree ◎strongly disagree
	When I am to learn, I will know what method by learning.	◎strongly agree ◎a little agree ◎generally agree ◎a little disagree ◎strongly disagree
	……	……

Since the number of evaluation index in each dimension of evaluation varies, the reasoning mechanism requires the scores achieved in each dimension to be standardized, making sure that every dimension has the same total grade. The result is presented in a visualized form of radar chart. The result interface can be referred to in Fig. 4.

According to the analysis of users' need, the ISA's target users, students and teachers, are offered with different design of work flow, which is showed in Fig. 3.

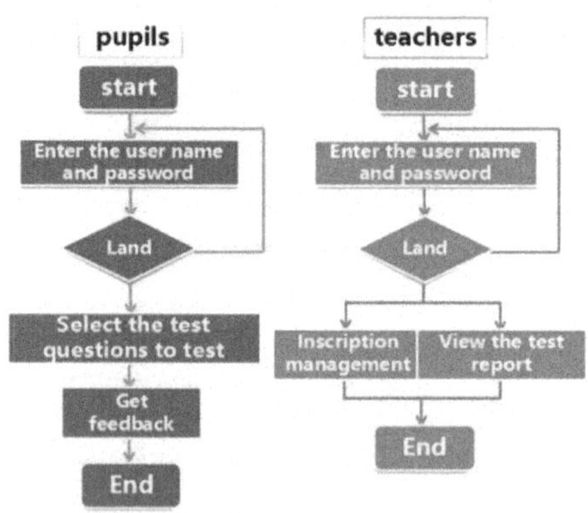

Fig. 3. Business flowchart of users

4.2.2 Design of Interface

Since the target user of ISA is pupils, quite a few cartoon-style designs are applied in the interface to cater to their interest. There are totally five screens in the interface, which are the welcome page, log-in page, question page, result page and ending page. The welcome page is designed in the form of power-on animation. Log-in page is for the users to input their accounts and log in. The question page is for the testing, which is showed in Fig. 4. The result page which is showed in Fig. 4 applies the visualized form of radar chart. The ending page is like the power-off animation with the information of the designer and copyright.

1. The log-in page 2. The question page 3.The result page

Fig. 4. A part of interface of ISA

4.2.3 Design of Logic Function

The projecting of an Android ISA on APP Inventor2 chiefly consists of two tasks, interface design and l blocks edit. After dragging the needed components and drop it to the screen and arranging their locations, it is time to switch to the blocks edit part where respective function is assigned to the components to make sure it works as commanded. The chief logic functions of the ISA include user administration (that is, to check the qualification of a user) and test evaluation.

(1) User Administration
The log-in page comes after the welcome page. According to the requirement of the system, the users should include both teachers and students. The pair of users are connected based on the design that one teacher is in charge of one teaching class. That is to say, a teacher can check out the testing results of all the students in a class. With this setting, screen initialization will be carried out first and then tags, buttons, background color and cartoon title will be dragged out and designated. The function of buttons will then be attached in the Blocks Editor, including log-in button and register button. Part of the design is showed in Fig. 5.

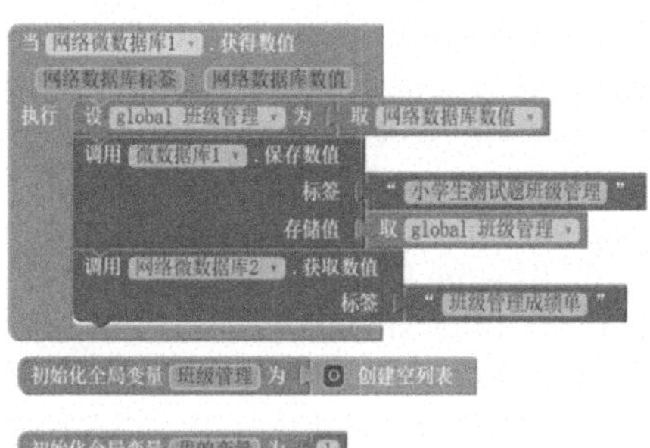

Fig. 5. Part of the logic function design

(2) Test Evaluation
As to the evaluation function, firstly, display all the components of the question page in the same screen. Secondly, define the screen content, set up tables, tags and check box, etc. Thirdly, decide the background color of the interface, and finally, initialize all the needed components. Part of the process of setting the interface components is showed in Fig. 5.

5 Test and Effect of the ISA

5.1 Test of the ISA

After finishing the logic function design, deliver the program package in the form of apk to the cloud server to get the output of APP and QR code for download. Then scan the code and install it in a smart phone with the help of MIT AI2 Companion. Conduct an experience test according to the functional design of the ISA. The result proves that the system works stably and functionally well.

ISA was then tested by the second class of Grade 5th in the Guangzhou Panyu Experimental Primary School, China. The class is in a e-schoolbag project and its system, Android, satisfies the system requirement of the ISA. The testing result shows that the ISA works functionally well with smooth screen switching and ideal display effect. Almost every tag can successfully carry out the tasks while react in a considerably fast speed. To conclude, the ISA program match the need of users as expected and the testing process is well conducted.

5.2 Analysis of the Acceptability and Satisfaction Degree of User

The design of the survey scale is based on the framework of UTAUT, which is proved to be satisfying in the acceptability tests. [22] The framework involves four core factors, Performance Expectancy, Effort Expectancy, Social Influence, Facilitating Conditions, with the complement of two others, Attitude toward Using Technology and Behavioral Intention to Use the System.

The research takes the form of questionnaire survey with 138 pieces delivered and 130 pieces received. The overall response rate is 94.2%. Among them, 128 pieces are valid, accounting for 92.7% of all. To check up the credibility of the questionnaire, Cronbach α coefficient in SPSS was used and the score was 0.733, which meant that it was of high credibility. The questionnaire was measured with a five-point Likert-type scale ranging from “strongly disagree (−2)” to “strongly agree (2)” [23]. The data was processed by the formula of two-dimensional scale: $Fi = \Sigma ajnij/2\,N$ is display in Table 3.

The statistics outcome shows that the Fi score for each category is $Fi > 0$, which means that the students are overall satisfied with the ISA. However, the score to the category that “the ISA offers effective advices” is $0 < Fi < 0.5$, which is lower than others. It seems that the advices offered in the ISA still need to be improved.

Table 3. Acceptability and user satisfaction degree of the ISA

Aspects	Questions	Value
Performance expectancy	1. The test result of the ISA is relatively scientific	0.68
	2. The ISA offers effective advices	0.48
Effort expectancy	3. The interface of the ISA is enjoyable and comfortable	0.64
	4. The ISA is easy to use for me	0.84
Personal attitude	5. I think it necessary to use the ISA regularly to do the test	0.59
	6. The ISA increases the pleasure of study	0.84
Behavior intention	7. I like using the ISA	0.66
	8. I expect to use the ISA continuously in the future	0.72

5.3 The Practical Design of the ISA

Under the ubiquitous learning condition, the app is designed to evaluate pupils' intellectual skills. And our research is to design the instructional applications of the ISA.

(1) under the ubiquitous learning condition, the students are required by teacher to download and install the ISA. Then, given a period of time, students accomplish the evaluation under the relaxed condition. After that, ISA will timely give the result and targeted suggestions to the students.
(2) Students can improve the intellectual skills according to the suggestions. Besides, teachers can train in a targeted way for each student according to the evaluation result.
(3) After a period of time, students can do the evaluation again under the ubiquitous learning condition to examine the promotion effect.

6 Conclusions

This research puts forward the index system for the pupils' intellectual skills through the literature research. And we establish the scale for evaluation of students' intellectual skills. Such research expands the theories about pupils' intellectual skills. Moreover, on the basis of this evaluation index system and App investor, our research designs ISA for evaluation of students' intellectual skills, and analyses the acceptability and user satisfaction degree of the ISA. ISA is not only conducive for teachers to evaluate the pupils' intellectual skills under the ubiquitous learning condition, but also provides a certain significant reference to others' evaluation App.

References

1. Jiang, H.: Promoting ubiquitous learning for anyone, at anytime and anywhere: a practice of SOU serving the construction of a learning city. J. Open Educ. Res. **4**, 24–30 (2014)
2. Gagné, R.M.: Conditions of learning, 227–265 (1970)
3. Gal'perin, P.Y.: Study of the intellectual development of the child. J. Russ. East Eur. Psychol. **27**(33), 26–44 (1987)

4. Feng, Z.L.: Structured and Targeted Teaching Psychology Principle. Beijing Normal University Press, Beijing (1998)
5. Johnson, S.D.: Learning technological concepts and developing intellectual skills. Int. J. Technol. Des. Educ. **7**(1), 161–180 (1997)
6. Xie, Y.R., et al.: Research on training of pupils' scientific inquiry intellectual skills in smart learning environment. J. Open Educ. Res. **22**(2), 104–112 (2016)
7. Marzano, R.J.: Dimensions of THINKING: A Framework for Curriculum and Instruction, p. 175 (1988)
8. Punturat, S., Suwannoi, P., Ketchatturat, J.: Intellectual skills assessment for the teacher students at the faculty of education, Khon Kaen university. Procedia Soc. Behav. Sci. **116**, 1704–1708 (2014)
9. Paul, R., Elder, L.: Critical Thinking: Tools for Taking Charge of Your Professional and Personal Life. Prentice Hall, Upper Saddle River (2011). Sony Reader
10. Li, J.Z.: Research on the development of the sports college students' teaching ability and intellectual skill training. Inner Mongolia Sports Technol. 91–94 (2016)
11. Zhu, X.: Research on Chemical Intellectual Skills Training Junior High School Students. Capital Normal University (2008)
12. Ma, Z.Y.: The Research on Developing Student's' Intellectual Skills of Flash Animation Making under the Information Technology Environment. South China Normal University (2010)
13. Vagale, V., Niedrite, L.: Intellectual ability data obtaining and processing for e-learning system adaptation. In: Niedrite, L., Strazdina, R., Wangler, B. (eds.) BIR 2011. LNBIP, vol. 106, pp. 117–129. Springer, Heidelberg (2012). doi:10.1007/978-3-642-29231-6_10
14. Flavell, J.H.: Metacognition and cognitive monitoring: a new area of cognitive-develop intellectual inquiry. J. Am. Psychol. **34**(10), 906–911 (1979)
15. Dong, Q.: The Theory of Metacognition. J. Beijing Normal Univ. **01**, 68–74 (1989)
16. Huang, X.: The properties, structure and characteristics of learning strategies. J. East China Norm. Univ. **04**, 85–92 (1990)
17. Cao, J.C.: Experimental study on professional sports in basketball teaching "interaction" intellectual sills teaching. J. Shanghai Sports Inst. **27**(6), 114–115 (2003)
18. Wang, Z.M., Wang, H.: Pay attention to intellectual skills smart talent cultivation. J. Occup. Circle **3**, 44 (2007)
19. Royer, J.M., Cisero, C.A., Carlo, M.S.: Techniques and procedures for assessing cognitive skills. J. Rev. Educ. Res. **63**(2), 201–243 (1993)
20. Marzano, R.J.: Dimensions of Thinking: A Framework for Curriculum and Instruction. The Association for Supervision and Curriculum Development, 125 N. West St., Alexandria, VA 22314-2798 (1988)
21. Torrance, E.P.: Creativity testing in education. Creative Child Adult Q. **1**, 136–148 (1976)
22. Venkatesh, V., Morris, M.G., Davis, G.B., et al.: User acceptance of information technology: toward a unified view. J. Mis. Q. **27**(3), 425–478 (2003)
23. Ni, M., Kwok, L.-f., Zhen, L., Xie, Y., Long, H., Zheng, X., Li, W.: A study of an e-schoolbag supporting flipped classroom model for junior mathematics review class. In: Cheung, S.K.S., Kwok, L.-f., Yang, H., Fong, J., Kwan, R. (eds.) ICHL 2015. LNCS, vol. 9167, pp. 243–254. Springer, Cham (2015). doi:10.1007/978-3-319-20621-9_20

Assessment for Blended Learning

Online Learning Activity Index (OLAI) and Its Application for Adaptive Learning

Jiyou Jia[1(✉)] and Yueyang Yu[2]

[1] Graduate School of Education, Peking University, Beijing 100871, China
jjy@pku.edu.cn

[2] Department of Computer Science, Beijing Foreign Studies University, Beijing 100089, China
yuyueyang@bfsu.edu.cn

Abstract. We propose a model, Learning Activity Index (LAI) to describe learners' learning activities comprising three components, i.e., speed, quality and quantity. We then concretize this model into online learning and propose the Online Learning Activity Index (OLAI). With the example of a web-based mathematics learning system, OLAI can be calculated by the summarization of standardized and dimensionless speed, quality and quantity. So OLAI is also a dimensionless value and can comprehensively describe the learner's online learning behavior. We use OLAIMAA (OLAI Mean of All Activities) to measure one learner's online learning activities during a certain period on average and OLAISAA (OLAI Sum of All Activities) to measure those from a summative perspective. Similarly, the performance of a group, such as a class or a school, can also be described by those indexes. Furthermore, we design the personalized instructional strategies adaptive to the learner's OLAI and the OLAI of the learning group. The instructional strategies include the feedback corresponding to numerical intervals of three components of OLAI, bonus based on longitudinal comparison with the learner's own activity profile, bonus based on locally horizontal comparison with learner's classmates or partners in the same online group, and bonus based on globally horizontal comparison with all learners in the same system. We suggest that OLAI should be taken into consideration for the design of online learning platforms or course management system, and be referred as a basic approach to individualized instruction by both teachers and parents.

Keywords: Learning analytics · Learning activity index · Online learning activity index · Mathematics · Adaptive learning

1 Introduction

The past few years have witnessed a rapid growth of online learning, and specially, MOOCs (Massive Open Online Courses). Subsequently, online learning activity analysis has become one of the hottest issues [1, 2]. However, the definitions of learning activity and online learning activity are still ambiguous. In a traditional learning environment, the learning activity of a student generally consists of three parts: before-class activity, in-class activity, and after-class activity. Before class, students are

S.K.S. Cheung et al. (Eds.): ICBL 2017, LNCS 10309, pp. 213–224, 2017.
DOI: 10.1007/978-3-319-59360-9_19

expected to preview the work, such as finishing readings and preliminary exercises. During class, students are supposed to listen, think, answer questions, complete quiz, join discussions and attend periodical exams. After class, students need to do homework and review the work.

Online learning activities are often interpreted as activities in online learning context, including browsing pages, watching videos, viewing documents, writing online quizzes or tests, posting in forums, submitting homework and evaluating the peers. Among all the activities, online quiz may be the most widespread-used one, and generally consists of a set of questions in forms such as multiple-choices and fill-in-the-blanks. Because the answers to multiple-choices and fill-in-the-blanks questions are predefined, the learner can instantly get a score and corresponding feedbacks from the platform, just after submitting the answers. Most platforms record learners' quizzing data, such as the answers they submitted, the time they spent, and their attempts on the questions. Those data can be reviewed by the students, the teachers or the parents later. Those data can be analyzed and can play a fundamental role in the study of online learning activity.

2 Related Work

As an emerging and interdisciplinary area, learning activity analysis requires expertise not only from education, but also from learning science and data mining [3, 4]. Many researchers have focused on the analysis of learning data, in an effort to understand its importance and implication to education. Mukala et al. [4] employ process mining techniques on MOOC data to analyze the underlying learning process, which helps understand the learning processes students follow, the timing of the processes and the deviation from an ideal process. Arnold and Pistilli [5] point out that with meaningful feedbacks produced by Learning Analytics, Course Signals (CS) can increase students' success in academic work. Ren et al. [6] use Multi-Regression Models to identify key features that are related with the study habits and learning behaviors of students.

However, there is a deficiency of existing research literature on quantitative methods to describe online learning activity including online quizzes. This paper thereby attempts to propose the Learning Activity Index (LAI) and Online Learning Activity Index (OLAI) model, a new viewpoint to present references.

3 Three Dimensions of Learning Activity

Assessment on learning activity falls under three dimensions, i.e. adequacy, efficiency and accuracy. To achieve adequacy, learners should complete enough activities to reach learning goals; to efficiency, learners should master the expected skills; to accuracy, learners should complete activities with fair quality. For example, if a student has finished enough homework to understand what is taught in class with good quality represented by high scores at a well-timed pace, then it is not hard to predict this student's success on the subject.

Therefore, we propose an index, LAI (Learning Activity Index), to combine and quantify the three dimensions, adequacy, efficiency and accuracy, to better depict students' learning activity, which works similarly as BMI (Body Mass Index). BMI is the weight in kilograms divided by the square of the height in meters, to measure the degree of body fat, indicating the according nutritional status. It can offer a comprehensive assessment from both weight and height for body figure and is thus relatively reliable.

In a traditional learning environment, such as a classroom, the accuracy and adequacy of students' learning activities are accessible to teachers. The adequacy is indicated by the numbers of activities the students have completed, and the accuracy is indicated by the correctness rate. But the efficiency is often lack of evidence, because it is difficult for the teachers to record every student's time spent on the learning activities, for example, writing the quizzes. Thus the LAI within traditional learning environment is difficult to be calculated.

By comparison, the online learning platforms offer a more convenient way to assess all three dimensions by recording the necessary information more completely and systematically than any human labor. Thus the online version of LAI, OLAI (Online Learning Activity Index), can be defined and calculated precisely through using the online data of the learners. In the following sections we will exemplify the OLAI formula with an interactive web-based online mathematics learning system.

4 OLAI Formula of an Online Mathematics Learning System

"Lexue 100" (Happy Learning for 100 Points, http://www.lexue100.com) is a web-based interactive learning system for school mathematics, developed by Beijing Lexue 100 Online Education Co., Ltd. with 16-year practice in multimedia education software and blended learning. A large number of corresponding quizzes are designed for the different versions of mathematics textbooks that are used in different provinces and metropolis in China. Each quiz is composed of a series of gap-filling or single-choice questions. So the question's standard answer is predefined and can be compared with the user's trial answer. The quiz score and feedback are instantly provided to the user, as soon as he or she submits the trial answers. Answering quizzes is the main learning activity in this system. Users are allowed to pass only if every answer gets right, meaning that if the first try is wrong, they will have to try again until the answer hits the point.

Based on behaviorism and other learning theories, three learning strategies are adopted by this system: Individualized Adaptation, Incremental Mastery and Interactive Discovery. According to the system's website, they are defined as the following: "Individualized adaptation means that every student can select the quizzes according to his or her own demand. Incremental mastery means that in every quiz, the students should correctly answer every composing question in the sequence, otherwise he or she cannot go on to answer next question. Interactive discovery means that the student can ask for help from the online teaching assistant by answering difficult questions."

On the server backend, for each completed quiz activity of every learner, the system generates a record for this quiz activity, including usetime (the time spent on the whole test, measured by seconds), difference (the amount of time ahead of or behind the dimension time, which is already computed by the system for each distinct test, measured by seconds, positive for shorter than the dimension time and negative for longer), and result (details of a learner's answers to this test). After scrutinizing the result data, we retrieve further information about the quiz: question_number (count of the questions), wrongs (count of the questions in which the user has tried more than once), tries (count of the wrong attempts in all questions), and guesses (the count of the questions in which the user has tried more than three times. A user may guess the right answer. Since most questions in the system are multiple choices with 4 options, we set the default threshold as 3. The threshold can be set other values correspond to other kinds of questions.)

Based on the information above, we quantify the dimensions of OLAI, i.e. efficiency, accuracy, adequacy into values called speed, quality, and quantity respectively.

4.1 Speed

The speed is inversely proportional to the time spent on completing an activity. A time frame with a start threshold and an end threshold is allowed for a specific activity. If one learner completes the activity within the time frame, we normally describe the completion speed as normal. If the learner completes the activity ahead of the time frame, we can define the difference from the actual use time to the start threshold of the frame as positive, and the difference from the end threshold of the frame to the actual use time as negative. The dimensionless speed for completing one learning activity can be defined as the following formula.

$$\text{Speed} = \text{difference} \;/\; (\text{usetime} + \text{difference})$$

whereas usetime is the time a user spends on a certain activity recorded by machine, and difference is the deviation, that is, the time ahead of (with a positive value) or behind (with a negative value) the time frame. Both parameters are provided by the learning platform.

For example, given one online quiz with a time frame [200 s, 400 s],

When the learner No. 1 registers 100 s on the quiz, the difference is +100 s, and the speed is calculated by speed1 = 100/(100 + 100) = 0.5.

When the learner No. 2 spends 300 s on the quiz, within the time frame, the difference is 0, then the speed is calculated by speed2 = 0/(300 + 0) = 0.

When the learner No. 3 spends 500 s on the test, the difference is −100 s, and the speed is calculated by speed3 = −100/(500−100) = −0.25.

Those calculation examples demonstrate that the bigger the speed value is, the more efficiently the learner completes the activity. Two extreme cases are that speed is 1, meaning null second is spent on the activity, and speed is an infinite negative number, meaning the user never completes the activity. The speed's value is limited to the frame $(-\infty, 1]$.

4.2 Quality

Results of a learning activity, especially test scores, are often considered as significant evidence to assess the accuracy of completing this activity. However, the score can be affected by many chance factors and often hide important process details, so it alone is insufficient to reflect the real quality of users' learning activity. For example, when unfamiliar with a multiple-choice question, the user is prone to guess the answers for many times, what is not encouraged for effective learning. Therefore, we define the quality as follows:

$$\text{quality} = (\text{question\_number} - \text{guesses})/(\text{question\_number} + \text{tries}).$$

As mentioned above, when a user tries more than once on a question, the question will be flagged as wrong and if the times of attempts outnumber three, it will further be flagged as guess. In the formula, "question_number − guesses" refers to the number of questions that are not flagged as guess; "question_number + tries" refers to the total times of a user confirming an answer, whether right or wrong.

For example, assuming that a test consists of 10 questions, thus question_ number = 10.

Given guesses = 0, tries = 10, we can calculate quality by quality = 10/ (10 + 10) = 0.5, meaning none has been flagged as guess but at least four questions are flagged as wrong.

The best case is when a user completes the whole quiz without any mistake, that is, tries = 0, guesses = 0, then we get the quality of 100%, while the worst case of quality, 0, is produced by a user who tries over three times on each question. Generally, the bigger the quality is, the better the result of this quiz activity is. The quality's value is limited in the frame [0, 1].

4.3 Quantity

A learning activity is composed of sub tasks. For example, a quiz activity is composed of a number of questions. Answering one question means one interaction between the learner and the quiz. Granularity refers to the amount of interactions required of learners between opportunities to interact. The larger the granularity of an online quiz, the more interactions between the user and the system are required in the quiz, and more details should be considered to answer the whole quiz. Vanlehn demonstrated that as the granularity of an intelligent tutoring system increases, the system's effectiveness increases [7]. Therefore the quantity of a learning activity should be proportional to the number of sub tasks of the activity, in the case of a quiz, to the number of questions which should be answered. In order to get a dimensionless value for the adequacy, we define the quality of a quiz as the following:

$$\text{quantity} = \text{question\_number}/\text{mean\_question\_number},$$

where the question_number is the number of questions in the quiz, and the mean_ question_number is the average question number of all quizzes which the learners have written with the speed greater than null and the quality equal to 100%. In the "Lexue 100" mathematics online course, the mean_question_number between Sept. 1st 2013 and May 5th, 2016 equals 26.7.

The mean_question_number can also be defined by other ways, for example, can be the average question number of all quizzes in a course.

The quantity's value is limited to the frame (0, Qmax], where QMax is the maximum quality of a given online course.

4.4 Online Learning Activity Index (OLAI)

Considering that all the three features above are dimensionless real numbers, we sum the three values as the value of the online learning activity index (OLAI) for a completed online activity such as a quiz as follows:

$$\mathrm{OLAI} = \ \mathrm{speed} + \mathrm{quality} + \mathrm{quantity}$$

It is expected that a bigger OLAI represents a better overall and comprehensive performance consisting of three dimensions, namely adequacy, efficiency and accuracy, because three dimensions may interrelate to each other, and a single one cannot indicate the overall performance.

A single OLAI only describes one learning activity of a learner on completing one quiz. In order to depict one learner's long-time performance, a mean or a summary of all the learner's activities during a certain period, for example, one term or one school year, can be further calculated. Therefore, we define two other significant concepts, OLAIMAA (OLAI Mean of All Activities), the mean values of all OLAIs of one learner for a certain period, and OLAISAA (OLAI Sum of All Activities), the sum of all OLAIs of one learner for a certain period. To some degree, OLAIMAA denotes the average performance of one learner, while OLAISAA denotes the accumulative achievements of the learner.

For each of the three components of OLAI, the average and cumulative performance can also be calculated for a certain period with the following concepts: speedMAA (speed mean of All Activities), speedSAA (speed Sum of All Activities), qualityMAA (quality mean of All Activities), qualitySAA (quality Sum of All Activities), quantityMAA (quantity mean of All Activities) and quantitySAA (quantity Sum of All Activities).

OLAI is designed for reusability and applicability. Not only individual analysis but also collective analysis can use OLAI to capture learners' activity performance. In order to describe the learning activity of a group during a period, such a class or a school, we further define four concepts: OLAIMAP, OLAISAP, OLAIMAAAP, and OLAISAAAP.

OLAIMAP (OLAI Mean of All Participants) is the mean value of all learners within a certain group for a certain activity, and denotes the average performance of all group members for a specific activity.

OLAISAP (OLAI Sum of All Participants) is the sum value of all learners within a certain group for a certain activity, and denotes the summative performance of all group members for a specific activity.

OLAIMAAAP (OLAI Mean of All Activities of All Participants) is the mean value of OLAIMAA of all learners within a certain group, and denotes the average performance of all activities of all group members during a period.

OLAISAAAP (OLAI Sum of All Activities of All Participants) is the sum of OLAISAA of all learners within a certain group, and denotes the accumulative achievements of the group.

5 The Adaptive Learning Bonus System Based on OLAI

As the OLAI depicts the accuracy, adequacy and efficiency of online learners' performance, instructional strategy including reward system and functional interface adaptive to the learner's OLAI can be designed to facilitate the learner's individualized learning. The reward can be in the form of credits or virtual currency.

After one learner completes one learning activity, the online system can calculate the values of three components and the value of OLAI for this activity, the OLAISAA and OLAIMAA for already completed activities. Each completed activity is rewarded proportionally to the OLAI value of the learner. If the learner completes the same activity for many times, only the highest OLAI will be rewarded. The "Many Attempts, Highest Adopted" mechanism is similar to the ordinary examination system in schools, and is aimed to encourage the learner to efficiently complete one quiz, not to repeat the same quiz only for obtaining rewards. Furthermore, the system can also evaluate the learner's performance at four different levels as follows.

5.1 Level 1: The Feedback Corresponding to Numerical Intervals of Three Components of OLAI

The three components of OLAI, i.e. speed, quality and quantity, can be divided different frames as in Table 1. The speed can be divided into three intervals: high within [0.5, 1], medium within [0, 0.5], and low within $(-\infty, 0]$. The quality can be divided into two intervals: high within [0.5, 1], and low within [0, 0.5]. The quantity can be divided into 3 intervals: high within [1, Qmax], medium within [0.5, 1], and low within [0, 0.5], where Qmax is possible maximum value of the quantity in an online system. Therefore the combination of those three intervals counts 18. Every combination represents one status of the learner for one learning activity, and requires diverse instructional feedback.

5.2 Level 2: Bonus Based on Longitudinal Comparison with the Learner's Own Activity Profile

If the learner in the latest activity achieves the best performance in the learning history, i.e. obtains the highest OLAI value, the bonus for "Personal Best Performance" should

Table 1. Interval combinations of the values of three components of OLAI and its pedagogical implication

No.	Speed Quality Quantity	OLAI	Learning performance	Feedback
1	[0.5, 1] high [0.5, 1] high [1, Qmax] high	[2, Qmax + 2]	Best	Highest reward
2	[0.5, 1] high [0.5, 1] high [0.5, 1] medium	[1.5, 3]	Very good	Higher reward
3	[0.5, 1] high [0.5, 1] high [0, 0.5] low	[1, 2.5]	Good, but fewer questions are answered	Suggest to do more difficult quiz
4	[0.5, 1] high [0, 0.5] low [1, Qmax] high	[1.5, Qmax + 1.5]	Good, but the correctness should be improved	Suggest to do the quiz more carefully, or to do easier quiz
5	[0.5, 1] high [0, 0.5] low [0.5, 1] medium	[1, 2.5]	Not good	Suggest to do the quiz more carefully to get better accuracy
6	[0.5, 1] high [0, 0.5] low [0, 0.5] low	[0.5, 2]	Poor	Suggest to do the quiz more carefully
7	[0, 0.5] medium [0.5, 1] high [1, Qmax] high	[1.5, Qmax + 1.5]	Very Good	Suggest to improve the speed, or do easier quiz
8	[0, 0.5] medium [0.5, 1] high [0.5, 1] medium	[1, 2.5]	Good	Suggest to improve the speed
9	[0, 0.5] medium [0.5, 1] high [0, 0.5] low	[0.5, 2]	Not bad	Suggest to improve the speed and do more difficult quiz
10	[0, 0.5] medium [0, 0.5] low [1, Qmax] high	[1, 1 + Qmax]	Word hard to attempt the difficult quiz	Suggest to do easier quiz
11	[0, 0.5] medium [0, 0.5] low [0.5, 1] medium	[0.5, 2]	Ordinary	Suggest to improve the correctness
12	[0, 0.5] medium [0, 0.5] low [0, 0.5] low	[0, 1.5]	Ordinary	Suggest to improve the correctness and difficulty
13	(−∞, 0] low [0.5, 1] high [1, Qmax] high	(−∞, 1 + Qmax]	Pretty good	Suggest to improve the speed, or be concentrated on learning

(*continued*)

Table 1. (*continued*)

No.	Speed Quality Quantity	OLAI	Learning performance	Feedback
14	(−∞, 0] low [0.5, 1] high [0.5, 1] medium	(−∞, 2]	Good	Suggest to improve the speed, or be concentrated on learning
15	(−∞, 0] low [0.5, 1] high [0, 0.5] low	(−∞, 1.5]	Good	Suggest to improve the speed, or be concentrated on learning, or to improve the difficulty
16	(−∞, 0] low [0, 0.5] low [1, Qmax] high	[−∞, 0.5 + QMax]	Not good	Suggest to do easier quiz and to improve the quality and speed
17	(−∞, 0] low [0, 0.5] low [0.5, 1] medium	[−∞, 1.5]	Not good	Suggest to improve the quality and speed and to get help from teachers
18	(−∞, 0] low [0, 0.5] low [0, 0.5] medium	[−∞, 1]	Worst	Suggest to improve the quality and speed and to get help from teachers

be rewarded to the learner. Similarly, the bonus for "Personal Highest Speed", "Personal Highest Quality", or "Personal Highest Quantity" should be rewarded if the learner achieves highest value of speed, quality or quantity in his or her own activity history. Otherwise, if the OLAI this time does not achieve the best historical value, but is just higher than that in previous activity, the bonus for "Overall Step Progress" should also be rewarded. The bonus for "Speed Step Progress", "Quality Step Progress", or "Quantity Step Progress" should be rewarded if the learner achieves higher value of speed, quality or quantity than that in his or her previous activity.

If the OLAI this time is higher than the learner's OLAIMAA in the history, or in other words, the learner improves his or her mean performance after completing this activity, the bonus for "Personal Overall Progress" should be rewarded. Similarly, the bonus for "Personal Speed Progress", "Personal Quality Progress", or "Personal Quantity Progress" should be rewarded if the learner achieves higher value of speed, quality or quantity than the average value in his or her learning history.

5.3 Level 3: Bonus Based on Locally Horizontal Comparison with the Learner's Classmates or Partners in the Same Online Groups

If the learner in the latest activity obtains the highest OLAI value among all the classmates or learning partner in the same group who have completed the same activity, the bonus for "Class Activity Best Performance" for this activity can be rewarded to this learner. Similarly, the bonus for "Class Activity Highest Speed", "Class Activity

Highest Quality", or "Class Activity Highest Quantity" should be rewarded if the learner achieves highest value of speed, quality or quantity among the classmates or learning partners in the same activity.

Otherwise, if the OLAI this time does not achieve the best horizontal value, but is higher than the previous OLAIMAP of the group members in that activity, or in other words, this learner contributes to the average performance improvement of the whole group, the bonus for "Class Activity Performance Contribution" should be rewarded. The bonus for "Class Activity Speed Contribution", "Class Activity Quality Contribution", or "Class Activity Quantity Contribution" should be rewarded if the learner achieves higher value of speed, quality or quantity than the average value in the whole class or group.

If the learner after completing the latest activity obtains the highest OLAIMAA value among all the classmates or learning partner in the same group, the bonus for "Class Best Average Performance" can be rewarded to this learner. Similarly, the bonus for "Class Best Average Speed", "Class Best Average Quality", or "Class Best Average Quantity" should be rewarded if the learner achieves highest mean value of speed, quality or quantity among the classmates or learning partners in all activities.

Otherwise, if the OLAIMAA this time does not achieve the best horizontal value, but is higher than the OLAIMAAAP of all group members, or in other words, this learner contributes to the average performance improvement of the whole group, the bonus for "Class Average Performance Contribution" should be rewarded. The bonus for "Class Average Speed Contribution", "Class Average Quality Contribution", or "Class Average Quantity Contribution" should be rewarded if the learner achieves higher mean value of speed, quality or quantity than the average value in the whole class or group.

5.4 Level 4: Globally Horizontal Comparison with All Learners in the System

If the learner in the latest activity obtains the highest OLAI value among all the learners in the system who have completed the same activity, the bonus for "Globally Activity Best Performance" for this activity can be rewarded to this learner. Similarly, the bonus for "Globally Activity Highest Speed", "Globally Activity Highest Quality", or "Globally Activity Highest Quantity" should be rewarded if the learner achieves highest value of speed, quality or quantity among all learners in the system.

Otherwise, if the OLAI this time does not achieve the best horizontal value, but is higher than the OLAIMAP of all learners in the system in that activity, or in other words, this learner contributes to the average performance improvement of all learners in the system, the bonus for "Globally Activity Performance Contribution" should be rewarded. The bonus for "Globally Activity Speed Contribution", "Globally Activity Quality Contribution", or "Globally Activity Quantity Contribution" should be rewarded if the learner achieves higher value of speed, quality or quantity than the average value of all learners in the system.

If the learner after completing the latest activity obtains the highest OLAIMAA value among all learners in the system in all activities, the bonus for "Globally Best

Average Performance" can be rewarded to this learner. Similarly, the bonus for "Globally Best Average Speed", "Globally Best Average Quality", or "Globally Best Average Quantity" should be rewarded if the learner achieves highest mean value of speed, quality or quantity among all learners in the system in all activities.

Otherwise, if the OLAIMAA this time does not achieve the best horizontal value, but is higher than the OLAIMAAAP of all learners in the system, or in other words, this learner contributes to the average performance improvement of all learners in the system, the bonus for "Globally Average Performance Contribution" should be rewarded. The bonus for "Globally Average Speed Contribution", "Globally Average Quality Contribution", or "Globally Average Quantity Contribution" should be rewarded if the learner achieves higher mean value of speed, quality or quantity than the average value of all learners in the system.

5.5 Overall Bonus Adaptive to OLAI

Summarizing all the bonus result at above four levels, the overall bonus can be presented to the learner. This positive bonus system based on longitudinal, locally horizontal and globally horizontal comparison is designed to encourage the learner to keep on surpassing both himself or herself and the other learning mates, but not to punish those retrogressive learners. Moreover, the positive bonus system presents bonus reward and feedbacks corresponding to both the learner's individual activity performance and the collective performance of the group the learner belongs to, and thus is not individualized and personalized, but also collectively.

6 Conclusion and Future Work

In this work, we start out with analyzing learners' learning activity in three dimensions, namely speed, quality and quantity. Then based on them, we propose a model, Learning Activity Index (LAI) and its online version–Online Learning Activity Index (OLAI), to describe learning activities in a quantitative approach. We concretize the OLAI model with a web-based mathematics instruction system "Lexue 100" by defining the calculation formula for three components speed, quality and quantity. The OLAI value is the sum of the three dimensionless values, and can be used to describe the performance of a learner who completes one learning activity such as a quiz.

For a certain activity, OLAIMAP (OLAI Mean of All Participants) denotes the average learning performance of all learners, and OLAISAP (OLAI Sum of All Participants) denotes the accumulative achievements of all learners. For a certain period, OLAIMAA (OLAI Mean of All Activities) of a learner denotes the average learning performance, and OLAISAA (OLAI Sum of All Activities) denotes the accumulative achievements of the learner. OLAIMAAAP (OLAI Mean of All Activities of All Participants) denotes the average learning performance of all group members, and OLAISAAAP (OLAI Sum of All Activities of All Participants) denotes the accumulative performance of all group members.

Individualized or personalized instruction adapted to students' learning activities and learning performance is of great theoretical and practical values. But it is far studied how to implement adaptive personalized instruction. We start from the OLAI definition and calculation formula with the example of a web-based mathematics learning system "Lexue 100", and design the personalized instructional strategies corresponding to the learner's OLAI and the OLAI of the learning group. The adaptive instructional strategies include the feedback corresponding to numerical intervals of three components of OLAI, bonus based on longitudinal comparison with the learner's own activity profile, bonus based on locally horizontal comparison with learner's classmates or partners in the same online group, and bonus based on globally horizontal comparison with all learners in the same system.

We suggest that OLAI should be taken into consideration for the design of online learning platforms or course management system, and be referred as a basic approach to individualized instruction by both teachers and parents. Of course the calculation of the three components of efficiency, accuracy and adequacy for other activities different from the popular quiz activity should be explored in depth.

In the future, we will seek to implement the instructional strategies designed in this paper adaptive to the learner's activity represented by OLAI, and to evaluate its pedagogical effect through robust empirical research such as quasi-experiments.

Acknowledgement. This research is supported by the project, "Lexue 100, Smart Education", of Beijing Lexue 100 Online Education Co., Ltd. The authors thank also all the teachers and students who have participated in the project.

References

1. Elbadrawy, A., Polyzou, A., Ren, Z., Sweeney, M., Karypis, G., Rangwala, H.: Predicting student performance using personalized analytics. IEEE Comput. **49**(4), 61–69 (2016)
2. Moissa, B., Gasparini, I., Kemczinski, A.: A systematic mapping on the learning analytics field and its analysis in the massive open online courses context. Int. J. Distance Educ. Technol. **13**(3), 1–24 (2015)
3. Hughes, G., Dobbins, C.: The utilization of data analysis techniques in predicting student performance in massive open online courses (MOOCs). Res. Pract. Technol. Enhanced Learn. **10**(1), 10–15 (2015)
4. Mukala, P., Buijs, J.C.A.M., van der Aalst, W.M.P.: Exploring students' learning behaviour in moocs using process mining techniques. Technical report, Eindhoven University of Technology, BPM Center Report BPM-15-10 (2015). BPMcenter.org
5. Arnold, K.E., Pistilli, M.D.: Course signals at Purdue: using learning analytics to increase student success. In: Proceedings of the 2nd International Conference on Learning Analytics and Knowledge, pp. 267–270. ACM, April 2012
6. Ren, Z., Rangwala, H., Johri, A.: Predicting performance on MOOC assessments using multi-regression models. arXiv preprint arXiv:1605.02269 (2016)
7. VanLehn, K.: The relative effectiveness of human tutoring, intelligent tutoring systems, and other tutoring systems. Educ. Psychol. **46**(4), 197–221 (2011)

Analysis on the Effect of Knowledge Sharing in Network Learning Space - A Case Study of Teachers' Workshop

Qingtang Liu[1], Hong Wang[1(✉)], and Si Zhang[2]

[1] School of Educational Information Technology, Central China Normal University, Wuhan 430079, Hubei, China
1511821107@qq.com

[2] College of Information Science and Engineering, Hunan First Teachers College, Changsha 410205, Hunan, China

Abstract. During the period of 13th five-year plan, the guideline for education informatization emphasizes on construction of network learning space to promote the reform of learning and teaching methods. The construction of network learning space can provide teachers with a platform for training and learning. And all teachers' activities can be completed on this platform. Recently, contents about knowledge sharing of teachers have drew attention of researchers. To best understand the effect of knowledge sharing on network learning space, this paper chooses a typical example teacher workshop as research object. Based on statistical analysis, content analysis and social statistical analysis, this paper performs research on quantity, content and features of social interaction of knowledge sharing. The results show that: (1) Teachers are generally very active on network learning space; (2) Teachers' posts are closely related to topics; (3) Teachers have built strong connections with each other; (4) Communications often involve more than 2 people. Therefore, this result can be a reference to other related research works.

Keywords: Network learning space · Knowledge sharing · Social interaction

1 Introduction

With the rapid development of information technology, it provides technical support for the construction of an online learning environment, and promotes online collaboration and interaction. During the period of the 13th five-year plan, the guideline for education informatization clearly points out the construction of "three channel two plat-form", and emphasizes on construction of network learning space to promote the reform of learning and teaching methods [1]. The construction of network learning space is conducive to the formation of teachers' new training, interaction, etc. The nine ministries and commissions takes the lead in putting forward the platform based on the network learning space to organize the teachers to carry out online training activities [2]. Since 2013, the primary and middle school teachers' information technology application ability improvement project has been started. And it puts forward carrying out teacher training combined field practice with network training on the base of network training

S.K.S. Cheung et al. (Eds.): ICBL 2017, LNCS 10309, pp. 225–235, 2017.
DOI: 10.1007/978-3-319-59360-9_20

community, and points out that the network training community should open the personal space for the teachers and open the workshop for the trainers [3]. Teacher's network training activities, such as curriculum learning, workshop activities and school-based training activities, are all based on the network learning space. Therefore, the effect of knowledge sharing and social interaction among teachers in the network learning space has caught the attention of researchers. Take into account this situation, this study makes an in-depth analysis of the effect of knowledge sharing and social interaction, and explores the quantity, content and social interaction characteristics of knowledge sharing aimed to provide some reference for teacher training.

2 Theoretical Framework

2.1 Network Learning Space

Learning space is learning environment for learners, which is divided into three kinds consist of formal, informal and virtual learning space. Virtual learning space generally includes network learning space, virtual reality and social platform [4]. The network learning space is run on the learning support service platform, and supports the virtual space of teaching and learning [5]. Network learning space is generally from broad and narrow sense to understand its connotation. The generalized network learning space includes not only the learning management system, online education platform and virtual platform, but also QQ, WeChat, blog and other various social software and network platform; the narrow sense of network learning space only refers to the virtual space, which is specially designed for online teaching and learning, such as The national educational resources public service platform and the world university city [6]. With the further development of educational informatization and the "three channel two platform", the research of network learning space becomes more and more active. Although the researchers carried out theoretical research on the concept [7], principles [8], design [9] and evaluation system [10] of network learning space, but on the whole, the research of network learning space is still scattered, so it is necessary to carry out the research on the effect of network learning space, especially the learning effect, learning style and so on.

2.2 Related Research on Knowledge Sharing

Knowledge sharing is an important aspect of knowledge management, and it is the exchange and discussion of knowledge through various ways within the organization in order to achieve the goal of expanding the value of knowledge utilization [11]. Knowledge sharing has traditionally been the focus of scholars, and scholars have a wealth of theoretical contributions in the connotation of knowledge sharing, and they from the different theoretical point of view to understand the connotation of knowledge sharing. The scholars of communication theory emphasize that knowledge sharing is a two-way communication between the owner of knowledge and the knowledge demanders; the scholars of the theory of common knowledge emphasize that knowledge sharing is the process of knowledge sharing and knowledge transfer; knowledge sharing is defined as knowledge transfer and knowledge explanation by scholars of transfer and learning theory; Behavioral scholars point out that knowledge sharing is the behavior set of information exchange [12]. The theme and resource of knowledge sharing are frequent in different theories. The scholars actively set out from their own point of view and use their own language to depict the process of knowledge sharing, and the wide range of knowledge sharing model is a spiral model proposed by Japanese scholar Nnaka Fujiro. That is included with four processes: (1) the socialization of knowledge. Individual shares implicit knowledge in the organization and it is a process of transformation from implicit knowledge to implicit knowledge; (2) the externalization of knowledge. Owners of knowledge explicitly transfer implicit knowledge and it is a process of transformation from implicit knowledge to explicit knowledge; (3) the combination of knowledge. The owners of knowledge integrate the scattered explicit knowledge into a knowledge system and it is a process of transformation from explicit knowledge to explicit knowledge; (4) the internalization of knowledge. The knowledge demanders apply learned explicit knowledge to practice and it is a process of transformation from explicit knowledge to implicit knowledge [13]. As to the influence factors of knowledge sharing, scholars do research based on discrete learning environments. Founded on the theory of planned behavior and the theory of humanism, some scholars construct a conceptual model of influencing factors of knowledge sharing in virtual communities [14]. In the course of the study to explore the theoretical framework of knowledge sharing of College Teachers, some scholars find the result is that sharing atmosphere, sharing intention and sharing effect has the greatest impact [15]. Chen, Gao & Zhang [16] do a study on factors of knowledge sharing in the blog environment.

With the development of information technology, the knowledge sharing of network learning space has been widely concerned. Based on diverse theoretical perspectives, scholars use different methods to analyze the knowledge sharing in network learning space. Although scholars use many method including with the social network analysis method [17], content analysis method [18], interview method [19] and empirical research method [20] to study the relevant situation about knowledge sharing in network learning space, but the research on the level of knowledge sharing and the network structure of social interaction is of great significance to the promotion of teacher training and learning.

3 Research Design

3.1 Participants

Network learning space provides training learning platform for teachers, and teacher workshop is staffed by teachers from the same subject across the region by the "national training plan" demonstration of network training and school-based training, which has the general characteristics of network learning space. In order to examine the effect of knowledge sharing in the network learning space, the teacher workshop is selected as the research object to study the effect of knowledge sharing and the network structure of social interaction. The selection of the sample teacher workshop is based on the following: the number of teachers is moderate; all the staff participate in activities; and activities are carried out in accordance with the plan. According to the selection principle, the study select Chinese workshop as the specific research object of many of the teachers' workshop. This Chinese Workshop launched three research themes, the theme "how good the dull as ditch water phonetic teaching" is selected to make three aspects of analysis contained in knowledge sharing quantity, content analysis and social interaction network structure analysis.

3.2 Research Ideas

The study selects the theme of the Chinese workshop to study the content, content and social interaction of the network learning space. In the data collection phase, the platform can record all the data in the process of teachers' participation in training, consist of collect posting number, replies etc.; in the data analysis phase, the study from three aspects of quantity, knowledge sharing from the content and structure of the network makes a detailed analysis. In detail, that is to say, the method of statistical analysis, content analysis and social network analysis method are used to analyze the network learning space of teachers' participation in training in knowledge sharing, and data analysis results are summarized to obtain the conclusions of the research, and moreover some suggestions on teacher training and knowledge sharing are put forward.

3.3 Research Method

In order to analyze the quantity and content of knowledge sharing in network learning space and the network structure of social interaction, the method of combining qualitative analysis with quantitative analysis is used. In the analysis of the amount of knowledge sharing and the number of social interaction in the network learning space, the data statistical analysis method is used to analyze the quantity, and at the same time, quantitative analysis of the data is obtained; as for the analysis of network learning space knowledge sharing content, content analysis method is used to analyze the types and content of each post and reply for studying knowledge sharing level, and the post replies are classified by encoding and encoding framework; in the analysis of network structure characteristics of network learning space in social interaction, analysis of density and centrality of social interactive features with the social network is get through social network analysis method, and core personnel and personnel on the edge is classified.

4 Results

4.1 Quantitative Analysis of Knowledge Sharing

In the course of the training study, the number of teachers' knowledge sharing to some extent indicates how the initiative and actively teachers participate in the training study. Through the statistics on the number of teachers to post and reply, we find that there are a total of 91 teachers to participate in discussion to the first theme in the process of the training study. Other data is: total of posts (included with replies) is 679; posts (first post) is 230; replies (reply to posts) is 449; the number of posts per teacher is 7.46; the number of first post per teacher is 2.53; the number of replies is 4.93 and the number of replies to each post is 1.74. Statistics data show that the number of posts and replies is better, teachers is initiative and enthusiastic to participate in the training study, and teachers is active to express their own views and opinions and actively communicate and interact with other members, creating a more intense training learning atmosphere.

4.2 Content Analysis of Knowledge Sharing

In the process of training and learning, high-quality knowledge sharing effect not only shows in the number of teachers posting and replies, but also reflects teachers involved posts and replies content level and interactive depth, thus there is a need to classify and deep analyze the content of posts and replies. In this study, content analysis is utilized to study the content and depth of knowledge-sharing. The content analysis framework is based on the coding framework of Hou & Wu [21] and adapts to the characteristics of network learning space. Content analysis is a way to make effective inferences and conclusions on the basis of procedural analysis of text and other materials [22]. This framework (as showed in Table 1) has undergone the process of adaptation - modification - to communicate with experts to discuss modification - the reliability test then is finalized. It detailed codes and classifies the content of posts and replies, and elaborates on each category.

According to the content coding framework of knowledge sharing, we category and analyze the first theme in the Chinese teachers' workshop. In order to circumvent the subjectivity of coding, the study adopts two-person coding method, and then calculate its consistency to determine the reliability of coding framework. The process of coding is follow: (1) researchers lonely code a part of posts of the first theme; (2) compute consistency; (3) communicate with each other for the doubt points of the content analysis coding framework; (4) researchers lonely code again other some part of posts according to the revised framework; (5) calculate consistency again. Built on the value of 0.4–0.75 for a reasonable value [23], F value is 0.82, indicating that the framework of good reliability. The rest of the posts is complete coding by one researcher.

The coding results are presented in Fig. 1. Through the content analysis method, we find that when teachers training and learning. They mainly take subjective statement of personal views and objectively narrate the teaching practice process and knowledge sharing accounted for a higher proportion. So it can be inferred that teachers' training learning has been the level of knowledge sharing, and teachers are willing to share personal knowledge and experience and to actively digest the views of other members. However, some of the content is not relevant to the theme. We carefully check these content, and then find that these posts are related to other themes. It is possible that some teachers do not pay attention to the theme when they train and learn. As for social interaction, there is most interaction to posts when teachers communication, few no interaction. It again from the side shows that teachers interact frequently when they train and learn, creating a strong knowledge sharing and communication interaction atmosphere.

Table 1. The content analysis coding framework for knowledge sharing

Dimensions	Item	Definition	Description	Example
IM1 (Related Theme)	IM11	Information sharing/ Comparison	Statement of observation and opinion (subjective)	I think to highlight the main role of the students…
	IM12	Inconsistent discovery and exploration among participants	Different identity and area; through questions and answers to clarify the differences or problems (that is, descript the phenomenon, including the characteristics of cognitive characteristics of students, but also proposed solutions to the problem)	As a teacher, all know… but in specific teaching activities… I think…
	IM13	Meaning negotiation/ knowledge sharing	The significance of relational negotiation, and the relative weights applied to diversification protocols (objective) (The phenomenon, the objective description of the problem; put forward common sense, etc.)	Listening is the basis and prerequisite for effective education…
	IM14	Advice on shared knowledge	Views on shared knowledge (consent or objection, etc.)	I think Li is right
	IM15	Off-theme	It has nothing to do with the theme	
IM2 (Social Interaction)	IM21	(Teacher-to-theme interaction)	(Discussion with theme)	(As the basic level of social interaction)
	IM22	(Interaction between teachers)	(Posted Replies, there are divergent discussions and other interaction)	(As the sublimation level of interaction)
	IM23	No-interaction	Neither with the theme of interaction, nor the interaction between teachers	

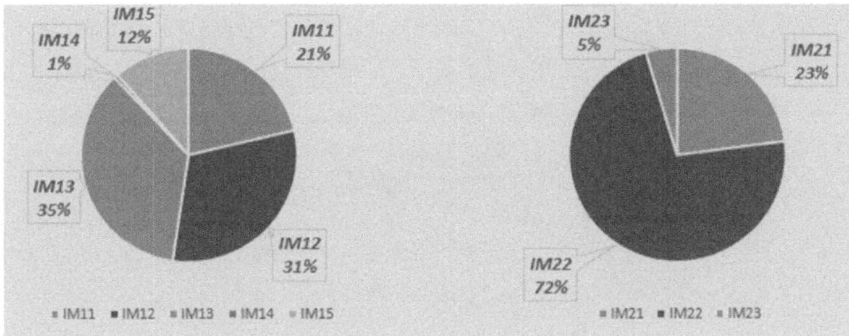

Fig. 1. Content analysis encoding results

Note:
On Left (theme-related dimension encoding results)

IM11: Information sharing/Comparison; IM12: Inconsistent discovery and exploration among participants; IM13: Meaning negotiation/knowledge sharing; IM14: Advice on shared knowledge; IM15: Off-theme
On Right (social interaction dimension coding results)
IM21: Teacher-to-theme interaction; IM22: Interaction between teachers; IM23: No-interaction

4.3 Analysis of Social Interaction Network Structure

When research the effect of knowledge sharing, we pay attention to the quantity and content of knowledge sharing in addition, we need to pay attention to the social interaction between teachers in the process of group, that is, the social network formed by the teachers during the process of training and learning. In the study, social network analysis method is used to study the characteristics of the social interaction in the process of knowledge sharing. The data of the training and learning process is analyzed by Ucinet software, and the social network structure and related parameters such as density and centrality were obtained. The formation of interactive relationship model shown in Fig. 2. (The vertex that interactive teachers, vertex connection between teachers that the post, replies and other interactive behavior). From the diagram of interaction pattern, it can be seen that (1) Teachers have different degrees of interaction; (2) some teachers are located at the center of the network, indicating that they actively participate in interaction; (3) the degree of participating in the interaction of marginal teachers is relatively low; (4) a small part of teachers is isolated, indicating that the teacher does not interact with other teachers.

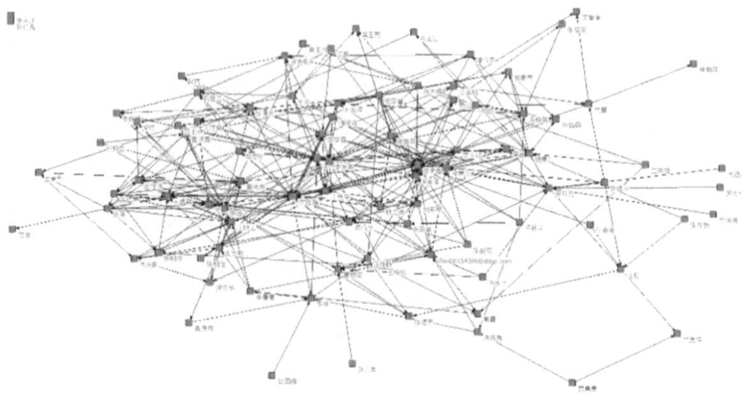

Fig. 2. The interactive network structure of network learning space

The index most frequently used to measure the network connectivity is density. And the value of density is greater. The link between group members is closer. In this study, the value of density in network learning space is 0.0415, and there are many social interactions between teachers, which have formed a relatively close social network.

Generally, centrality is used to measure whether the actor is in the center of the social network, and usually contains four centrality: Eigenvector Centrality, Local Centrality, Betweenness Centrality and Closeness Centrality. Eigenvector Centrality is a standardized measure of the centrality of the actors and the central potential of the network. The goal of Eigenvector Centrality is to find the core members of the net-work in the overall structural sense; Local Centrality describes the actor's local center index, and is used to measure the network of actors of their own interactive ability; Betweenness Centrality is a measure of the extent to which the actor lies between the other two actors; Closeness Centrality is just the opposite of Betweenness Centrality, taking into account the extent to which the actors are not affected by other actors [24]. The mean value of eigenvector centrality, local centrality, betweenness centrality and closeness centrality of the network in network learning space is 11.507, 8.278, 1.60 and 22.332. As for the eigenvector centrality, the actor with the higher value is the core figure of the network, and the number of teachers in the core figure is relatively more, however there are many teachers whose value is 0, which belongs to the marginal character.

From the perspective of social interaction network structure, the interaction of teachers in the network learning space is relatively high, and the relatively tight social net-work has been established. The teachers have a high degree of centrality, and among them the maximum of centrality degree is 36.667; teachers' interaction exists intermediary centers, that is, the interaction between teachers is not confined to two teachers, and the interaction of many teachers is more common.

5 Conclusion and Suggestion

5.1 Conclusion

Based on the analysis of the number and the content of knowledge sharing and social interaction and structure of the network social interaction in the process of the training study in Chinese teacher workshop, we draw the conclusion for the effect of knowledge sharing in network learning space:

- The teachers' initiative and enthusiasm in participating in the training study activities are higher. In the process of training and learning, teachers actively post and reply, have good data about the average value of posts and replies, and show a high degree of active training and learning. However, we also see that some teachers simply reply to the post of others, and only to achieve a shallow learning.
- Teachers post positively and interactively communication with theme, but there are some posts beside the theme. In the process of training and learning, teachers brainstorm and express personal views, and learn the knowledge shared by others to practice further into their own knowledge. But we also see that some teachers do not pay attention to the theme, then freely express their opinions. Off-topic posts also lead other teachers' replies discussion, the social interaction is invalid.
- There is a relatively tight social network has formatted between teachers. And the interaction of teachers also exists intermediary center. That is to say the interaction is not only limited between 2 teachers, which is a certain extent of the teachers' interactive knowledge sharing process.

5.2 Suggestion

- There is a need to construct learning scaffolding in order to promote deep knowledge sharing. In the learning process, teachers have high initiative and enthusiasm in participating in learning activities. However it still stays in the shallow to share knowledge with others, and thus there is a need for assistants aimed at the characteristics of network learning space to design process, construct training learning scaffolding such as training log and reflection to promote the internalization and depth knowledge sharing of teachers' knowledge.
- Assistants shall be concerned about the content of teachers in the process of training learning study, and give tips to the content and the teacher which shows the off-theme post. Through analysis of the content of posts, we find that some teachers ignore the theme of the training causing unrelated to the topic of personal views to submit to the extent to affect others post and replies. Thus assistants need to pay close attention to the process of teacher training learning, and timely give tips to the submitted off-topic post teacher.
- Shall take measures to enhance the communication of teachers, aimed at creating an interactive atmosphere. The network learning space provides teachers with a good training and communication platform. Teachers frequently interact with others to form contention and thought collision, in order to achieve the goal of the growth of teachers' own professional knowledge. At the same time, it is necessary to take some

measures to encourage the teachers to communicate with other teachers through the multi-dimensional interactive way for improving the shallow interaction and create a good interactive atmosphere in network learning space.

Acknowledgments. This paper is supported by Chinese Education Ministry's New Century Excellent Talents Supporting Plan (No. NCET-13-0818) and "the Fundamental Research Funds for the Central Universities" (No. CCNU16A05023).

References

1. Liu, Y.D.: (2015). http://www.moe.edu.cn/publicfiles/business/htmlfiles/moe/s3342/201211/144240.html
2. The nine ministries and commissions (2015). http://www.nxzyk.com/s_nxjyxxh/2013_6_26/A5514A9E09A6146E580_2013626_1149.html
3. Education Department (2015). http://guopei.ncet.edu.cn/detail-announcement-10590.html
4. Zhang, S., Liu, Q.T., Huang, J.X., et al.: A study on the influence factors of primary and secondary school teachers' use of online learning space - Based on the survey of the UTAUT model. China Educ. Technol. **3**, 99–106 (2016)
5. Liang, Y.Z., Zhao, C.L., Ruan, Y.J., et al.: An empirical study on the interactive behavior in the network learning space: based on the perspective of social network analysis. China Educ. Technol. **7**, 22–28 (2016)
6. Yang, X.M., Zhao, X.S., et al.: Development of network learning space: connotation, stage and suggestion. China Educ. Technol. **4**, 30–36 (2016)
7. Hu, Y.B., Huang, R.M., Liu, D.Y.: Classification of online learning space: framework and enlightenment. China Educ. Technol. **4**, 37–42 (2016)
8. Huang, L.H., Zhou, Y.F., Chen, X.J.: The construction of network learning space in class under the background of class. China Educ. Technol. **3**, 86–90 (2014)
9. Zhang, Z.S., Jin, Y.F., Wu, T.: Planning and design of network learning space platform. China Educ. Technol. **4**, 47–53 (2015)
10. Li, Y.B., Wang, Y.Y., et al.: Study on the evaluation index system of teachers' online learning space. E-education Res. **6**, 100–106 (2015)
11. Wang, W.J., Guan, S.F., Li, Y.F.: Visual analysis of hot spots and frontiers of knowledge sharing. Libr. Inf. Sci. **1**, 115–123 (2012)
12. Shen, Z.Q.: Study on the mechanism of knowledge sharing in virtual learning community. Qufu Normal University (2013)
13. Nonaka, I., Takeuchi, H.: The Knowledge – Creating Company. Oxford University Press, New York (1995)
14. Wang, G., Li, X.B.: Investigation and analysis of the influencing factors of knowledge sharing in virtual community. China Educ. Technol. **4**, 56–61 (2010)
15. Zhao, L., Wang, R.C.: Research on implicit knowledge sharing model and evaluation index system of University Teachers Based on AHP. China Educ. Technol. **10**, 100–105 (2014)
16. Chen, X.D., Gao, D.D., Zhang, W.: The application of Blog in the interdisciplinary knowledge sharing. China Educ. Technol. **8**, 17–20 (2004)
17. Wang, L.: Study on the relationship between social network position and knowledge construction of virtual learning community. China Educ. Technol. **8**, 18–23 (2010)
18. Lai, W.H., Ye, X.D.: Social network analysis of knowledge sharing in virtual learning community. Mod. Educ. Technol. **10**, 97–101 (2010)

19. Zhang, M.X., Liu, S.: Research on the knowledge management behavior of teachers in the online practice community. China Educ. Technol. **9**, 120–125 (2014)
20. Liu, X.M., Sun, W., Wang, L.: A study on the knowledge sharing behavior of primary and secondary school teachers' network peer mutual aid organizations. Mod. Prim. Secondary Educ. **9**, 82–86 (2014)
21. Hou, H.T., Wu, S.Y.: Analyzing the social knowledge construction behavioral patterns of an online synchronous collaborative discussion instructional activity using an instant messaging tool: a case study. Comput. Educ. **57**(2), 1459–1468 (2011)
22. Rourke, L., Anderson, T., Garrison, D.R., et al.: Methodological issues in the context analysis of computer conference transcripts. Int. J. Artif. Intell. Educ. **11**(3), 8–22 (2001)
23. Banerjee, M., Capozzoli, M., Mcsweeney, L., Sinha, D.: Beyond kappa: a review of interrater agreement measures. Can. J. Stat. **27**(1), 3–23 (1999)
24. Wang, L.: Social Network Structure of Virtual Learning Community, pp. 37–38. Peking University Press, Beijing (2011)

Topic Classification on Short Reflective Writings for Monitoring Students' Progress

Leonard K.M. Poon[1(✉)], Zichao Li[2], and Gary Cheng[1]

[1] Department of Mathematics and Information Technology, The Education University of Hong Kong, Hong Kong SAR, China
{kmpoon,chengks}@eduhk.hk

[2] Department of Computer Science and Engineering, The Chinese University of Hong Kong, Hong Kong SAR, China
zcli@cse.cuhk.edu.hk

Abstract. Reflection has been widely considered as an important element in student learning in higher education. Among different forms of reflective writing, one-minute papers can quickly and easily get students to reflect on their learning. Unlike short quizzes, the responses to one-minute papers could cover a wide open range and could require more time to review and summarize. When one-minute papers are administrated online, their responses are available in electronic form and this facilitates a computational approach for analysis. In this paper, we propose a machine learning approach to analyzing the students' responses to one-minute papers. We build a text classifier to identify the topics discussed in the responses. Our results of a preliminary study conducted in a blended learning course demonstrate that the classifier can effectively detect the topics and the proposed method can be used to monitor student progress based on the detected topics.

Keywords: Topic classification · One-minute papers · Reflective writings · Blended learning · Learning analytics

1 Introduction

Reflection has been widely considered as an important element in student learning in higher education [16, 23–25]. Reflective writing is usually used to promote reflective learning [12, 19]. It is different from the traditional writing in assessment, sometimes called substantive writing. Substantive writing attempts to present information and ideas the writer has about a topic. In contrast, reflective writing attempts to identify the significance and meaning of a given learning experience for the writer [13].

Reflective writing can be classified into three forms [13], namely one-minute papers [26], regular journal writing [10], and learning portfolios [31]. Among the three forms, one-minute papers can quickly and easily get students to reflect on their learning. They are usually conducted weekly at the end of a class with a short reflection question that is expected to be completed in a minute or two. In addition to those advantages of reflective writing, this kind of weekly short written responses may also encourage active student participation and regular class attendance, hear student voice, and inform teaching for the next class [8].

S.K.S. Cheung et al. (Eds.): ICBL 2017, LNCS 10309, pp. 236–246, 2017.
DOI: 10.1007/978-3-319-59360-9_21

The one-minute paper was originated by Charles Schwartz in the early 1980s and has been popularized by Angelo and Cross [2] in the 1990s [26]. The technique has been considered as one of the most effective innovations for learning and teaching [20]. It has been used in higher education for various subjects, including business study [15], economics education [32], healthcare programs [1], library research support [34], medical training [3, 33], and other areas [20, 30].

Unlike short quizzes, the responses to a one-minute paper could cover a wide open range. Therefore, it could require more time to review and summarize them than to grade the quizzes [17]. Often, the one-minute paper is administrated online [29, 34] and hence the responses are available in electronic form. This allows teachers to conveniently adopt a computational approach to facilitate the analysis on the responses.

In this paper, we propose a machine learning approach to analyzing the students' responses to one-minute paper for monitoring students' progress. We use a text classifier to identify the topics discussed in the responses. Since the responses are often short and do not contain any topic labels, we train the text classifier using textual content extracted from different sections of lecture notes. This paper shows also the results of a preliminary study using our proposed method in a blended learning course, in which face-to-face lessons are supplemented by the online activity of one-minute papers. The results demonstrate that the classifier can effectively detect the topics and the proposed method can be used to monitor student progress based on the detected topics.

The contributions of this paper are threefold. First, it proposes a text classification method to detect topics in one-minute papers. The issue of short responses for training classifier is addressed by using lecture notes as training data. Second, it demonstrates how to use the detected topics to monitor student progress. Third, it shares the experience of conducting a blended learning course where online one-minute papers are used to supplement traditional face-to-face classes.

In the remaining of this paper, we first review background and related work in Sect. 2. We then describe our methods and the preliminary study in Sect. 3. After that we present the results of the preliminary study in Sect. 4 and conclude the paper in Sect. 5.

2 Background and Related Work

2.1 One-Minute Paper

The one-minute paper is usually conducted at the end of a class. Two questions are typically asked:

1. What is the most important thing you learned today?
2. What question remains unanswered?

Other questions are also possible. For example, Fink [13] suggests the question can be one of the above questions as well as one of the following two:

- What is the most unclear thing today?
- How would you describe the relationship between topic X and Y in your own words?

Many variations on the basic format of the one-minute paper is possible [26]. For example, the paper can be conducted with hardcopy or online. Besides, the students' responses can be anonymous or signed and they can be graded or ungraded.

Stead [26] points out several benefits of using one-minute paper. First, the questions require students to rank the relative importance of what they have heard. This encourages active listening in class and provides a chance for reflecting what they have learned. Second, the questions train a higher order cognitive skill by requiring the students to ask questions. Third, the responses allow quick feedback for the class and the teachers. Fourth, the one-minute paper show to the students that the instructor values their opinions and learning needs. This may further improve student motivation.

2.2 Automatic Assessment

Automatic assessment refers to some computational methods to automatically grade students' assignments. Burrows et al. [7] categorizes such techniques based on the types of questions they address with three levels of organization. The first level distinguishes between recognition and recall questions. Examples of recognition questions include multiple-choice questions. The second level divides the recall questions based on the form of answers, namely natural language text, structured text (e.g. mathematics and source code), and speech. The third level further divides the natural language text questions based on the length of answers. Fill-the-gap answers may have one to a few words. Short answers generally have one phrase to one paragraph. Essays have two paragraphs to several pages. The one-minute papers can be considered as short answer questions according to the above categorization.

Burrows et al. [7] recently review 35 automatic short answer grading (ASAG) systems. Four approaches are identified among them. First, the concept mapping approach detects whether each of the expected concepts exist or not in the student answers during grading. Second, the information extraction approach performs fact finding in student answers using a series of pattern matching operations including regular expressions and parse trees. Third, the corpus-based approach exploit statistical properties of a large collection of documents using techniques such as Latent Semantic Analysis (LSA) [18] and BiLingual Evaluation Understudy (BLEU) [22], which can be useful for identifying synonyms for correct answers in short text. Finally, the machine learning approach grades or scores answers typically using a classification model or regression built on features extracted using natural language processing techniques. The machine learning techniques often used include decision tree, k-nearest neighbors, support vector machine, linear regression, logistic regression, and a combination of them (see [4] for an introduction to those techniques).

The ASAG systems in general aim to score the answers based on correctness [7, 11, 21]. However, correctness may not be important in reflective writings and so those systems may not be appropriate for such writings. Our proposed method is based on a machine learning technique, namely naive Bayes classifier, but it aims to detect topics in the answers and does not require manually graded answers as training data. Similar to the corpus-based methods we build our model with a collection of documents. However, we use lecture notes rather than answers as the corpus and use a supervised rather than an unsupervised method.

Recently, some automatic assessment systems have been proposed for reflective writings. Unlike our method, those systems have different aims from ours. Some of those methods aim to detect whether a writing is reflective or not [25, 28]. Some aim to detect in reflective writings the reflective parts [27] or anomalous features, such as sarcasm, humor, and emotional tone [14]. Chen et al. [9] aim to detect topics in reflective journals and their work is most similar to ours. However, our study uses shorter texts obtained from responses to one-minute papers and could be more challenging. Besides, their work uses an unsupervised method called latent Dirichlet allocation (LDA) [6] and shows only 10 topics in their results. In contrast, our method uses a supervised method and allows predefined and also significantly more topics.

3 Methods

We conducted our study in a 13-week course in the Education University of Hong Kong. The course was an introductory programming course for undergraduate students. It had two sessions and 66 students in total. Face-to-face classes were held weekly.

3.1 One-Minute Paper

Students in the course were required to complete a one-minute paper in each of 11 weeks. They had to submit their responses on Moodle and their names were recorded. We set the deadline of each paper to be exactly the starting time of the following class. The reason was that this allowed students to have more time to complete the paper based on previous feedbacks. At the same time, we did not want the students to write the answers during the following class.

The one-minute papers were given a weight of 10% of the overall grade to encourage students to complete them. Three possible grades could be given for each answer. Full marks would be given when an answer addressed the reflection question and showed significant reflection. Half marks would be given when an answer addressed the reflection question but did not show significant reflection. No marks would be given when an answer did not address the reflection question. The significance of reflection was usually indicated by the presence of explanation.

Following the suggestion by Fink [13], we used only one question for reflection each time. Some questions asked students to identify the most important, most difficult, most useful, or most confusing thing about any topic in a class. Some questions required students to point out the most confusing thing, most surprising thing, or the biggest advantages of a specific programming construct. The other questions asked students to identify the similarities or dissimilarities between two or three related concepts.

3.2 Topic Classification

Topic modeling techniques are often used to detect topics among a collection of documents and classify documents into those topics [5]. They are unsupervised and detect topics based on the co-occurrence of words in a document. One example of topic modeling methods that is widely used is LDA [6]. There are two possible issues when such techniques are used for responses to one-minute paper. First, the responses are short and hence words belonging to the same topic may co-occur less frequently than in longer texts. This may lead to fewer or less meaningful topics. Second, topics unrelated to course content may be detected due to the unsupervised approach. This may be a problem if the objective of the study is to check the discussed topics against some predefined ones. As a matter of fact, we tested two LDA-based methods on the responses to one-minute papers in a preliminary experiment. The topics detected were not satisfactory.

To address the above two issues, we adopt a supervised approach for topic classification. One issue of using a supervised method is that it requires labeled data for training. To reduce the manual effort needed to provide labels, we extract labeled data from lecture notes based on the existing sections. Specifically, we assume that lecture notes are organized by sections and consider each section of lecture notes as a topic with a single document. In the course under study the lecture notes were divided into 51 sections. Hence, we used 51 documents, each with a unique topic label, as data for training the text classifier.

Each document in the training data is converted to a word vector. It is considered as one training sample labeled with the section heading as the topic. We removed the stop words using the NTLK package.[1] Since the course under study was a programming course, the lecture notes contained source code as examples. To improve the classification performance, in the source code examples we substituted all variable names with the token `variablename` and all comments with the token `comment`. Each section of lecture notes is then converted to a binary word vector, where each element indicates the presence or absence of the corresponding word. The resulting training data contain 51 documents as samples and 1280 words as attributes.

It is likely that a response to a one-minute paper belongs to more than one topic. Therefore, we consider the topic classification problem as a multi-label classification problem rather than a multi-class classification problem. In other words, we assign possibly multiple labels to each response. Consequently, we build a text classifier for each topic. Each classifier gives a binary output and is used to determine whether a response belongs to the corresponding topic.

Suppose we are training the classifier for topic t. Each topic classifier is built with the same collection of documents as training data. However, different labels are used for training different topic classifiers. The document with topic t is used as a positive example, while the other documents are used as negative examples.

We use naive Bayes classifier [4] for topic classification. Let D be the number of distinct words in data. Use $\boldsymbol{w} = (w_1, \cdots, w_D)$ to denote a word vector, where

[1] http://www.nltk.org.

$w_i \in \{0, 1\}$. Further denote the class variable by c_t, which takes the value of 1 when the topic is t and 0 otherwise. The naive Bayes model for topic t is defined by:

$$P(c_t|\boldsymbol{w}) = \frac{P(c_t)\prod_{i=1}^{D} P(w_i|c_t)}{\sum_{c_t \in \{0,1\}} P(c_t)\prod_{i=1}^{D} P(w_i|c_t)}.$$

Consider the training data with n documents. Let N_i be the number of documents that contain the i-th word and $N_{c_t i}$ be the number of documents that belong to class c_t and contain the i-th word. The parameters $P(w_i|c_t)$ are estimated by relative frequency counts in the training data as follows:

$$P(w_i|c_t) = \frac{N_{c_t i} + \alpha}{N_i + n\alpha},$$

where α is known as the smoothing parameter. In our experiment, we used $\alpha = 1$ and used `scikit-learn`[2] for the implementation of the Naive Bayes classifier.

To assign topic labels to a response, we first convert the response to a word vector $\boldsymbol{w}$ using the same set of words in the training data. We then compute the probability $P(c_t|\boldsymbol{w})$ for each topic t and assign the topic label t to $\boldsymbol{w}$ if $P(c_t = 1|\boldsymbol{w}) > 0.5$.

4 Results of Preliminary Study

We received 565 responses to the one-minute papers assigned in the 11 weeks from the 66 students in the course. On average, each student submitted responses to 75% of the papers assigned. Figure 1 shows the percentage of responses by the week when the paper was assigned. It shows a downward trend in completion rate. This was possibly caused by a heavier workload towards the end of a semester.

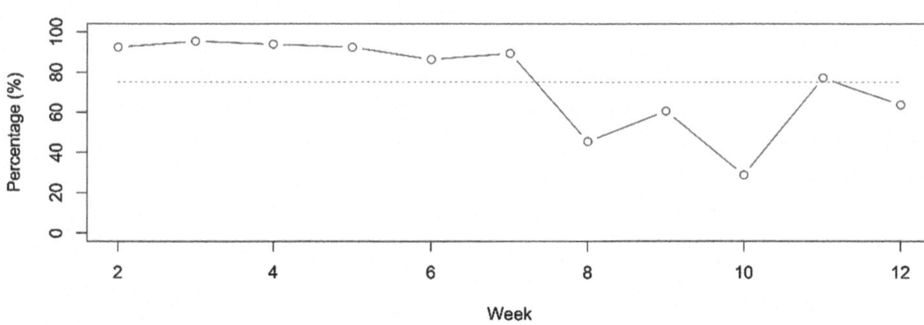

Fig. 1. Percentage of students giving responses to one-minute paper against the week number in the course. The average (75%) is indicated by the dotted line.

[2] http://scikit-learn.org.

We next test the performance of the classifier. The course instructor, who is also the first author, manually labeled the 262 responses submitted by the students in one of the sessions in the course. Each response was labeled by 1.84 topics on average. Note that these labels were not used in training since such labels are usually not available in practice. We then used the Naive Bayes classifier to assign the labels of the 262 responses. The classifier attained a precision rate of 0.69 and a recall rate of 0.39. In other words, 69% of the predicted topics were correct whereas 39% of the manually labeled topics were detected. The rates are evidently higher than those obtained by a random guess. They show that the classifier is effective in detecting topics.

Figure 2 shows a heat map indicating the number of responses by the detected topic for each week. The topics, indicated by the section headings, are listed along the horizontal axis. The topics are ordered according to the week they were covered. We see from the figure that the detected topics have a higher number along the diagonal. This is reasonable because the topics discussed in responses are more likely to be the topics covered in class that week.

We see also that some off-diagonal cells have a relatively large number. One possible reason was that the classifier was inaccurate. However, there could also be two other reasons. First, some students might discuss topics that were covered in earlier weeks. For example, the topic "variables" was mainly discussed in weeks 2 and 3, but it was also discussed in weeks 7 to 9. Similar pattern can be observed for the topic "console input". Both topics are core concepts in programming and could be discussed along with other more advanced topics. Second, some topics are similar and could be difficult to be distinguished correctly by using words only. For example, the topic "instance variables and methods" can be similar to the topic "variables". Therefore, some responses in week 3 were misclassified. Overall, the distribution of topics by week looks reasonable.

To monitor the students' progress, we plot the number of responses by their detected topics for each student. Figure 3 shows a heat map that can be used for such purpose. It may help the course instructor to identify students needing concern. For example, we see that some students, e.g. students 24, 25, and 59, discussed few topics throughout the course. This may suggest that those students showed little understanding on various topics.

We may also look at some important topics and look for students who do not discuss those topics. For example, the "variables" and "methods" are important concepts in a programming course. We see from Fig. 3 that some students, e.g. students 22, 60, and 65, did not discuss those topics in any of their responses. This may suggest that those students did not grasp the important topics in the course.

Figures 2 and 3 can also provide possibly useful feedbacks to the instructor. The instructor may look for any topics that are seldom discussed. For example, we see that some topics related to "operators", "expressions", and "strings" had not been discussed in the responses. The instructor may then check whether the importance of topics has been appropriately perceived in class or whether the questions cannot cover some important topics well.

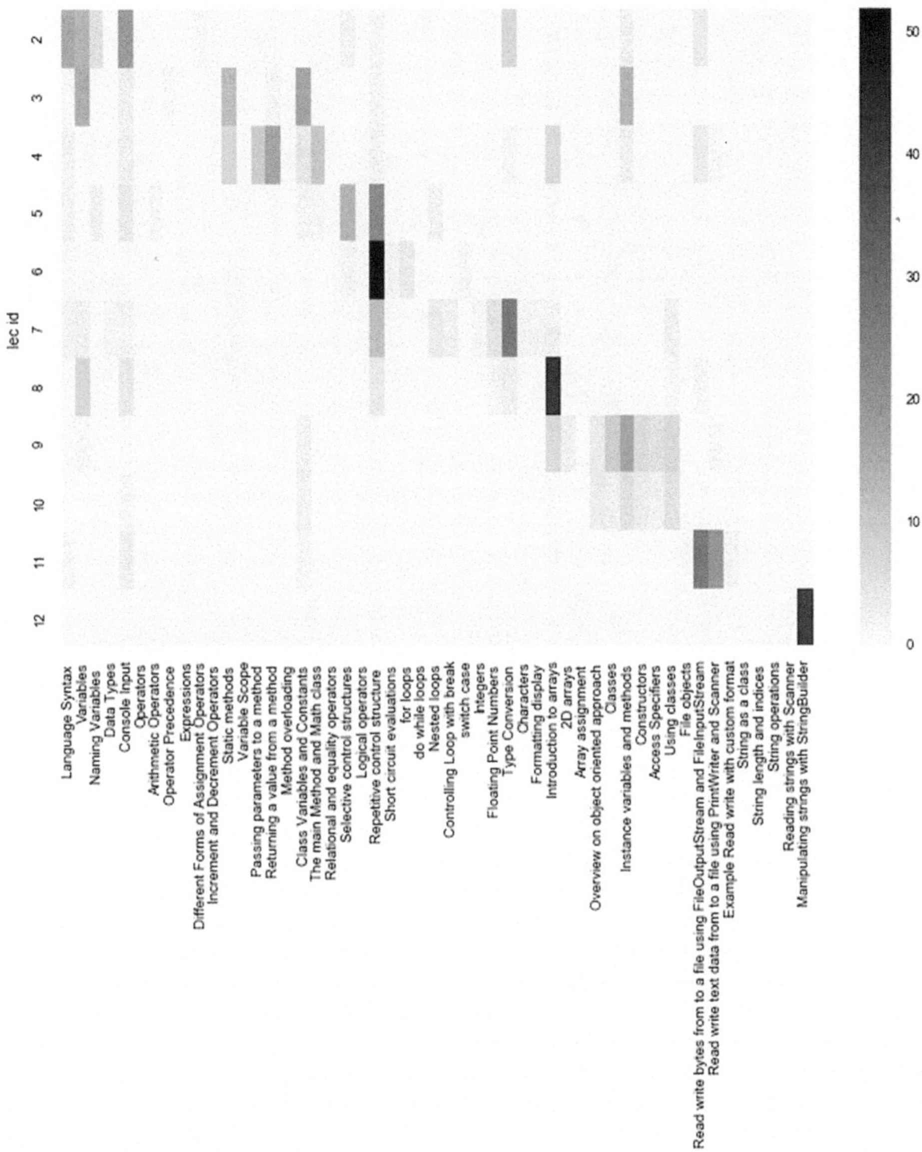

Fig. 2. Number of one-minute paper responses per week (vertical axis) and per topic detected (horizontal axis). The topics are ordered according to the week when they were covered in class.

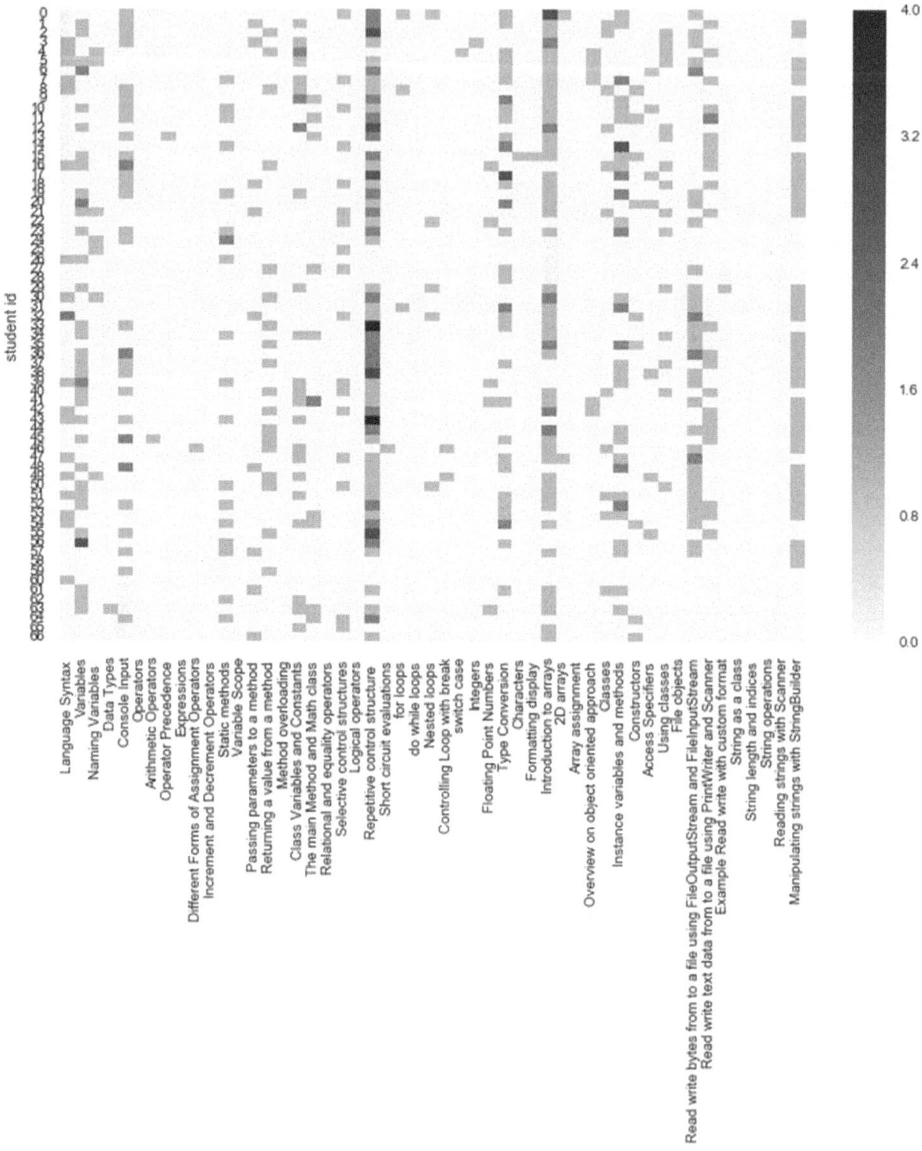

Fig. 3. Number of one-minute paper responses per student (vertical axis) and per topic (horizontal axis).

5 Conclusion

In this paper, we propose to use a text classifier to detect topics in students' responses to one-minute papers. We tested our proposed method in a blended learning course where the one-minute papers were administrated on Moodle. The results of our preliminary study shows that the text classifier can effectively detect topics in the responses. We also show that the detected topics can be used to monitor students' progress and provide feedback to course instructors. Our current study demonstrates that the proposed approach is feasible. In the future, we plan to improve the performance of the topic classifier and conduct more extensive experiments to evaluate our approach.

References

1. Anderson, D., Burns, S.: One-minute paper: student perception of learning gains. Coll. Stud. J. **47**(1), 219–227 (2013)
2. Angelo, T.A., Cross, K.P.: Classroom Assessment Techniques: A Handbook for College Teachers. Jossey-Bass, San Francisco (1993)
3. Ashakiran, S., Deepthi, R.: One-minute paper: a thinking centered assessment tool. Int. J. Med. Update **8**(2), 1–9 (2013)
4. Barber, D.: Bayesian reasoning and machine learning. Cambridge University Press, Cambridge (2012)
5. Blei, D.M.: Probabilistic topic models. Commun. ACM **55**(4), 77–84 (2012)
6. Blei, D.M., Ng, A.Y., Jordan, M.I.: Latent Dirichlet allocation. J. Mach. Learn. Res. **3**, 993–1022 (2003)
7. Burrows, S., Gurevych, I., Stein, B.: The eras and trends of automatic short answer grading. Int. J. Artif. Intell. Educ. **25**(1), 60–117 (2015)
8. Carless, D., Zhou, J.: Starting small in assessment change: short in-class written responses. Assess. Eval. High. Educ. **41**(7), 1114–1127 (2016)
9. Chen, Y., Yu, B., Zhang, X., Yu, Y.: Topic modeling for evaluating students' reflective writing: a case study of pre-service teachers' journals. In: Proceedings of the Sixth International Conference on Learning Analytics & Knowledge, pp. 1–5 (2016)
10. Cowan, J.: Noteworthy matters for attention in reflective journal writing. Act. Learn. High. Educ. **15**(1), 53–64 (2014)
11. Dos Santos, J.C.A., Favero, E.L.: Practical use of a latent semantic analysis (LSA) model for automatic evaluation of written answers. J. Braz. Comput. Soc. **21**(1), 21 (2015)
12. Farrell, T.S.C.: Does writing promote reflective practice? In: Renandya, W.A., Widodo, H.P. (eds.) English Language Teaching Today. ELE, vol. 5, pp. 83–94. Springer, Cham (2016). doi:10.1007/978-3-319-38834-2_7
13. Fink, L.D.: Creating Significant Learning Experiences: An Integrated Approach to Designing College Courses. Jossey-Bass, San Francisco (2003)
14. Gibson, A., Kitto, K.: Analysing reflective text for learning analytics: an approach using anomaly recontextualisation. In: Proceedings of the Fifth International Conference on Learning Analytics and Knowledge, pp. 275–279 (2015)
15. Halverson, J.: Minute paper and interdisciplinary studies: pre-test/post-test study. J. High. Educ. Theory Pract. **14**(3), 44 (2014)
16. Hatton, N., Smith, D.: Reflection in teacher education: towards definition and implementation. Teach. Teach. Educ. **11**(1), 33–49 (1995)
17. Kwan, F.: Formative assessment: the one-minute paper vs. the daily quiz. J. Instr. Pedagogies **5**, 1–8 (2011)
18. Landauer, T.K., Foltz, P.W., Laham, D.: An introduction to latent semantic analysis. Discourse Process. **25**(2–3), 259–284 (1998)
19. Lengelle, R., Meijers, F., Poell, R., Post, M.: The effects of creative, expressive, and reflective writing on career learning: an explorative study. J. Vocat. Behav. **83**(3), 419–427 (2013)

20. Lucas, G.M.: Initiating student-teacher contact via personalized responses to one-minute papers. Coll. Teach. **58**(2), 39–42 (2010)
21. Mittal, H., Syamala Devi, M.: Computerized evaluation of subjective answers using hybrid technique. In: Saini, H.S., Sayal, R., Rawat, S.S. (eds.) Innovations in Computer Science and Engineering. AISC, vol. 413, pp. 295–303. Springer, Singapore (2016). doi: 10.1007/978-981-10-0419-3_35
22. Papineni, K., Roukos, S., Ward, T., Zhu, W.J.: BLEU: a method for automatic evaluation of machine translation. In: Proceedings of the 40th Annual Meeting on Association for Computational Linguistics, pp. 311–318 (2002)
23. Rogers, R.R.: Reflection in higher education: a concept analysis. Innov. High. Educ. **26**(1), 37–57 (2001)
24. Ryan, M., Ryan, M.: Theorising a model for teaching and assessing reflective learning in higher education. High. Educ. Res. Dev. **32**(2), 244–257 (2013)
25. Shum, S.B., Sándor, Á., Goldsmith, R., Wang, X., Bass, R., McWilliams, M.: Reflecting on reflective writing analytics: assessment challenges and iterative evaluation of a prototype tool. In: Proceedings of the Sixth International Conference on Learning Analytics & Knowledge, pp. 213–222 (2016)
26. Stead, D.R.: A review of the one-minute paper. Act. Learn. High. Educ. **6**(2), 118–131 (2005)
27. Ullmann, T.D.: Keywords of written reflection – a comparison between reflective and descriptive datasets. In: Proceedings of the 5th Workshop on Awareness and Reflection in Technology Enhanced Learning, vol. 1465, pp. 83–96 (2015)
28. Ullmann, T.D., Wild, F., Scott, P.: Comparing automatically detected reflective texts with human judgements. In: Proceedings of the 2nd Workshop on Awareness and Reflection in Technology-Enhanced Learning, pp. 101–116 (2012)
29. Vonderwell, S.: Assessing online learning and teaching: Adapting the minute paper. TechTrends **48**(4), 29–31 (2004)
30. Vonderwell, S.K., Boboc, M.: Promoting formative assessment in online teaching and learning. TechTrends **57**(4), 22–27 (2013)
31. Wade, R.C., Yarbrough, D.B.: Portfolios: A tool for reflective thinking in teacher education? Teach. Teach. Educ. **12**(1), 63–79 (1996)
32. Whittard, D.: Reflections on the one-minute paper. Int. Rev. Econ. Educ. **20**, 1–12 (2015)
33. Wolff, M., Wagner, M.J., Poznanski, S., Schiller, J., Santen, S.: Not another boring lecture: Engaging learners with active learning techniques. J. Emerg. Med. **48**(1), 85–93 (2015)
34. Wolstenholme, J.: Evidence based practice using formative assessment in library research support. Evid. Libr. Inf. Pract. **10**(3), 4–29 (2015)

Evaluation of Stress Conditions for FIM UHK Students in Order to Improve Blended Learning and Flexibility of Educational Process

Věra Strnadová(✉), Petr Voborník, Jiří Haviger, and Kateřina Provazníková

University of Hradec Králové, Rokitanského 62, 500 03 Hradec Králové, Czech Republic
{vera.strnadova,petr.vobornik,jiri.haviger,
katerina.provaznikova}@uhk.cz

Abstract. The aim of this study is to clarify the current theoretical background of the issues dealing with stress factors as well as to introduce the course and statistical evaluation of our own research. It focuses on the connection between stress load and behaviour of university students. In the research the following areas are monitored: life style, living and social conditions and the influence of negative emotions on stress increase. The method of the research is subjective questioning and statistical processing of correlations in the field of frustration tolerance, handling stress and psychosomatic symptoms.

The first empirical survey was going on in the years 2011–2013 among 1322 university students in total, They were from the Faculty of Informatics and Management in Hradec Králové – the study branches of Applied Informatics, Financial Management, Information Management, Management of Tourism and Sport Management – and also from the Faculty of Pharmacy of Charles University in Prague. In the area of psychosomatic symptoms significant correlations have been found for all items in relation to health damaging strategies, so called malcoping strategies.

The second empirical survey monitored the sample of respondents in the years 2015–2016. 191 students participated in the research, all of them studying at the Faculty of Informatics and Management in Hradec Králové – the branches Applied Informatics, Financial Management, Information Management and Management of Tourism. Statistical evaluation was carried here with the help of correlation of handling stress area in relation to other monitored items. In the items directed to the section of psychosomatic symptoms significant correlations have been found again almost in all questions in relation to malcoping strategies. Of all types of items the best correlation was in the vulnerability section. The electronic online application which enabled subjective questioning and classification into stress factors was set up and placed on the web.

Keywords: Frustration tolerance · Handling stress · Psychosomatic symptoms · Life style · Statistical correlations

S.K.S. Cheung et al. (Eds.): ICBL 2017, LNCS 10309, pp. 247–258, 2017.
DOI: 10.1007/978-3-319-59360-9_22

1 Importance of Wider Social Context for Quality of Life

In their study Gillernová and the team of authors [1] present the importance of a wider social context for the quality, harmony and sound functioning of the family, in which the individual lives. There is a focus on Bronfenbrenner's model of '*the development of an individual in social context*' which distinguishes several system levels. They include both the aspect of a setting and the aspect of an individual's activity.

Macro system represents the widest social environment where a family lives (geographic conditionality, a socio-economic formation, a nationality, an ethnic group, a village, a city, a socio-economic status or a class membership of the family).

Mezzo system deals with a varied social environment where the family members belong (a kind of relationship between partners, their original families, institutions, peer groups, previous relationships).

Eco system represents the social factors that do not affect the family members directly outside the family, but they only affect the settings to which individuals belong (e.g. the change of education system may influence the atmosphere in the family).

The types of social factors that influence an individual imminently are united in *micro system* (specific ways of family communication, mutual perception of family members, particular family philosophy, applied principles of upbringing, the way of spending free time, managing financial matters, distribution of activities associated with running a household). The following issues can also be included in this system: education and intelligence of family members as well as their state of health, the feeling of satisfaction, sexual particularities, but also recognized values, the relationship to an extended family and the society as a whole [2, 3]. The subject of our research, which is related to the influence of stress factors on the quality of life of an individual, could also be included in the micro system level.

The current research indicates that the ways of a person's behaviour and the level of social conditions can significantly increase the susceptibility to mental disorders or physical illnesses. For instance, when a university student is preparing for a very hard exam until late night, in fact he/she threatens his/her performance during the actual exam due to lack of sleep [4, 5].

2 Coping Strategies of University Students

When carrying out research studies at FIM UHK in 2011 [6, 7] the following *options of coping strategies* were identified. These are strategies of coping with stress or releasing stress tension among students at the age of 20–25: talking to a good friend, a partner or a sibling, or on the contrary a momentary retreat into solitude, unwinding through physical activities and sport, the ability to cry it off or on the contrary the experience of laugh and staying in a merry company, listening to favourite music, various cultural activities or the possibility of peaceful undisturbed sleep.

3 Statistical Correlations of Items from the Years 2011–13

3.1 Monitored Period and Characterization of Respondents

Statistical evaluation with the help of correlations monitored the sample of 1322 respondents in the period of 2011–2013. They were university students of Faculty of Informatics and Management in Hradec Králové – the study fields of Applied Informatics, Financial Management, Information Management, Management of Tourism and Sport Management and students of the Faculty of Pharmacy at Charles University in Prague (see the graph in Fig. 1 and the table in Table 1).

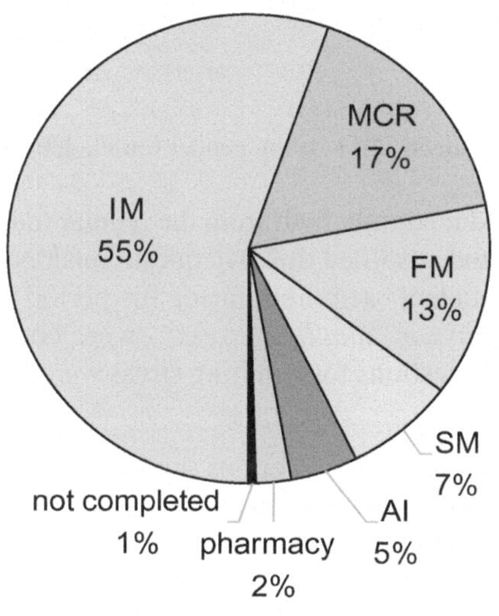

Fig. 1. Division of respondents 2011–13 by field of study

Table 1. Division of respondents 2011–13 by fields

Abbreviation	Number	%	Field and university
IM	734	55%	Information management – UHK
MCR	222	17%	Management of tourism – UHK
FM	177	13%	Financial management – UHK
SM	97	7%	Sport management – UHK
AI	60	5%	Applied informatics – UHK
pharmacy	31	2%	Faculty of pharmacy – Charles university in Prague
Not completed	7	1%	Field not completed in questionnaire
In total	**1 328**	**100%**	There are 1322 persons, i.e. 6 of them changed the field in one of the phases of the research

In the monitored sample there were 652 men and 669 women, one person did not fill in his/her gender (see Fig. 2 on the left). All students ranged between the age of 17 to 27 with the average age 19.932 years (see graph in Fig. 2 on the right).

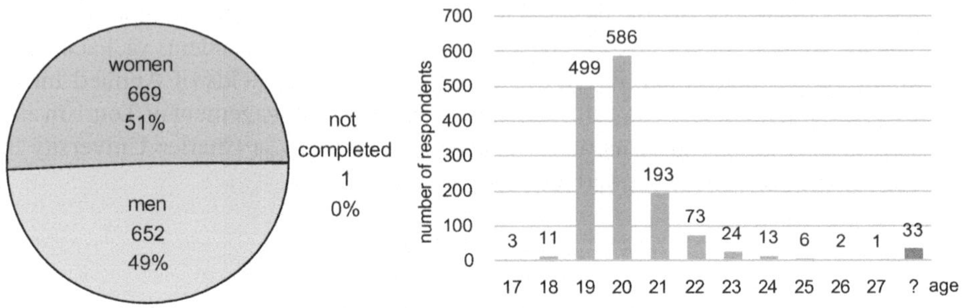

Fig. 2. Division of respondents 2011–13 by gender (on the left) and by age (on the right)

Students were selected randomly both from the regular (daily) and combined forms of studies. These 1,322 students filled in 2,046 questionnaires in the years 2011–2013.

From the sample of students acquired during the period of 2011–2013 the correlations of section B – *Ways of handling stress* – were compared against the other answered questions. The questions for handling stress were divided into the following groups [8, 9]:

- A – Procedures arousing negative emotions (malcoping)
- B – Damaging (malcoping) ways of behaviour
- C – Coping strategies (healthy stress management)

With the help of IBM SPSS program Spearman's rank correlation coefficient was carried out and significant correlations were selected and confirmed mutually on the level of probability at least 0.05. The correlation coefficient (r) determines the degree of relation between two variables and it is expressed by the number with the value between 0 and 1. No relation is 0, total dependency is indicated by 1. With the increase of the value from 0 to 1 the degree of relation is rising [10, p. 26].

3.2 Section A - Frustration Tolerance

The item: '*I can estimate work for myself and I do not feel the urge to think through all the essentials properly*'.

In the first question significant correlations were found with the use of procedures of type A (−0.212) and type B (0.177). A negative correlation means that **people who cannot plan their work also tend to use these malcoping strategies**. This was a probably the reason why students using malcoping strategies A and B chose the item saying 'They sometimes have more work than they are able to manage', A (0,173), B (0,182).

Other important correlations of malcoping strategies were found in the item '*I know I am as good as anyone else*'. Here a significant negative correlation (−0.193 and −0.219) can be found while positive correlation can be found in coping strategies

(0.119). **This proves that students using malcoping methods underestimate themselves and on the contrary, students who use coping strategies have healthy self-esteem.**

3.3 Section C – Life Style

In the *Life style* section there is the most important correlation with malcoping and coping strategies. It appears that students who use malcoping strategies of A type sleep much less than they need (0.226) and similarly in malcoping strategies of B type (0.190). On the other hand, students who **can use strategies of C type – coping strategies, have the length of sleep reflecting their need** (negative correlation −0.134).

3.4 Section E - Psychosomatic Symptoms

In section *Psychosomatic symptoms* significant correlations were found in all items in relation to malcoping strategies of A and B type. Specifically, in 14 correlations 10 correlations were found with the coefficient above 0.2, from which all were confirmed on 0.01 level of significance.

In the items '*I feel the tension in the neck and back muscles*', '*I have a headache at times*', '*I have a stomach ache*', '*I have a fast heart beat (sometimes connected with heart palpitation)*', '*I feel tired and feel lack of energy*', '*I suffer from insomnia*' **a significant correlation with malcoping strategies of A and B type with the coefficients from 0.215 to 0.331 was found in all the cases.**

3.5 Statistical Correlations of Coping Strategies

Unlike significant correlations found in malcoping strategies (type A and B strategies), **no important rank coefficients were found in using coping strategies (C type)**. This brings us to the conclusion that if we want to improve our mental state we must stop using malcoping strategies in the first place. If we succeed, we can devote time and effort to the development of physical and mental potential using coping strategies.

4 Statistical Correlations of Items from the Years 2015–16

4.1 Monitored Period and Characteristics of Respondents

The statistical evaluation, which was done with the help of correlation of *Handling stress* section in relation to the other items, followed the sample of respondents at the end of winter term 2015–2016.

191 students of the Faculty of Informatics and Management participated in the research. Their fields of study were Applied Informatics, Financial Management, Information Management and Management of Tourism (see the graph in Fig. 3 and table in Table 2).

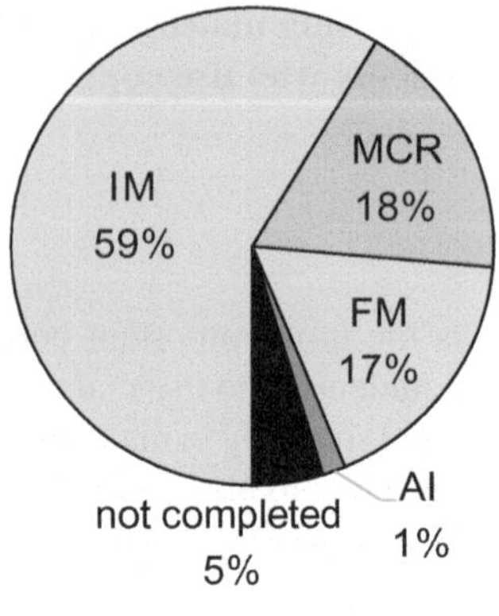

Fig. 3. Division of respondents 2015–16 by field of study

Table 2. Division of respondents 2015–16 by fields

Abbreviation	Number	%	Field and university
IM	112	59%	Information management – UHK
MCR	34	18%	Management of tourism – UHK
FM	33	17%	Financial management – UHK
AI	3	1%	Applied informatics – UHK
Not completed	9	5%	Field not completed in questionnaire
Total	**191**	**100%**	

In the monitored sample there were 92 men and 98 women, one person did not fill in his/her gender (see Fig. 4 on the left). All students ranged between the age of 17 and 41 with the average age of 20.78 years (see graph in Fig. 4 on the right).

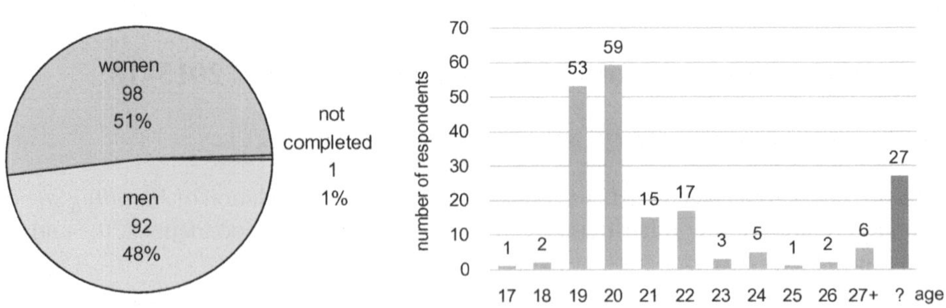

Fig. 4. Division of respondents 2015–16 by gender (on the left) and by age (on the right)

Students were selected randomly, both from daily and combined forms of studies.

From the sample of students gained in the research at the end of winter semester 2015–2016 the correlations of *Ways of handling stress* section were compared to the other answered questions. The questions for handling stress were again divided into the following groups:

- A – Procedures arousing negative emotions (malcoping)
- B – Damaging (malcoping) ways of behaviour
- C – Coping strategies (healthy stress management)

With the help of the statistical program IBM SPSS – version 21 at FIM Spearman's coefficient of rank correlation was carried out, significant correlations were selected and confirmed mutually on the level of probability 0.05.

4.2 Section A - Frustration Tolerance

The item: '*I can estimate work for myself and I do not feel the urge to think through all the essentials properly*'.

In the first item significant correlations with using malcoping strategies of A type (−0.171) and B type (−0.200) were found. Negative correlation means that **students who cannot plan their work also tend to use these malcoping strategies**. Possibly for the same reason students using the method B chose the item which says that '*They sometimes have more work than they are able to manage*' (0.271).

Even more distinctive correlation was in the item of similar type: '*I can concetrate on one thing and yet to clear the mind from other things although they are also important*'.

There is a very distinctive negative correlation with strategies of type A (−0.353) here. It is becoming evident that **students who, use these malcoping procedures evoking negative emotions are not able to ease their mind and fully concentrate on vital matters**.

4.3 Section C – Life Style Versus Section D – Living and Social Conditions

In the items directed at the section *Life style* and *Living and social conditions* no significant correlations with the section *Handling stress* (strategies of type A, B, C) were found.

4.4 Section E – Psychosomatic Symptoms

In the items directed at the section *Psychosomatic symptoms* significant correlations were found almost in all questions in relation to malcoping strategies A and B. Specifically, in 14 correlations there were found 11 correlations with the coefficient above 0.2, all of which were confirmed at a significance level of 0.01.

In the items '*I have a headache at times*', '*I have a stomach ache*', '*I have a fast heart beat (sometimes connected with heart palpitation)*', '*I feel tired and feel lack of energy*', '*I suffer from insomnia*' **a significant correlation with malcoping strategies of A and B type with coefficients from 0.24 to 0.358 was found in all the cases**.

In the item related to '*Pain in the neck muscles*' only correlation with malcoping strategies of B type was found.

4.5 Section F – Vulnerability

However, of all types of items the biggest correlation was found in the section *Vulnerability to stress*. **The total vulnerability reaches very important correlations in malcoping strategies of A type (0.609) and B type (0.558)**. It means that the more students use these malcoping strategies the more vulnerable they are to affecting stress factors. These correlations were again confirmed on the level of significance of 0.01.

4.6 Statistical Correlations of Coping Strategies

Unlike found significant correlations in malcoping strategies **no significant correlations were found in using coping strategies**. From this fact we can conclude that if we want to improve our physical and mental state, first of all we must stop using malcoping strategies (A and B type). If we succeed, we can devote time and effort to the development of physical and mental potential of our personality with the help of coping strategies (C type). The result of the research in 2015–16 thus statistically confirmed the results already obtained from the research in previous years 2011–13.

4.7 Statistical Correlations in Items of Section E – Psychosomatic Symptoms and Items of Section C – Life Style

Items E5–C1

- Items: *I have normal memory – I sleep as much as I need*
- Correlation: **0.232**
- Explanation: This correlation of two items refers to the link between sleep duration and memory. **It is confirmed that sufficient sleep time (depending on individual needs) positively affects memory functions**.

Items E6–C1

- Items: *I feel tired and feel lack of energy – I sleep as much as I need*
- Correlation: **0.414**
- Explanation: We can see that there is a high correlation, a high level of importance. This correlation confirms the fact that **sleep duration affects the physiological state of respondents (fatigue, exhaustion level, current amount of mental and physical energy**).

Items E6–C2

- Items: *I feel tired and feel lack of energy – I eat at regular time*
- Correlation: **0.301**
- Explanation: This correlation is an interesting result because a high degree of significance shows the connection between the time of receiving food and mental and

physical state of monitored individuals. It is thus confirmed that **the students who eat at regular times are less tired and physically exhausted than the students who do not have a regular routine and appropriate regimen.**

Items E6–C5 and E7–C2

- Items: *I feel tired and feel lack of energy – During the day I have sufficient fluid intake*
- Correlation: **0.197**
- Items: *I suffer from insomnia – I eat at regular time*
- Correlation: **0.266**
- Explanation: These two correlations indicate that **sufficient fluid intake and regular consumption of food affect healthy or unhealthy functioning of the organism** – they have significant impact on the degree of mental and physical fatigue, the feeling of sufficiency or lack of energy and the quality of sleep.

Partial summary of correlation C–E. Comparing two sections of the questionnaire – section E – *Psychosomatic symptoms* and section C – *Life style* (see Table 3) confirmed our expectation, that **sufficient sleep time** has a direct impact on the state of **energy, the level of memory and the amount of fatigue**.

Table 3. Statistical correlation in items of sections E and C

Item of questionnaire E	Correlation	Question of questionnaire C
E5	0.232	C1
E6	0.414	
	0.197	C5
	0.301	C2
E7	0.266	

The research also confirmed that a regular diet (or regular eating time and regular sufficient fluid intake) positively affects the ability to fall asleep, it ensures a sufficient supply of energy for students and prevents feelings of fatigue.

4.8 Statistical Correlations in Items of Section D – Living and Social Conditions and in Items of Section C – Life Style

The correlation between individual items of section D and C is shown in Table 4. The correlation of the last item in this table (D5–C7) indicates the fact that students who **have opportunity to relax in their free time have also time to devote it to their hobbies** (nobody organizes their free time).

In the comparison of these two sections *Living and social conditions* and *Life style* we are not able to identify clear connection. Although statistically significant correlations appeared here, we cannot confirm proper statistical interconnection.

Table 4. Statistical correlation in items of sections D and C

Question of questionnaire D		Item of questionnaire C		Correlation
N.	Item	N.	Item	
1	*All my things have their place*	2	*I eat at regular time*	0.357
		4	*I eat in a hurry*	0.242
		6	*I spend my free time outdoors and in the open air*	0.194
2	*I like homely atmosphere*	2	*I eat at regular time*	0.187
		6	*I spend my free time outdoors*	0.323
		7	*I have a hobby for relaxation*	0.258
3	*I feel I would need more space at home*	1	*I sleep as long as I need*	0.233
		4	*I eat in a hurry*	0.231
5	*When at home I can have a rest*	4	*I eat in a hurry*	0.259
		7	*I have a hobby for relaxation*	0.194

4.9 Statistical Correlations in Items of Section D – Living and Social Conditions and in Items of Section E – Psychosomatic Symptoms

We assume that students who live in a peaceful household, where a regular routine is set up, with a pleasant atmosphere and where every member has his/her own personal space, will widthstand the effect of stress factors and should not feel tired and exhausted.

Items D3–E6

- Items: *I feel I would need more space at home – I feel tired and feel lack of energy*
- Correlation: **0.279**
- Explanation: Here the correlation confirms the assumption that **little living space leads to a feeling of fatigue, exhaustion and lack of energy**. There is a high correlation importance.

Items D5–E6

- Items: *When at home I can have a rest – I feel tired and feel lack of energy*
- Correlation: **0.242**
- Explanation: Assumption confirmation is high importance of correlation here. Students who **can use their free time for relaxation at home will feel less tired** than students who do not have this possibility.

Items D6–E6

- Items: *I feel that there are a lot of us living under one roof – I feel tired and feel lack of energy*
- Correlation: **0.221**
- Explanation: Students who **lack sufficient living space are more susceptible to energy losses**. It is confirmed by high level of correlation.

Items D6–E1

- Items: *I feel that there are a lot of us living under one roof – I feel tension in neck and back muscles*
- Correlation: **0.192**
- Explanation: This correlation indicates a connection between **sufficient living space for a person and psychosomatic symptoms of physical nature that a person states.**

Partial summary of correlation D–E. There is clear interconnectivity between section D – *Living and social conditions* and section E – *Psychosomatic symptoms* (see Table 5). If respondents have enough living space, they are less susceptible to physical and mental symptoms, which negatively influence their life. On the other hand, lack of living space leads to a higher degree of occurrence of psychosomatic symptoms in students.

Table 5. Statistical correlation in items of sections D and E

Item of questionnaire D	Correlation	Question of questionnaire E
D3	0.279	E6
D5	0.242	
D6	0.221	
	0.192	E1

5 Conclusion

The aim of the study was in the first place to clarify theoretical background of the issues dealing with stress factors. Also the process and statistical evaluation of our own research were described. Statistical correlations of the questionnaire survey carried out in 2011–2013 were compared. 1,322 university students participated in the survey. In the section of psychosomatic symptoms a significant correlation with malcoping strategies of A and B type with coefficients from 0.215 to 0.331 was found in selected items.

Statistical correlations of a questionnaire survey conducted in 2015–2016 among 191 students indicated that of all types of items the biggest correlation was found in the section vulnerability – vulnerability to stress. Overall vulnerability reaches very significant correlations in malcoping strategies of type A (0.609) and B (0.558). It means that the more strategies damaging their health the students use the more vulnerable they are in relation to affecting stress factors, These correlations were confirmed on the level of importance 0.01.

On the address http://qol.alltest.eu/stress the original electronic application was created [11] in the Czech and English versions thanks to which it is possible to reach much larger sample of respondents because besides the ones directly involved in the project other "anonymous" volunteers can participate in the research. All the recorded data is available immediately after it is entered and thus it can be automatically continuously evaluated.

Acknowledgments. This article was supported by the projects SPEV 2017 by the Faculty of Informatics and Management, University of Hradec Králové. We thank J. Cabal, J. Petružálek, L. Režný, and D. Šefara for their help in data collecting.

References

1. Gillernová, I., Kebza, V., Rymeš, M., et al.: Psychologické aspekty změn v české společnosti. Grada Publishing, pp. 24–25 & 119–120 (2011)
2. Bronfenbrenner, U.: The Ecology of Human Development: Experiments by Nature and Design. Harvard University Press, Cambridge (1996)
3. Goleman, D.: Emočníinteligence, p. 348, Prague, Columbus (1997)
4. Wolfson, A.R.: Bridging the gap between research and practice: What will adolescents' sleep-wake patterns look like in the 21th century? In: Carskadon, M.A. (ed.) Adolescent Sleep Patterns: Biological, Social and Psychological Influences, pp. 198–219. Cambridge University Press, New York (2002)
5. Fishbein, M., Triandis, H.C., Kanfer, F.H., Becker, M., Meddlestadt, S.E., Eichler, A.: Factors influencing behavior and behavior change. In: Handbook of Health Psychology (1998)
6. Strnadová, V.: Interpersonální komunikace, p. 543. Gaudeamus, Hradec Králové (2011)
7. Strnadová, V., Voborník, P.: Effective online education system for first year students at the university. In: 2015 International Symposium on Educational Technology (ISET), Wuhan, China, pp. 35–39. IEEE (2015)
8. Micková, E., et al.: Nepodléhejte stresu, Manuál poradce pro práci s videoprogramem. Regionální zaměstnanecká agentura, Ostrava (2004)
9. Beech, H.R.: The use of behavioral therapy in somatic stress reactions. In: Kalimo, R., El Batawi, M.A., Cooper, C.L. (eds.) Psychosomatic Factors and Work. WHO, Geneva (1987)
10. Strnadová, V.: Kurz psychologie, vol. 4, p. 309. Gaudeamus, Hradec Králové (2015)
11. Strnadová, V., Voborník, P.: Business intelligence application for analyses of stress potential zones in the population doing sports. In: Information and Software Technologies, pp. 16–28. Springer, Berlin (2015)

Effects of Mobile Apps on Learning Motivation and Study Performance of Nursing Students

Kam Cheong Li, Linda Yin-King Lee, Suet-Lai Wong, Ivy Sui-Yu Yau, and Billy Tak-Ming Wong(✉)

The Open University of Hong Kong, Hong Kong, China
{kcli,yklee,slwong,isyyau,tamiwong}@ouhk.edu.hk

Abstract. This paper reports a study on the effects of mobile apps on the learning motivation and study performance of nursing students. A total of 20 students participated in focus group interviews for collecting qualitative feedback on their learning motivation and use of mobile apps for learning. Two consecutive cohorts of students in a nursing programme, each with about 200 students, were recruited for the quantitative part of the study for assessing their learning motivation through a survey and study performance by two tests. The results showed that the students actively used the mobile apps for studying supplementary learning materials. The students maintained a relatively high level of motivation for performing and learned well, but they had relatively low perceived satisfaction and self-efficacy with mobile learning. They showed better study performance after practising mobile learning. Positive correlation was found between students' motivation in terms of intrinsic value and the improvement in learning performance after practising mobile learning. This study also suggests that students' perceived intrinsic value with mobile learning has to be enhanced for improving their study performance.

Keywords: Mobile learning · Nursing education · Learning motivation · Study performance

1 Introduction

The use of mobile technology is becoming an integral part of education. According to a McGraw-Hill Education's report in 2015 [1], almost two-thirds of US college students used mobile devices for learning purposes — a 20% increase since 2014 and a 69% increase since 2013; and the advantage mentioned most frequently by these students (64%) was mobility. Also, additional benefits of mobile learning have been widely reported, such as enhancing interaction and collaborative learning [2], and student engagement and access for learning [3]. Together with the availability of network infrastructure, these advantages serve as the key reasons for educational institutions to practise mobile learning [4].

However, the reports on such benefits are less clear about in what ways, and to what extent, mobile learning, compared with conventional classroom learning, can enhance learning motivation and study performance. Motivation has for long been identified as a necessary precondition for students to engage in learning activities and a factor

S.K.S. Cheung et al. (Eds.): ICBL 2017, LNCS 10309, pp. 259–269, 2017.
DOI: 10.1007/978-3-319-59360-9_23

influencing learning effectiveness [5]. Vogel et al. [6] also emphasize the significance of students' motivation in engaging in and sustaining the use of mobile devices for learning. However, despite findings on the overall changes in learning motivation after practising mobile learning being widely reported [e.g. 7–9], the amount of attention given to the potential relationship between specific aspects of motivation and mobile learning has been minimal [10, 11]. Also, how student performance is influenced by motivational factors in mobile learning practices has yet to be established.

This paper presents the results of a study on the effects of mobile learning on students' learning motivation and study performance. It focuses on the use of mobile apps in nursing education, which features a diversity of learning environments from classrooms to laboratories and wards, and a substantial part of clinical practicums. The results of this study contribute to the effective design and implementation of mobile learning for motivating students to engage in learning activities.

2 Related Studies

Prior research on mobile learning has shown that its effect on students' learning motivation is a critical, yet understudied, issue. Although students' attitudes towards the use of mobile devices for learning have been found to be positive in general, this does not guarantee the sustainable practice of mobile learning [12, 13]. For example, Vogel et al. [6], in an eight-week study of students' use of mobile devices for learning, found that the usage rate could be maintained at a high level only at the beginning of the study period. Li and Wang [14] pointed out that "all such efforts and research are futile or at least substantially discounted, if students are disengaged" (p. 1).

Another issue that remains inadequately explained is how mobile learning can enhance study performance. There is a paucity of empirical evidence on this matter and existing studies have only produced weak and inconclusive findings. For instance, Vogel et al. [6] found significantly improved performance in examinations for students who had actively used mobile devices for learning, compared with those who had not. However, in contrast, Williams [15] did not obtain significant results to support the superiority of mobile learning over conventional face-to-face classroom learning.

There were at least two limitations in the settings of these previous studies. First, the participants did not have a strong incentive to use mobile devices throughout a long period of time — their motivation to keep using the mobile devices seemed weak [6]. To conduct such studies effectively, students must be placed in a real learning environment in which their learning outcomes are important. Second, the significance of these research studies was often limited by not having a large enough group of participants practising mobile learning over a sufficiently long period of time, thus not getting results close to real-life practices and with sufficient statistical power. For instance, Park et al. [16] found that the students were not even able to master the use of mobile devices for learning over a five-week period of time. Therefore, there is a need to assess the effectiveness of mobile learning which is implemented in a real setting for an extended time period among a relatively large group of students [17]. The present study, in which mobile learning was situated in a real setting among over 200 students and had been practised for at least one academic semester, represents an effort to fill the gap in previous research.

Learning motivation has not been well-elaborated as a concept in models related to mobile learning. For example, in Koole's FRAME model [18], mobile learning is effective when three aspects — the device, learner and social factors — are all covered, and where motivation is only one of the attributes in the learner aspect without further specification. Similarly, Yau and Joy [19] propose a model consisting of five dimensions relevant to students' preferences for mobile learning. Learners' level of motivation is one of the dimensions where possible factors are suggested, such as intrinsic and extrinsic motivations, without further validation.

On the other hand, there have been extensive studies on learning motivation. It has been viewed as central to engagement in learning [20, 21], and consists of a variety of components following two dominant theories in explaining motivation, namely achievement goal theory and expectancy-value theory [22]. In the achievement goal theory, students have different purposes or goal orientations for engaging in academic tasks, including (1) performance goal orientation — demonstration of competence relative to others, and (2) mastery goal orientation — the development of competence and mastery of tasks [23, 24]. The expectancy-value theory suggests that students' achievement and engagement are influenced by their perceived value of tasks and expectations of success [25]. The perceived value of a task includes three components, namely the (1) intrinsic value — the enjoyment gained from doing the task; (2) attainment value — how important it is to do well in the task; and (3) utility value — how useful the task is in relation to one's future [26]. This conceptualization of learning motivation is adopted in the present study.

3 Methodology

This project aims to identify the effects of mobile learning on students' learning motivation and study performance in the context of nursing education. It was conducted in a university in Hong Kong, which has been extending the provision of mobile learning to its nursing courses [27, 28]. For learning purposes, each new nursing student is given a tablet which includes mobile learning apps developed for the nursing courses, with specific features such as a clinical glossary, videos of nursing procedures and real-time quizzes.

This research examines students' learning motivation and study performance before and after using mobile learning. With their written consent, two cohorts (2014 and 2015) of undergraduate nursing students from a course on Health Assessment were recruited for this study. Unlike the 2015 cohort, the 2014 cohort had not yet practised mobile learning.

Data on the learning motivation were collected through (1) a focus group interview with 20 participants focusing on their experiences after practising mobile learning; and (2) a questionnaire survey (225 participants) after using mobile learning for a semester. The questionnaire was adopted from a validated instrument from a previous study by Wong and Li [29], which was adapted to the mobile learning context for this study. It consisted of 12 items covering six motivational factors, i.e. performance goal orientation, mastery goal orientation, intrinsic value, attainment value, utility and self-efficacy.

The students' study performance was examined using a test of their knowledge, which included 30 questions on the comprehension and application of nursing concepts, which were taught in class and covered in their mobile learning apps. The test was conducted at the end of the course for the 2014 cohort (184 students, without practising mobile learning); and at both the start and end of the course for the 2015 cohort (225 students, before and after practising mobile learning).

4 Results

The results are based on both qualitative analysis of the students' responses in the focus group interview, and quantitative analysis of the questionnaire survey data, together with assessment of the students' study performance. The findings address three major areas: (1) the effect of mobile apps on students' learning motivation; (2) the effect of mobile apps on students' study performance; and (3) the relationship between students' learning motivation and study performance.

4.1 Students' Learning Motivation

To understand the students' motivation and/or obstacles to practising mobile learning, a triangulation method was adopted, covering both qualitative analysis of the interview data from the students, and quantitative analysis of survey data about students' motivation in mobile learning.

Focus Group Interview. The responses of students with experience of mobile learning revealed the benefits from and obstacles in using mobile learning, and improvements which could be made to help in transforming positive attitudes towards mobile learning, if any, to actual practice among the students. Three aspects of the responses from the students are summarized below.

First, the students were generally satisfied with the nursing videos provided in the mobile app for revisiting relevant skills in clinical practicums. They pointed out that the video content helped them to visualize the procedures in real practice and facilitated their retention of the content. The mobile app was seen to be useful throughout the whole learning cycle, from engaging in in-class quizzes to after-class revision. Student 'ES' said:

> I will use [the nursing video app] for review purposes, because the app contains a lot of videos and then I can practise the nursing skills using the app.

Second, the mobile app used for clinical assessment in wards promoted interaction between students and mentors. Student 'CH' explained:

> The clinical mentor can use the assessment app to monitor our study progress and give feedback immediately. When we are practising wound dressing, for example, the clinical mentor can check which students have passed the assessment on that item through the mobile app, and focus more on helping those students who need more assistance.

Third, institutional support, such as technical assistance and warranty of the devices throughout the students' study period, was highly recommended by the students, as this motivated their use of the mobile devices without worrying about bearing the maintenance cost on their own. The students indicated the technical problems they encountered, such as unstable connection of the device to the server. For example, student 'M' talked about his experiences:

> There was a time I have completed a clinical assessment using the app, but the system displayed that I have not completed the assessment items. I needed to call the technical support staff for help. This is important as sometimes there are technical problems with the mobile app we cannot solve.

Questionnaire Survey. The students' motivation in mobile learning was also shown in their ratings on 12 questionnaire items on various motivational factors. Table 1 shows the mean ratings of the items (using a 7-point Likert scale ranging from 1 "strongly disagree" to 7 "strongly agree"). Table 2 shows the mean ratings on the six motivational factors.

Table 1. Mean ratings on items about students' motivation in mobile learning

Rank	Item #	Item content	Mean	SD	n
1	11	It is important for me to have an outstanding academic performance	4.92	1.14	225
2	10	If I am interested in the course, I still want to learn no matter whether the course content is difficult or not	4.86	1.18	225
3	7	I think these mobile apps can be used as supplementary materials for other nursing courses	4.76	1.23	223
4	9	I want to learn as much as possible in this course	4.73	1.06	224
5	4	I enjoy self-paced learning by using the mobile apps	4.68	1.13	225
6	12	Outperforming my classmates is my learning motivation	4.65	1.16	225
7	5	Using these mobile apps for study can enhance my understanding of health assessment	4.61	1.13	225
8	3	These mobile apps arouse my interest and motivate my self-study	4.59	1.24	225
9	6	My learning experience with these mobile apps adds value to my overall academic performance	4.53	1.07	225
10	2	My level of satisfaction with these mobile apps for health assessment is high	4.47	1.19	224
11	1	I have learnt a lot from these mobile apps	4.40	1.22	224
12	8	I think mobile learning is better than classroom learning	4.09	1.37	225

The results showed various extents of effects of the mobile learning practice on the motivational factors. The students gave relatively high ratings for both mastery goal orientation and performance goal orientation. They considered it was important to obtain outstanding academic performance and to outperform others. They also showed strong motivation to master the content of the course and learn as much as possible.

Table 2. Average ratings on items about students' motivation in mobile learning

Rank	Items #	Factor	Mean	SD	n
1	9, 10	Mastery goal orientation	4.79	1.01	225
2	11, 12	Performance goal orientation	4.79	1.05	225
3	3, 4	Attainment value	4.63	1.12	223
4	5, 6	Self-efficacy	4.57	1.02	224
5	1, 2	Intrinsic value	4.55	1.06	225
6	7, 8	Utility	4.42	1.11	225

The factors related to the perceived value and expectation of success in mobile learning — intrinsic value, utility and self-efficacy — were rated relatively low. While the students enjoyed the self-paced learning through the mobile apps, the perceived level of self-efficacy and the added value to learning interest and performance were ranked at a medium level. In addition, the students' satisfaction with the mobile apps, the overall good learning outcome from using it, and the relative advantage of mobile learning over classroom learning were rated lowest.

There is a statistically significant difference between the high and low ratings for motivational factors. For example, comparing the ratings for mastery goal orientation and utility using an independent sample t-test, $t(448) = 3.70, p < .01$, the result suggests that the students' practice of mobile learning would have varying degree of effect on different aspects of their learning motivation.

4.2 Study Performance

The study performance of students practising mobile learning was shown by group comparison of the test scores between the students who had not practised mobile learning (2014 cohort) and those who had practised mobile learning (2015 cohort). A pretest-posttest analysis of the test scores was also conducted for the same group of students (2015 cohort) before and after using mobile learning.

Group Comparison. Table 3 shows the test scores for the conventional learning group and the mobile learning group, and the results of an independent sample *t*-test. Of the three types of scores, only the application score showed a significant group differences — $t(384) = 3.15, p < .01$ — indicating that the mobile learning group outperformed the conventional learning group in terms of the application of nursing concepts.

Table 3. Comparison of test scores between two learning groups

Test score*	Conventional learning group (n = 184)		Mobile learning group (n = 202)		t	p
	M	SD	M	SD		
Comprehension	9.66	2.37	9.57	1.86	−0.44	.66
Application	9.82	2.12	10.46	1.87	3.15	<.01
Total	19.48	3.91	20.03	3.03	1.54	.12

* Full score: 15 for comprehension and application, and 30 in total.

Pretest-posttest Analysis. A pretest-posttest analysis was conducted on the same group of students before and after practising mobile learning. It addresses the limitations of the group comparison between two different cohorts — the differences in test scores might be due to other between-group differences that are relevant to the study performance, for example different learning ability of two naturally occurring groups, but not the effect of mobile learning.

Table 4 presents the results for a paired sample t-test for the test scores. The results show that the students had a significant improvement in all test scores after using mobile learning. The mobile learning practice helped the students to obtain a better learning outcome.

Table 4. Pretest-posttest analysis of test scores before and after mobile learning

Test score*	Before mobile learning		After mobile learning		n	t	p
	M	SD	M	SD			
Comprehension	8.56	2.01	9.60	1.88	180	5.21	<.01
Application	8.86	2.02	10.46	1.86	180	7.86	<.01
Total	17.33	3.67	20.07	3.05	181	7.75	<.01

* Full score: 15 for comprehension and application, and 30 in total.

4.3 Relationship Between Students' Motivation and Study Performance

A correlation analysis was carried out between students' motivation ratings and their learning performance in order to determine whether the students' study performance after practising mobile learning was related to students' motivation in mobile learning.

Correlations between Learning Motivation and Study Performance. A correlation analysis was conducted between the students' motivation and the test scores for the students after practising mobile learning. Table 5 presents the Pearson correlation coefficients for each pair of variables, including the correlations of each of the three test scores with the aggregate score for motivation rating (taking the mean of the 12

Table 5. Correlations between students' learning motivation and study performance

Motivation ratings	Test score		
	Comprehension	Application	Total
	r(200)	*r*(200)	*r*(200)
Motivation (aggregate)	.05	.08	.08
Mastery goal orientation	.08	.03	.06
Performance goal orientation	.09	.06	.06
Attainment value	−.01	.10	.05
Self-efficacy	.03	.07	.06
Intrinsic value	.04	.11	.10
Utility	−.01	.01	−.00

questionnaire items) and the sub-score for each of the six factors. No significant correlations were found, indicating that the test performance may be predicted better by other variables.

Correlations between Motivation and Improvement in Study Performance. Another correlation analysis was conducted to test whether the students' motivation was related to the extent of improvement in study performance. This analysis focused on the amount of progress made by each individual participant after practising mobile learning, which may be more specifically related to motivation to practise mobile learning. The improvement of each participant's study performance was measured by subtracting the test scores before mobile learning from the scores after mobile learning. The improvement in test scores was then correlated with the motivation scores.

Table 6 presents the Pearson correlation coefficients for each pair of variables. The results show a significant correlation between improvement in total scores and the sub-score for intrinsic value: $r(179) = .15$, $p < .05$. Despite the weak positive association indicating that such improvement may be related to other variables, the result suggests that it is important for motivating students in terms of their perceived intrinsic value — the enjoyment gained from practising mobile learning — to gain improvement in study performance.

Table 6. Correlations between students' motivation and study performance improvement

Motivation ratings	Improvement in test score		
	Comprehension	Application	Total
	$r(178)$	$r(178)$	$r(179)$
Motivation (aggregate)	.140	.08	.13
Mastery goal orientation	.15	−.00	.09
Performance goal orientation	.12	.02	.05
Attainment value	.11	.12	.15
Self-efficacy	.13	.09	.13
Intrinsic value	.12	.11	.15*
Utility	.10	.07	.11

* $p < .05$.

5 Discussion

The findings showed the potential effect of mobile apps on students' learning motivation, particularly in terms of overcoming the limitations of conventional classroom learning. The participants, who were situated in a real learning context, maintained a relatively high motivation for practising mobile learning. This addresses the limitations in previous research where mobile learning was practised in an experimental setting [6, 17]. The students' feedback highlighted the advantages of mobile learning over conventional face-to-face classroom learning, which provided them with incentives to engage in mobile learning. For example, the students' expectations for multimedia and interactive learning materials and features for facilitating student-teacher interactions were satisfied according to those who had practised mobile learning. Particularly in clinical practicums, the students deemed the learning content and quick feedback between students and mentors useful and significant. This confirms the effectiveness of the use of mobile technologies in promoting just-in-time and contextual learning which have been emphasized in nursing education [10, 30]. The mobile learning practice was shown to have tackled the technological and policy challenges as stated in Khaddage et al. [11] regarding the need for apps developed for specific courses and the provision of technical support. The positive students' experience suggests how the effectiveness of the practice enhanced their motivation in learning.

The students had a better study performance after practising mobile learning. The findings showed that such improvement was correlated with the students' intrinsic value in mobile learning, highlighting the importance of students' enjoyment in achieving better academic performance. This finding enriched the present understanding of the impact of mobile learning on students' motivation. Instead of enhancing motivation in general [6, 8, 9], mobile learning may improve one or more specific aspects of motivation. In this regard, the design of mobile learning activities could have more specific objectives in relation to motivating students to learn. Also, as only one motivational factor was found to be associated with improvement in performance, there are potentially other factors leading to the improvement. This suggests that there should be future work on exploring the effect of having higher student motivation in mobile learning and its influence on students' learning outcomes.

This study also points out possible linkage between relevant frameworks of mobile learning and motivation theories. While motivation has yet to be well-elaborated in mobile learning models such as Koole's FRAME model [18] and Yau and Joy's five dimensional model [19], the findings in this study showed that motivational factors as identified in the achievement goal theory and expectancy-value theory [22–25] can serve to categorize students' motivation in mobile learning and thus potentially extend the relevant models or frameworks in this aspect.

6 Conclusion

The study presented in this paper has highlighted the potential effects of mobile apps on learning motivation and study performance in the context of nursing education. It has shown the importance of conducting mobile learning research in a real setting for an extended period of time and the significance of implementing mobile learning practice with the potential technological and policy challenges taken into consideration. These factors would affect students' experience in and incentives for engaging in mobile learning activities. The results of this study reveal possible effect of mobile learning on different motivational factors, and show that not each motivational factor may be related to study performance.

These findings contribute to advancing mobile learning research in refining aspects of both theory and implementation. They suggest possible links between existing frameworks of mobile learning and theories of motivation, and their influence on study performance. Future work in this regard will lead to a better theoretical foundation for mobile learning and more effective measures for motivating student engagement.

Acknowledgement. The work described in this paper was substantially supported by a grant from the Research Grants Council of the Hong Kong Special Administrative Region, China (UGC/FDS16/H10/14).

References

1. McGraw-Hill Education: Are learning analytics the new 'Likes'? 87% of college students perform better with access to personalized data, new research finds (2015). http://www.mheducation.com/news-media/press-releases/learning-analytics-new-likes-college-better-access-personalized-data-new-research.html
2. Project Tomorrow: Project K-Nect evaluation report. Irvine: Project Tomorrow (2010). http://www.tomorrow.org/docs/Project_k-Nect_Evaluationreport_Final_Jul7.pdf
3. Aderinoye, R.A., Ojokheta, K.O., Olojede, A.A.: Integrating mobile learning into nomadic education programmes in Nigeria: issues and perspectives. Int. Rev. Res. Open Distance Learn. **8**(2) (2007). doi:10.19173/irrodl.v8i2.347
4. UNESCO: Policy guidelines for mobile learning. The United Nations Educational. Scientific and Cultural Organization (2013). http://unesdoc.unesco.org/images/0021/002196/219641e.pdf
5. Malone, T.W., Lepper, M.R.: Making learning fun: a taxonomy of intrinsic motivations for learning. In: Snow, R.E., Farr, M.J. (eds.) Aptitude, Learning, and Instruction: III. Conative and Affective Process Analyses, pp. 223–253. Erlbaum, Hillsdale (1987)
6. Vogel, D., Kennedy, D.M., Kwok, R.: Does using mobile device applications lead to learning? J. Interact. Learn. Res. **20**(4), 469–485 (2009)
7. Ciampa, K.: Learning in a mobile age: an investigation of student motivation. J. Comput. Assist. Learn. **30**, 82–96 (2014). doi:10.1111/jcal.12036
8. Gregory, K.H., Crompton, H.: The relationship between mobile learning, instructional delivery, and student motivation in a large undergraduate science class. In: Crompton, H., Traxler, J. (eds.) Mobile Learning and STEM: Case Studies in Practice, pp. 162–172. Routledge, New York (2016)
9. Koole, M., McQuilkin, J.L., Ally, M.: Mobile learning in distance education: utility or futility? J. Distance Educ. **24**(2), 59–82 (2010)
10. Chan, D.: Development of the clinical learning environment inventory: Using the theoretical framework of learning environment studies to assess nursing students' perceptions of the hospital as a learning environment. J. Nurs. Educ. **41**(2), 69–75 (2002)
11. Khaddage, F., Christensen, R., Lai, W., Knezek, G., Norris, C., Soloway, E.: A model driven framework to address challenges in a mobile learning environment. Educ. Inf. Technol. **20**(4), 625–640 (2015). doi:10.1007/s10639-015-9400-x
12. Garrett, B.M., Jackson, C.: A mobile clinical e-portfolio for nursing and medical students, using wireless personal digital assistants (PDAs). Nurse Educ. Today **26**, 647–654 (2006). doi:10.1016/j.nedt.2006.07.020
13. Kenny, R.F., Park, C.L., van Neste-Kenny, J.M.C., Burton, P.A.: Mobile self-efficacy in Canadian nursing education programs. In: 9th World Conference on Mobile Learning (mLearn 2010), Valletta, Malta (2010)
14. Li, K.C., Wang, F.L.: Student engagement: meanings, approaches and ideas for educators interested in ICT. In: Li, K.C., Wang, F.L., Yuen, K.S., Cheung, S.K.S., Kwan, R. (eds.) Engaging Learners through Emerging Technology. CCIS, vol. 302, pp. 1–10. Springer (2012)

15. Williams, P.W.: Assessing mobile learning effectiveness and acceptance. Ph.D. thesis, George Washington University (2009)
16. Park, C., van Neste-Kenny, J.M.C., Burton, P.A., Kenny, R.F.: A model of mobile faculty presence in nursing education practise. Can. J. Nurs. Inf. **5**(3), 21–42 (2010)
17. Kenny, R.F., van Neste-Kenny, J.M.C., Park, C.L., Burton, P.A., Meiers, J.: Mobile learning in nursing practise education: applying Koole's FRAME model. J. Distance Educ. **23**(3), 75–96 (2009)
18. Koole, M.L.: A model for framing mobile learning. In: Ally, M. (ed.) Mobile Learning: Transforming the Delivery of Education and Training, pp. 25–47. AU Press, Edmonton (2009)
19. Yau, J.Y.K., Joy, M.S.: Proposal of a mobile learning preferences model. Int. J. Interact. Mob. Teach. **4**(4), 49–51 (2010). doi:10.3991/ijim.v4i4.1445
20. Appleton, J., Christenson, S.L., Furlong, M.: Student engagement with school: critical conceptual and methodological issues of the construct. Psychol. Schools **45**, 369–386 (2008). doi:10.1002/pits.20303
21. Furrer, C., Skinner, E.: Sense of relatedness as a factor in children's academic engagement and performance. J. Educ. Psychol. **95**(1), 148–162 (2003). doi:10.1037//0022-0663.95.1.148
22. Liem, A.D., Lau, S., Nie, Y.: The role of self-efficacy, task value, and achievement goals in predicting learning strategies, task disengagement, peer relationship, and achievement outcome. Contemp. Educ. Psychol. **33**(4), 486–512 (2008). doi:10.1016/j.cedpsych.2007.08.001
23. Elliot, A.J.: Approach and avoidance motivation and achievement goals. Educ. Psychol. **34**(3), 169–189 (1999). doi:10.4324/9780203888148.ch13
24. Linnenbrink, E.A., Pintrich, P.R.: Achievement goal theory and affect: an asymmetrical bidirectional model. Educ. Psychol. **37**(2), 69–78 (2002). doi:10.1207/s15326985ep3702_2
25. Pintrich, P.R., Schunk, D.H.: Motivation in Education: Theory, Research, and Applications, 2nd edn. Merrill/Prentice-Hall, Englewood Cliffs (2002)
26. Berger, J.L., Karabenick, S.A.: Motivation and students' use of learning strategies: evidence of unidirectional effects in mathematics classrooms. Learn. Instr. **21**, 416–428 (2011). doi:10.1016/j.learninstruc.2010.06.002
27. Li, K.C., Lee, L.Y.K., Wong, S.L., Yau, I.S.Y., Wong, B.T.M.: Preparing for mobile learning in nursing education: perspectives of students and teachers. In: 29th Annual Conference of the Asian Association of Open Universities (AAOU), Kuala Lumpur, Malaysia (2015)
28. Li, K.C., Lee, L.Y.K., Wong, S.L., Yau, I.S.Y., Wong, B.T.M.: Mobile learning in nursing education: preference and readiness of nursing students. In: 2nd International Conference on Open and Flexible Education (ICOFE), pp. 313–323, Hong Kong, China (2015)
29. Wong, S.N., Li, K.C.: Learner engagement and motivation: a study of distance learning students in Hong Kong. In: 25th World Conference of the International Council for Open and Distance Education, Tianjin, China (2013)
30. Rees, S., Moloney, C., Farley, H.: Mobile learning initiatives in nursing education. In: Zhang, Y. (ed.) Handbook of Mobile Teaching and Learning, pp. 275–289. Springer, Heidelberg (2015)

Computer-Support Collaborative Learning

Empirical Study on Google Earth (GE)-Integrated Science Lessons: Cases from Two Chinese Elementary Schools

Xiuli Cheng[1], Yuqing Guo[2(✉)], and Yan Li[2]

[1] National Center for Educational Technology, Room 609, No. 160 Fu Xingmen Nei Street, Beijing, China
Xiuli_c1217@126.com

[2] Zhejiang University, Room 118, Shao Yifu Building, No. 148 Tian Mushan Road, Hang Zhou, Zhejiang Province, China
Niki.y.guo@gmail.com, yanli@zju.edu.cn

Abstract. The goal of the study is to investigate the effectiveness of applying Google Earth (GE) in an elementary science lesson by comparing the academic results between GE-integrated instruction and traditional instruction. The teaching practice was implemented in two Chinese elementary schools located in Hangzhou, Zhejiang Province. The GE-integrated and traditional inquiry activities were both designed based on 5E learning cycle and qualitative and quantitative methods were used to test the effectiveness of GE-integrated instruction. Data analysis found that: (1) students shown great interests in GE-integrated science lesson; (2) teachers held positive attitude toward the application of GE in science teaching; (3) there were no significant differences in academic results between traditional instruction and GE-integrated instruction. Suggestions and proposals were put forward at the end of the study.

Keywords: 5E learning cycle · Elementary science · Google Earth (GE) · Integrating

1 Introduction

With the positive influence of information technology on education being recognized by more and more people, the integration of geospatial technologies in K-12 science education becomes increasingly popular. As one of geographical technologies to some extent, GE has captured much attention of researchers and educators. According to Britt and LaFontain [1], lessons incorporating GE attract students in a deeper understanding of their place in the world. With the help of GE, students can explore the earth in a more interactive, meaningful and dynamic manner, learning their locale in the context of the globe [2]. Empirical studies focusing on integrating GE in middle school science teaching found that the software played important role in promoting students' academic results, spatial literacy and other aspects. The study of Kulo and Bodzin integrated GE into the teaching of Energy in the science curriculum of eighth grade [3]. The results of the experimental classes showed that students' knowledge about energy were enriched, their ability of spatial thinking enhanced through integrating GE into science teaching. Besides, the software provided better learning experience compared with traditional

S.K.S. Cheung et al. (Eds.): ICBL 2017, LNCS 10309, pp. 273–283, 2017.
DOI: 10.1007/978-3-319-59360-9_24

teaching. To find a better way to use GE to improve learning geographic features, Bodzin and Cirucci integrated GE into the middle school science teaching [4]. The results showed that students' science learning interests and the ability to analyze remote sensing images were highly improved. The same results were found in the research of Almquist et al. [5]. In their empirical research of integrating GE into teaching plate tectonics unit of grade seven, they found that students' comprehension capacity and spatial thinking ability were greatly improved; moreover, students' attitude toward science learning were transformed through the application of GE.

It can be seen that applying GE in science teaching has attracted the attention of educators and practitioners, and most results of the studies indicated that the software promotes students' science study in many aspects, such as the knowledge acquisition, spatial literacy or inquiry ability. Another important thing found through analyzing existing studies is that the studies mostly focus on integrating GE in middle school science teaching. Researches on implementing the software in elementary science teaching, nevertheless, are relatively scarce.

The aim of the study was to answer two questions: (1) Is it feasible to apply GE in elementary science lessons? (2) Is there any difference in students' performances in academic tests after taking GE-integrated instruction and traditional instruction?

To answer the first question, the study investigates elementary school students and teachers' attitude toward using GE in their science classroom. For the second question, the study adopts comparing the academic results of traditional teaching classes and the classes applying GE.

2 Theoretical Base-5E Learning Cycle

The GE-integrated activities were designed based on 5E learning cycle in the study. 5E learning cycle is an instruction mode widely used in education, especially in science

Table 1. Summary of the 5E learning cycle

Phase	Summary
Engagement	The teacher accesses to learners' prior knowledge and helps them engage in a new concept by providing an attractive activity or a question.
Exploration	The teacher provides learners with inquiry activities, within which learners' existing concepts and skills are identified.
Explanation	The explanation phase provides opportunities for learners to demonstrate their conceptual understanding or process skills through the inquiry activities. After learners' demonstration, the teacher corrects their misunderstandings and directly introduces the new concept or skill.
Elaboration	Challenging activities or questions are proposed in the elaboration stage to extend learners' utility of new concepts or skills.
Evaluation	The evaluation stage of 5E learning cycle encourages learners to assess their concept learning and provides opportunities for teachers to evaluate the performance of the learners through the four stages.

Notes: *Summary of the BSCS 5E Instructional Model*

education. Basically, it is inquiry-based, grounded in the constructivist philosophy of learning. The model consists of five phases: engagement, exploration, explanation, elaboration and evaluation. Each phase has a specific function and helps teachers' instruction and learners' acquisition of a better understanding of science and technology [6]. The following table shows the functions and tasks of each phase of 5E learning cycle (Table 1).

5E learning cycle instructional model can be applied at different levels of designing curriculum materials [7]. The effectiveness of the model on science education has been demonstrated by researches. Learners' performance on subject knowledge is better compared with those taught by traditional or other instructional modes [8–10]. In addition to the effect on learners' subject knowledge achievements, instructions based on 5E learning cycle is found to be fun and interesting, and motivated learners' science learning and improved their thinking ability [11]. Besides, teachers and learners' attitude toward science learning are promoted with the help of the model. Researches have confirmed that the sustained use of an effective and research-based instructional model is helpful for learners to learn fundamental concepts in science [12]. 5E learning cycle is a relatively mature one in science education and its effectiveness has been demonstrated by amount of studies. In view of this, the study chooses the mode to guide the design of GE-integrated inquiry activities.

3 5E Learning Cycle-Based Instructional Design

The GE-integrated activity design of the study focuses on two modules of the unit The Surface and Its Change of the Earth in the textbook of fifth grade: The Surface of the Earth and The Topographical Change Caused by the Interior Movement of the Earth. Taking module one: The Surface of the Earth as an example, the following elaborates the 5E learning cycle based activity design on GE. The sequence of the activity is designed following the procedure of 5E learning cycle, i.e. engagement, exploration, explanation, elaboration and evaluation. Concrete procedures of teaching are provided in Fig. 1 in accordance with the five steps of 5E learning cycle to guide science teachers to implement their teaching.

The whole sequence of teaching The Landforms of the Earth consists of five activities, each of which corresponding to one procedure of 5E learning cycle. The activities are designed concrete and practical, following the rules of 5E learning cycle and implemented on GE. The key point of the module is to learn the concept of landform. Three questions relevant to landforms are proposed to arouse students to recall and demonstrate their prior knowledge about the surface of the earth. Inquiry activities on GE are assigned to explore the surface of the earth after students were engaged in the learning content. The exploration of landforms on GE takes the five basic terrains of China as an example. In the stage of exploration, students first learn the five basic terrains of China on GE. With the help of the various functions of GE, students explore the features of the five basic terrains and others ones of China.

To explore a terrain, students firstly learn about the brief introduction of it. Figure 2 showed the landmark of Tibet Plateau developed on GE through the "landmark" function of the software.

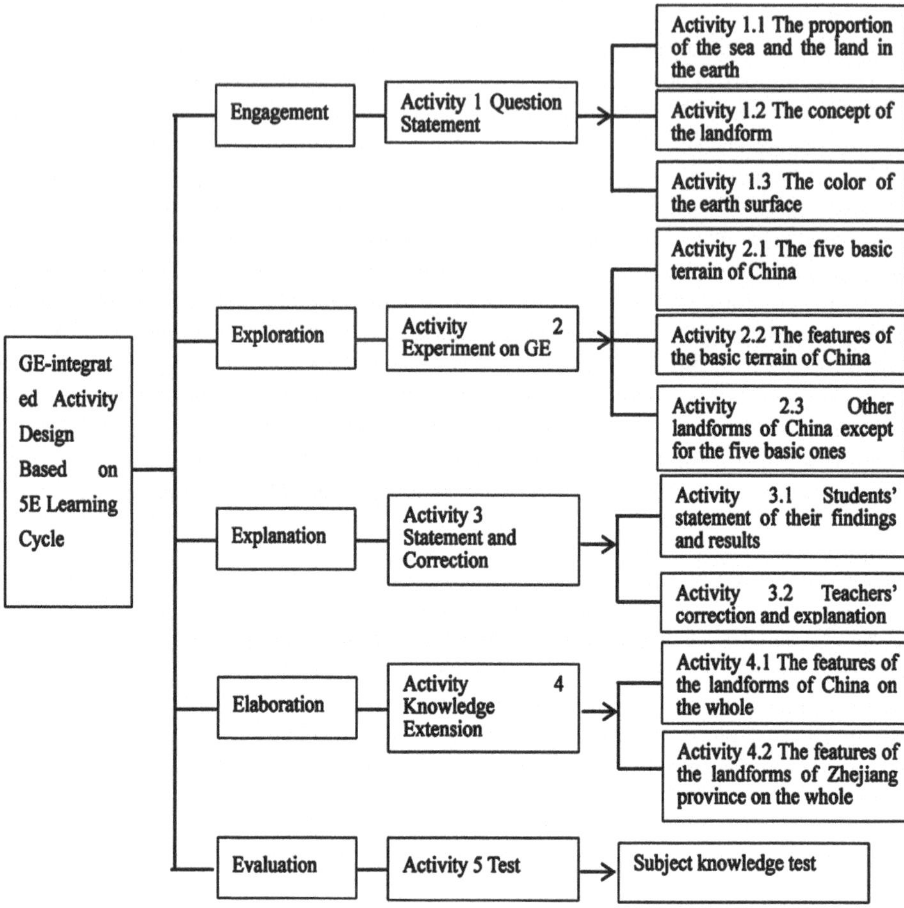

Fig. 1. Activity design based on 5E learning cycle for learning the landforms of the Earth

Figure 3 is the Tibet Plateau highlighted on GE for students to learn plateau in detail in the study. Overlay function of GE was used to outline the plateau. The location, elevation and profile of terrains are the data students should collect in their exploration on GE.

To deepen their understanding of plateau and provide help for their exploration on GE, the study requires students to explore the topography of plateau using the function of setting up profile map of Tibet Plateau of GE (Fig. 4).

There are mainly two tasks in the explanation stage: firstly, students state their findings through exploration activities on Google Earth. Proofs are required to demonstrate their results. After students' demonstration, teacher corrects their faults and illustrates the concept of landform and relevant knowledge directly. Activities in elaboration stage are designed to deepen students' understanding of the concept of landform and extend their knowledge. The main task in the elaboration stage is to learn the features

Fig. 2. Landmark of Tibet Plateau on GE

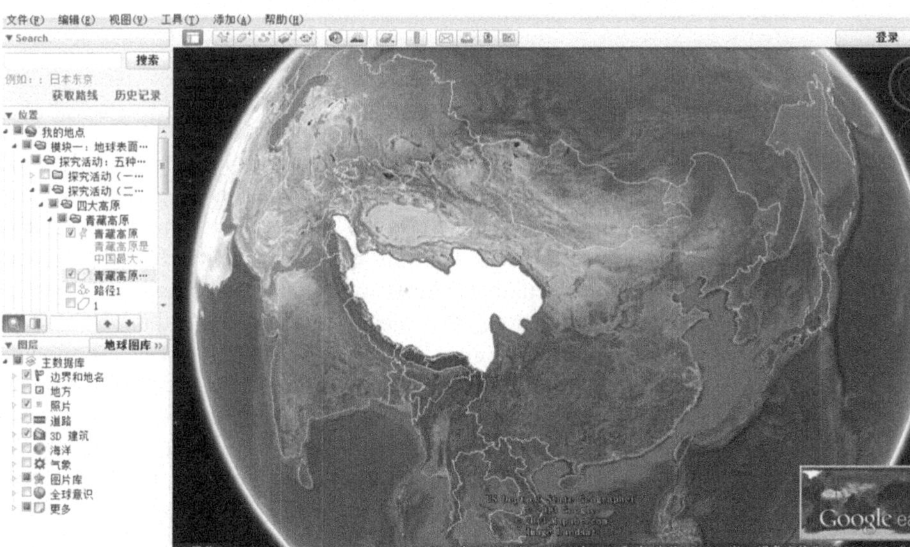

Fig. 3. The Profile of Tibet Plateau highlighted on GE

of the terrains of China and Zhejiang province as a whole on GE, applying students' new knowledge about landforms. Tests are carried out after all the activities are implemented.

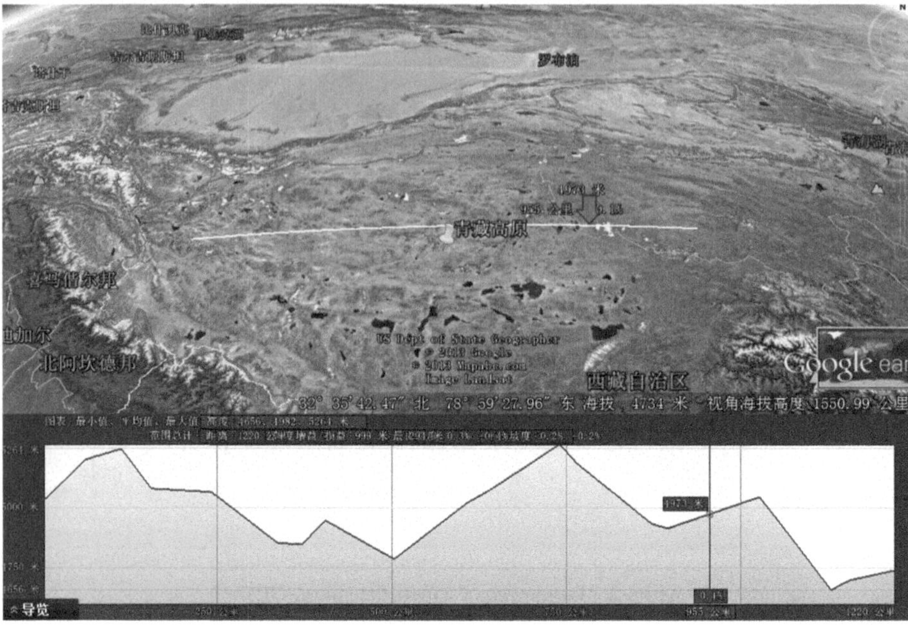

Fig. 4. The profile map of Tibet Plateau on GE

4 Methodology

Quantitative and qualitative methods were used to collect data in the study. Quantitative analysis refers to the pre-and post-test of students in both controlled and experimental classes. In order to compare the results between traditional class and experimental class objectively, the instruction were both designed on the base of 5E Learning Cycle. The purpose of the tests is to measure students' learning status and the results of traditional teaching as well as GE-based instruction. The tests were composed of two patterns: the multiple choice and true or false questions. The questions were designed on the basis of analyzing the key points of the two modules. There were twelve questions in module one and eleven questions in module two. Each question was assigned to one point. Therefore, there are twelve points in total of module one and eleven points in module two. The pre-test was carried out in October, 2014, when the two modules were not started yet. The post-test, questionnaire and interview were carried out in December, 2014 when participating students and science teachers finished both of the two modules.

Questionnaire survey and interview were used as qualitative analysis in order to get a deeper understanding of the result and feeling of using GE. The questionnaire was adapted from Davis, which was structured in three parts [13]. The first part aimed at collecting data about the usefulness of GE in science learning, which was measured by four items, including "using GE would enhance my effectiveness in science learning", "using GE would improving my performance in science learning", "I think GE is useful in science learning" and "using GE in science classroom would enhance my productivity". The second part aimed at collecting data about the usability of using GE, which were measured by four items, including "I would find GE easy to use", "it takes short time for me to master operation of GE", "it would be easy for me to become skillful at using GE" and "I would find it easy to use GE to do what I want to do". The third part was used to collect data about students' satisfaction of GE, which measured by six items. The sample statements were "I am glad that I could have the chance to use GE to learn science", "if I had an opportunity to take another course by using GE, I would gladly to do so", "I was very satisfied with the course". For these items, there was a five-point Likert scale for students to express their views: 1 = Strongly Disagree; 2 = Disagree; 3 = Neutral; 4 = Agree; 5 = Strongly Agree.

Interview was used to analyze the experience of two science teachers of using GE in their science teaching, which mainly focused on three questions:

Q1: What's the advantage of using GE in the science classroom?
Q2: Are there any difficulties in using the software?
Q3: What's the main problem in promoting the application of GE in science classroom?

5 Instructional Implementation

Four natural classes of fifth grade from two elementary schools (named School W and School T in the study) located in Hangzhou, Zhejiang Province were randomly selected as controlled and experimental class. Both of the two selected schools are typical urban elementary schools. In each of the two selected schools, one class was randomly selected as experimental class and the other the comparing one. The Table 2 below gives the detailed information about these four classes.

Table 2. Target students in the study

Class	Number of students	
	School W	School T
Experimental class	41	21
Control class	40	24

GE-integrated instruction was used in the two experimental classes, while traditional teaching method applied in the two controlled classes. The study involved two science teachers from the two schools. In each school, the same science teacher taught both the experimental and the controlled class. Therefore, except for GE, other variables were the same in both the experimental and controlled classes in each school. The target students had experience in "Group Cooperative Learning" in their daily learning, and were qualified with basic computer skills. Experimental and control classes were tested by the same questions and comparison between them was carried out. The results of both the pre-and post-test were analyzed by T-test through SPSS software to compare the result between applying GE and traditional instruction in elementary science teaching.

6 Findings

Pre-and post-test data analysis

Table 3 summarized the comparative results of pre- and post-test of experimental and controlled classes in module one. In pre-test, no significant differences were found in students' performance between the experimental and controlled classes in both School T and School W. In the post-test, results of t-test found that there were no significant differences between students' performance between the experimental class and control class in School T while there was significant difference between students' performance between the experimental class and control class in School W. The mean score of experimental class in the post-test of module one was 8.56, while the controlled class was 9.75 and the P value was 0.00 (<0.05). The result of the controlled class in the post-test was significantly superior to the experimental.

Table 3. Comparison between students' performance in pre-and post-tests in module one (n = 126)

Module one	School	Class	N	Mean	SD	DF	T	P
Pre-test	T	Experimental class	21	8.10	1.76	43	1.96	.06
		Controlled class	24	7.04	1.83			
	W	Experimental class	41	7.51	2.06	79	.82	.41
		Controlled class	40	7.88	1.91			
Post-test	T	Experimental class	21	9.10	1.84	43	1.96	.06
		Controlled class	24	8.04	1.76			
	W	Experimental class	41	8.56	1.98	68	3.24**	.00
		Controlled class	40	9.75	1.26			

Table 4 summarized the comparative results of pre- and post-test in module two in experimental and controlled classes. In pre-test, no significant differences were found in students' performance between the experimental and controlled classes in both School T and School W. In the post-test, results of t-test found that there was no significant difference between students' performance between the experimental class and control class in School W while there was significant difference between students' performance between the experimental class and control class in School T. The mean score of experimental class in the post-test of module one was 8.38, while the controlled class was 7.21 and the P value was 0.03 (<0.05). The result of the experimental class in the post-test was significantly superior to the controlled class.

Table 4. Comparison between students' performance in pre-and post-tests in module two (n = 125)

Module two	School	Class	N	Mean	SD	DF	T	P
Pre-test	T	Experimental class	21	6.38	1.60	43	.45	.66
		Controlled class	24	6.58	1.44			
	W	Experimental class	41	6.66	1.37	78	1.60	.11
		Controlled class	39	7.18	1.54			
Post-test	T	Experimental class	21	8.38	1.99	43	2.27*	.03
		Controlled class	24	7.21	1.47			
	W	Experimental class	41	8.22	1.78	78	1.18	.24
		Controlled class	39	8.64	1.37			

6.1 Students' Attitude Towards GE-Integrated Science Lessons

As indicated in Table 5, students held positive attitude toward using GE in their science class ($M > 3.5$). Students showed high recognition toward "usefulness of GE" ($M = 4.13$, $SD = 1.00$) and the "usability of GE" ($M = 4.12$, $SD = 1.04$) of GE; on the other hand, students were relatively satisfied with the software in their science classroom ($M = 4.12$, $SD = 0.92$).

Table 5. Students' attitude towards GE-integrated science lessons

Dimensions	N	M	SD	Minimum	Maximum
Usefulness of GE	62	4.13	1.00	1	5
Usability of GE	62	4.12	.92	1	5
Satisfaction	62	4.11	1.04	1	5

Note: 1 = strongly disagree, 2 = disagree, 3 = neutral, 4 = agree, 5 = strongly agree

6.2 Interview with Science Teachers

Interview was used to understand the experience of two science teachers who first tried GE in their instruction. As for the Q1, the two teachers proposed some advantages of using GE in science classroom. Firstly, the application of the software could provide more knowledge for students, broadening their horizon. Second, it's very handful for teacher to teach the focus and difficulties of science knowledge. Third, students' inquiry interests could be greatly aroused by the interactivity and immediacy of GE. Fourth, students' information technology capacity can be promoted by the means of using GE. Moreover, the application of GE is helpful to motivate science teachers to improve their information technology capacity as well.

According to the two science teachers, there were not too many difficulties in operating GE in their science classroom. The software was equipped with many powerful features, yet only some simple ones were needed in teaching elementary science. It was easy for them to integrate GE to their teaching. Even though, the two teachers pointed out that time and energy were necessary to learn the software well to provide more help to science teaching. For the main problems in promoting GE in elementary science classroom, two teachers stated that the workload of instructional design was aggravated by applying GE in their teaching. Second, as the classroom teaching time was limited, it was difficult to fully play the role of the software. Third, students' attention was easy to distract as the GE provided many functions, such as the street view function.

7 Discussion

The empirical study focuses on applying GE in elementary science classroom. Quantitative and qualitative analysis showed that though there was no significant differences between the results of applying the software and traditional teaching, elementary school students and science teachers held positive attitude toward the application of GE in their science learning and teaching. Applying GE in elementary science classroom is feasible.

Researchers reflected the reasons why the academic results of applying GE didn't show advantages over traditional instruction in the study. That might be explained by several reasons. Firstly, the time for GE-integrated instruction was relatively short. Two modules were taught applying GE in the study, each of which taking one class. The chances for students and teachers to learn and use the software were therefore, fairly limited, which hindered the software to fully play its role in science classroom to a large extent. Learning itself is a long and gradual process and the ability of learning to use a new technology in learning also needs time. Students and teachers indicated that there were few difficulties in applying GE in their science learning and teaching though, according to data analysis and interview, the use of the software in their learning doesn't become a natural part of their science classroom in the study. Secondly, traditional test method for academic results can't reflect the effect of GE-integrated instruction well. Traditional pencil and paper test was employed to measure students' achievement of GE-integrated instruction and compare the results of applying GE and traditional teaching in the study. This kind of test is a good way to measure students' knowledge acquisition, but it's hard to reflect their improvement in the ability of using information technology in science learning. The information technology capacity is somewhat abstract compared with knowledge acquisition and its improvement is difficult to measure. It's a hard work to find a right testing method to examine the effect of GE-integrated science teaching.

According to analyzing the factors that affected the role of GE in science teaching, some suggestions are put forward to solve the problems in later researches. First of all, systematic and long-term teaching practice is necessary. On-going and long-term practice is essential, combining the application of the software in and after science class is important as well. Only in this way, can the software become a part of the science teaching and exert its role fully. Besides, systematic and scientific instructional design is equally important. There is no need to emphasize the role instructional design plays in teaching practice. In integrating GE into elementary science teaching therefore, a set of scientific instructional design is especially crucial. Second, well-diversified test methods should be used to assess the results of applying GE in elementary science teaching relatively correctly and objectively. To measure the result of GE-integrated instruction and students' improvement of information technology capacity more objectively, several new testing methods should be utilized besides traditional ones. As mentioned above, to find such testing methods are difficult in practice, which needs trial and error.

Integrating GE into elementary science teaching practice is a relatively new domain in China. There are difficulties on the way to better play the role of the software in the teaching, which on the other hand provides more chances and possibilities in the future study. Combining systematic and long-term practice with diversified testing methods in integrating GE into elementary science will be the main direction of further studies in the future.

Acknowledgement. This work was supported by the Fundamental Research Funds for the Central Universities (DCL001), and grant from the Instructional Reform funding from Department of Education of Zhejiang Province (KG2015001) and Department of Education Online Learning funding (2016YB143).

References

1. Britt, J., LaFontain, G.: Google Earth: a virtual globe for elementary geography. Soc. Stud. Young Learner **21**, 20–23 (2009)
2. Ratinen, I., Keinonen, T.: Student-teachers' use of Google Earth in problem-based geology learning. Int. Res. Geogr. Environ. Educ. **20**, 345–358 (2011)
3. Kulo, V.A., Bodzin, A.M.: Integrating geospatial technologies in an energy unit. J. Geogr. **110**, 239–251 (2013)
4. Bodzin, A.M., Cirucci, L.: Integrating geospatial technologies to examine Urban land use change: a design partnership. J. Geogr. **108**, 186–197 (2013)
5. Almquist, H., Blank, L., Estrada, J.: Developing a scope and sequence for using Google Earth in the middle school earth science classroom. Geol. Soc. Am. **492**, 403–412 (2012). Special Papers
6. The BSCS 5E Instructional Model and 21st Century Skills: A commissioned paper prepared for a workshop on exploring the intersection of science education and the development of 21st century skills. http://www7.nationalacademies.org/bose/Bybee_21st%20Century_Paper.pdf
7. The BSCS 5E Instructional Model: Origins and Effectiveness. http://science.education.nih.gov/
8. Piyayodilokchai, H., Panjaburee, P., Laosinchaim, P., Ketpichainarong, W., Ruenwongsa, P.: A 5E learning cycle approach–based, multimedia-supplemented instructional unit for structured query language. Educ. Technol. Soc. **16**, 146–159 (2013)
9. Sadi, Ö., Çakiroğlu, J.: Effects of 5E learning cycle on students' human circulatory system achievement. J. Appl. Biol. Sci. **4**, 63–67 (2010)
10. Liu, T.C., Peng, H., Wu, W.H., Lin, M.S.: The effects of mobile natural-science learning based on the 5E learning cycle: a case study. Educ. Technol. Soc. **12**, 344–358 (2009)
11. Boddy, N., Watson, K., Aubusson, P.: A trial of the five Es: a referent model for constructivist teaching and learning. Res. Sci. Educ. **33**, 27–42 (2003)
12. Bransford, J.D., Brown, A.L., Cocking, R.R.: How People Learn: Brain, Mind, Experience, and School. National Academy Press, Washington, D. C. (2003)
13. Davis, F.D.: Perceived usefulness, perceived ease of use, and user acceptance of information technology. MIS Q. **13**, 319–340 (1989)

A Study on Grouping Strategy of Collaborative Learning Based on Clustering Algorithm

Qingtang Liu, Shen Ba(✉), Jingxiu Huang(✉), Linjing Wu, and Chuanyuan Lao

School of Educational Information Technology, Central China Normal University, Wuhan, 430079 Hubei, China
shenba@mails.ccnu.edu.cn, jimsow@163.com

Abstract. As educational informatization develops continuously, blended learning has become the focus of increasing amount of research works. Among these studies, researchers indicate that collaborative learning, as an important teaching strategy, is of great effectiveness in promoting students' learning performance either in E-learning or classroom teaching. However, due to the fact that different students may have different learning styles, it is crucial for teachers to take this factor into consideration. Therefore, to enhance the validity of grouping in collaborative learning, this paper proposes a grouping strategy based on the analysis results of students' learning styles using K-Means and hierarchical clustering. Results of clustering analysis can provide a valuable reference no matter for homogeneous grouping or heterogeneous grouping.

Keywords: Collaborative learning · Learning style analysis · Clustering analysis · Education data mining · Grouping strategy

1 Introduction

With the rapid development of educational informatization, various emerging teaching strategies and innovative technologies are employed to improve traditional lecture-type teaching. Constructivism learning theory indicates that new teaching methods should be student-centered. Instead of being the recipient of external stimulus and knowledge, students should be equipped with the ability to process information on their own initiatives. Only in this way will they become constructors of knowledge [1, 2]. In order to achieve this purpose, it is necessary for teachers to reform traditional lecture-type teaching. There is a trend in both E-learning and classroom teaching to apply collaborative learning as a dominant teaching method. Based on modern social psychology, educational sociology and cognitive psychology, collaborative learning has redefined the relationship between teachers and students [3]. In a collaborative learning group, several students study and work together to solve a problem or to complete a task given by teachers. It has been proved in many studies that students tend to perform better in collaborative learning than individual learning through discussing and sharing ideas with each other [4, 5]. However, in a lot of collaborative learning cases at present, students are divided randomly into study groups, which have limited group performance on some level and led to uneven development among group members.

S.K.S. Cheung et al. (Eds.): ICBL 2017, LNCS 10309, pp. 284–294, 2017.
DOI: 10.1007/978-3-319-59360-9_25

Hence, to improve existing grouping mechanism, we proposed a grouping strategy that can be utilized to analyze and classify students base on their learning styles. Due to different data collecting mechanism of E-learning and classroom teaching, we further designed a questionnaire to collect necessary data according to the learning style theory of Rita Dunn [6] for classroom collaborative learning. Then K-Means and hierarchical clustering were applied to analyses processed data to classify students according to their learning styles. To verify the effectiveness of grouping results, 46 students who are in the same class were treated as research objects.

The rest of this paper is organized as follows: Sect. 2 briefly reviews basic theories and related works. Section 3 illustrates the process of data collecting and clustering analysis. Section 4 provides the conclusion and outlook of our study.

2 Related Works

2.1 Grouping Strategy in Collaborative Learning

Collaborative learning is closely related to a learning concept by Lev Vygotsky called the zone of proximal development. He denotes that there are tasks students can accomplish and tasks they are incapable of accomplishing individually. The zone of proximal development represents tasks in between, which students can fulfill through cooperating with each other [7]. His theory has drawn increasing number of researchers' attention to the field of collaborative learning. A learning style classification mechanism for e-learning is proposed by Wen-Yan Kao in 2009. This mechanism improves k-NN classification and combined it with genetic algorithm to analyses data of students collected from an E-learning system [8]. Tang Jie proposes a peer-model for collaborative learning in Mobile Computer Supported Collaborating Learning (mCSCL) to help students find suitable learning partners [9]. Base on the attributes of learning ability, interests and understanding level, Hu Hui proposes an Enhanced Ant Colony Optimization (EACO) algorithm to compose cooperative learning [10]. And in 2016, Ma Yanyun focuses on measuring students' cooperative ability on the purpose of improving the effect of network collaborative learning [11].

This paper is inspired by these works in terms of improving effectiveness and efficiency of grouping. However, data resources of these studies are mainly acquired from E-learning systems which can automatically record data of students' learning behaviors and learning habits. But in classroom teaching circumstances, teachers usually do not have such means to collect students' data. Therefore, to scientifically gather information that can be processed and analyzed on the purpose of improving grouping strategy in real classroom teaching scenarios. This paper designed a questionnaire according to Dunn's learning style theory. Then K-means and hierarchical clustering algorithm was employed to analyses collected data.

2.2 Clustering Analysis

Clustering analysis can be defined as a process that several data objects get divided into different clusters. Data points come from the same cluster are similar with each other while different from those from another cluster [12]. Clustering analysis has been applied to a lot of areas. In business and market research, clustering analysis is used to partition customers into different groups to better understand their shopping habits to generate marketing strategies. In the field of image segmentation, clustering can be utilized to divide a digital image into distinct region for border detection or object recognition [13]. In Web searching, clustering analysis can be applied to classify Web files according to their subjects. As mentioned in Sect. 2.1, clustering analysis is also widely employed in E-learning. For example, it can be used for mining group features of distant learners to support adaptive learning and learning resources recommendation [14].

Clustering analysis itself is not an algorithm. The process of it is completed through series of different algorithms according to what kind of clustering result is required. Generally, clustering algorithms may be classified into four categories: Exclusive Clustering, Overlapping Clustering, Hierarchical Clustering and Probabilistic Clustering [15–17]. In this paper, we combined K-means with hierarchical clustering. With a large number of variables, K-means algorithm can be computationally faster than other clustering algorithms. Even if the number of students is very larger, it is still very efficient to use K-means clustering for rough classification. And this algorithm is also easy to implement. Therefore, we employed K-means algorithm to roughly classify students into several clusters first. However, since many studies have proved that study group consists of 3–5 students tend to work better. It is necessary to achieve a more detailed classification. Hierarchical clustering algorithm combines the two most similar data points of all data points and iterates this process again and again. In other words, the merging algorithm of hierarchical clustering is to determine the similarity between two data points by calculating the distance between them and all data points. The smaller the distance is, the higher the similarity is. And the nearest two data points or categories are combined to generate a cluster tree. However, using hierarchical clustering can be time consuming if sample amount is too big. So, we applied hierarchical algorithm after K-means clustering to further divide students into smaller clusters.

3 Learning Style Analysis Using Clustering Algorithm

In the process of data mining, collecting students' data from e-learning system and traditional classroom is distinctly different. E-learning system can be utilized as an efficient tool to record factual data like sex, age, hobby, etc. However, in traditional classroom environment, teachers are usually lack of means to collect students' learning information in standard from. Therefore, we collected information of learners by questionnaires designed according to the learning style model of Dunn. On the one hand, this method is simple, convenient, efficient and highly effective. On the other hand, with only little 'dirty' data and noise data, data collected this way can have higher integrity. Thus, it will make data pre-processing part much easier. During data pre-processing, we mainly focused on converting data into the standard form for clustering analysis. At last, K-means clustering algorithm and hierarchical clustering algorithm are used to perform clustering analysis on the pre-processed data respectively. The result will be valuable for formulating personalized learning strategies, for improving teaching strategies and especially for grouping strategies in classroom teaching in primary and secondary schools.

3.1 Data Collecting

Data preparation is critical to the success of data mining. It comprises many aspects. First of all, data should be collected from multiple data sources to guarantee comprehensiveness, usability, quality and time-validity of data. This may require applying the theories and technologies of data warehouse. The other question lies on how to derive necessary indexes, which mainly depends on the experience of data miners and convenience of tools. In Dunn's theory of learning style, the formation of learning style is thought to be affected by various factors on different levels shown in Table 1. Therefore, the questionnaire designed in this research has 30 questions where every factor corresponds to one or two questions and every question has three choices as shown in Table 2.

Table 1. Elements of learning style

Stimulation level	Elements of learning style
Environment	Sound, Light, Temperature, Arrangement of Learning Space
Emotion	Motive, Learning Persistence, Character
Society	Collectiveness, Independence, Peer, Group, Learning Partners
Physiology	Perception, Temporal Rhythm, Activity, Sitting Position
Psychology	Analysis and Synthesis, Left Brained and Right Brained Type, Meditation and Impulse

Table 2. Learning style questionnaire

Questions	Choices	Answers
1. What background sound do you prefer while studying?	A. Exciting music B. Gentle music C. I prefer it to be quiet	
2. What kind of light you prefer while studying?	A. Gentle B. Bright C. Dim	
⋮	⋮	⋮
30. What will you do when you need to make a decision while shopping?	A. Make the decision right away B. Make the decision after deep consideration C. Hesitate to make the decision	

Questionnaires were handed out to 46 students from the School of Educational Information Technology, Central China Normal University. And 43 of questionnaires were collected with a collecting rate of 93.5%.

3.2 Data Pre-processing

Data pre-processing is of great necessity in data mining because low-quality data will lead to low-quality data mining results. Moreover, data can easily get interfered by noise, missing value and inconsistent data. Data pre-processing usually takes four steps: data cleaning, data integration, data reduction and data conversion. Each step completes different tasks. In consideration of learning style data gathered in this study, this paper conducted data conversion and principal component analysis on the original data.

Data Conversion

It is shown in Table 3 that every data tuple S has 30 attributes from A_1 to A_{30}. The data range of attribute A is {a, b, c}. Thus $S_i = \{A_1, A_2, A_3, \ldots\ldots, A_{28}, A_{29}, A_{30})$, i = {1, 2, 3, 4, ……, 43}. That is to say, Question A of every questionnaire has three choices a, b and c. For the reason that clustering algorithm only takes numeric values while a, b and c are not. Therefore, a, b and c is given the value of 1, 2 and 3 respectively as shown in Table 4.

Table 3. Original data

Student	Attribute							
	A_1	A_2	A_3	…	A_{10}	…	A_{29}	A_{30}
S_1	a	b	c	…	c	…	a	c
S_2	b	b	a	…	c	…	a	b
S_3	c	a	c	…	a	…	b	b
⋮	⋮							
S_{10}	b	b	a	…	b	…	c	b
⋮	⋮							
S_{42}	a	c	c	…	c	…	b	a
S_{43}	a	b	a	…	a	…	a	c

Table 4. Converted data

Student	Attribute							
	A_1	A_2	A_3	…	A_{10}	…	A_{29}	A_{30}
S_1	1	2	3	…	3	…	1	3
S_2	2	2	1	…	3	…	1	2
S_3	3	1	3	…	1	…	2	2
⋮	⋮							
S_{10}	2	2	1	…	2	…	3	2
⋮	⋮							
S_{42}	1	3	3	…	3	…	2	1
S_{43}	1	2	1	…	1	…	1	3

Principle Component Analysis

Principle Component Analysis (PCA) is to simplify data with multiple variables with least data loss. More specifically, PCA is to proceed dimension reduction for high dimension variable spaces. The basic steps are: (1) Standardizing original data to eliminate differences among variables on order of magnitudes and dimensions; (2) Calculating correlation matrixes of standardized data matrixes; (3) Calculating eigenvalues and eigenvectors of the correlation matrix; (4) Calculating variance contribution rates and accumulated variance contribution rates and determining principle component C1, C2……Cm according to the rule that the sum of variance contribution rates of principle component is greater than 80%; (5) Building synthesizing evaluable function; (6) Calculating total scores based on synthesizing function, ranking total scores and evaluating.

As it is shown in Fig. 1, variance contribution rate of first 10 components takes greater proportion. And according to Fig. 2, the accumulated variance contribution of first 14 components is 81% by calculation. Therefore, original data can be reduced to 14 principle components through dimensionality reduction. $S_i = (A_1, A_2, A_3, \ldots\ldots, A_{12}, A_{13}, A_{14})$. This result further proves that learner's learning style is mainly influenced by environment, emotion and society.

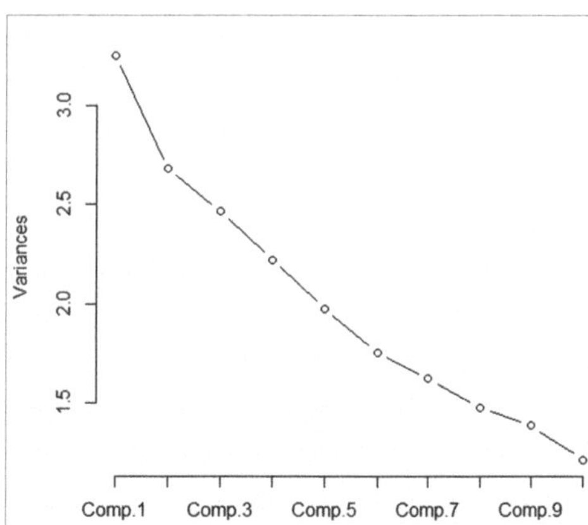

Fig. 1. Scree plot of PCA

```
 [1] 3.25206176 2.68221001 2.46674381 2.22221590 1.97664891 1.75393436
 [7] 1.62282440 1.47580227 1.38582401 1.21400192 1.18807090 1.12576423
[13] 1.03824586 0.89338675 0.77069829 0.72772904 0.68965024 0.58087102
[19] 0.53240883 0.42762883 0.36767569 0.35494251 0.27420567 0.25580893
[25] 0.20185953 0.14951148 0.13504120 0.11705521 0.07285417 0.04432427
```

Fig. 2. Eigenvalue of each component

3.3 Clustering Results Analysis

Examine Areal Distribution of Data Object Using K-means

K-means clustering is also known as dynamic clustering. It is relatively easy to calculate. And it does not require users to input distance matrix. The basic steps of K-means clustering are to assign the clustering number N first. Then N sample points are chosen randomly as initial center points. After that, the distance between every sample point and every center point is calculated to classify samples. Last, repeating this process until all center points are fixed. Therefore, it can be concluded that the key to K-means clustering is to determine the number of clusters.

In this paper, 10 sample values were extracted from data first to calculate their Euclidean distance matrix. Then we drew a heat map of the matrix. As it can be seen from Fig. 3, the darker the color is, means the shorter the distance is. So, there is approximately 4 to 5 Euclidean distance block. Thus, N = {4, 5}. Since silhouette coefficient contains condensation and degree of separation, it can be used to determine the superiority of cluster. The superiority value varies from −1 to +1 (+1 represents the highest superiority). According to the theory, this paper calculated silhouette coefficient repeatedly using different cluster numbers to determine what the best one is.

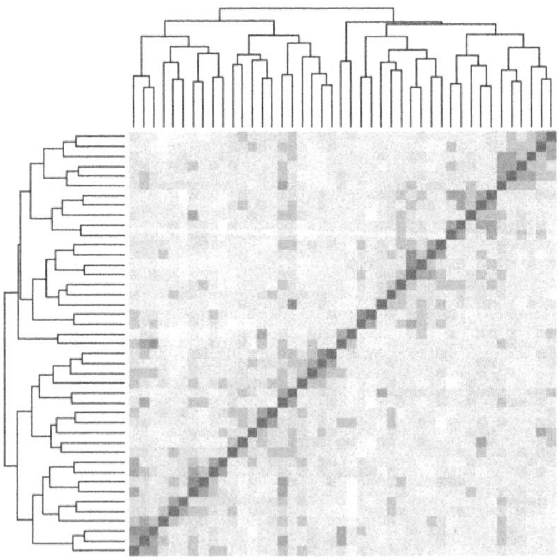

Fig. 3. Sample heat map

After calculating the silhouette coefficient corresponds to each cluster number, N = 4 is discovered to have the highest silhouette coefficient value (Table 5). To demonstrate the effect of clustering analysis, we used MDS to reduce data dimensions. Then we used different shapes to represent original classifications. And the result of clustering is displayed using different colors as it is shown in Fig. 4. The figure also shows that the clustering result is relatively distinct but there are still intersections among cluster 1, 3, 4. These intersections may imply that students' learning styles have polytonality. And some students are more easily to get affected by internal and external factors.

Table 5. Cluster silhouette coefficient

Cluster number N	Silhouette coefficient S(o)
4	0.05760475
5	0.05482903

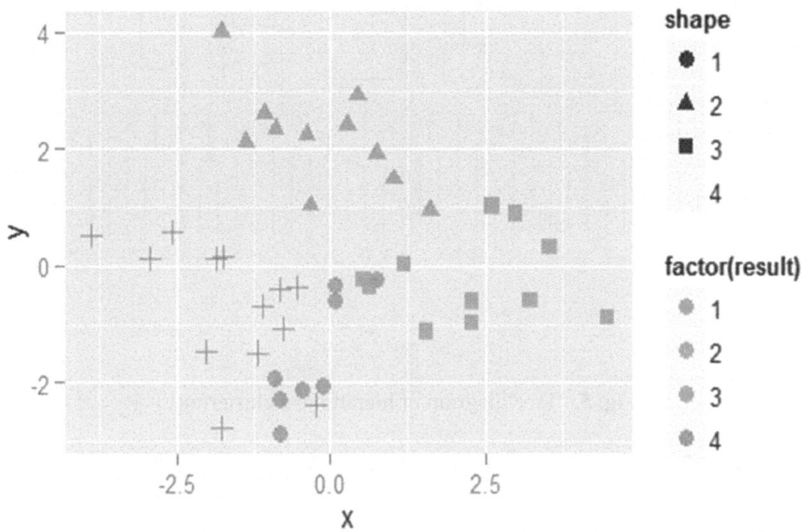

Fig. 4. Result of K-means clustering

Examine Areal Distribution of Data Object Using Hierarchical Clustering
Hierarchical clustering can convert data objects into hierarchical structure or tree structure to display features of hidden parts when data objects are small clusters for example (all data objects in that cluster can be treated as outliers). This paper utilized hierarchical clustering to classify data objects. The result of this algorithm can provide significant guidance to personalized learning strategy making and teaching strategy improving especially grouping strategy for group study in classroom teaching. Teachers often need to adopt homogeneous grouping strategy or heterogeneous grouping strategy according to different learning tasks when carrying out group studies. Homogeneous grouping is the base of heterogeneous grouping. And hierarchical clustering can provide references to homogeneous grouping. Therefore, we divided data objects into 4 clusters using hierarchical clustering. As it is shown in Fig. 5, every cluster represents a homogeneous group. But because the size of every cluster is different, we split bigger cluster (2, 3, 4) into small ones. In other words, this process is to split the homogeneous groups with larger number of learners to make the capacity of every group more even.

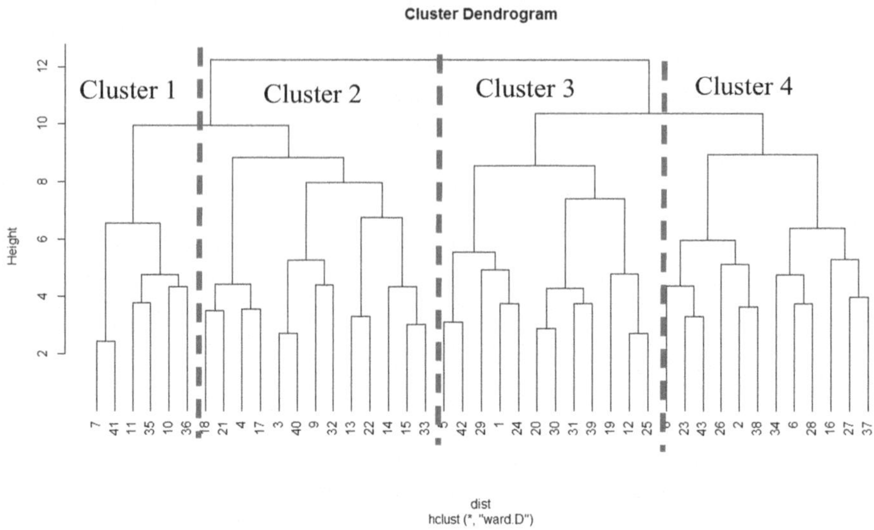

Fig. 5. Tree diagram of hierarchical clustering

According to learners' preference towards learning process, Kolb has drew a conclusion that there are four dominant learning styles: convergent thinking style which mainly comprises abstract conceptualization and active experiment; convergent-divergent style which mainly comprises practical experience and reflecting observation; assimilative style which mainly comprises reflecting observation and abstract conceptualization and adaptive style which mainly comprises active experiment and practical experience [18]. Therefore, it is reasonable and scientific to divide learning style data objects into four clusters using K-means and hierarchical clustering according to Kolb's learning style model (Fig. 6).

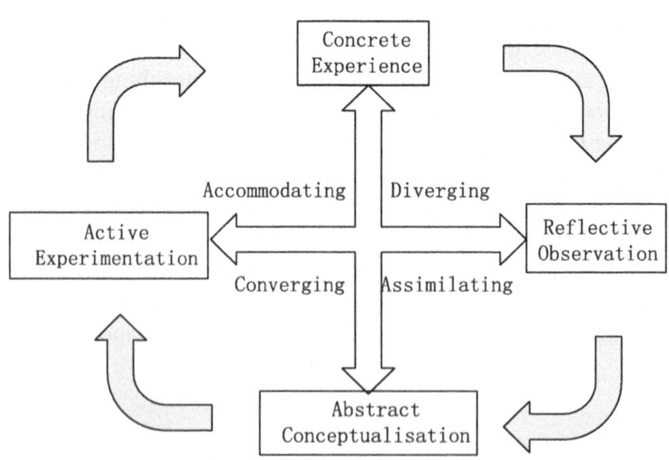

Fig. 6. Kolb's learning style model

4 Conclusion and Outlook

With the rapid development of educational informatization, a reform to traditional lecture-type classroom teaching method is commonly agreed to be necessary. Collaborative learning has been proved by a lot of empirical research works to be effective in promoting students' learning outcomes and learning initiatives. The first step to designing a successful collaborative learning activity is to divide students into groups in which every student can fully release their potentials. However, most studies on grouping strategy aim at E-learning while classroom teaching still plays a major part in today's schools. Therefore, this paper designs a learning style questionnaire according to Dunn's learning style theory to help teachers collect students' information. Then we applied K-means and hierarchical clustering to analyses pre-processed data to classify students according to their learning styles. The results of clustering analysis show that there are generally four types of students. In Kolb's learning style theory, he also divides students' learning styles into four categories. Therefore, our study conformed to the mainstream learners' classification model. By referring to the results of this paper, teachers can effectively and efficiently conduct homogeneous and heterogeneous grouping in classroom teaching scenarios to promote students' learning performance.

In the future, further researches will be conducted on improving efficiency of existing algorithms to promote the quality of clustering. And the size of sample class in this study is relatively small. Therefore, more studies should also be focusing on verifying and improving the validity of this strategy by enlarging sample quantity and sample variety.

Acknowledgment. This research is supported by the National High-tech Research and Development Program (No. 2015AA015408) and the Fundamental Research Funds for the Central Universities (No. CCNU16A05023).

References

1. Piaget, J., Mays, W.: The principles of genetic epistemology. Philos. Q. **24**(94), 87 (1997)
2. He, K.K.: The teaching mode, teaching method and teaching design of Constructivism. J. Peking Univ. (Soc. Sci. Ed.) **5**, 74–81 (1997)
3. Chiu, M.M.: Adapting teacher interventions to student needs during cooperative learning. Am. Educ. Res. J. **41**(2), 365–399 (2004)
4. Prince, M.: Does active learning work? A review of research. J. Eng. Educ. **93**(3), 223–231 (2004)
5. Zhao, J.H., Li, K.D.: Collaborative learning and collaborative learning mode. Chin. Educ. Technol. **10**, 5–6 (2000)
6. Dunn, R.: Learning style: state of the science. Theory Pract. **23**(1), 10–19 (1984)
7. Vygotsky, L.: Interaction between learning and development. Mind Soc. 79–91 (1978)
8. Chang, Y.C., Kao, W.Y., Chu, C.P., Chiu, C.H.: A learning style classification mechanism for e-learning. Comput. Educ. **53**, 273–285 (2009)
9. Tang, J., Li, H.J., Qiu, F.Y.: A research on collaborative grouping peer-model in mCSCL. Distant Educ. China **2**, 48–51 (2012)
10. Hu, H., He, J.H.: Research of composing cooperative learning group based on enhanced ant colony optimization algorithm. Comput. Eng. Appl. **50**(13), 137–141 (2014)

11. Ma, Y.Y., Yuan, J.: Based on GSDBK – means grouping algorithm research for networked collaborative learning. Electron. Sci. Technol. **29**(12), 89–92 (2016)
12. Han, J.W., Kamber, M., Pei, J.: Data Mining, 3rd edn. Morgan Kaufmann Publishers Inc., San Francisco (2004)
13. Bewley, A., Upcroft, B.: Advantages of exploiting projection structure for segmenting dense 3D points clouds. In: Proceedings of Australasian Conference on Robotics and Automation. University of New South Wales (2013)
14. Lin, C.F., Yeh, Y.C., Hung, Y.H., Chang, R.I.: Data mining for providing a personalized learning path in creativity: an application of decision trees. Comput. Educ. **68**, 199–210 (2013)
15. Andrew, M.: K-means and hierarchical clustering – tutorial slides. http://www-2.cs.cmu.edu/~awm/tutorials/kmeans.html
16. Osmar, R.Z.: Data clustering. In: Principles of Knowledge Discovery in Databases. http://www.cs.ualberta.ca/~zaiane/courses/cmput690/slides/Chapter8/index.html
17. Dunn, J.C.: A fuzzy relative of the ISODATA process and its use in detecting compact well-separated clusters. J. Cybern. **3,** 32–57
18. Kolb, D.A.: The Learning Style Inventory: Technical Manual. McBer and Company, Boston (1999)

The Study on the Roles in the Practical Applying Oriented Asynchronous Collaborative Learning Network

Bo Liu(✉), Huijie Cui, Xiao Liu, and Changqin Huang

School of Education Information Technology,
South China Normal University, Guangzhou 510631, China
gavinliu2003@126.com

Abstract. Asynchronous collaborative learning network (ACLN) makes the process of collaboration learning more convenient. In ACLN there are various roles, e.g., group leader, group member including positive member and negative member etc. They play different parts in group learning, especially each person. This work explored how the personal member enact relationship in the regular collaborative learning and influence the direction of the group, and how their interaction is enabled and constrained by personal role. This study considers four aspects of ACLN: the design, cohesion, roles and power network structures. The design is evaluated by the Social Interdependence Theory of Cooperative Learning. The network structures are analyzed by Social Network Analysis of the response relations among participants during online discussions. After analyzing data for three years from one ACLN academic university courses, we found that the knowledge construction process reached the setting aim and developed cohesive cliques in ACLN.

Keywords: CSCL · Collaborative learning · Comprehensive practice · Educational technology

1 Introduction

The research of Computer Supported Collaborative Learning (CSCL) is an important subfield of the Educational Technology discipline. There has been great development of CSCL in virtue of computer internet and multimedia technique. Johnson. D. and Johnson. R. has firstly presented the concept of Cooperative Learning (CL), one kind of theory and strategy to implement teaching with the students in a group or group.

At present cooperative learning has been widely used in different level education cosmopolitan for improving the class atmosphere, effectively enhancing scores and motivating student's non-cognitive skills. The students are divided into groups and under the common learning target and certain incentive mechanism they maximize respective achievement and then learn collaboratively and co-adjutant, known as Group Collaborative Learning. Many researchers have carried out deep studying about it. Huaide Chen etc. has intensively studied virtual learning partner system "Integration-Kid", in which two simulated agents, teacher and partner, were established virtually. Researchers in Educational Technology Research Institute of South China

S.K.S. Cheung et al. (Eds.): ICBL 2017, LNCS 10309, pp. 295–306, 2017.
DOI: 10.1007/978-3-319-59360-9_26

Normal University has designed and developed a comprehensive CSCL platform "CSCLEP", which can not only provide collaborative learning environment for students but also collaborative researching platform for teachers.

The platform Web-based Collaborative Learning was developed in Network Education Laboratory of College of Information Science in Beijing Normal University, which can survey learner's style and follow the tracks of learning activities and then supply task based teaching model. In the project STEP (Secondary Teacher Education Project), a web-based collaborative learning environment has been developed for pre-teacher students, in-service teachers, pedagogues and subject experts to experience instructional design and analytical skill in real teaching and studying surroundings.

Apart from those collaborative learning platforms, many researches have made the beneficial exploration of influence factors in group collaborative learning. Jia-hou Li etc. used case studying of educational blog community and knowledge innovating, obtaining the results that there were three notably positive factors affecting the innovation ability, e.g., density, centrality and multi-object; Jian-hua Zhao described the sociality of network-based CSCL activities; KuiXie etc. used opening coding and content analysis to open out the model of social conflict evolution in authentic online learning.

However, there must be many different roles in CSCL that should be deeply studied. As the classical perspective of Benne and Sheats's (1948) group roles theory, there were three kinds of roles in CSCL, e.g., Group Task Roles, Group Building and Maintenance Roles and Personal Roles. And there were many different sub-classes in each kind of the role mentioned above, some being positive, some being negative, but all these different roles have different effect on the collaborative learning.

2 A Review of Relative Studies

In 1990 Hiltz and Mason suggested that analyzing transcripts of asynchronous communication could enable quality assessment of the learning process and its outcomes. Henri provided a detailed model for the analysis. His model relies on breaking down the transcript into "units of meaning" (a message or a part of it), and classifying these units into categories and sub-categories according to expressions within the units. In particular, two of the categories express critical-thinking phases of knowledge construction: cognitive and meta-cognitive actions. This model has been used successfully in several transcript analyses to identify high phases of critical thinking.

Specifically, the Interaction Analysis model specifies that Knowledge Construction Process proceeds through five phases; accordingly, messages (or parts thereof) should be classified into the associated phases of critical thinking.

The model defines five phases: sharing/comparing knowledge; discover/explore disagreements; synthesis via negotiating meaning; testing/modifying proposed synthesis vs. schemas, theory, facts, beliefs; proofs of reaching agreements or meta-cognitive admitting change of knowledge.

Thus, knowledge construction processes of different cooperative scenarios will differ in the phases they reach, as expressed in the associated transcripts. One should not expect the Knowledge Construction Process to reach phase 4 (testing) if it was not designed to do so. We use SNA methods to analyze the two ACLNs described in Sect. 4.

Recently Garton, Haythornwaite and Wellman suggested using SNA methods for analyzing online networks, in particular learner networks. Several authors have demonstrated the applicability of SNA to specific learning situations. In these studies, the collaborating persons (students, tutors, experts, and so) are the actors. Links between a pair of actors represent the amount of communication between them. Most researchers concentrated on analyzing the distribution of power (or centrality) in the resulting network. Martinez and colleagues compared the centrality of inter-group and intragroup communication. Power distribution characteristics of multi-relation networks have been analyzed by Haythornthwaite. Cho, Stefanone and Gay found that powerful actors in web-based communication are also more influential than others as referrals. Reffay and Chanier concentrated on the evolution of cohesion in learning groups. De Laat combined SNA with Content Analysis and demonstrated that the interaction patterns in the analyzed course were centralized and that the Knowledge Construction Process focused on sharing and comparing information.

3 Research Design

3.1 Object of Study

Historical data was collected from three semesters. The participants were junior students who were enrolled in an online course related to instructional technology in the university. The examined course was a 16-week course in Multi-media classroom that covered topics related to the integration of instructional technology in elementary education settings. This course was designed based on constructivist instructional principles and student centered learning approaches. It was delivered through the Moodle course management system. With the arrangement of teacher, students must discuss their group task, also include personal homework, all of these discussions were posted. Students were also encouraged to comment on each other's reflections as an on-going discussion.

3.2 Research Methods

Questionnaire survey

This study used questionnaire method to obtain the individual characteristics of group members, according to the principle of homogeneity between heterogeneous, groups in the group building. Questionnaire survey is based on written questions way to collect information related to a research method. Researchers will have to research into the problem of the form, you can use the mail, to answer or tracking access method of distribution and the collection, thereby gaining subjects views and opinions on this question, the use of questionnaire investigation, the key lies in the choice of questionnaire, subjects and the results analysis.

This method aims to get the relevant information about the research themes by searching for and analyzing the present literature in order to get a general picture of the research questions. The relevant concepts in the research need to be defined by reviewing and analyzing the relevant research publications.

Case study method

A case study is a research methodology common in educational science. It is based on an in-depth investigation of a single individual, group, or event. Case studies may be descriptive or explanatory. Case studies emphasize detailed contextual analysis of a limited number of events or conditions and their relationships. They provide a systematic way of looking at events, collecting data, analyzing information, and reporting the results. As a result the researcher may gain a sharpened understanding of why the instance happened as it did, and what might become important to look at more extensively in future research. In my research, I will choose one to two cases of group collaborative learning courses conducted in the university and keep tracking, recording and investigating personal roles and collect the relevant information and data, and then analyze the data to reach reasonable conclusion.

This study is given priority to the case study method, paying close attention to the research object in the individual performance, group assistance, community features. Exactly as Shepard Greene believes that case study is engaged in one of the basic method of social science research, and it can be a example of individuals or time to explore, in-depth and vertical to observe events, collect data, analyze information, and report the results to provide the research route of system; the case study can help the researchers find that the related factors of events to reveal the relationship between these factors and the dominant elements (Shepard, J., & Greene).

Content analysis method

Content analysis method is a systematic, replicable technique for compressing many words of text into fewer content categories based on explicit rules of coding. During the forum transcript analysis, online discussion posts were coded using the analysis framework of Online Interaction Model that denotes and categorizes the purpose and content of an individual post. Each online discussion post was classified into one analytic category for the certain personal role.

Social Network Analysis

Social Network Analysis (SNA) is a useful tool for studying relations. It is a collection of graph analysis methods that researchers developed to analyze networks in social sciences, communication studies, economics, political science, computer networks, and others. SNA methods provide precise mathematical definitions of five groups of characteristics of the actors and of the network itself: cohesion, equivalence (role-groups), power of actors, range of influence, and brokerage. These characteristics are expressed in terms of corresponding Network-Structure parameters derived from the relations among the actors. An introduction to SNA can be found in Scott and Hanneman. Burt elaborates on the insights that can be obtained from the various values of the network structures.

A "social network" is defined as a group of collaborating (and/or competing) entities that are related to each other. Mathematically, this is a graph (or a multi-graph); each participant in the collaboration is called an actor and depicted as a node in the graph. Valued relations between actors are depicted as links between the corresponding nodes. Actors can be persons, organizations, or groups—any set of related entities.

SNA is used in a wide range of applications, from analyzing relations within families to analysis of a Military C4ISR (Command, Control, Communications,

Computers and Intelligence, Surveillance, and Reconnaissance) network; from analyzing the positions of adolescents in social networks and their sexual experience to analyzing political power networks; from analyzing management structures in multi-national corporations to analyzing terrorist networks. The website of the association of researchers, INSNA, provides links to journals, mailing lists and other resources.

4 Data Collection and Analysis

4.1 Data Collection

The analysis in this research is based on recorded data from discussing forum that was the part of the bilingual class, Computer Based Education (243 participants) ran during the falls semester from 2009 to 2011. The original data included articles posted amounted to 2749, the group test scores, group's displaying of courseware design, case teaching, classroom teaching, practice writing and reporting.

After preliminary statistic of data, the basic situation of the group discussion is shown in Table 1. Surrounding the curriculum content and organization the teacher has designed 32 theme topics forums (referring Table 1), shorted as TTF. There are 24 groups of students to participate in this discussing forum with total posting number 2749, and 85.91 on each topic, group average posting article being 119.5. Total clicking number is 33275, 1039.8 of the TTF average click in each topic and 1446.7 of TTF average click on each group.

Table 1. Forum survey

	Forum theme	Learning group	Posting number	Total clicks
Scale	32	24	2749	33275

As shown in Fig. 1, in 32 theme topics, there are four topics in which the number of posting is below20, because their contents are relevant to the outside practicing, belonging to the practical activities of the operation, mainly presenting by a report open. Number of posting article within the scope of 20 to 110 there are 18 theme topics, belonging to common level. There are ten theme topics in which the posting count is over 100. Furthermore, in the theme topic "Welcome and Greeting!" they have posted up to 241 messages, just a hot TTF! Statistical standard deviation is 55.61 of the entire theme TTF, and it illustrates the posting is very different from some theme TTF to the others. If the lower four topics and the hot topics TTF are removed and, statistics show that the standard deviation is 41.1, at this time that every subject TTF Posting data deviation can be passable.

As shown in Fig. 2, it is focused on the 24 group posting in the whole forum, the posting number ranges from 25 to 245, including 16- group posting 245, the highest one and 22- group posting 25, the minimum one. The statistical standard deviation is 54.07, of all group TTF posts how each theme TTF Posting data deviation is larger, if the removal of the lower two groups and the higher two groups, statistics show that the

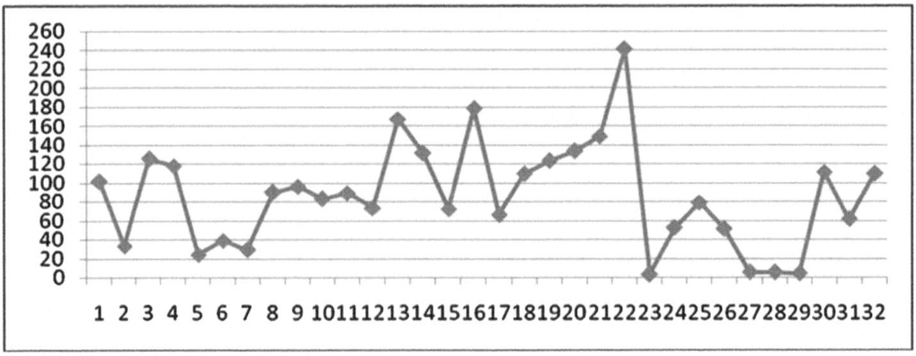

Fig. 1. Forum posting distribution

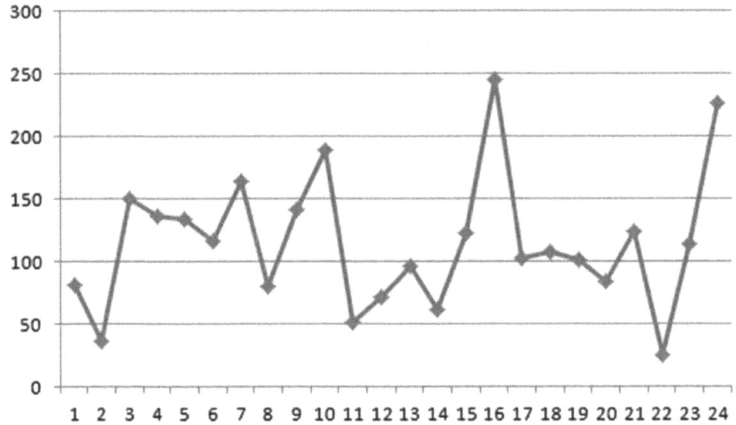

Fig. 2. Group posting distribution

standard deviation is 42.36, at this point that most of the group to participate in the TTF Posting data deviation can be normal.

4.2 Data Analysis

Degree of node center

Using the "Network Centrality and Power - Degree" function of UCINET, it can been calculated for each group collaboration Network of the every topic. According to the teaching design of 32 theme topics, there are 24groups to participate in learning and we have gotten 736 group collaborative learning networks, limited space, here only listed part of those networks (as shown in Table 2) to analyze the degree of node center, such as one hot TTF F-11 and two middle TTF F-16, F-22 from which three different level of groups being selected to represent as an example for analysis. Due to the direction of the cooperation TTF posting, namely being replying and been replied in the network,

Table 2. Degree of node center (partial)

Group \ Topic		F-11		F-16		F-22	
	node	Outdegree	Indegree	Outdegree	Indegree	Outdegree	Indegree
K-group	61	22	19	16	13	15	13
	89	11	13	10	12	8	9
	36	7	9	6	4	6	9
	39	6	4	5	5	3	6
	45	5	3	6	5	2	4
	44	1	2	6	4	4	3
	64	1	1	3	2	3	0
M–group	73	16	13	14	12	11	9
	85	11	8	10	9	8	6
	92	10	4	9	3	7	5
	93	6	2	5	4	5	4
	127	1	3	4	5	4	0
	27	1	1	4	2	3	4
H-group	29	15	14	14	13	16	11
	38	6	9	9	5	12	9
	54	5	4	6	3	3	0
	55	4	3	2	0	2	0
	57	3	2	1	1	1	0

therefore the collaboration networks of this researching field are asymmetric digraph, and it is necessary to divide the degree of those nodes in the network into two kinds: indegree and outdegree, when discussing node center and the mediation center.

From the information in the Table 2 it shows there is at least one person in each three groups, for example, 61 in K-group, 73 in M-group, 29 in H-group, played a "core" status in three kinds of TTF, and apparently served as the role of their group leader. Most of the members of the first two groups of F-16 and F-22 in Table 2 can actively participate in to collaboration learning, but H-group shows a little more weak interesting in the last two topics, needing to give more attention. In addition, there are 5 people (for instance, the node of 64, 127, 54, 55, 57) just to participate in reply, but not been replied, which means they didn't reach effective interactive learning.

Degree of node mediation center

Using the function of "Network Centrality and Power - Freeman Betweenness - Node Betweenness" in UCINET, it can been calculated for each Node of the mediation center degree (seeing Table 3) in general, all the 18 students from three groups have intermediary participation rate up to 83.33%, and only five students (64,54,127,55,57) have not worked intermediary effect. Throughout the three TTFs, the standard deviation of TTF mediation center degree is as following, F-11 being 5.483, F-16 being 4.215, F-22 being 4.317, so the TTFF-11reached the highest interactive learning, and the member have effectively participated in the information communication between individuals. But there is not much difference between the left two TTFs and both of them are less than the former.

Table 3. Degree of node mediation center (partial)

Group \ Topic		F-11	F-16	F-22
	Node	Degree	Degree	Degree
K-group	61	20.5	15.0	12.5
	89	11.2	10.2	8.1
	36	8.0	5.0	7.0
	39	4.0	4.5	2.5
	45	3.0	5.0	2.0
	44	1.0	4.0	3.0
	64	1.0	2.0	0.0
M–group	73	12.5	10.8	10.0
	85	8.0	9.2	6.0
	92	5.5	4.0	5.0
	93	3.0	4.0	6.0
	127	1.0	4.0	0.0
	27	1.0	2.0	2.0
H-group	29	14.5	13.0	11.0
	38	6.5	5.0	8.5
	54	4.0	3.0	0.0
	55	3.0	0.0	0.0
	57	2.0	1.0	0.0

4.3 Overall Characteristic of the Collaborative Network

Condensation of network density

The condensation value scope is between the field of [–1, +1], when the value is closer to –1, it means that the network is greater condensed and the group is more in the centralized state. On the contrary it means the whole network is very much fragmented. Using the function of "Network - Cohesion - E - I Index" in UCINET, it can calculate condensation of network density (seeing Table 4). Those values show all the three groups' collaborative learning in TTF F-11 is satisfying. And the collaboration of the first group is better, but the other two groups' collaboration has a certain scattered, but the difference is not too much, achieving collaborative communication with more attention later. Unfortunately, all these three groups' collaboration in the other two TTF, F-16 and F-22, is much more incompact than it in F-11, maybe for some other reasons.

Table 4. Condensation of network density statistics (partial)

Group	Topic		
	F-11	F-16	F-22
K-group	0.028	0.108	0.125
M-group	0.041	0.25	0.29
H-group	0.072	0.32	0.44

Groupuscule

Using the function of "Network - Subgroups - Cliques" in UCINET can find in the Network communication group, calculated results as shown in Table 5. The selection of sample size is not big (the number of the group is not more than 7), but from the result it can be found there is a certain amount of small groups, 70 ones al together. In the topic forum of F-11 there are 5 groupuscules with 4 students, 2 in K-group and M-group, 1 in H-group. There exists two-person or three-person collaborative learning subgroup in all those groupuscules. In TTF these collaborative learning subgroup, therefore, being due to reasons such as direction, interest group formation, have realized the overall coordination of propellant function effectively, and this pattern should be actively promoted in CSCL.

Table 5. Network subgroups (partial)

Group	Topic		
	F-11	F-16	F-22
K-group	2(4), 4(3), 6(2)	3(3), 6(2)	3(3), 5(2)
M-group	2(4), 3(3), 5(2)	4(3), 5(2)	2(3), 4(2)
H-group	1(4), 4(3), 5(2)	3(3), 4(2)	1(3), 5(2)

Noting presentence x(y) indicates that the network contains, x groups in which there are y persons.

Overall comment analyzing

In this section the overall comment of each learning group is summarized through the six dimensions measuring data, courseware design, the courseware developing, class presenting, practice reporting, thesis writing, examination, the calculated results as shown in Table 6. The value of the first four dimensions is the average of the mutual score from all the groups, and the thesis writing is reviewed by the graduate assistant, and the final examination score is obtained from exam-paper according to the teaching plan.

Table 6. Group examination (partial)

Group	Topic						
	Design	Developing	Report	Practice	Thesis	Exam	Overall comment
K-group	84	84	83	93	87	85.67	86.07
M-group	80	83	82	90	87	89.17	85.59
H-group	82	82	82	89	82	83	83.30

Overall comment comes from the weighted average of the six dimensions data obtained above, namely referring to the Eq. 1.

$$y = x_1 * 0.15 + x_2 * 0.15 + x_3 * 0.15 + x_4 * 0.15 + x_5 * 0.15 + x_6 * 0.25 \qquad (1)$$

y means overall comment; x_1 means courseware design;
x_2 means courseware developing; x_3 means class presenting;
x_4 means practice reporting; x_5 means thesis writing; x_6 means examination

The results showed that the first five scores of K-group are top in a leading position except the test scores is general because one student of the group has gotten the lowest test score about 78.5. But the group overall strength is strongest. All the three groups perform well in practice reporting, which means their group practice is efficient and these groups act with stronger operational ability.

Microsoft Excel analysis tool is used mainly for raw data statistics and finishing, and the social network analysis software UCINET is used to explore the inherent characteristics of group collaboration network, characterization of individual characteristics and characteristics of the whole group. To research the individual characteristics of the network focusing on the individual core in the network, it is mainly based on the analysis of the following two properties: (1) network centrality and power degrees: referring to the connection with the individual nodes of the total number of all the other nodes, the greater the degree number, the more compact relations among collaborative learning; (2) the degree of mediation center: referring to the information or resources for the dependence of the nodes in the flow of network. That the numerical value is greater means the intermediary of the nodes is stronger.

To research the characteristics over all group collaboration network the network overall characteristic will be dug out and then some advices will be put out to optimize the overall network structure. There are two indexes to be studied: (1) the network condensation density: it is one of the key factors affecting the performance of group collaborative learning. According to the situation of condensed density, size, and the number of overlapping, we can assess the close degree of group collaboration; (2) the network subgroups clique: if a small group of people is particularly close relationship of collaborative groups, can be combined into a secondary collaboration group. It reflects the group cooperation study, different interests and the change of group collaboration. Due to the directional posting in cooperation TTF, namely replying and replied, therefore in this researching the collaboration networks are asymmetric digraph, when discussing the node center and the mediation center degrees there are two kinds of degrees: outdegree (replying) and indegree (replied).

5 Conclusion and Expectation

5.1 Conclusion

In this paper, the empirical study on the influence group cooperative learning effect on two kinds of method, virtual and reality of collaborative learning, has been done based on empirical research of case analysis. According to the train of thought for designing and studying the problem drive type four factors have been analyzed as following:

Overall coherence of collaborative learning network
The high condensation density of the network reflects the strong interaction among the group members, and it directly affects the coordination of the group collaboration and effectively conveys information and communication;

Groupuscule of collaborative learning network
Small active group embodies the network of local high cohesion, in the process of collaborative learning group, and local cohesion can efficiently achieve collaborative focus, then for whole concentration plays a good role in promoting;

Individual core of collaborative learning network
There is always a center person in the collaborative learning network, so he(she) bears a guiding role in the process of collaboration, making the collaborative learning always around a central theme, although how the discussing spreads out, in the end it cannot deviate from the topic;

Intermediary of collaborative learning network
Every people in the group as one molecule of collaborative learning must be able to truly participate in the collaboration among activities, so the index of the mediation of the individuals is setup to measure the network centricity. It shows that the member not only assist each other with two-way communication skills, and also can communicate between the parties, achieving mutual benefit, sharing of information. These factors for collaborative learning effects play a crucial role.

5.2 Expectation

In this study we used the case studying method, but limited to the case studying, the future we will continue to carry out the follow-up study, and continuously strengthen exploration in the following several aspects: Constructing a standardized group cooperative learning evaluation system and perfecting the existing evaluation index framework. Strengthen teachers' involvement in the process of group cooperative learning into additional teacher, to found that positive information, inspiration and to promote the benign development of collaboration. The personal self-evaluation mechanism will be introduced so that group members are able to clear objectives, always clearing their own situation, accomplishing the enemy and know you, and fight.

Acknowledgments. This work is supported by 2014 Guangzhou philosophy and social science "12th Five-Year" planning project (14Y15), the National Science Foundation of China (Grant No. 61370229), the National Key Technology R&D Program of China (Grant No. 2014 BAH28F02), and the S&T Projects of Guangdong Province (Grant No. 2014B010117007, 2015B010109003, 2015B010110002, 2016B010109008).

Using Blended Learning for Collaborative Learning in Herbal Medicine

Verayuth Lertnattee(✉) and Bunyapa Wangwattana

Faculty of Pharmacy, Silpakorn University, Nakhon Pathom 73000, Thailand
{lertnattee_v,wangwattana_b}@su.ac.th,
verayuths@hotmail.com

Abstract. The objectives of this research are to apply and evaluate the KUIHerbRx2016, a blended learning tool for collaborative learning in herbal medicine. The 167 third year pharmacy students were assigned to contribute their opinions in topics of local names in several languages, indications, precaution/toxicity, additional information, images of herbs, products, and links to herbs. Opinions provided to the KUIHerbRx2016 should be evidence-based information and avoid copyright violations. Three domains of learning were evaluated. For cognitive skills, students can collaborative work and contribute knowledge on all topics. However, the average percentage of opinions with references on three topics, i.e., indications, precaution/toxicity, and additional information was 63.89. From the results, students could provide adequate information to the system. However, the number of opinions with references and citations for opinions should be improved. For responsibility, students could do their assignment completely in terms of the number of herbs, topics of herbal information and time used. They expressed their information technology skills to search herbal information, put opinions into the tool, and share information among students.

Keywords: Blended learning · Collaborative learning · Herbal medicine · Knowledge management

1 Introduction

In Thailand, herbal medicines are highly popular. Products from natural herbs are frequently used for improved health. It is necessary for pharmacists and other healthcare professionals to learn about knowledge of traditional medicine for their professional practices [1, 2]. In pharmacy curriculum, most courses can be classified as a modern medicine. Only some courses are provided for traditional medicines. Several topics in herbal information, e.g., herbal nomenclature system and medicinal usages, are useful in professional practice. However, ways to use and apply herbs may be distinct according to cultural background. This kind of data should be contributed by practitioners or experts from different regions. With Web 2.0 technologies, they give us an opportunity for sharing and distributing information from a group of members on a topic of interest [3, 4]. The Knowledge Unifying Initiator for Herbal Information (KUIHerb), a system for gathering herbal information, is used as a

S.K.S. Cheung et al. (Eds.): ICBL 2017, LNCS 10309, pp. 307–318, 2017.
DOI: 10.1007/978-3-319-59360-9_27

platform for building a Web community [5]. To encourage students to learn herbal medicine, the KUIHerb had been planned to use as a computer-mediated activity in a blended learning. However, some reasons that it is not suitable to use as a learning tool. For example, different concepts of information provided by members in KUIHerb and students. Members in the KUIHerb may contribute their opinions based on their experiences while pharmacy students should contribute herbal information related with scientific evidences. In the KUIHerb, herb names are usually contributed in Thai. However, students in the 21st century should be handled herb names in several languages, especially English and languages that are frequently used in the Southeast Asian countries. This feature is not implemented in the KUIHerb. Furthermore, several errors in content from contributed opinions may occur during the learning process. The consequent is that members and visitors of the KUIHerb, may receive incorrect information. In the academic year of 2015, we created a new and clean Website based on the KUIHerb. The KUIHerb was modified to be a Web-based and social network-based learning tool on herbal medicine, which is called KUIHerbRx2016. Information of herbs in several regions can be distributed and exchanged among groups of students. Multi-lingual names of herbs should be collected. Regions of applying the name and methods of assigning the name can be input. Furthermore, opinions given to the KUIHerbRx2016 should be evidence-based opinions. To support this concept, a set of reliable references should be suggested. The quantitative and qualitative evaluations had been done to proof contributions from students.

In the rest of this paper, the detail of herbal information is described in Sect. 2. The concept of blended learning is provided in Sect. 3. Section 4 presents the concept of the KUIHerbRx2016, a blended learning tool in herbal medicines. Section 5 gives the learning process design, settings, and evaluations. The results and discussions are given in Sect. 6. A conclusion and future work are made in Sect. 7.

2 Herbal Information

Herbal information is information about medicinal herbs. Normally, students learn herbal medicines in both lecture and practice classes. In a course of health informatics, a topic of knowledge management is set for applying to herbal knowledge. A supplement-learning tool in herbal medicine is created and used to improve knowledge and skill in herbal medicine with scientific methods and support multi-lingual and multi-script herb names. Therefore, this tool may be applied for both blended learning and knowledge management in herbal information. Some topics are emphasized, i.e., herb names, medicinal uses (indications), precautions and toxicities, as well as additional information. Herb names and medicinal uses, which may be different among cultures, are still problems. The scientific name of an herb and its images are usually used for common understanding. However, scientific names are not usually used as common term in communication between healthcare professionals and patients. In Thailand, Traditional Thai Medicine (TTM) has been developed for a long time. Due to the fact that significant number of Chinese people and their descendants settle in Thailand,

Traditional Chinese Medicine (TCM) is also popular. In a Chinese drug store, the names of crude drugs are called in Chinese languages, normally in Chaozhou (Teochew) dialect. However, the standard dialect of Chinese languages, Mandarin, is increasing in popularity among this region [6]. Only two alphabets are usually used in Thailand, i.e., Thai and English. Therefore, names of herbs and crude drugs are presented in Thai, English, or Latin and/or transliterated into Thai and English. Some problems occur when names of these herbs and crude drugs are in other languages, e.g., Chinese. The name in Chaozhou and Mandarin dialects are still important to use for identifying a Chinese herb or a crude drug. However, it is hard for a new generation pharmacist to recognize herbs or crude drugs with these dialects.

At this moment, pharmacy students should be studied more about herbal medicines. Due to Asian Economic Community (AEC) has been established [7], students may be faced with a harmonized healthcare system. For raw materials about herbs and herbal products, students should be able to understand their names in several languages. Traditional and modern applications of herbal medicines for each country should be studied. Moreover, information in herbal medicine provided to professionals and patients should be based on scientific evidences.

3 Blended Learning

Blended learning is a kind of learning which combines some useful methods to enhance the learning by traditional methods. With traditional teaching and learning methods, these are given by simple methods, e.g., orally or a pen. In blended learning, online courses should be combined with the traditional learning and the proportion of online courses should be in range of 30–79% [8]. The great advantage of blended learning is the flexibility to applied learning processes to students [9]. In the twenty-first century, flexibility of teaching and learning methods based on individual students. Students can manage their time and place for learning. Blended learning may be applied on both individual and collaborative learning. Collaborative learning defines learners as a group or team. Learners in a group help each other to search for understanding something. Trend in the 21st century, collaborative learning environment is supported by technology [10].

4 KUIHerbRx2016: A Tool for Collaborative Learning in Herbal Medicine

This KUIHerb's version, which was used as a tool for collaborative learning in herbal medicine, is called KUIHerbRx2016. In this version, two types of contributions could be applied, i.e., text and non-text information. For non-text, images and links external sources could be used. Six main topics of opinions are described as follow.

4.1 Herb Name

The thing should be kept in their mind is that an herb may have several names for each naming system and one name may be referred to several herbs. The relationship between herbs and their names is many-to-many. In the KUIHerbRx2016, is modified to be able to input herb names in multiple languages with a systematic pattern. Top 50 most widely spoken languages were used. Although Laos and Khmer (language of Cambodia) languages are not in the top 50 languages, they were added into the system because they are languages in ASEAN. Four methods of inputting are defined, i.e., characters, Romanization, transliteration and combination among these three methods.

4.2 Medicinal Usage

This component is composed of parts used, indication, and how to use for this indication. Medicinal uses may be different among cultures. For example, the aqueous extract of *Tinospora crispa* has been used for treatment of stomach trouble, diarrhea, and indigestion for Filipinos and Malays [11]. In Thailand, the decoction from its stems, leaves, and roots has been used to treat fever, cholera, etc. Opinions are given by pharmacy students here should cite to reliable sources of information, e.g., scientific research, standard textbooks, and information from the Internet. References can be given in the tab of References. Although information from articles in journal and books is more reliable than information from articles on the Internet, some websites published reliable sources [12], which can be used for references.

4.3 Precaution/Toxicity and Additional Information

These two topics are free text without majority voting. For a precaution, any suggestions will be kept for warning when someone would like to use the herb. For additional information, other valuable information such as cultivation may also be given.

4.4 References for Each Opinion

This space can be applied for suggesting references for an opinion in order to make the opinion more reliable. In KUIHerb, this topic is allowed only an administrator. However, students can access this topic in KUIHerbRx2016. When students contributed their opinions in other topics, each component should be cited by a set of reliable information sources, e.g., scientific research papers, standard textbooks, etc.

4.5 Images of Herbs and Links

A set of images for an herb is an important feature. We can identify the herb from its images. Several herbs can be found in a botanical garden of Faculty of Pharmacy. The images should relate to the whole plant and the parts, which are important for medicinal uses and identifying (e.g., leaves, flowers). A set of keywords should be given to the system. Students were encouraged to take their own photos of herbs (from real herbs). These images should not be taken from the Internet. However, some herbs are rarely found. Therefore, this topic is an optional. To alleviate this problem, the topic of link was created. Only links to images of herbs were kept in the system.

4.6 Images of Health Products from Herbs

In order to introduce herbal products to students, a task of finding herbal products from herbs was assigned to students. The products may be traditional or modern medicines. These products can be normally found in the drug stores.

5 Learning Process Design, Settings and Evaluations

5.1 Learning Process Design and Settings

The third year pharmacy students in Faculty of Pharmacy, Silpakorn University that registered the course "health informatics" in the academic year of 2015 (Jan, 2016 to May, 2016), were assigned to contribute their opinions in KUIHerbRx2016. The number of students was 167. The KUIHerbRx2016 was initialed with information of 911 herbs. The 200 herbs began with information on all topics to use as samples. The rest were initialed in topics of scientific name, English names, and general characteristics (for some herbs). Three assignments were given to students: (1) each student was an initiator on two herbs (assigned by a professor) in all topics (herb images, products and links are optional) as much as possible (2) each student was a participant for at least one herb (can vote or input their opinions), and (3) the student should do the questionnaire about the KUIHerbRx2016. Only the first and the second assignments were input into the KUIHerbRx2016 and reported in electronic documents. These two assignments were discussed in this paper. The students were encouraged to contribute local names in Thai and multi-lingual names especially, languages in ASEAN. Opinions provided to the KUIHerbRx2016 should be evidence-based information and avoid copyright violations. Students can searching herbal information for create their own opinions or vote to existing opinions which they belief to be correct. Herbal information, formats of input, methods to prepare pictures for herb images, and methods for tagging languages can be exchanged. Their tacit knowledge will be transformed into explicit knowledge.

5.2 Evaluations

Three domains of learning were used to evaluate students after an assignment was completed. Details of an evaluation for each domain are described as follow.

Cognitive Skills. Students' cognitive skills were evaluated by ability to apply knowledge and understanding of principles for analyzing various situations, especially new situations. In this topic, students were able to apply principles for searching and summarizing herbal information with evidence-based information. Reliable references for an opinion should be given. Quantitative and qualitative analysis of opinions were used for evaluating the cognitive skills.

Responsibility. Students' responsibilities were evaluated by the ability to work effectively in groups and social responsibility. In this domain of learning, maximum, minimum, and average numbers of herbs contributed to the KUIHerbRx2016 were used as indicators.

Information and Communication Technology Skills. These kinds of skills were evaluated by the ability to use information and communication technology. Students should apply information technology for contributing their opinions into KUIHerbRx2016. The tool was use for exchanging information among students. Furthermore, contributions for each student were reported in an electronic document and sent into the Google Classroom for this topic. The numbers of students, which contributed their opinions in KUIHerbRx2016 and send reports into Google Classroom were used as indicators for the domain of learning.

6 Results and Discussions

6.1 Process Design for Knowledge Management in Herbal Information

The process of using blended learning for knowledge management in herbal information was designed as described in the previous section. The diagram of the process is presented in Fig. 1.

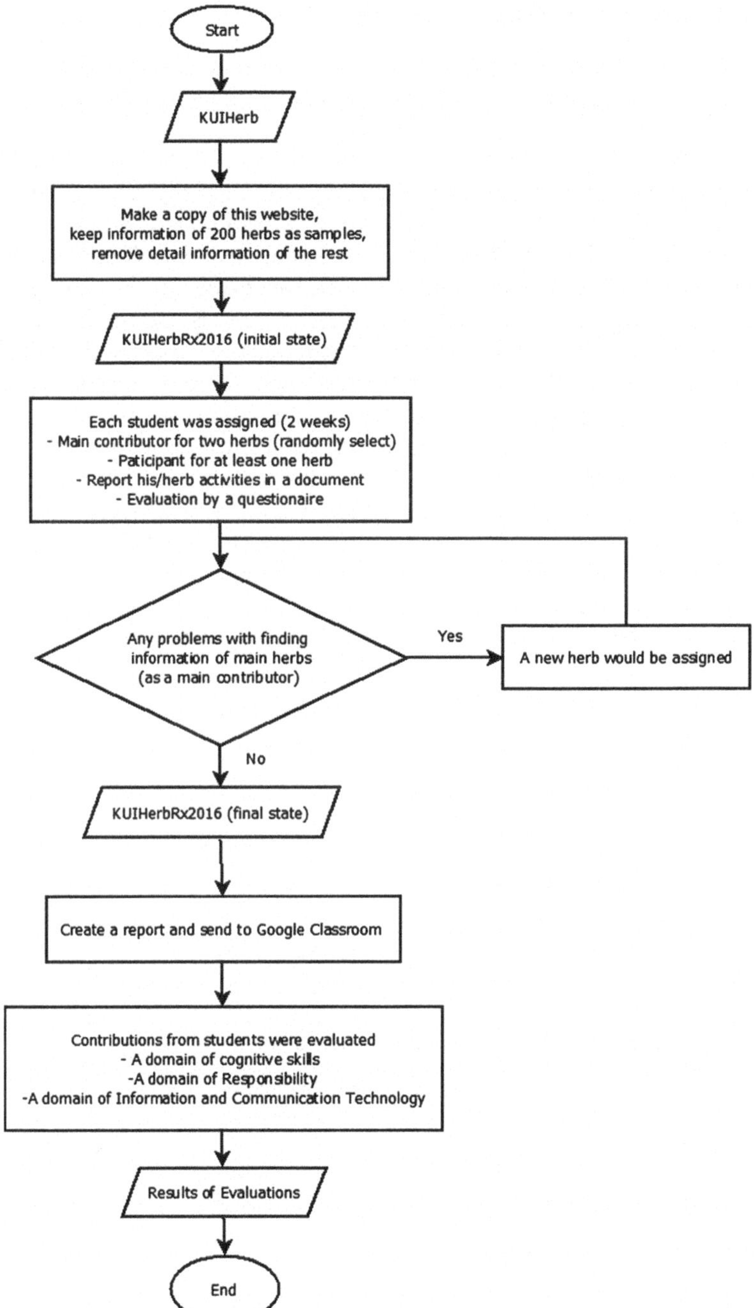

Fig. 1. The process of using blended learning for knowledge management.

6.2 Evaluations of Domains of Learning

Evaluations were grouped into 3 parts based on related domains of learning, i.e., (1) cognitive skills, (2) responsibility and (3) information and communication skills. The results for each domain are described in detail here.

Domain of Cognitive Skills In this research, only opinions in text, i.e., local and multi-lingual names, medicinal usage, precaution/toxicity, additional information and references, were used to perform analysis in both quantitative and qualitative analysis. The result is shown in Table 1. Two patterns of statistics are taken into account, i.e., the total opinion and the total herb. The total opinion (Opinion) is the number of opinions contributed from the students for each topic. The total herb (Total Herb) is the number of herbs that students provide information for each topic. Moreover, the numbers of herb names in top ten languages are shown in Table 2. In order to assess quality of contributions from students, 10 herbs were randomly selected. The numbers of references contributed to each topic for each herb are reported in Table 3. Values in Table 3 are represented in form of *a/b*, where *a* is the number of opinions which references are given and *b* is the total number of opinions for that topics. For contributions of pictures, examples of health products from an herb were shown in Fig. 2.

Table 1. Distributions of students' opinions on each topic

Topic	Opinion	Total herb
Local and multi-lingual name	1487	307
Medicinal usage	1383	317
Precaution/Toxicity	164	271
Additional information	581	289
Images of herbs	369	181
Images of products	108	69
Images from links	939	303
References	912	325

Table 2. The numbers of herb names in top ten languages

Language	# of herb names
Thai	391
English	229
Chinese	131
Hindi	72
Japanese	59
French	53
Malay	51
Spanish	50
Vietnamese	47
Russian	34

Table 3. The ratio of opinions with references/all opinions.

SCI name	Indication	Precaution/ Toxicity	Add. Infor.
Annona squamosal	3/3	1/1	0/0
Cinnamomum camphora	0/1	1/2	0/2
Citrus aurantifolia	1/2	1/1	2/2
Colocasia esculenta	0/3	1/1	0/1
Diospyros areolata	3/3	0/0	2/2
Elephatopus scaber	4/4	2/2	4/4
Euphorbia pulcherrima	3/3	3/3	3/3
Michelia alba	0/8	0/0	0/9
Streblus asper	3/3	1/1	2/2
Total	21/34	10/11	15/27
Percentage	61.76	90.91	55.56

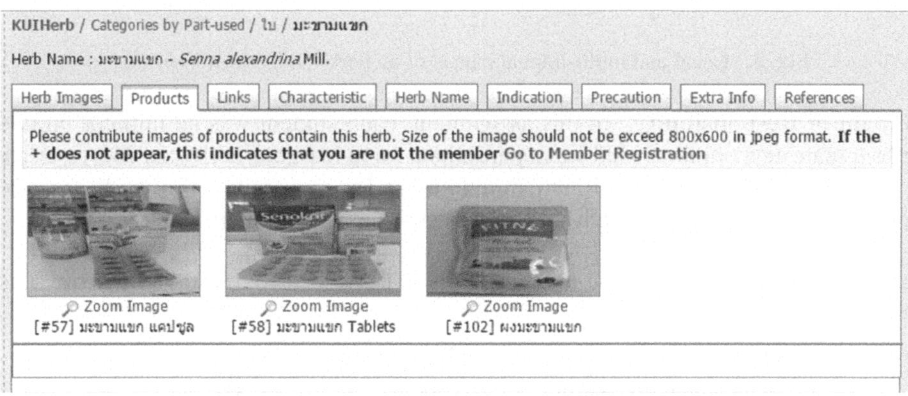

Fig. 2. Images of health products from an herb (*Senna alexandrina*).

From the results of quantitative analysis, some observations can be made. Students can collaborative work and contribute knowledge on all topics. Topics of multi-lingual and local names as well as medicinal usage were the most and the second contributed opinions, respectively. Several references had been suggested. For local and multi-lingual names (Fig. 3), a large number of names were given in Thai and other languages. From the Table 2, English and Chinese names are commonly used in Thai. For other ASEAN languages, Malay and Vietnamese are also frequently found. Several suggestions about precaution/toxicity and additional information were also contributed. The result of qualitative analysis is given in Table 3, the average percentage of opinions with references on three topics, i.e., indications, precaution/toxicity, and additional information (Add. Infor.) was 63.89. Therefore, approximately one-third of opinions on these topics were given without any references. From the results, students could provide adequate information to the system. However, the number of opinions with references and citations for opinions should be improved.

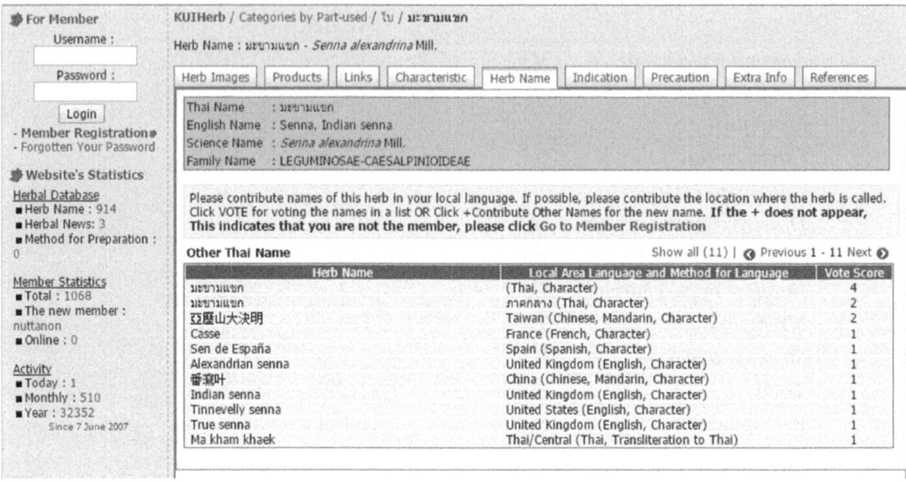

Fig. 3. Local and multi-lingual names of an herb (*Senna alexandrina*).

Domain of Responsibility. In this assignment, each student was an initiator on two herbs (create new opinions) and was a participant for at least one herb (can vote or create new opinions). Therefore, maximum, minimum, and average numbers of herbs contributed to the learning tool for each student were used as indicators in Table 4.

Table 4. Maximum, minimum and average numbers of herbs contributed to the KUIHerbRx2016 for each student.

Topic	New opinion	Vote
Maximum number of herbs	7.00	7.00
Minimum number of herbs*	1.00	1.00
Average number of herbs	2.52	3.07

From the result, the average number of herbs given new opinions and vote for the existing opinions were 2.52 and 3.07, respectively. Students had good responsibility and do their assignment above expectation. For the minimum number of herb, two students did not do their assignment. The asterisk (*) means, the values are reported minimum number of herbs for students who contributed their opinions in the KUIHerbRx2016. Two students had not been completed their assignment, the number of herbs for new opinions was 1.00. In summary, students could do their assignment completely in terms of the number of herbs and time.

Domain of Information and Communication Technology Skills. From 167 students in this class, the numbers of students, which contributed their opinions in KUIHerbRx2016 and send reports into Google Classroom were 165 and 163, respectively. Therefore, two students did not contribute any opinion in the KUIHerbRx2016 while four students did not send their reports. Using date/time stamp on opinions recorded in a database, there is no late for inputting students' opinions. With the monitoring system in Google Classroom, there was also no late for receiving reports. From the results, students had ability to use information and communication technology to do their assignments.

7 Conclusion and Future Work

In this work, the KUIHerbRx2016 was used as a Web-based blended learning tool in herbal medicine to improve three domains of learning, i.e. cognitive skills, responsibility as well as information and communication technology skills. Several topics in herbal information were assigned to students, e.g., local and multi-lingual names, medicinal usages, precaution/toxicity, additional information, references, images of herbs (from their both cameras, and link to images on the Internet), and herbal products. Activities of searching, collecting, contributing new opinions and/or vote to exist opinions, and providing comments to the system with evidence-based information, enhanced skills in herbal medicine, including information and communication. Students gained more experience on herbal medicines. Both quantitative and qualitative contributions from students were evaluated. From the results, students could provide adequate information to the system. However, the number of opinions with references and citations for their opinions should be improved. For responsibility, students could do their assignments completely in terms of the number of herbs, topics of information and time used for contributing their opinions. They expressed their information technology skills to search herbal information, put opinions into the tool, and share information among students.

For references of contributed opinions, sources of information should be categorized and analyzed. Furthermore, the correctness of assigning languages in herb names should be evaluated. We leave these for our future work.

Acknowledgments. This work was supported by the Higher Education Research Promotion and National Research University Project of Thailand, Office of the Higher Education Commission, and supported by Instructional Innovation Development Project, Silpakorn University (2014).

References

1. Dvorkin, L., Gardiner, P., Whelan, J.: Herbal medicine course within pharmacy curriculum. J. Herbal Pharmacother. **4**, 47–58 (2004)
2. Murtaz, G.: An evaluation of Pakistani pharmacy students' knowledge of herbal medicines in Pakistan. Afr. J. Pharm. Pharmacol. **6**, 221–224 (2012)
3. Lin, K.: Building web 2.0. Computer **40**, 101–102 (2007)
4. Gruber, T.: Collective knowledge systems: where the social web meets the semantic web. Web Semant. Sci. Serv. Agents World Wide Web **6**, 4–13 (2008)
5. Lertnattee, V., Chomya S., Sornlertlamvanich V.: Applying collective intelligence for search improvement on Thai herbal information. In: Proceedings of 9th International Conference on Computer and Information Technology, Xiamen, pp. 178–183 (2009)

6. LaPolla, R.: Language contact and language change in the history of the sinitic languages. Procedia Soc. Behav. Sci. **2**, 6858–6868 (2010)
7. Supakankunti, S., Herberholz, C.: Transforming the ASEAN Economic Community (AEC) into a global services hub: enhancing the competitiveness of the health services sector in Thailand. J. Bus. Econ. **6**, 1128–1135 (2015)
8. Allen, I.E., Seaman, J.: Changing course: ten years of tracking online education in the United States. Sloan Consortium. PO Box 1238, Newburyport, MA 01950 (2013)
9. Nizkodubov, G., Evseeva, A.: Planning and implementation of the process aimed at teaching English to adult learners. Mediterr. J. Soc. Sci. **6**(2), 643 (2015)
10. Keser, H., Özdamli, F.: What are the trends in collaborative learning studies in 21st century? Procedia Soc. Behav. Sci. **46**, 157–161 (2012)
11. Quisumbing, E.: Medicinal Plants of the Philippines. Katha Publishing Company, JMC Press, Quezon City (1978)
12. Kräenbring, J., Monzon Penza, T., Gutmann, J., Muehlich, S., Zolk, O., Wojnowski, L., Maas, R., Engelhardt, S., Sarikas, A.: Accuracy and completeness of drug information in Wikipedia: a comparison with standard textbooks of pharmacology. PLoS ONE **9**, e106930 (2014)

Interactive Whiteboard-Based Instruction Versus Lecture-Based Instruction: A Study on College Students' Academic Self-efficacy and Academic Press

Yinghui Shi[1], Changling Peng[1], Xue Zhang[1], and Harrison Hao Yang[1,2(✉)]

[1] Central China Normal University, Wuhan 430079, China
yhshi@mail.ccnu.edu.cn, pengchangling@mails.ccnu.edu.cn,
zhangxue0112@yeah.net

[2] State University of New York at Oswego, Oswego 13126, USA
harrison.yang@oswego.edu

Abstract. The purpose of this study was to investigate the effects of interactive whiteboard (IWB)-based instruction on students' academic self-efficacy and academic press. A quasi-experiment study was conducted using a sample of 103 freshmen from a university in central China. While students in one class employed the IWB-based instructional approach, students in the other class employed the traditional lecture-based instructional approach. Students in both classes studied English for three months. The pre- and post- surveys showed that the students with the IWB-based instructional approach had a higher level of academic self-efficacy and academic press than did the students' with the lecture-based instruction approach, which indicated that the use of IWB can increase students' self-efficacy and academic press when cooperated with an appropriate instructional approach.

Keywords: Interactive whiteboard · English teaching · Academic self-efficacy · Academic press

1 Introduction

The interactive whiteboard (IWB) is a touch-sensitive board that works in conjunction with a computer and a digital projector, and it is an all-in-one teaching tool with multiple capabilities that combined the functions of traditional chalkboards, flipcharts, dry-wipe boards, and video players [1]. The IWB witnessed a large spread and implementation in different forms of education at all levels within a number of countries and regions all over the world in recent years, and it has appeared as a technological innovation that used widely in teaching and learning in k-12 education [2]. It offers opportunities for teachers and students to interact with instructional materials and each other in a collaborative learning environment, and provides a variety of features that supported and extended by additional

S.K.S. Cheung et al. (Eds.): ICBL 2017, LNCS 10309, pp. 319–328, 2017.
DOI: 10.1007/978-3-319-59360-9_28

software to improve technical interactivity [3], such as dragging and dropping, hiding and revealing, shading and highlighting, moving and animating, retrieving of material, immediate feedback and indefinite storage [4–6].

Benefited from these functions and features, the IWB has the potential to enhance demonstration and presentation of teaching materials, to improve the quality of interactions among teacher, students and teaching contents [7]. Previous studies have highlighted several potential advantages of IWBs use, such as enhancing students' learning and retention and increasing students' learning engagement, interest and motivation (e.g., [8–11]).

In china, a growing body of teachers is taking several potential advantages of IWBs use, such as improving student learning motivation, increasing the interest of classroom teaching, enhancing the interaction and creation of classroom instruction. While lots of studies have been done on the effects of IWB on students' learning achievement, motivation, and attitudes toward the IWB etc., relatively little attention has been received with respect to the effects of IWB-based instruction on college students' academic self-efficacy and academic press, which were considered as two important predictor of or mediator for students' learning achievement or outcomes (e.g., [12, 13]). Thus, this study was aimed to investigate the effects of IWB-based instruction on students' self-efficacy and academic press, in order to have a better understanding on the IWB-based instruction in higher education.

2 Literature Review

2.1 IWB and Academic Self-efficacy

Self-efficacy, defined as "a person's own judgment in regarding to realize the capacity to successfully organize necessary events to achieve the objectives given", has a power that can affect individuals' preferences towards a specific area and their behaviors [14]. The impact of students' self-efficacy on their preferences and behaviors can be positive or negative. Individuals have self-efficacy on many issues including the behaviors that they should show in their daily life [15]. In this context, academic self-efficacy can be regarded as a special type of self-efficacy [16]. Academic self-efficacy is defined as the belief of the students through own their ability to perform activities relating to the school [17]. In other words, academic self-efficacy refers to an individual's expectations and confidence in his/her academic ability or learning ability, which indicates the relationship between learning and self-efficacy. In higher education, academic self-efficacy specially means college students' judgment of their confidence to complete a learning task.

A considerable amount of studies about academic self-efficacy are derived from the field of psychology, and the findings of these studies show that academic self-efficacy, as a predictors of academic achievement, plays a decisive role on learning performance in a certain extent (e.g., [18, 19]). However, there has been little research identifying the relationships between IWB-based instruction and academic self-efficacy from the pedagogic perspective, despite that it is widely believed IWB-based instruction can improve students' self-efficacy, enhance the instructional outcome and increase students' learning motivation. A study conducted by Castagnaro (2012) might be one of the few. From the results of his survey, it's concluded that significant and positive correlations emerged among variables within the established self-efficacy domain and the use of IWB in the classroom [20].

2.2 IWB and Academic Press

As a part of students' perception, academic press has been defined from different perspectives. Shouse (1996) argued that academic press is the extent to which school organizations are driven by achievements oriented values, goals, and norms, which is found both within and outside the school [21]. In the studies of Midgley et al. (2000), academic press referred to students' perceptions that their teacher pressed them for understanding [22].

According to Shouse, academic press served not only as a prerequisite for improving student achievements, but also as a basis for meaningful communality within schools [21]. Middleton and Midgley (2002) found that academic press was positively associated with self-efficacy [23], which was a considered as an important predictor of students' learning achievement [13]. In addition, Deng (2008) found that the level of academic press for ambitious learners is significant higher than those are satisfied with staying where they are [24]. It seems that a certain degree of academic press is more likely to have a positive impact on individual learning achievement and motivation. Despite that academic press plays a vital role in the process of students' learning, little attention has been paid on students' academic press under the IWB-based instructional circumstance. Based on the definition that proposed by and the scale developed by Midgley et al. (2000), this study applies a quantitative questionnaire to assess college students' academic press for understanding within the IWB-based teaching environment.

2.3 The Research Questions

Previous studies have explored self-efficacy and academic press from theoretical and practical aspects in the development of e-Education. However, there have been few studies that have addressed the effects of IWB-based instruction on students' academic self-efficacy and academic press. Therefore, the main purpose of this study will cover the following research questions:

1. Was there a significant difference in students' academic self-efficacy between the IWB-based instruction and the traditional lecture-based instruction?
2. Was there a significant difference in students' academic press between the IWB-based instruction and the traditional lecture-based instruction?

3 Method

3.1 Participants

The participants of this study were 103 freshmen from two classes of non-English major of a university that located in central China. Two classes were randomly divided into two groups: the experimental group (n = 52) and the control group (n = 51), with each group consisting of one class.

English was taken as the learning subject. The same instructor was involved in this study, who taught both the experimental group and the control group. The instructor was trained to be proficient in using IWB and had substantial teaching experiences and corresponding pedagogy to conduct IWB-based instruction.

3.2 Instructional Approaches

A quasi-experimental study was conducted to examine the difference of the effects of IWB-based classroom instruction and traditional lecture-based classroom instruction on student academic self-efficacy and academic press. Students in the experimental group employed the IWB-based instructional approach, while students in the control group employed the traditional lecture-based instructional approach.

Traditional lecture-based instructional approach. The traditional lecture-based instructional approach refers to the traditional classroom teaching with the jointly use of projector, screen and chalkboard. Traditional lecture-based instruction is generally considered as teacher-centered and teaching content-oriented, which promoted by practices and drills with less classroom interaction between teachers and students. The framework of the traditional lecture-based instructional approach is shown in Fig. 1.

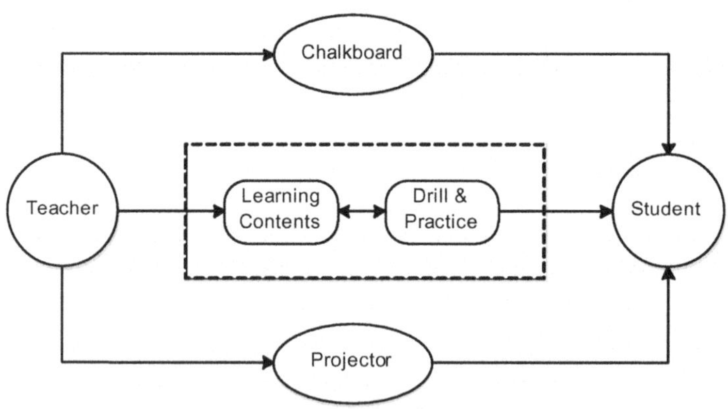

Fig. 1. Framework of the traditional lecture-based instructional approach.

In the traditional lecture-based instructional approach, teachers usually use the projector to display multimedia teaching resources for students, such as video and audio files, and various types of documents. As teachers and students cannot operate and write directly on the projector, and thus they have to write contents on the chalkboard, by which the interaction between teachers and students can be achieved. In the traditional lecture-based classroom, the chalkboard is mainly used for the teacher's handwriting and students' answers to exercise questions, while the projector is used only for the presentation of course material.

IWB-based instructional approach. IWB-based instructional approach refers to the use of IWB in the classroom to display teaching contents, to carry out teaching activities, to realize instructional interaction between teachers and students, and to complete the whole process of classroom teaching. In order to cultivate students' abilities to understand concepts and solve problems, the IWB-based instructional approach emphasizes the student-centered learning environment to help students complete the self-construction of knowledge. The framework of the IWB-based instructional approach is shown in Fig. 2.

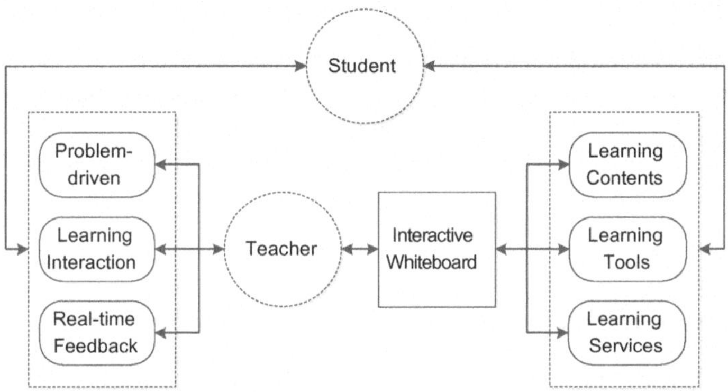

Fig. 2. Framework of the IWB-based instructional approach.

In the IWB-based classroom, the IWB was mainly used for three aspects: one was for the demonstrations of multimedia courseware; second one was for the whiteboard-writing and annotation of teaching contents; and the third one was for the interaction among the teacher, students and the IWB. With the help of the IWB, teachers can provide students with abundant learning contents and a variety of learning services to satisfy the different needs of students, as well as implement deep interaction with students. In addition, the interaction can also happen among students or between students and the IWB with the help of the built-in learning tools and learning services of the IWB. Moreover, teachers can provide instant feedback and evaluation for students via the IWB.

3.3 Measures

To measure the effects of IWB-based instruction on students' academic self-efficacy and academic press, two scales were applied in this study. One is the Academic Efficacy Scale (AES), and the other is the Academic Press Scale (APS). Both of the two scales are a part of the Patterns of Adaptive Learning Scales (PALS), which is developed by Midgley et al. (2000) to explore the relation between the learning environment and students' motivation, affect, and behavior.

The AES consists of five items, which are expressed with a five-point Likert scale, ranging from 1 (strongly disagree) to 5 (strongly agree). A sample item of this scale is 'I'm certain I can figure out how to do the most difficult class work'. The APS consists of seven items, which were also expressed with a five-point Likert scale. A sample item of this scale is 'My teacher doesn't let me do just easy work, but makes me think'.

The AES and the APS were translated into Chinese with the help of two educational experts. Results from the factor analysis indicated that all the items within the APS and the AES fell into one single factor respectively. The reliability alpha for the AES and the APS were 0.78 and 0.79, which indicated that the two scales were deemed to be sufficiently reliable for assess students' academic self-efficacy and academic press.

3.4 Procedure

All participants were required to take APS and AES surveys at the beginning and at the end of course. One week before the start of the experiment, the pre-survey was conducted. After a three-month long teaching experiment, the post-survey was carried out simultaneously in the two groups. Data analysis was conducted using SPSS software.

4 Results

4.1 Students' Scores on the AES, APS in the Pre-survey

To explore the effects of two different instructional approaches on students' academic self-efficacy and academic press, an independent sample T-test was conducted to examine the significance of the difference between the control group and the experimental group students who participated in the pre-survey. The independent sample T - test results were shown in Table 1.

Table 1. The results of t-test for students' AES and APS scores in the pre-survey

Scale	Group	N	Mean	SD	t	p
AES	Experimental group	51	3.35	0.81	−1.59	0.116
	Control group	52	3.56	0.52		
APS	Experimental group	51	3.55	0.62	−1.04	0.303
	Control group	52	3.66	0.48		

As shown in Table 1, the control group had a slightly higher mean than those of the experimental group with respect to the AES and APS scores in the pre-survey. But the t-test result indicated that there was no significant difference between the experimental group and the control group, which means that the experimental group and the control group students have the same level of academic self-efficacy and academic press.

4.2 Students' Scores on the AES, APS in the Post-survey

After a three-months teaching experiment, the analysis of covariance (ANCOVA) was conducted to examine the difference between the control group and the experimental group with respect to students' academic self-efficacy and academic press in the post-survey, by using the pre-survey scores as covariate and the post-survey scores as dependent variables, in order to decrease the interference of the pre-survey scores on the experimental results. The adjusted mean and standard error (SE) for the two groups, as well as the F-value are revealed in Table 2.

Table 2. The results of ANCOVA for students' AES and APS scores in the post-survey

Scale	Group	N	Adjusted mean	SE	F	p
AES	Experimental group	51	3.57	0.08	4.43	0.038*
	Control group	52	3.35	0.07		
APS	Experimental group	51	3.74	0.07	9.253	0.003**
	Control group	52	3.47	0.06		

*p < 0.05, **p < 0.01.

According to the results, there were significant differences between the experimental group and the control group on the mean scores of AES ($F = 4.43$, $p < 0.05$) and APS ($F = 9.253$, $p < 0.01$), as shown in Table 2.

The results indicated that the students with the IWB-based instructional approach had a significantly higher level of academic self-efficacy and academic press than did the students' with the lecture-based instruction approach, which indicated that the use of IWB can increase students' academic self-efficacy and academic press when cooperated with an appropriate instructional approach.

5 Discussion and Conclusion

The purpose of this study was to investigate the effects of IWB-based versus traditional lecture-based classroom instruction on students' academic self-efficacy and academic press. It was found that there were statistically significant differences on students' academic self-efficacy and academic press between the experimental group and the control group, with the experimental group had significantly higher scores toward the academic self-efficacy and academic press than did the control group. The result suggested that the IWB-based classroom instruction could improve students' academic self-efficacy. It might be because students in the experimental group have a higher learning interest and motivation, and they have more chance to interact with the instructor, peers and the teaching contents. During the learning process, students' interests become more diversified, and the accumulation of experience will contribute to develop abilities, engagement and confidence of learning, which were thought to be positively related to students' self-efficacy [25, 26]. Another major reason may arise from the experienced teacher's instructional design, which can provide students with strong learning activities and learning support [27]. In this study, the teacher has been trained to use the IWB skillfully before the experiment.

The results also indicated that IWB-based instruction improved the students' academic press effectively. It is important to note that the academic press in this study is a press for understanding or thoughtfulness, and the measure of academic press was focused on students' perceptions of the instructor's behavior. By the nature of the instructional approaches, students in the IWB-based approach have more opportunities to interact with their instructors comparing to the students in the traditional instructional approach, and students in the IWB-based approach are required to engage in higher order thinking skills. This might explain why the experimental group students' academic press is significantly higher than that of the control group students.

As previous studies have revealed that academic press was positively associated with students' learning achievements and stood as a statistically significant predictor of school achievements [21], and therefore educators should pay more attention to the role that students' academic press plays in students' learning, considering the widespread implementation of IWB-based instruction in educational settings. For example, education administrators and instructors can strengthen the supervision and communication with students within the IWB-based instruction, in order to improve their academic press appropriately.

It is noteworthy that control group students' academic self-efficacy and academic press were both declined in the post-survey. The decline of academic self-efficacy might because control group students have less confidence to complete the learning task as more learning content being taught during the experiment. While the decline of academic press might mainly due to the nature of traditional lecture-based instructional approach, in which the instructor showed less demanding on students' thoughtful academic behaviors and fewer high level questions [28]. Specific reasons for these issues need to be further investigated hereafter.

It should be noted that this study only examined the effects of IWB-based classroom teaching and learning in college English course, and the findings of this study may not fully reflect the efficiency of the use of IWBs in other subject areas. To this end, future studies are suggested to explore the effects of IWB-based instruction on some other disciplines besides English, such as mathematics, education, arts. In addition, more attention should be paid to the design and implementation of appropriated instructional approaches for IWB-based instruction, in order to achieve an improvement in student's academic self-efficacy and academic press.

Acknowledgement. This work was supported by the specific funding for education science research by self-determined research funds of CCNU from the colleges' basic research and operation of MOE (ccnu16JYKX037).

References

1. Kennwell, S., Higgins, S.: Introduction to IWBs. Learn. Media Technol. **32**, 207–212 (2007)
2. Shi, Y.H., Yang, Z.K., Yang, H., Liu, S.Y.: Study on the research hotspots of interactive whiteboards in education. In: 4th International Conference on Internet Multimedia Computing and Service, pp. 209–212. ACM ICPS (2002)
3. Smith, H., Higgins, S., Wall, K., Miller, J.: Interactive whiteboards: boon or bandwagon? A critical review of the literature. J. Comput. Assist. Learn. **21**, 91–101 (2005)
4. Glover, D., Miller, D., Averis, D., Door, V.: The interactive whiteboard: a literature survey. Technol. Pedagogy Educ. **14**, 155–170 (2005)

5. Kennwell, S.: Reflections on the interactive whiteboard phenomenon: a synthesis of research from the UK. BERA (British Educational Research Association), UK (2006)
6. Mercer, N., Hennessy, S., Warwick, P.: Using interactive whiteboards to orchestrate classroom dialogue. Technol. Pedagogy Educ. **19**, 195–209 (2010)
7. BECTA (British Educational Communications and Technology Agency).: Getting the most from your interactive whiteboard: a guide for secondary schools. BECTA, Coventry (2004)
8. Schroeder, R.: Active learning with interactive whiteboard: a literature review and a case study for college freshmen. Commun. Inf. Literacy **1**, 64–73 (2007)
9. Hall, I., Higgins, S.: Primary school students' perceptions of interactive whiteboards. J. Comput. Assist. Learn. **21**, 102–117 (2005)
10. Smith, F., Hardman, F., Higgins, S.: The impact of interactive whiteboards on teacher-pupil interaction in the national literacy and numeracy strategies. Br. Edu. Res. J. **32**, 443–457 (2006)
11. Shi, Y.H., Yang, Z.K., Yang, H., Liu, S.Y.: The impact of interactive whiteboards on education. In: 4th International Conference on Internet Multimedia Computing and Service, pp. 213–218. ACM ICPS (2002)
12. Lee, J.: Universals and specifics of math self-concept, math self-efficacy, and math anxiety across 41 PISA 2003 participating countries. Learn. Individ. Differ. **19**, 355–365 (2009)
13. Vogel, F.R., Human-Vogel, S.: Academic commitment and self-efficacy as predictors of academic achievement in additional materials science. High. Educ. Res. Dev. **35**, 1298–1310 (2016)
14. Bandura, A.: Self-efficacy — toward a unifying theory of behavioral change. Psychol. Rev. **84**, 191–215 (1997)
15. Kutluca, T., Ekici, G.: Examining teacher candidates' attitudes and self-efficacy perceptions towards the computer assisted education. Hacettepe Univ. J. Educ. **38**, 177–188 (2010)
16. Etem, Y., Ulas, A.H., Akan, D.: Teacher self-efficacy, academic self-efficacy, and computer self-efficacy as predictors of attitude toward applying computer-supported education. J. Comput. Hum. Behav. **64**, 591–601 (2016)
17. Linnenbrink, E.A., Pintrich, P.R.: Achievement goal theory and affect: an asymmetrical bidirectional model. Educ. Psychol. **37**, 69–78 (2002)
18. Zajacova, A., Lynch, S.M., Espenshade, T.J.: Self-efficacy, stress, and academic success in college. J. Res. High. Educ. **46**, 677–706 (2005)
19. Liew, J., McTigue, E.M., Barrois, L., et al.: Adaptive and effortful control and academic self-efficacy beliefs on achievement: a longitudinal study of 1st through 3rd graders. J. Early Child. Res. Q. **23**, 515–526 (2008)
20. Castagnaro, A.V.: Evaluating sixth graders' self-efficacy in response to the use of educational technology. http://scholarship.claremont.edu/cgi/viewcontent.cgi?artle=1070&context=cgu_etd
21. Shouse, R.C.: Academic press and sense of community: conflict, congruence, and implications for student achievement. Soc. Psychol. Educ. **1**, 47–68 (1996)
22. Midgley, C., Maehr, M.L., Hruda, L.Z., Anderman, E., Anderman, L., Freeman, K.E., et al.: Manual for the Patterns of Adaptive Learning Scales. University of Michigan, Ann Arbor (2000)
23. Middleton, M.J., Midgley, C.: Beyond motivation: middle school students' perceptions of press for understanding in math. Contemp. Educ. Psychol. **27**, 373–391 (2002)
24. Deng, Q.: A practical research on the learning pressure among college students. J. Nerv. Dis. Ment. Health **8**, 20–23 (2008)
25. Bandura, A.: Adolescent development from an agentic perspective. In: Pajares, F., Urdan, T. (eds.) Self-efficacy Beliefs of Adolescents, pp. 1–43. Information Age Publishing, Greenwich (2006)

26. Zimmerman, B.J., Cleary, T.J.: Adolescents' development of personal agency: the role of self-efficacy beliefs and self-regulatory skill. In: Pajares, F., Urdan, T. (eds.) Self-efficacy Beliefs of Adolescents, pp. 307–337. Information Age Publishing, Greenwich (2006)
27. Shi, Y.H., Yang, H., Wu, D., Zhu, S.: Interactive whiteboard-based instruction versus Lecture-based instruction: a study on students' learning achievement. In: 4th International Conference of Educational Innovation through Technology, pp. 231–235. IEEE Computer Society, CPS (2015)
28. Middleton, M.J., Blumenfeld, P.: Types and sources of academic press in middle school science classrooms. http://www-personal.umich.edu/~krajcik/Types%26Sources.pdf

Improved Flexibility of Learning Processes

Investigation of the ICT Situation in Chinese Primary School: The Role of School Characteristics

Congcong Li[1], Wenting Zhou[1], Chun Lu[1], and Di Wu[2(✉)]

[1] National Engineering Research Center for E-Learning,
Central China Normal University, Wuhan, China
licongcong693@126.com, zhouwenting_eisr@163.com,
luchun_et@163.com

[2] Collaborative & Innovative Center for Educational Technology,
Central China Normal University, Wuhan, China
dr.wudi@gmail.com

Abstract. The development of ICT in schools was influenced by many external environment factors and internal ICT factors. To identify the school-level factors linked with schools ICT situation, and the differences of the ICT implementation stages of rural and urban schools, a survey of 4,357 was conducted. Four subscales including *environment*, *support*, *application*, and *fund allocation* were extracted from the Features of School ICT Situation (FSIS). Through stepwise regression analysis, it is revealed that the ICT literacy of teacher is the most important predictor for schools' FSIS. In addition, there are more Essential Elements of School Characteristics (EESC) items that can make significant prediction of FSIS for rural schools than for urban schools, and their predictive power for FSIS of rural schools is stronger than that of urban schools. The result reflects that EESC items which evaluate background and basic situation of ICT development in schools have stronger positive predictive power for schools in rural areas and the number of predictive indicators is larger. EESC items have relatively weaker predictive power and fewer predictive indicators for urban schools.

Keywords: Development of ICT in education · Essential elements of school construction · Teachers' ICT competence · Rural-urban divide

1 Introduction

Over the past decade, information and communication technology (ICT) has a pervasive impact on education. The question about what variables determine the development of ICT in education has been repeatedly put forward. Countries and researchers begun to rethink school characteristics and investigated the situation of ICT in education. Both of the STaR (School Technology and Readiness) charts developed by American CEO Forum on Education & Technology and the SRF (The self-review framework) assessment scale released by British Educational Communications and Technology Agency emphasize the ICT development indexes at the school level.

S.K.S. Cheung et al. (Eds.): ICBL 2017, LNCS 10309, pp. 331–342, 2017.
DOI: 10.1007/978-3-319-59360-9_29

With the integration of ICT in education, the factors influencing the development of ICT in schools are not limited to the basic ICT construction situation such as ICT infrastructure, but also closely linked with some external environment such as basic school conditions. For the primary school, the external environment for ICT development mainly consist of both the schools' general background and basic information of ICT construction in the present research. Schools' background refers to the basic information of schools' characteristics [1, 2], including school location, education stage and school size. The basic ICT construction situation includes ICT competence of staff, ICT integrated classrooms, digital instruction materials, school policies on ICT, and so on. Previous studies have confirmed the importance of teacher ICT literacy [3, 4]. Teachers' ICT competence not only constitutes one of the keys to guaranteeing ICT application at the school level, but also contributes to students' ICT skills and their own professional development [5–7]. Besides human resources, classroom construction is an important component in the ICT program of schools. Students can experience critical thinking and learn communication skills through multimedia learning [8]. Through multimedia application, students have shown improvement in both their behavioral development and reading comprehension [9, 10]. Apart from teachers' competence and learning environment, the use of digital resources helps students cultivate the habits of self-regulated learning and enquiry-based learning [11]. It has a significant effect on students' reading and writing abilities [12]. Furthermore, school policies on ICT development are one of the crucial factors influencing execution and sustainability of schools' ICT development [13].

Previous researches on the evaluation of ICT in education development generally involved four aspects, namely the learning environment, resource support, application in learning and teaching, and the allocation of funds. The researches on ICT environments for teaching and learning probably consider both physical computers or multimedia classrooms and cyber learning spaces. Many governments and organizations have issued one-to-one computing programs [14]. The implementation of such programs has positive impacts on both the interaction between students and teachers and the teaching and learning practices [15]. As for resource support, previous studies show that it requires more specific and diversified facilities and forms of support that appropriately change educational objectives and contents, as well as materials and infrastructure [16], which would be conducted to provide the required information to help both schools and educational policy-making. The index of budget for ICT in schools was found to have the strongest impact on the ICT materials index compared with the other indices [5]. Besides, ICT competence training for teachers has been found to help improve their use of ICT [17]. When it comes to ICT application, the use of ICT has aroused much attention [18, 19]. It is important to make efforts to improve ICT application in schools to raise their ICT composite index because ICT application correlates strongly with the composite index [5]. The level of students' and teachers' ICT usage is one of the factors that impacts ICT application in classrooms. Studies based on the Japanese National Curriculum have reported that students using ICT more often in their learning show higher enhanced abilities of solving problems [20]. Besides the above-mentioned topics, previous research on teacher ICT literacy training has asserted that training alone without ongoing support is unlikely to be effective, and that a supportive environment is important [21]. Targeting funding to support mentors contributes to helpful tutorials

[22]. In addition, constant and rapid ICT construction and integration in education in China has brought about a corresponding increase in training fees and technology support costs; therefore, the allocation of schools' ICT funds could reflect, at least to some extent, the level and stage of schools' ICT development.

Although research interests in the external environment and the internal factors of ICT has increased [23], the rapid development of ICT in schools and the rural-urban disparities make it necessary to carry out further exploration of the latent factors affecting ICT situation. This study aims to identify the school-level factors linked with schools ICT situation, and the differences of the ICT implementation stages of rural and urban schools. The findings could be particularly useful for policy makers in setting up school ICT strategic plan.

The research hypotheses of this study are therefore as follows:

1. The indices concerning teachers' ICT competence have the greatest impact on the development of ICT in Chinese primary schools.
2. The essential elements of school characteristics have different impact on the rural and the urban school ICT situation.
3. The predictive relationship between school ICT situation and the essential elements of school construction is different in rural schools and urban schools.

2 Method

2.1 Participants and Questionnaires

This study, which was conducted from January 2016 to March 2016, aimed to assess the ICT development of primary schools. The research was based on survey response data from 4,357 schools of various provinces in China. The number and scale of the samples meet the standard for correlation and stepwise regression analysis. Among all of the valid samples, 1,011 schools are in urban areas, accounting for 23% of the total, and 3,346 schools are in rural areas, making up 77% of the total.

Essential Elements of School Characteristics (EESC)
The EESC was composed of school background information and basic ICT characteristics. School background information referred to school locality, school size, and education stage. Basic ICT characteristics referred to network access, school-based resources, ICT classroom, teacher ICT training, and school ICT plan. The indices and descriptions were shown in Table 1.

Features of School ICT Situation (FSIS)
The items referred to the construction of an ICT learning environment and digital terminals for instruction and learning, technical support for material and human resources, students' and teachers' time length of learning with ICT and the way of allocating ICT funds. The indices and their short descriptions was shown in Table 2.

Table 1. Indices of EESC

Indicators	Short description
School locality	Rural school or urban school
School size	Number of classes
Education stage	Primary school (grades 1 to 6), junior high school (grades 7 to 9)
Campus network	Bandwidth of campus network
School-based resources	Whether there are school-based resources
Multimedia classrooms	Proportion of multimedia classroom
Computer classrooms	Number of computer classrooms
Full-time technicians	Number of full-time technicians
ICT qualified teachers	Proportion of ICT qualified teachers
ICT plan	Whether there are any ICT plans

Table 2. Indices of FSIS

Indicators	Short description
Computer classroom usage	Computer classroom usage rate
Multimedia classroom usage	Multimedia classroom usage rate
Students' VLS enrollment	Students' virtual learning space enrollment rate
Teachers' VLS enrollment	Teachers' virtual learning space enrollment rate
PC/student ratio	The ratio of computers to students
PC/teacher ratio	The ratio of computers to teachers
Total network	Bandwidth of total network
ICT construction expenditure	Spending on ICT construction
ICT investment proportion	% total ICT expenditure
Teachers attending ICT training	% teachers attending ICT training
Students' ICT learning time	Students' average online learning time per week
Teachers' ICT learning time	Teachers' average online teaching time per week
Technical support expenditure	Spending on ICT technical support
ICT workshops expenditure	Spending on ICT training and workshops

2.2 Data Analysis

In this study, a series of statistical techniques was applied. First, to identify the factor structure of the FSIS, an exploratory factor analysis was conducted. Then, the correlations within and between the EESC items and the extracted FSIS factors were analyzed. Subsequently, the items of the EESC influencing the FSIS were analyzed through stepwise linear regression. The EESC were considered as predictor variables, whereas the FSIS were processed as dependent variables. Finally, stepwise linear regression analysis of the rural group and the urban group was conducted to identify the differences in the predictive relationships of the two groups.

3 Results

3.1 Factor Analysis

This research employed exploratory factor analysis to validate the factors of the FSIS questionnaire. The indicators in this study included different types of information, such as *ICT construction expenditure*, and *students' ICT learning time*. Therefore, to obtain reasonable results, the values of 14 quantitative indicators were standardized according to their Z scores while utilizing the factor analysis method. Principal component analysis was used as the extraction method, and the rotation method was Varimax with Kaiser Normalization. An item was retained only when its loading was greater than 0.50 on the relevant factor and less than 0.50 on the non-relevant factor.

The factor analysis shown in Table 3 revealed that indices of school ICT situation were grouped into four scales named *environment*, *support*, *application*, and *fund allocation*. The reliability coefficients (α) for these scales were 0.78, 0.74, 0.67, and 0.52, respectively, with an overall reliability coefficient of 0.76. Therefore these scales were deemed to be sufficiently reliable for assessing the development of ICT in schools. Since the ICT environment included intrinsic complex elements and covers various aspects, the *environment* had relatively more items, and played a heavier role than other subscales. It was revealed that at the current stage the main part of schools' ICT situation was still the environment.

Table 3. Rotated factor loadings and Cronbach's α values for the FSIS (n = 4357)

Items of the FSIS	Environment	Support	Application	Fund allocation
Environment α = 0.78				
Computer classroom usage	0.78			
Students' VLS enrollment	0.70			
Multimedia classroom usage	0.69			
PC/student-ratio	0.65			
PC/teacher-ratio	0.60			
Teachers' VLS enrollment	0.58			
Total network	0.43			
Support α = 0.74				
ICT construction expenditure		0.74		
ICT investment proportion		0.71		
Teachers attending ICT training		0.65		
Application α = 0.67				
Students' ICT learning time			0.87	
Teachers' ICT learning time			0.78	
Fund allocation α = 0.52				
Technical support expenditure				0.85
ICT workshops expenditure				0.73

Total variance explained is 53.87%, overall α = 0.76

3.2 Correlations Between the EESC and the FSIS

In this study, the Pearson's correlation was applied to show the relationships between the EESC and the FSIS, as shown in Table 4. There were statistically significant positive correlations between the EESC and the FSIS. *Environment* had a stronger relationship with the EESC than other factors (r = 0.052 ~ 0.685, $p < 0.01$). All the relationships between *fund allocation* and the EESC (r = 0.024 ~ 0.151, $p < 0.05$) were relatively low. Among the EESC items, *ICT qualified teachers* had the strongest relationships with the FSIS. It indicated that *ICT qualified teachers* played an important role in the development of ICT, especially in the construction of an ICT instruction environment.

Table 4. The Correlations between items of the EESC and factors of the FSIS (n = 4357)

Items of EESC	Environment	Support	Application	Fund allocation
School locality	.367**	.087**	.204**	.048**
School size	.399**	.126**	.228**	.070**
Education stage	.285**	.131**	.172**	.074**
Campus network	.258**	.048**	.126**	.024*
School-based resources	.433**	.118**	.241**	.080**
Multimedia classroom	.633**	.199**	.382**	.111**
Computer classroom	.524**	.142**	.245**	.084**
Full-time technicians	.154**	.287**	.144**	.096**
ICT qualified teachers	.685**	.285**	.431**	.151**
ICT plan	.052**	.265**	.082**	.087**

Notes: $^{*}p < 0.05$; $^{**}p < 0.01$

3.3 Stepwise Regression Analysis for Predicting the FSIS

Stepwise linear regression was employed to make predictions about the four FSIS factors, as shown in Table 5. First, seven EESC items can make significant and positive predictions of *environment*, and two items are significant but negative predictors for *environment* (R^2 = 0.64). Second, *support* could be significantly explained by six EESC items, five positively and one negatively (R^2 = 0.18). Third, *application* can be significantly and positively explained by eight EESC items (R^2 = 0.23). Lastly, six EESC items can serve as positive predictors of *fund allocation* (R^2 = 0.03).

According to the results, it should be noted that *ICT qualified teachers* is the major predicting factor for FSIS factors, especially for the *environment* factor. At the same time, the regression results suggest that *full-time technicians* is highly linked with *supporting*. Last but not least, *education stage* plays a minor part in schools' FSIS.

Table 5. Stepwise regression model of predicting schools' FSIS by EESC items (n = 4357)

FSIS	Predictor(s)	*B*	*S.E.*	β	*T*	R^2
Environment						
	ICT qualified teachers	.007	.000	.387	52.392***	.64
	Multimedia classroom	.475	.012	.284	39.221***	
	Computer classroom	.139	.004	.251	33.617***	
	School-based resources	.190	.010	.122	19.031***	
	Campus network	.000	.000	.053	8.727***	
	School size	–.005	.000	–.097	-11.919***	
	School locality	.155	.014	.078	11.181***	
	Full-time technicians	.016	.003	.030	4.957***	
	ICT plan	–.033	.015	–.014	-2.283*	
	Constant	–.939	.015		-63.604	
Support						
	Full-time technicians	.114	.005	.203	22.392***	.18
	ICT qualified teachers	.004	.000	.213	19.978***	
	ICT plan	.498	.023	.195	21.731***	
	Education stage	.076	.016	.045	4.878***	
	Multimedia classroom	.065	.019	.037	3.471**	
	Campus network	–.000	.000	–.024	–2.675**	
	Constant	–.557	.033		–16.895	
Application						
	ICT qualified teachers	.006	.000	.276	25.401***	.23
	Multimedia classroom	.339	.021	.168	15.845***	
	Full-time technicians	.040	.006	.061	6.926***	
	School-based resources	.109	.018	.058	6.185***	
	Computer classroom	.024	.007	.037	3.687***	
	ICT plan	.081	.026	.028	3.152**	
	School locality	.066	.022	.028	2.969**	
	Education stage	.045	.018	.023	2.500*	
	Constant	–.780	.043		-18.050	
Fund allocation						
	ICT qualified teachers	.002	.000	.102	8.605***	.03
	Full-time technicians	.037	.006	.059	6.010***	
	ICT plan	.170	.028	.059	6.046***	
	Education stage	.061	.019	.032	3.192**	
	Multimedia classroom	.056	.023	.029	2.444*	
	School-based resources	.040	.019	.022	2.125*	
	Constant	–.337	.040		-8.370	

Notes: *$p < 0.05$; **$p < 0.01$; ***$p < 0.001$

3.4 Comparison of the Stepwise Regression Results for Rural and Urban Schools

The above passages examined the relation between EESC items and FSIS factors of all types of primary schools in areas of different administrative levels. However, there is an overall development gap between rural and urban schools at practice. In order to investigate the predictions within both types of schools, step regression analysis was further applied to determine the EESC items predicting the FSIS. The outcome variables are the EFA scores of the FSIS factors, and the EESC items are adopted as predictors.

Table 6. Comparative stepwise regression model analysis of rural and urban schools

FSIS	R^2		Predictor(s)		β	
	Rural	Urban			Rural	Urban
Environment	.62	.41	ICT qualified teachers	Similarity	.375	.384
			Multimedia classroom		.278	.288
			Computer classroom		.246	.262
			School-based resources		.122	.101
			School size		–.050	–.171
			Education stage	Difference	.020	–.049
			Campus network		.110	–
			Full-time technicians		.029	–
			ICT plan		–.013	–
Support	.20	.07	Full-time technicians	Similarity	.207	.175
			ICT qualified teachers		.208	.103
			ICT plan		.208	.121
			Education stage	Difference	.044	–
			Multimedia classroom		.042	–
			Campus network		–.033	–
			Computer classroom		.024	–
Application	.23	.07	ICT qualified teachers	Similarity	.278	.216
			Multimedia classroom		.185	.100
			Full-time technicians		.062	.063
			School-based resources	Difference	.064	–
			Computer classroom		.050	–
			ICT plan		.034	–
			Education stage		.036	–
			School size		–.022	–
Fund allocation	.04	.01	ICT qualified teachers	Similarity	.103	.054
			ICT plan		.056	.088
			full-time technicians	Difference	.062	–
			Education stage		.035	–
			Multimedia classroom		.027	–
			School-based resources		.027	–

The comparisons are focused on exploring the similarities and differences between rural and urban schools, as is shown in Table 6. Among all of the EESC items, *ICT qualified teachers* is the most successful for predicting almost all FSIS factors. In addition, this item likely plays a relatively more influential role than other EESC items. *School size* only negatively predicts *environment*, and shows no predictive power for *supporting* and *fund allocation*. *Full-time technicians* can positively predict all for rural schools, but demonstrates no predictive power for *environment* or *fund allocation* for urban schools. *Multimedia classroom* shows strong positive predictive power for rural schools, but no predictive power for *supporting* or *fund allocation* for urban schools. *Computer classroom* has strong and positive predictive power for *supporting* and *application* for rural schools, but significant predictive power only for *environment* for urban schools. *School-based resources* can positively predict both *application* and *fund allocation* for rural schools, but only *environment* for urban schools. *ICT plan* can predict *environment* negatively and *application* positively for rural schools, but demonstrates no significant predictive power for these two factors for urban schools. *Campus network* only positively predicts the factor of *environment* for rural schools, but shows no predictive power at all for any of the four FSIS factors for urban schools. *Education stage* shows significant positive predictive power for all four FSIS factors for rural schools, but for urban schools it has only negative predictive power for *environment* and no significant predictive power for the other three factors. To sum up, in both groups, *environment* can be significantly predicted by the largest number of predictors, and the number of predictors for rural schools is comparatively more than that for urban schools.

4 Discussion

This study reveals the relationship between school ICT situation and the essential elements of school construction.

The results indicate that *ICT qualified teachers* was the strongest predictor of the FSIS, especially for *environment*, *supporting*, and *application*. The level of this index has a significantly positive relation to *environment*. First, it may bring more teachers to master and apply the ICT skills of the staff. With the gradual popularization of the ICT-assisted instruction, it can increase the usage rate of schools' multimedia classrooms, recording-broadcasting classrooms, computer classrooms, and other ICT infrastructure. Corroborated in some previous studies, developing teachers' ICT integration capability is benefit for making full use of infrastructure [5], and teachers can improve their TPACK scores and professional development by sustainable ICT training [24]. Meanwhile students' usage rate and acceptance degree are affected by teachers' ICT capability obviously [25–27].

Three observations can be made from the comparative analysis between rural and urban schools. First, for both rural and urban schools, *ICT qualified teachers* showed strong predictive power of all FSIS factors. Second, the EESC factors showed much stronger predictive power of *environment* than any of the other factors. Third, there was still a significant rural-urban gap in the development stage.

Although rural and urban schools share some commonalities to some extent in their ICT development as the above mentioned two points, there is still a significant gap in development stage between rural schools and urban schools as the following third observation: EESC items have stronger predicative power of FSIS factors of rural schools. EESC items which evaluate background and basic situation of ICT development in schools have stronger positive predictive power for schools in rural areas and the number of predictive indicators is larger. EESC items have relatively weaker predictive power and fewer predictive indicators for urban schools. It indicates that since Chinese rural schools and urban schools are now at different stages in their ICT development. Since schools in rural areas are devoted to solving the environment construction issues [28, 29], whereas schools in urban areas have benefited from the application of mature software and hardware infrastructure, adequate staff with ICT capability [30]. They are faced with development of higher-order individual abilities like design thinking and creativities. Further exploration of the key factors related to the differences of ICT development in rural and urban schools needs to be conducted in order to narrow the gap.

5 Conclusion

This study confirmed that there are predictive relationships between the FSIS and the EESC. Teachers' ICT capability is closely related to the composite of ICT situation in both rural and urban schools. Improving teachers' ICT competence can be an effective way of promoting schools' ICT development. EESC have a stronger connection with ICT situation in rural school than in urban school, which means Chinese rural and urban schools are now at different stages in ICT development.

There are still some limitations for indices adopted in this study. Further studies are required to explore the key factors related to the rural-urban gap in school ICT development.

Acknowledgements. This research was supported by National Science & Technology Pillar Program during the Twelfth Five-year Plan Period under grant (No.2014BAH22F01).

References

1. Valcke, M.: Understanding structural and cultural school characteristics in relation to educational change: the case of ICT integration. Educ. Stud. **35**(2), 223–235 (2009)
2. Tondeur, J., Valcke, M., Braak, J.V.: A Multidimensional approach to determinants of computer use in primary education: teacher and school characteristics. J. Comput. Assist. Learn. **24**(6), 494–506 (2008)
3. Law, N., Chow, A.: Teacher characteristics, contextual factors, and how these affect the pedagogical use of ICT. In: Law, N., Pelgrum W.J., Plomp, T. (eds.) Pedagogy and ICT Use: In Schools Around the World Findings from the IEA Sites 2006 Study, pp. 181–219. Springer, Netherlands (2008)

4. Prestridge, S.: The beliefs behind the teacher that influences their ICT practices. Comput. Educ. **58**(1), 449–458 (2012)
5. Aoki, H., Kim, J., Lee, W.: Propagation & level: factors influencing in the ICT composite index at the school level. Comput. Educ. **60**(1), 310–324 (2013)
6. Chuang, H.-H., Weng, C.-Y., Huang, F.-C.: A structure equation model among factors of teachers' technology integration practice and their TPCK. Comput. Educ. **86**, 182–191 (2015)
7. Wastiau, P., Blamire, R., Kearney, C., Quittre, V., Van de Gaer, E., Monseur, C.: The Use of ICT in education: a survey of schools in Europe. Eur. J. Educ. **48**(1), 11–27 (2013)
8. Mai, N., Tse-Kian, N.: Engaging students in multimedia-mediated constructivist learning - students' perceptions. J. Educ. Technol. Soc. **12**(2), 254–266 (2009)
9. Cano, M.-D., Sanchez-Iborra, R.: On the use of a multimedia platform for music education with handicapped children: a case study. Comput. Educ. **87**, 254–276 (2015)
10. Lysenko, L.V., Abrami, P.C.: Promoting reading comprehension with the use of technology. Comput. Educ. **75**, 162–172 (2014)
11. Kong, S.C.: An empirical study of school-based planning for the use of information technology to improve the quality of education in the twenty-first century. Technol. Pedagogy Educ. **36**(3), 343–359 (2009)
12. Li, Q., Ma, X.: A meta-analysis of the effects of computer technology on school students' mathematics learning. Educ. Psychol. Rev. **22**(3), 215–243 (2010)
13. Vanderlinde, R., Van Braak, J., Tondeur, J.: Using an online tool to support school-based ICT policy planning in primary education. J. Comput. Assist. Learn. **26**(5), 434–447 (2010)
14. Nielsen, W., Miller, K.A., Hoban, G.: Science teachers' response to the digital education revolution. J. Sci. Educ. Technol. **24**(4), 417–431 (2015)
15. Bateman, D., Oakley, C.: The Classmate PC 1:1 ELearning Project in Australia. Deakin University Faculty of Arts and Education (2009)
16. Mooij, T., Smeets, E.: Modelling and supporting ICT implementation in secondary schools. Comput. Educ. **36**(3), 265–281 (2001)
17. Kim, J.H., Jung, S.Y., Lee, W.G.: Design of contents for ICT literacy in-service training of teachers in Korea. Comput. Educ. **51**(4), 1683–1706 (2008)
18. Hermans, R., Tondeur, J., van Braak, J., Valcke, M.: The impact of primary school teachers' educational beliefs on the classroom use of computers. Comput. Educ. **51**(4), 1499–1509 (2008)
19. Leask, M., Pachler, N.: Learning to Teach Using ICT in the Secondary School. Routledge, New York (2013)
20. MEXT: Section 8 Technology and Home Economics New Course of Study for Junior High School. Ministry of Education, Culture, Sports, Science and Technology, Japan (2008)
21. Williams, D., Coles, L., Wilson, K., Richardson, A., Tuson, J.: Teachers and ICT: current use and future needs. Br. J. Edu. Technol. **31**(4), 307–320 (2000)
22. Haydn, T.A., Barton, R.: Common needs and different agendas: how trainee teachers make progress in their ability to use ICT in subject teaching. some lessons from the UK. Comput. Educ. **49**(4), 1018–1036 (2007)
23. Tearle, P.: ICT implementation: what makes the difference? Br. J. Edu. Technol. **34**(5), 567–583 (2003)
24. Dong, Y., Chai, C.-S., Sang, G.-Y., Koh, J.H.L., Tsai, C.-C.: Exploring the profiles and interplays of pre-service and in-service teachers' technological pedagogical content knowledge (TPACK) in China. J. Educ. Technol. Soc. **18**(1), 158–169 (2015)
25. Rodríguez, P., Nussbaum, M., López, X., Sepúlveda, M.: A monitoring and evaluation scheme for an ICT-supported education program in schools. J. Educ. Technol. Soc. **13**(2), 166–179 (2010)

26. Cox, M.J., Marshall, G.: Effects of ICT: do we know what we should know? Educ. Inf. Technol. **12**(2), 59–70 (2007)
27. Pi-Sui, H., Priya, S.: A systemic plan of technology integration. J. Educ. Technol. Soc. **9**(4), 173–184 (2006)
28. Bandung, Y., Gani, A.M., Tanuwidjaja, H.C., Sembiring, J.: The challenges of delivering multimedia-based learning services in rural areas. In: International Conference on Information Technology Systems and Innovation, pp. 1–6. IEEE, Indonesia (2015)
29. Lv, J.: ICT education in rural areas of southwest china: a case study of Zhongxian County, Chongqing. In: International Conference on Computer Science & Education, pp. 681–685. IEEE, Singapore (2011)
30. Looker, E.D., Thiessen, V.: Beyond the digital divide in canadian schools: from access to competency in the use of information technology. Soc. Sci. Comput. Rev. **21**(4), 475–490 (2003)

Blended Learning for Improving Flexibility of Learning Structure Query Language (SQL)

Verayuth Lertnattee(✉) and Perayot Pamonsinlapatham

Faculty of Pharmacy, Silpakorn University, Nakhon Pathom 73000, Thailand
{lertnattee_v,pamonsinlapa_p}@su.ac.th, verayuths@hotmail.com

Abstract. The Structural Query Language (SQL) is the popular language used for managing and retrieving data and information from relational databases. To support the decision making for healthcare professionals including pharmacists, learning SQL is one of an important topic in a database course. The objective of this research was to introduce blended learning for improving flexibility of learning SQL. The learning process was discussed and planned. Contents in this topic and examples of relational databases were designed and implemented. The SQLite was selected as a relational database management system due to its flexibility of using and managing. After a face-to-face class, students could practice their exercises with any of their computing devices, i.e., computers, tablets and smartphones. Moreover, these devices could operate with or without Internet connection. Students could practice and manage their exercises at any time and from anywhere. With evaluations from students, the results showed that the flexibility of the system enhanced their ability for learning SQL.

Keywords: Blended learning · Structure query language (SQL) · SQLite · Mobile device

1 Introduction

In healthcare information system, a database keeps information about healthcare professionals, patients, medicines, medical equipment, etc. For healthcare professionals, basic attributes such as name, address, contact phones, area of specialization, and so on while attributes for patients may be name, address, contact phones, health record number, date of birth, history of appointments, prescriptions, physical examination, laboratories tests, diagnoses from doctors, etc. If these data and/or information were stored in a relational database, the language, which is usually used to store and retrieve data from the database, is Structure Query Language (SQL). Several researches applied SQL for retrieving or managing health and medicine data. For example, in the process of developing a decision tool for identifying abuse of controlled substances, the pattern analysis logic for the measures was encoded into SQL [1]. In development of query strategies to identify a histologic lymphoma subtype, SQL-based query was applied [2]. A method to construct fine-grained access control for personal health record based on SQL in a relational database was introduced [3]. From these examples, SQL is an important language to learn

S.K.S. Cheung et al. (Eds.): ICBL 2017, LNCS 10309, pp. 343–353, 2017.
DOI: 10.1007/978-3-319-59360-9_30

not only in information technology professional but also in other professionals who need SQL to generate information.

Health professionals including pharmacy are needed who are well educated in health informatics. The curricula of health and/or pharmacy informatics would lead to raise the quality and efficiency of healthcare. Health informatics involves the study, design, and implementation of information and information systems in health care. In Faculty of Pharmacy, Silpakorn University, Thailand, Master Degree Program in Pharmacy (Health informatics) was introduced in 2008. A course about database management was set. Classical teaching, i.e., face-to-face has been applied in the course. A topic of the SQL is always taught in the course. In the second semester, academic year of 2016, the face-to-face teaching was blended with an assignment to improve students' skills in this topic. Students had flexibility to select various tools on both computers and mobile devices, i.e., smartphones and tablets with or without Internet connection. Students could do an assignment from everywhere and every time. To improve the flexibility, contents of this topic were designed. A set of hardware and software was selected. An assignment was given to students. Finally, an assessment by students' satisfaction was done.

In the rest of this paper, the detail of Structure Query Language is described in Sect. 2. Section 3 presents the concept of the blended learning. Section 4 gives the concept of improving flexibility for learning Structure Query Language. Section 5 explains our blended learning design and evaluations. The results from students' evaluations and discussions are given in Sect. 6. A conclusion and future work are made in Sect. 7.

2 Structure Query Language

Structured Query Language (SQL) is a popular query language for relational database management systems (RDBMS) according to ANSI (American National Standards Institute). In the course for beginner, two types of SQL are usually introduce to learners, i.e., DDL and DML [4]. Data Definition Language (DDL) statements are used to define the database structures in a relational database model. CREATE, ALTER and DROP are examples of DLL that are used for creating objects, altering structure of objects and deleting objects in a database, respectively. For Data Manipulation Language (DML), the set of statements is used to manage data within schema objects. For example, SELECT is applied for retrieving data from a database. INSERT, UPDATE and DELETE are used for modifying data in a database. Main RDBMSs such as Oracle, Microsoft SQL Server, PostGreSQL and MySQL use SQL as a language for managing their databases. Although these RDBMSs use SQL as their primary language, most of them also have their some proprietary extensions that are normally only applied on their system. However, standard SQL commands can be applied on most of RDBMSs.

3 Blended Learning

Blended learning is a kind of learning which combines some useful methods to enhance the learning by traditional methods. Several perspectives of blended learning were given and discussed [5]. In blended learning, online courses should be combined with the traditional learning and the proportion of online courses should be in range of 30–79% [6]. Key principles for designs and practices on each model of blend learning based on Maslow's and Vygotsky's educational theory, were reviewed [7]. Using blended learning in higher education was discussed [8]. The great advantage of blended learning was the flexibility to applied learning processes to adult learners [9]. Blended learning was introduced to teach programming languages [10]. The advantages and disadvantages of blended learning were also given. In this study, some techniques using modern technologies were blended into the traditional method for teaching and learning general programming languages. However, mobile technologies were not mentioned at that time of study. In the twenty-first century, flexibility of teaching and learning methods based on individual students. Students can manage their time and place for learning. With modern technologies, Internet connection and mobile devices make students can be improved their knowledge and skills at anytime from anywhere.

4 Improving Flexibility for Learning Structure Query Language

For a face-to-face class, knowledge about SQL is provided and discussed. Lecturers should focus on theory of the topic. Blended learning is used for improving students' skill in SQL. With traditional methods, students can practice SQL in two approaches. The first approach is that they have to install a set of software into their computers. With this approach, a student may have high skill in software installation and configuration. The other approach, network connection (usually the Internet) should be available to students for connecting to a database server. Some rigidities are found in the traditional method, i.e., rigidities in hardware, software and network connection. The hardware of choice to learn programming language is computer platform (desktop and laptop). Although mobility of a computer is possible, especially the laptop computer, its mobility is far from that of mobile devices. For software, an enterprise level of RDBMS is usually used for learning SQL. Therefore, the high performance computers are normally utilized. If the small RDBMS can be used for learning SQL, the less performance devices, which are usually smaller in size, may be applied. If students do not want to install a set of software into their computers, small client software may be used for connecting the client to the RDBMS server. Internet connection has to be persistence and stable. Moreover, when students applied some mistaken commands, data stored in a database may be incorrect. Students may wait an administrator to correct or recover a database. These limitations interrupt students' learning processes. In this paper, a blended learning system was designed to alleviate these problems. To improve flexibility of a blended learning system, a set of hardware and software were selected and learning contents were designed.

4.1 Hardware and Operating Systems

To improve flexibility of learning process, mobile smartphones and tablets were included for practicing devices. Nowadays, students use their smartphones (including tablets) to do comprehensive functions. It is easy to train students using them as powerful tools in blended learning systems. Three popular operating systems for smartphones and tablets are Android, IOS and Windows Mobile [11] while the top three operating systems in computers are Windows, Mac OS and Linux. In both computers and smartphones, Web browsers and applications for each platform can be found. Flexibilities for selecting a device, an operating system, and a set of software to perform SQL commands are possible. The flexibility to choose between desktop and laptop computers, which have more powerful in computing and normally bigger screen size. Compare to the smaller size, less weight, and less computing power from smartphones, they are more portable than desktop computer and even laptop computers. Furthermore, if standalone applications which use low resources and easy to manage are set, the Internet connection will be not necessary to perform the task of blended learning.

4.2 Database Management Systems

The SQLite is originally design as an embedded relational database management system for resource-limited devices. From this concept, it can be used in small computing devices, e.g., tablets and smartphones. Of the three popular operating systems in tablets and smartphones, a set of software, which has a feature of managing SQLite databases, can be found. The SQLite has some advantages. It is an ACID-compliant and implements most of the SQL standard [12]. It can be considered as zero-configuration database management system because no setup and administration needed. Furthermore, data in a database is completely stored in single cross-platform disk file. With these two features, students can easy to manage databases even they are not a technology expertise or a computer scientist. Flexibility from moving a database file from several platforms helps students to continue their practice. The SQLite is not designed for a production system from client-server database engine. High volume data with high concurrency access is not suitable for loading into a database of SQLite. However, it is suitable in a learning system with small volume of data and low concurrency access to a database. Therefore, a client-server system for teaching and learning SQL is possible.

5 Blended Learning Design and Evaluations

5.1 Blended Learning Instructional Design

The first year graduate students in Master Degree Program in Pharmacy (Health informatics), Faculty of Pharmacy, Silpakorn University that registered the course "Database Design and Implementation for Health Information Management" in the second semester, academic year of 2016 (Aug, 2016 to Jul, 2017). The number of students was four. In this course, blended learning was used approximately 50%. In the topic of Structure Query Language, the face-to-face teaching was blended with practicing an assignment. Various tools on both computers and mobile devices, i.e., smartphones and tablets with or without Internet connection, may be used to do an assignment. To improve flexibility of learning, i.e., students could do an exercise from everywhere and every time, contents of this topic was designed. A set of hardware and software was selected.

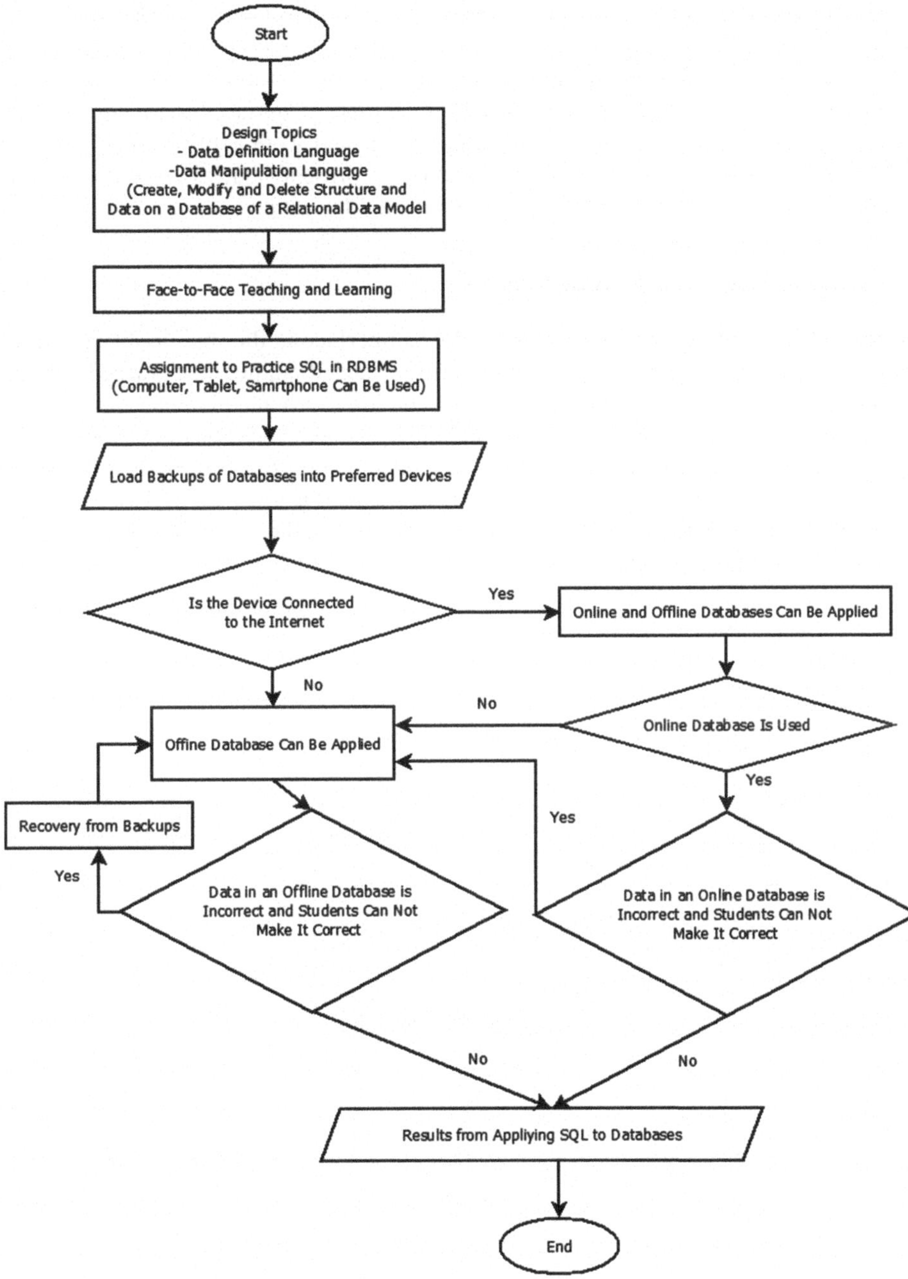

Fig. 1. The process of using blended learning for improving flexibility of learning.

An exercise was assigned to students. The SQLite, an open source software was used as a relational database management system. It might be applied as a client-server system or standalone system. In a client-server system, a terminal software with command line interface and a Web-based application could be applied. For a standalone system, a set of software was selected based on an operating system in a device. Three operating systems were used. Microsoft Windows 10 was used in desktop computers, laptop computers, and Windows phones. The IOS and Android were applied on iPhone and Android-based smartphone, respectively. The Fig. 1 presents a diagram of the process of using blended learning for improving flexibility of learning.

5.2 Various Tools for Learning SQL

Command Line Interface. The command line interface is the traditional system to learning SQL. A simple command-line utility named sqlite3 (or sqlite3.exe on Windows) is provided by the SQLite. It allows the user to manually enter and execute SQL statements against a SQLite database. All SQL commands for the version of the SQLite are fully supported by this utility. The example presents the command line for using the learnsql.db (a database that is created by the SQLite). The SQL statement is typed and it is terminated by a semicolon, press "Enter" and the SQL will be executed. The result was shown in Fig. 2.

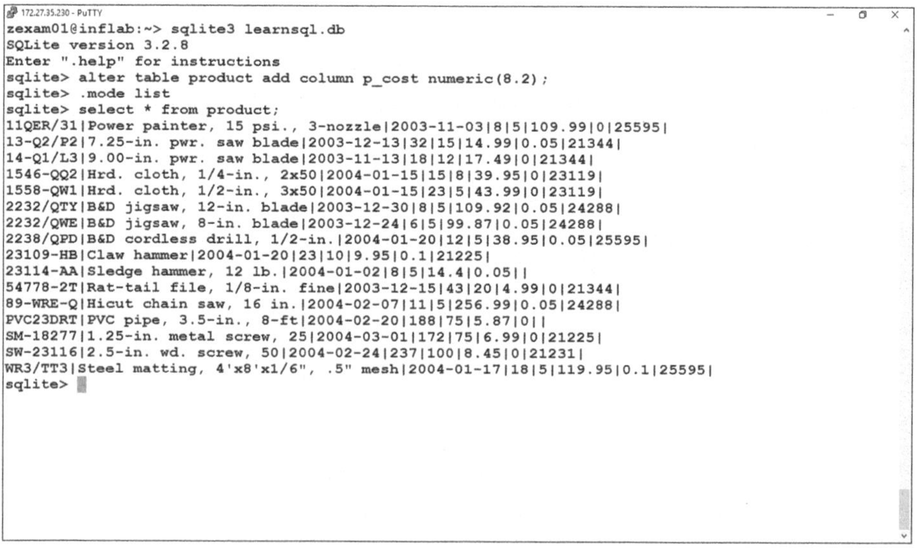

Fig. 2. The sqlite3, a command line utility for using SQLite databases.

Web-based Application. The phpLiteAdmin is used as a web-based application for managing SQLite databases. It is written in PHP with support for SQLite3 and SQLite2. As mention in previous section, a database of the SQLite is stored in a flat-file, phpLiteAdmin can be dropped into a directory on a server. With a bit of setting up, it will be accessed by users via a Web browser from any computing devices. However, if teachers prepared the system on the Internet, the Internet connection is required to use this system for practicing. Furthermore, some SQL commands will be not execute correctly based on the version of software. The GUI of the phpLiteAdmin is shown in the Fig. 3.

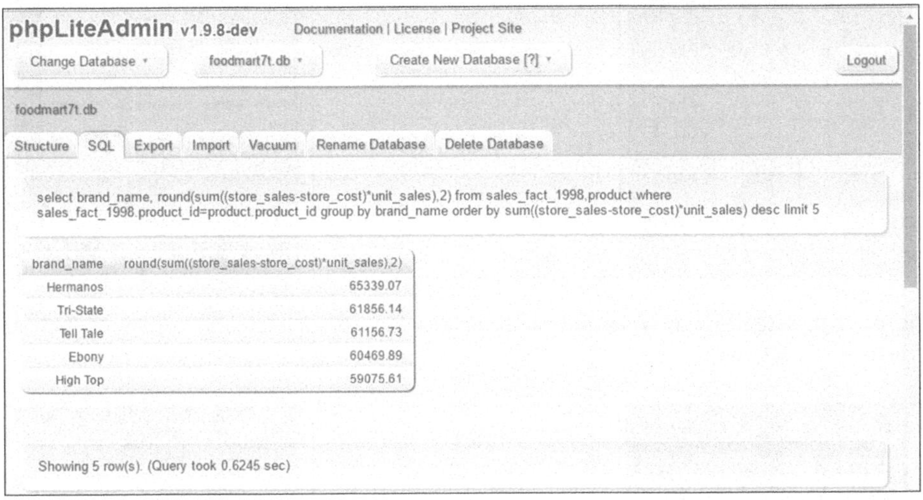

Fig. 3. The phpLiteAdmin, a Web-based application for administration of SQLite databases.

Mobile Applications on Mobile Devices. For a computer (desktop computers and laptop computers), most of utilities for using SQLite databases can be installed and used to practice SQL. However, it is hard to bring a computer to everywhere. Nowadays, mobile devices are used for daily life. Tablets and smartphones are usually applied for communication and other tasks. Although less computing power compares to a computer, it is fast enough to execute SQL commands for learning SQL. When Internet connection is available, a browser may be used to access to the phpLiteAdmin for practicing SQL. However, if the connection is not available or limited in speed, local mobile applications can be applied. In our design, three popular operating systems for smartphones were used. For each operating system, a utility that may be either open source or free software for SQL databases was installed and tested. The aSQliteManager, Private DB and COM-SQL were selected as utilities for managing SQLite databases on Android, IOS and Windows 10 Mobile smartphones, respectively. This powerful and colorful software was easy to use. In Fig. 4, SQL statements are input to these applications in Android, IOS and Windows Mobile 10 and the results from executing are shown in Fig. 5, respectively.

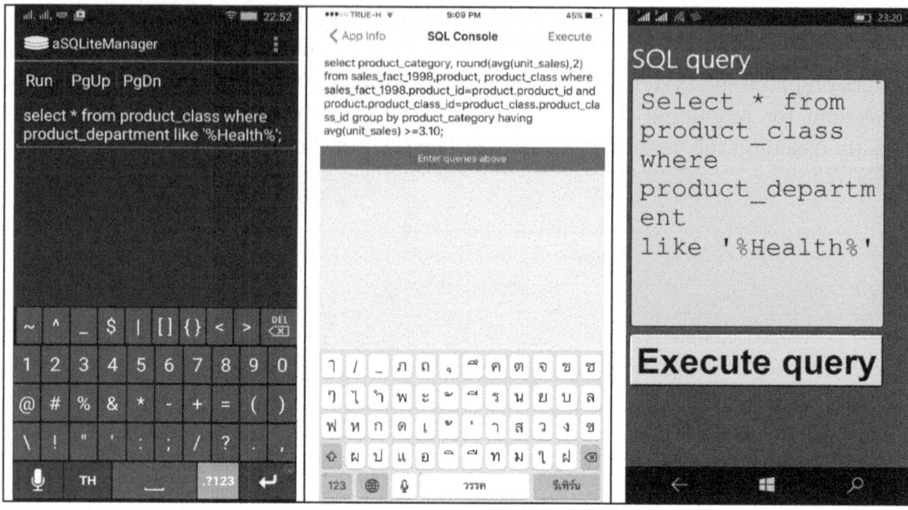

Fig. 4. SQL statements are types into mobile applications (From left to right: Android, IOS and Windows 10 Mobile).

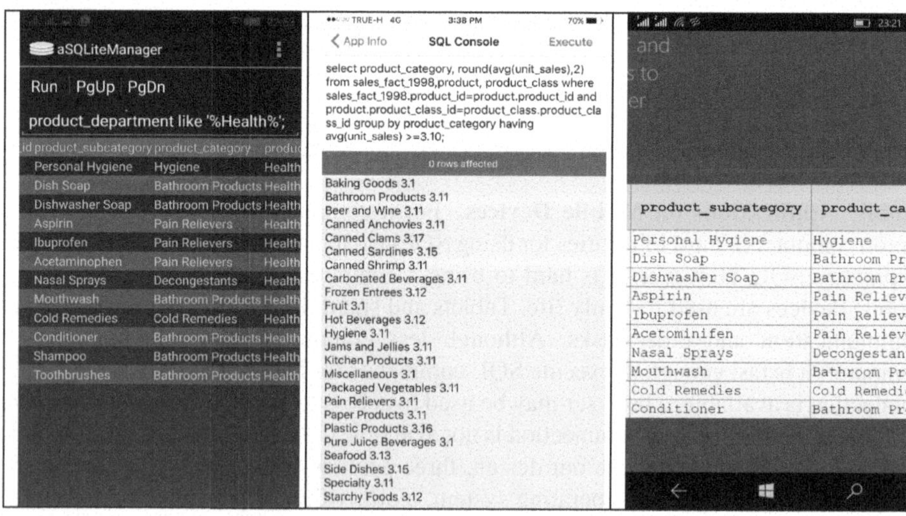

Fig. 5. Results from executing SQL statements (From left to right: Android, IOS and Windows 10 Mobile).

5.3 Evaluations

When an assignment was given to students, students managed their time and equipment to practicing SQL. A questionnaire about hardware and software that students used during the period of learning was used. Moreover, students' satisfaction about the flexibility of the blended learning designed system was included in the questionnaire.

6 Results from Students' Evaluations and Discussions

With four graduated students in this course, all of them have their own laptop computers and smartphones. Three of them use iPhones as their primary smartphone and the other one has an Android smartphone. Hardware and software used for doing the assignment is given in Table 1. The assignment had been done and then students did their questionnaires. The five-level Likert scale was used in this questionnaire. Students' satisfactions in the blended learning are presented in Table 2. Furthermore, the effectiveness of blended learning for improving students' learning on three domains of learning is shown in Table 3.

Table 1. Hardware and software used in the blended learning.

Device	# of student	
	Browser	Application
Computers	2	2
Mobile devices (Smartphones and Tablets)	0	2

Table 2. Students' satisfactions in the blended learning.

Topic	Average score ± SD	
	Computers	Mobile devices
Easy to use	4.50 ± 0.50	4.25 ± 0.43
Use for doing assignment	4.50 ± 0.50	4.25 ± 0.83
Necessary for blended learning	4.50 ± 0.50	4.00 ± 1.00

Table 3. Improving students' learning on three domains of learning.

Domain of learning	Average score ± SD
Knowledge	4.25 ± 0.43
Cognitive skills	4.25 ± 0.43
Information technology skills	4.25 ± 0.43

From the results, some observations can be made. Both computers and smartphones including tablets were used to do the assignment. Computers were important tools for students due to their large screen and easy to type SQL commands. Mobile devices were used when computers were not available in some situations. When computers were used, Web browsers were usually applied because the graphical user interface of the phpLiteAdmin was easy to use. On the opposite, mobile applications were more preferable on mobile devices compare to Web browsers. The RDBMS was installed on the Linux server. Pharmacy students were not familiar with command lines on the server. Therefore, no student used terminal clients to connect the RDBMS server. Three domains of learning were assessed. The result suggested that the blended learning was effective to improve students' learning on these three domains.

7 Conclusion and Future Work

In this research, improving flexibility of learning SQL to students was introduced. Students should practice and manage their exercise at any time and from anywhere. In order to improve flexibility, the learning process was planned. Contents for this topic and examples of relational databases were designed and implemented. Selections of hardware, software and the Internet connection were taken into account. For hardware, computers and mobile devices were selected. Operating systems were determined based on their hardware. The SQLite was chosen as a relational database management system due to its flexibility of using and managing. After a face-to-face class, students could practice their exercise with any of their computing devices, i.e., computers, tablets and smartphones. Several methods could be applied to utilize the SQLite, i.e., command line interface, Web-based applications, including mobile applications. Moreover, these devices could operate with or without Internet connection. With the evaluation of students' satisfactions in the designed learning system, the results were shown that the flexibility of the system enhanced their ability for learning SQL.

Acknowledgments. This work was supported by Instructional Innovation Development Project, Silpakorn University (2016).

References

1. Mailloux, A., Cummings, S., Mugdh, M.: A decision support tool for identifying abuse of controlled substances by forwardhealth medicaid members. J. Hosp. Mark. Public Relat. **20**, 34–55 (2010)
2. Graiser, M., Moore, S.G., Victor, R., Hilliard, A., Hill, L., Keehan, M.S., Flowers, C.R.: Development of query strategies to identify a histologic lymphoma subtype in a large linked database system. Cancer Inform. **4**(3), 149–158 (2007)
3. Sujansky, W., Faus, S., Stone, E., Brennan, P.: A method to implement fine-grained access control for personal health records through standard relational database queries. J. Biomed. Inform. **43**, S46–S50 (2010)
4. Foster, E.C., Shripad, G.: Overview of SQL. In: Database Systems, pp. 205–209 (2016)
5. Kaur, M.: Blended learning - its challenges and future. Procedia – Soc. Behav. Sci. **93**, 612–617 (2013)
6. Allen, I.E., Seaman, J.: Changing Course: Ten Years of Tracking Online Education in the United States. Sloan Consortium, PO Box 1238, Newburyport, MA 01950 (2013)
7. Chew, E., Jones, N., Turner, D.: Critical review of the blended learning models based on maslow's and vygotsky's educational theory. In: Proceedings of the 1st International Conference on Hybrid Learning and Education, pp. 40–53 (2008)
8. Okaz, A.: Integrating blended learning in higher education. Procedia – Soc. Behav. Sci. **186**, 600–603 (2015)
9. Nizkodubov, G., Evseeva, A.: Planning and implementation of the process aimed at teaching english to adult learners. Mediterr. J. Soc. Sci. **6**(2), 643 (2015)

10. Wang, F.L., Fong, J., Choy, M., Wong, T.L.: Blended teaching and learning of computer programming. In: Proceedings of the 6th International Conference on Advances in Web Based Learning, pp. 606–617 (2007)
11. Grønli, M., Hansen J., Ghinea, G., Younas, M.: Mobile application platform heterogeneity: Android vs Windows Phone vs IOS vs Firefox OS. In: IEEE 28th International Conference on Advanced Information Networking and Applications, pp. 635–641. IEEE Press (2014)
12. Owens, M.: The Definitive Guide to SQLite (Definitive Guide). Apress, Berkeley (2006)

A Hand-Waving Dance Teaching System Based on Kinect

Qingtang Liu, Shufan Yu(✉), Yang Wang, Huixiao Le, and Yangyang Yuan

School of Educational Information Technology, Central China Normal University, Wuhan 430079, Hubei, China
yushufan1993@gmail.com

Abstract. Hand-waving dance is the essence of Tujia culture. Whereas it is facing the danger of dying out. Following a choreographer's direct demonstration or watching videos recorded by dancers is the traditional learning method. Though there will be a certain degree of effect, the preciseness and feedbacks are often not so satisfying. In this paper, by analyzing the application of motion sensing technology in dance teaching, we designed and developed a set of interactive teaching system based on Kinect for Tujia traditional Hand-waving dance. In this system, not only can users learn dance skills, but they can also get an intuitionistic evaluation and review their learning process. Our study aims to solve the problem in Hand-waving dance teaching and provides a new method for Hand-waving Dance learning. Finally, we can see that the interactive learning based on computer is gradually becoming a new popular learning style.

Keywords: Interactive learning · Kinect · Motion sensing · Hand-waving dance

1 Introduction

Hand-waving dance, known as the wonderful work in Tujia culture, is the essence of Tujia minority culture. Nowadays, there are two main ways to carry out the teaching and inheritance of the dance. One way is to learn the hand-waving dance from a choreographer face-to-face instruction. Another is to collect the motions of professional dancers then organize them into texts, images, videos and other multimedia teaching materials for learning. Nevertheless, for the former one, hiring dance coaches can be costly, which is not acceptable to most of the public. For the latter one, the learning effect is not ideal. Let alone conducting scientific analysis of learners. Consequently, we are urgently in need of an effective method to teach hand-waving dance, an endangered intangible cultural heritage.

Motion sensing, also known as motion sensing control technology, is a kind of technology that directly uses body motions, sound, eye rotation and other means to interact with the surrounding devices or environment. During the process, the user's action is identified and analyzed by computers so that feedback can be made [1]. In 2007, Nintendo launched Wii Remote. After the release of this product, the concept of "somatosensory game" appeared. The majority of gamers are very keen on this "farewell game controller" gameplay and they give good feedbacks. Then in 2010, Microsoft launched Kinect and opened the SDK in the Windows platform [2], which provides some

S.K.S. Cheung et al. (Eds.): ICBL 2017, LNCS 10309, pp. 354–365, 2017.
DOI: 10.1007/978-3-319-59360-9_31

examples of the human body three-dimensional posture tracking. Microsoft has been promoting and training a number of potential developers until Kinect began public. Kinect v2.0 launched in 2014 made motion-sensing technology really popular. Compared to the first-generation Kinect product, it enhances the depth sensing capability, improves the Output Resolution, reduces the latency of the system and improves the body tracking algorithm [3]. Gradually, in such fields as medical fitness, retail industry, education, training and scientific research, Kinect begins to be widely used [4]. With the further development of motion sensing technology, more and more studies focuses on computer interactive learning. Interactive learning refers to all the human-computer interactions that contribute to learning. It is widely used in various fields such as enterprise innovation, communication ability training, teaching and cultivating, and has achieved good results [5]. As a branch of interactive learning, computer interactive learning makes use of intelligent interactive system and learners in the virtual environment for "human-machine" interaction. For it is interactive and immersive, this computer-based two-way communication is becoming the mainstream learning style.

Therefore, for the teaching of hand-waving dance, motion sensing technology has become a feasible solution. This paper sorts out and analyzes the relevant researches of somatosensory technology in the application of dance education. We will verify that "motion sensing technology can provide a better solution for Tujia hand-waving dance teaching" and design and develop a set of hand-waving dance teaching system based on Kinect. In order to solve the problem exists in traditional hand-waving dancing, the system needs to accomplish the following goals:

1. To avoid being as boring as the traditional teaching method of hand-waving dance.
2. Realizing the real-time scoring of the user's dance motions, to provide timely feedback to the learners.
3. Learners are able to look back at their performance so that learners can self-correct their motions.

The rest of this paper is organized in the following order: The second part briefly summarizes the theoretical basis of this paper and the relevant work already carried out domestically and abroad. The third part introduces the Tujia hand-waving dance teaching system in detail. The fourth part is the summary and prospect of this paper.

2 Relative Work

Although motion-sensing technology has only developed just a few years, it has a good application prospects. In this section, we reviewed the researches on dance teaching and motion evaluation to prove our study was feasible and necessary.

2.1 Studies on Dance Teaching Based on Kinect

According to a great deal of literature, we can see that most works about dance teaching by motion sensing technology relate to Ballet. Matthew kyan's study is a typical sample. He uses the trainer's movement data captured by Kinect cameras to conduct ballet dancing training [6]. The system creates a virtual reality environment consisting of three projectors, where learners can learn ballet with the help of Kinect.

Wang Tong et al. from Harbin Institute of Technology, invented a multi-screen interactive folk dance entertainment system based on Kinect [7]. Similar to Kyan's system. They built a square lab and projected to the four walls. Kinect is placed in the center of the lab. Users can get an immersive experience in this system.

Kar R's work extends the dance application of Kinect to the field of Indian dance. He uses Kinect to discover visually fascinating dance fragments for "Odissi" (an Indian dance) creation and teaching [8].

It is obvious that dance teaching based on Kinect has the characteristics of immersion and interactivity which Tradition dance teaching doesn't possess. So "Kinect provides a better way for interactive teaching of dance" proves to be feasible. However, rarely can we find relevant researches of applying motion sensing technologies to hand-waving dance teaching and Intangible Cultural Heritage protection, so our team mainly focus on the somatosensory teaching and then design a set of dance system to solve the problem in traditional hand-waving dance teaching.

2.2 Studies on Motion Evaluation Based on Kinect

The motion evaluation also becomes a research hotspot recently. Kang shuchen utilized Kinect "Bone Tracking" technology to evaluate the child's static sitting posture and dynamic behavior. This study aimed to test the mobility coordination of children [9]. Wang wenyuan's study realized table tennis teaching based on Kinect, after the four groups of basic action training, their system evaluates the posture of the learners [10].

There are also some researches on dance evaluation. Alexiadis et al. used Kinect's skeletal tracking technique to do dance evaluation [11]. Their program compares the joint positions and joint velocities (the output of the skeleton tracking module) and the 3D Flow-Error by "aligning dance movements from two different users and quantitatively evaluating their performance" to provide feedback to the dancer. Huang et al. from the National Dong Hwa University of Taiwan exploit the Kinect to evaluate a dancer's performance compared to the sample motions of the "teacher". Different from Alexiadis's study. Their criteria are based on posture and tempo accuracy [12].

More Studies show that Motion Evaluation based on Kinect will become a trend. Nevertheless, we haven't found any work related to real-time dance evaluation. Let alone self-assessment. Hence designing a set of dance system which owns good evaluation mechanism will become the focal point of our work.

3 Hand-Waving Dance Teaching System

3.1 Design of the System

Considering the development state of the traditional hand-waving dance, the masses who need to learn the dance are mostly young people from Tujia minority. For young people, the traditional hand-waving dance teaching is boring. The advantage of somatosensory teaching is the natural operation behavior of a user in the process of teaching.

This teaching model is conducive to increase the user's physical and psychological pleasure. In the process of designing motion-sensing application, points should be noted are as follows: the user group, the number of users, user characteristics. The teaching system we designed is mainly for young people. So, when designing functions, interfaces, modules, we should take into account their characteristics.

3.1.1 Interface and Model Design

Consider hand-waving dance as a treasure of Tujia. Elements that carry characteristics of Tujia Minority are mainly employed in the progress of designing the background interface, such as Tujia clothes and jewelry.

For the modeling part, We used the "poly by poly" technique to display the charisma of Tujia boys and girls. In order to improve the operating efficiency, we appropriately reduced some useless vertexes and polygons. The following Fig. 1 shows the 3D models in this systems.

Fig. 1. Models in this system.

3.1.2 Interaction Design

The system interacts with the user's somatosensory manipulation, which is divorced from the shackles of third-party tools such as the mouse and keyboard. By recognizing the position of your hands, you can move your hand in front of the Kinect instead of mouse movement and click operation. The learner uses the palm to operate the system and choose the module function. Considering the usability of the system, the mouse interacts with the "hover" operation by which you can choose a function after Staying on a button for 3 s. Figure 2 below shows the functional interaction of the system.

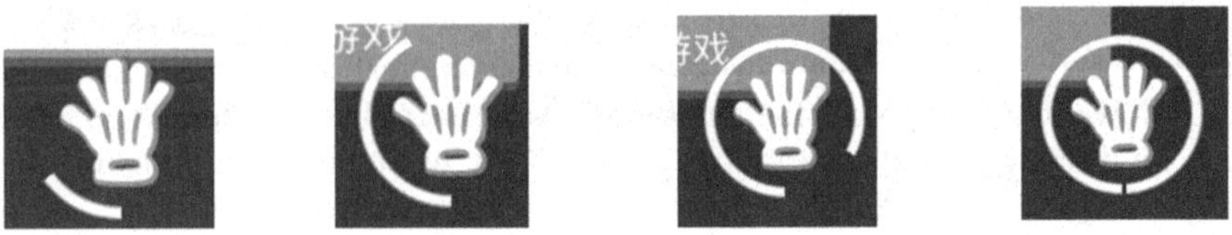

Fig. 2. Interactive method

3.1.3 Module Design

In the progress of designing hand-waving dance teaching system module, the education and entertainment should combine effectively. In an interactive system, the user is both a learner and an Instructor. The purpose of the system is to enable users to learn hand-waving dance in a happy mood. So, we try to accomplish the following points when designing different teaching modes:

- To be inspired in learning
- To learn in different ways
- To get feedback in real time
- To do self-correction
- To compete with friends

Of course, all of these must correspond with the learner's knowledge and age. Hence we set up four teaching modes in this system, they are practice mode, feedback mode, double mode and playback model. Specific features will be shown in Sect. 3.3.

3.2 Implementation of the System

3.2.1 Operation Process of the System

We designed the basic framework of this system according to the characteristics of Kinect and Hand-waving dance. Functions are as follows: 1. Data collection 2. Data analysis of skeletons 3. Interaction with system 4. Evaluation of dance (Fig. 3).

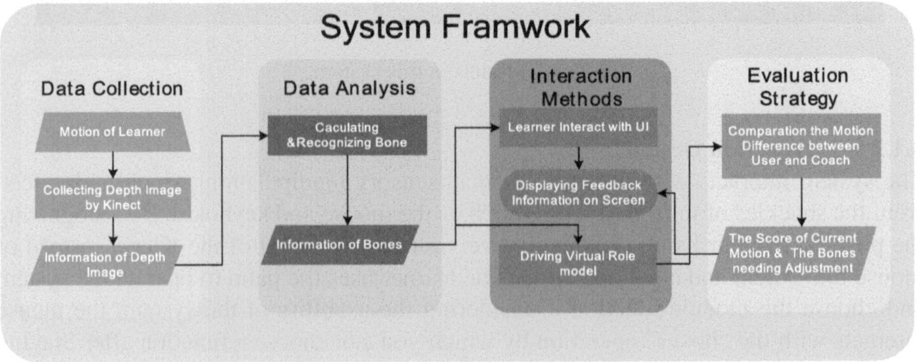

Fig. 3. System framework

Steps 1, 2, 3 are mainly as follows: Kinect identifies and captures the Learner's depth image. The position of the current user's each joint can be recognized by running the background-clipping and bone recognition algorithms on the image. User's joints location information collected by the system controls the virtual characters in the scene to interact with the scene.

After a simple interaction with the system, we need to get real-time feedback.

Therefore, Step 4's core idea is to evaluate the user's dance posture in real time. The actions involved in the system are divided into two categories and bound to two types of 3D body model respectively. One of them is coach's action. The action performed by the professional hand-waving choreographer pre-collected and bound to the coach model. Another is user's action. Users can utilize Kinect to control their own character model, perform Tujia hand-waving dance motion.

3.2.2 Key Techniques

(1) **Motion Capture.**

Motion capture technology can measure, track and record the position of users' various parts of the body during exercise, then convert the position into computer-recognized data coordinates, and coherent data coordinates can be applied in the field of 3D animation [13]. Common motion capture techniques include mechanical motion capture, electromagnetic motion capture, active optical motion capture, and passive optical motion capture. Though these technologies have high accuracy, they are always expensive and have a complex operating process. So, to correspond to the original design intention. we still use Kinect to capture virtual choreographer's movements. The camera in Kinect can obtain user's 20 joints (19 bones) information, including the location and rotation and some other information in the three-dimensional space.

In the system, we invited a professional Hand-waving choreographer to participate in the process of action recording. And exported action model which is in .dae format can be assigned in unity to the Tujia Coach for they have the same skeleton. As for learners, they study the dance in front of the camera. The system compares learner's gesture and posture with the virtual coach and then give feedback to the learner. Figure 4 is the process of action capture and model binding.

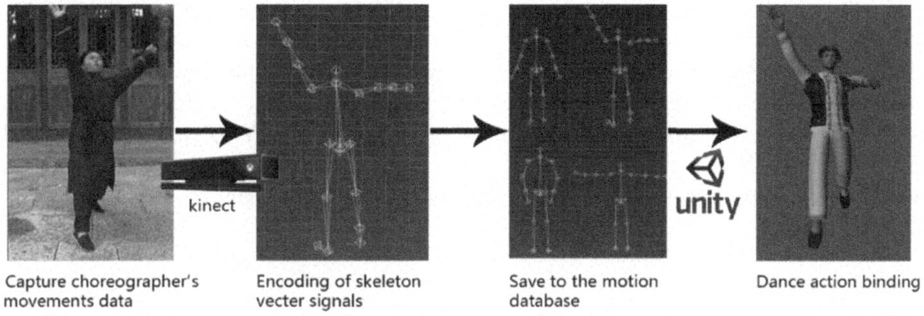

Fig. 4. Motion capture & Action binding

(2) **Dance Real-time Evaluation**.

In Unity, each joint of the character model is seen as a game object. The property "Transform" can be used to get the position and movements information of these key skeleton points in the world coordinate system. Therefore, the difference between the skeletal eigenvector matrix can be calculated by extracting the skeletal vector information on the user model and the coaching model. Kinect V2 can recognize 25 joints data of the human body. Considering the feature of Hand-waving dance, we removed five unrelated joints. The remaining 20 joints make up 19 skeletons. Figure 5 is the skeletal structure that can be recognized in Kinect (the red points are removed joints).

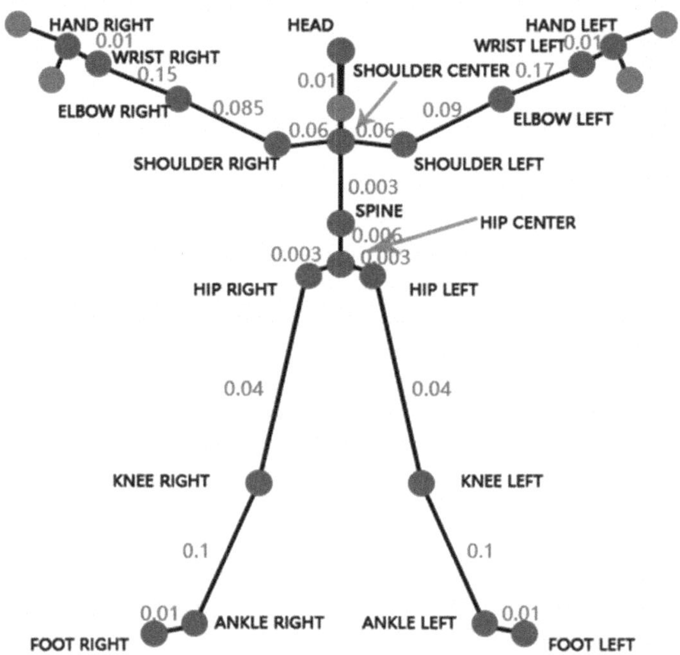

Fig. 5. Structure of human skeleton (Color figure online)

Each bone has its own position and angle information when a person takes some actions [14]. In this system, the coach and the learner may not have the similar figure. Thus, we characterized one specific motion by exploiting cosine features of 19 bones we defined. For example, for the bone between Left Shoulder and Center Shoulder joint, assuming that their spatial coordinates are (X_1, Y_1, Z_1) and (X_2, Y_2, Z_2), then the skeletal space vector is $(X_1-X_2, Y_1-Y_2, Z_1-Z_2)$, the cosine of the vector relative to each axis can be obtained by calculation. Figure 6 shows the calculation step.

$$\cos\alpha = \frac{x_2 - x_1}{\sqrt{(x_2 - x_1)^2 + (y_2 - y_1)^2 + (z_2 - z_1)^2}}$$
$$\cos\beta = \frac{y_2 - y_1}{\sqrt{(x_2 - x_1)^2 + (y_2 - y_1)^2 + (z_2 - z_1)^2}}$$
$$\cos\gamma = \frac{z_2 - z_1}{\sqrt{(x_2 - x_1)^2 + (y_2 - y_1)^2 + (z_2 - z_1)^2}}$$
$$(\sqrt{(x_2 - x_1)^2 + (y_2 - y_1)^2 + (z_2 - z_1)^2} \neq 0)$$

Fig. 6. Steps of calculating cosine eigenvalue

Three cosine eigenvalues (cosα, cosβ, cosγ) of each bone severe as an eigenvector and save on a matrix. So, we can get a 19*3 characteristic matrix. After extracting the eigenvector of each bone in Instructor's model and learner's model. We innovatively use the Euclidean distance to compare the similarity of the feature matrix. Then the difference degree $\mathbf{e}_i$ of eigenmatrix in each bone can be calculated.

There are eight motions in hand-waving dance. Each motion has its own characteristics. Different parts of a body have different frequency. So, we can achieve the frequency of the use of each bone according to a Hand-waving dance video, and then determine each bone's weight $\boldsymbol{w}_i$. The weight of each bone marked with orange numbers in Fig. 7. We use $\boldsymbol{d}_{max}$ and $\boldsymbol{d}_{min}$ represents maximum difference and the minimum difference degree of the motion. And finally, through the following algorithm to obtain real-time scores.

$$\text{socre} = \frac{d_{(u,c)} - d_{max}}{d_{min} - d_{max}} * 100 \qquad (d_{(u,c)} = \Sigma_1^{19}(w_i * \mathrm{e}_i))$$

Fig. 7. Key Algorithm

At the same time, we extracted the least standard four parts of each frame and displayed on the screen. This allows the user to get timely feedback. The Fig. 8 below shows the evaluation result of one motion.

The frame rate of Kinect v2 upgrades to 30 fps compared to 15 fps of its first generation which makes the amount of data updated per second become much larger and real-time evaluation become much more referential.

Fig. 8. The evaluation results of one motion.

3.3 Function Module Introduction

Based on the characteristics of Kinect and Hand-waving dance, the teaching system is divided into the following four modes: practice mode, feedback mode, double mode and playback mode, Fig. 9 below shows the system function module, with a variety of methods to realize basic exercises of Tujia Hand-waving dance and reflective learning.

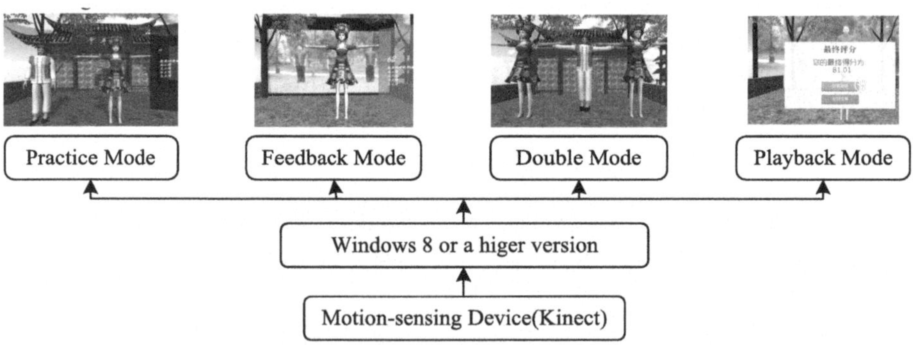

Fig. 9. Function module of this system

3.3.1 Practice Mode

Practice mode is the first scene of this system. Hence, users can dance following the virtual choreographer just like following the real choreographer beside them. This mode can help new learners of hand-waving dance know more about the basic moves of hand-waving dance and its essentials since the basic movements of each dance are determined by the professional choreographer. In addition, each basic movement contains several frames of the static move and the movement database contains almost all the basic movements of hand-waving dance for evaluation of the user's movement. Moreover, the method for movement evaluation has been illustrated above. Players can imitate the moves of virtual choreographer in practice mode eventually. The player can go into the next movement only if the score of this movement reaches 65. Otherwise, the player cannot go ahead until this movement is qualified.

3.3.2 Feedback Mode

Learners can master the basic movements of hand-waving dance after practice mode. But the continuity of the whole dance needs to be improved. Hence, feedback mode is designed and developed based on this. Users can learn the whole continuity of hand-waving dance by following the virtual choreographer in feedback mode. What's more, each movement of the player can be recognized and scored according to the movement compared to the corresponding standard ones in movement database. More importantly, the substandard four important parts can be demonstrated to help the user adjust immediately. Therefore, learners can get the essentials of each movement and the whole continuity of dance after feedback mode.

3.3.3 Double Mode

The double mode is an integration of learning partner, competitiveness and enjoyment. Kinect can be used to track two learners at the same time. It means that two users can learn hand-waving dance together following the same virtual choreographer. And they are learning companions who can learn from each other. The evaluation results are the final evaluation of their overall dance movements and there will be scores to enhance the enjoyment at the end of the dance. Above all, two users can learn together and enhance learning enjoyment by competition and cooperation.

3.3.4 Playback Mode

Playback mode makes it possible for reflective learning of the dance, which is not easy in the traditional dance learning. After learning a passage of dance, users may need to check the learning outcome and find out the problems existing in the learning process. The recording and replaying function can be used to record and replay the learning process of the user to promote his/her reflective learning. Being aware of the shortage of their own learning, learners can improve their learning correspondingly.

Figure 10 shows the system used by a learner.

The initial application site of this system locates in Changyang, Yichang, Hubei Province. After our guidance, the staffs in Tujia Museum learned the Hand-waving dance in front of the Kinect. They grasp some key motions of this dance and expressed their satisfaction with this system.

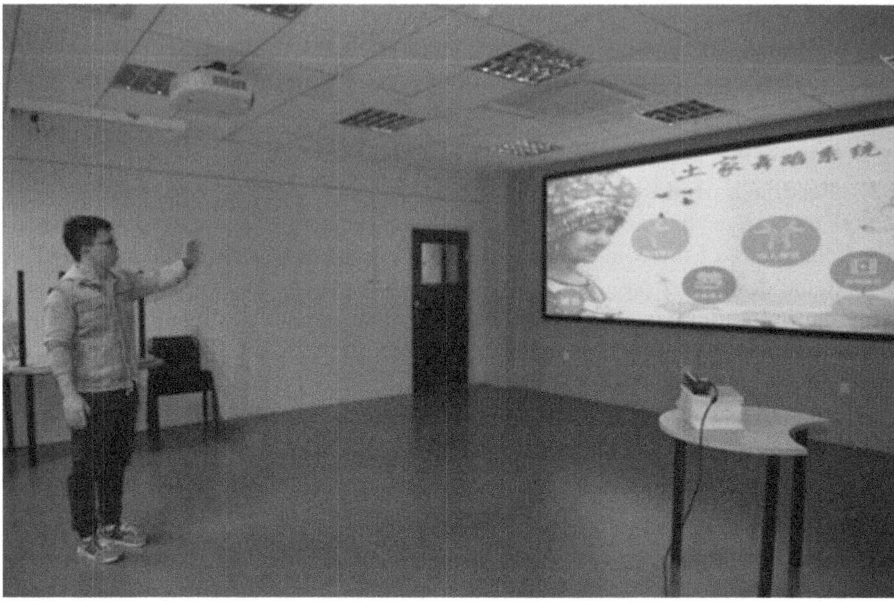

Fig. 10. Learning experience

4 Conclusion

Hand-waving dance is a national Intangible Cultural Heritage. It is the essence of Tujia ethnic culture and the evidence showing that Tujia is different from other minorities. While the developing condition is not ideal. Hand-waving dance teaching and heritage are facing a challenge. Therefore, this article analyses the application of motion sensing technology in dance education and design and develop an interactive Hand-waving dance teaching system to improve current dancing teaching. It also fills the gaps in relative researches. At the same time, the study also plays an important role in the protection of Hand-waving dance and the intangible cultural heritage.

It is observed that the interactive blended learning has gradually become a mainstream in education through this study of interactive dance teaching. More and more researches have proved that computer-based interactive learning will become a trend for future education. We believe that motion sensing technology will integrate with the intelligent wearable device and virtual reality technology to open up an "Anybody at any time, in any place, by any way, learn any content" wisdom learning era.

Acknowledgement. This work was funded by National Science and Technology plan project, Key Technology Research and Demonstration of Tujia music culture digital protection and display (2015BAK03B03).

References

1. Li, Q., Wang, Q.: Motion sensing technology in education. Distance Educ. J. **1**, 48–55 (2015)
2. Li, R., Wang, L.: A survey of human body action recognition. Pattern Recogn. Artif. Intell. **27**(1), 35–48 (2014)
3. Li, D.: The Application of Kinect's Human Body Pose Recognition Method in Dance Training. Heilongjiang University, Heilongjiang Province (2015)
4. Yuan, X.: An analysis on the present situation of the application of motion sensing technology in education. Chin. J. ICT Educ. **10**, 85–86 (2016)
5. Du, X.: Research on teaching method based on interactive learning. J. Educ. Inst. Jilin Province **2015**(04), 77–80 (2015)
6. Kyan, M., et al.: An approach to ballet dance training through MS Kinect and visualization in a CAVE virtual reality environment. ACM Trans. Intell. Syst. Technol. (TIST) **6**(2), 1–37 (2015)
7. Wang, T., Wang, J., Liu, X.: A Multi-screen Interactive Folk Dance Entertainment System Based on Kinect. Chinese Patent CN104808798A, 29 July 2015
8. Kar, R., Konar, A., Chakraborty, A.: Dance composition using microsoft kinect. In: Gavrilova, Marina L., Tan, C.J.Kenneth, Saeed, K., Chaki, N., Shaikh, S.H. (eds.) Transactions on Computational Science XXV. LNCS, vol. 9030, pp. 20–34. Springer, Heidelberg (2015). doi: 10.1007/978-3-662-47074-9_2
9. Kang, S.: Research on Contextual Assessment Method of Children 's Sports Coordination Ability Based on Kinect. Nanjing Normal University, Jiangsu Province (2015)
10. Wang, W.: Research on the Application of Courseware Based on Motion Sensing Technology in Primary School's Table Tennis Teaching. Shanghai Normal University (2014)
11. Dimitrios, S.A., et al.: Evaluating a dancer's performance via Kinect based skeleton trackinga dancer's performance via kinect-based skeleton tracking. In: 19th ACM International Conference on Multimedia, November 2011
12. Huang, T.-C., et al.: Automatic dancing assessment using Kinect. In: Proceedings of the International Computer Symposium ICS, December 2012
13. Shi, L.: Digital Protection of Non-material Cultural Heritage Dance by Motion Capture Technique. Yunnan Arts University, Yunnan Province (2015)
14. Zhu, G., Cao, L.: Human motion recognition based on skeletal information of kinect sensor. Comput. Simul. **31**(12), 329–345 (2014)

Design of a Mobile Handwriting Test Revision System for Cognitive Apprenticeship Instruction Model in Mathematics Learning

Hung-Hsu Tsai[1(✉)], Jie-Yan Peng[1], You-Ming Yong[1], Chun-Shan Wang[1], and Pao-Ta Yu[2]

[1] Department of Information Management, National Formosa University, Huwei Township, Yunlin County, Taiwan
thh@nfu.edu.tw

[2] Department of Computer Science and Information Engineering, National Chung Cheng University, Minhsiung Township, Chiayi County, Taiwan

Abstract. The purpose of the paper is to develop a MObile Handwriting TEst Revision (MOHTER) system which can be applied in an instructional design called a cognitive apprenticeship instruction model for mathematics learning in higher education. The MOHTER system offers a mobile-device APP for students who use the APP in uploading their image version of answer sheets to the cloud server of the system. Subsequently, teachers utilize the proposed system to revise answer sheets via teachers' handwriting through web interface or web APP. Here, a significant feature of the system is to integrate four operations, revising answer sheets with handwriting, assigning scores for answer sheets, writing teachers' comments on students' answer sheets, and selecting answer sheets to be modelling on class, in a single window as well as to operate these four actions through web applications. The system can support a cognitive apprenticeship instruction model for mathematics learning.

Keywords: Cognitive apprenticeship · Mobile learning · Handwriting · Instructional design · Mathematics learning · Higher education

1 Introduction

Cognitive apprenticeship is an approach in which learning is embedded in activates and makes deliberate use of the social and physical context [10]. Recently, cognitive apprenticeship theory has been applied to devise instructional designs in diverse research fields for learning in educations. An article presents an alternative instructional model for clinical skills teaching which utilizes the principles of cognitive apprenticeship [2]. The results show the proposed model can help to solve the problem that an increased number of learners leads to a reduced emphasis on traditional apprenticeship learning. The principles of a cognitive apprenticeship model was applied in the design of a teacher-student interaction during classroom teaching and learning while imparting modern technological thinking and problem-solving skills to seventh grade students [1]. An attempt of a paper is to integrate a cognitive apprenticeship model in a Web-based educational

S.K.S. Cheung et al. (Eds.): ICBL 2017, LNCS 10309, pp. 366–378, 2017.
DOI: 10.1007/978-3-319-59360-9_32

technology course to construct a methodological framework for fostering teacher education students. The results of the paper revealed that students found the use of cognitive apprenticeship methods cultivated an understanding of integrating technology for teaching and learning [3]. Cognitive apprenticeship model is also applied to develop a learning environment for a computer programming course [4]. The learning environment is devised via exploiting cognitive apprenticeship and pair programming approaches as the primary instructional strategies. It is a visual programming environment so that teachers who have no prior experience in computer programming are enable to develop their own software applications to meet their instructional requirements. An objective of an article is to apply the cognitive apprenticeship methods in developing classroom instruction and then to investigate what implications while drawing upon the proposed classroom instruction for cultivating industrial and technical teachers [8]. How to foster students' problem-solving abilities has become an important and challenging issue. An article develops a learning mechanism by integrating cognitive apprenticeship and collaborative learning approaches [7]. The article aims at investigating the effects of human factors on problem-solving effectiveness in the cognitive apprenticeship model.

Cognitive apprenticeship theory was also applied in mathematics learning [5, 6, 9]. A paper presents a cognitive apprenticeship learning environment for a course in mathematical modelling and problem solving [5]. Students are supervised in the learning environment where the teacher adopts a range of techniques to cultivate student thinking with expert thinking. A pedagogical framework based on the cognitive apprenticeship for the development and use of a 3D virtual environment in mathematics learning [9]. This paper explores how to employ the 3D virtual environment to facilitate the teaching of mathematics in primary education.

Many articles have proposed integrating the use of information technology in mathematics learning to have outstanding results. However, most mathematics instructions are still in traditional classrooms with some instructional equipment such as personal computer, projector, projection screen, etc. Moreover, the learning management system (LMS) is also a common software to help learners in mathematics learning. Nowadays, it is ubiquitous to find that students have their own mobile devices in school campus. Accordingly, how to integrating cognitive apprenticeship instruction and mobile learning in mathematics instruction in classroom is an important and emerging research topic recently. Here the paper proposes a mathematics instructional design based on cognitive apprenticeship theory. Additionally, the MOHTER system, a mobile handwriting test revision system, is developed to support the mathematics instructional design. Several papers have proposed to show using handwriting to assist learners in mathematics learning has positive learning performance [13, 14]. In [14], the paper proposed an approach to adapting, deploying and testing handwriting-based interfaces in the domain of intelligent tutoring systems for algebra equation solving. The paper found that using handwriting input can offer benefits to students in learning mathematics in higher education. In [13], the article integrates a digital pen learning system in the collaborative problem solving for investigating learning achievement and learning motivation in a conventional mathematics courses. In the learning process, using handwriting to explain students' answer obtains satisfying results. Therefore, the paper also involves the use of handwriting on revising students' answer sheets to devise an instructional design to carry out the modelling and reflection methods of cognitive apprenticeship model.

In the paper, the mathematics instruction in classroom focuses on handwriting quizzes. Once students finish a handwriting quiz, they photo their own answer sheets of the quiz and then upload them to the LMS via mobile devices. Unfortunately, many popular LMSs do not provide teachers user-friendly functions to revise the image version of answer sheets by handwriting revision. For example, e3 campus (http://e3.nfu.edu.tw/EasyE3P/LMS2/), an LMS is exploited in National Formosa University, Taiwan. Up to date, it still has several limits and drawbacks when teachers revise the handwriting answer sheets, and students turn in their handwriting answer sheets as well as watch their answer sheets teacher revised. Theses limits and drawbacks are stated as follows.

- Teacher does not readily download students' answer sheet for revision, an example as shown in Fig. 1.

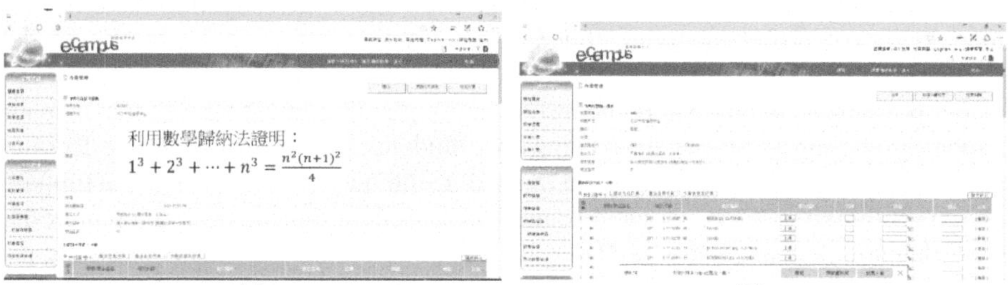

(a) (b)

Fig. 1. (a) and (b) show teachers download students' answer sheets for revision by batch and one for each processes, respectively.

- Teacher needs to use other software, for example, paint (mspaint.exe in Microsoft windows), to revise students' answer sheet by handwriting, an example as shown in Fig. 2.

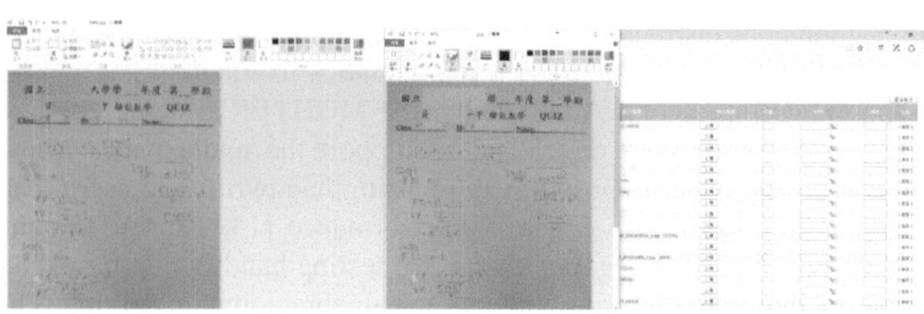

(a) (b)

Fig. 2. (a) Teachers revise answer sheets by handwriting using painting software which have to be installed in teachers' computers or mobile devices. (b) Teacher needs to switch two individual windows while getting students' answer sheets and revising them by handwriting.

- Teacher is not easy to upload revised students' answer sheet to LMS. That is, the revision of the current answer sheet and upload the revised answer sheet are in separated windows, an example as shown in Fig. 3.

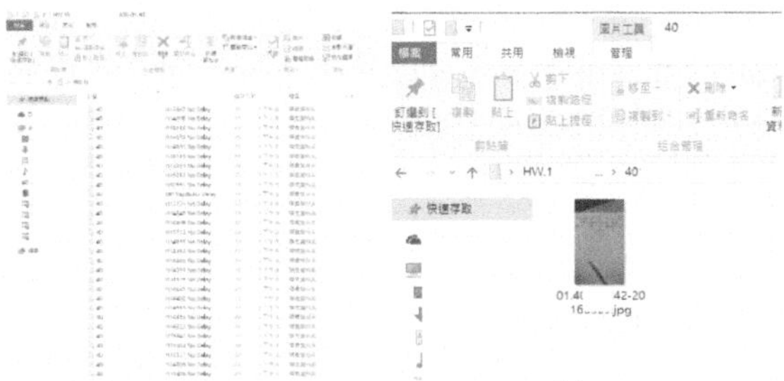

(a) (b)

Fig. 3. (a) and (b) show the revived answer sheets have to be saved in teachers' computers and upload them to LMS.

- E3 campus do not offer functions to record the answering mistakes, and then to analyze these records.
- Teacher is not easy to mark or select revised answer sheets for modelling or reflection, two teaching methods of cognitive apprenticeship model.

Hence, this motivates us to develop the MOHTER system which offers teachers cross-platform functions to revise answer sheet by handwriting, to assign types of mistakes or errors in which students write answers, and to analyze results of students' answers based on Bloom's cognitive domain. A significant characteristic of the MOHTER system is to operate these functions with web apps and within in the same windows without switching windows. It also provides students functions, realized by APPs, to upload students' answer sheets with image version, to inquire the results of answer sheets, to obtain answer sheets teachers revise via handwriting, and to study teaching materials. The functions mentioned above can be utilized in the development of an instructional design according to cognitive apprentice theory for mathematics leaning.

In Sect. 2, some related literatures are reviewed. In Sect. 3, the MOHTER system is briefly described. In Sect. 4, an instructional design according to cognitive apprenticeship theory is proposed for mathematics learning, and some discussions are given. Finally, conclusions are drawn in Sect. 5.

2 Literature Review

2.1 Cognitive Apprenticeship

'Cognitive apprenticeship' is proposed by [10], which is a kind of an instructional model derived from the metaphor of the apprentice working under the master craftspeople in traditional societies. In the traditional master-apprentice model, the master craftsperson will typically perform a psycho-motor skill which is first observed by the apprentice.

The apprentice then continues to learn the skill under guidance and help from the master. A chief difference between this traditional model and the cognitive apprenticeship model is in the opinion of task visibility. In traditional apprenticeship, the process of performing a task or skill to be learned is usually easily observable. In cognitive apprenticeship, while carrying out the task or skill probably is observable. Meanwhile, an emphasis is placed upon the thinking that must precede and be part of the task, and accompany any necessary observations made after its completion [10, 11]. There are six main learning methods for learning activity within the cognitive apprenticeship model, which are briefly stated as follows.

- Modelling: The expert carrying out the skill so that the learner can observe and build a conceptual model of the processes required to do it.
- Coaching: The expert observes the learner accomplish the skill and provides hints, feedbacks, reminders, and perhaps further modelling - focuses on promote the learner's performance closer to that of the expert.
- Scaffolding: Learning is supported to assist learners to progress to the next level. Support is gradually removed until learners is able to complete the skill by themselves.
- Articulation: Any method of aiding learners to articulate their knowledge, reasoning, or problem-solving processes.
- Reflection: Enabling learners to compare their results with those of an expert, another learner, and ultimately, an internal cognitive model of expertise.
- Exploration: Pushing learners into a mode of problem solving on their own so that learners are able to adapt to new problems in the real world.

2.2 Bloom's Taxonomy of the Cognitive Domain

Bloom et al. developed to a classification system for three domains: the cognitive, the affective, and the psychomotor [12]. For the cognitive, it is commonly referred to as Bloom's Taxonomy of the Cognitive Domain. The major concept of the taxonomy is that statements of educational objectives can be arranged in a hierarchy from less to more complex. The six domains from less level to more complex level are given as the follows, knowledge, comprehension, application, analysis, synthesis, and evaluation [12]. The definitions for each level can be found in the following [12].

- Knowledge: Students recall or recognize information, ideas, and principles in the approximate form in which they were learned.
- Comprehension: Students translate, comprehend, or interpret information based on prior learning.
- Application: Students select, transfer, and use data and principles to complete a problem or task with a minimum of direction.
- Analysis: Students distinguish, classify, and relate the assumptions, hypotheses, evidence, or structure of a statement or question.
- Synthesis: Students originate, integrate and combines ideas into a product, plan or proposal that is new to them.

- Evaluation: Student appraise, assess, or critique on a basis of specific standards and criteria.

3 System Descriptions

The MOHTER system is developed to assist teachers in classroom to accomplish an instructional design based on cognitive apprenticeship theory. Figure 4 exhibits an example to illustrate an instruction using the modelling method of cognitive apprenticeship model in classroom. Students use mobile devices to watch teaching materials or their answer sheets teacher revises.

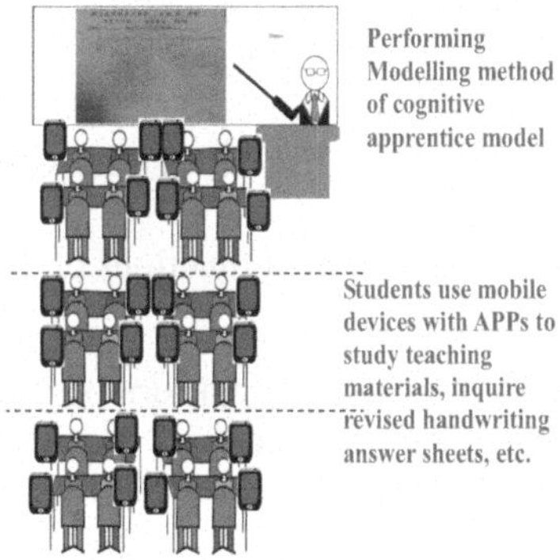

Fig. 4. An example to illustrate an instruction using the modelling method of cognitive apprenticeship model in classroom. Students use mobile devices to watch teaching materials or their answer sheets teacher revised.

3.1 System Architecture

Figure 5 shows the system architecture of the MOHTER system. It provides cross-platform services by mobile devices with large screen or personal computers with touch screen or digital pen. First, the MOHTER system offers administrator to perform course, class, user, and authentication managements. Teacher can employ the MOHTER system to manage/maintain teaching materials with multimedia format, to maintain quizzes for editing question sheets, setting quiz schedules, revising answer sheet, assigning types of mistakes or errors for answer sheets, getting the analysis results of students' answer sheets, and to manage/maintain announcements for classes. Students can exploit the proposed system to watch teaching materials, to photo students' answer sheets, to query quizzes for turning in answer sheets to the cloud server of the MOHTER system, and to inquire the results of revised answer sheets.

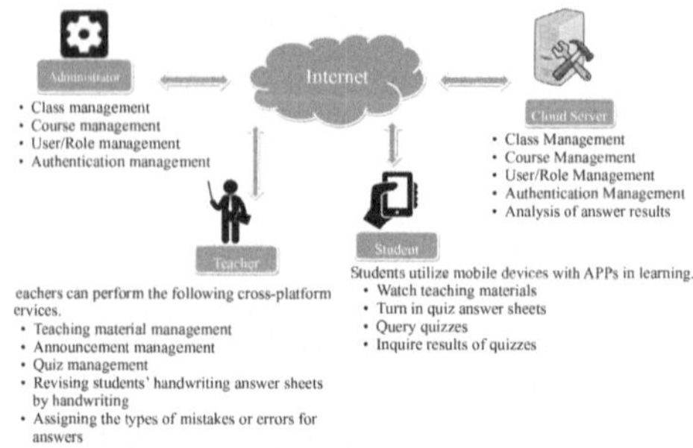

Fig. 5. The system architecture of the MOHTER system.

3.2 System Functions

There are three categories of functions the MOHTER system offers for three roles, teacher, student, and administrator.

Figure 5 presents these three categories of functions of the MOHTER system, which are briefly stated as follows.

- Teachers can perform the following cross-platform services.
  - Teaching material management: Teacher uses the function to edit and to maintain teaching units or the teaching materials related to quizzes such as the teacher's answers for quizzes.
  - Announcement management: Teacher uses the function to send notifications to students.
  - Quiz management: Teacher uses the function to edit and to maintain quizzes for quiz schedule, question sheet, what level of cognitive domain a quiz is on, etc.
  - Revising students' handwriting answer sheets by handwriting: Teacher uses the function to revise students' handwriting answer sheets by handwriting over web-based interface, and also upload the revised version of students' answer sheets in the same window with answer sheet revison.
  - Assigning the types of mistakes or errors for answers: Teacher uses the function to assign the types of mistakes or errors occurred in students' answer sheets. These records can be analyzed to deeply understand student learning status.
- Students utilize mobile devices with APPs in learning via the following services.
  - Watch teaching materials: Students employ the function to watch teaching units or the teaching materials related to quizzes such as the teacher's answers for quizzes.
  - Turn in quiz answer sheet by mobile devices with APPs: Students employ mobile devices to enable the function to photo their answer sheets by handwriting and then turn in the photo to cloud server of the MOHTER system.
  - Query quizzes: Students employ Apps to query quizzes for coming or passed quizzes.
  - Inquire the results of quizzes: Students employ Apps to inquire the results of their answer sheets.

- Administrator carries out the following functions realized by web APP before class.
  - Class management: Administrator exploits the function to edit and to maintain class information. For example, a class contains what courses.
  - Course management: Administrator utilizes the function to edit and to maintain course information. For example, the records students take the course.
  - User/Role management: Administrator employs the function to edit and to maintain users and roles information.
  - Authentication management: Administrator uses the function to edit and to maintain authentication information for keeping security to prohibit illegal users.

4 An Instructional Design Based on Cognitive Apprenticeship Theory

In the paper, an instructional design based cognitive apprenticeship theory is developed via exploiting the functions of the MOHTER system. Figure 6 depicts an instructional procedure while carrying out the modelling or reflection methods of cognitive apprenticeship model. The instructional procedure is summarized as follows.

Step1: Administrator creates a class and import a list of courses the class has.

Step2: For each course, administrator imports a list of students who take the course and creates teachers who teach their course.

Step3: Teacher prepares teaching materials before class by web APP. Teacher edits course descriptions, imports teaching materials and quizzes for each course. Teacher schedules quizzes.

Step4: Students employ mobile devices with by APPs in learning. Students watch teaching units outside classroom. Students query quizzes in classroom. Students start to write down their answers of quizzes in answer sheets on class in classroom once a quiz is issued. Once students accomplish writing answers on answer sheets, they upload the image version of their answer sheets.

Step5: Teacher uses computers (web interface) or mobile devices (web APP) in answer sheet revision by handwriting. Note that computers needs the function, touch screen or digital pen, for convenience in answer sheet revision. Teacher use either mobile device or web interface (web App) on computer to revise the image version of answer sheets by handwriting, and then to evaluate these answer sheets. Teacher sends revised image version of students' answer sheets to cloud server by web App. Teacher chooses which answer sheets be candidates while carrying out the modelling method of cognitive apprenticeship model.

Step6: Students utilize APPs to inquire the results of quizzes for getting the following. The image version of the revised answer sheets by teacher's handwriting revision. What mistakes or errors that students usually make. Scores for the quiz.

Step7: Teachers exploit teaching methods within cognitive apprenticeship model to devise an instruction on class in classroom. Teacher carries out the modelling method of cognitive apprenticeship model. Teacher models (or display) representative revised answer sheets on classroom, and then explain the mistakes or errors students usually make. Teacher executes the reflection method of cognitive apprenticeship model via displaying representative revised answer sheets on classroom, and then asking students to think what findings can be obtained for inspecting these representative revised answer sheets.

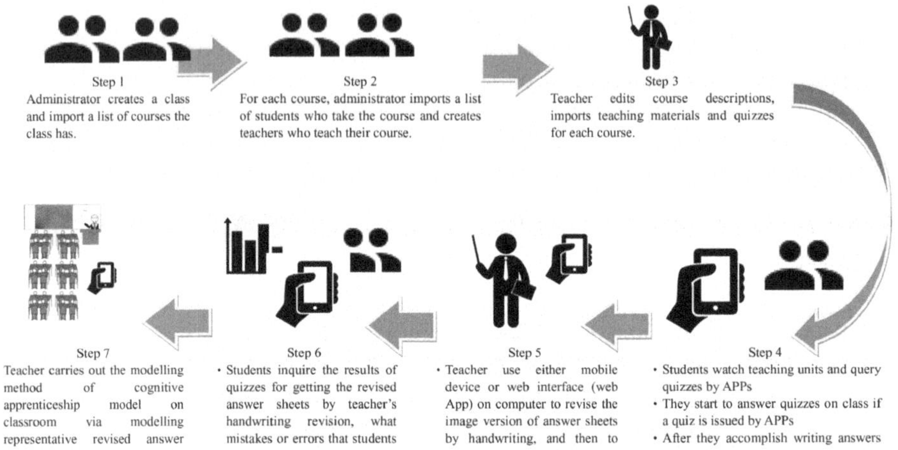

Fig. 6. An instructional procedure while carrying out the modelling method of cognitive apprenticeship model.

Figures 7, 8 and 9 express an example for learning mathematics via an instructional design based on cognitive apprenticeship theory. The learning activities during the instruction can be conducted in classroom. Here the MOHTER system is involved to support learning activities in the instruction. Figure 7 show an example for accomplishing Step 3. Figure 8 illustrates the process of performing Step 4. Figure 9 depicts in doing the answer sheet revision process, as executing Step 5. Observing Figs. 7, 8 and 9, the MOHTER system can facilitate learning activities during the instruction to realize cognitive apprenticeship model for learning mathematics. A significant feature of the system is to integrate four operations, revising answer sheets with handwriting, assigning scores for answer sheets, writing teachers' comments on students' answer sheets, and selecting answer sheets to be modelling on class, in a single window as well as to operate these four actions through web applications. Therefore, teachers readily revise answer sheet by handwriting instead of other existing systems that teachers require to switch several separate windows while revising answer sheets by handwriting and through web operation. Note that, another feature of the system is to offer cross-platform services for teachers.

(a) (b)

Fig. 7. (a) Teacher edits a quiz. (b) A schedule of quizzes.

(a) (b)

(c) (d)

Fig. 8. (a) Students exploit Apps to enter the MOHTER system. (b) Students query quizzes for getting starting quizzes. (c) Students enter a starting quiz. (d) Students get the photo version of their answer sheets, and upload them to cloud server.

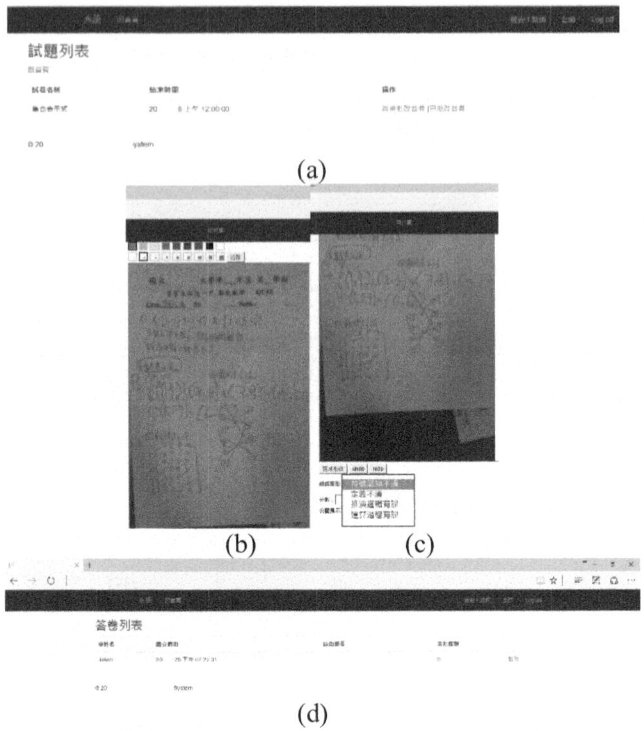

Fig. 9. (a) Teacher enters the MOHTER system for getting quizzes that are not yet revised. (b) Teacher uses web APP to revise answer sheets by handwriting, which might be supported by the touch-screen function. Teacher revises answer sheets over web interface. (c) Teacher evaluates the answer sheet, assigns the types of mistakes or errors occurred in the answer sheet, and select whether the sheet is a candidate to be used in modelling phase on class. (d) Teacher can query the analysis results of types of mistakes or errors.

5 Conclusions

The paper has developed the MOHTER system which can be applied in an instructional design based on the cognitive apprenticeship model for mathematics learning in higher education. The MOHTER system offers students the APP to upload the image version of their answer sheets to cloud server on class after they accomplish their answer sheets by handwriting. The MOHTER system provides functions to revise answer sheets by adding teachers' comments on answer sheets by handwriting and to record the types of mistakes or errors students unusually make for these answer sheets. Moreover, teacher selects candidate answer sheets for giving more explanations to them on class, which can be referred to as modelling and reflection methods within cognitive apprenticeship model. A significant characteristic of the system is to integrate four operations, revising answer sheets with handwriting, assigning scores for answer sheets, writing teachers' comments on students' answer sheets, and selecting answer sheets to be modelling on class, in a single window as well as to operate these four actions through web applications. Therefore, teachers readily revise answer sheet by handwriting instead of other existing systems that teachers require to switch several separate windows while revising answer sheets by handwriting and through web operation. Another feature of the system is to offer cross-platform services for teachers. Hence, the MOHTER system can be definitely support the learning activities based on cognitive apprenticeship theory for learning mathematics.

In future study of the paper will examine more teaching methods within cognitive apprenticeship model in instructional design, conduct experiments via questionnaires to predict and to investigate the performance of the MOLFAS system according to students' acceptance for the ease of use and usefulness, and also investigate the impact on learning effectiveness when deriving the proposed instructional design supported by the MOLFAS system in mathematics learning.

Acknowledgements. This work has been supported by the Ministry of Science and Technology of Taiwan under Contract nos. MOST 105-2511-S-150-003-MY2, 105-2511-S-194-002-MY3, and 105-2511-S-194-001.

References

1. Järvelä, S.: The cognitive apprenticeship model in a technologically rich learning environment: interpreting the learning interaction. Learn. Instr. **5**(3), 237–259 (1995)
2. Woolley, N.N., Jarvis, Y.: Situated cognition and cognitive apprenticeship: a model for teaching and learning clinical skills in a technologically rich and authentic learning environment. Nurs. Educ. Today **27**(1), 73–79 (2007)
3. Dickey, M.D.: Integrating cognitive apprenticeship methods in a web-based educational technology course for P-12 teacher education. Comput. Educ. **51**(2), 506–518 (2008)
4. Lee, Y.J.: Empowering teachers to create educational software: a constructivist approach utilizing Etoys, pair programming and cognitive apprenticeship. Comput. Educ. **56**(2), 527–538 (2011)
5. Wedelin, D., Adawi, T.: Teaching mathematical modelling and problem solving - a cognitive apprenticeship approach to mathematics and engineering education. Int. J. Eng. Pedagogy **5**(4), 45–55 (2014)
6. Brown, J.S., Collins, A.: Situated cognition and the culture of learning. Educ. Res. **18**(1), 32–42 (1989)
7. Kuo, F.-R., et al.: A cognitive apprenticeship approach to facilitating web-based collaborative problem solving. Educ. Technol. Soc. **15**(4), 319–331 (2012)
8. Duncan, S.L.S.: Cognitive apprenticeship in classroom instruction: implications for industrial and technical teacher education. J. Ind. Teach. Educ. **33**(3), 66–86 (1996)
9. Bouta, H., Paraskeva, F.: The cognitive apprenticeship theory for the teaching of mathematics in an online 3D virtual environment. Int. J. Math. Educ. Sci. Technol. **44**(2), 159–178 (2013)
10. Collins, A., Brown, J.S., Newman, S.E.: Cognitive apprenticeship: teaching the craft of reading, writing and mathematics. Thinking J. Philos. Child. **8**(1), 2–10 (1988)
11. Collins, A., Brown, J.S., Holum, A.: Cognitive apprenticeship: making things visible. Am. Educ. **15**(3), 6–11 (1991)
12. Huitt, W.: Bloom et al.'s taxonomy of the cognitive domain (2011). http://www.edpsycinteractive.org/topics/cognition/bloom.html

13. Huang, C.S., et al.: A collaborative digital pen learning approach to improving students' learning achievement and motivation in mathematics courses. Comput. Educ. **107**, 31–44 (2016)
14. Anthony, L., Yang, J., Koedinger, K.R.: Adapting handwriting recognition for applications in algebra learning. In: Proceedings of the International Workshop on Educational Multimedia and Multimedia Education, pp. 47–56 (2007)

The Remote Synchronous Classroom in China

Jin Cai[1,4], Harrison Hao Yang[2,3(✉)], Yanhong Li[1], and Jason MacLeod[2]

[1] Collaborative & Innovative Center for Educational Technology, Central China Normal University, Wuhan, China
[2] School of Educational Information Technology, Central China Normal University, Wuhan, China
[3] School of Education, State University of New York at Oswego, Oswego, NY, USA
harrison.yang@oswego.edu
[4] College of Computer, Hubei University of Education, Wuhan, China

Abstract. The purpose of this study is to provide an overview of the remote synchronous classroom, which is a newly developed and unique blended learning method in the Chinese K-12 education system. The study consists of three main parts: the description and comparison of key synchronous learning, the review of innovative developments and the modern significance of the remote synchronous classroom in China, and key issues that must be addressed to improve implementation of the remote synchronous classroom.

Keywords: Synchronous learning · Remote synchronous classroom · Synchronous virtual classroom · Education equality · K-12 education

1 Introduction

Information and communications technologies (ICT) support the capacity for synchronous distance education in lieu of traditional education approaches [1–3]. Distance education has gained popularity for a variety of reasons, including factors supporting education equality [4]. In modern China, the migration of young people to urban centers and uneven distribution of economic develop has resulted in educational disadvantages for students located in rural and remote geographic regions. Therefore, methods of synchronous distance education are a topic gaining much attention in recent year. Furthermore, with the increasing availability and reliability of telecommunication tools, the Remote synchronous classroom (RSC) has specifically become an important method of distance education.

This study describes the RSC, provides a review of the innovative developments and modern significance of the RSC in China, and identifies key issues that must be addressed to improve implementation of the RSC.

S.K.S. Cheung et al. (Eds.): ICBL 2017, LNCS 10309, pp. 379–386, 2017.
DOI: 10.1007/978-3-319-59360-9_33

2 Conceptual Overview of Synchronous Learning Methods

Synchronous learning refers to the simultaneous education of students, with or without a similar geographic location [5]. Synchronous learning can occur when students and a teacher are in the same physical classroom or when the teacher telecommunicates with the students from a remote location. Synchronous learning technology can include, one-way audio (radio broadcasting), one-way audio-video coupled with two-way written communication (email, chat rooms, discussion groups, etc.), and two-way audio-video (video conference systems).

Davidson-Shivers, Tanner, and Muilenburg [6] found that asynchronous responses were more focused and content specific than synchronous responses in text-based communication. Murphy, Rodriguez-Manzanares, and Barbour [7] found that asynchronous learning was better for cognitive learning among the more independent learners because it provided more time for reflection; while synchronous learning was more motivational in facilitating individuals' participation. Therefore, the use of synchronous learning methods can offer opportunities for social interaction in technology-supported learning environments [8]. In order to best describe the RSC, this section provides an overview and comparison of the three major forms of synchronous learning, including the face-to-face classroom, the synchronous virtual classroom, and the RSC.

2.1 The Face-to-Face Classroom

The face-to-face (F2F) classroom is known as the traditional delivery method of synchronous learning. The F2F classroom provides a shared physical space where learning can take place uninterrupted by outside distractions [9]. In the traditional F2F classroom, students participate in synchronous learning that is leaded by a single teacher [10]. All students in the F2F classroom are taught via the same learning methods and materials and interact only in the shared physical space.

2.2 The Synchronous Virtual Classroom

The synchronous virtual classroom (SVC) is commonly recognized in relation to web-conferencing or e-conferencing systems [11], which allows students and the teacher to communicate synchronously using technological features such as audio, video, chat, interactive visual display, and application sharing [12]. The use of a SVC enables students to learn from anywhere, without having to physically travel to a shared F2F classroom [13]. The SVC is an approach to distance education that has many benefits, such as providing immediate feedback, strengthening social presence, enhancing student interaction, encouraging the exchange of multiple perspectives, and fostering the exchange of emotional supports [14].

2.3 The Remote Synchronous Classroom

The RSC enables delivery of a teacher's instruction to a parallel remote classroom through technology [15]. The RSC typically has two groups of students, in two geographically separated locations [16]. However, sometimes more than two classes are connected. One group of students, referred to as the F2F class, is located in the same classroom as the teacher. The secondary student group(s), referred to as the remote class, is connected through technology. All remote classes can hear the teacher and see the instructional content being conveyed in real-time [17]. The main goal of the RSC is to maintain as many traditional F2F classroom interactions as possible and provide the same high quality educational experience in all locations. In that sense, the teacher must consider the remote students' involvement and psychological needs when preparing and delivering instruction.

2.4 Comparison of the Main Synchronous Learning Methods

Table 1 shows a comparison of the relevant aspects of the main three synchronous learning methods, including teachers, students, technology, pedagogy, and environment.

Table 1. Comparison of synchronous learning methods

	F2F	SVC	RSC
Teacher	Single teacher	Single teacher	Multiple teachers
Students	Single F2F class	Single virtual class	Multiple classes; (single F2F, one or more remote classes)
Technology	Traditional multimedia (projector and whiteboard)	Online learning platform	Telecommunication technology and traditional multimedia
Pedagogy	Considers only F2F classroom learners	Considers only distance learners	Considers both F2F and distance learners
Environment	Physical	Virtual	Physical & virtual

As opposed to the F2F classroom or SVC, the RSC has two or more teachers. One teacher leading their F2F classroom, while the other teacher(s) is connected remotely facilitating their respective class. Through the use of telecommunication technology, the teacher in the F2F classroom delivers the learning content to all classrooms.

3 Implementation of the RSC in China

3.1 Timeline of Innovative Developments with the RSC

This section reviews the development of the RSC in respect to three stages of growth:

Stage 1 – Explorative Period from 2009-2012. The first case of the RSC appeared in Guangdong province in 2009, followed by additional cases appearing in Zhejiang and

Jiangsu provinces. During this time period, the RSC was primarily exploratory teaching attempts, with few well developed teaching mechanism.

Stage 2 – Rapid Growth Period from 2013-2015. As benefits of the RSC became recognized, the RSC experienced a period of rapid growth in many academic disciplines and geographic regions of China. For example, music and art courses were taught through the RSC in a regular teaching schedule at schools in Shandong province since September 2013. Students joined together between a rural and urban region for synchronous learning at least 8 lessons per week.

Stage 3 – Stable Growth Period from 2016-Present. Since the establishment of successful case studies and the introduction of more effective teaching strategies, the RSC has continued to be more frequently adopted. For example, Hainan province planned to increase the number of schools using the RSC to 200 in 2016. The main implementation of the RSC is among 16 urban schools and 26 rural schools in Hubei Province. In Chuzhou city, the amount of urban school using the RSC increased from 34 to 50 connecting with more than 200 rural school between 2013 and 2015. However, to date, few cases of the RSC have been documented in far western regions of China.

3.2 Current Status of the RSC Implementation

Based on a review of all documented cases of the RSC, there are 61 cases of the RSC in China, including 53 primary schools and 8 secondary schools. Figure 1 shows the subject distribution of RSC usage. So far, the RSC is most frequently used for teaching

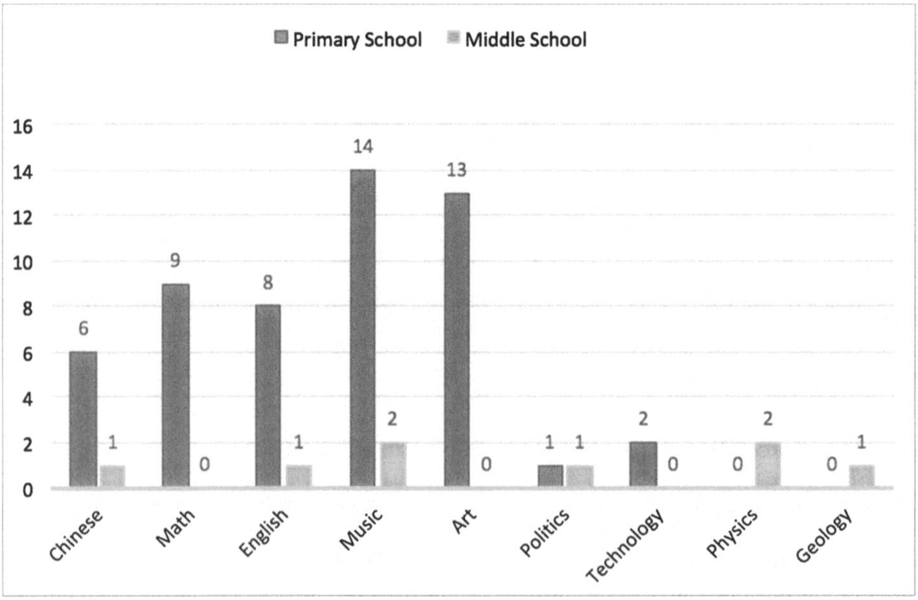

Fig. 1. Subject distribution of RSC usage cases

music and are, however, the RSC has been applied across almost every subject discipline. RSCs are the most popular in primary schools. To date, no cases of the RSC exist at the high school level.

3.3 Primary Demand for the RSC

The primary demand for the RSC is derived from small schools in rural regions of China. These schools are the weakest members of the educational sector, with regards to technological, curricular, and human resources. Due to the deficit of teachers in their rural regions, the quality of their education systems are comparatively much lower than their urban counterparts. Therefore, the RSC has been most recognized as a vehicle to share resources and improve the quality of education in rural schools. Figure 2 shows a diagram of the primary model of RSC implementation.

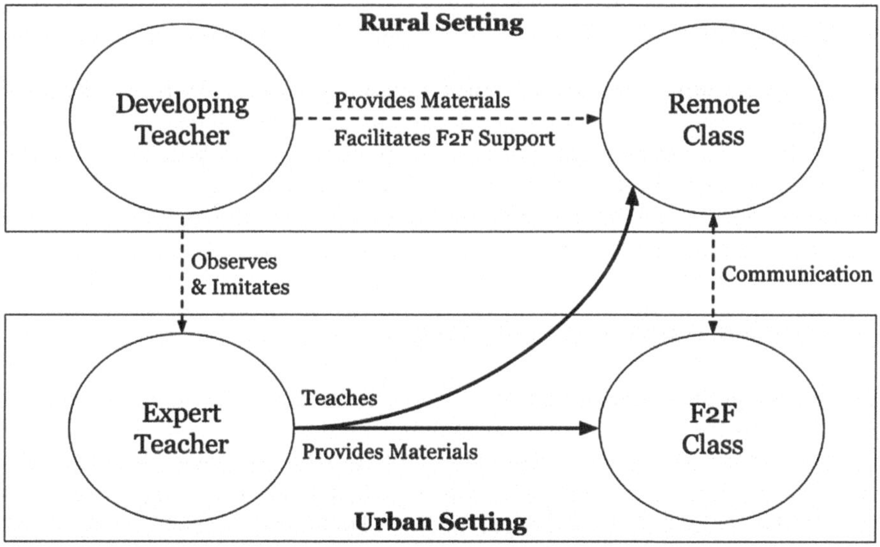

Fig. 2. Primary model of RSC implementation in China

Within the primary model of RSC implementation, the expert teacher at an urban school teaches both the urban and rural students. Meanwhile, the developing rural teacher facilitates F2F support in their respective class and learns through cooperation with the expert urban teacher. In some cases, students even communicate between the two different geographic settings.

3.4 Significance of the RSC

The RSC provides a positive strategy for the transitioning equity issues prevalent in the Chinese K-12 education system. Through the ability to more easily share resources, the

RSC improves education equity among geographically divided regions [18]. More specifically, the following key benefits have been realized from the RSC in China.

Improves Access to High Quality Learning Material. Through sharing resources within the delivery process of the RSC, disadvantaged rural areas are able to benefit from the high quality resources available in more urban settings.

Improves Access to High Quality Teachers. Similar to the sharing of high quality learning materials, the RSC also shares access to high quality teachers, which is a major issue among rural areas. For example, Before January 2014, the children of Liuci School in Hubei Province never had formal music lessons due to a lack of teachers qualified in that subject matter. The RSC changed this situation and by providing new opportunities for students that were never before possible. Through using the RSC, there are many opportunities to enhance students' opportunities in specialized subject matters, such as music, art and English, which have all been historically difficult to teach in the disadvantaged rural regions of China.

Improves Communication and Cultural Relations between Different Regions. Within China, there still remain issues of communication and understanding between the many different cultural regions. The RSC provides not only benefits of education equity, but also societal benefits. Through establishing educationally based collaboration projects, the RSC is providing opportunities for the people of different Chinese regions to accelerate their understandings of one another and promote unity among the nation.

4 Conclusion and Future Challenges

Despite being an underrepresented topic within the research literature, the RSC has clearly established a value contribution. Within China, the primary significance of the RSC is derived in the educational method's ability to promote education equity, particularly among the most disadvantage individuals. Much has been accomplished with the RSC since the exploratory period began in 2009. However, the limited penetration of the RSC into far west regions of China suggests that much value is left to be gained from this educational approach. This final section highlights the key technological and pedagogical challenges of the RSC requiring additional research.

4.1 Technical Challenges

The stability of communication remains a problem for the RSC. For example, delay of signal, clarity of image and sound, etc. These technical challenges are believed to have very negative effects on the engagement of remote students. If technical hardware and network speeds reduce the quality of connection, the full potentials of the RSC cannot be realized. Other technical issues that remain relate to camera positioning and classroom organization. For example, how to design the most appropriate table and chair layout which encourages the most positive interaction and exchange of information. Lighting and color of the classroom are other factors which require careful consideration.

4.2 Pedagogical Challenges

Considering Individual Student Differences. The geographic separation of the RSC creates new difficulties for the teacher to equally recognize remote students. When traditional teaching is put into a digital format, some of the value of message transmission can be lost, such as gestures, facial expressions, eye contact, body movements and other nonverbal symbols of communication. It may be difficult for the students to achieve the same learning goals by only watching a remote demonstration of a teacher. Therefore, further research is necessary regarding the learning achievement and affective comparisons between the F2F and remote student classes.

Widening Ranges of Student Skill Levels. When combining more students into a single class, the potential for differing skills levels increases. This is particularly true when you are connecting regions of differing educational equality. Therefore, the challenge to align appropriate content for students' varying skill levels will be an issue that requires careful investigation and planning.

Repositioning Teacher Roles and Responsibilities. Many changes are required between the roles of the two (or more) teachers involved in the RSC. How do they adapt to the new roles? How do they work together to ensure the effectiveness of synchronous classroom teaching? Who is responsible for assessment? There is probably not one solution to these questions. The RSC is a decentralized educational initiative, which means individual school partnerships are what drive collaboration. Thus, the answers to these questions are likely to vary based on the terms of each scenario. In any case, how to design the most appropriate teaching model remains an area requiring further research.

Acknowledgments. The work was supported by the Key Project of Philosophy and Social Science Research, Ministry of Education of China (14JZD044).

References

1. Branon, R.F., Essex, C.: Synchronous and asynchronous communication tools in distance education. TechTrends **1**, 36 (2001)
2. Yang, Z.K., Yang, H., Wu, D., Liu, S.Y.: Transforming K-12 Classrooms with Digital Technology. Information Science Reference/IGI Global, Hershey (2013)
3. Yang, H., Wang, S.: Cases on Formal and Informal e-Learning Environments: Opportunities and Practices. Information Science Reference/IGI Global, Hershey (2012)
4. Beldarrain, Y.: Distance education trends: integrating new technologies to foster student interaction and collaboration. Distance Educ. **2**, 139–153 (2006)
5. Chen, N.S., Ko, H.C., Kinshuk, Lin, T.: A model for synchronous learning using the Internet. Innov. Educ. Teach. Int. **42**(2), 181–194 (2005)
6. Davidson-Shivers, G., Tanner, E., Muilenburg, L.: Online discussion: how to students participate? Presented at the Annual Meeting of the American Education Research Association, New Orleans, LA, 26 April 2000

7. Murphy, E., Rodríguez-Manzanares, M.A., Barbour, M.: Asynchronous and synchronous online teaching: perspectives of Canadian high school distance education teachers. Brit. J. Educ. Tech. **4**, 583–591 (2011)
8. Hiltz, S.R., Wellman, B.: Asynchronous learning networks as a virtual classroom. Comm. ACM **9**, 44–49 (1997)
9. Holley, L.C., Steiner, S.: Safe space: student perspectives on classroom environment. J. Soc. Work Educ. **1**, 49–64 (2005)
10. Johnson, S.D., Aragon, S.R., Shaik, N., Palma-Rivas, N.: Comparative analysis of learner satisfaction and learning outcomes in online and face-to-face learning environments. J. Interact. Learn. Res. **1**, 29 (2000)
11. McBrien, J.L., Cheng, R., Jones, P.: Virtual spaces: employing a synchronous online classroom to facilitate student engagement in online learning. Int. Rev. Res. Open Distr. Learn. **3**, 1–16 (2009)
12. Martin, F., Parker, M.A.: Use of synchronous virtual classrooms: why, who, and how? J. Online Learn. Teach. **2**, 192–210 (2014)
13. Morrow, J., Phillips, D.J., Bethune, E.: Teaching and learning: flexible modes and technology applications. Brit. J. Midwifery **15**(7), 445–448 (2007)
14. Park, Y.J., Bonk, C.J.: Is online life a breeze? A case study for promoting synchronous learning in a blended graduate course. J. Online Learn. Teach. **3**, 307–323 (2007)
15. Warriem, J.M., Murthy, S., Iyer, S.: A model for active learning in synchronous remote classrooms: evidence from a large-scale implementation. In: Wong, L.H., Liu, C.C., Hirashima, T., Samedi, P., Lukman, M. (eds.) Proceedings of the 21st International Conference on Computers in Education (2013)
16. Lin, J.F., Yu, S.Q.: Reflections on the present situation and problems of network course in China. Distance Educ. Ch. **2**, 55–59 (2001)
17. Yang, G.X., Zhang, R.L.: A bird's-eye view of the modern distance education project in rural primary and middle schools. Inf. Tech. Educ. Prim. Sec. **10**, 4–7 (2006)
18. Zhao, D., Fan, X.Z.: Promoting equal opportunity and inclusive education: the future trend and development strategy of rural teaching. Mod. Educ. Manag. **1**, 22–25 (2013)

Open Educational Resources

Distance-Learning Students' Perception on the Usefulness of Open Educational Resources

Simon K.S. Cheung(✉)

The Open University of Hong Kong, Good Shepherd Street, Homantin, Kowloon, Hong Kong
kscheung@ouhk.edu.hk

Abstract. Open educational resources or OER have been widely used for teaching and learning in higher education. This paper investigates the distance-learning students' perception on the usefulness of OER for learning purposes. Through a survey conducted to the distance-learning undergraduate students at the Open University of Hong Kong, it is revealed that OER are often used and generally considered useful as supplementary learning materials for acquiring relevant knowledge and doing assignments and projects. Among other types of OER, open access textbooks and reference books, and openly shared lecture notes and video clips are considered in particular useful. Massive open online courses and tutorials are considered to be more useful than small-scale mobile learning modules. For online learning tools, online dictionaries and encyclopedia are considered to be very useful. It is also revealed that the reliability, quality and comprehensiveness of OER are key concerns for distance-learning students to use OER for learning purposes.

Keywords: Open educational resources · Open access textbooks · Massive open online courses · Online dictionary · Distance learning · Student perception

1 Introduction

In the past two decades, with the broad penetration of information and communication technologies, the prevalence of digital cultures, and the formal establishment of open license such as Creative Commons [1], vast amount of open and free online resources have been available through the Internet. They include online news, e-books, games, images, audio and video clips, and open-source software. Among many others, open educational resources or OER are referred to the "digitized materials offered freely and openly for educators, students, and self-learners to use and re-use for teaching, learning and research" [2]. It is of no doubt that OER have evolved as a major source of resources for teaching and learning, initially in higher education and now extended to cover primary and secondary education or K-12. Official policies on the adoption of OER for teaching and learning have been established at both the government and institution levels [3]. Nowadays, OER have been widely admitted as useful learning resources by students, especially distance-learning students who are more accustomed to self-learning based on a collection of learning materials.

S.K.S. Cheung et al. (Eds.): ICBL 2017, LNCS 10309, pp. 389–399, 2017.
DOI: 10.1007/978-3-319-59360-9_34

Like many other open resources in the Internet, the OER contents are continuously growing in various formats and various ways at a compound rate. For the vast amount of OER available from the Internet, Cheung, et al. attempted to categorize OER for higher education into four categories, namely, open courseware, open online courses, open e-books, and open-source learning tools to support teaching and learning [4]. Open courseware refer to the complete sets of self-contained course materials which are organized for self-study, such as OpenCourseWare [5], OpenLearn [6], CORE [7] and iTunes U [8]. Open online courses refer to the online courses openly and freely accessible through the Internet. Not only providing the course materials, open online courses allow online interactions between the instructors and students. Massive open online courses or MOOCs, such as EdX [9], Coursera [10], OER University [11] and FutureLearn [12], are good examples. Open e-books are the self-contained textbooks or reference books in electronic format that are openly and freely accessible online and downloadable for offline usage. There are many well-established open textbook platforms, for example, OpenStar CNX [13], College Open Textbooks Collaborative [14], Flat World Knowledge [15] and Project Gutenberg [16]. Open-source learning tools include online dictionaries and encyclopedia, and learning platforms, such as Wikipedia [17], Wiktionary [18], Moodle [19], and Google for Education [20].

While OER are generally admitted as useful learning resources by the students in higher education, it is worthwhile to study the usefulness of OER from the students' perspectives. Confining the scope of study to the distance-learning students in higher education, this paper investigates the students' perception on the usefulness of OER for learning purposes. Through a survey conducted to distance-learning undergraduate students at the Open University of Hong Kong in December 2016 [21], the students' perception on the usefulness of each of the four categories of OER (open courseware, open online courses, open e-books, and open-source learning tools) is analyzed. The frequency of usage, and the preference of devices for accessing OER, as well as the concerns on the shortcomings of OER are also reported. The results devise some findings on the students' perception on how OER can be effectively used for learning purposes. This serves as a good reference for educational researchers and practitioners in the adoption of OER for teaching and learning.

The rest of this paper is organized as follows. Section 2 is an overview of OER for teaching and learning. Section 3 reports the above-mentioned survey in details. Key findings from the survey results are also discussed. Section 4 briefly concludes this paper with some suggestions.

2 Overview of OER for Teaching and Learning

This section gives an overview of OER for teaching and learning in higher education. According to Cheung et al., these OER can be grouped under four categories, namely, open courseware, open online courses, open e-books, and open-source software and tools to support teaching and learning [4]. In the following, each category of OER is defined with well-known examples, and then discussed on how the OER are usually used for teaching and learning.

2.1 Open Courseware

Open courseware are self-contained learning materials in electronic format, consisting of learning objects and modules, which are coherently organized for a course of study. Usually provided by higher education institutions and open learning institutions by openly sharing some of their existing courseware or learning materials, these open courseware are mainly targeted for higher education and distance-learning students. Some representative examples are cited as follows.

- The OpenCourseWare or OCW was initiated by the Massachusetts Institute of Technology to make its course materials openly and freely available through the Internet [5]. Learning materials of a total of 2,340 courses are offered, and there are over 2 million visits every month.
- The OpenLearn was initiated by the Open University to offer open and free learning materials of its courses to the public [6]. Learning materials of over 850 courses (around 12,000 study hours) under 12 subject areas are offered. Open Learn has attracted over 44 million visitors.
- The China Open Resource for Education or CORE was established by a group of universities in China to offer open courseware in Chinese medium [7]. Some open courseware were translated from the existing English-based open courseware. Currently, there are over 10 million visitors.
- iTunes U was launch by Apple Incorporation for universities to deliver open and free university-level learning materials [8]. The materials are mainly audio and video contents, covering lectures, tutorials and demonstrations. Currently, over 1 million learning items are available.

Open courseware usually take the forms of course texts, lecture notes, audio and video clips. Distance-learning students usually use these open courseware contents to supplement their learning materials, acquire relevant knowledge as study reference, and get more resources for doing assignments or projects and preparing for quizzes, tests and examinations.

2.2 Open Online Courses

Open online courses are typically online courses that are freely and openly available through the Internet. They are characterized by the interactive participation between the instructors and students. Many open online courses provide the necessary learning materials. In recent years, massive open online courses or MOOC have grown rapidly. Many MOOC are offered by the renowned universities such as Harvard University, Stanford University, Princeton University, Cornell University, Massachusetts Institute of Technology and University of Toronto. For this reason, they are described as the door to the "Ivy League for the Masses" [22].

Some representative examples are cited as follows.

- EdX is a MOOC platform hosting open online courses of over 90 renowned universities around the world [9]. It aims to offer the best higher education opportunity to anyone who wants to achieve, thrive and grow. Over 1,300 courses under 30 subjects are openly and freely available.

- Similar to the EdX, Coursera is another MOOC platform hosting open online courses of renowned universities [10]. It aims to empower people with world-class education that would improve their lives and the communities they live in. Almost 2,000 from 148 universities are offered.
- OER University was established by a collaboration of 33 distance-learning or open learning and like-minded institutions [11]. It provides a MOOC platform, aiming to offer open and free learning opportunities using OER with pathways to attain credible and recognized qualifications.
- FutureLearn is a MOOC platform hosting hundreds of open online courses mainly from the universities in United Kingdom and other European countries [12]. It aims to pioneer the best social learning experiences for everyone. Over 5 million people have joined the FutureLearn.

Different from the open courseware, open online courses emphasize the interaction between the instructors and students. Enrollment is required, and students have to attend online classes regularly. They are instructor-led courses in a virtual classroom setting. Students usually take open online courses to acquire relevant knowledge and reinforce their understandings of the studied concepts.

2.3 Open E-Books

Open e-books are e-books, openly and freely accessible online or downloadable for offline usage. Open e-books broadly cover open textbooks and open reference books. Not only consisting textual contents, as e-books, open e-books contain a variety of digital contents such as audio, video and multimedia elements. Besides providing multimedia-rich contents, open e-books have many advantageous features over the traditional printed books. Revisions and updates of the e-book contents can be made efficiently. Open e-books allow easy adaptation and customization by the instructors to cater for the students' learning difference and specific learning needs. Some representative examples are cited as follows.

- Openstar CNX was initiated by Rice University with a mission to improve the students' accesses to education [13]. Open textbooks at the post-secondary level in Mathematics, Science, Social Sciences and Humanities are openly and freely offered to hundreds of thousand students.
- College Open Textbooks Collaborative is a consortium of 29 educational organizations with a focus to drive awareness and adoption of open textbooks by offering hundreds of open textbooks, providing training to the instructors, and conducting peer-review of open textbooks [14].
- Flat World Knowledge provides a platform of college-level open textbooks with video contents [15]. The open textbooks are written by experts, and peer-reviewed, edited and highly developed. The open textbooks are also supported by test banks, presentation slides and printed copies.

- Project Gutenberg offers 53,000 open e-books, most of which were previously published by bona fide publishers [16]. These open e-books can be read online or downloaded in various formats, including e-Pub, Kindle and plan texts. The e-books have been diligently proof-read by volunteers.

Although many open e-book projects claim that open e-books are as good as the traditional printed books, the quality of open e-books is still a key concern for many instructors and students. The open e-books, especially open textbooks, are often used as alternative textbooks or reference books by students to acquire relevant knowledge and reinforce their understandings of studied concepts.

2.4 Open-Source Learning Tools

Open-source learning tools are different from open courseware, open online courses and open e-books. They are online tools or open-source software that support teaching and learning, such as online dictionaries, online encyclopedia and other learning tools, as well as open learning platforms for self-learning and collaborative learning. Some representative examples are cited as follows.

- Wikipedia is a well-known multilingual, web-based, free-content encyclopedia project [17]. It adopts a model of openly editable contents that can be written collaboratively by anonymous volunteers. At present, Wikipedia has collected over 41 million articles in 294 languages.
- Like Wikipedia, Wiktionary is an online dictionary, supporting 172 languages [18]. Wiktionary collects over 5 million English words, over 3 million French words, and over 1 million words in other languages such as Deutsch, Pulaski, Portuguese, Japanese, and Italian.
- Modular Object-Oriented Dynamic Learning Environment or Moodle is an open-source learning platform for learning management, such as in hosting learning materials, supporting interaction between the instructors and students, other administrative activities [19].
- Google for Education is a bundle of free applications provided by Google for teaching and learning [20]. These applications include e-mail, calendar, word processing, and presentation software, as well as free online cloud storage. Collaborative learning is well supported.

Open online dictionaries and encyclopedia are often used for checking definitions and meanings of terms. They have many advantages over the traditional dictionaries and encyclopedia, such as quick and convenience in access. Open learning platforms are often used by the instructors and students in learning management. Students often use the shared cloud storage for collaborative learning and working on team projects and assignments. Other learning tools are also used in learning activities, for example, constructing mind maps, and preparing presentation slides.

3 Survey on the Usefulness of OER

This section reports a survey on the usefulness of OER from the perspectives of distance-learning students [21]. The survey was conducted to the distance-learning undergraduate students at the Open University of Hong Kong in December 2016.

The Open University of Hong Kong is a well-established public university in Hong Kong that offers both undergraduate and postgraduate programmes in two modes, namely, the traditional face-to-face learning mode and distance-learning mode. The university currently has 19,600 students, about half in face-to-face learning mode and the other half in distance-learning mode [23]. In the distance-learning programmes, the students are given a full set of self-contained course materials for each enrolled subject. Based on the learning materials together with some reference materials, the students should be able to learn the concepts individually. Although the students can seek helps from the instructors, the course materials are principally considered to be sufficient enough for the students' self-learning.

The survey was randomly sent to the distance-learning undergraduate students of all programmes via e-mails. It was conducted in the format of online questionnaires. The students are asked to respond within 2 weeks. A total of 191 valid responses were received. The questionnaire consists of 3 parts. The first part focus on the general pattern and perception of using OER, such as the frequency of usage and preferred devices. The second part focus on the usefulness of each category of OER for learning purposes. The third part focus on the shortcomings of OER.

3.1 General Pattern and Perception of Usage

Table 1 shows the frequency of accessing OER for learning purposes. It is shown that 73% often or very often access OER (every day or more than once per week) while 23% sometimes access OER (once per week). It is also shown that only 4% seldom access OER (less than once per week).

Table 1. Devices often used for accessing OER for learning purposes.

	Desktop computer	Notebook computer	Table devices	Smart phones
Yes	86%	78%	57%	85%
No	14%	22%	43%	15%

Table 2. Frequency of accessing OER for learning purposes.

	% of responses
Very often (every day)	27%
Often (more than once per week, but not every day)	46%
Sometimes (once per week)	23%
Seldom (less than once per week)	4%
Never	0%

Table 2 shows the devices used for accessing OER. It is shown that the majority (around 80%) use desktop computers, notebook computers and smart phones while 57% use tablet devices.

Table 3 shows the students' overall perception on the usefulness of OER, where the majority (75%) generally consider OER very useful or useful for supplementing the course materials, acquiring relevant knowledge, doing assignments and projects. About half (57%) generally consider OER also very useful or useful for preparing tests and examinations.

Table 3. General usefulness of OER for learning purposes.

	Very useful	Useful	Neutral	Less useful	Not useful
To supplement the existing course materials	38%	37%	19%	3%	2%
To acquire more knowledge as learning reference	34%	40%	20%	3%	2%
To get resources for doing assignments or projects	34%	40%	22%	4%	0%
To get resources for preparing tests or examination	28%	29%	29%	8%	5%

3.2 Usefulness of OER in Learning Activities

The following tables report the students' perception on the usefulness of OER under different categories. Table 4 focus on the usefulness of open courseware. As shown in Table 4, all types of open courseware are considered very useful or useful by the majority (around 70%).

Table 4. Usefulness of open courseware or course materials for learning purposes.

	Very useful	Useful	Neutral	Less useful	Not useful
Openly shared complete sets of course materials	45%	28%	24%	3%	1%
Openly shared lecture notes or class notes	45%	33%	20%	2%	1%
Openly shared video clips of lectures or classes	44%	30%	21%	4%	1%
Other supplementary course or learning materials	40%	29%	26%	4%	1%

For open online courses, it is shown in Table 5 that self-contained MOOC and open online tutorials on specific topics are considered very useful or useful by the majority (around 70%) but less than 50% considers small-scale mobile learning modules and interactive discussion forums very useful or useful.

Table 5. Usefulness of open online courses, tutorials or forums for learning purposes.

	Very useful	Useful	Neutral	Less useful	Not useful
Massive open online courses (self-contained full courses)	47%	23%	21%	8%	1%
Open online tutorials on specific topics	34%	33%	24%	8%	2%
Small-scale mobile learning courses or apps	20%	26%	39%	10%	5%
Open online interactive help desks or discussion forums	20%	27%	38%	11%	5%

Table 6 shows the perception on the usefulness of open e-books and e-journals. It is shown that the majority (80%) consider open e-textbooks and reference books very useful or useful, while half (56% to 61%) also consider open e-journals, e-magazines and other open documentation also very useful or useful.

Table 6. Usefulness of open e-books and open e-journals for learning purposes.

	Very useful	Useful	Neutral	Less useful	Not useful
Open access e-books (self-contained textbooks)	58%	22%	16%	3%	2%
Open access e-books (self-contained reference books)	51%	29%	16%	3%	2%
Open access e-journal, e-periodicals or e-magazines	32%	24%	30%	11%	3%
Open access reports or other open access documentations	38%	23%	25%	9%	4%

Table 7. Usefulness of open-source software or tools for learning purposes.

	Very useful	Useful	Neutral	Less useful	Not useful
Open online dictionaries or encyclopedia	47%	25%	20%	5%	3%
Online anti-plagiarism checker and grammar checker	39%	19%	27%	11%	4%
Other open learning software (mind map, slide builder, etc.)	23%	26%	36%	11%	3%
Online learning platform for self or collaborative learning	32%	33%	26%	8%	1%

Table 7 shows the perception on the usefulness of open-source learning tools, where online dictionaries, online encyclopedia and online learning platforms are considered very useful or useful by the majority (65% to 72%). About half (49% to 58%) consider online anti-plagiarism checkers, grammar checkers and other learning software very useful or useful.

3.3 Shortcomings or Concerns of OER

In the literature, there are studies on the criticism of adopting OER for teaching and learning [24, 25]. OER are regarded to be inferior to the traditional learning resources in subject coverage, comprehensiveness and organization of the learning resources, quality and accuracy of the contents. From the students' perspective, OER are often criticized on whether the contents are accurate, comprehensive, well organized, and updated. Table 8 shows the students' perception on these shortcomings or concerns of using OER for learning purposes. It is shown that almost half (38% to 50%) strongly agree or agree with these shortcomings or concerns. Inaccurate and incomprehensive contents are the major shortcoming or concerns.

Table 8. Shortcomings and concerns of using OER for learning purposes.

	Strongly agree	Agree	Neutral	Disagree	Strongly disagree
Contents may not be accurate	22%	28%	34%	12%	4%
Contents may not be up-to-date	8%	30%	42%	15%	5%
Contents may not be comprehensive	19%	28%	39%	11%	3%
Contents may not be well organized	15%	29%	38%	12%	6%

3.4 Key Findings from the Survey Results

The survey results devises the following key findings on the students' perception on the usefulness of OER for learning purposes.

- The popular devices for accessing OER include desktop computers, notebook computers and smart phones, but not tablet devices.
- OER are very often or often used (every day or more than once per week) by the students for learning purposes.
- OER are generally considered to be very useful or useful for supplementing the course materials, acquiring relevant knowledge and getting more resources or materials in doing assignments or projects.
- Open courseware (including the complete set of course materials, lecture notes and video clips) are considered to be very useful or useful.
- Self-contained open online courses and online tutorials on specific topics are considered to be very useful or useful. Small-scale mobile learning modules are not considered as useful as typical open online courses.
- Open textbooks and reference books are considered to be very useful while open e-journals and other documentations are also considered to be useful.
- Online dictionaries and encyclopedia are considered to be very useful while online learning platforms are also considered to be useful.

- The accuracy, quality and comprehensiveness of contents are considered to be key concerns for using OER for learning purposes.

4 Conclusion

It is of no doubt that OER have been developed into a major source of educational resources in higher education. While understanding the advantages and shortcomings of OER, higher education students generally admit that OER is useful for learning purposes. It is believed that the level of acceptance for distance-learning students are even higher. Based on a survey conducted to distance-learning undergraduate students at the Open University of Hong Kong, this paper analyzes the students' perception on the usefulness of OER. It is affirmative that distance-learning students often access OER and generally consider OER useful for learning purposes.

The survey results essentially devise a number of key findings. The findings show that OER are considered useful for supplementing the course materials and acquiring relevant knowledge, but less useful for preparing tests and examinations. Distance-learning students mostly consider open courseware, open online courses and tutorials more useful than small-scale mobile learning modules. Open e-textbooks and open reference books as well as open online dictionaries and encyclopedia are in particular useful resources for learning purposes. It is also revealed that the accuracy, quality and comprehensiveness of contents are key concerns of using OER for learning purposes. All these findings would provide a practical reference for distance-learning institutions in the adoption of OER for teaching and learning.

References

1. Creative Commons: Website of creative commons (2017). http://creativecommons.org
2. OECD: Giving Knowledge for Free: The Emergence of Open Education Resources, Centre for Educational Research and Innovation. Organization for Economic Cooperation and Development (2007)
3. Hoosen, S.: Survey on Governments' Open Educational Resources Policies. World OER Congress, Commonwealth of Learning and UNESCO (2012)
4. Cheung, Simon K.S., Li, K.C., Yuen, K.S.: An overview of open education resources for higher education. In: Lam, J., Li, K.C., Cheung, Simon K.S., Wang, F.L. (eds.) ICT 2013. CCIS, vol. 407, pp. 26–34. Springer, Heidelberg (2013). doi:10.1007/978-3-642-45272-7_3
5. MIT: Website of MIT OpenCourseWare (2017). http://ocw.mit.edu
6. OpenLearn: Website of OpenLearn (2017). http://www.open.edu/openlearn
7. CORE: Website of China Open Resource for Education (2017). http://www.core.org.cn
8. Apple: Website of iTunes U (2017). http://www.apple.com/itunes-u
9. EdX: Website of EdX (2017). http://www.edx.org
10. Coursera: Website of Coursera (2017). http://www.coursera.org
11. OERU: Website of OER University (2017). http://www.oeru.org
12. FurtureLearn: Website of FutureLearn (2017). http://www.futurelearn.com
13. CNX: Website of OpenStar CNX (2017). http://www.cnx.org
14. CCOTC: Website of college open textbooks collaborative (2017). http://www.collegeopentextbooks.org

15. FlatWorld: Website of flat world knowledge (2017). http://flatworldknowledge.com
16. Gutenberg: Website of Project Gutenberg (2017). http://gutenberg.org
17. Wikipedia: Website of Wikipedia (2017). http://www.wikipedia.org
18. Wiktionary: Website of Wiktionary (2017). http://www.wiktionary.org
19. Moodle: Website of Moodle (2017). http://www.moodle.org
20. Google: Website of Google for Education (2017). http://www.google.com/edu
21. OUHK: Survey on the students' perception on the use of open educational resources for learning purposes. Internal Report, Information Technology Unit (2016)
22. Time: College is Dead. Long Live College! Time Magazine. http://nation.time.com/2012/10/18/college-is-dead-long-live-college/. Accessed 18 October 2012
23. OUHK: Website of Open University of Hong Kong (2017). http://www.ouhk.edu.hk
24. Educause: 7 Things You Should Know About Open Educational Resources. Educause Learning Initiative (2010)
25. Allen, I.E., Seaman, J.: Opening the Curriculum: Open Educational Resources in U.S. Higher Education. Babson Survey Research Group, Babson Park (2014)

Learning Experience Questionnaire for Multimedia Case-Based Instruction: Development, Validation and Implications for Design

Tingting Yang and Heng Luo(✉)

School of Educational Information Technology,
Central China Normal University, Wuhan 430079, China
luoheng@mail.ccnu.edu.cn

Abstract. To explore the key constructs of multimedia case-based instruction (MCBI), this study developed and validated a questionnaire to examine learners' learning experience with MCBI with tests for reliability and validity. Based on the literature review, the questionnaire was initially designed with 39 questions and was administered to 86 graduate students taking an instructional design course. Item analysis and exploratory factor analysis were conducted sequentially with the questionnaire data, and the statistical results informed the deletion of 13 problematic questions from the overall scale. The revised questionnaire yielded a strong internal reliability, and can be further reduced into four distinct factors measuring MCBI's contextuality, effects, design features and explorative nature respectively. The study results are expected to enhance people's understanding of MCBI and provide implications for the design, development and delivery of multimedia cases for instruction.

Keywords: Multimedia case-based instruction · Questionnaire development · Reliability · Validity · Instructional design

1 Introduction

Case-based instruction (CBI) is a well-established instructional theory that actively engages learners in real or hypothetical situations with the purpose of developing their higher-order thinking skills through context-specific activities such as problem solving, decision making, critical reasoning, reflection and discussion [1, 2]. CBI is known to be quite effective in preparing learners for what they will encounter in their future professions by exposing them to similar scenarios or problems [3–5], and has been widely practiced in disciplines such as law, business, medicine, and teacher education [6, 7]. Recent development of multimedia technologies has provided new opportunities for case development and presentation: videos and images often include more contextual information and thus can increase the authenticity of case description; interactive design functions such as prompt questions, automated feedback, and navigation control allow learners to actively reflect on case problems and customize their learning process. Thus, multimedia case-based instruction (MCBI) has become increasingly popular and

S.K.S. Cheung et al. (Eds.): ICBL 2017, LNCS 10309, pp. 400–411, 2017.
DOI: 10.1007/978-3-319-59360-9_35

has led to a growing body of research investigating its impact on learners' learning experiences since mid-1990s [8–13].

Despite the growing research interest in MCBI, there seems to be a lack of research instruments that examine the related case-based learning experience. Although many researchers have discussed critical characteristics of MCBI in the literature such as authenticity, contextuality, provocativeness, interactivity, rich media and promotion of higher-order thinking [14–16], most discussions were theoretically based, without empirical validation of learner perception collected from survey research. A few exceptions were found during the literature review as some studies attempted to measure learners' MCBI learning experience by creating their own questionnaires. For example, Choi et al. [9] developed an 8-item Likert Scale questionnaire to assess learners' perceived learning effects, motivation, and preference in an MCBI lesson, and Luo [6] developed a 24-item Likert Scale questionnaire to collect learners' opinions regarding different design features of an MCBI tutorial. However, none of the questionnaires were subject to reliability and validity verification, and the relationship between different constructs of MCBI was rarely examined. Such problem undermines the credibility and interpretability of survey research findings regarding MCBI.

To address this research problem, this study aims to develop and validate a questionnaire that provides a reliable, valid, and efficient measure of learners' MCBI learning experience and operationalize its key constructs such as case affordances, media preference, instructional scaffold, and perceived effects. The research findings are expected to enhance people's understanding of MCBI and provide implications for the design, development and delivery of multimedia cases.

2 Questionnaire Development

2.1 Key Constructs of MCBI

Although CBI has been widely practiced and researched in the past, it was often vaguely denoted in the literature without clear definition and examination of its key constructs. As Dooley and Skinner [17] pointed out, "the phrase 'case method' embraces such an array of pedagogic practice that the term itself has no precise connotation. There are as many varieties of the case method as there are practitioners" (p. 277). To understand MCBI, it is important to first understand the construct of *case affordances*: various benefits that good cases can bring to teaching and learning. Summarizing findings from literature review, the key affordances of a good case include:

- Authenticity and credibility of case narratives that not only present contextual details but also enhance learning engagement and motivation [6, 9];
- Complexity that captures controversy and ambiguity of the real-world problems to inspire rich discussions and reflections [5, 14, 18];
- Vicarious experiences that prepare learners for their future professions by presenting similar scenarios and problems [3, 16];
- Reflective activities such as analysis, problem solving, decision making, critical reasoning that promote higher-order thinking [19, 20];

- Opportunities for theory application that aim to bridge the vast chasm between principles and practice [10, 16].

Compared to traditional CBI relying on text narratives, MCBI is unique for its extensive use of multimedia technology in case development and delivery, and thus makes *media preference* and *instructional scaffold* two important constructs to explore in this study. Our review of literature reveals that learners have a strong preference for studying multimedia cases, and has reported several benefits of MCBI such as greater interest, enhanced authenticity, better comprehension [8, 10, 11]. A few studies also investigated instructional scaffold for MCBI, exploring ways to design better guiding questions, interactive elements, feedback mechanism, and learner control to promote more meaningful case learning experience [21, 22]. Lastly, the construct of *effects* was also examined in this study to identify various perceived benefits of MCBI and explore their relationships with the other constructs.

2.2 Overview of Questionnaire Items

Based on the literature review findings, this study tentatively developed a questionnaire to examine learners' learning experience with MCBI. The learning experience questionnaire (LEQ) consists of three parts with a total of 39 questions. Part One includes 5 questions that collect learners' personal data such as gender, age, major and initial motivation to learn. Part Two includes 32 five-point Likert scale questions that have learners rate statements regarding the four constructs of MCBI as previously discussed: (1) various case affordances including sense of authenticity, real-world complexity, vicarious experience, reflective opportunities and theory application (No. 6–21), (2) media preference based on the appeal and effectiveness of multimedia usage (No. 22–25), (3) instructional scaffold in the forms of guiding questions, interactions and learner control (No. 26–31), and (4) perceived effects of MCBI on learners' motivation, cognitive and metacognitive presence (No. 32–37) (see Table 1). Part Three of the questionnaire consists of only 2 dichotomous questions, asking learners whether they consider their learning experience to be positive and would recommend it in the future. Those two questions were designed to provide a summative overview of learners' opinions on MCBI.

3 Methods

3.1 Research Context

The research data were collected from 86 first-year graduate students who enrolled in an instructional design (ID) course offered by a research university located in central China. The course is mandatory for graduate students majored in educational technology, and is usually offered in the first semester of their graduate program. An essential instructional activity of this course is to have students explore various ID scenarios in the form of multimedia case modules where students can apply their ID knowledge and skills to analyze instructional problems, design instructional solutions and practice their ID related problem-solving and decision-making skills. A complete case study session usually includes three phases: investigation of the case module, completion of the case study report and participation in case discussion in the next class. The LEQ was administered on the 5th class of the course, after students completed their first case study session. The students used their mobile phones to scan the QR code for the questionnaire link and submitted their responses online. A total of 86 questionnaires were collected electronically and downloaded as an Excel worksheet, which was later converted into an SPSS data file to allow future analysis using IBM SPSS Statistics 19.

3.2 Multimedia Case Module

The multimedia case module for the first case study session describes an instructional problem in a hospital setting: the weekly one-hour seminars held by a hospital were not well received by its pediatric residents, and many residents failed to pass the pediatric boards at the end of their residency. Students would take the role of an instructional designer hired by the hospital director to analyze the reasons behind such problem, and suggest instructional or non-instructional interventions to solve the problem. Students could interview different characters in the case module (e.g., the hospital director, two seminar lecturers and three resident students), examine the materials used by the lecturers, and inspect the facilities and resources for the seminars (Fig. 1). The case module was based on a real instructional event and was developed using Articulate Storyline 2.

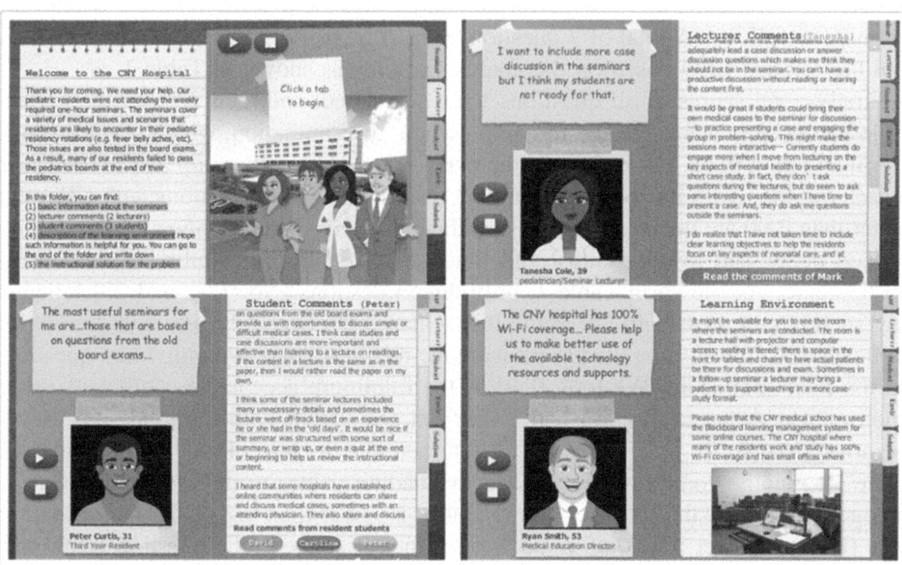

Fig. 1. Screen captures of the multimedia case module

3.3 Procedures of Analysis

To formulate a LEQ with desirable survey reliability and validity to describe and explain MCBI learning experience, two major procedures of data analysis were conducted in this study: item analysis and exploratory factor analysis (EFA). Item analysis investigated the performance of each questionnaire item in relation to external criterion or in relation to the remaining items. It was conducted first in this study to ensure that all questions in the LEQ have met the statistical requirements for acceptable item reliability and quality. The questions that failed to meet the requirements were removed from the LEQ and data analysis in latter phases. Exploratory factor analysis (EFA) was conducted later as the means for data reduction and structure detection. After deleting questions disqualified to be included into a single factor and reconsidering factors with less than three questions, the number of variables were reduced, and structure in the relationships between variables was detected. The results of EFA provide evidence for the internal consistency of the LEQ, and inform the development and interpretation of the final questionnaire.

4 Results

4.1 Item Analysis

The quality of the questions determines the quality of a questionnaire. In this study, we consider the following criteria as important for ensuring the quality of LEQ questions: it should possess sufficient discriminating power to be meaningful; it should be congruent with the overall LEQ testing objectives; and it should acquire strong internal consistency. Consequently, we performed three statistical tests, and the results are presented as follows. A total of 7 questions (No. 6, 7, 9, 17, 22, 23, 29) were removed from the original LEQ based on the analysis results, as shown in Table 1.

Firstly, total scores of all questions were calculated, and then 27% of the highest and lowest scorers were selected to compute item discrimination, which was measured by critical ration (CR). CR compares the performance of upper group and lower group on each question with independent-sample t test. Statistically, questions with CR value greater than 3.00 are deemed to possess sufficient discriminating power to differentiate between upper and lower groups, and thus can promote the stability of the overall questionnaire. As shown in Table 1, only three questions (No. 7, 9, and 23) failed to meet such requirement with CR value lower than 3.00. Secondly, Pearson correlation coefficient (PCC) was computed to measure the relevance between individual questions and the total sum score. We took 0.40 as the minimum acceptable coefficient value, which indicated that a question had a medium correlation with the total sum. Seven questions (No. 6, 7, 9, 17, 22, 23, 29) turned out to have PCC lower than 0.40 (Table 1). Finally, communalities and factor loading values were computed as part of homogeneity test. If the value of communality is lower than 0.2 or the factor loading value (FLV) is lower than 0.45 in such case, then it suggests the question has a poor correlation with the common factor and should consider deletion. As shown in Table 1, the seven questions with low correlation coefficient (No. 6, 7, 9, 17, 22, 23, 29) also failed to pass the homogeneity test in this study, therefore were removed from the LEQ.

4.2 Exploratory Factor Analysis

Item analysis has identified seven questions in the initial LEQ that were deemed to be poorly designed due to their low reliability measures and incongruence with the overall questionnaire scale. After removing those questions, the LEQ consisted of 25 questions and its internal reliability increased to 0.94, as measured by Cronbach's alpha. The revised LEQ was then subjected to exploratory factor analysis (EFA) with the purpose of identifying key factors that explain learners' MCBI learning experience.

Firstly, an initial EFA without fixed number of factors extracted was conducted in order to check sampling and data adequacy. The correlation matrix showed that the questionnaire data were suitable for factor analysis with large correlation values mostly higher than 0.45. Bartlett's test of sphericity ($\chi 2 = 1263.06$, df = 85, $p < .001$) and the Kaiser-Meyer-Olkin (KMO) measure (0.85 > 0.8) also indicated that the statistical assumptions of EFA were met in this study. The EFA procedure was then repeated iteratively with the purpose of extracting meaningful factors. Only factors with eigenvalues larger than 1.00 and included more than three question items would be extracted. During such process, an additional 6 questions (No. 8, 10, 30, 31, 36, 37) with low and scattered factor loading values were further deleted from the LEQ.

Table 1. Item analysis results for the LEQ questions (N = 86)

Question		CR	PCC	Communalities	FLV
6	I feel the case is based on real events and characters	3.04	#.33	#.09	#.30
7	I feel the case story is fictitious, fabricated by the case designer	#2.01	#.20	#.03	#.16
8	I think the case reflects the real-world complexity of instructional design	3.98	.48	.21	.46
9	Conflicting perspectives and contradictive information are commonly presented in the case	#.28	#.03	#.00	#–.04
10	I think I might encounter similar instructional design task as introduced in the case	5.51	.50	.22	.46
11	The case narratives include plenty of rich description of contextual details	6.85	.48	.24	.49
12	The case provides many useful details for instructional analysis and decision-making	6.73	.62	.41	.64
13	I feel the characters in the case are vivid and alive	5.94	.58	.33	.58
14	I had an immersive experience when studying the cases	6.62	.62	.40	.63

(continued)

Table 1. (*continued*)

Question		CR	PCC	Communalities	FLV
15	The character conversations and event descriptions in the case often made me reflect how I would react and proceed in such situation	5.75	.57	.33	.57
16	The case module provided me with an opportunity to apply instructional design knowledge and theories into practice	9.14	.77	.61	.78
17	I would consciously review previously learned knowledge and theories when investigating the case	3.04	.44	#.19	#.43
18	I would compare different ideas or different solutions when investigating the case	5.24	.54	.30	.54
19	I would contemplate and evaluate different solutions for the case problem	7.39	.67	.47	.69
20	I found my case learning experience quite explorative: I can investigate freely, collecting information from multiple sources to seek the solution	5.53	.65	.43	.66
21	I found the case module quite appealing and can inspire my interest to learn	7.67	.74	.56	.75
22	The case module has successfully utilized different media forms such as graphics, audios, videos and animations	3.35	.42	#.17	#.41
23	Compared to the case module, I would rather study the case description in text (reversed)	#2.71	#.36	#.12	#.35
24	I have learned much useful information from the multimedia content (e.g., images, audios and videos) in the case	7.40	.66	.43	.66
25	I wish that the future case modules would include even more multimedia content such as images and videos	6.93	.61	.37	.60
26	My case learning process is not arbitrary and chaotic as I felt I	4.96	.64	.46	.68

(*continued*)

Table 1. (*continued*)

Question		CR	PCC	Communalities	FLV
	have received adequate guidance for learning				
27	I found the guiding questions in the case quite useful, guiding me to conduct meaningful reflections	6.62	.71	.54	.73
28	I would carefully consider the embedded guiding questions when investigating the case	8.18	.74	.58	.76
29	Compared to instructor-led case learning experience, I prefer the self-directed, explorative case learning experience like this one	3.72	.42	#.16	#.40
30	I can fully control my case learning process (e.g., selection of content, learning order and learning pace)	4.03	.49	.23	.48
31	I sometimes felt I was having a conversation with my instructor or my peers when studying the cases	6.91	.60	.35	.59
32	The case learning experience is a fun learning experience	9.04	.74	.57	.76
33	Such form of case learning can inspire my interests towards the course content	8.85	.80	.67	.82
34	The case learning experience made me have deeper understanding about the related knowledge and theories introduced in the course	6.07	.67	.46	.68
35	The case learning experience improved my skills to apply theoretical knowledge into solving real instructional problems	5.92	.61	.39	.63
36	I had moments of enlightenment and inspiration where I came up with creative design ideas.	5.57	.62	.36	.60
37	Through such case learning experience, I have realized the deficiency of my existing knowledge and skills, and thus have a more specific goal for future study	5.84	.62	.38	.62
Criterion		> = 3.0	> = .40	> = .20	> = .45

stands for short of the standard.

At last, four factors were successfully extracted from the questionnaire data with eigenvalues of 8.75, 1.73, 1.25 and 1.09 respectively, and accounted for 46.04%, 9.11%, 6.55%, 5.74% of the variance. Altogether, the four factors could explain 67.43% of the total variance, which is larger than the suggested minimum proportion of 60%. Cronbach's α was computed for the 19-question LEQ to provide reliability estimation. The α value for the entire questionnaire was 0.93, and for the four factors were 0.84, 0.88, 0.85, and 0.81 respectively. Therefore, the LEQ was deemed to meet the acceptable reliability standard of 0.70 and above, and can be interpreted as internally consistent when measuring MCBI learning experience. Table 2 lists the four factors and the LEQ questions within each factor.

Factor 1 consists of 5 questions initially designed to examine the case affordances such as sense of authenticity, vicarious experience, reflective opportunities and appeal. It is the most important factor and emphasizes a key construct of MCBI–*contextuality*: rich, contextualized case narratives are essential for MCBI to be effective, and are the foundation for various case-related learning benefits. Factor 2 focuses on the construct of *effects*: it consists of 4 questions (No. 32–35) initially designed to measure MCBI effects such as the deeper understanding of theories, increased problem-solving skills and higher motivation to learn; it also includes two questions (No. 12, 16) about case affordances to link theories with practice by engaging learners in activities such as analysis and decision making. Factor 3 combines the questions on media preference and instructional scaffold, and can be referred to as a single construct: *useful design features*. Factor 4 singles out *explorative nature* as a key construct for MCBI, with all three questions focusing on the exploration and comparison of different ideas and solutions for the case problem.

Table 2. Factors extracted from the LEQ and factor loading value for each question

Questions		Factor loading
Factor 1: *Contextuality - contextualized case narratives as key element of MCBI*		
13	I feel the characters in the case are vivid and alive	.83
14	I had an immersive experience when studying the cases	.77
15	The character conversations and event descriptions in the case often made me reflect how I would react and proceed in such situation	.68
11	The case narratives include plenty of rich description of contextual details	.67
21	I found the case module quite appealing and can inspire my interest to learn	.62
Factor 2: *Effects - perceived effects of MCBI to promote meaningful learning*		
34	The case learning experience made me have deeper understanding about the related knowledge and theories introduced in the course	.75
35	The case learning experience improved my skills to apply theoretical knowledge into solving real instructional problems	.74

(*continued*)

Table 2. (*continued*)

Questions		Factor loading
33	Such form of case learning can inspire my interests towards the course content	.68
32	The case learning experience is a fun learning experience	.65
16	The case module provided me with an opportunity to apply instructional design knowledge and theories into practice	.59
12	The case provides many useful details for instructional analysis and decision-making	.50
Factor 3: *Design features–use of multimedia and scaffolding features to enhance MCBI*		
27	I found the guiding questions in the case quite useful, guiding me to conduct meaningful reflections	.72
25	I wish that the future case modules would include even more multimedia content such as images and videos	.72
26	My case learning process is not arbitrary and chaotic as I felt I have received adequate guidance for learning	.70
28	I would carefully consider the embedded guiding questions when investigating the case	.68
24	I have learned much useful information from the multimedia content (e.g., images, audios and videos) in the case	.68
Factor 4: *Explorative nature–exploration and comparison of different ideas and solutions*		
18	I would compare different ideas or different solutions when investigating the case	.85
19	I would contemplate and evaluate different solutions for the case problem	.71
20	I found my case learning experience quite explorative: I can investigate freely, collecting information from multiple sources to seek the solution	.60

5 Discussion and Conclusion

Our work in this study has led to the development and validation of a questionnaire instrument that can be used to measure different aspects of people's learning experience with MCBI. The statistical results helped us identify and remove a total of 13 problematic items in Part Two of the questionnaire to optimize its reliability and validity as a research instrument. The refined LEQ consists of 19 questions that yield a quite strong internal reliability (Cronbach's $\alpha = 0.93$), and can be further reduced into four distinct factors focusing on MCBI's contextuality, effects, design features and explorative nature respectively. The EFA results also offer interesting insights to re-examine MCBI, which are discussed in below.

First, it appears that many well-acknowledged benefits and affordances of CBI can be attributed to one unique feature: case narratives with rich, contextual details. The contextual details can help increase the sense of authenticity, provide immersive experience, and capture the complexity of real-world problems, which in turn engage learners in meaningful learning activities such as review, analysis, application, and problem-solving. Such finding is consistent with what Luo [6] suggests: contextualized case stories could facilitate case comprehension, support case demonstration, promote higher-order thinking and enhance the appeal of CBI.

It is also interesting to note that multimedia use and scaffolding design were initially considered as two constructs for MCBI but were later combined as one factor of the LEQ. One possible explanation is that multimedia technology nowadays has become increasingly interactive and is no longer limited to content delivery. Take the case module for example, many scaffolding features such as guiding questions and learner control were embedded in the multimedia content in the forms of visual cues, hyperlinks, action triggers and interactive quizzes. It might become increasingly difficult to separate multimedia use and scaffolding design in future case development.

Lastly, multiple perspectives and open-ended inquiry are considered as two important characteristics of effective CBI [5, 23]. EFA results in this study supported such argument since the fourth factor extracted from the LEQ highlights open and explorative learning experience as another key construct for MCBI. Such finding has several important design implications: first, cases should be presented in a non-linear fashion to allow different investigating approaches and solution proposals; second, conflicting viewpoints and information should be presented simultaneously to allow analysis and interpretation from different perspectives; and finally, various scaffolding features and instant feedback should be integrated to guide learners to contemplate, evaluate and compare possible solutions to the case problem.

However, two caveats need to be considered when interpreting the study findings. First, the sampling method of this study was convenient and the sampling size was far from the appropriate size of 300 cases, which undermines both the external and statistical validity of the research findings. Also, the data analyzed were based on the learning experience with one multimedia case module. Whether the results of LEQ reliability and validity can be applied to other types of MCBI remains largely unknown. These limitations should be addressed in future research in order to get deeper insights into the measurement and factor structure of MCBI.

Acknowledgment. This study has been supported by the research project named "Crowdsourcing-based assessment research in the context of large-scale online education" (Project No. 16YJC8 80054), funded by China's Ministry of Education's Youth Scholar Research Funding Grant in the fields of humanities and Social Sciences.

References

1. Ertmer, P.A., Russell, J.D.: Using case studies to enhance instructional design education. Educ. Technol. **35**(4), 23–31 (1995)
2. Jonassen, D.H., Hernandez-Serrano, J.: Case-based reasoning and instructional design: using stories to support problem solving. Educ. Tech. Res. Dev. **50**(2), 65–77 (2002)
3. Andrews, L.: Preparing general education pre-service teachers for inclusion: web-enhanced case-based instruction. J. Spec. Educ. Technol. **17**(3), 27–35 (2002)
4. Christensen, C.R., Hansen, A.J.: Teaching and The Case Method. Harvard Business School Press, Boston (1987)

5. Merseth, K.K.: Cases and case methods in teacher education. In: Sikula, J. (ed.) Handbook of Research on Teacher Education, 2nd edn., pp. 722–741. Macmillan and the Association of Teacher Educators, New York (1996)
6. Luo, H.: Applying the case-based method in designing self-directed online instruction. Syracuse University (2015)
7. Williams, S.M.: Putting case-based instruction into context: examples from legal and medical education. J. Learn. Sci. **2**(4), 367–427 (1992)
8. Baker, E.A.: Multimedia case-based instruction in literacy: pedagogy, effectiveness and perceptions. J. Educ. Multimedia Hypermedia **18**(3), 249–266 (2009)
9. Choi, I., Lee, S., Jung, J.: Designing multimedia case-based instruction accommodating students' diverse learning styles. J. Educ. Multimedia Hypermedia **17**, 5–25 (2008)
10. Choi, I., Lee, K.: Designing and implementing case-based learning environments for enhancing ill-structured problem solving skills: classroom management problems for prospective teachers. Educ. Tech. Res. Dev. **57**, 99–129 (2009)
11. Jarz, E.M., Kainz, G.A., Walpoth, G.: Multimedia-based case studies in education: Design, development, and evaluation of multimedia based case studies. J. Educ. Multimedia Hypermedia **6**(1), 23–46 (1997)
12. Linn, M.C., Songer, N.B., Eylon, B.S.: Shifts and convergences in science learning and instruction. In: Calfee, R., Berliner, D. (eds.) Handbook of Educational Psychology, pp. 438–490. Macmillan, Riverside (1996)
13. Risko, V.J., Yount, D., McAllister, D.: Preparing preservice teachers for remedial instruction: teaching problem solving and use of content and pedagogical knowledge. In: Padak, N., Rasinski, T.V., Logan, J. (eds.) Inquiries in literacy learning and instruction, pp. 179–189. College Reading Association, Pittsburg (1992)
14. Barnes, L.B., Christensen, C.R., Hansen, A.: Teaching and the Case Method, 3rd edn. Harvard Business School Press, Boston (1994)
15. Berg, E.V.D., Jansen, L., Blijleven, P.: Learning with multimedia cases: An evaluation study. J. Technol. Teach. Educ. **12**(4), 491–509 (2004)
16. Shulman, L.S.: Toward a pedagogy of cases. In: Shulman, J.H. (ed.) Case Methods in Teacher Education, pp. 1–30. Teachers College Press, New York (1992)
17. Dooley, A.R., Skinner, W.: Casing case method methods. Acad. Manag. Rev. **2**(2), 277–289 (1977)
18. Boling, E.C.: Linking technology, learning, and stories: Implications from research on hypermedia video-cases. Teach. Teach. Educ. **23**(2), 189–200 (2007)
19. Doyle, W.: Case methods in the education of teachers. Teach. Educ. Q. **17**(1), 7–16 (1990)
20. Sykes, G., Bird, T.: Teacher education and the case idea. In: Grant, G. (ed.) Review of Research in Education, pp. 457–521. American Educational Research Association, Washington, DC (1992)
21. Luo, H., Koszalka, T.: Making Design Decisions Visible: Applying the Case-Based Method in Designing Online Instruction (2011). http://scholarworks.iu.edu/journals/index.php/ijdl/article/view/1102/1296
22. Scott, K.M., Kitching, S., Burn, D., Koulias, M., Campbell, D., Phelps, M.: "Wherever, whenever" learning in Medicine: Interactive mobile case-based project. In: Steel, C.H., Keppell, M.J., Gerbic, P., Housego, S. (eds.) Curriculum, Technology & Transformation for an Unknown Future. Proceedings Ascilite Sydney 2010, pp. 888–890 (2010)
23. Lee, S.H., Lee, J., Liu, X., Bonk, C.J., Magjuka, R.J.: A review of case-based learning practices in an online MBA program: a program-level case study. Educ. Technol. Soc. **12**(3), 178–190 (2009)

Research on Open University Online Courses Learning Support Service (OCLSS) from the Perspective of Ubiquitous Learning

Xianyue Wu[1], Yi Qiu[2(✉)], Youru Xie[2], Huiyan Zhang[2], and Lihong Wu[2]

[1] The Open University of Guangdong, Guangzhou, China
xywu@gdrtvu.edu.cn
[2] South China Normal University, Guangzhou, China
654285537@qq.com, 1284756092@qq.com, 797361157@qq.com,
xieyouru@aliyun.com

Abstract. Along with the gradual promotion of information education, the emerging information technology provides a broad and innovative platform for online learning services of Open University, and significantly advances the integration of the ideas of Ubiquitous learning (U-Learning) and blended learning. This research, based on the online courses of Open University, established a system of evaluation index for learning support services. Based upon the twenty-two online courses of the Open University of Guangdong (OUGD), an evaluation and analysis was conducted to explore the status quo and problem of the learning support services in these open universities. On this basis, combining with relevant research and empirical surveys this research found that the learning support services were moving along the trend towards personalization, ubiquitous and intelligence, which might provide a useful reference to the diverse development and innovative application of OCLSS in our country.

Keywords: Online courses · Learning support service · Ubiquitous learning

1 Introduction

With the development of Cloud Computing, Big Data and Internet of Things and other new technologies, it will become a trend that online courses will be constructed applying the ideas of blended learning and ubiquitous learning in open universities. In June 2016, *The 13th Five Year Plan of Educational Informationization* published by the Ministry of Education of the People's Republic of China clearly states that the exploration of support service model of digital educational resources need to be expedited [1], and the level and capacity of digital educational resource services need to be significantly

This article is the research result of national education science "Twelfth Five - Year Plan" key topic "*Education Informatization and Massive Open Online Course (MOOCS) strategic research in 2014*" (Project approval number: ACA140009).

S.K.S. Cheung et al. (Eds.): ICBL 2017, LNCS 10309, pp. 412–424, 2017.
DOI: 10.1007/978-3-319-59360-9_36

promoted. All these can provide a baseline and orientation to the construction and application of online courses of open universities. At present, the China Radio and TV University is moving along with the strategic direction towards an open university. Open University will play an important role in the lifelong education system in China which will be set as the pivot of the construction of this system [2]. Because of the separation and the remoteness of teachers and students in this system, the quality of learning support services (LSS) has a direct influence on the learning outcomes [3]. However, there is little research on learning support service.

Ding said that "*the learning support service is the sum of the support services provided to students in various forms from information, resource, personnel to facilities which based on two-way communications between teachers and students/students and the media*" [4]. For Open University online courses, LSS include the provision of learning resources, counseling on the learning process, publishing and feedback to teaching information, monitoring homework and conducting examinations, the implementation of teaching plan [5] etc., in order to help promoting learning autonomy and ultimately improving the quality and effectiveness.

Ubiquitous learning is considered as a new learning method consisting of ample learning opportunities in which learners can learn anytime and anywhere without specific equipment but can enjoy the ubiquitous learning supports [6]. The features of ubiquitous learning include personalization, contextualization, immersion and intelligence which provide an excellent reference in establishing a framework for OCLSS in the Open University. This research aims to analyze the OCLSS in OUGD to explore the status quo and problems of OCLSS in Open University and to propose recommendations to these questions.

1.1 A Review of the Application of Ubiquitous Learning in Open University

The Open University is a new type of higher education, which is supported by the modern information technologies for both obtaining academic qualifications or to a certain extent, without the academic qualifications [7]. Recent researches in ubiquitous learning for Open University focus on learning space modeling, learning resources development, strategic planning, technical architecture and other aspects of social service reform under the concept of Ubiquitous Learning. Xiao *et al.* [8] constructed a seamless learning space model based on the idea of Ubiquitous Learning. Based on the analysis of the characteristics of Open University resources and ubiquitous learning, Wang [9] put forward the construction model of micro learning resources for Open University. He [10] combining the concept of ubiquitous learning with the characteristics of an Open University, identified the path of cultivating the core competence in the perspective of ubiquitous learning. Fan [11] reformed the information technology platform for educational services by combining the concepts of ubiquitous learning and cloud computing technology. Moushir *et al.* [12] built a dynamic knowledge map for learning based on computer supported ubiquitous learning environment. Jiang [13] suggested that the services provided by Open University might provide valuable experience in developing a learning-oriented city by combining the concept of ubiquitous learning with the requirements of a learning society.

Based on the above analysis, we found that there are a lot of researches on the application of ubiquitous learning in Open University, but there are few researches on the online courses of Open University, especially the learning support service.

1.2 A Review of Learning Support Services for Online Courses in Open University

The learning support service starts from the summation of the practical experience of distance open education, which does not only have a great impact on distance education, but also on the field of Education [14]. The main focus of research in learning support service is on its theory, the system construction, the comparative study and the development trend. Xiang *et al.* [14] examined the evolution of learning support services from the ideological enlightenment to its maturity. Based on the practice of Shanghai Open University, Shi *et al.* [15] analyzed the problems in the process of open education by means of questionnaire survey, and constructed a learning support service system in five dimensions. Howard Spoelstra *et al.* [16] built a model of optimizing learning support services through the collection of key data in the learning network. Philipp Bitzer *et al.* [17] designed and developed an efficient blended learning support system through literature analysis, case practice and expert advice.

We found that there are a lot of researches in the field of Open University resource development, strategic planning, technology innovation and social services, and there are also researches in learning support services but on learning support service for online courses in open universities.

2 Research Design

2.1 Research Purpose

The purpose of this study is to evaluate the online courses of OUGD with the concept of Ubiquitous Learning, to identify the status quo and problems, and to suggest ways to enhance the level of Online Course Learning Support Service (OCLSS) and the developing courses with good branding, with the hope to provide useful reference for the OCLSS of Open University in China.

2.2 The Evaluation Index System

In order to evaluate the online courses in terms of learning service support, we need to determine the evaluation index of the OCLSS for OUGD, and to conduct systematic evaluation and analysis on selected samples according to the index. The evaluation index system of Learning Support Service is the key to the success of this study.

An LSS includes the learning guides, scaffolding supports for learning problems, learning management and other services related to learning. In other words, the design and implementation of learning support services should be based on the learner's learning activities, not only to provide a clear learning path and related learning recommendations, but also to provide different channels for learners to solve the problems encountered in the learning process. At the same time, we should also do a good job on the curriculum update, curriculum announcement, and technical support management services relating to curriculum. We thus, used "learning guidance", "consulting help" and "management service" as the primary indices of OCLSS evaluation index system on Open University.

Through literature research, system analysis and other methods, we further refine the primary indices into 7 s level indicators and detailed evaluation criteria, as shown in Table 1.

Table 1. Evaluation index system of OCLSS in Open University

Primary indices	Secondary indexes	Indicator description
Learning guidance	Learning path	Course have Clear learning path guidance
	Learning suggestions	Provide advice or guidance for self-learning
Consulting help	Common problem	Specific module for common problem and provide solution
	Artificial help	Artificial support for adult learners to provide timely and effective help
	Technical support	Technical systems provide timely and effective help for adult learners
Management service	Course management	Timely release, update on the curriculum arrangement, content Q & A, teaching management notice, reminders, documents, etc.
	Team support	The course is equipped with high quality staff, providing teaching guidance, technical support, student management and consulting services

In order to ensure the reliability of the evaluation index system, two independent experts grade the LSS for 10 online courses, and then compare the two scores for reliability calculation.

$$\text{reliability} = \frac{n \times \text{Average mutual agreement}}{1 + [(n-1) \times \text{Average mutual agreement}]}$$

$$\text{Average mutual agreement} = \frac{2M}{N1 + N2}$$

Where n is the number of coders; M is number of two experts having the same scores; $N1$ represents the total scores for the first expert and $N2$ for the second expert. In this study, n was 2, M was 59, $N1$ and $N2$ were all of the order of 70, the calculated reliability was 0.84 (>0.7); which shows the higher consistency of judgment using the same index by the two experts. Thus the index system was considered having high reliability; we can then apply the evaluation index system in this study.

2.3 The Evaluation Objects

After careful examination on the available courses, we finally selected 22 courses in 5 different areas in OUGD. These courses were contributed from School of Economic Management and Standardization, School of Cultural Communication, School of Information and Engineering, School of Law and Administration and The Ministry of Public Education Foundation. These online courses were listed and shown in Table 2.

Table 2. Study sample list of online courses LSS research in OUGD

College	Course name
School of Economic Management and Standardization	Theory and method of standardization
	Standardized laws and regulations
	Basic knowledge of Metrology
	Principles of management
	Quality Assurance
	Systems engineering
School of Cultural Communication	Development and protection of cultural resources
	Culture Industry Introduction
	Intercultural communication
	The general theory of Chinese culture
School of Information and Engineering	Mathematical foundations of information security
	Java programming
	Computing Thinking
School of Law and Administration	Introduction to Sociology
	Labor and Personnel Dispute Settlement Act
	Contract law
	Labor psychology
	Labor Contract Law
The Ministry of Public Education Foundation	Introduction to political theory and civic culture
	College English (B)
	Fundamentals of computer application
	Learning Guide for OUGD

3 Analysis the Learning Support Service of Open University Online Course

3.1 Current Status

3.1.1 General Analysis

According to the evaluation index, 22 online courses were analyzed in this study. A summary of the results is shown in Table 3.

Table 3. Results of analysis on Open University online courses learning support service

Primary indices	Secondary indexes	Indicator description	Number of courses	Proportion
Learning guidance	Learning path	Course have Clear learning path guidance	18	81.8%
	Learning suggestions	Provide advice or guidance for self-learning	17	77.3%
Consulting help	Common problem	Specific module for common problem and provide solution	4	18.2%
	Artificial help	Artificial support for adult learners to provide timely and effective help	9	40.9%
	Technical support	Technical systems provide timely and effective help for adult learners	4	18.2%
Management service	Course management	Timely release, update on the curriculum arrangement, content Q & A, teaching management notice, documents, etc.	4	18.2%
	Team support	The course is equipped with high quality staff, providing teaching guidance, technical support, student management and consulting services	10	45.5%

In general, most of the 22 courses do not only provide a clear learning path for learners but also self-study advice and guidance. Help support services and management services are relatively weak, a few courses are using a variety of ways to provide help and support to learners, the services in course management are still very limited. In general, the learning support services for the 22 courses are unable to support ubiquitous learning for the time-being and will need to improve.

3.1.2 Dimensional Analysis

At the beginning of a learning process, learning guide services are designed to help learners understanding precise characteristics of distance open education, preparing to adapt to the new learning environment, at the same time to provide personalized learning advice and help. Our statistical results show that 81.8% courses provide a clear learning path guide, 77.3% courses provide learners with a personalized learning advice and help, in which the course *Standardized laws and regulations* provides learners with a clear learning guide through linkages on simple but orderly learning pages; *Culture Industry Introduction* sets up learning guidance for each unit to help learners immersing into the situation of each unit and visually guided learners to participate in learning activities; *Computer Thinking* provides learners with learning path guides by using the platform features similar to xMOOC; *Labor Contract Law* provides learners with a clear and orderly learning guide via a carefully designed course interface by means of features in FLASH; *Learning Guide for OUGD* provides personalized learning guide and interactive courseware to learners following the SCORM standard. Based on the requirements of OUGD, 22 courses are generally providing detailed study guides to learners by supplying learning help and learning suggestions. It is worth noting that *Labor Contract Law* course also provides platform operating suggestions to learners, as shown in Fig. 1, so that learners may focus on learning the course content by reducing the threshold of technical operations. In summary, 80% learning guidelines have their own characteristics.

Fig. 1. *Labor Contract Law* course provides platform operating suggestions

About consulting help, 18.2% online courses provide auto-answering service for common issues in learning via technological support; 40.9% of the courses offer artificial help for learners. Among these courses, *Intercultural communication* set FAQs for common questions in the curriculum, *Mathematical foundations of information security* set FAQs for platform operation. In addition to providing auto-answers to some common problems, the hybrid use of technical systems and manual intervention (artificial help) supports and provides learners with personalized help and guidance. *Principles of management* using social networking tools such as QQ establishes a communication channel for learners and the teaching team; *Culture Industry Introduction* provides a variety of communication means to learners to ask questions via mailbox, telephone number and QQ number; *Introduction to political theory and civic culture* provides WeChat Official Accounts, integrating artificial support and technical support to help learners; with an interface shown in Fig. 2. Generally, only 40% of the 22 courses provide consulting help service, <20% courses can use artificial and technology system together to provide help service for learners, there is still much room for improvement.

Fig. 2. *Introduction to political theory and civic culture course* consulting help

Management service is the command center of Open University Online Courses, including curriculum management and team support. Course management services include timely release of information, updating curriculum arrangement, organizing contents of Q & A, issuing a notice of teaching management, announcements, reminders, documents, etc. Team support services primarily for the smooth implementation of courses include teaching counseling, technical support, student management and consulting services, etc. Statistical results show that 18.2% online courses have management services and 45.5% have team support. Notification and announcement is the portal window of course management services, including course plan and arrangements, study schedule and alert, test and assignment submission. *Theory and method of standardization* provides announcement reminding learners to participate in learning activities with time and venue data; *Labor Contract Law* reminds learners via announcement to participate in learning activities; *Introduction to political theory and civic culture* sends curriculum arrangements and event notification via WeChat Official Accounts and announcements simultaneously. In addition to timely announcements allowing learners adjusting their learning rhythm, a strong course team is an important element to support curriculum implementation. *Java programming* takes advantage of platform features to provide services for learners such as technology FAQ, as shown in Fig. 3. *Learning Guide for OUGD* sets FAQs for learners to solve the problems of examination, teaching, student affairs, technology, etc.

Fig. 3. *Java programming* course management service

3.2 Problems and Solution Strategies

Open University online course learning support service is very important. With the continuous development of Ubiquitous Learning, it is a trend to provide learners with sustainable, adaptive, personalized, roamed and multi-dimensional learning support services. Through the above analysis, it is not difficult to find that the current online course learning support service concept of Open University is relatively lack behind with limited forms of services and still has a large space for improvement.

3.2.1 Singular Support Channel not Good to Developing Collaborative Services

Less than half of the 22 courses offer course help and support, in which artificial help is the most common form. Although artificial help has the characteristic of high personalization and strong pertinence, this singular channel provides services with poor effect and low efficiency, and is unable to cope with increasing number of learners. Some learner's information literacy is poor, but the curriculum platform does not provide visual operation guidance; some learners have difficulties in their study and cannot adapt to the artificial help, but the curriculum platform has no intelligent Q&A area. One of the urgent problems to be solved in the OCLSS of Open University is thus the singular support channel without collaborative services.

In order to solve this problem, we need to explore various means of help support, for example, establishing a curriculum FAQ edition for answering common questions automatically, providing learners with a variety of contact methods, adopting technology supports to optimize help support services, providing learning guide pages for easy operations, using robots for answering simple questions in a personalized manner, adopting social networking tools to reduce the threshold of seeking help, promoting the formation of mutual aid groups. All these may help improve the channels of support and eventually leading to the provision of smarter support services.

3.2.2 Course Management not Effectively Supporting Learning Interactions

As found in this study, only <20% of the 22 courses provide timely release of updated contents and information of course arrangements, teaching management, reminders etc., only 45% courses providing teaching guidance, technical support, management and consulting services to help students. Thus, how to build a learning community and to improve the management service level of Open University so as to effectively promote online learning interaction is an issue that needs to be solved.

In order to solve this problem, the course team should actively guide the learners to participate in online discussions and provide timely feedback and support learners in completing their homework assignments and examinations. For example, in addition to joining in curriculum discussion areas, learners can also use social networking tools to interact teachers and other learners anytime and anywhere. Learners can also to enrich the learning content collaboratively by means of Wiki entries and use cloud notes to complete the learning report. Teachers can watch the learning situation of students through the platform data, and give students personalized learning guidance. Making use a learning dashboard to show the learning situation of learners, teachers can provide targeted guidance. The teacher may use visual means to quantify a learner's ability to learn, giving the learner an award to improve their sense of self-efficacy during the learning progression. The curriculum team should improve the efficiency and accuracy of management services constantly through advanced technology, provide synchronous, seamless and ubiquitous learning management, and actively guide learners to form learning community for effectively promoting the online interactive learning.

3.2.3 Support Service Concept not Meeting Needs of Ubiquitous Learning

Effective ubiquitous learning depends on the creation of a seamless learning space supported by technology. [18] At present, the interface of the 22 courses cannot be displayed on different resolution devices, mobile learning experience is poor. Although more than half of the 22 courses provide a learning guide for learners, the guidelines provided ignore the characteristics and learning styles of different learners. So the current OCLSS concept of Open University cannot meet the needs of ubiquitous learning.

In order to solve this problem, we proposed an adaptive page design concept to the technical support team of Open University online course platform which is widely used at this stage to optimize the course interface encoding, to continuously improve the visual experience, and to construct an interactive mode, so interfaces for each course can be personalized and humanized on different devices. In addition, it is necessary to develop a unified design standard for curriculum interface and to provide guidance for compiling curriculum interface design with this standard. Teachers can analyze the learner's learning style and information literacy through a pre-class assessment and provide targeted learning guide. In order to meet the different learners' learning habits and style, teachers can provide learners with different forms of learning suggestions, such as text, video, animation, comics and other different types for learners to choose.

4 The Development Trend of Online Learning Support Service in Open University

Based on above analysis and examining recent researches in this area, this study suggests the following trends for OCLSS in Open University.

4.1 Towards Personalize Learning Guidelines

A learning path is a selection of various sequential possibilities of effective learning between learning units in a given subject [19]. In the Open University online courses, learners select course contents by clicking on different hyperlinks. Combining each hyperlink in a sequential order constitutes the learning path of online courses. Analyzing study data and page selection data may facilitate the provision of adaptive learning path which puts learner preferred units together in a page zone for better learning path planning. Compared with a fixed learning path, the adaptive learning technology can be used to have a personalized learning path for each learner, to improve the learning effect and to optimize the learning experience. Providing personalized learning path planning will gradually become a trend of learning support service in Open Universities.

4.2 Integrate Concept of Ubiquitous into the Support Process

With the development in cloud computing, big data, mobile Internet and other emerging information technologies, it would be difficult to use the original learning support services to satisfy with the reform demands on education in this “Internet plus” era. The concept of Open University online course management service has been quietly changing. In addition to the use of the learning platform to deliver learning support services, social networking tools have also been applied in curriculum announcement and curriculum discussion. Ubiquitous learning aims to create a learner centered, intelligent and ubiquitous learning environment that learners can learn with a variety of devices whenever and wherever possible. Information can be automatically passed to the learner in the right way. Supporting services should also be learner centered intelligently at anytime and anywhere. The idea for the development of OCLSS in Open University should be enriched to optimize the existing service processes, to explore new service modes, and to ensure the effectiveness of curriculum implementation.

4.3 Moving Towards Smart Learning Management

The future Open University Online Courses will aim to provide a more personalized learning and emotional support services for learners, which will be based on integrating the concept of providing learning-centered services and its associated management process intelligently into a smart learning environment. Smart education is based on the Internet of things, Cloud Computing, Wireless Communication, and other new generation of information technologies to create an intelligent, perceptive, ubiquitous educational information ecosystem. Smart education can provide new technical support for Open University Online Course Learning Support Service [20]. For example, virtual learning assistants can help learners complete course learning and reduce the loneliness of learners. The learning dashboard can help learners quantify and analyze the level of self-learning with timely adjustment on learning strategies. Thus, it would be a future direction for providing high quality courses in Open University via smart online course learning support services, which will be based on the smart education concept with application of smart learning techniques and tools to promote learner interaction and thus enhance learning.

5 Conclusion

Based on the strategic plan of Education Information Communications Technology in China, this study suggested an evaluation index system of OCLSS in Open University, evaluated the 22 courses of the OUGD and analyzed the features and problems of support services in the implementation of these courses. This paper suggests that the future OCLSS in Open University will be personalized, ubiquitous and intelligent. We hope that this study can help Open University in identifying its problems of online learning support services, provide recommendations for improvement, and improve the quality and effectiveness of the online learning support services in Open University.

References

1. The Ministry of Education of the People's Republic of China: The 13th Five Year Plan of Educational Informationization. EB/OL, 6 July 2016. http://www.moe.gov.cn/srcsite/A16/s3342/201606/t20160622_269367.html
2. Chen, L., Zheng, Q.H., Lin, S.Y.: Opportunities and challenges of chinese open universities in the era of "Internet+". J. Open Educ. Res. **23**(1), 15–20 (2017)
3. Xie, Y.R., Zhang, H.Y., Wu, L.H., Sheng, C.X., Ni, M.S.: Theoretical analysis of the teaching and learning models of online education represented by MOOCs. J. e-Educ. Res. **3**, 50–58 (2016)
4. Ding, X.F.: Student learning support services in distance education (part I). J. China Educ. Technol. **3**, 55–59 (2002)
5. Pang, H.Y., Wen, W.D.: Reflections on the learning support service system in Open University. J. Changchun Educ. Inst. **24**, 114–116 (2015)
6. Yang, Y.B., Wu, L.H.: The innovative application model of network learning space from the perspective of ubiquitous learning. J. China Educ. Technol. **07**, 29–35 (2016)
7. Zhu, L.C.: Research on the integration strategy of adult education and non academic education in Open University——a case study of Hebei Open University. J. Contemp. Educ. Res. Teach. Pract. **12**, 270–271 (2015)
8. Xiao, J., Jiang, B.Q., Xu, Z.: The design and application of learning space characterized by seamless integration in u-learning. J. Mod. Distance Educ. Res. **6**, 96–103 (2015)
9. Wang, H.B.: Analysis of digital micro-resource development in open university. J. Guangzhou Open Univ. **11**(6), 37–41 (2011)
10. He, X.F.: Thoughts on cultivation of core competitiveness in perspective of ubiquitous learning. J. Nanjing Radio TV Univ. **2**, 1–5 (2015)
11. Fan, J.X.: The strategies of virtual digital campus architecture and connotation construction in Open University. J. Jiangsu Open Univ. **1**, 23–28 (2014)
12. El-Bishouty, M.M., et al.: Social knowledge awareness map for computer supported ubiquitous learning environment. J. Educ. Technol. Soc. **13**(4), 27–37 (2010)
13. Jiang, H.: Promoting ubiquitous learning for anyone, at anytime and anywhere: a practice of sou serving the construction of a learning city. J. Open Educ. Res. **4**, 24–30 (2014)
14. Xiang, G.X., Zhang, X.H.: The origin of learning service thought. J. Distance Educ. China **9**, 23–26 (2005)
15. Shi, C.J., Chen, H.J.: A study on the construction of open and distance education learning support service system: practice and exploration of Shanghai Open University. J. Open Educ. Res. **5**, 112–120 (2013)
16. Spoelstra, H., Rosmalen, P.V., Vrie, E.V.D., et al.: A team formation and project-based learning support service for social learning networks. J. Univers. Computerence **19**(10), 1474–1495 (2014)
17. Bitzer, P., Söllner, M., Leimeister, J.M.: Design principles for high-performance blended learning services delivery. Bus. Inf. Syst. Eng. **58**(2), 135–149 (2016)
18. Yu, S.Q., Yang, X.M., Cheng, G.: Learning resource designing and sharing in ubiquitous learning environment——the concept and architecture of leaning cell. J. Open Educ. Res. **15**(1), 47–53 (2009)

19. Qu, J.: Analyze and design of adaptive hypermedia tutorial system. Master's thesis, Beijing University of Posts and Telecommunications (2007)
20. Yang, X.M., Liu, Y.Q., Zhong, X.L., Song, S.Q.: The development strategy and path choice of smart education in China. Mod. Educ. Technol. **1**, 12–19 (2014)

Analysis on the Development of Educational Resources in the Open Universities in China

Shijie Li[1(✉)], Xianyue Wu[2], Yi Qiu[1], Lihong Wu[1], and Pengyu Chen[2]

[1] School of Information Technology in Education, South China Normal University, Guangzhou, China
491963653@qq.com, 654285537@qq.com, 1797361157@qq.com
[2] The Open University of Guangdong, Guangzhou, China
{xywu,pychen}@gdrtvu.edu.cn

Abstract. Cloud computing, big data and other emerging technologies have been commonly applied to education nowadays. Although these subversive technologies has brought new opportunities to many open universities, new challenges have been created from the new models, forms and demands, which have a strong impact on the existing distance educational framework and mechanisms. This paper proposes an evaluation index on the educational resources developed by open universities, based on the analysis on some online courses offered by the Open University of Guangdong and the Open University of China. The evaluation index is then applied to study and evaluate the current development of educational resources for open universities in China.

Keywords: Open universities · Educational resources · Resource analysis

This article is the research result of national education science "Twelfth Five - Year Plan" key topic "*Education Informatization and Massive Open Online Course (MOOCS) strategic research in 2014*" (Project approval number: ACA140009).

1 Introduction

In China, open universities can be regarded as a new type of high school supported by modern technology, which promotes both curricular and non-curricular education through open and distance education [1]. As mentioned in the *State Planning outline for medium and long term education reform and development (2010–2020)*, continuing education was an important part of the life-log education system, and the development of curriculum resources was identified as a strategic task for open universities [2]. *The 13th Five-Year plan for the national economic and social development of the People's Republic of China* emphasized the sharing of educational resources, developing online & distance education, and integrating digital educational resources for the society [3]. These indicated that the development and sharing of curriculum resources has become an important measure for open universities.

S.K.S. Cheung et al. (Eds.): ICBL 2017, LNCS 10309, pp. 425–432, 2017.
DOI: 10.1007/978-3-319-59360-9_37

However, many open universities have not made the corresponding changes [4, 5]. There are significant variations in quality on the educational resources between local open universities (e.g. the Open University of Guangdong) and national open universities (e.g. the Open University of China) [6]. In this paper, online courses from the Open University of Guangdong and the Open University of China are compared and the qualities of the educational resources are analyzed, so as to study and evaluate the current development of educational resources in open universities in China.

2 Related Work

Educational resources refer to the teaching and learning resources which are used for both distance education and full-time education. They include textual contents, audio, video, multimedia, virtual training courseware and other media resources [7]. There are research studies on the development of educational resources for open universities, such as on content design, sharing mechanism, case analysis, and comparative aspects. Zhao and Luo [7] carried out the modular content design of Yunnan Open University, according to the requirements of standardization, integration, diversification and networking. Zhang [8] explored the development and sharing of educational resources between schools and enterprises. Bai et al. [9] used the concept of OBE and constructive post-modern philosophy to develop a structural framework for open online courses. Xu and Sun [10] offered suggestions for the Open University of China in accordance with the comparative results generated from the open education practice between the Open University in UK and the Open University of China. Mtebe [11] investigated the use of online educational resources in 11 institutions of higher education in Tanzania. Among the research studies on educational resources for open universities, only a few were conducted on comparing and evaluating educational resources between the local open universities and the national open universities in China. This motivates our study on the evaluation of educational resources for open universities in China.

3 Framework for Analysis and Evaluation

Figure 1 outlines the framework for analyzing and evaluating the educational resources of open universities, based on the relevant studies. In April 2015, the "*Opinions on Strengthening the Application and Management of Online Open Courses in Colleges and Universities*" examined and evaluated the educational resources on the contents, instructional design and methods, teaching activities and evaluation, teaching effects and impact, team support and services. Li [12] developed an evaluation index system with a number of criteria on comprehensiveness, integrity, and rationality of the educational resources. Xie and Ke [13] also conducted a study on evaluating the educational resources for open universities on their relevance, comprehensive and diversity [13].

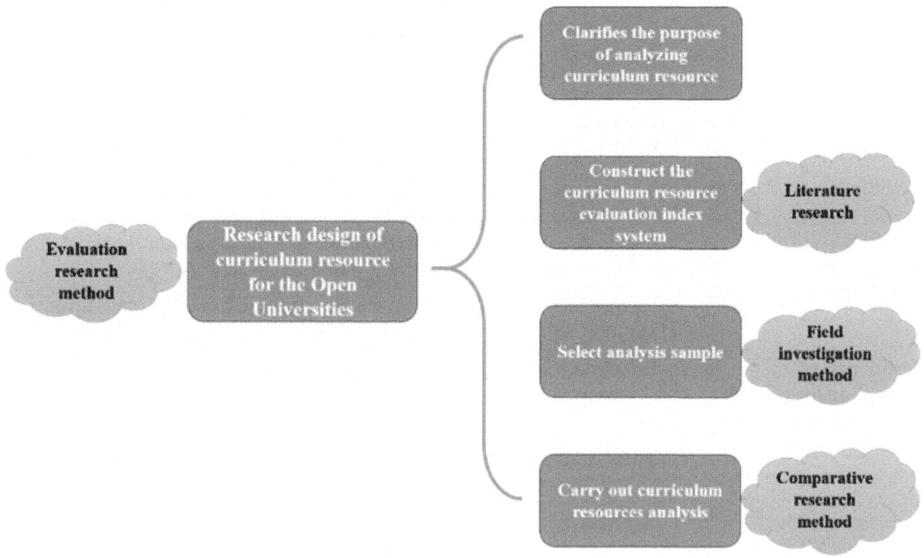

Fig. 1. Framework for analysis and evaluation of educational contents

Educational resources can be characterized by the diversity, relevance, rationality and comprehensiveness. Based on these characteristics, an evaluation index system is proposed, as shown in Table 1.

Reliability analysis of the evaluation index system was carried out. Two experts independently evaluated the online courses. Reliability of the results are calculated according to the following formula.

Reliability $= (n \times \text{average mutual agreement})/(1 + [(n-1) \times (\text{average mutual } agreeability)])$, where average mutual agreement $= 2M/(N1 + N2)$, n is the number of sample, M is the number of scorings, N1 is the total number of scoring for the first expert, and N2 is the total number of scoring for the second expert.

In our study, 12 online courses (6 from the Open University of Guangdong and the other 6 from the Open University of China) were selected. They cover subject areas in economic management, cultural industry management, information engineering, laws and regulations, foreign languages, learning guidance. Table 2 lists these online courses. Reliability analysis was conducted. Given that n is 2, M is 59, N1 and N2 are 84, the reliability is 0.83. The two experts are highly consistent with the same indicators, thus implying a high reliability of the evaluation index system.

4 Analysis of Curriculum Resource for the Open Universities

This section analyzes the evaluation results of the selected online courses from the Open University of Guangdong and the Open University of China.

Table 1. The evaluation index system

First level index	Second level index	Evaluation standard
Category and quality of the educational resources	Content Specification	Contents are presented in accordance with the course objectives, and the structure is logical and reasonable.
	Resource Category	Courses can provide resources, which are related to the curriculum, comprehensive, and well integrated.
	Resource Quality	Resources are presented in a proper form. They should be easy to read and understand.
Pertinence of educational resources	Resource Content	Resources can address the specific teaching problems, and meet the curriculum requirements.
	Individualization	Innovative, personalized learning resources can be provided.
	Audience	Resources are presented in accordance with the existing cognitive ability and learning needs.
	Resource Allocation	Resource allocation is reasonable and conforming to the requirements of the study.

Table 2. Selected online courses

Curriculum nature	The open university of Guangdong	The open university of China
Economic management	Standardization theory and method	Western Economics
Culture industry management	Introduction to Cultural Industry	Modern Chinese literature
Information engineering	Advanced Programming for JAVA	C Language Programming
Laws and regulations	Labor Dispute Processing	Labor Law and Social Security Law
Foreign languages	College English(B)	Interactions Listening & Speaking
Learning guidance	The Open University of Guangdong Learning Guidance	The Open University of China Learning Guidance

4.1 Evaluation Result

According to the evaluation index system, Tables 3 and 4 show the results for the online courses in the Open University of Guangdong and the Open University of China, respectively.

Table 3. The open university of Guangdong data analysis

First level index	Second level index	Evaluation standard	Number	Value
Category and quality of the teaching resources	Content Specification	Contents are presented in accordance with the course objectives, and the structure is logical and reasonable.	5	83.3%
	Resource Category	Courses can provide resources, which are related to the curriculum, comprehensive, and well integrated.	5	83.3%
	Resource Quality	Resources are presented in a proper form. They should be easy to read and understand.	5	83.3%
Pertinence of resource	Resource Content	Resources can address the specific teaching problems, and meet the curriculum requirements.	4	66.6%
	Individualization	Innovative, personalized learning resources can be provided.	2	33.3%
	Audience	Resources are presented in accordance with the existing cognitive ability and learning needs.	5	83.3%
	Resource Allocation	Resource allocation is reasonable and conforming to the requirements of the study.	3	50%

From the tables, it is shown that the evaluation results of online courses in the Open University of Guangdong is better than that in the Open University of China. This is because of the frequency and renewal process of the curriculum resources. However, the Open University of China is better than the Open University of Guangdong in pertinence of resource, particularly in resource content, individualization and resource allocation.

The educational resources of the Open Universities are mainly composed of online courses, with other resources as supplement. As for the Open University of Guangdong, the statistical results showed that 83.3% of the content structure is scientific and reasonable. 83.3% of the course is rich in resources. 83.3% of the curriculum resource is presented in a proper form, with vivid video resources. Text resources meet the course requirements and are easy to read. As for the Open University of China, 83.3% of the content structure is scientific and reasonable, 66.6% of the course is rich in resources, but only 33.3% of the curriculum resource is presented in a proper form, with vivid video resources. Text resources meet the course requirements and are easy to read.

Table 4. The open university of China data analysis

First level index	Second level index	Evaluation standard	Number	Value
Category and quality of the teaching resources	Content Specification	Contents are presented in accordance with the course objectives, and the structure is logical and reasonable.	5	83.3%
	Resource Category	Courses can provide resources, which are related to the curriculum, comprehensive, and well integrated.	4	66.6%
	Resource Quality	Resources are presented in a proper form. They should be easy to read and understand.	2	33.3%
Pertinence of resource	Resource Content	Resources can address the specific teaching problems, and meet the curriculum requirements.	5	83.3%
	Individualization	Innovative, personalized learning resources can be provided.	3	50%
	Audience	Resources are presented in accordance with the existing cognitive ability and learning needs.	5	83.3%
	Resource Allocation	Resource allocation is reasonable and conforming to the requirements of the study.	4	66.6%

It can be seen that only 33.3% of the sample courses in the Open University of China meet the standards. Most of the course videos have no subtitles. Video screen is blurred and fuzzy that affected the learner's viewing. Most of the video are too long in length (exceeding 40 min). The Open University of Guangdong is better than the Open University of China on this indicator.

For the Open University of Guangdong, the statistical results showed that 66.6% content of teaching resources could address the specific teaching problems and meet the requirements of curriculum teaching. 83.3% of the resources are in accordance with the existing cognitive ability and learning needs. As for the Open University of China, 83.3% content of teaching resources can address the specific teaching problems and meet the requirements of curriculum teaching. 83.3% of the resources are in accordance with the existing cognitive ability and learning needs. In contrast, only 50% of the learning resources can provide innovative, personalized learning resources.

It can be seen that 66.6% of the sample courses in the Open University of Guangdong are in accordance with the existing cognitive ability and learning needs. 83.3% of the sample courses in the Open University of China meet the above requirements.

4.2 Problems and Countermeasures

Through the above study, a number of problems in the development of educational resources are identified.

There is a lack of integrity in designing the educational resources. The curriculum resources structure is too fragmented. Therefore, the open universities should continue to strengthen the integration of curriculum resources. The course team should seek to improve the existing educational resource in the resource structure. In addition, the team should strengthen the link between the curriculum and the resources.

Most of the learning resources are mainly based on instructional videos. There is a lack of other forms or supplements. Besides, the courses are too dependent on external resources. There are insufficient original resources. These original resources and external resources are not well integrated. The course team should seek to provide more original resources, and to improve the integration of the original and external resources, such as eliminating the duplication.

5 Conclusion

It is one of the main directions for open universities to adjust the original curriculum resources, introduce and integrate effectively the external resources related to the teaching content, and then build the diversified curriculum with rich content and reusable resources. The advance of technologies and the concept of lifelong education make online open courses continue to evolve. Open universities should optimize the educational resources, improve the quality of courses, and support personalized learning. The curriculum structure should be adjusted accordingly.

In this paper, an evaluation index system is proposed for the open universities in China. Based on the evaluation index, a comparative study for 12 online courses of the Open University of Guangdong and the Open University of China is conducted. Problems and shortcomings are identified. It is found that the educational resources should be more diversified and reusable. The content should be more personalized. The results can provide a good reference for open universities in China in developing educational resources of online courses.

References

1. Zhu, L.C.: A study on the integration strategy of adult education and non-diploma education in the open university - A case study of Hebei Radio and TV university. J. Contemp. Educ. Res. Teach. Pract. **12**, 270–271 (2015)
2. Ministry of Education of the People's Republic of China: State Planning outline for medium and long term education reform and development (2010–2020). EB/OL. 29 July 2010. http://www.moe.edu.cn/publicfiles/business/htmlfiles/moe/moe_838/201008/93704.html
3. Xinhua News Agency: The 13th Five - Year plan for the national economic and social development of the people's republic of China. EB/OL. 7 March 2016, http://news.xinhuanet.com/politics/2016lh/2016-03/17/c_1118366322_21.htm

4. Ren, W.M., Shi, Z.Y.: Several urgent problems in the construction of the open university of China. Mod. Distance Educ. Res. **2**, 9–13 (2011)
5. Huo, S.P.: Reflections on instructional design in the construction of the open university resources. J. Yunnan Open Univ. **4**, 7–9 (2013)
6. Ding, W.Y.: An analysis of the difficulties facing the transformation from local universities to national universities. J. Open Univ. Guangdong **2**, 6–9 (2013)
7. Zhao, Y., Luo, J.: Construction of three - dimensional curriculum resource system of the open university. Mod. Distance Educ. Res. **4**, 89–96 (2014)
8. Zhang, Y.C.: Research on the construction of the open university curriculum for enterprise education. J. Distance Educ. **3**, 93–98 (2013)
9. Bai, J., Xie, Y.R., Li, W., Wu, L.H.: Research on the resource structure model of online open course based on OBE concept in "Internet+" era. China Educ. Technol. **1**, 64–70 (2017)
10. Xu, J.P., Sun, F.W.: Comparison and enlightenment of the basic characteristics of the open university in China and Britain. Distance Educ. China **9**, 38–45 (2015)
11. Mtebe, J.S.: Investigating perceived barriers to the use of open educational resources in higher education in Tanzania. Int. Rev. Res. Open Distance Learn. **2**, 43–66 (2014)
12. Li, W.: Research on Evaluation Index System of Network Course. Master's thesis, Tianjin Normal University (2009)
13. Xie, Y.R., Ke, Q.C.: Development and Application of Network Course. Publishing House of Electronics Industry, Beijing (2005)

Improving Video Engagement by Gamification: A Proposed Design of MOOC Videos

Yun Zhu[1], Leisi Pei[2(✉)], and Junjie Shang[3(✉)]

[1] College of Creative Studies, Shanghai Theater Academy, Shanghai 200040, China
zhuyun@sh163.net
[2] Beijing Academy of Educational Sciences, Beijing 100101, China
peileisi@pku.edu.cn
[3] Graduate School of Education, Peking University, Beijing 100871, China
jjshang@pku.edu.cn

Abstract. MOOCs have rapidly been a predominant form of distance learning recently. Through high-speed internet, students in MOOCs can not only enjoy best learning resources around the world, but also connect closely with others. However, it is worrying that completion rate of MOOCs is only 10% on average, which reflects the low engagement of learning in MOOCs. Confronted with such problem, this paper proposed a gamification design of MOOC videos by adding implicit feedback into mechanics and updating existing delivery media from lecture-style to narrative-style.

Keywords: Video engagement · Gamification · MOOC · MDA · Flow theory

1 Introduction

Described as "the educational buzzword" [1], Massive Open Online Courses (or MOOCs for short), have been sweeping across the whole world since 2012, which is regarded as the year of MOOC [2]. As a promising knowledge delivery model in distance learning, MOOCs provide potential learners not only the free but high-quality and unlimited learning opportunities, like OER (Open Educational Resources) and OCW (OpenCourseWare) projects, but also a worldwide connected learning environment, which enables students with diverse backgrounds [3] from all over the world to interactively work together online at any time and place according to their individual learning interests [4].

Although MOOCs providers (namely Coursera, edX and Udacity) afford students with sufficient learning supports, researchers have disappointedly found that the completion rate on average is less than 10% [5, 6]. To improve student engagement, a variety of empirical studies have been conducted by redesigning MOOC contents, such as video lectures, quizzes and assessments, discussion board, course structure, weekly reminders and etc. Among all of these contents, video lectures are predominant learning materials that students spend majority of their time in MOOCs studying [7]. Besides, video lectures also play a significant role in course design, which generally cost course staff considerable time and money to produce [8].

S.K.S. Cheung et al. (Eds.): ICBL 2017, LNCS 10309, pp. 433–444, 2017.
DOI: 10.1007/978-3-319-59360-9_38

Considering the importance of videos, we propose a gamification design for the MOOC "*How to Teach by Gamification*", which is running on the *Chinese University MOOC* (the only official MOOC provider in China, www.icourse163.org).

2 Literature Review

Video lectures are the pre-recorded learning materials to deliver knowledge in MOOCs, which integrate audio, image and text of all kinds, such as figure and voice of instructors, background music and subtitles, into one package. Although the number of MOOC providers are booming worldwide, it makes no difference in the basic system architecture of most MOOC providers [9], especially in video lectures. A study has scrutinized how video production style affects student engagement in MOOC studying, for instance, various video styles, different speaking rate, video duration, and watching intensity [8, 10].

This paper concentrates particularly on video content, which means, how to increase student engagement with video lectures by using gamification elements in video content design.

2.1 Engagement and Motivation

Student engagement refers to the state of student being wholly involved, occupied, retained, and intrinsically interested in something [10]. It is believed that student engagement relates closely to students' learning attitude and academic achievements and is the prerequisite for any kind of learning, including MOOCs [11]. However, the innate properties of MOOC, especially massiveness and openness, make engaging learning in MOOCs more challenging. Lots of empirical studies have been conducted to explore effective MOOC design strategies to improve engagement, for example, promoting interactions among instructors and students [12], connecting course structure and content with students' real life [13], setting clear learning goals [14].

Student engagement is commonly identified as a construct with three components: behavioral engagement, emotional engagement and cognitive engagement [11]. Behavioral and emotional engagement underline the extrinsic participation in an activity and intrinsic feeling towards people involved in, meanwhile, cognitive engagement implies the thinking strategies applied in the specific task solving [15, 16]. These three components are closely interrelated and work with each other as a whole.

In some extent, motivation fundamentally determines student engagement. Self-determination theory (SDT), as an extremely influential work, defines intrinsic and extrinsic motivation [17]. Intrinsic motivation is conceptualized as inherently enjoyable experience and driven by psychological need satisfaction. While, extrinsic motivation emphasizes more on external rewards from external environment, which means, people are motivated to complete tasks to other rewards [18]. Intrinsic motivation reflects the natural human propensity that allowing people to perform more productively and efficiently. While, extrinsic motivation, contrasting not always with intrinsic motivation, can be internalized into intrinsic motivation when well-designed, and therefore alters people behavior in expected way [19].

These two classes of motivation relate closely to three human psychological needs (shown as Fig. 1): autonomy, relatedness and competence [19], which can be describes as Fig. 1 [20]. Autonomy is the need to make own choices with freedom, lays the foundation of behavioral and emotional engagement; Competence refers to the need to master learning, hence, it is perceived as the vital basis of cognitive engagement and also offers motivation to behavioral and emotional engagement; Relatedness, generally, is considered as the need to connect with others, which contributes a lot to emotional engagement [11].

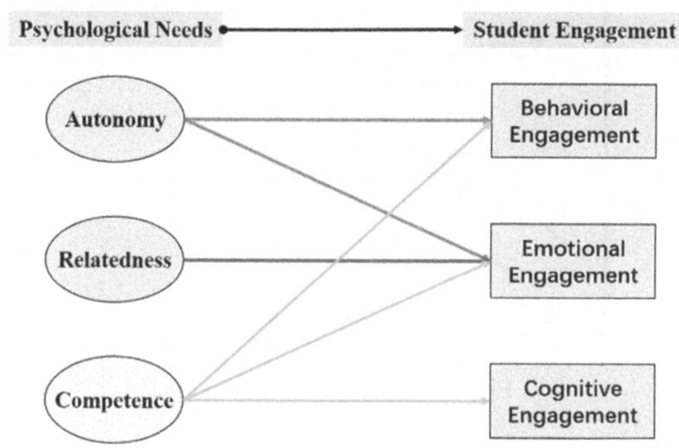

Fig. 1. The relation between motivation and engagement

2.2 Design by Gamification

Gamification is well-known for its mystic power in evoking fabulous feeling of experience [21]. As an academic concept, gamification is "the use of game design elements in non-game contexts" to improve user experience and engagement [22]. The emergence of gamification dates back to 2008, when this concept was employed in digital media industry. It was until the half of 2010 that gamification had received widespread adoption of the public [23]. At present, gamification has been flourishing beyond entertainment business [24], and gradually grabs the attention of school teachers to improve student motivation. Studies report that many university courses have been gamified by adding narrative elements, "experience points and levels" and records of student achievements. These modifications by gamifying make courses more engaging for learners [18].

The core value of gamification is enhancing people's intrinsic motivation through instant feedback in activity. Malone, a distinguished researcher in both game design and motivation, analyzed behaviors in video games and finally constituted three general principles to improve intrinsic motivation: challenge, fantasy, and curiosity [25]. Challenge refers to the goal, uncertain attainment and self-esteem in actual tasks. Fantasy is the imagination of physical environment which can remind people of engaging emotion experience. And curiosity can be divided into two classes: sensory curiosity to attract attention and cognitive curiosity to form better knowledge structure [26]. By applying these principles in design, the activities will be much responsible like gameplaying.

Csikszentmihalyi, from the perspective of interaction, describes how activities make it possible for engaging experience to occur, which is academically known as "flow".

To achieve flow experience, designers should pay high attention in balancing action and skills [27]. Because people are more likely to quit when required higher-level action, and otherwise, people will get bored (depicted as Fig. 2). Besides that, clear goals and responsive feedback inspire the feeling of control, which also contribute to flow experience.

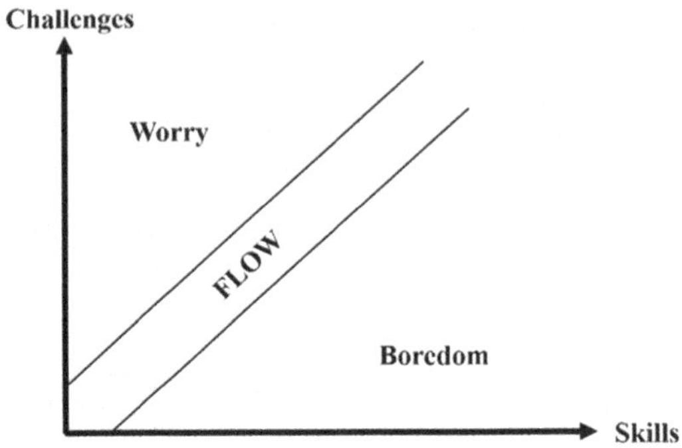

Fig. 2. Model of flow state

3 Limitation of MOOC Videos

3.1 MOOC Overview

"*How to Teach by Gamification*" is a free MOOC produced by *Educational Game Research Group of Peking University*, which is intended for school teachers, especially in elementary schools. In this course, registered students can learn the concept and latest researches of gamification, and how to do instructional design by gamification stepwise in practice. Certainly, students have to complete all of assessment and discussion tasks to attain course certificate.

This MOOC lasts five weeks in total, excepting for the preparation week at the start and final test week in the end. So far, it has been successfully opened twice. The first iteration started in August, 2016, the second iteration began in November, 2016. According to the social background investigation, the majority of registered students in the first irritation are school teachers, and others are game-related university students and product managers.

In contrast with the first irritation, the second one is totally redesigned by gamification in mechanics of MOOC videos. However, even though these two irritations appear completely different at first glance, the knowledge and sequence are all the same, including words spoken by instructors.

3.2 Analysis Framework

Before utilizing gamification design principles to enhance video engagement, it is fundamental to locate exact limitation of current videos in MOOC "*How to Teach by*

Gamification". Here, we adopt MDA framework, a pervasively accepted game design structure, to analyze target videos.

MDA is a formal approach to figuring out how game works, which consists of three core components: *Mechanics*, *Dynamics* and *Aesthetics*. Mechanics refers to a collection of game rules, data and algorithms, which form the core skeleton of game. Dynamics refers to the run-time player inputs and game outputs during interactions. Aesthetics represents the emotional responses of players in gameplay [28].

The working flow of MDA is shown as Fig. 3. From designer's viewpoint, mechanics determine the dynamic interaction system and therefore lead to a particular aesthetic experience. However, from player's view, aesthetic experience comes first, and they are getting close to core mechanics step by step through interacting with dynamics [28].

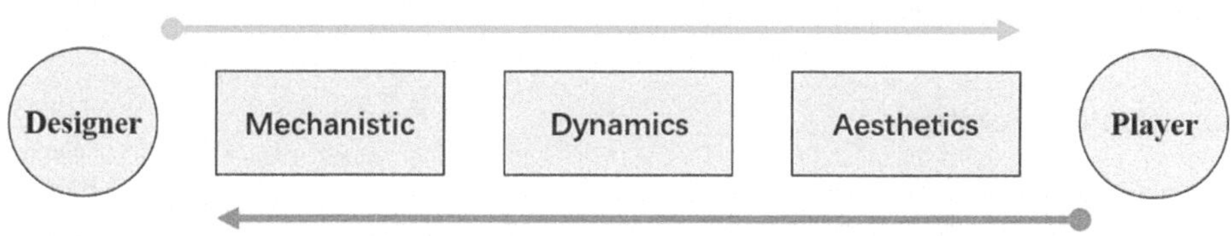

Fig. 3. MDA framework

3.3 MOOC Videos in MDA

On the purpose of redesigning MOOC videos, it is reasonable to conduct analysis from the designer's perspective of MDA. The analysis is carried out as follows.

First, the mechanics of MOOC videos concentrate mainly on the knowledge and sequence, delivering media and self-directed learning. Knowledge and sequence belong to psychological need- competence, which contribute to all three types of engagement. Delivering media, like talking head and PowerPoint slides, is more related to the need-relatedness, which has impact on emotional engagement. And self-directed learning gives students the full right to watch whatever video they would like to, which satisfies their need of autonomy and makes it possible for behavioral and emotional engagement in video watching.

Second, the dynamics of MOOC videos are highly depended in video interfaces, such as play, pause, stop, increase/decrease speed and volume, and toggling to full screen [9]. It is apparent that the dynamic interactions between students and videos are too basic to generate engaging experience.

Finally, the particular aesthetic experience is created for students in MOOC based on first two steps. That is to say, the video engagement relies mainly on the design of mechanics and dynamics.

Figuring out the workflow above, it is obvious that the key to enhance video engagement is scientifically redesigning mechanics and dynamics. Nevertheless, the dynamics of MOOC have already been fixed by MOOC providers, and it is unrealistic for course instructors to add extra functions on existed MOOC platform. In addition, self-determined learning in mechanics is also fixed by MOOC system, which cannot be easily modified by course designers as well.

Considering all of these limitations, the most appropriate way is redesigning mechanics of MOOC videos, in other words, reproducing videos by adding new engaging mechanics or updating existing mechanics to more attractive ones.

4 Improvement of MOOC Videos

Based on the limitation analysis, it is feasible to improve video engagement in MOOCs via two gamification approaches: one is adding new engaging mechanics in MOOC videos; the other is updating existing mechanics to more engaging ones. In the second irritation, therefore, we add implicit feedback into the *knowledge and sequence* mechanics and update the *delivery media* from formal lecture-style to informal narrative-style, which matches the implicit feedback.

4.1 Implicit Feedback

Almost every game has its own well-designed feedback system, such as points, badges and levels. When interaction happens between players and game, feedback system responses quickly to notify players whether they get closer or further to the targeted goal. However, when watching a sequence video lectures, students hardly ever get any responsive feedbacks about learning goals: what kind of benefits can students acquire from achieving goals. That's the reason why it is difficult for students to maintain motivation on video lectures.

Unlike games, MOOC providers only publish the video playing function. Thus, it is impossible to apply explicit feedbacks, like points or badges, into original MOOC systems based on watching times or duration. In view of such facts, we finally choose implicit feedbacks, which means, the learning goals are carefully set based on students' authentic needs in physical world, so that students can easily transfer what they watch to their real work.

Since most of registered students are school teachers, we first analyze the learning needs of school teachers, specially the psychological needs on relatedness and competence in school teaching. Then, we rearrange the learning content in the order of professional development of school teachers. Finally, the learning sequence and goals are structured across two dimensions: competence and relatedness.

4.1.1 Competence

Competence is the core of professional development of school teachers. Teaching by gamification, as an emerging and potential teaching strategy, certainly cannot be mastered overnight. On the basis of the Five-Stage Skill-Acquisition Model [29], we establish a five-level learning sequence: novice, advanced beginner, competence, proficiency and expertise. The learning becomes more demanding as students level up weekly. In this way, students can clearly know where they are in the competence achieving.

Novice. It's the first-level competence in teaching by gamification and arranged in week one. In this level, students need to roughly know the concept and typical cases of gamification.

Advanced beginner. It refers to the second-level competence in teaching by gamification and is shown in week two. In this level, students will get a glance at teaching by gamification.

Competence. Coming into the third-level competence in week three, students start to put teaching-by-gamification strategy individually into some teaching steps, for example, ice-breaking, reviewing, class-exercising.

Proficiency. It's an advanced process after the third-level competence. In week four, students learn how to flexibly integrate teaching-by-gamification strategies with other strategies, for instance, inquiry-based learning, flipped-class leaning and collaborative learning.

Expertise. After previous four-week learning, students finally master teaching-by-gamification. To become expert, students should continue expanding their horizon on gamification and evaluate this strategy by critical thinking, which are the key points in week five.

4.1.2 Relatedness

With the competence improving in reality, people will get more opportunities to expand social network. In the second irritation, students will not only experience the development of competence, but also get to know more people involved and interested in teaching-by-gamification strategy. By means of expanding social network, MOOC students can obtain more emotional engagement based on SDT. And meanwhile, the development of social network is also a kind of emotional feedback for MOOC students, which is more explicit than feedback deriving from competence gaining.

Novice stage. School leader and junior researcher, whom school teachers are most acquainted with at work, share their ideas on how to teach by gamification.

Advanced beginner stage. Product manager, who is specialized in educational game developing, give lectures in the meeting room of his company.

Competence stage. Senior researchers, working in an educational research institute, exchange ideas with students on how to teach by gamification.

Proficiency stage. The leader of the educational game committee, which is an official organization focus on teaching by gamification, shows up and help students comprehend teaching-by-gamification strategy much deeper.

Expertise stage. An authoritative professor in a well-known university, who is an expert in teaching-by-gamification, presents his prospective opinions on educational games and teaching-by-gamification strategy and points out the essence of this research field.

By integrating these two dimensions together, the psychological needs of MOOC students, which contribute to the intrinsic motivation, are well embedded into videos, and also build up the implicit feedback system in the video watching. With no doubt, MOOC students are more likely to engage into watching such responsive MOOC videos.

4.2 Narrative-Style Delivery Media

The production style of most videos published in MOOC providers, currently, can be coded by labels, including slides, code, Khan-style, classroom, studio and office desk [8].

In spite of different production styles, MOOC videos function as a direct knowledge delivery media in nature, which strongly resemble classroom teaching in practice. To enhance engagement, we update the knowledge delivery media by bringing into narrative element.

Narrative, pervasively known as story, indicates a logical sequence of realistic or imaginary events, which is presented by spoken or written words, still photographs or dynamic images [30]. In fact, every narrative can be distinguished as two layers: the level of the world represented in the story (story level) and the level at which this representation takes place (representation level) [31]. In the second irritation, we attempt to wrap narrative element around MOOC videos based on these two layer.

Story level. An overwhelming majority of registered students in MOOC "*How to Teach by Gamification*" are school teachers in physical world. Taking these students' actual demands into consideration, we make up a story about the learning adventure of a female green-hand school teacher (named Teacher Zhang), who exerts great efforts in learning teaching-by-gamification strategy and achieves success eventually. The story begins with a typical conflict between Teacher Zhang and her students, that students have no interest in cramming method of teaching. Teacher Zhang, one day, heard that it is effective to teach by gamification in class. Since then, she set out her journey of learning teaching-by-gamification strategy. Five different plots, in total, are designed in accordance to five-level implicit feedback system. The opening and closure of the narrative are respectively inserted in the beginning of week 1 and end of week 5. And between two neighboring plots, we also design transition videos of "*preview of the next week*"

Table 1. Five different plots in MOOC videos design

Week	Settings	Characters	Events
Week 1	School	School Leader Nie Junior Researcher Pei	Teacher Zhang is frustrated by cramming method of teaching in school and presents interest in teaching-by-gamification
Week 2	Game company	Product Manager Xiao Junior Researcher Pei Company CEO Zhu	Teacher Zhang visits game company
Week 3	Research institute	College Lecturer Qu Senior Researcher Cao	Teacher Zhang attends teacher training program
Week 4	Committee	Committee Leader Jiang Senior Researcher Cao	Teacher Zhang attends lectures in educational game committee
Week 5	University	PhD Candidate Zhang Professor Shang	Teacher Zhang meets the top professor in teaching-by-gamification and finally succeeds

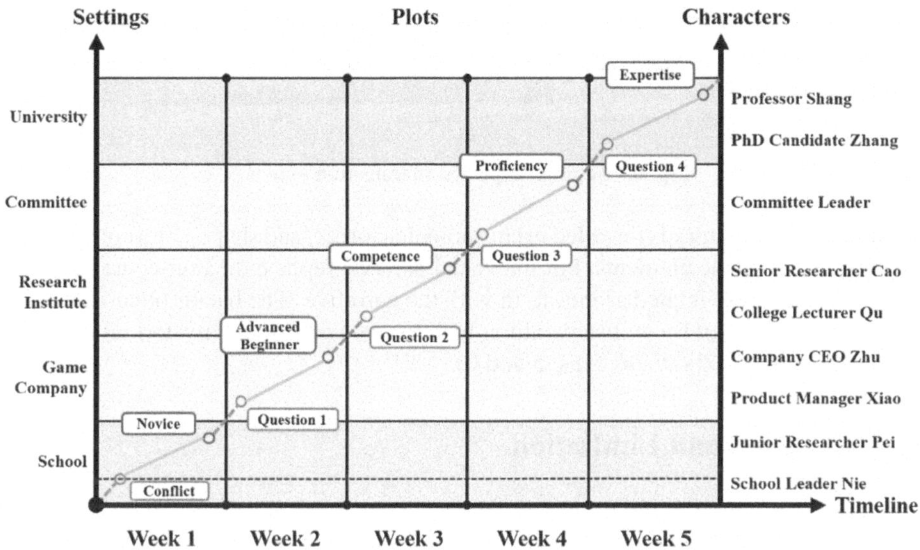

Fig. 4. Five-level plots and its relation with implicit feedback system.

and "*previously on last week*". The logic of story is fully described below in Table 1 and Fig. 4.

Representation level. To engage MOOC students more strongly into the learning adventure of Teacher Zhang, we present this narrative from the first-person perspective, which brings greater focus on the cognition and emotion variation of a particular character and makes it easy for audience to feel the sense of immersion. The figure of the narrator, Teacher Zhang, doesn't appear in videos until the week 5. All of her opinions and feelings about this learning adventure are completely present via her voice-over. In

Fig. 5. Photographic non-context-related VS mouse-painted context-related.

Fig. 6. Settings appeared in transition videos.

addition, the whole story is threaded in chronological order, and shaped by a combination of visual and acoustic elements. For the visual part, we replace the non-context-related settings into context-related scenes to fit with the narrative. The background scenes are entirely accomplished by mouse painting, which create additional mysterious aesthetic feeling for viewers (shown as Figs. 5 and 6).

5 Conclusion and Limitation

In this paper, a gamification design of MOOC videos in "*How to Teach by Gamification*" has been proposed and implemented. By scrutinized analysis of student engagement and gamification related theories (SDT and FLOW) and industry design methods (MDA), we eventually come up with two available approaches to gamify MOOC videos and engage registered students: one is adding implicit feedback into the *knowledge and sequence* mechanics of MOOC videos; the other is updating the existing delivery media from formal lecture-style to informal narrative-style.

To our knowledge, this MOOC is the first gamified online course all over China, which marks a significant step forward in gamification of education. However, more empirical studies are needed to scientifically evaluate the actual effect of this gamification design in MOOC videos.

Acknowledgements. This work has been fully supported by MOE Research Center for Online Education Foundation (Project NO. 2016ZD101). We should also give thanks to Ximei Qu, Minmin Zhong, Yang Zhang, Xiao Ma, Ruonan Hu, YangChunxiao Wang, Xiaowei Zhao and Weijia Jin for video recording and editing in the MOOC, *"How to Teach by Gamification"*.

References

1. Daniel, J.: Making sense of MOOCs: musings in a Maze of Myth, Paradox and possibility. Open Educ. Res. **2012**, 18 (2013)
2. Pappano, L.: The Year of the MOOC. The New York Times (2012)
3. Liu, M., Kang, J., Cao, M., Lim, M., Ko, Y., Myers, R., Weiss, A.S.: Understanding MOOCs as an emerging online learning tool: perspectives from the students. Am. J. Distance Educ. **28**, 147 (2014)
4. Liyanagunawardena, T.R., Adams, A.A., Williams, S.A.: MOOCs: a systematic study of the published literature 2008-2012. Int. Rev. Res. Open Distance Learn. **14**, 202 (2013)
5. Jordan, K.: Initial trends in enrolment and completion of massive open online courses. Int. Rev. Res. Open Distance Learn. **15**, 133 (2014)

6. Coffrin, C., Corrin, L., Barba, P.D., Kennedy, G.: Visualizing patterns of student engagement and performance in MOOCs. In: International Conference on Learning Analytics and Knowledge, vol. 83 (2014)
7. Breslow, L.: Studying learning in the worldwide classroom research into edX's first MOOC. Res. Pract. Assess. **8**, 13 (2013)
8. Guo, P.J., Kim, J., Rubin, R.: How video production affects student engagement: an empirical study of MOOC videos. In: ACM Conference on Learning @ Scale Conference, vol. 43, p. 41 (2014)
9. Goel, A., Chauhan, J.: An analysis of video lecture in MOOC. In: International Conference on ICT in Education, Research and Industrial Applications: Integration, Harmonization and Knowledge Transfer, ICTERI 2015, vol. 1356 (2015)
10. Giannakos, M.N., Jaccheri, L., Krogstie, J.: How video usage styles affect student engagement? Implications for video-based learning environments. In: The International Conference on Smart Learning Environments (2016)
11. Hew, K.F.: Promoting engagement in online courses: what strategies can we learn from three highly rated MOOCS. Br. J. Educ. Technol. **47**, 320 (2016)
12. Freitas, S.I.D., Morgan, J., Gibson, D.: Will MOOCs transform learning and teaching in higher education? Engagement and course retention in online learning provision. Br. J. Educ. Technol. **46**, 455 (2015)
13. Hone, K.S., El Said, G.R.: Exploring the factors affecting MOOC retention: a survey study. Comput. Educ. **98**, 157 (2016)
14. Hew, K.F., Cheung, W.S.: Students' and instructors' use of massive open online courses (MOOCs): motivations and challenges. Educ. Res. Rev. **12**, 45 (2014)
15. Helme, S., Clarke, D.: Cognitive Engagement in the Mathematics Classroom. Springer, Netherlands (2001)
16. Christenson, S.L., Reschly, A.L., Wylie, C.: Handbook of Research on Student Engagement. Springer (2012)
17. Deci, E.L., Ryan, R.M.: Intrinsic Motivation and Self-Determination in Human Behavior. Springer, US (1985)
18. Landers, R.N., Rachel, K.N.B., Armstrong, M.B.: Psychological Theory and the Gamification of Learning. Gamification in Education and Business, 165 p. Springer International Publishing (2015)
19. Ryan, R.M., Deci, E.L.: Intrinsic and extrinsic motivations: classic definitions and new directions. Contemp. Educ. Psychol. **25**, 54 (2000)
20. Hew, K.F.: Towards a model of engaging online students: lessons from MOOCs and four policy documents. Int. J. Inf. Educ. Technol. **5**, 425 (2015)
21. Sailer, M., Hense, J.U., Mayr, S.K., Mandl, H.: How gamification motivates: an experimental study of the effects of specific game design elements on psychological need satisfaction. Comput. Hum. Behav. **69**, 371 (2017)
22. Deterding, S., Khaled, R., Nacke, L., Dan, D.: Gamification: toward a definition. In: CHI 2011 Gamification Workshop Proceedings, vol. 12 (2011)
23. Dyer, R.: A Conceptual Framework for Gamification Measurement. Gamification in Education and Business, 47 p. Springer International Publishing (2015)
24. Curtis, V.: Motivation to participate in an online citizen science game: a study of Foldit. Sci. Commun. **37**, 723 (2015)
25. Malone, T.W.: Toward a theory of intrinsically motivating instruction. Cogn. Sci. **5**, 333 (1981)

26. Malone, T.W.: What makes things fun to learn? Heuristics for designing instructional computer games. In: ACM SIGSMALL Symposium and the First SIGPC Symposium on Small Systems, vol. 162 (1980)
27. Csikszentmihalyi, M.: Flow and the Foundations of Positive Psychology. Springer, Netherlands (2014)
28. Hunicke, R., Leblanc, M., Zubek, R.: MDA: a formal approach to game design and game research. In: Challenges in Games AI Workshop, vol. 1 (2004)
29. Dreyfus, H.L.: The ethical implications of the five-stage skill-acquisition model. Bull. Sci. Technol. Soc. **24**, 251 (2004)
30. Abbott, H.P.: The Cambridge Introduction to Narrative. Cambridge University Press, Cambridge (2002)
31. Fludernik, M.: An Introduction to Narratology. Routledge, London (2009)

Pedagogical and Psychological Issues

A Review on Recent Development of the Involvement Load Hypothesis

Haoran Xie[1], Di Zou[2(✉)], Fu Lee Wang[3], and Tak-Lam Wong[1]

[1] Department of Mathematics and Information Technology, The Education University of Hong Kong, Tai Po, New Territories, Hong Kong
[2] Department of English Language Education, The Education University of Hong Kong, Tai Po, New Territories, Hong Kong
dizoudaisy@gmail.com
[3] Caritas Institute of Higher Education, Tseung Kwan O, New Territories, Hong Kong

Abstract. The Involvement Load Hypothesis, proposed by Laufer and Hulstijn in 2001, has been widely adopted and applied to estimate effectiveness of word-focused tasks in promoting word learning. With the development and shift of learning contexts, models and technologies in the past sixteen years, the involvement load hypothesis has been researched from various aspects. This review investigates the applications and theoretical developments of the hypothesis, focusing on two main areas: examination of the three components of the hypothesis, and comparison or integration of the hypothesis with other hypothesis or theories, for example, the technique feature analysis. Future developments in related fields are also discussed.

Keywords: Involvement Load Hypothesis · Vocabulary learning · Incidental learning · Second language acquisition

1 Introduction and Background

The Involvement Load Hypothesis (ILH), proposed by Laufer and Hulstijn in (2001), has been widely adopted and applied to estimate the effectiveness of word-focused tasks in promoting the learning of target words. The basic idea of this hypothesis is to examine the involvement load induced by each learning task from three dimensions: search, evaluation and need. Search denotes whether a task involves finding the meaning or form of a target word, evaluation is induced when a task requires comparing different target words against a given context or creating original contexts for the target words, and need refers to the motivation of a learner to learn the target words (Hulstijn and Laufer 2001).

The involvement load hypothesis is quite valuable for designing word learning tasks and estimating their effectiveness in facilitating vocabulary acquisition (Eckerth and Tavakoli 2012; Lu 2013). With the development and shift of learning contexts, models and technologies in the past sixteen years, the involvement load hypothesis has been researched from various aspects. This review investigates the applications and theoretical developments of the hypothesis, focusing on two main areas: examination of the three components of the hypothesis, and comparison or integration of the hypothesis with other

S.K.S. Cheung et al. (Eds.): ICBL 2017, LNCS 10309, pp. 447–452, 2017.
DOI: 10.1007/978-3-319-59360-9_39

hypothesis or theories, for example, the technique feature analysis. Future developments in related fields are also discussed. There are several studies (Kim 2011; Eckerth and Tavakoli 2012; Lu 2013; Huang and Lin 2014; Zou 2016; Zou 2017; Lee and Pulido 2017) along the first research direction. Kim (2011) investigated the impact of learner proficiency on the ILH by conducting the experiments on English-as-a-second-language learners at two different proficiency levels (i.e., matriculated undergraduate students vs. students in an Intensive English Program). The findings of the experiments indicated that (i) a higher level of learner involvement during task performance promoted more effective initial learning and retention of target words; (ii) different tasks with the same involvement load resulted in a similar amount of vocabulary learning; and (iii) as long as L2 learners' cognitive and language abilities allow them to complete vocabulary tasks in a given time, a deeper level of processing of the new words, especially the evaluation component of task-induced involvement during tasks, promotes better L2 vocabulary learning (Kim 2011). Eckerth and Tavakoli (2012) studied the differential effects of the variables 'word exposure frequency' and 'elaboration of word processing' on the initial word learning and subsequent word retention of advanced English learners, and found equal effects of both variables on initial word learning, but subsequent word retention was more contingent on elaborate processing of form–meaning relationships than on word frequency. Lu (2013) examined the effectiveness of four vocabulary tasks (i.e., single blank filling, triple blank filling, blank filling of a summary, and summary writing) in promoting the learning of meanings and forms of nine newly learned words and using them to generate original sentences. Huang and Lin (2014) compared the three approaches (the inference-gloss-gloss condition, the gloss-retrieval-gloss condition and the full glossing condition) to glossing and their effects on vocabulary learning. Zou (2016) compared two typical approaches to search: dictionary consultation and inferencing, and found that dictionary consultation was significantly more effective than inferencing although they were supposed to promote similarly effective word learning according to the original matrix of the involvement load hypothesis. A possible extension of the search component of the hypothesis was therefore indicated. Zou (2017) proposed an augmented evaluation framework based on the involvement load hypothesis, further classifying it by employing psychological and cognitive terms like chunking and hierarchical organization, and suggested an additional degree of prominence for evaluation so as to obtain a more precise measurement of the involvement load of a word learning task. Compared to the matrix of the original model which allocates two degrees of prominence to the evaluation component: moderate when comparisons of word meanings or forms are involved and strong when generation of original contexts is induced, Zou's (2017) extension is more accurate while assessing the effectiveness of a certain task. Her extended evaluation component further takes the associations among various learner-generated contexts into account and suggests that "evaluation induced by cloze-exercises be allocated with 'moderate evaluation' as it involves no use of chunking, hierarchical organization or pre-task planning, evaluation induced by sentence-writing with 'strong evaluation' as it involves chunking and pre-task planning at the sentence level, and evaluation induced by composition-writing with 'very strong evaluation' for it involves chunking, hierarchical organization and pre-task planning at the composition level" (Zou 2017, p. 1). Lee and Pulido (2017) investigated the impact of topic interest, alongside L2 proficiency and gender, on L2 vocabulary acquisition through reading. The findings of this study indicated that there may be another way, which involves high-level and low-level interests in the topics of learning materials, to distinguish different degrees of prominence of the need component of the ILH.

Another stream of studies (Haratmeh 2012; Chen and Yang 2013; Khoii and Sharififar 2013; Fatalaki 2014; Hu and Nassaji 2016; Ansarin and Bayazidi 2016) focuses on the comparison or integration of the hypothesis with other hypothesis or theories concerning word learning. Haratmeh (2012) attempted to study the relative effectiveness of tasks with different involvement loads on both receptive and productive vocabulary knowledge of learners, and argued that involvement load is not the only determining factor for estimating task effectiveness, but input/output-orientation of tasks is also a decisive parameter in task effectiveness. Khoii and Sharififar (2013) studied the effects of two cognitive strategies, rote memorization and semantic mapping which can be integrated in the ILH, on vocabulary acquisition. Chen and Yang (2013) examined the influence of a commercial adventure video game on foreign language learning and suggested that adventure video games can provide useful input to help college students enhance their English listening, reading, vocabulary skills and learning motivation. Fatalaki (2014) investigated which modality has greater effect on task involvement load through examining word learning of Iranian Intermediate EFL learners while doing listening and reading tasks. The impact of modality-based activities was discussed. Hu and Nassaji (2016) compared two frameworks which operationalize the construct of elaborate processing of L2 vocabulary learning: Involvement Load Hypothesis (ILH) and Technique Feature Analysis (TFA), the results of which showed that the TFA had a better explanatory power in predicting vocabulary learning gains than the ILH. In addition, Ansarin and Bayazidi (2016) investigated the facilitative effects of repetition and the relationships between repetition and task-induced involvement load, and suggested that incidental vocabulary learning is more affected by repetition of encounters than by elaboration of meanings.

2 Comparison Framework

The comparison framework of extant studies is consisted of three parts: classification of generic approaches, the research focus of different studies (i.e., which of the three components of the ILH is mainly investigated), and the related theoretical frameworks.

2.1 Classification of Generic Approaches

In this subsection, the extant studies will be classified according to their generic approaches. There are mainly three categories of methodologies which are widely adopted in educational research.

- **Positivism.** The approaches of this category are empirical and quantitative in nature. The results are obtained through comparing the performance of different groups of participants in various experimental settings (Goldin 2000; Cohen et al. 2013).
- **Interpretivism.** The approaches following the interpretivism use the case study paradigm to obtain better understanding of individuals first, and then draw some

portraits under the research contexts (Heshusius and Ballard 1996). Qualitative evidence are the main focus of the studies in this category.

- **Critical theory.** The critical social theory is concerned in particular with issues of power and justice and the ways that the economy; matters of race, class and gender; ideologies; discourses; education; religion and other social institutions; and cultural dynamics interact to construct a social system (Young 1990; Kincheloe and McLaren 2002) (Table 1).

Table 1. The classification of the ILH related studies

Research studies	Classification
Kim (2011)	Positivism
Haratmeh (2012)	Positivism
Eckerth and Tavakoli (2012)	Positivism
Lu (2013)	Positivism
Chen and Yang (2013)	Positivism
Khoii and Sharififar (2013)	Positivism
Huang and Lin (2014)	Positivism
Fatalaki (2014)	Positivism
Hu and Nassaji (2016)	Positivism
Zou (2016)	Positivism + Interpretivism
Ansarin and Bayazidi (2016)	Positivism
Zou (2017)	Positivism + Interpretivism
Lee and Pulido (2017)	Positivism

As shown in Table 2, the extant studies mainly follow the positivism as their research methodology. A few studies adopt a hybrid framework which includes both positivism and interpretivism. In addition, we can observe that no studies use critical theory.

Table 2. The research focus of different studies

Need	Search	Evaluation
Lee and Pulido (2017)	Huang and Lin (2014) Zou (2016)	Kim (2011) Eckerth and Tavakoli (2012) Lu (2013) Zou (2017)

2.2 The Research Focus of Different Studies

Concerning the research focus of different studies (i.e., which of the three components of the ILH is mainly investigated), we categorized the main studies on the involvement load hypothesis into three groups as follows.

There is only one study on the need component, so far as we know. Lee and Pulido (2017) suggested an expansion of need after investigating the impact of topic interest on vocabulary acquisition. Two studies, Huang and Lin (2014) and Zou (2016) examined the search component, and proposed possible development of this dimension. More researchers are interested in the evaluation component, for example, Kim (2011), Eckerth and Tavakoli (2012), Lu (2013) and Zou (2017). They inspected the effectiveness of different approaches to evaluation and provided suggestions for potential extension of the involvement load hypothesis.

2.3 The Related Theoretical Frameworks

In this subsection, we summarize the related theoretical frameworks of the studies (Haratmeh 2012; Chen and Yang 2013; Khoii and Sharififar 2013; Fatalaki 2014; Hu and Nassaji 2016; Ansarin and Bayazidi 2016) that focus on the comparison or integration of the hypothesis with other hypothesis or theories. As shown in Table 3, various related theoretical frameworks, such as the Input Hypothesis (Krashen 1989), the Output Hypothesis (Swain 1993), and the Technique Feature Analysis (Nation and Web 2011) have been compared to the involvement load hypothesis. Such a diversity of theoretical frameworks indicates a wide research field in the integration of the ILH with other theories.

Table 3. The related theoretical frameworks

Research studies	Theoretical frameworks
Haratmeh (2012)	Input & output hypothesis
Chen and Yang (2013)	Game-based learning
Khoii and Sharififar (2013)	Semantic mapping
Fatalaki (2014)	Task modality
Ansarin and Bayazidi (2016)	Repetition theory
Hu and Nassaji (2016)	Technique feature analysis

3 Conclusion

In this paper, we reviewed recent studies on the involvement load hypothesis. We focuse on two main areas: examination of the three components of the hypothesis, and comparison or integration of the hypothesis with other hypothesis or theories. Our comparison framework is consisted of three parts: classification of generic approaches, the research focus of different studies (i.e., which of the location in three components of the ILH is mainly investigated), and the related theoretical framework. This review is likely to shed light on future research on the involvement load hypothesis and in the fields related to vocabulary acquisition.

Acknowledgment. The work described in this paper was fully supported by a grant from the Research Grants Council of the Hong Kong Special Administrative Region, China (UGC/FDS11/E06/14). This article is based on part of Haoran Xie's course essay (EDUCD0011 Understanding Educational Research) for the fulfillment of the Doctor of Education programme, which was submitted to University of Bristol in 2017.

References

Ansarin, A.A., Bayazidi, A.: Task type and incidental L2 vocabulary learning: repetition versus task involvement load. South. Afr. Linguist. Appl. Lang. Stud. **34**(2), 135–146 (2016)

Chen, H.J.H., Yang, T.Y.C.: The impact of adventure video games on foreign language learning and the perceptions of learners. Interact. Learn. Environ. **21**(2), 129–141 (2013)

Cohen, L., Manion, L., Morrison, K.: Research Methods in Education. Routledge, New York (2013)

Eckerth, J., Tavakoli, P.: The effects of word exposure frequency and elaboration of word processing on incidental L2 vocabulary acquisition through reading. Lang. Teach. Res. **16**, 227–252 (2012)

Fatalaki, J.A.: Involvement load hypothesis: word meaning retention across oral and written task types. Int. Lett. Soc. Humanistic Sci. **37**, 29–45 (2014)

Goldin, G.A.: A scientific perspective on structured, task-based interviews in mathematics education research (2000)

Haratmeh, M.S.: Involvement load and task type in task effectiveness: two aspects of vocabulary knowledge. Int. J. Acad. Res. **4**(4), 86–95 (2012)

Heshusius, L., Ballard, K. (eds.): From Positivism to Interpretivism and Beyond: Tales of Transformation in Educational and Social Research (the Mind-Body Connection). Teachers College Press (1996)

Huang, L.L., Lin, C.C.: Three approaches to glossing and their effects on vocabulary learning. System **44**, 127–136 (2014)

Hulstijn, H., Laufer, B.: Some empirical evidence for the involvement load hypothesis in vocabulary acquisition. Lang. Learn. **51**, 539–558 (2001)

Hu, H.C.M., Nassaji, H.: Effective vocabulary learning tasks: involvement load hypothesis versus technique feature analysis. System **56**, 28–39 (2016)

Khoii, R., Sharififar, S.: Memorization versus semantic mapping in L2 vocabulary acquisition. ELT J. **67**(2), 199–209 (2013)

Kincheloe, J.L., McLaren, P.: Rethinking critical theory and qualitative research. In: Ethnography and Schools: Qualitative Approaches to the Study of Education, pp. 87–138 (2002)

Kim, Y.: The role of task-induced involvement and learner proficiency in L2 vocabulary acquisition. Lang. Learn. **61**(s1), 100–140 (2011)

Krashen, S.: We acquire vocabulary and spelling by reading: additional evidence for the input hypothesis. Mod. Lang. J. **73**(4), 440–464 (1989)

Lee, S., Pulido, D.: The impact of topic interest, L2 proficiency, and gender on EFL incidental vocabulary acquisition through reading. Lang. Teach. Res. **21**(1), 118–135 (2017)

Lu, M.: Effects of four vocabulary exercises on facilitating learning vocabulary meaning, form, and use. TESOL Q. **47**, 167–176 (2013)

Nation, I.S., Webb, S.A.: Researching and Analyzing Vocabulary. Cengage Learning, Heinle (2011)

Swain, M.: The output hypothesis: just speaking and writing aren't enough. Can. Mod. Lang. Rev. **50**(1), 158–164 (1993)

Young, R.E.: A critical theory of education: Habermas and our children's future (1990)

Zou, D.: Vocabulary acquisition through cloze exercises, sentence-writing and composition-writing: Extending the evaluation component of the involvement load hypothesis. Lang. Teach. Res. **21**(1), 54–75 (2017)

Zou, D.: Comparing dictionary-induced vocabulary learning and inferencing in the context of reading. Lexikos **26**(1), 372–390 (2016)

A Curriculum Design to Cultivate Creative Thinking Through Educational Games

Sijie Ma[1], Junjie Shang[1(✉)], and Haiming Xiao[2]

[1] Graduate School of Education, Peking University, Beijing 100871, China
{masijie,jjshang}@pku.edu.cn
[2] Boyat (Beijing) Culture Technology Co., Ltd., Beijing 100871, China
haiming-1990@163.com

Abstract. As creativity is important for innovation and future success in the global competition, the cultivation of students' creative thinking has been a heated research topic in the field of education. Educational games can effectively support teaching and learning in many ways, and this paper presents a curriculum design with game-based learning. On the basis of this curriculum, the topic of balance between education and entertainment in gamed-based learning curriculum design, and the six principles on curriculum design for cultivating creative thinking through educational games have been discussed.

Keywords: Creative thinking · Educational games · Curriculum design

1 Introduction

Creative thinking is one of the core competitiveness for students to be successful in the modern society. Worldwide, people are aware of the issues when it comes to preparing the next generation for a changing future. Both educators and researchers have been working hard to find possible ways to cultivate students' creativity. However, games do provide them with a source of inspiration.

The digital native, especially when we refer to the generation born after 2000, grow up and live a life with rich media and digital devices all around. Students are familiar with games, and many of them are fond of playing different kinds of games. As educational games began to emerge and become popular in recent years, it is accepted gradually that games can be not only entertaining, but also instructive. Students learn academic content and new skills from games, some of which might be achieved better than learning in traditional teaching approach.

In the United States, educational games have attracted much attention as a new way of teaching and learning. The National STEM Game Design Challenge for increasing students' learning interest in science, technology, engineering and math, as well as improving their innovation and collaboration skills, was launched in September, 2010. Quest Atlantis, the educational game developed by Sasha Barab, professor of Indiana University, has been registered by thousands of students around the world since it was released for free in 2002. Teachers in the United State, Australia, Singapore, Denmark and other countries have used it in teaching. More than 50,000 global students have

S.K.S. Cheung et al. (Eds.): ICBL 2017, LNCS 10309, pp. 453–463, 2017.
DOI: 10.1007/978-3-319-59360-9_40

finished 50,000 quests and more than 100,000 tasks. With government support, the scientific research on educational game theory and practice has been flourishing.

Educational games provide ill-structured problem solving situations and open space for students to explore. They need to think deeply, challenging the existing knowledge and experience, which helps to improve their innovative thinking and problem solving skills. Research into this problem has identified several areas, including the concept of creative thinking, the value of educational games, as well as the assessment of game-based learning. Based on perception, memory, thinking, association, and understanding, creative thinking is the activity that people come up with new ideas during learning and research process. It is the advanced procedure developed on the basis of human general thinking. The core factor of innovation ability lies in creative thinking, which is of great importance in problem solving process. A comparison study focused on the effect of educational games on improving students' creativity was conducted by Eow et al. Results show that students who learn by playing educational games perform better on the Khatena-Torrance Creative Perception Inventory, which means game-based learning is more effective on the cultivation of creativity than the traditional way, though it doesn't work as for increasing students' confidence [1]. Educational experiments have been conducted to study how educational games support teaching and learning. Results show that educational games are effective tools for construction of meaning and creative learning, as games encourage students to use prior knowledge and help to make connection with new knowledge. And self-designed games are more challenging and competitive, which motivate students to learn intrinsically [2].

How to cultivate students' creative thinking with the help of educational games? Internationally, the two approaches to creative thinking cultivation are learning in games and learning about games.

Learning in games refers to that researchers develop or choose the games supporting students as learning environment, and students are immersed in it learning knowledge, skills, and reconstructing understanding. Computer games and traditional games are both included. Clements [3] evaluated the impact of LOGO, which is the programming environment developed for students to learning programming, and found that LOGO has improved students' creativity significantly. Subhi [4] concluded that LOGO had positive effect on students' creative thinking after reviewing researches on the application of LOGO in teaching and learning before 1999.

Learning about games refers to developing games to cultivate students' creativity. Researchers provide students with game-developing tools and encourage them to develop games individually or in group, so as to improve creativity. Some courses are based on a particular subject while some are game developing curriculum. Cheng [5] analyzed students' learning effect in interactive multimedia curriculum with game making pedagogy, and results show that this pedagogy model is effective to help students improve problem solving skills and creative thinking, stimulate and maintain their learning motivation as well.

This paper is taking an integrated approach towards creative thinking, which is designing the game-based learning curriculum, Cultivating Creative Thinking through Educational Games. This curriculum with sixteen lessons is designed mainly for primary school students aged from ten to twelve years old. The curriculum objectives, the curriculum content with a sample lesson, the interpretation of game-based learning, the instructional strategy, and the experimental research of this curriculum construct the body of this paper. After discussing the topic on the balance between education and entertainment in game-based learning curriculum design, the six basic principles on curriculum design for cultivating creative thinking through educational games are described in the last part of this paper.

2 Curriculum Design for Cultivating Creative Thinking Through Educational Games

2.1 The Curriculum Objectives

Creative thinking is a comprehensive ability that involves knowledge, intelligence, attitude, and social and cultural environment. It takes longer time to accumulate and practice creative thinking skills. This curriculum is not only aiming at improving students' creativity, but also teaching students the way of how to learn creativity.

The curriculum objectives are as follows:

(1) Students understand the basic concept of creative thinking and subordinate skills.
(2) Students develop a sense of innovation as well as creativity tendency.
(3) Improve students' learning interest and motivate them to learn.
(4) Students master the basic skills of game-developing and are able to develop games with tools.

2.2 The Curriculum Content

This curriculum consists of four relevant modules, including the introduction to creative thinking, the basic training of creative thinking, the advanced training of creative thinking, and the comprehensive training of creative thinking. These modules comply with the instructional mode of creative problem solving process, which was edited by Isaksen and Treffinger in 1991. The creation process is divided into three main compositions with six steps as Fig. 1 shows below. The first part is understanding the problem, including three steps that are mess-finding, data-finding, and problem-finding. The second part is generating ideas, including the step of idea-finding. And the third part is planning for action, including two steps, solution-finding and acceptance-finding. Each part or step is essential in creative activities.

Parts	Steps
Understanding the problem	Mess-finding
	Data-finding
	Problem-finding
Generating ideas	Idea-finding
Planning for action	Solution-finding
	Acceptance-finding

Fig. 1. The instructional mode of creative problem solving process

As divergent thinking is the core of creative problem solving, it directs thinking towards the contrary of traditional concepts and to challenge old ideas [6]. Since there has been sufficient training of convergent thinking in students' daily learning, this curriculum suggests that the training of divergent thinking should be particularly emphasized. Besides divergent thinking, there are some other ways of thinking that are considered to have potentials to produce creative ideas such as horizontal thinking, reverse thinking, and lateral thinking. These ways of thinking support the problem solving process with techniques and methods from different dimensions and directions. For the above reasons, this curriculum starts with the cultivation of fundamental observation ability and memory ability, and proceeds with the integration of divergent thinking, horizontal thinking, reverse thinking, and lateral thinking. Figure 2 shows the sample training program of the curriculum design in general, and it takes about one lesson for each game or activity to be finished.

Module	Aimed Skills	Games or Activities Recommended
Introduction to creative thinking	No particular	Crayon Physics, Draw the Matchstick Men
		RGP Maker
Basic training of creative thinking	Observation	Mysteries House
		Find Fault
	Memory	Crazy Ball
		Memorize the Chess Map
Advanced training of creative thinking	Reverse thinking	The Hardest Game
		Think in Reverse
	Horizontal thinking	Rory's Cubes
		Six Thinking Hats
	Lateral thinking	Scientist Mash-up
		Random Quiz
Comprehensive training of creative thinking	Thematic story design	Theme and question
		Prototype and game
	Game development	Conversation
		Scene change

Fig. 2. The training program of the curriculum design

Here is a sample lesson on divergent thinking training with Crayon Physics. This is a 2D physics puzzle/sandbox game, in which players get to experience what it would be like if their drawings would be magically transformed into real physical objects. Players need to move the ball to touch the star so as to proceed. In this lesson, students are encouraged to come up with as many solutions as they can in one game (Fig. 3).

Ways of Thinking	Screen Shot
Regular thinking. Most students get passed in this way.	
Reverse thinking. Encourage students to think if they can move the ball from the left side.	
Horizontal thinking. Encourage students to think how to use the triangle bracket to get passed.	
Lateral thinking. Encourage students to make use of math knowledge they learned, such as a line is defined by two dots.	

Fig. 3. Different ways of thinking and the results of it in a game of Crayon Physics

Each game of Crayon Physics is an open-ended problem. In order to pass it, students have to think of solutions based on their prior knowledge. Although they may remember one solution already, this lesson encourages students to put forward more solutions. For divergent thinking, students may use horizontal thinking, reverse thinking, and lateral thinking as different ways to solve the problem creatively.

2.3 The Interpretation of Game-Based Learning

Based on the previous work done by our research team, this paper holds two different views on the cultivation of students' creativity with game-based learning. One view takes educational games as tools that support teaching, while the other integrates designed game mechanics into the curriculum.

Educational games can support teaching in several parts, including the introduction, situational simulation, drill practice, and comprehensive applications. In this curriculum, for example, the game Think in Reverse is used for leading in, and motivates students to learn. Situational simulation games are where students choose to play different roles, as this type of games helps to think over a problem from other aspects. The game Memorize the Chess Map is used for practice the knowledge just learned. And the famous classic comprehensive game Crayon Physics can be used either for increasing students' motivation or drill practice.

As for the game mechanics, points, badges, and leaderboards are mostly and widely used in daily practice. These elements are helpful to motivate students, so the learning tasks get some points for reward in each lesson. When the group's points reach a certain number of level, the group will get promoted. In the curriculum, each level is named after students' favorite characters in the famous traditional Chinese story. Although the rule of points and reward has been set before class, the teacher could adjust the rule based on specific conditions with flexibility.

2.4 The Instructional Strategy

One strategy is to reward curiosity and the thirst for knowledge. Curiosity is one of the essential factors in the expression of creativity. The ability to see things differently, especially from an original or unconventional perspective, the willingness and ability to change personal view, and to re-examine the problem in time, these are all important aspects of creative thinking emphasized by researchers. Therefore, curiosity is the emotional element of creativity that needs to stimulate firstly.

The core feature of game is entertaining, which means the fun and attraction of playing games. On one hand, games provide an open and safe virtual environment for learning, while making students curious about the curriculum and creativity. On the other hand, games can convey a way of thinking. When students play Crayon Physics, they might learn some physics knowledge. And when a student comes across similar mechanisms in daily life, he or she might try it in the game next time. Games help to lead the curiosity to life out of class, which is the significance of games in the curriculum. According to Csikszentmihalyi [7], there are two contradictory directives inside each human. One is the conservative tendency consisting of self-protection instinct, self-expansion instinct and energy-saving instinct. Another is the tendency to expand, and it consists of instincts such as interest for inquiry, novelty and adventure. However, the motivation to do creative activities will be suppressed if it lacks chances for curiosity to play a role. Therefore, there is reward but no punishment in this curriculum and every creative work deserves a reward during the learning process.

The other strategy is to provide opportunities for choice and discovery. Research has found that people are more intrinsically motivated if the work is chosen by themselves, compared to work chosen by others or work they are forced to do. Students usually deal with problems mostly chosen by others other than themselves at school. But if they are allowed to make their own choice and decide which problem is the first to deal with, they can develop the potential of creativity. As Finke stated [8], it is an important means to promote creativity by providing students with the opportunity to make a real discovery. For this consideration, two dimension of the instructional strategy is designed in this curriculum. The first dimension is the design of curriculum content. Based on the creative problem solving model, the module of introduction to creative thinking consisting of two lessons for students to learn problem finding. They can find problems by themselves out of class with what they have learned in class. The second dimension is the task-oriented learning method of this curriculum. Students have to finish a thematic campus design and use RPG Maker to present. This task is open-ended which allows for personal choice and creation.

2.5 The Experimental Research of the Curriculum

To implement the curriculum, our research team has conducted a quasi-experiment at a primary school in Beijing. A class of 21 students participate in the pre-test while 16 of them (4 girls and 12 boys) has finished the experiment. Most of the students have rich experience in playing games and all of them are able to operate computers, which reach the basic requirements of the course. Students complete the Williams Creativity Tendency Scale and the Creative Thinking Measurement Scale before class and do these two scales again after the course teaching based on the curriculum design.

The results of paired samples T test in creative thinking, creative personality, and learning motivation of students show that the course can increase students' curiosity and make them love challenges more. It also finds that the students who care more about the performance in knowledge learning show less curiosity in exploring the unknown. Otherwise, students who are in higher level of motivation to success give worse comment on the course. Based on these findings, this paper comes up with six basic principles of designing game-based curriculum for cultivating students' creative thinking, which will be discussed in the last part of this paper.

3 The Balance Between Education and Entertainment in Game-Based Learning Curriculum Design

When using educational games to cultivate students' creative thinking, the game-based learning curriculum design has to take the factors of both education and entertainment into account. Many educational game researchers and front-line teachers are concerning about the question that how to balance between education and entertainment. Followings are suggestions from this curriculum.

3.1 Educational Games Should Meet the Curriculum Objectives

This paper suggests that educational games are games with educational value, including the ones based on curriculum guidelines as well as developed for commercial purposes. However, from the theory and practice of educational game research currently, it can be concluded that the independent design and development of educational games cost too much and take longer time, which will be hard to benefit scientific research. Therefore, choosing the off-the-shelf games meeting with the curriculum objectives is a better choice for research.

Education is in the first place of consideration when choosing educational games, in other words, we should consider how much is the game fit for the curriculum objectives. It is accepted by researchers and practitioners that educational games do not work well under some learning circumstances. If we choose a game without thinking about the curriculum objectives, but for adding to teaching or trying a new media, it will never reach the balance between education and entertainment.

3.2 Educational Games Should Consider Students' Cognitive Load

Considering students' cognitive load means we should choose the educational game that fits cognitive characteristics. If the game exceeds students' cognitive load, like being too complex to operate, it will have side effect on the achievement of instructional objectives and damage the entertainment of the game at the same time. All the educational games used in this curriculum are quick to get started for the targeted students. Take this game, Think in Reverse, as an example. Students only need to move the mouse to complete the game, and the game perfectly reflects the concept of reverse thinking. On the one hand, it stimulates students' interest in learning, on the other hand, students have a chance to experience reverse thinking.

3.3 Entertainment Lies in the Applying of Educational Games and the Design of Game Mechanics

There are two ways for the curriculum to cultivate creative thinking through educational games, as entertainment lies in the applying of educational games and the design of game mechanics. A well-designed game mechanic can turn the boring educational activity to an entertaining learning experience. The games in this curriculum bring game elements to the traditional classroom, such as earning points and using random cards. These features appeal to students and engage them to learn and play with initiative.

3.4 Reflection Is a Way to Balance Education and Entertainment

It is a good habit to reflect in learning. Reflection facilitates students to think out of the game and get back to knowledge and method when they learn creative thinking with educational games. Students are fully immersed in game when they are playing. But if it goes too far, the learning will be prone to be inefficient. This is where the teacher is needed. The teacher leads student to reflect and summarize, which will ensure students still adhere to learning during their playing. There is a session for reflection after each game-playing on this curriculum. Students are asked to share the questions they found during their playing or along the game process, and these inspire everyone to think deeply in mind. However, it is demanding for teachers to organize the reflection session. As teachers should not only take the pace of a class and know when it is time to move on, but also be aware of students' problems and ask them what they have learned in the game.

4 The Six Basic Principles on Curriculum Design for Cultivating Creative Thinking Through Educational Games

4.1 Define Creative Thinking Skill Training and Creative Personality Building in Terms of Curriculum Concept

As for the curriculum concept, it is necessary to define clearly the cultivation of creative thinking as creative thinking skill training and creative personality building, and the output of students' creative products should be emphasized, which is the ultimate representation of creative thinking. During school education, students' creative thinking is mainly manifested in the fluency, novelty, and suitability of problem finding, problem analyzing and problem solving. Creative thinking is related to certain learning activities and has special methods and tools [9]. Students can learn it and get improved by specific training. Creative personality is the inner motivation of creative thinking. Only when students are encouraged to innovate and make it a habit to think creatively, can they produce creative outputs after finding, analyzing, and solving problems in a novel and unique way.

4.2 Design Reasonable Game Mechanics for the Curriculum and Remain Flexible

The points of students' task performance in game-based learning are immediate feedback which motivates students to learn. The leaderboards help to enhance the sense of competition among students, and encourage them to fully reach their learning potentials. The badges can visualize learning process and students' progress, strengthen the sense of identity, and improve understanding on the importance of success. These core elements of game mechanics should be consistent with each other, as to ensure the equity of game mechanics in the curriculum.

As teachers and students interact in teaching and learning, the game-based activities are dynamic process that produces generative resources. The teacher should modify the game reward level based on students' performance during the interaction so as to engage students in learning.

4.3 Set Observable and Operational Curriculum Objectives

The curriculum objectives should be observable and operational learning objectives, so that students have a clear expectation on their learning outcomes. For the curriculum of cultivating creative thinking, the learning objectives include understanding the definition and assessment of creative thinking, mastering useful creative thinking methods such as the Six Thinking Hats and Brainstorming, using related tools to present creative thinking process, as well as designing and developing creative products like games with game-developing tools. Learning with clear goals helps students to find the right road to move forward. When they realize the progress they are making step by step, the intrinsic motivation will be increased accordingly.

4.4 Arrange More Engaging Learning Activities for Curriculum Content

The curriculum emphasizes that students experience creative thinking by themselves and get trained in participation, with fewer requirements on the definition or basic theory of creative thinking. As the curriculum is designed for primary school students in senior grades, it is more effective for them to learn creative thinking in games or other learning activities. For example, discussion topics like how many ways to use a paperclip or a pencil, how to design better envelope, inspire them to ask why and come up with new ideas. By this way can they experience the fluency, novelty, and suitability of creative thinking. Students learn creative thinking methods from educational games and other learning tasks. They get to know how to visualize their thinking and use tools to develop games. In a word, students master creative thinking skills and develop creative personality through participatory learning.

4.5 Choose Appropriate Media Resources for the Curriculum

As for the media resources used in the curriculum, it is better to choose imaginative pictures, easy-to-operate educational games also meeting the curriculum objectives. And education is the primary factor to considerate.

There are three types of media resources used in game-based learning curriculum that cultivates creative thinking, the pictures, the games, and the videos. For pictures, the abstract pictures encouraging students' divergent thinking are recommended. Since educational games are the main media resources in the curriculum of cultivating creative thinking, the games for primary school students should be easy to operate, and try to avoid the side effect on the curriculum objectives. As a higher order thinking, creative thinking is developed on the basis of simple thinking. The educational games for creative thinking skills should also support the basic skills and keep small steps in training.

4.6 Create a Good Learning Atmosphere Through Proper Teaching Methods

It is necessary to provide students with free, open and safe classroom atmosphere during teaching and learning. The teacher should keep the balance between a lively class and a disciplined class. If there are too many rules, teaching will be dull; but few rules, learning will be inefficient.

When it comes to questions, the teacher should prepare questions for individual thinking and group discussion in proper proportion. Given the difficulty of getting everyone fully participated in group discussion during classroom teaching as well as the collaboration skill level of primary school students, they need teacher's instruction with more practice in order to improve group discussion. For teacher questioning and students think individually, this kind of classroom participation will benefit most of the students if the teacher pays attention to the quiet students and engage more of them in active learning.

Acknowledgements. This work has been supported by Key project of The Beijing 13th Five Year Plan in 2016 for Education Science (No. CAHA16052) and Emergency Management Project of National Natural Science Foundation of China in 2016 (No. L1624017).

References

1. Eow, Y.L., Ali, W.Z.B.W., Mahmud, R.B., Baki, R.: Computer games development and appreciative learning approach in enhancing students' creative perception. Comput. Educ. **54** (1), 146–161 (2010)
2. Vos, N., Meijden, H.V.D., Denessen, E.: Effects of constructing versus playing an educational game on student motivation and deep learning strategy use. Comput. Educ. **56**(1), 127–137 (2011)
3. Clements, D.H., Gullo, D.F.: Effects of computer programming on young children's cognition. J. Educ. Psychol. **76**(6), 1051–1058 (1984)
4. Subhi, T.: The impact of LOGO on gifted children's achievement and creativity. J. Comput. Assist. Learn. **15**(2), 98–108 (1999)
5. Cheng, G.: Using game making pedagogy to facilitate student learning of interactive multimedia. Australas. J. Educ. Technol. **25**(2), 204–220 (2009)
6. He K.: Modern educational technology and the innovative cultivation of talents. e-Education Res. 06, 3–7 (2000)
7. Csikszentmihalyi, M.: Creativity: flow and the psychology of discovery and invention. Adult Educ. Q. 43(12), 823–824. (1997).
8. Finke, R.A., Ward, T.B., Smith, S.M.: Creative Cognition: Theory, Research, and Applications. MIT Press, Cambridge (1992)
9. Zhao S., Zhao G, Wu Y.: Thinking skills training: a technological catalyst to effectively enhance learning. Mod. Distance Educ. Res. **04**, 28–34+78 (2012)

Deployment of Cognitive and Affective Determinants in Blended Learning - Case Study

Miloslava Černá(✉)

Department of Applied Lingusistics, Faculty of Informatics and Management,
The University of Hradec Králové, Rokitanského 62, 500 03 Hradec Králové, Czech Republic
miloslava.cerna@uhk.cz

Abstract. The paper discusses psycho-didactic framework which is applied to stimulate language development and test language competence in students of bachelor study programmes within Blended learning concept. Cognitive and affective determinants are unique to each student. When this perspective is simplified to the core it is possible to state that each student has his/her learning prerequisites like knowledge and has his/her attitudes, interests and self-esteem. In this presented research we tried to demonstrate the concept of determinants with real participants on the real teaching-learning stage. The goal is to maternize theory and visualize how theory aligns with practice.

Keywords: Psychodidactics · Placement test · User satisfaction · Blended learning · Cognitive · Motivation

1 Introduction

The paper discusses psycho-didactic framework which is applied to stimulate language development and test language competence in students of bachelor study programmes within Blended learning concept. Psychodidactic approach in this study doesn't fully contradict traditional subject centred teaching/learning system. The effectiveness of the process of education is still assessed by gained knowledge and competences in particular subject.

But learner's personality, his/her cognitive and affective determinants are in focus and form a kind of basis for organizing the teaching/learning process in the psychodidactic approach and form a core of inhere demonstrated case study.

The paper strives to introduce an innovative approach, while maintaining the traditional need for knowledge acquisition and skills development. The innovative approach is demonstrated on the case study which was conducted with sophomore students of Applied Informatics, Information and Financial Management bachelor study programmes within professional English language subject this winter semester where two-hour language classes are run weekly and supported with an e-course in the Blackboard learning management system.

The research which is presented in this paper belongs to the university specific project "The Influence of Mobile Technologies and Social Networks on the Development of Cognitive Processes". A broad cognitive learning theory explores human

S.K.S. Cheung et al. (Eds.): ICBL 2017, LNCS 10309, pp. 464–474, 2017.
DOI: 10.1007/978-3-319-59360-9_41

thinking. The specific project as well as the discussed research build on last year research [1] and provide this research with highlighted cognitive and affective perspective. Cognitive and affective determinants are unique to each student. When this perspective is simplified to the core it is possible to state that each student has his/her learning prerequisites like knowledge and has his/her attitudes, interests and self-esteem.

2 Methodological Frame

This chapter provides readers with literature review, state of art, research goals, hypotheses and applied methods.

2.1 Literature Review

Main part of literature review is devoted to Psychodidactics, history and selected examples of applied theory, stating definitions to key words like psychodidactics, cognitive and affective determinants. The lesser part of the literature review deals with user testing methods of web-sites.

The standard approach to exploration of teaching/learning process is run from two perspectives: the content perspective in other words from the didactics perspective and from the process perspective i.e. from the perspective of psychology [2]. Psycho-didactics interconnects approaches and knowledge mainly from general didactics, psychology of learning and cognitive psychology. Kholodnaya and Gelfman stated the following definition: "Psychodidactics is the area of pedagogy that designs content, forms, and methods of teaching based on integrated psychological, didactic, methodological and subject-matter knowledge while focusing specifically on the mental patterns of personality development as a basis for organizing the teaching process" [3]. The same authors applied this poly-functional psychological approach when creating materials for math learners. Researchers believe that their innovative teaching technology which is based on development-focused educational texts will foster development of mental experience consisting of cognitive, conceptual, metacognitive and intentional components and that this kind of texts will reflect students' personal learning styles [4].

Among famous representatives of psychodidactics theory belongs Benjamin Bloom who is known to most academicians in the pedagogy field as an author of Taxonomy of educational objectives [5]. In this paper we would like to mention his education - philosophical work "Learning for Mastery" as the starting point of the paper. This kind of instructional strategy was written 50 years ago but its ideas are valid up to now and perfectly fit e-learning concept. A category of time and the access to additional supportive learning material are key characteristics of this strategy [6]. Bloom [7] defines in his following work cognitive and affective determinants in student's learning process.

- *Each student has his/her unique experience and prerequisites for learning which represent the cognitive determinants like kind of knowledge, skills and abilities.*
- *The other component called affective characteristics explores different attitudes of students to accomplishing learning tasks. Affective characteristic is a complex of interests, attitude, stances and self-assessment* [7].

In this paper we try to demonstrate the concept of determinants with real participants on the real teaching-learning stage. The goal is to maternize theory and find out whether it is possible to align theory with practice.

Bloom's strategy got developed, innovated and is reflected in e.g. Individualised instructions [8], Flipped mastery, Flipped Classrooms [9]. Miao and Qu define flipped classroom: "The flipped classroom means that students complete learning the knowledge at home, and the classroom becomes a place of interaction, communication, collaboration and support among peers or from teachers" [9] (p. 126). In the quoted study the flipped classroom is narrowed to videos which serve as main students' learning source. Researchers explore learning strategies: Learning plans, Taking notes and Repetition [9].

An interesting finding was revealed and is definitely worth further discussion. It will be incorporated among main thoughts in the Conclusion chapter. The finding relates to general view of success, to what the real goal of learning process is. And if we overlap the borders of psychodidactics in this case we could get to the Philosophical issue – what values more 'the way' or 'the goal'. Researches claim that students from Flipped classroom case study pay much more attention to the test scores, whether they have mastered the knowledge itself [9]. The attitude fully corresponds with main global trend in testing which is primarily based on multiple –choice questions, languages including. As an example can be mentioned The ACT (American College testing) [10] can be mentioned. The ACT was designed for assessing high-school students' readiness to study at the university or college. There is a worked out system of standardized multiple choice tests covering assessment of skills in 4 areas: English, Mathematics, Reading, and Science.

Rather sceptical to that format of a multiple choice unit test were researchers already two decades ago. Lai and Biggs [11], argue that this kind of testing fits learners interested in the surface of the information, learners whose approach to gaining knowledge doesn't go to the core of the knowledge via thorough deep information processing.

A deep insight into the 'Cognitive Science' is provided in Mohanty's literature review [12]. She widens the psychodidactics approach with an importance of a linguistics factor. Mohanty defines Cognitive science as the interdisciplinary branch of science which draws from linguistics, computer science, psychology and neuroscience. Knowledge, cognition, understanding and their interrelationships which are considered to be key mental phenomena of Cognitive science are discussed from various perspectives; how they are perceived, explained, categorized and developed by various experts within last sixty years. She starts with Bloom the guru in Pedagogy, as already mentioned above, who became immortal with his "taxonomy of educational objectives" [5], via Piaget to contemporary cognitive psychology with two distinctive approaches: Information – processing approach and Connectionist approach [12].

Expectancy-value theory/model of motivation is another example of psycho-didactic concept which has been widely utilized, developed and modified by researchers and which fully corresponds to the focus of this contribution [13, 14]. The Choice of tasks, persistence, vigour and performance of students are influenced by motivation which is defined by three components: by their beliefs about how well they are able to accomplish the task, how they value the activity itself which refers to the students' goals and how they perceive the importance of the task and the third component which is called affective component refers to emotional responses to the tasks.

Last section of literature review refers to technical part of usability testing. Methodology of web usability draws from Jacob Nielsen [15]. Most of his wisdom is spread and systematically updated on his websites [16].

2.2 State of Art

Blended learning concept enables wide utilization of psychodidactic theory; reflects the importance of TIME category [6] which enables students work at their own pace, highlights necessity of creation of adapted content material which fits variety of students learning styles.

Blended Learning as a main concept in teaching/learning English language as a second language has more than 15 years long history at the Faculty of Informatics and Management, University of Hradec Kralove [17]. At the beginning of new millennium our young faculty invested into the purchase of learning management system WebCT; since its establishment it has insisted on utilization of ICT in education, blended learning concept is imbedded in the policy. Within two decades teachers and academicians gained a profound professional experience in this combined way of work with students in face-to-face classes and virtual space as well as in the field of Blended teaching/learning theory [8, 18].

All subjects of Professional English for both full-time students and part-time students are accompanied by e-courses which enlarge study environment. E-courses are actively and systematically used as a source of study material, as an information noticeboard and as a forum. These e-courses are living bodies; they are enriched with students and teacher's contributions. Students contribute on both compulsory and voluntary basis [1]. Structure of individual lessons in the language e-course is based on didactics rules [5]: objectives of the lesson and development of desired competences are thoughtfully formulated, see Fig. 1.

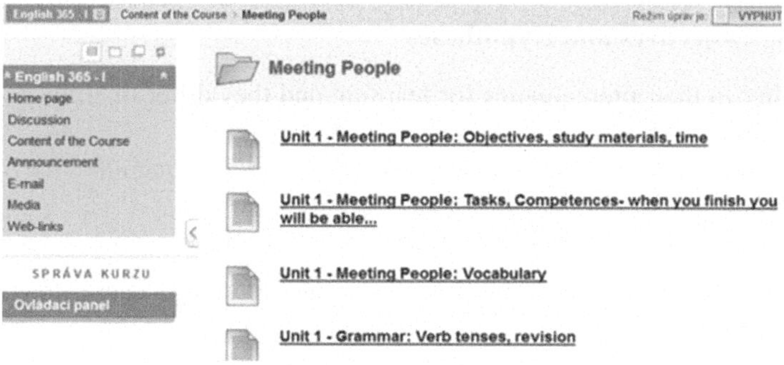

Fig. 1. Structure of a language lesson in an e-course

The *factor of time* is stated but it serves as an indicator of possible time needed for the accomplishment of the unit. As mentioned above – study material is worked out by the teacher and enriched with students' contributions. Students are instructed which part of the study content represents the basis of their study which might be considered as the cognitive component of their learning process. But at the same time they are offered supplementary language material for development of language skills. Work in this section reflects either that students themselves feel that practising and improvement of language skills (e.g. reading, listening or grammar) are needed or just students feel interest in them (e.g. writing) – which fits the affective component of the learning process. Figure 2 brings an extract from the e-course Announcement section. It is the first announcement to students which was made after the first face-to-face introductory lesson at the beginning of the semester. Students are in the e-course systematically instructed what to prepare for the next face-to-face classes including the elementary duty – just to bring their text book. Students are offered a set of tasks including the task on Placement test which belongs to one of basic building blocks of this study.

10 +11 October - Tasks

Zaslal(a): **Miloslava Černá**
Posláno: **English 365 - I**

Tasks - 10 and 11 October

1) **News** - *will you prepare at least 10 sentences?*
2) Will you do the placement test? See **DIALANG in the section "Content"** *(don´t forget to write the final score you have reached in the vocabulary test)*
3) Will you prepare **10 expressions** to the topic – **University environment,** you can place this task into the Discussion section, as well.
4) Will you bring the textbook English 365/ student´s book 3, please?

Fig. 2. First announcement in the e-course with tasks

The approach to design and organization of language classes corresponds to psycho-didactics theory because both cognitive and affective components of learning process are taken into consideration in face-to-face classes as well as on the virtual platform.

2.3 Setting Objectives and Hypotheses

Students differ in their prerequisites for learning and they differ in attitudes to accomplishing learning tasks.

The main goal is to demonstrate the concept of cognitive and affective factors with real participants on the real teaching-learning stage.

The accomplishment of the goal will be approached from:

- exploration of students' needs analysis in language learning (where affective component dominates)
- from students' belief in their language competences (affective component)
- from students' score reached in repetitive language placement tests (cognitive component)

The sub-goal is to work out a comparative study on students' needs analysis in language learning with focus on language educational web-sites.

Hypotheses stem from the presented individual steps:

Hypothesis H1: Needs analysis on students' language requirements will be comparable with the needs analysis which was made 2 years ago.
Hypothesis H2: More than two thirds of students will be interested into the activity connected with web design, because applied linguistics matches their specialisation.
Hypothesis H3: Students belief in own competences will be higher than real competences.

2.4 Research Sample and Applied Methods

The accessible research sample consisted of sophomore students of Professional English subject. Students were of the same age, same year at the university, same specialization and with the similar length of school English study history. In the initial face-to-face part of the research all students (61) from three language subject groups participated. About two thirds (39) of them participated also in the second part which was run in the virtual place.

Semi-structuralized discussion, needs analysis, user-testing of web-sites, placement test and expectancy model of motivation were applied in this research. Some methods will be described in detail some only briefly. The process was complex due to that the use of methods overlaps and isn't always presented in individual steps as individual entities.

3 Procedure and Findings

3.1 Semi-structuralised Discussion and Needs Analysis

A semi-structuralized discussion was applied. It was based on Students needs analysis on web design of educational language website hence reflecting also their needs in language learning. Within the semi-structuralized discussion an updated needs analysis was made. Data were discussed and visualised in the graph. Comparative study showed significant changes. The discussion consisted of two main sections: students' needs analysis relating to language web sites and the other part drew ideas from Expectancy model of motivation. Students language needs were in this research explored at two levels: at the level of web design and at the level of modified expectancy model. Needs analysis depicts the trend in students' needs related to features and functionalities which language web-site should have and provide.

Requirements on web sites combine exploration of cognitive and affective determinants where affective factor focuses on interests and cognitive component reflects students' own belief in their competence.

Two years ago a survey was run with an accessible sample of ninety four students from the second year of Bachelor study programme at the Faculty of Informatics and Management during Professional English language classes. Students were asked to discuss, then identify and write down three to five requirements on web sites; what service and activities they should provide to meet their demands in studying languages.

Key findings, where 'Revision of grammar' and 'Preparation for international language exams domineered, follow: two thirds of students called for revision and practicing grammar, half of students expressed interest in international exams; 11 of them namely in the First Certificate and 3 in computer based IELTS test (the International English Language Testing System. Surprisingly there was low or nearly no interest in practicing and testing listening skills; 57 students stated that they could master that skill via watching movies, 46 students insisted on tests with explanation of results, only 12 students mentioned on-line dictionary and finally 9 students insisted on updated sites.

Findings from two years old survey were used as the starting point for the semi-structured discussion which was run during the first organizational meeting with three groups of 61 sophomore full-time students of the Professional English language subject at the beginning of winter semester in October 2016.

Requirements on language web-sites reflect both cognitive and affective needs in the area of desirable functionalities like incorporated on-line dictionary, updated sites or version for mobiles and then there needs to practice individual language skills.

The Fig. 3 illustrates findings which were gained from the repetitive analysis, see comparison of the "Old" Needs analysis with the "New" Needs analysis. Abbreviation "NA" stands for Needs analysis. The first finding, which raised surprise, relates to the significant drop in interest in gaining certificates in international language exams. Why two years ago half of students were ready to sit for an international language exam to gain globally recognized certificate? Only one third of current students are considering taking an international language exam. This finding calls for discussion. Students' major is "informatics" so, maybe they can see future just in their field and are going to focus on gaining certificates in their field, in spite of the fact that valid language certificate opens the door to career opportunities.

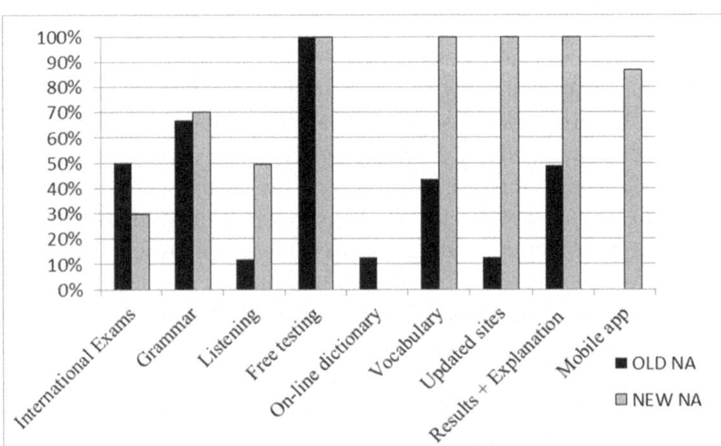

Fig. 3. Comparison of findings on Needs analysis

As for the need to practice grammar the results are comparable. About 70% of students believe that grammar section should be on the menu of language website. All participants in both groups consider Free testing in language website as a must. There is a considerable increase in students' awareness of the importance of listening skills development. One half of current students perceive development of listening skills important and believe that it shouldn't be omitted. Like the previous group all students prefer watching films with subtitles, even if our country is be highly rated in dubbing. None of current students demanded on-line dictionary as a part of web. All students use translator and only about 15 language enthusiasts use monolingual explanatory dictionary like The FreeDictionary or Merriam-Webster. *There was an enormous increase in the need of practicing vocabulary.* All 61 students stressed the importance of vocabulary acquisition. All students consider updated sites as a standard feature, "ageing" websites without innovations and updated news will lose its visitors-they mean. All current students want immediate response and explanations of the reached results in on-line tests within the selected educational language web-sites. They are not willing to search for explanation anywhere else. Once they are doing the test they nearly instant response, if possible they like the format when they fill in the tasks then click and check whether they were right or even only click to see the answers. A great deal of students approach their learning tasks from their tablets and mobile devices. It was no surprise that they expected websites to be well designed to match the specifics of these frequently used devices.

3.2 Expectancy Model of Motivation

Expectancy-value model of motivation [13, 14] as a psychodidactic concept was applied and slightly modified to match the university environment because originally it was discussed within primary and secondary levels of education. Nevertheless motivation with all its colourful components influences performance not only of students: belief in ability, expectancy items connected with perceived value of stated tasks and goals and finally affective component referring to emotional part when completing tasks, like usefulness and satisfaction.
These three components were adapted into the following model:

1. *Belief in own (students') abilities* was expressed in question "What is the level of your language competence?" The answers were recorded during the semi-structured discussion with all students.
2. *Perceived value of stated tasks and goals* was based on their willingness to participate in usability testing of web-sites together with completing the placement test based.
3. *Affective component* was discussed within the frame of the user testing of the language web site. In focus was satisfaction of user's with the web sites.

Out of 61 students 39 students participated in the other part of the research. Three-component expectancy model is built on findings from the semi-structuralised discussion during face-to-face classes at the introductory lesson and then on findings from user testing of web sites.

39 students completed user testing of language diagnostic website. Satisfaction as one of the expectancy model component was a followed category. On the scale, reaching

from minus five to plus five points, students were asked to select the level of satisfaction. None gave negative assessment but no one gave absolutely positive assessment. The mean of the level of satisfaction in this group of students was plus 2 points.

When it comes to time category it was related to completing the placement test, the time span was narrow. The mean was 5 min to complete the test. 15 min which was spent on the test was maximum, nearly half students managed to complete the placement test in 3 min.

Last graph Fig. 4 concludes the exploration on affective and cognitive components. Striped bar represents students' belief in their language competence, black bar represents the reached score in the placement test and the grey bar shows reached score in the placement test at the end of the semester. Students assessed their competences according to standardized 6 level language competence scale CEFR (Common European Framework): A1 up to C2. Assessment in the selected placement vocabulary test is divided in the following way: A1 (100 points), A2 (101–200), B1 (201–400), B2 (401–600), C1 (601–900) C2 901–1000). Median of students' scores was in the first run of the placement test at the start of the semester 656 points and at the end the median increased to 700 points, it means level C1.

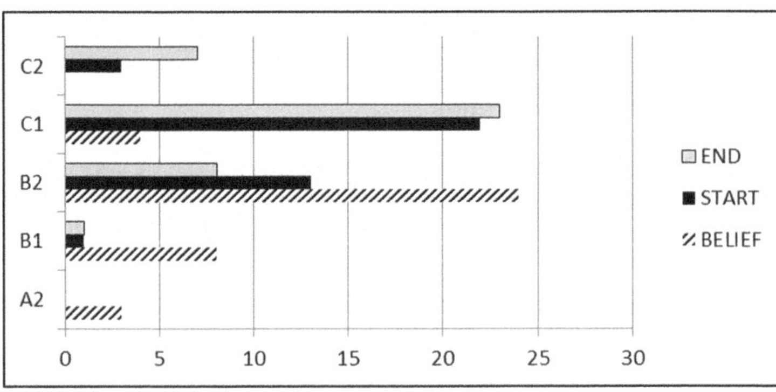

Fig. 4. Self-evaluation, level of language competence – start and end of the semester

Students assessed their competences according to standardized 6 level language competence scale CEFR (Common European Framework): A1 up to C2. Assessment in the selected placement vocabulary test is divided in the following way: A1 (100 points), A2 (101–200), B1 (201–400), B2 (401–600), C1 (601–900) C2 901–1000). Median of students' scores was in the first run of the placement test at the start of the semester 656 points and at the end the median increased to 700 points = level C1.

Students undervalued their competences: 3 students - A2, 8 students B1, the biggest deal 24 students assessed themselves as B2 and only 4 believed in their language skills as placed themselves into category C1. In reality they were by one level higher: there was only 1 student B1, 13 students B2, 22 students C1 and there were even three students with the score reaching the highest level C2.

4 Conclusion and Discussion

The objective and a sub-goal were reached. Needs analysis was run and expectancy model was designed for the purposes of this research. Both methods will be again applied in language classes.

Hypothesis H1 has to be rejected. Students' requirements got changed significantly. They demand more vocabulary practising and they show much lower interest in international exams even if their language competences reach high level on the language competence scale.

It is highly recommended to check students' needs in their subject. All stakeholders profiteer. Students are made to think about their prerequisites, interests and are made to formulate expectations. Teacher shows his/her respect to students' needs and can reflect findings into the modification of learning content.

Hypothesis H2 has to be rejected. 39 out of 61 students participated in web usability testing part. (One more student and the hypothesis could be accepted). But those students who participated, they worked responsibly. All of them submitted thoroughly filled form on web usability and completed placement test in it at the beginning of the semester and consequently repeated the test at the end of the semester.

Hypothesis H3 also has to be rejected in this study. Students belief in own competences was much lower than achieved scores in the placement test. It was bright motivating moment for students to find out that their level of competence is higher. This affective factor worked also in case when 8 students reached slightly lower amount of points but anyway stayed at the same competence level. They focused more on the concept of testing and web-design than on their skills. Here we are approaching the issue which was described in the Flipped classes case study (119). This group of students was more interested in the "way" than in the score of the placement test. They appreciated new experience with placement tests, with the way of scaling language competences and exploring learning from knowledge-motivation perspective where not only cognitive part counts.

There is no pure teaching/learning concept which could be 100% accepted by professional audience. We can speak about strategies or philosophy but teaching/learning process will always be a mixture of strategies where some will dominate and others will wait for their moment of glory, some will become "immortal" and some will have just an ephemeral life.

Acknowledgment. The paper was supported by project of Students Grant Agency – FIM, University of Hradec Kralove, Czech Republic (under ID: UHK-FIM-SP-2017). Authors express thanks to Jan Freiberg for help with collection of data.

References

1. Černá, M.: User evaluation of language websites as a way of students' engagement into Blended learning process – case study. In: Cheung, S., Kwok, L., Shang, J., Wang, A., Kwan, R. (eds.) Blended Learning: Aligning Theory with Practices, ICBL 2016. LNCS, vol. 9757, pp. 269–280. Springer, Heidelberg (2016)

2. Průcha, J.: Modern Pedagogy. Portal, Praha (2009). ISBN 978-80-7367-503-5
3. Kholodnaya, M.A., Gelfman, E.G.: The Routledge International Handbook of Innovation Education. In: Shavinina, L.V. (ed.) Routledge 2013, School Textbooks as a Medium for Intellectual Development of Children During the Mathematics Teaching Process, pp. 315–318 (2013)
4. Kholodnaya, M.A., Gelfman, E.G.: Development-focused educational texts as a basis for learners' intellectual development in studying mathematics. Psychol. Russ. State Art, **9**(3), 24–37 (2016)
5. Bloom, B.S., et al.: Taxonomy of Educational Objectives: Cognitive Domain. David McKay Company, Inc., New York (1956)
6. Bloom, B.S.: Learning for Mastery. UCLA, Berkeley (1968)
7. Bloom, B.S.: Human Characteristics and the School Learning. McGraw-Hill, New York (1976)
8. Klimova, B.: Teacher's role in a smart learning environment—a review study. In: Uskov, V., Howlett, R.J., Jai, L.C. (eds.) Smart Innovation, Systems and Technologies, vol. 59, pp. 51–59. Springer (2016). ISBN 978-3-319-39689-7, ISBN 978-3-319-39690-3 (eBook) doi: 10.1007/978-3-319-39690
9. Miao, R., Qu, X.: Research of learning strategies in flipped classroom a case of extra-curricular english study. In: Cheung, S., Kwok, L., Shang, J., Wang, A., Kwan, R. (eds.) Blended Learning: Aligning Theory with Practices, ICBL 2016, LNCS, vol. 9757. Springer, Heidelberg, pp. 118–127 (2016)
10. The ACT (2017). http://www.act.org/aboutact/history.html
11. Lai, P., Biggs, J.: Who benefits from mastery learning? Contemp. Educ. Psychol. **19**, 13–23 (1994). doi:10.1006/ceps.1994.1002
12. Mohanty, A.: Cognition, affection and conation: implications for pedagogical issues in higher education (2010). http://pedagogy.iitkgp.ernet.in/downloads/Cognition_Pedagogy.doc
13. Jacobs, P.A., Newstead, S.E.: The nature and development of student motivation. Br. J. Educ. Psychol. **70**, 243–254 (2000)
14. Wigfield, A., Eccle, J.: Expectancy-value theory of achievement motivation. Contemp. Educ. Psychol. **25**, 68–81 (2000)
15. Nielsen, J.: Design Web Usability: The Practice of Simplicity. Pearson Education Inc., Upper Saddle River (2000)
16. Nielsen, J: Nielsen Norman Group (2015). http://www.nngroup.com/articles/
17. Poulova, P., Simonova, I.: eLearning at Czech Universities in 1999–2010. In: Proceedings of the 9th European Conference on E-learning, vol. 1, pp. 488–496 (2010)
18. Frydrychova Klimova, B.: Blended learning. In: Vilas, A.M. et al. (eds.) Research, Reflections and Innovations in Integrating ICT in Education, vol. 2, FORMATEX, Spain, pp. 705–708. ISBN 978-84-692-1790-0 (2009)

The Influence of Different Personality Traits on Learning Achievement in Three Learning Situations

Lu Wang[1], Yuan Tian[2], Yuju Lei[2], and Zongkui Zhou[2(✉)]

[1] National Engineering Research Center for E-Learning, Central China Normal University, Wuhan 430079, China
[2] School of Psychology, Central China Normal University, Wuhan 430079, China
zhouzk@mail.ccnu.edu.cn

Abstract. In order to explore the relationships among learning achievement, personality characteristics and learning context, and to test what kind of personality characteristics are suitable for what kind of learning situation, an experimental study was conducted on 45 college students (24 women, 21 men) in China. Participants were randomly assigned to 6 days of instruction in one of three learning situations: traditional classroom, online learning, and flipped classroom (blended learning). Personality was assessed in terms of the Big Five traits, and achievement scores reflected learning of the course material. Results showed that (1) There were no significant differences in the influence of the three learning situations on learning achievement; (2) Among the Big Five personality traits, Conscientiousness had a significant impact on learners' academic performance, and positively predicted learning achievement; (3) There was a significant interaction between Openness and learning situation: students with high Openness showed the best performance in the online learning situation, and did worst in the traditional classroom; students with moderate Openness did best in the flipped classroom. The results of this study suggest that in the process of personalized education, we should attach importance to the matching of learning situation and individual differences. This may be especially true in online learning and flipped classroom environments, in order to optimize the learning effect in learners with different personality characteristics.

Keywords: Big five personality traits · Traditional classroom · Online learning · Flipped classroom · Learning achievement

1 The Definition of Related Concepts

1.1 The Traditional Classroom

The traditional classroom is a knowledge-based classroom, which, although it can strengthen knowledge, may ignore other aspects of students' lives and development. In the traditional classroom students passively accept knowledge through teachers' indoctrination, with an emphasis on completing the teaching task and achieving the teaching goal.

S.K.S. Cheung et al. (Eds.): ICBL 2017, LNCS 10309, pp. 475–488, 2017.
DOI: 10.1007/978-3-319-59360-9_42

1.2 Online Learning

The definition of online learning has been controversial. Terry Anderson and Randy Carrison proposed in 2004 that the process of online learning is one in which the learners could interact with learning content, teachers and other learners to acquire knowledge. Learners thus get support, gain knowledge, and construct personal meaning in the learning process. Students can grow with learning [1].

Ding (2006) thought that the term online learning had a narrow sense and generalized sense. The narrow sense of online learning referred to all the participants of teaching and learning being online at the same time and in contact with each other; it essentially was a kind of learning based on real-time synchronous communication interactions on computer networks. Generalized online learning referred to a context in which all the teaching and learning activities would be classified as online learning. These activities were realized through computer networks, especially the Internet, and included real-time synchronous communication learning and non-real-time asynchronous communication learning on computer networks [2].

1.3 The Flipped Classroom

The Flipped Classroom has also been named the Inverted Classroom or the Reversed Classroom. It can be seen from the name that it was developed as a teaching mode with reforms and changes from the traditional classroom.

The teaching process in the flipped classroom usually includes knowledge impartment and knowledge internalization, in two stages. In the traditional classroom, the knowledge impartment was done through teachers teaching in the classroom, and knowledge internalization required students to do assignments or practice after class.

In contrast to the traditional classroom, in the flipped classroom, teachers first create short teaching videos according to the knowledge content, and learners watch the teaching videos by themselves outside the classroom. In this way the process of knowledge impartment becomes a process of self-completion with the help of videos outside the classroom. After learners return to class, the emphasis becomes the interaction between teachers and students and between students and students. Teachers help students complete the internalization of knowledge by organizing links; some links include resolving doubts and discussing problems or application of knowledge [3].

Therefore, in this study we defined the Flipped Classroom as a kind of teaching mode in which learners watch teaching videos to realize knowledge impartment, and then in the classroom communicate with teachers and companions and complete assignments to implement knowledge internalization.

The Flipped Classroom is essentially a combination of the traditional classroom and online learning, that is, blended learning. It includes the advantages of both online learning and the traditional classroom. Compared with the traditional classroom, online learning was significantly different in that learners and teachers were separated in the space. Learners could control and grasp their own learning content, learning process and learning methods. At the same time, online learning was designed not only to impart knowledge, but also to foster an exploring and innovative spirit, self-learning ability, information processing skills and integration ability [4]. These characteristics are maintained in the flipped classroom format.

2 Literature Review

2.1 The Big Five Personality Model

In the late 1980s a new personality classification system was introduced: the Big Five personality model. This model has gradually become recognized by researchers as the dominant model for conceptualizing personality [5]. According to Costa and McCrae's nomenclature, the five factors of personality are: Extroversion, Agreeableness, Conscientious, Neuroticism, Openness. Each dimension of the Big Five personality model can be divided into three levels, Table 1 shows descriptions of individuals at high, moderate, and low levels of each trait.

Table 1. Descriptions of high, medium and low scores on the Big Five Personality Questionnaire [6].

Five personality traits	High score description	Medium score description	Low score description
Neuroticism	Very sensitive and emotionally fragile, easily upset	Able to cope with pressure, but sometimes experience the feelings of guilt, anger or sadness	Carefree, generally can function well even in the face of pressure
Extroversion	Outgoing, cheerful, lively, have their tail up, willing to work with people most of the time	Maintain a tepid personality, willing to get along with people, but also pay attention to personal privacy	Introverted, serious, like to be alone or with a few close friends
Openness	Like to experience new things and have extensive interests and rich imaginations	Practical, but also willing to try new methods and can seek a balance between the old and the new	Hardheaded, traditional and can stick to own principles
Agreeableness	Gentle, caring, desire cooperation, avoid conflict	Compassionate, easygoing, but sometimes are opinionated and do not lack of sense of competition	Haggle over every ounce, incredulous, arrogant, competitive and straightforward
Conscientious	Have a strong sense of responsibility, methodical, have high standards, strict, make efforts to achieve their goals	Reliable, organized, have clear goals, but sometimes also can put the work aside	Are idle by nature, lack organization, sometimes are sloppy, do not want to make plans

2.2 The Influence of Personality on Academic Achievement

Personality is a stable behavior tendency that is thought to reflect differences in individuals' thoughts and emotions. Many studies have demonstrated that there is a significant relationship between personality and academic achievement. **The Relationship Between Conscientiousness and Learning Achievement.** In studies of the Big Five personality traits and academic achievement, the most consistent conclusion has been that conscientiousness could predict academic achievement, with a strong and stable positive correlation between them (Blickle [7], 1996; Chamorro-Premuzic & Furnham [8], 2003; Lounsbury, Sundstrom, Loveland, & Gibson [9], 2003). In addition, conscientiousness has been found to predict specific and more accurate measures of academic achievement, such as a university course final grade (Lounsbury, Sundstrom, Loveland, & Gibson, 2003), and graduation thesis research achievements (Chamorro-Premuzic & Furnham, 2003b).

Conscientiousness has also been shown to be positively correlated with behaviors important for academic achievement. This trait is positively correlated with learning adaptability, learning motivation, and learning strategy, and negatively correlated with learning burnout. Students high in conscientiousness are diligent, more rigorous, and more persistent, and they show more initiative for learning.

The Relationship Between Openness and Learning Achievement. Farsides and Woodfield (2003) found that openness to experience was positively correlated with academic achievement [10]. Gray et al. (2002) selected 334 college students as subjects, and found that openness to experience was significantly associated with college performance ($r = 0.18$) [11]. This dimension was also found to predict final course grades (Lounsbury et al., 2003) and psychological test scores (Dollinger & Orf [12], 1991). Openness may reflect the intelligence component of personality, because openness is often found to be positively related to intelligence (Chamorro-Premuzic & Furnham [13], 2007); therefore the significant correlation between openness and academic achievement is usually interpreted to be related to competence factors.

However, many studies have found no significant correlation between openness and academic achievement. O'Connor and Paunonen (2007) found that the correlation coefficient between them was only $r = .06$, a nonsignificant value; at the same time, it was found that the correlation coefficient fell within a confidence interval of $r = -.10$ to $r = .22$, suggesting that there were unknown variables that played a moderating role in the relationship between openness and academic achievement [14].

The Relationship Between Agreeableness and Learning Achievement. Some studies have found that there was a positive correlation between agreeableness and academic achievement. For instance, Gray et al. (2002) chose 334 college students as the subjects, and found agreeableness was significantly associated with college grades ($r = 0.15$). However, other studies found that there was a negative correlation (Rothstein et al. [15], 1994) or no correlation (Chamorro-Premuzic & Furnham, 2003). Based on element analysis, O'Connor and Paunonen (2007) concluded that agreeableness was not an important determinant of academic achievement.

The Relationship Between Extroversion and Learning Achievement. Research on the relationship between extroversion and academic achievement has produced a wide variety of results. These can be summed up in three views:

The first view is that there is no correlation between the two. Ehrman found that students with good grades were both introverted and extroverted, and concluded that students with good grades did not have a specific personality [16].

The second view is that extraversion is correlated positively with academic performance. For example, Zhang (1989) found that the outgoing, stable, and gregarious person tended to have good academic achievement [17]. Excessively introverted students often did not resolve contradictions within themselves or between themselves and the external environment, and were generally psychologically immature. These characteristics could negatively affect academic achievement.

The third view is that there is a negative correlation between the two, perhaps related to the uncertainty of external factors. Song et al. [18] (2001) found that although highly extroverted people were more likely to have a positive emotional experience, and this positive experience was helpful in improving learning achievement, they were very sociable and not always able to work independently and quietly, resulting in lower learning achievement.

The Relationship Between Neuroticism and Learning Achievement. Some studies have shown a negative correlation between neuroticism and academic achievement. For example, De Raad et al. [19] (1996) showed that high neuroticism was associated with significantly lower academic achievement. Neuroticism was defined as low confidence, high levels of arousal and anxiety, and pressure tendency; people with this personality trait were seen as likely to experience anxiety and stress, interfering with academic achievement.

However, O'Connor and Paunonen's (2007) meta-analysis found a very weak correlation between neuroticism and academic achievement. The correlation fell within a relatively narrow range, from $r = -.10$ to $r = .04$, suggesting that neuroticism might not be an important determinant of academic achievement.

2.3 The Influence of Learning Situations on Learning

The Influence of Online Learning on Learning. Many researchers have found that online learning, as an effective supplement to traditional learning, could promote learning. For example Zhong and Yang (2002) summed up the influence of online learning environments on learning. (1) Online learning not only made autonomous learning become a reality, but also made autonomous learning popular, and as learners had full choice in the content, time and space, autonomous learning became a necessity. (2) Online learning fully achieved interactive cooperative learning; learners could download handouts and related information from the Internet, and could communicate with other students through the Internet, and this enhanced learning initiatives [20]. Gosper et al. [21] (2008) also described some of the advantages of online learning: learners could have exam review through the network technology; the online learning could help learners to solve complex concepts; learners could control the speed and place of learning; learners could preview before the lectures through online learning; it also could help learners make systemic notes. An Australian survey found that 80% of students believed that online courses could make learning easier (Flores & Savage [22], 2007).

Online learning indeed has many advantages, but is the effect of online learning really better than the traditional classroom? Some researchers have found that learning achievement in the traditional classroom was higher than that in online learning (Gratton-LaVoie [23], 2009; Figlio, Rush & Yin [24], 2010). Parsons-Pollard et al. [25]. (2008) found that in an entry-level criminal justice course, the students' performance in the traditional classroom was higher than that of students in the online learning course, a difference that was small but statistically significant. At the same time, many scholars have found no significant difference in learning outcomes in the traditional learning and online learning settings. In an introduction to biology course, Lents and Cifuentes [26] (2009) compared the achievement of students in a traditional classroom and in an online learning setting, and found no significant difference between the two.

The Influence of the Flipped Classroom on Learning. From the theoretical view, the teaching mode of the flipped classroom provides an effective external support for the students' acquisition of knowledge and promotion of ability. This mode has been described as: learning first, teaching after learning, learning to teach. According to Bergmann and Sams [27] (2012), through the implementation of the flipped classroom, teachers no longer needed to speak for two hours in class; they could make full use of classroom time to discuss and solve problems. Long et al. [28] (2014) found that learning experience before class could improve students' interest in learning and their understanding of the learning situation.

However, many studies have found that there were not many differences between the learning effect of the flipped classroom and the traditional classroom. Snowden's [29] (2012) study found that in the traditional and flipped learning experience, there were no significant differences in students' perception and achievement. Mason et al. also found that there was no significant difference in student scores in the two learning situations.

3 Research Hypotheses

In summary, the personality characteristics of learners have been shown to be powerful predictors of learning and behaviors that promote learning; meanwhile, different teaching situations might have a differential impact on learning, and personality and learning situations may interact to predict learning. The hypotheses of this study were as follows:

Hypothesis 1: Learners' personality traits would affect individual academic achievement

H1a: conscientiousness would positively predict academic achievement;
H1b: openness would positively predict academic achievement;
H1c: extraversion would positively predict academic achievement;

Hypothesis 2: there would be no significant differences between the three learning situations in terms of academic achievement

Hypothesis 3: individual personality traits would affect the academic achievement of learners in different learning situations

H3a: highly conscientious individuals would show similar academic achievement in all three learning situations;

H3b: individuals with high extroversion and low openness would show higher academic achievement in the traditional classroom than in the other two settings;

H3c: individuals with low extraversion and highly open individuals would show higher academic achievement in the online learning setting than in other settings;

H3d: individuals with high extroversion and high openness would show higher academic achievement in the flipped classroom than in other settings.

4 Research Methods

4.1 Participants

Participants were selected based on their lack of previous exposure to the topic of the learning materials. And last we recruited 45 undergraduate participants (21 men and 24 women, 7:8 ratio) through advertising. Their ages ranged from 20 to 23 years old, and they were from the Huazhong University of Science and Technology and the Central China Normal University. Participants had no basic knowledge of psychology before the experiment, and this was the first time that they had participated in a psychological experiment. All participants volunteered, and informed consent was obtained in advance. Participants were paid after the experiment.

4.2 Experimental Procedure

We used the Latin square experimental design. The participants were randomly divided into three groups (A, B, and C), each with 8 women and 7 men. The experiment took place over six days. Before the beginning of the experiment, participants filled out the Big Five Personality Questionnaire. Each participant learned in the same situation for each of the six days (either the traditional classroom, online learning, or the flipped classroom). Participants in the traditional classroom condition listened to instruction for 15-20 min, then completed a test of what they had learned. Participants in the online learning situation watched an instructional video that was recorded in the traditional classroom, then completed a test of what they had learned. Participants in the flipped classroom watched the same video, solved problems in a classroom setting, then completed a test of what they had learned. The participants learned a new knowledge point of the basic psychology every day according to the Latin square design. The design of these six days was ABC, CAB, BCA, ACB, CBA, BAC.

4.3 Measuring Tools

Basic information questionnaire: This questionnaire collected information about the participants' gender, date of birth, year in school, major, QQ username (a form of social media), email, telephone number, previous online learning experience, and previous psychology course experience.

Previous Knowledge Test. This test was developed by Homer et al. (2008) using questions from the test bank of a developmental psychology textbook. The previous knowledge test consisted of 16 multiple-choice questions, each worth 1 point for a correct response. The higher the score, the more knowledge of developmental psychology the participant had. Participants' previous knowledge was evaluated prior to the experiment in order to select participants without prior exposure to the learning materials.

Big Five Personality Questionnaire. The questionnaire used in this study had 44 questions that measured the five personality dimensions. Participants responded on a 5-point scale (1 = strongly disagree, 5 = strongly agree), and 16 items were reverse scored. The reliability of the five subscales of neuroticism, extraversion, openness, agreeableness, and conscientiousness were 0.90, 0.87, 0.80, 0.82, and 0.91, respectively.

Learning Achievement Tests. The six tests consisted of 41 questions, including not only the single selection but also the multiple-choice.

4.4 Data Processing

We conducted multivariate analyses of variance (ANOVAs) using the five dimensions of the Big Five Personality and learning situations as independent variables. The correct rate of answers on the learning achievement six tests was the dependent variable. First, the five dimensions were translated into standard scores, then each dimension was divided into three groups (high, medium, and low) according to previous studies (Costa & McCrae [30], 1985; Bindu Gupta [31], 2008).

5 Results

5.1 Analysis of the Correct Rate

Comparison of Learning Achievement for Individuals with Different Levels of Conscientiousness in Different Learning Situations. We analyzed the conscientiousness dimension of the big five personality questionnaire. We then completed a 3 (learning situation: traditional classroom, online learning, flipped classroom) × 3 (conscientiousness: high, medium, low) ANOVA with learning achievement test performance as the dependent variable. The results showed that the interaction between learning situation and conscientiousness was not significant ($F(4, 84) < 1$), as shown in Table 2.

The main effect of conscientiousness was significant ($F(2,42) = 3.18, p<0.05$, $\eta_p^2 = 0.13$). LSD comparison showed that those with higher levels of conscientiousness showed more learning (*M* high = 0.80, *M* medium = 0.74, *M* low = 0.73). And High significantly greater than Low, they reached a significant level ($p < 0.05$).

The main effect of learning situation was not significant ($F(2,84) = 2.00$, $p > 0.05, \eta_p^2 = 0.045$). Thus, the online learning or the flipped classroom had no advantage over the traditional classroom on learning achievement test performance.

Table 2. The learning effect of individuals with different levels of conscientiousness in the three learning situations.

	Conscientiousness		
	High group (*n* = 15) *M* (*SD*)	Medium group (*n* = 13) *M* (*SD*)	Low group (*n* = 17) *M* (*SD*)
Traditional classroom	0.78 (0.14)	0.78 (0.11)	0.72 (0.16)
Online learning	0.72 (0.16)	0.70 (0.13)	0.71 (0.11)
Flipped classroom	0.83 (0.10)	0.75 (0.11)	0.76 (0.10)

Note: The numbers in brackets are the standard deviation of the correct rate

Comparison of Learning Achievement for the Individuals with Different Levels of Openness in the Different Learning Situations. We analyzed the openness dimension of the big five personality questionnaire. We then completed a 3 (learning context: traditional classroom, online learning, flipped classroom) × 3 (openness: high, medium, low) ANOVA with learning achievement test performance as the dependent variable. The results showed that the interaction between learning situation and openness was significant ($F(4,84) = 3.03, p<0.05, \eta_p^2 = 0.13$). The simple effect analysis showed that when the learner's openness level was higher, the impact of the three kinds of learning situations on learning achievement was significant ($F(4,84) = 3.03, p<0.05, \eta_p^2 = 0.13$). When openness was high, learning achievement with online learning was greater than learning achievement with the flipped classroom, which was greater than learning achievement with the traditional classroom (see Table 3 for means and standard deviations). When the learner's openness was in the middle level, the effect of the flipped classroom on learning achievement was the best, whereas the students who watched the videos alone had the worst learning achievement. When the learner's openness was low, learning achievement was the least for online learning. The results showed that the higher the openness of the learners, the better the outcome of the online learning, and they were more suitable for other teaching situations that were different from the traditional face-to-face teaching.

Table 3. The learning effect of individuals with different levels of openness in the three learning situations.

	Openness		
	High group (n = 15) M (SD)	Medium group (n = 13) M (SD)	Low group (n = 17) M (SD)
Traditional classroom	0.70 (0.13)	0.79 (0.13)	0.77 (0.14)
Online learning	0.78 (0.08)	0.75 (0.14)	0.64 (0.13)
Flipped classroom	0.76 (0.10)	0.83 (0.11)	0.74 (0.08)

Note: The numbers in brackets are the standard deviation of the correct rate

Comparison of Learning Achievement for Individuals with Different Levels of Extroversion in Different Learning Situations. We analyzed the extroversion dimension of the Big Five Personality Questionnaire. We then completed a 3 (learning situation: traditional classroom, online learning, flipped classroom) × 3 (extroversion: high, medium, low) ANOVA with learning achievement test performance as the dependent variable. The results showed that the interaction between learning situation and extroversion was not significant ($F(4, 84) < 1$; see Table 4 for means and standard deviations). The main effects of learning situation and extroversion were also not significant (extroversion: $F(2, 42) < 1$; learning situation: $F(2,84) = 1.78, p > 0.05$, $\eta_p^2 = 0.041$).

Table 4. The learning effect of individuals with different levels of extroversion in the three learning situations.

	Extroversion		
	High group (n = 15) M (SD)	Medium group (n = 17) M (SD)	Low group (n = 13) M (SD)
Traditional classroom	0.74 (0.14)	0.77 (0.14)	0.76 (0.13)
Online learning	0.70 (0.16)	0.71 (0.12)	0.79 (0.09)
Flipped classroom	0.79 (0.14)	0.78 (0.05)	0.78 (0.13)

Note: The numbers in brackets are the standard deviation of the correct rate

Comparison of Learning Achievement for Individuals with Different Levels of Agreeableness in Different Learning Situations. We analyzed the agreeableness dimension of the big five personality questionnaire. We then completed a 3 (learning situation: traditional classroom, online learning, flipped classroom) × 3 (agreeableness: high, medium, low) ANOVA with learning achievement test performance as the dependent variable. The results showed that the interaction between learning situation and agreeableness was not significant ($F(4, 84) < 1$; see Table 5 for means and standard deviations). The main effects of learning situation and agreeableness were also not significant (agreeableness: $F(2, 42) < 1$; learning situation: $F(2,84) = 1.78, p > 0.05$, $\eta_p^2 = 0.041$).

Table 5. The learning effect of individuals with different levels of agreeableness in the three learning situations.

	Agreeableness		
	High group (n = 15) M (SD)	Medium group (n = 17) M (SD)	Low group (n = 13) M (SD)
Traditional classroom	0.82 (0.12)	0.72 (0.12)	0.75 (0.16)
Online learning	0.76 (0.13)	0.72 (0.12)	0.72 (0.15)
Flipped classroom	0.80 (0.09)	0.75 (0.13)	0.80 (0.08)

Note: The numbers in brackets are the standard deviation of the correct rate

Comparison of Learning Achievement for Individuals with Different Levels of Neuroticism in Different Learning Situations. We analyzed the neuroticism dimension of the big five personality questionnaire. We then completed a 3 (learning situation: traditional classroom, online learning, flipped classroom) × 3 (neuroticism: high, medium, low) ANOVA with learning achievement test performance as the dependent variable. The results showed that the interaction between learning situation and neuroticism was not significant ($F(4, 84) = 1.47$, $p > 0.05$; see Table 6 for means and standard deviations). The main effects of learning situation and neuroticism were also not significant (neuroticism: $F(2, 42) = 2.35, p > 0.05, \eta_p^2 = 0.10$; learning situation: $F(2, 84) = 2.30, p > 0.05, \eta_p^2 = 0.052$).

Table 6. The learning effect of individuals with different levels of neuroticism in the three learning situations.

	Neuroticism		
	High group (n = 15) M (SD)	Medium group (n = 17) M (SD)	Low group (n = 13) M (SD)
Traditional classroom	0.74 (0.13)	0.76 (0.10)	0.76 (0.09)
Online learning	0.71 (0.12)	0.68 (0.17)	0.79 (0.12)
Flipped classroom	0.83 (0.14)	0.74 (0.13)	0.80 (0.11)

Note: The numbers in brackets are the standard deviation of the correct rate

6 Summary and Discussion

This study explored the relationship between personality characteristics and learning achievement assessed in three learning situations (the traditional classroom, online learning and flipped classroom), in order to test which kind of personality was more suitable for which kind of learning situation. These results have implications for the design of personalized learning environments.

The results showed that the three kinds of learning situations produced similar learning achievement. This suggests that online learning and blended learning settings are not more effective than traditional classroom settings. This finding may have been due to the nature of the course in this study, because this course belongs to the nature of liberal arts, if other courses such as the nature of the operation and the nature of science may have different results. However, the more important findings concerned learning settings and learning achievement in relation to characteristics of the learner. The two characteristics that stood out as important were the personality traits of conscientiousness and openness.

Conscientiousness was directly related to higher learning achievement, regardless of learning setting. This finding supported Hypothesis 1 and was consistent with earlier research showing that conscientiousness effectively predicted learning behaviors important for achievement. It is possible that other Big Five traits are not as important for learning; past research has shown that agreeableness and extroversion mainly predicted the nature of interpersonal relationships, and neuroticism mainly predicted individual mood.

Openness was directly related to better learning achievement, and also showed a significant interaction with learning setting in predicting learning achievement. Previous studies found that openness was significantly associated with thirst for knowledge, cognitive need and cognitive ability (Chamorro-Premuzic & Furnham [32], 2005). In fact, it was interpreted as the main "investment characteristic," having a causal relation with the acquisition of knowledge and skills.

The learning characteristics associated with openness also help explain the nature of the interaction between setting and personality in predicting learning achievement found in the current study. The higher the openness, the higher the acceptance of the online learning setting in which the person was more able to adapt to the new teaching situation; the person with a low level of openness showed higher learning achievement in the traditional classroom. These results confirmed Hypothesis 2.

7 Educational Enlightenment

In the context of modern information technology, the use of information technology in education provides many convenient learning opportunities to meet the personalized needs of learners. In order to best make use of this technology, we must understand individual differences related to learning. As the American psychologist Bloom said, personalized teaching within the classroom context depends on personalized guidelines for individual learning, and this is not simply a change in the role of teachers and students or a reversal of the teaching order. This study showed some personality traits indeed predicted learning achievement, especially in certain learning environments, suggesting the importance of matching learners with appropriate learning settings.

This study gave us several insights, namely that it is important: (1) to make teaching methods, learning situations and individual differences match as far as possible; (2) to develop effective interventions based on students' personality, and to improve students' conscientiousness and openness; and (3) to adapt online learning and flipped classrooms to be more consistent with personalized learning; (4) to design corresponding learning activities according to different learners' personality characteristics, so that all learners feel accommodated.

Acknowledgements. This research is supported by the Research Program Funds of the Collaborative Innovation Center of Assessment toward Basic Education Quality at Beijing Normal University (2016-04-013-BZK01), (2016-04-003-BZK01) and Financially supported by self-determined research funds of CCNU from the colleges' basic research and operation of MOE (CCNU15A05047).

References

1. Anderson, T., Carrison, R.: Theory and Practice of Online Learning. Athabasca University Press (2004)
2. 丁兴富. 论远程学习的理论和模式. 开放教育研究 **03**, 17–27 (2006)
3. 曹莉. 翻转课堂及其在我国的应用研究. 华中师范大学 (2015)
4. 崔彩英, 孙红卫. 在线学习方式与传统学习方式的对比分析研究. 科技展望 **06**, 220–221 (2016)
5. 姜梅芳. 大五人格, 对上司批评的反应和工作绩效的关系研究—从员工可教练性视角. 广东外语外贸大学 (2009)
6. 陈少华.人格与认知. 北京: 社会科学文献出版社 (4), 10–12 (2005)
7. Blickle, G.: Personality traits, learning strategies, and performance. Eur. J. Pers. **10**(5), 337–352 (1996)
8. Chamorro-Premuzic, T., Furnham, A.: Personality predicts academic performance: Evidence from two longitudinal university samples. J. Res. Pers. **3**(4), 319–338 (2003)
9. Lounsbury, J.W., Sundstrom, E., Loveland, J.M., et al.: Intelligence, "Big Five" personality traits, and work drive as predictors of course grade. Pers. Individ. Differ. **35**(6), 1231–1239 (2003)
10. Farsides, T., Woodfield, R.: Individual differences and undergraduate academic success: the roles of personality, intelligence, and application. Pers. Individ. Differ. **34**(7), 1225–1243 (2003)
11. Gray, E.K., Watson, D.: General and specific traits of personality and their relation to sleep and academic performance. J. Pers. **70**(2), 177–206 (2002)
12. Dollinger, S.J., Orf, L.A.: Personality and performance in "personality": conscientiousness and openness. J. Res. Pers. **25**(3), 276–284 (1991)
13. Chamorro-Premuzic, T., Furnham, A., Lewis, M.: Personality and approaches to learning predict preference for different teaching methods. Learn. Individ. Differ. **17**(3), 241–250 (2007)
14. O'Connor, M.C., Paunonen, S.V.: Big Five personality predictors of post-secondary academic performance. Pers. Individ. Differ. **43**(5), 971–990 (2007)
15. Rothstein, M.G., Paunonen, S.V.: Personality and cognitive ability predictors of performance in graduate business school. J. Educ. Psychol. **86**(4), 516–530 (1994)
16. Ehrman, M.E.: The role of personality type in adult language learning: an ongoing investigation. In: Parry, T.S., Stansfield, C.W. (eds.) Language Aptitude Reconsidered. Englewood Cliffs, pp. 126–178. Prentice Hall Regents, N.J. (1990)
17. 张理义, 高柏良, 黄箭星, 李斌. 学习成绩与青少年个性特征及有关因素的研究. 中国校医 **01**, 19–21 (1994)

18. 宋专茂, 吴强, 赵风雪. 学习成绩优良与学习成绩落后大学生的人格特征研究. 社会 心理科学 **01**, 41–44+24 (2001)
19. Raad, B.D., Schouwenburg, H.C.: Personality in learning and education: a review. Eur. J. Pers. **10**(5), 303–336 (1996)
20. 钟志贤, 杨蕾. 论在线学习. 现代远距离教育 **01**, 30–34 (2002)
21. Gosper, M., Green, D., Mcneill, M., et al.: The Impact of Web-Based Lecture Technologies on Current and Future Practices in Learning and Teaching (2008)
22. Flores, N., Savage, S.J.: Student demand for streaming lecture video: empirical evidence from undergraduate economics classes. Int. Rev. Econ. Educ. **6**(2), 57–78 (2007)
23. Gratton-Lavoie, C., Stanley, D.: Teaching and learning principles of micro economics online: an empirical assessment. Res. Econ. Educ. **40**, 3–25 (2009). Winter
24. Figlio, D.N., Rush, M., Yin, L.: Is it live or is it internet? Experimental estimates of the effects of online instruction on student learning. Working paper 16089, National Bureau of Economic Research, Cambridge (2010)
25. Parsons-Pollard, N., Lacks, T.R., Grant, P.H.: A comparative assessment of student learning outcomes in large online and traditional campus based introduction to criminal justice courses. Crim. Justice Stud. **21**, 239–251 (2008)
26. Lents, N.H., Cifuentes, O.E.: Web-based learning enhancements: video lectures through voice-over powerpoint in a majors-level biology course. J. Coll. Sci. Teach. **39**, 38–46 (2009)
27. Bergmann, J., Sams, A.: Flipped Your Classroom: Reach Every Student in Every Class Every Day. International Society for Technology in Education, USA (2012)
28. Long, T., Logan, J., Waugh, M.: Students' perceptions of pre-class instructional video in the flipped classroom model: a survey study. In: Searson, M., Ochoa, M. (eds.) Proceedings of Society for Information Technology & Teacher Education International Conference 2014, pp. 920–927. AACE, Chesapeake (2014)
29. Snowden, K.E.: Teacher perceptions of the flipped classroom: using video lectures online to replace traditional in-class lectures. Thesis Prepared for the Degree of Master of Arts (2012). Accessed from http://digital.library.unt.edu/ark:/67531/metadc149663/m2/1/high_res_d/thesis.pdf
30. Costa Jr., P.T., McCrae, R.R.: The NEO Personality Inventory. Psycho-logical Assessment Resources, Odessa (1985)
31. Gupta, B.: Role of personality in knowledge sharing and knowledge acquisition behaviour (2008)
32. Chamorro-Premuzic, T., Furnham, A.: Personality and Intellectual Competence. Lawrence Erlbaum Associates, Mahwah (2005)

Author Index

The manufacturer's authorised representative in the EU is Springer Nature Customer Service Centre GmbH, Europaplatz 3, 69115 Heidelberg, Germany. If you have any concerns regarding our products, please contact ProductSafety@springernature.com

Printed and bound by CPI Group (UK) Ltd, Croydon, CR0 4YY
22/09/2026
02220983-0009